KU-345-115

Earth's Last Frontiers

Introduction

Man has always been fascinated by the challenge of the unknown. To learn more about the world, adventurers have braved great dangers, and faced terrible hardships. It is to such men of courage and endurance that we owe our knowledge today. But, and this is particularly true in an age when little of the earth remains unknown, exploration is not simply a question of finding new lands, or of charting unknown seas. It can involve man pitting his strength against the elements, in a hostile and unfamiliar environment, to build up a true picture of the world in which he lives.

This is the story of man's struggle with the elements, as he has sought to break down the barriers to a complete knowledge of the earth. The first part tells of the opening up of the polar regions, and this is true exploration as we understand it. But it is also exploration in a new dimension, that of a frozen, arctic world. The challenge and the conquest of that world became an obsession with adventurers, and gradually, through their efforts, the Arctic and Antarctic were explored.

The barrier of altitude is the subject of this book's second section, as mountaineers strive to conquer the world's highest peaks. No discovery this, but rather man testing his strength against nature in the battle to do what no man has done before. Finally, in the third part of the book, we turn to the world's waters, to the seas and the oceans that have always interested man. His interest has been two-fold—first, that of scientific investigation into the seabed, and the waters and life in them; second, that of challenging a new environment itself. As his efforts have been increasingly successful, man has become more able to live in the ocean. Slowly, he is on the way to conquering the last of earth's frontiers.

A HISTORY OF DISCOVERY AND EXPLORATION

Earth's Last Frontiers

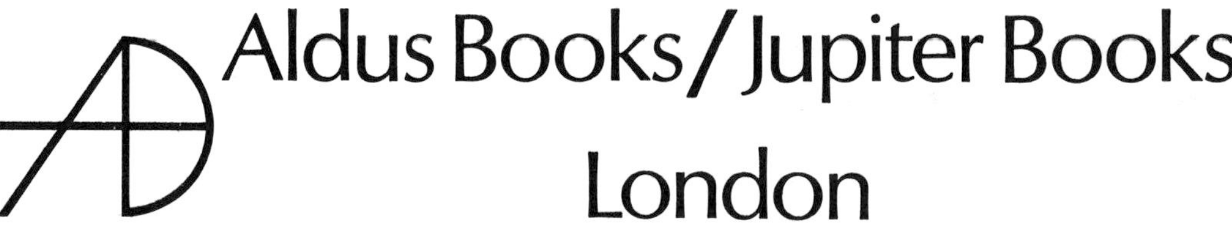

Aldus Books / Jupiter Books
London

Contents

Part 1 The Frozen World

Part 2 The Roof of the World

This edition published in 1973 by
Aldus Books and Jupiter Books, London
SBN 490 00294 3
Distributed by Jupiter Books
9-13 Cowcross Street, London EC1M 6DR

Printed and bound in Yugoslavia by
Mladinska Knjiga, Ljubljana

Part 3 Secrets of the Sea

Below: the crewmen of Willem Barents' expedition to the Arctic in 1596 shooting a polar bear. They were unsuccessful in their desperate attempt to hack a path for their ship out of the ice to the open water, and they had to spend the winter in the Arctic.

PART ONE

The Frozen World

BY THAYER WILLIS

The Ends of the Earth

1

By mid-morning on April 6, 1909, a United States naval officer, Robert E. Peary, accompanied by his Negro servant and four Eskimos, had reached a position on the ice that they estimated to be just three miles south of the North Pole. Although they were only a few miles from their goal, both the men and their dogs were too exhausted to continue. After 20 years of Arctic exploration and the last 12 years trying to reach the pole, Peary was on the brink of success. But he was too tired to realize that his life's purpose had almost been achieved. The accumulated weariness of six days and nights of forced marches and the constant anxiety of the journey seemed to roll across him. As soon as the Eskimos had constructed *igloos* (snow houses) for everyone, and the men had eaten and given a double ration to the dogs, Peary crawled into his igloo for a few hours' rest.

Weary though he was, Robert Peary could not sleep for long.

Left: men and dogs in the remote icy expanses at the ends of the earth, still the most successful combination for polar journeys. Here the dog teams of the transarctic expedition led by Wally Herbert in the winter of 1968–1969 cross the endless Arctic ice fields.

Right: Commander Robert E. Peary, the first man to reach the North Pole. Peary said, "The arctic brings a man face to face with himself. If he is a man, the man comes out; and if he is a cur, the cur shows as quickly."

Above: icebergs and pack ice float in the ghostly desolation of the ocean surrounding the frozen continent of Antarctica. The polar regions have a haunting, austere beauty that has proved irresistible to many explorers.

When he awoke a few hours later, he picked up his diary and wrote these words: "The Pole at last! I cannot bring myself to realize it. It seems all so simple and commonplace."

Then Peary and two Eskimos loaded some food and navigation instruments aboard a sledge and pushed on northward for about 10 miles to a position beyond the pole. After a march of only a few hours, Robert Peary became the first man to actually stand at the North Pole—the summit of the world. There was nothing there to mark the magical point—that invisible spot on the Arctic ice where the directions of east, west, and north disappear and only one direction remains—south.

The following day the small party of six men turned their sledges toward the south and began to race toward the northern coast of Ellesmere Island and their ship that was waiting at Cape Columbia.

Peary knew that if they were to reach land again they would have to hurry. What worried him most was the possibility of a gale that could break up the ice over which they traveled. Once broken the *floes,* or floating sheets of ice, would become separated by *leads*, or areas of open water. The breaking up could in turn speed up the drift of the ice eastward in the direction of the tepid North Atlantic. The comparative warmth of the water in that region would melt the solid ice from beneath them. The safe return of Peary and his companions to Cape Columbia 16 days later ended one of the greatest success stories of man against the elements.

Peary's triumph in overcoming the problems of getting to and from the North Pole tells us a great deal about the Arctic. First of all, there is the region of continuous cold around the North Pole. Here, there is no land, just a solid surface of ice in the midst of the Arctic Ocean. In his earlier travels Peary had been to, or very near, the other parts of the Arctic. These include the Arctic Ocean and its thousands of islands, and the northern parts of the continents of Europe, Asia, and North America.

Like every explorer who has tried to get to the North Pole, Peary had to leave land behind him and travel over the ice. Moreover, he had to do this at the coldest and darkest time of the year when the ice was firm and no open water barred his way. He also had to contend with the drift of the ice that is always moving. This meant that Peary had to allow for this drift in setting his course northward. There was also the difficulty of establishing supply depots along the route. A cache of food left at a particular spot on the march northward would not be at that spot when the expedition returned south. The drifting pack ice was again the explanation for this. Even if he took the chance of locating a supply of food he had left behind several weeks before, he still faced the risk of finding that it had been raided by foxes or polar bears in the meantime.

The first European known to have ventured into the Arctic region was Pytheas, a Greek mathematician and explorer. In 325 B.C., he sailed around Britain and headed north in search of a land

Right: part of the *Carta Marina* drawn by the Swedish bishop Olaus Magnus (1490–1558), showing Iceland and Greenland—the first map to give an accurate picture of the far north.

Above: a bronze Viking plaque of the 600's, showing two bears attacking a man. Greenland, where Eric the Red established his colonies, had a milder climate than it has today, and Viking settlers were able to grow vegetables and feed their stock in pastures in the summer. Even during the winter they could hunt the animals that roamed the wild areas beyond the settlements.

called Thule (which may have been Norway or Iceland), which he had learned about from the Britons. For hundreds of years, however, no one believed Pytheas' story or his description of the continuous daylight that occurs around the area from May through July. Europeans, and in particular the Romans, thought that ice covered everything in the north and that no ships could travel there.

About 300 years after the Roman Empire had lost its influence in the world (during the A.D. 400's) Europeans again began to sail north to the Arctic. The first to do so were Christian monks from Ireland. They were looking for a place of solitude as they sailed in their small, open, round-bottomed boats and followed the path of migrating geese to Iceland. The date of their arrival there was about 770. A hundred years later the first Norsemen, or Vikings, reached Iceland to settle there. These were bands of Scandinavian sea rovers who were the ancestors of today's Norwegians, Swedes, and Danes.

Then about the year 900, a Norseman named Gunnbjørn was blown off course on his way to Iceland. After drifting for days through the dangerous Arctic waters he at last sighted land—the black, ice-studded cliffs of east Greenland. When the storm finally abated, he made his way back to Iceland with stories of a new land that lay six days' sail to the west.

The adventurous Vikings were excited by the tale. They had

Above: the problems of taking ships to the polar regions are as difficult today as they were for the earlier explorers. Here the U.S.S. *Atka* lies at McMurdo Sound, Antarctica. In both Arctic and Antarctic waters ships can quickly become locked in the ice.

already colonized Iceland and were now eager to find new lands. Still, it was a risky voyage and Gunnbjørn's descriptions of drifting ice and dense fog soon damped their enthusiasm. About 82 years passed before a Norseman set out with some companions to retrace Gunnbjørn's westward voyage. This was Eric the Red. After he first sighted the east coast of the island Gunnbjørn had seen, he sailed around the dangerous belt of icebergs that hugged the coast. Eric then rounded the southern tip of the island and landed near the present-day port of Eriksey at the entrance to Eriksfjord.

Much of the new land he saw looked like Iceland: rocky islets covered with seabirds, deep fiords cutting into the coastline, an abundance of seals, fish, and whales. Inland, at the protected heads of the fiords, Eric found grassy meadows and hills, dotted with dwarf-juniper and willow trees. In the summer it was warm enough to raise vegetables and there was plenty of pastureland. Along the coast Eric and his companions found the fishing excellent. Seals and walruses were also numerous and provided both food and clothing.

From the time of Eric until the early 1900's, Greenland became much colder, and today most of this largest island in the world is covered by ice. But with the exception of Greenland, explorers and scientists have found that in summer nine-tenths of all Arctic lands have no snow and ice. Berries, vegetables, and a large variety of

Above: the crosier of a Viking bishop, found in a Greenland grave, probably that of Jon Smyrill (which means "sparrow-hawk"), who died in 1209. It was during the 900's that the Viking colonies in remote Greenland were converted to the Christian faith.

Opposite: a map of the world from a psalter of the 1200's, showing it as a flat disk with the holy city of Jerusalem at the center. It was believed that an impassable ocean lay encircling the disk, which long discouraged exploration into the seas around Europe.

flowers grow along the North American coast, northern Siberia, and the northernmost parts of Norway, Sweden, and Finland. During the winter the sun never shines on much of the Arctic. But in some Arctic regions it shines at midnight at certain times in the summer. This phenomenon, known as the midnight sun, occurs at the Arctic Circle on June 22, and farther north the periods of midnight sun last longer. For example in northern Norway there is continuous daylight from May through July.

Many of the animals that Eric the Red saw on Greenland in 982 still roam the Arctic. The reindeer and the caribou are the most common, and they generally come in great herds to the summer pasturelands. Bears, foxes, hares, and squirrels also provide both food and fur for the people living in the Arctic. Three species of seals live year-round in Arctic waters, and they are joined by herds of walruses, and schools of belugas and narwhals. Arctic *char* (a variety of trout) choke the far northern rivers and streams in spring, when they return to spawn. In the ocean off the coasts of North America, Siberia, and the Scandinavian countries there are halibut, salmon, and above all cod. To those skilled in hunting and fishing the north supplied almost everything needed for life.

In the summer of 985 about 500 Icelanders followed Eric the Red to the wonderful island to the west that he called Greenland. Most of them established villages around the fiords along the milder southwestern coast, the first colony being in the region of the present-day port of Julianehab.

Word of their successful landing on Greenland reached Iceland and eventually Norway. Other emigrants began to risk the cold and stormy journey by open boat to join the colonists on Greenland. Many people built farms for themselves out of stone and peat, and generally the settlers appear to have flourished in their new homeland. In the summer they farmed, and during the winter months kept themselves supplied with food and clothes by fishing and hunting. According to ancient Norse records, it was not long before the Greenlanders began trading with the Eskimos, exchanging their corn and the iron they imported from Norway for ivory walrus tusks and the skins of bears and seals that the Eskimos had for sale.

Christianity was already established in Greenland by the 1100's, when a bishop was sent to the island to preside over the religious life. The Norwegian Vikings, by paying taxes, even helped to finance the early crusaders to liberate the Holy Land.

In 1261, the Greenlanders voted to become a crown colony of Norway. But by this time their prosperity was beginning to decline. The mild climate that had made farming possible in both Greenland and Iceland was changing. As temperatures dropped, ice began to cover more of the land. At the same time fewer Norwegian ships came to Greenland because of a depressed economy in Norway.

The Greenlanders had relied completely on Norway for their supplies of iron tools, salt, and other necessities. By the middle of the 1300's years would pass without the arrival of a single ship from the

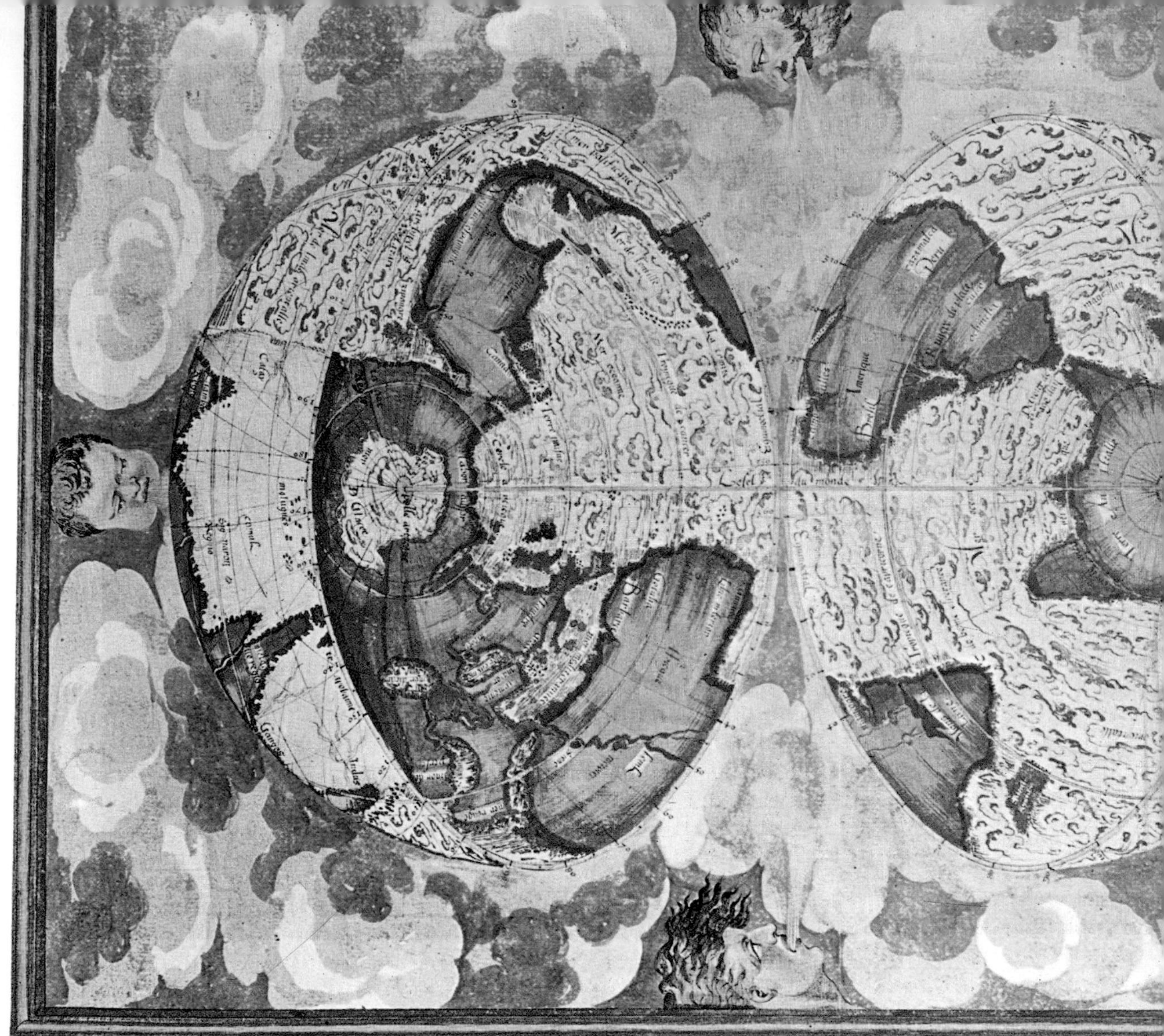

mother country. According to the evidence found by archaeologists the Norse colonies in Greenland seem to have died out in the 1400's. Bodies that have since been found show signs of starvation and scars from wounds. Perhaps when the economy declined and food became scarce, war broke out between the Greenlanders and the Eskimos. Because no records survived to give us a clue to their fate, no one really knows what happened to them.

In the second half of the 1200's, long before the Greenlanders vanished, Europe had been dazzled by the tales brought back by Marco Polo of the fabulous wealth of the Orient—the East Indies, China, and Japan. But the overland routes that Polo had followed were closed to the Christians by the Moslems whose empire, from about 750 to the 1200's, had extended from the Atlantic Ocean to the borders of India. Thus the rich profusion of Oriental silks, spices, tapestries, porcelain, and precious stones were protected—at least for a while. In the early Middle Ages many people in Western Europe

Above: a world map by a French cartographer, Guillaume Le Testu, for a 1555 atlas. It shows a globe cut in two, pulled open, and printed inside and out. Like most early maps, it is based mainly on supposition, but Le Testu's concept of polar geography is amazingly accurate. The Arctic (at left) is an icy sea, and Antarctica is a land mass.

Right: an Indian miniature of a European sailor. During the rush of exploration that began during the 1400's sailors from Europe probed the far reaches of the world, searching for a way to the famous wealth of the East. Their long journeys disproved the myths that frightened the medieval Europeans.

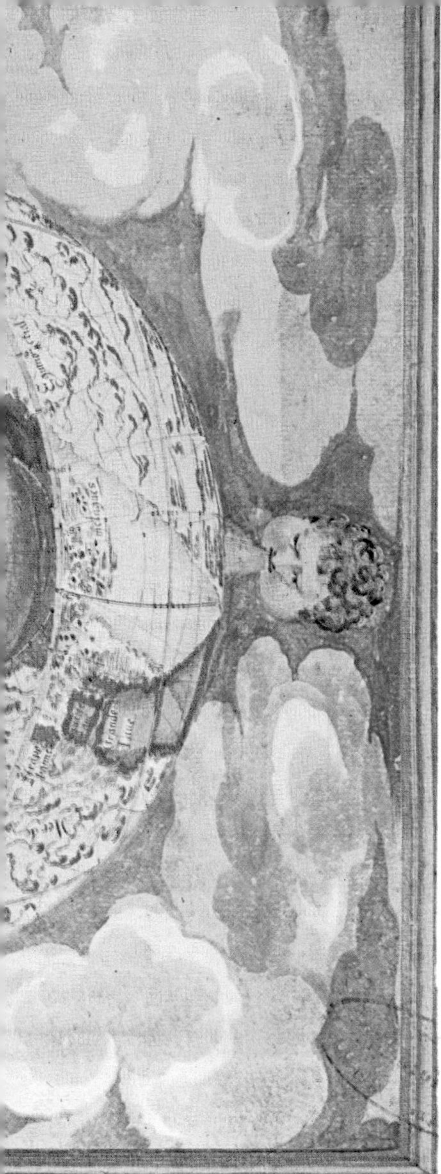

still believed that the earth was a flat disk centered on Jerusalem, and surrounded by a continuous and impassable ocean. They thought it was impossible to sail to the East. Gradually in the 1400's the idea that the earth was round began to be accepted by educated people. At this time the theories and observations of the Greek geographer and astronomer Ptolemy (who had lived in Alexandria, Egypt in about A.D. 150) were translated into Latin, the language used by most educated men. His eight-book *Geography* contained lists of latitude and longitude that provided mapmakers with a system of showing where a place existed on the globe. By the late 1400's the earth was thought of as a globe and divided into equal parts, the lines of longitude running north and south along the earth's surface, and those of latitude running around the earth parallel to the equator. Maps began to look like the maps of today, and explorers began to think of circumnavigating the earth.

In his *Geography* Ptolemy had also written about a vast land to the south that joined Africa and Asia together and stretched across the bottom of the world. For many hundreds of years this great unknown southern land, *Terra Australis Incognita* (unknown south land), was the setting for numerous frightening myths. Here was a place of ghosts where only Satan could feel at home, bounded on the north by terrific heat and in the south by bitter cold. A map made in the 1300's shows pictures of the terrible inhabitants that lived there. The Antarctic Ocean was thought by many sea captains to be a place of towering waves from which the hand of the Devil reached out to snatch at unwary ships.

Then in the 1400's seamen sailing under the rival flags of Spain and Portugal began to dispel these myths. As they made their way around the southern tip of Africa, they disproved the ancient theory that Africa was linked with a third continent to the south. Then Ferdinand Magellan on the first voyage around the world (1519–1521) saw, beyond the strait that bears his name, a land he called Tierra del Fuego (land of fire). This new land was soon included on maps as the northern tip of a continent. Magellan thought it was a group of islands, but as the years went by other seamen and geographers began to put Tierra del Fuego on maps as the northern tip of a vast Antarctic continent separated by the Strait of Magellan from the mainland of South America. For the next 200 years the idea of a fertile Southern Continent was the subject of speculation.

It was not until the late 1700's that men such as Captain James Cook actually set out to look for the mysterious land. Between 1800 and 1820, American and British seal hunters sighted islands around Antarctica, primarily about the area of the South Shetland Islands. One of the men, Nathaniel B. Palmer, from Stonington, Connecticut, may have been the first man to actually see the Antarctic Peninsula. When he returned from his search for fresh seal hunting grounds south of Deception Island he had a rather gloomy story to tell. He had sailed along the coast of "an extensive mountain

Above: emperor penguins on Ross Island, Antarctica, one of the varieties found on the Southern Continent. The Adélie penguin is another, named—like Adelie Land—for the wife of the French explorer Dumont d'Urville.

country, more sterile and dismal it possible and more heavily laden with ice and snow than the South Shetlands."

Explorers began to take an interest in the forbidding, storm-swept land during the 1800's. But it was not until the 1900's that anyone penetrated well into the frozen white wilderness that covers an area of about 5,100,000 square miles across the bottom of the world. Men like Robert Falcon Scott, Sir Ernest Shackleton, and Sir Douglas Mawson were among the first to give an accurate picture of this fifth largest continent on earth. They experienced the hurricane-force winds that scream across the Antarctic—winds that drive snow before them at speeds of up to 200 miles an hour. They suffered the agony of frost-bitten toes and hands when temperatures drop to around –40°F. along the coasts. Some of them even wintered in the Antarctic and managed to stay alive on this icebound continent where inland the mercury plunges sometimes as low as –100°F.

As they made their way from the Ross Ice Shelf, explorers found a range of mountains bordering the vast central plateau. These had to be crossed in order to get to the South Pole. Between the mountain peaks, which ranged from 6,000 to 12,000 feet in height, were great rivers of blue ice that moved slowly down to the sea.

It was a lonely land that these explorers risked their lives to discover. Separated from the nearest mainland by 600 miles of the most tempestuous ocean on earth, they found only a few hardy plants and insects on the rocky mountain sides. Although there were seals, whales, fish, and penguins along the coast, as they struggled inland the explorers were to find no animals to supplement the food they carried with them. Unlike the Arctic where each summer the tundra brightens with scores of plants, only three kinds of flowering plants grow on the Antarctic Peninsula.

For the explorer the difficulties of the Antarctic are great: the frightening temperatures, the physical strain imposed by the high

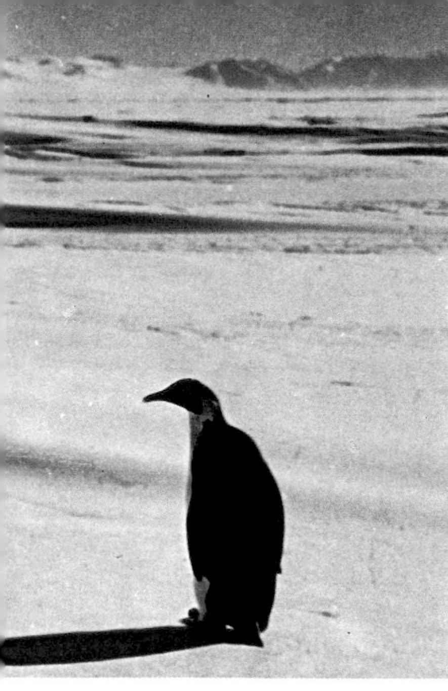

altitudes in the mountains, the menace of sudden blizzards, and the crevasses formed by slowly shifting ice sheets. Yet, despite these obstacles, it retained its lure.

In the story of exploration Antarctica is unique as the one continent whose real discoverers are known to us. Although we do not know definitely how prehistoric man migrated over the earth's surface, one of the earliest known migrations took place when prehistoric men moved from North Africa to Europe. Gradually people speaking an Indo-European language probably spread throughout Asia. Then, more than 20,000 years ago, men crossed the Bering Strait to North America and eventually worked their way southward into South America. Thus when explorers first reached these continents they had been preceded by Stone Age men. Even the most remote islands of the Pacific, such as Easter Island, were inhabited when the Dutch reached there in 1722. But the explorers and fishermen who first landed on Antarctica were, in fact, the first men to see this frozen world.

Right: the frozen world of the Antarctic is a place where scarcely anything blooms—except here, the Botanical Garden of Wilkes Station. As a relief from his scientific duties during Operation Deep Freeze, the station leader managed to fit a plexiglass dome to the side of the main building and planted vegetables.

A Northern Passage to Cathay 2

European explorers began to think about making voyages to the Arctic during the late 1500's. At that time they were trying to find a Northeast or Northwest Passage to Asia. The interest in finding a sea route to the East was particularly strong in England because of a decline in her trading with France and the Netherlands. An even more important incentive however, was the great wealth that Spanish and Portuguese merchants had acquired from the new trading partners they had discovered in America, India, and especially in China (or Cathay as it was then called by Europeans). London merchants and the ruling monarchs became increasingly

Left: the search for a northern passage to the riches of the East took European explorers into the Arctic regions. Here the ship of Willem Barents is caught in the ice, and the marooned crew members hunt for driftwood to build a hut. The illustration is from the official account of the expedition, taken from diaries, published in 1598.

Right: Sir Hugh Willoughby. He set out with Richard Chancellor, but was forced to winter on the coast of what is now Norway, where he and his men died. When their bodies were found by some Russian fishermen, his diary—in which Willoughby writes of their camp as the Haven of Death—was recovered. It ends abruptly.

interested in providing financial backing for English explorers who would search for a new route to the East.

The first question to be settled was the best route to the Orient. To the northeast, the sea was known to be ice-free as far as the northern tip of Norway. Even beyond the North Cape, Russian fishermen were known to take their boats eastward as far as the Ob River. The northwest route, on the other hand, seemed less hopeful. In 1497, the Italian navigator John Cabot had sailed the coast of Newfoundland for England without finding a single opening in the ice that might lead on to Cathay. Three years later the two Corte-Real brothers, who sailed under the Spanish flag, could find no limit to the northward stretching coast of America.

In 1551, "The Mysterie and Campanie of Marchants Adventurers for the Discoverie of Regions, Dominions, Islands, and Places unknowen" was founded in London. This company of merchant adventurers became the center of all activities directed toward the search for a Northeast Passage. Sir Hugh Willoughby was appointed by the company to command its first expedition. His pilot-general, a professional seaman named Richard Chancellor, was one of the best English navigators of his day. In May, 1553, these two men set out from Deptford, England on the first of many polar expeditions marked for tragedy.

A great storm off Norway separated their ships. The *Bona Esperanza,* Willoughby's ship, though crippled by the gale, finally made landfall on the northern coast of Norway, where they were forced to winter. In 1554 their bodies were found there—they had apparently died of scurvy, a wasting disease caused by faulty diet. This scourge was to claim the lives of polar explorers until the 1900's.

Meanwhile Richard Chancellor had weathered the storm and sailed his ship into the port of Vardo. There he met some Scottish traders, who tried to dissuade him from his search for a Northeast Passage to Cathay. Chancellor refused to be discouraged by their warnings, and headed his ship eastward again. It was midsummer, the days were long, and Chancellor held his course until he came to a place where there was no night at all, "but a continual light and brightness of the sun shining clearly on a huge and mighty sea."

Below: a map showing "Frobishers Straightes," which was supposed to confirm the discovery in 1576 by Martin Frobisher of a wide clear passage to Cathay, made when he sailed westward from Greenland to what is now Frobisher Bay.

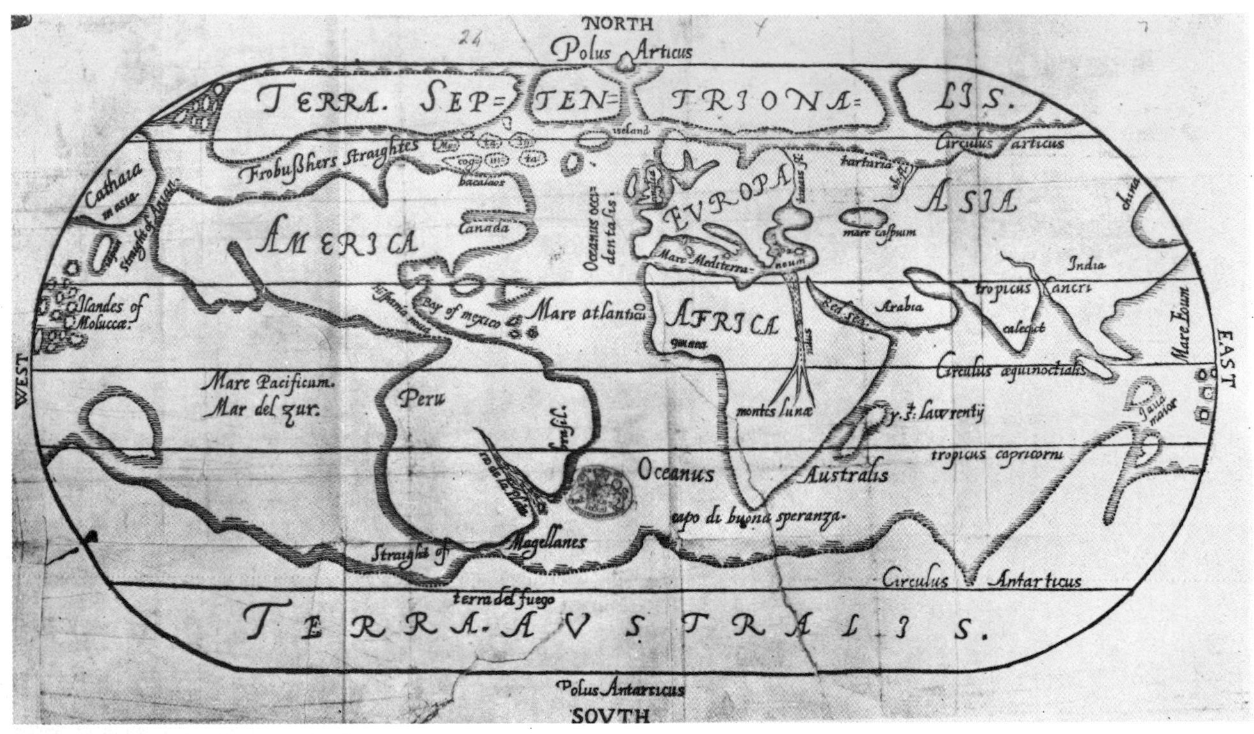

They put into a broad bay, "a hundred miles wide" at the mouth of the Dvina River, near the present-day port of Archangel.

When he went ashore Chancellor was met by emissaries of the Russian czar, Ivan the Terrible. They invited him to accompany them by sledge on the 700-mile journey to Moscow, and Chancellor agreed to do so. When, in the following summer of 1554, he returned to England, Chancellor carried with him a cordial letter from the czar to the King of England. Ivan was hopeful that his greetings would serve to open the way to mutual trade.

Chancellor's voyage led to the formation of the Muscovy Company which, from 1555, developed a lucrative trade with Russia and Persia. The search for a Northeast Passage was thereafter taken over by the Muscovy Company.

Then, during the reign of Queen Elizabeth I, the direction of the

Left: Martin Frobisher. He was convinced that he would find a northern passage to the Pacific like Magellan's southern route. When he sailed in 1576, Queen Elizabeth honored him by waving from her window as his ship sailed by.

search for a route to Cathay was changed to the northwest. In 1569, the publication of Gerhardus Mercator's new map of the world showed that a large land mass in fact blocked the way to the East but that in the West there was the start of a new passage that might lead to Cathay. Arctic exploration was therefore directed westward.

In 1576, the Englishman Sir Martin Frobisher set out from England to look for a Northwest Passage. His expedition, consisting of two small pinnaces, had as its first landfall the southern tip of Greenland. From Greenland he sailed on westward and dis-

Below: an incident from Frobisher's second voyage in 1577, when he mad‹ a triumphant return with men to mine the "gold" he found on Baffin Island.

covered Frobisher Bay, an indentation on Baffin Island. As the two ships sailed along the bay Frobisher thought that the land he saw off to the right must be Asia. As they approached the coast of this new land, Frobisher and his men were astonished to see small men in skin-covered canoes paddling toward them. With their Mongoloid features these men were surely inhabitants of the Indies. To prove that he had really reached Cathay Frobisher ordered that one of the Eskimos and a kayak were to be captured and taken in triumph back to London. Frobisher also took back to England some black rocks from Baffin Island that he thought might contain gold.

The return of the expedition to London with the "strange man of Cathay" was a joyful occasion, and Frobisher was treated as a hero. The Eskimo soon died of a cold he had contracted shortly after he arrived in England. But the black rock brought home from Baffin Island seemed to be a more sensational prize. When it was thrown into a fire, it gave off a goldish glow. And rumors of gold were what interested the queen and the merchants of London most. A Cathay Company was formed, gold miners were hastily recruited, and the queen sent Frobisher on another expedition to the Arctic.

On this 1577 voyage Frobisher again landed on Greenland, which he claimed for Queen Elizabeth and named West England. After establishing friendly relations with the Eskimos there, he

Above: the fleet of Willem Barents off Novaya Zemlya, on his first voyage in 1594. Barents was the chief pilot. The fleet was not able to continue farther because the winter was coming on, and so returned to Amsterdam to report on its progress eastward as well as to bring home a walrus.

Above: the exterior of the hut that Barents and his men built on Novaya Zemlya. The illustration shows the events of February 12, 1597, when they were able to shoot a bear from the hut, thus providing not only meat to eat, but also fat to light their lamps during the long dark nights of the winter.

Left: a navigation instrument from Barents' last voyage, discovered in 1871 in the hut that the men had built. Although in ruins, the ice covering it had preserved the objects inside: candlesticks, dishes, even books.

sailed on to Baffin Island for more gold collecting, returning to England as quickly as possible with 200 tons of rock.

His third and last voyage to Baffin Island was the first English colonizing expedition to the Canadian Arctic. There were 15 ships that sailed from London carrying miners to extract more gold, settlers, and a sufficient quantity of supplies for them to build houses and establish a colony on Baffin Island. But no sooner had the fleet entered Frobisher Bay than disaster struck. A storm arose that sent icebergs churning toward the ships. All but a few of them were sunk, thus ending the possibility of establishing a colony on Baffin Island. When Frobisher and the few remaining ships got back to England, they were confronted with even more devastating news. The Baffin ore had after all been wrongly identified as gold—it was nothing more than a worthless mineral called pyrite. Frobisher's claims of having found the Northwest Passage and the frontiers of Cathay were discredited.

In 1585, another English seaman, more modest than Sir Martin Frobisher, was put in charge of an expedition to chart the coasts of "West England" and Baffin Island. This was John Davis who was to make three Arctic voyages during the next three years. He made detailed journeys into the fiords of Greenland and then pushed northward into the unexplored waters of Baffin Bay. But always the

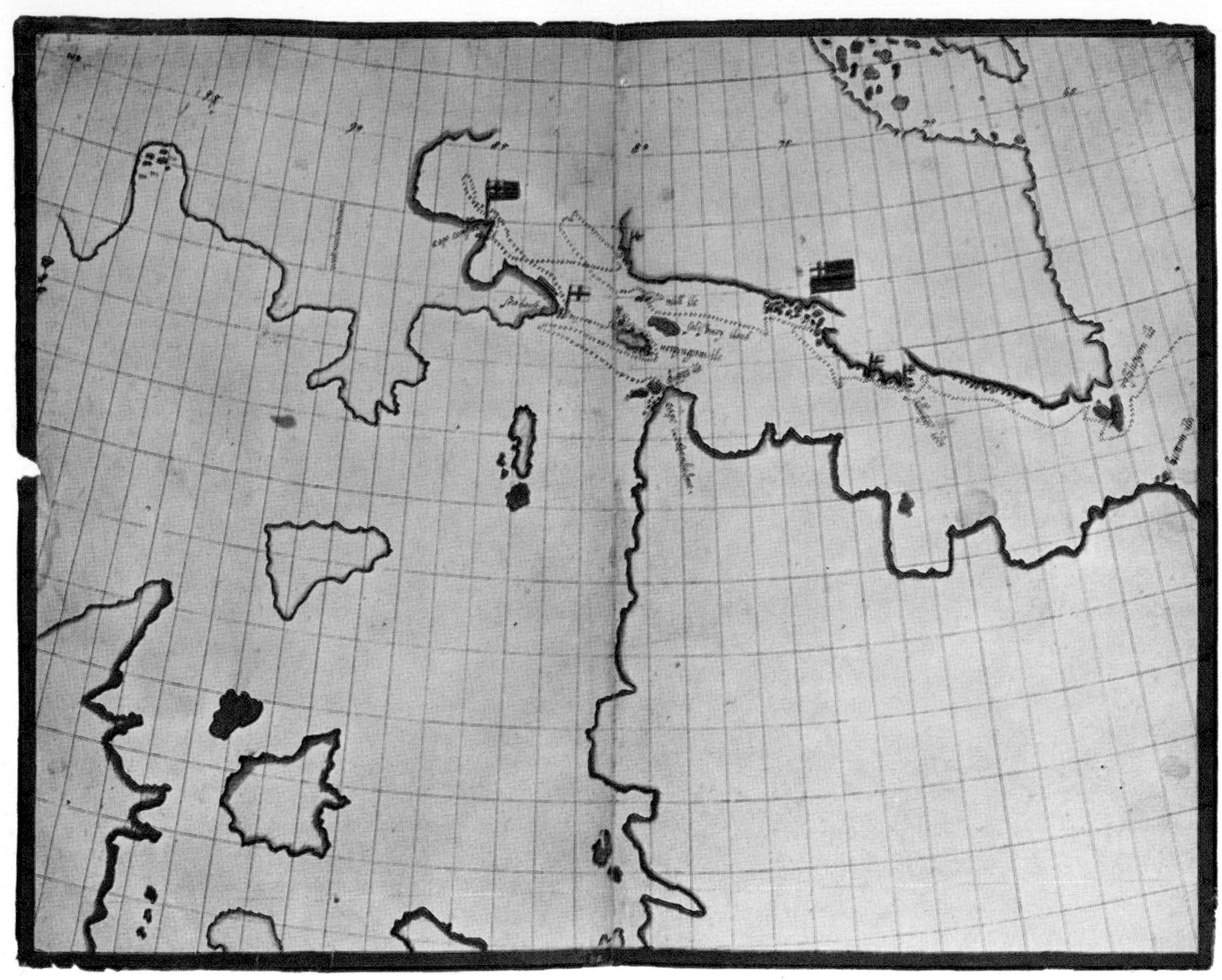

Above: Baffin's route chart of his 1615 voyage, showing by a "red prickle line" his route into Hudson Strait and the mouth of the Foxe Basin. The crosses show the places he landed "to make tryall of the tyde." The apparent lack of tides convinced him that Hudson Strait was not a passage to the west.

drifting icebergs pushed his ships back and hid any passage that might lead them through to the Orient.

Toward the end of the 1500's, Dutch seamen and merchants became the chief rivals of England in finding a land or sea route to the riches of Cathay. For them a northeastern passage was more desirable because along the way they could trade with the Russians. The most important person in these Dutch Arctic explorations was Willem Barents, who was the chief pilot on three successive voyages. On his third expedition, which left Amsterdam in 1596, Barents hoped to get to the Kara Strait by sailing around the northern tip of Novaya Zemlya. By following a very northerly route Barents piloted the ships of the expedition through unexplored seas, discovering West Spitzbergen, the largest island in a group now called Svalbard, before he turned eastward. But ice began to close in around his ship as it approached Novaya Zemlya, and gradually the ice pressed itself so hard around the ship that the hull was forced upward. When the ship finally burst out of the ice it was so cracked and damaged that the Dutchmen had to abandon it and seek shelter on the coast of Novaya Zemlya.

Thus began the first wintering of European explorers so far north and one we know about from the descriptions of one of the men who experienced it. From the timbers they had salvaged from their abandoned ship the Dutchmen built themselves a house, which they furnished with sleeping bunks, lamps, and all the remaining equipment they could haul from the frozen and disintegrating hull.

As the winter wore on the cold became so extreme that the wine froze and sheets became like stiff white boards. Then the supplies of bear fat began to run out. The smoke from the fire inside the house became so suffocating that the men had to stay in bed and keep warm as best they could from the hot stones that they put around their feet.

Somehow the Dutchmen managed to survive the winter but with little hope of ever being rescued. Willem Barents was convinced in fact that their only way of ever getting back to Amsterdam was to make a boat journey to the nearest mainland, which was the Kola Peninsula 1,600 miles away.

By mid-June the courageous men of his expedition managed to prepare themselves for another perilous experience. They loaded the ship's boats with all the cargo they could hold and set out. By using every means they knew—rowing, sailing, and even dragging the boats from one water channel to another—the Dutchmen completed the remarkable journey to the Kola Peninsula. But they arrived without Barents. A day or so after the start of the last stage of the expedition that he knew was so necessary, he had died.

With the return of Barents' expedition the Dutch interest in finding the Northeast Passage came to an end. It was left to the English to resume the search that they directed first to the east and then to the west. In 1610 Henry Hudson was commissioned by some English merchants to follow the inlets that John Davis had seen and to find for England a route through the northwest. As Hudson sailed through Hudson Strait and into the bay that was later named for him, he was convinced that this was the route to Cathay.

Six years later another English navigator and explorer, William Baffin came very near to solving the mystery of the Northwest Passage. He took his 50-ton ship the *Discovery* up the west coast of Greenland to Melville Bay before going westward. Then he sailed close by Jones Sound and into Lancaster Sound before being forced by the ice to turn back toward home. Both these sounds—although Baffin never knew this—lead into the open waters of the Beaufort Sea. From there to the Bering Sea would have been relatively easy going for the sturdy *Discovery*.

All during this period of Arctic exploration by the English and the Dutch, Russia was extending its power eastward across the enormous expanse of Siberia. By the late 1600's, Russian control stretched all the way to the Kamchatka Peninsula on the Pacific Ocean. Then, in 1725, Czar Peter the Great conceived the idea of a series of exploratory journeys by which he hoped the entire northern coast of Siberia would be discovered and mapped. To Vitus Bering,

Above: Peter the Great, who planned the Great Northern Expedition to map the northern Siberian coastline. He also commissioned the Dane Vitus Bering to discover if North America was joined to Asia, or if a passage separated them.

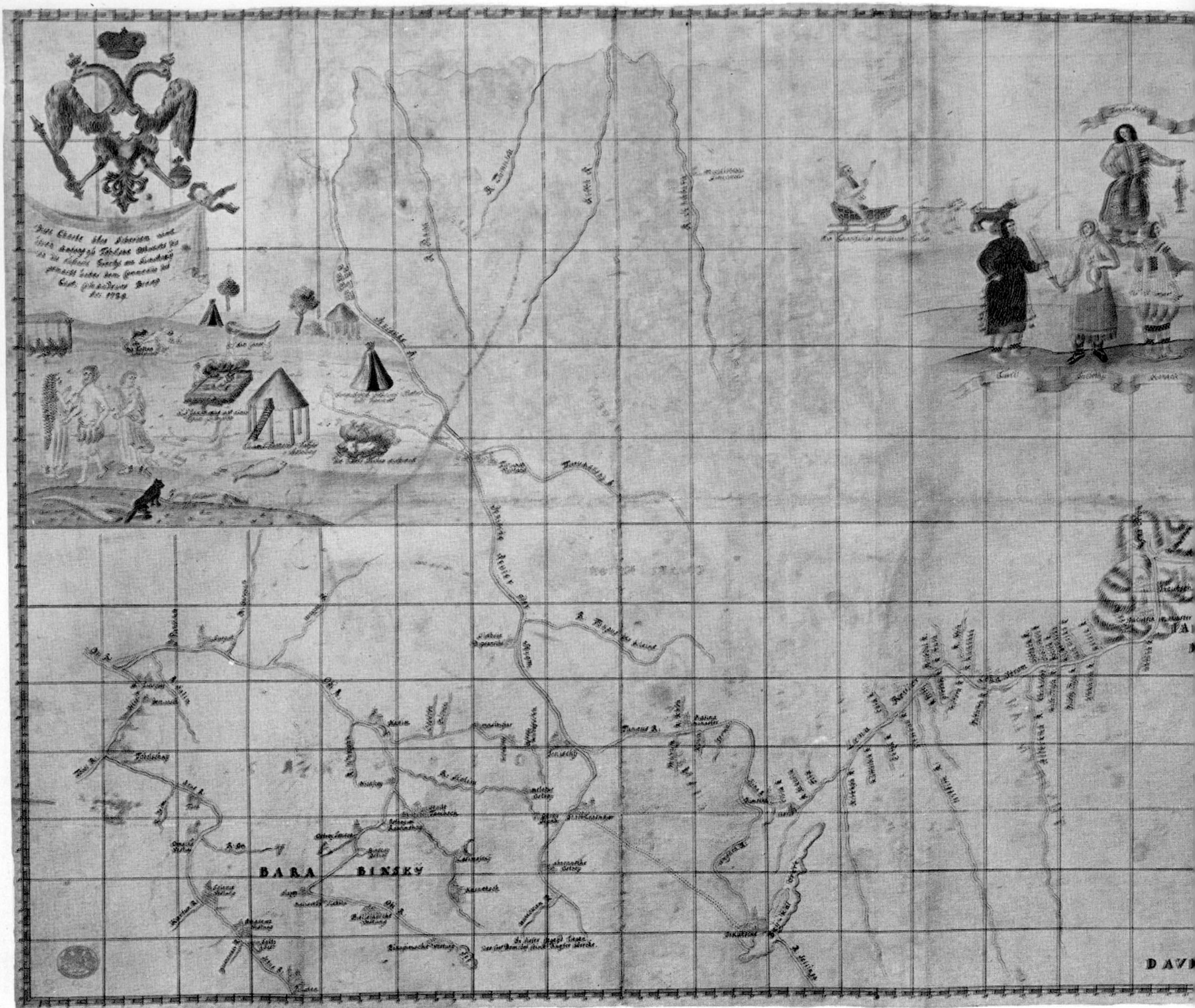

Above: a map drawn by order of Vitus Bering in 1729, illustrating his first expedition of 1727–1729. The map shows the people of Siberia as observed by Bering, and also records the line of soundings to above 67 degrees north. It was there that Bering decided "our task had been carried out and that the land did not extend farther north."

a Dane, he gave a formidable task. First of all Bering and 25 men would trek overland for more than 6,000 miles across Europe and Asia to Okhotsk on the Pacific Coast. From there they would make a sea voyage around the Kamchatka Peninsula and try to land on the American coast.

Despite the rigors of this vast expedition that involved the transportation of men and supplies over four of the largest rivers in Russia, Bering and his companions persevered. Once they managed to reach Okhotsk, they were then subjected to the frustration of waiting as ships for their voyage around Kamchatka Peninsula were made ready. Finally, in 1728, after nearly two years of waiting around, Bering was able to take ship with another Russian explorer named Alexei Chirikov from the east coast of the Kamchatka Peninsula. The expedition sailed northward as far as the Gulf of Anadyr. From there they passed an island that Bering named St. Lawrence and entered the Bering Strait. But because it was then

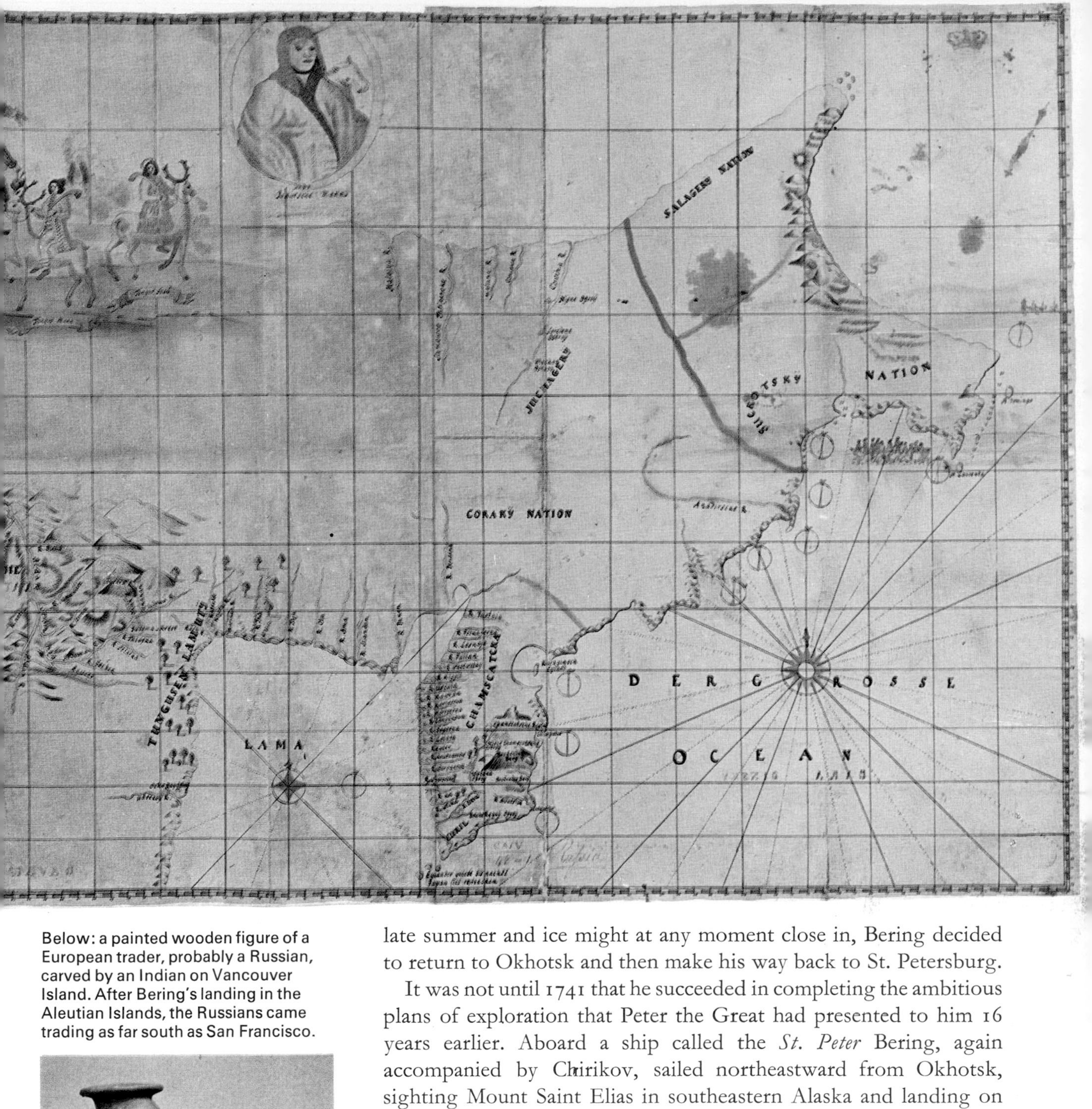

Below: a painted wooden figure of a European trader, probably a Russian, carved by an Indian on Vancouver Island. After Bering's landing in the Aleutian Islands, the Russians came trading as far south as San Francisco.

late summer and ice might at any moment close in, Bering decided to return to Okhotsk and then make his way back to St. Petersburg.

It was not until 1741 that he succeeded in completing the ambitious plans of exploration that Peter the Great had presented to him 16 years earlier. Aboard a ship called the *St. Peter* Bering, again accompanied by Chirikov, sailed northeastward from Okhotsk, sighting Mount Saint Elias in southeastern Alaska and landing on Kayak Island. Within a few years of Bering's landing on the American coast other Russians made contact with Alaskan Eskimos and were making trading voyages as far south as San Francisco.

During this same period, Englishmen were beginning to explore the Canadian interior and its coastline to the north. Yet it was not until the early 1800's that the golden age of Arctic exploration arrived. The British Navy took the lead in a general revival of interest in finding a Northwest Passage. What the British government hoped its navy would accomplish was the circumnavigation and exploration of the Arctic coast of Canada and the discovery of any new land to the north of North America.

This desire for more Arctic territories was in part due to Britain's fear of Russia's imperialistic interests in the Arctic. After Bering's landing on the Alaskan coast, Russian traders and hunters came to the region,and in 1784, established the first white settlement in Alaska on Kodiak Island. Then the Russians organized their own trading firm and this became the only governing power in Alaska.

So great was Britain's desire to counteract Russian operations in

Below: Sir John Ross, who commanded one of the naval squadrons that sailed north in 1818. He came to be called "Croker Mountain" Ross for the chain of mountains that he thought he saw just off Lancaster Sound, blocking his way to the west. He was mocked for lack of courage after his return. In 1829, Ross headed another expedition to find a Northwest Passage. It was during this voyage that his nephew, James Clark Ross located the North Magnetic Pole on Boothia Peninsula.

Left: Sir Edward Parry. At the time he was made commander of the new expedition in search of the Northwest Passage, he was only 29 years old. He was very ambitious, and had already won a fellowship to the Royal Society for his knowledge of hydrography, nautical astronomy, and magnetic research. He was also well known in the navy for his seamanship, navigation, and his sensitive leadership of men.

Below: the hand organ that Parry took along on all of his polar voyages. The organ helped to relieve the boredom of long months caught fast in the ice. The expedition members mounted amateur theatricals, and published their own regular weekly newspaper.

the Arctic that in 1818 Parliament offered a financial reward for the discovery of a Northwest Passage or for an attempt on the North Pole. By May of the same year a large Arctic expedition had been organized that involved two separate squadrons. One of these was to get as near to the North Pole as possible and the other was to sail up Davis Strait and search for an entrance to the Northwest Passage.

The man in charge of the latter squadron was Commander John Ross, and he had as his second-in-command a young officer who was to become an outstanding figure in Arctic exploration. This was Lieutenant Edward Parry. By the end of August, 1818, he and Ross had guided their two ships into Lanacaster Sound, which was considered to be the most likely route through to the northwest. The *Isabella* and the *Alexander* sailed westward through the sound for only a day when Ross suddenly gave the order to stop. Ahead of him he "distinctly saw land round the bottom of the bay forming a chain of mountains connected with those which extended along the north and south side." Parry and the other men on board could see nothing ahead but clear sea. So convinced was Ross that he saw mountains that he named them the Croker Mountains in honor of a secretary of the British Admiralty and gave the order for the *Isabella* and the *Alexander* to sail eastward to England.

When the expedition returned the story of Ross' Croker Mountains grew into a myth that many people considered had been nothing more than a convenient excuse for returning to safer waters. Gossip became so damaging to the navy's reputation that a second expedition was organized to settle the question of the Croker

Mountains in Lancaster Sound. This time Edward Parry was put in command. On May 11, the *Hecla* and the *Griper* left England.

This voyage, which was to last for over a year, was to be the greatest single forward stride made in the discovery of a Northwest Passage. Parry was to take the *Hecla* and the *Griper* into one of the most likely passages by which a seaway between the Atlantic and the Pacific could be established.

When the two ships reached Lancaster Sound, their crews listened for the reports from the men high up in the crow's-nests. Longitude 83° 12′ was reached with the shores of the sound miles apart and no Croker Mountains visible.

By the end of August, the *Hecla* and the *Griper* entered an even broader strait now known as Barrow Strait. They had a wide seaway to the west with room to maneuver between the large floes of ice. By early September, they had passed through Melville Sound and had crossed the meridian of 110° West from Greenwich England—a position in the Arctic Ocean that lies due north from the center of the state of Montana. All the men on board the *Hecla* and the *Griper* by having achieved this westward position became entitled to a reward of £5,000 (worth about $50,000 in today's money) under the Parliamentary Act of 1818. But there was little time for celebrations. Already Parry could see as he climbed to the crow's-nest of the *Hecla* an impenetrable barrier of ice stretching across their path. There was no sign of any open sea. The two ships anchored at a position slightly to the east of Cape Hearne. As they waited for the possibility that the ice might loosen up, the temperature continued to drop and the *Hecla* and the *Griper* were forced to put into a nearby bay to wait out the winter.

It was to be a long and dark one with 100 days of total darkness that began in the first week of November. However, in terms of good health and morale, it was to be a remarkable one. Parry made sure that the men had few idle moments for thoughts of home. A strict regime of work and exercise was established and in the evenings there was dancing and singing. Every two weeks a play was put on and every week the expedition's own newspaper—the *North Georgia Gazette and Winter Chronicle* was published.

In August 1821, Parry made one last attempt to take the *Hecla* and the *Griper* through the ice that had blocked their westward progress in the previous year. But the floes even in August were 50 feet thick and made impossible his plan to navigate the Northwest Passage. Parry was forced to return to England.

In 1824, however, Parry was back in the Arctic. This time he explored the waters to the south of Baffin Island and wintered over for two years. Still the ice defeated him.

The British for a while stopped thinking of reaching the Indies by way of a Northwest Passage. Instead, they started thinking of getting to the North Pole. Because he was the outstanding figure in Arctic exploration during this period, Edward Parry was the obvious man to make this first attempt on the pole.

Right: The Arctic Ocean, showing the routes of explorers who for almost 300 years tried to find a Northwest or a Northeast Passage to the Orient.

Line	Explorer	Route	Date
....	Willoughby & Chancellor	1	1553
	Willoughby	1A	1553–4
	Chancellor	1B	1553–4
— — —	Frobisher	2a	1576
		2b	1577
		2c	1578
....	Davis	3a	1585
		3b	1586
		3c	1587
———	Barents	4a	1594
	Barents	4A	1594
	Other members of expedition	4B	1594
	Barents (with Linschoten)	4b	1595
	Barents	4c	1596–7
	Expedition after death of Barents	4C	1597
— — —	Hudson	5a	1607
		5b	1608
		5c	1609
		5d	1610–1
———	Baffin (with Bylot)	6a	1615
		6b	1616
— — —	Bering	7a	1725–7
	Bering (with Chirikov)	7b	1728–9
	Bering (with Chirikov)	7c	1740–1
	Chirikov (after death of Bering)	7C	1741–2
....	Ross, John (with Parry & Ross, James C.)	8a	1818
	Buchan (with Franklin)	8b	1818
	Ross, John	8c	1829–33
———	Parry (with Ross, James C.)	9a	1819–20
		9b	1821–3
		9c	1824–5
		9d	1827

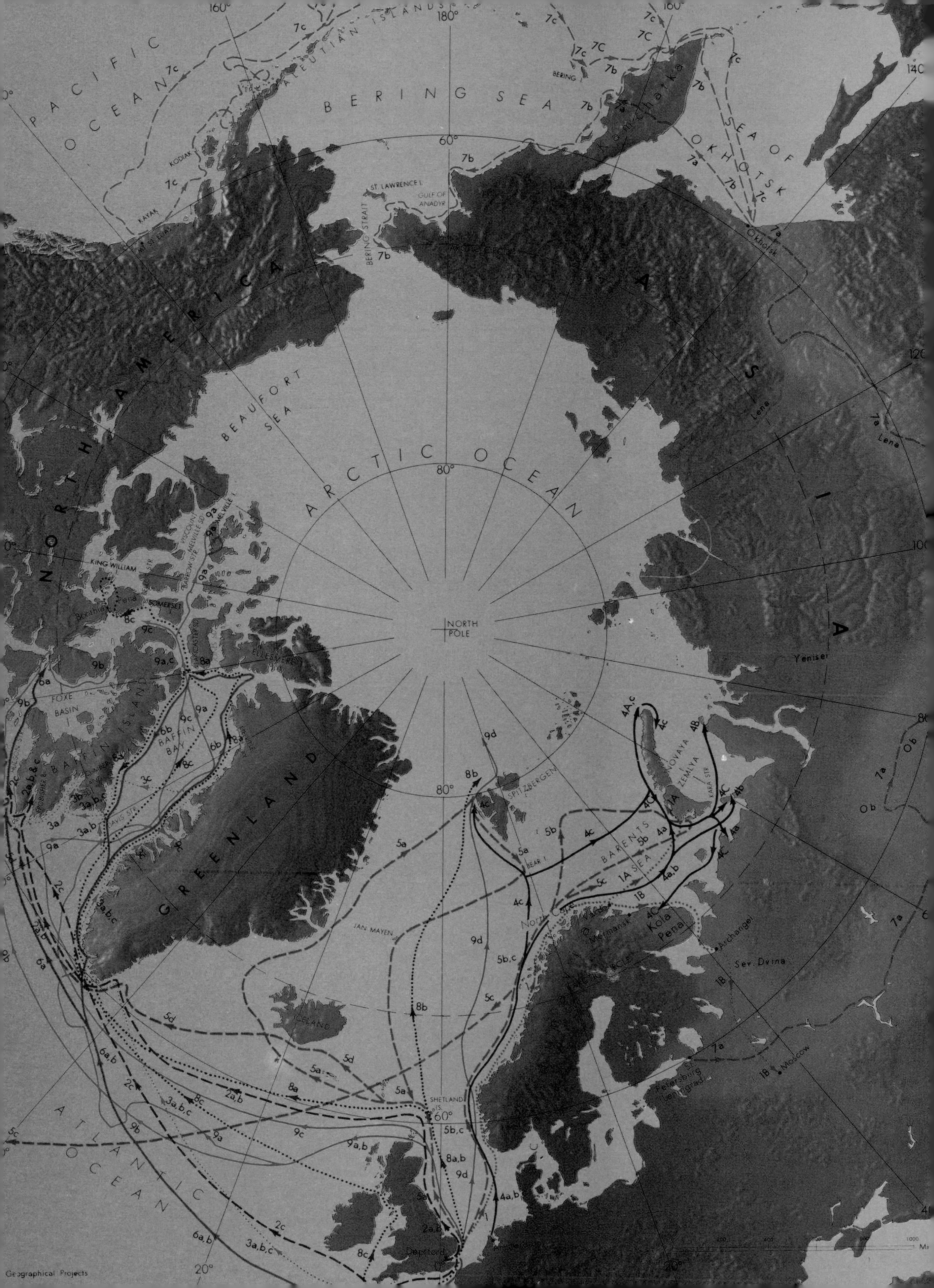

PACIFIC OCEAN
ALEUTIAN ISLANDS
BERING SEA
SEA OF OKHOTSK
Kamchatka
NORTH AMERICA
ASIA
ARCTIC OCEAN
BEAUFORT SEA
NORTH POLE
GREENLAND
BAFFIN ISLAND
BAFFIN BAY
FOXE BASIN
ELLESMERE
SPITZBERGEN
NOVAYA ZEMLYA
BARENTS SEA
JAN MAYEN
ICELAND
SHETLAND IS.
ATLANTIC OCEAN
North Cape
Murmansk
Kola Pena.
Archangel
Sev. Dvina
Moscow
Leningrad
Okhotsk
Lena
Yenisei
Ob
Deptford
KODIAK
KAYAK
ST. LAWRENCE I.
GULF OF ANADYR
BERING STRAIT
KING WILLIAM
SOMERSET
BEAR I.
KARA STR.
Geographical Projects

With an expedition of 28 men he sailed north to Spitzbergen in the late spring of 1827. From Trurenberg Bay in Spitzbergen he and his party proceeded over the ice. They took with them two boats shod along their keels with strips of iron. Whenever they had to cross ice the boats were dragged by the sturdiest men who accompanied Parry. When they came to open water the boats were launched and used as boats again.

In this way Parry and his men pushed on toward the pole until the end of July when they had reached latitude 82° 45′ N.—within

500 miles of the North Pole. At this point they were forced to turn back, but the record position they had achieved was to remain unbeaten for the next 48 years.

The year after this polar journey one more attempt was made to find a Northwest Passage. "Croker Mountain" Ross was in command of this expedition and he had with him as his second-in-command his nephew, James Clark Ross, a very talented commander who had made a number of previous Arctic journeys. Although the expedition ran into difficulties from the beginning because of the steam-powered engine used to propel the *Victory*, Ross managed to get the expedition to the east coast of Somerset Island. From here he turned south, sailing past Bellot Strait where he began to run into thick ice. As winter approached he was forced to make a landfall on the east coast of the Boothia Peninsula, where the *Victory* was to remain stuck for three winters. During the enforced stay James Clark Ross made good use of his time. He studied the dress and sledging techniques of the Eskimos who had a settlement near the *Victory*,

Above left: a watercolor by Sir John Ross showing two Eskimos, Ikmalik and Apelaglui, sketching the coast of King William Island while sitting on board the *Victory* when it was caught in the ice. This was painted during Ross' second voyage searching for the Northwest Passage, from 1829 to 1833.

Above: James Clark Ross on the ice, shooting musk ox, in a watercolor by his uncle, Sir John Ross, during their stay on the *Victory* in the Arctic. Both uncle and nephew spent a lot of time with the Eskimos. James Clark Ross used their sledging techniques to reach the North Magnetic Pole.

and with them he made long sledging journeys across the ice to King William Island. The younger Ross was also very interested in the study of magnetism and was eager to find the North Magnetic Pole. This he knew to be a mysterious spot in the Northern Hemisphere toward which the north-seeking compass needle points. The spot at that time lay somewhere in the region where the *Victory* was stuck. On May 31, 1831, James Clark Ross located the exact position of the North Magnetic Pole on Boothia Peninsula.

Eventually, after three winters had passed, the men on board the *Victory* were forced to abandon it and make their way by the ship's boats to Lancaster Sound. Here they were lucky enough to be picked up by a whaling ship and returned with it to England.

A Northwest Passage to Cathay had yet to be discovered. The dream of explorers for four centuries was to remain undiscovered until the summer of 1906. Nevertheless the idea of successfully traversing the northern route between the Atlantic and the Pacific was to continue to attract explorers during the intervening years.

Above: a Wedgwood portrait medallion of Captain James Cook, one of many such medallions of contemporary famous people made by the firm of Josiah Wedgwood. Cook's superb navigational abilities—as well as his gifts of leadership—were appreciated by the authorities, and he was the obvious choice to make the voyage in search of the Southern Continent.

The Great Southland 3

Even as late as the 1770's the idea of an unknown southern land—Terra Australis Incognita—still persisted. Somewhere below the bottom of Africa and the terrifying waters of Cape Horn there was a rich land, and the British government wanted to be the first to find it. In 1772 they commissioned Captain James Cook to begin the second of his famous voyages into the South Pacific—this time to solve the riddle of the great Southern Continent. He was given two ships, the *Resolution* and the *Adventure*, and in mid-July, 1772, they sailed from Plymouth, England. Because the two ships kept getting separated during the three-year voyage, most of what we know about the expedition concerns the *Resolution,* which Cook commanded.

Above: Cook's ships, the *Resolution* and the *Adventure,* collecting water by taking on ice at 61 degrees south. The watercolor is by W. Hodges, who was on Cook's voyages of 1773.

After passing south through the Atlantic and turning east around the Cape of Good Hope, Cook kept the ships as far south as the drifting ice permitted. On January 17, 1773, both of them crossed the Antarctic Circle, an imaginary circle of the earth parallel to the equator and forming the border of Antarctica. The men in Cook's expedition became the first to cross into the southern polar region—one of only a few genuine "firsts" in modern exploration. For after all, Stone Age men had preceded the explorers who first landed on places such as Iceland, Greenland, North America, Australia, and Easter Island.

The *Adventure* and the *Resolution* continued sailing south from the Antarctic Circle for a few hours but the seemingly endless

Above: a watercolor of a penguin by George Forster, a naturalist who accompanied Captain Cook on the 1773 journey when they were the first to cross the Antarctic Circle, although they did not sight Antarctica.

pack ice that stretched out before them forced Cook to turn northward and then to the east.

During the Antarctic "summers" of the two succeeding years the *Resolution* crossed the Antarctic Circle again and unknowingly got to within only 150 miles of the Antarctic shore. By the spring of 1775, when he rounded Cape Horn and headed for England, James Cook had sailed completely around the continent without sighting land. In his journal Cook made a forbidding prediction about Antarctica: "The risk one runs in exploring a coast in these unknown and icy seas is so very great that I can be bold enough to say that no man will ever venture farther than I have done, and that the lands which may lie to the south will never be explored."

James Cook's gloomy conclusions about Antarctic exploration were soon ignored by American and British seal and whale hunters. During the years between 1800 and 1820, they sighted many islands and parts of the Antarctic Peninsula as they pushed into Antarctic waters, testing tides and currents and ice conditions, always com-

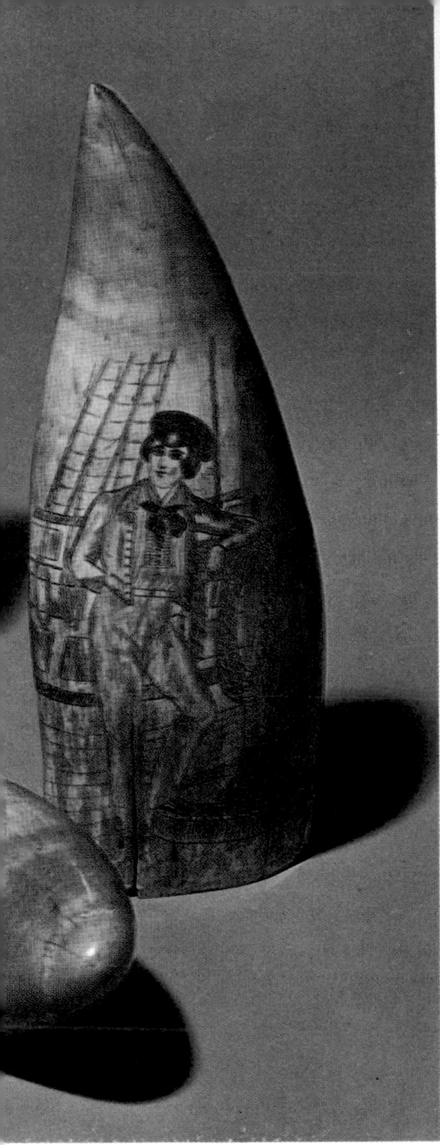

Above: decorated whales' teeth, one of the spare-time handicrafts, called scrimshaw, that occupied the sailors during the long whaling expeditions to the Arctic Circle. A jackknife was used to carve the outline, and the finest etching was done with a heavy sailcloth needle, the pickwick.

peting with each other to find new regions to fish and fresh breeding places for seals.

One of these men, Nathaniel B. Palmer of Stonington, Connecticut, discovered what is now called Deception Island (one of the South Shetland Islands) as he looked for new seal-hunting grounds. Then one day from the slopes of a mountain on Deception he saw another island (Trinity Island) and possibly also the Antarctic Peninsula. After he reported what he had seen, Palmer was commissioned by the captain of his seal-hunting fleet to explore in the direction of the distant island. Palmer, who may have been the first man to sight the mainland of Antarctica, found in his explorations "an extensive mountain country, more sterile and dismal if possible, and more heavily laden with ice and snow than the South Shetlands. There were sea-leopards on its shore but no fur seals. The main part of its coast was ice bound, although it was midsummer in this hemisphere, and a landing consequently difficult."

While on his way back to the South Shetland Islands to meet up again with the American sealing fleet, Palmer's ship, the *Hero,* became enveloped in a thick fog. Rather than risk a collision with an iceberg Palmer decided to anchor for the night. When he came on deck to stand watch and struck the ship's bell to toll the time, he heard through the fog the sound of an echoing bell. Half an hour later, the same thing happened again—Palmer struck two bells and heard the reply of two bells. Each half hour for the rest of the night came the ghostly echo.

Finally, in the morning, when the fog lifted, the men on board the *Hero* were amazed to see that their tiny sloop lay between two other sloops. When the American flag was hoisted, the other ships each hoisted an Imperial Russian flag.

Then a Russian sloop sent its boat to the *Hero* and invited Palmer aboard. He learned that the ships had been sent by the Russian czar to make a round-the-world voyage under the command of Captain Fabian von Bellingshausen. It is not clear from the records just how Palmer and Bellingshausen managed to converse, but presumably the Russians had an English-speaking person with them, or perhaps a few of the Russians could speak some English. On their way from Kronshtadt, on the Gulf of Finland, to the Antarctic Circle they had spent a month in England while they waited for charts and navigating instruments that were being prepared for them in London. They must have understood some English because during their stay they went sightseeing in London and even went to the theater.

The Russian expedition had sailed almost entirely around Antarctica, always within sight of the ice pack. Late in January, 1821, before his meeting with Palmer, Bellingshausen had discovered a small island in the Bellinghausen Sea and named it Peter I Island. At the end of January the *Vostok* and the *Mirnyi* sailing eastward had sighted land again and named it Alexander I Land after the czar. "I call this discovery 'land'," he wrote to the czar, "because its

Above: U.S. sealer Nathaniel B. Palmer, discoverer of Deception Island.
Below: James Weddell, who went 214 nautical miles farther south than Cook, searching for new sealing grounds. He found what is now called the Weddell Sea. Although his ship was fitted only for sealing, Weddell did what he could to make careful scientific observations, taking readings of the temperature of the water and observing the currents.

southern extent disappeared beyond the range of our vision." Later explorers were to find that what Bellingshausen had seen was really a large island separated from the mainland of Antarctica by a narrow strait 200 miles long.

During the next 15 years, the waters around the newly discovered continent were the scene of continued activity by the sealers. Another American seal-hunter, Captain John Davis of New Haven, may have been the first to actually set foot on Antarctica on February 7, 1821. After leaving Deception Island he found land to the south. Davis anchored his ship in Hughes Bay. The land, Davis noted in his log, was "high and covered entirely with snow." A party went ashore but found no seals. When he left, Davis wrote, "I think this Southern Land to be a Continent."

In the same year a British sealer named James Weddell sailed his two ships, the brig *Jane* and the smaller ship *Beaufoy*, to the South Orkney Islands and then turned south to look for new sealing lands. The two ships made their way through one of the most dangerous of Antarctic seas—made so by the great pressure of the circulating ice within it—until they reached the latitude 74° 15′ S.

Because the seal-hunting season was almost over and winter was just about to set in, Weddell decided to turn northward again. In order to cheer up his crew, who were disappointed that they had found no seals that in turn would pay their wages, Weddell made

Left: Palmer's little sloop between two big Russian sloops of war. Caught in the fog, Palmer had anchored, and when the fog lifted was astonished to find himself in between the two ships of Captain Bellingshausen.

Below: the Russian Captain Fabian von Bellingshausen, who commanded an Antarctic expedition to 70° S. latitude.

a little ceremony. The Union Jack was hoisted aboard both ships and the cannon were fired in honor of the men who had accompanied Weddell to the farthest south point so far attained—214 nautical miles nearer to the South Pole than Captain Cook had reached.

In the years between 1830 and 1850 exploration in both the Arctic and Antarctic became involved with the phenomenon of the earth's magnetism. This was the beginning of the era of larger and faster steamships that needed to be navigated by more precise compasses, which in turn involved a better understanding of magnetism. For centuries sailors and explorers had been aware of the north and south magnetic poles. A piece of magnetite hanging from a string would turn until it was pointing north and south, thus enabling sailors to tell in which direction they were sailing, even in a storm when they could not see the stars.

The earth has north and south magnetic poles in addition to its north and south geographic poles. But the magnetic and geographic poles are not located at the same places. The North Magnetic Pole that James Clark Ross located in 1831 was on the Boothia Peninsula in northern Canada, and about 1,000 miles from the North Geographic Pole.

It was predicted in the 1830's that the South Magnetic Pole would be discovered in the region of latitude 66°S. and longitude 146°E. Within a few years three expeditions were organized to find its exact location. Britain put James Clark Ross in charge of theirs, King Louis Philippe of France commissioned Dumont d'Urville to go to Antarctica for "the glory of France." The youthful United States made its first venture into large-scale exploration by dispatching Lieutenant Charles Wilkes and a squadron of ships to investigate the Antarctic.

D'Urville of France was the first to get away. He had been planning an expedition to the South Pacific, but when the king heard about Britain's plans he sent word to d'Urville saying that he must explore the Antarctic region. Because d'Urville was mainly inter-

Above: the French ships, the *Astrolabe* and the *Zelee*, in the dreaded storm belt between the latitudes of 50 and 60 degrees south. When the visibility was poor because of fog or snowstorms, the ships maintained contact by firing a gun every half hour or ringing bells. Left: Jules Dumont d'Urville, the commander of the French expedition in search of the South Magnetic Pole. A naval officer, he was a linguist, explorer, and ethnologist as well, who in the course of a varied career had rescued the Venus de Milo for posterity.

ested in studying the people who live on the Pacific Islands, he was not enthusiastic about the royal command.

Nevertheless, with two ships, the *Astrolabe* and the *Zelee,* the Frenchman set out in September, 1837. Since d'Urville's original plan had been to explore the tropics the vessels were not properly designed or outfitted for a voyage to Antarctica. As the *Astrolabe* and the *Zelee* pushed on through the southern ocean, their wide gunports admitted cascades of icy water into the holds. By January, 1838, however, they had reached the Weddell Sea and were making their way southward in an attempt to beat Weddell's record.

They got only as far as 63° 39′ S. when the pack ice closed in around them. For two frustrating months d'Urville's ships skirted the ice in an attempt to find a clear route, but they managed only to hover along the edge of the ice. Finally, they turned northward to spend the rest of the Antarctic summer of 1838 exploring the Graham Land tip of the Palmer Peninsula. Then for the remaining months of that year and for most of the following one d'Urville cruised the South Pacific.

On January 1, 1840, he turned his ships toward the Antarctic again, this time sailing south from Hobart, Tasmania. On January 19, Dumont d'Urville sighted land—a panorama of ice and snow fronted by towering ice cliffs that stretched far to the east and west, broken occasionally by deep recesses where the icebergs that littered the sea had fallen away. This he named Adelie Land after

Above: an engraving after a sketch by the expedition artist Louis Le Breton (who was also the ship's surgeon). It shows part of d'Urville's crew landing on the frozen shores of Adelie Land.

Right: the crewmen of the *Astrolabe* celebrating the discovery of Adelie Land. Dumont d'Urville wrote that the men "summoned *Father Antarctic* on deck. They presented all kinds of quaint scenes; there was a masked procession, a sermon, and a banquet, It all ended with dancing and a song."

his wife and dispatched a boat to explore France's Antarctic possession. Once they had got to the cliff, however, the Frenchmen found it too steep and icy for a landing. But they did manage to unfurl the French flag on a small rocky islet very near Adelie Land—to a chorus of squawks from a group of penguins—called Adélie penguins by d'Urville.

The South Magnetic Pole lay farther to the east and the spinning compass needle indicated that it could not be far away. While the *Astrolabe* and the *Zelee* were heading in the direction of the pole, they were involved in another of those chance encounters that seem to defy all odds. By 1841, the British and American expeditions to the South Magnetic Pole had got underway. Yet what were the chances of two of these expeditions meeting along the 13,800-mile coastline of the Antarctic? On January 29, the *Astrolabe* and the *Zelee* were wallowing through a heavy fog. Suddenly, the lookout spotted a man-of-war flying the Stars and Stripes bearing down upon them. It was the *Porpoise,* one of Lieutenant Wilkes' fleet that had been commissioned by the United States Navy.

Above: the *Astrolabe* leaving the icy polar sea. By this time the ship had been away from home for almost three years. Although d'Urville had been unable to go farther than Weddell, he had claimed Adelie Land for France.

D'Urville immediately ordered the sails raised so that he could meet the Americans. But the captain of the *Porpoise* misunderstood this maneuver. He thought that the French ships were trying to keep their exploration a secret by sailing away, so he gave orders for the *Porpoise* to make its way through the fog.

Shortly after this encounter d'Urville reached another icy coast that seemed to extend indefinitely and prevent further movement south. The men aboard the *Astrolabe* and *Zelee* had been away from home for almost three years, and must have welcomed the order to turn the ships away from the icy cliffs and head for France. Even though more than a century was to pass before another French expedition entered Antarctica, d'Urville's discoveries there did result in France's claim to the thin wedge of territory that extends from the coast of Adelie Land to the South Pole.

When Dumont d'Urville returned to France he claimed that he had first sighted the Antarctic on January 18. Lieutenant Wilkes was later to make the statement that he had been the first to find land in the same region of Antarctica—on January 19. Wilkes, it turned out, had been first after all. For d'Urville had crossed the International Date Line in his voyage but had failed to advance the date in his log. So land had been seen on the 19th by both explorers, but Wilkes had seen it first. According to his log, the young American lieutenant had sighted the continent some 10 hours before Dumont d'Urville.

The United States expedition commanded by Charles Wilkes had

Above: Charles Wilkes, the commander of the United States expedition that left in 1838. The expedition had been organized amid great rivalry and much argument, and the choice of Wilkes as the commander was very controversial

Right: a painting from an original sketch by Charles Wilkes after he had landed on Antarctica in 1840. The men did not have the proper clothing needed to withstand the extreme cold they encountered. Wilkes complained that "Although purchased by the Government at great expense, it was found to be entirely unworthy of service, and inferior in every way to the samples."

sailed from Hampton Roads, Virginia in August, 1838. It was the most ill-prepared and probably the unhappiest expedition that ever sailed to Antarctica. The ships selected were unsuitable and Wilkes proved to be an impetuous and over strict commander.

None of the ships was fortified against the ice and heavy weather and the large square gunports were left wide open for the surge of icy southern seas. There were three warships in the expedition—the *Vincennes,* the *Peacock,* and the *Porpoise*—together with two smaller ships, which served as tenders to the larger ones, and a supply ship, which proved to be so slow that it was sent home early in the expedition.

Six months after leaving Virginia the expedition assembled itself for the first push into the Antarctic at Orange Harbor, Nassau Bay in the south of Tierra del Fuego. The *Porpoise*, with Wilkes aboard, and one of the tenders made for the Weddell Sea, which proved to be much icier than it had been at the time of Weddell's voyage. At the same time the *Peacock* and another of the tenders, the *Flying Fish*, went westward in hopes of getting as far as Captain Cook's 105°W. By riding above the ice and slipping through narrow leads the *Flying Fish* only just failed to reach 71° 10'S., which had been Cook's most southerly point.

Then in May, 1839, when winter had come to the Antarctic, the United States expedition made its way into the warmer waters of the Pacific Ocean. It was to be seven months before the ships were able to go south again. When they again entered the Antarctic

Above: Sir James Clark Ross. He was experienced in arctic conditions, and had two ideal ships to cope with the ice. It was his ambition to match his discovery of the North Magnetic Pole by claiming the southern one as well.

region early in 1840, the men on board got their first glimpse of land when they sighted one of the Balleny Islands, which of course had already been claimed by the British sealer John Balleny.

The *Peacock* and the *Vincennes* then went westward, following the coast of a belt of packed ice. Along the way the *Peacock* was wrecked and broken up by a collision with an iceberg, so the westward push that Wilkes was so keen to accomplish was made by the *Vincennes* and the *Porpoise.* He was convinced that if he could penetrate the ice belt that lay to the south he would reach land. At the end of January he saw his chance to take the ships safely between the massive islands of ice into a bay. This bay, which he calculated to be 140° 30′ E. and in latitude 66° 45′ S., was backed up by land rising to the south, and stretching east and west for 60 miles (probably in the vicinity of Adelie Land). Here Wilkes confidently announced the existence of the Antarctic continent, and called the bay they had sailed into Piner's Bay, after one of his crewmen. It was during this period that the *Porpoise,* sailing independently of the *Vincennes,* met Dumont d'Urville's ships.

For most of the time they cruised along the Antarctic continent the men on board the *Vincennes* were in great discomfort. Every rope and every inch of deck was thickly encrusted with ice and the hold of the ship was too small to accommodate the men properly. Moreover, the clothing issued to them was absurdly inadequate for polar weather. It is not surprising that the crewmen shown in the illustrations of the journey look white and chilled and scantily dressed for the occasion.

By mid-February, 1840, the *Vincennes* encountered a vast peninsula of ice that jutted out into the sea and blocked any further progress. Wilkes had nevertheless managed to get west of Sabrina Land to longitude 97° 37′ E., even though he had now to give up his idea of getting as far west as Enderby Land. The *Vincennes* turned northeast again with the *Porpoise* trailing it. In his journal Wilkes remarked, "I have seldom seen so many happy faces or such rejoicing as the announcement of my intention to return produced." By mid-March, Wilkes was in Sydney Harbour, Australia, having completed a remarkable voyage despite the frailty of the ships and the poor food and the flimsy clothing that had been supplied for the expedition. Wilkes and his men had traveled along 1,500 miles of Antarctic coast, by far the most important cruise to the south polar region yet undertaken.

Even though the idea of searching for the South Magnetic Pole had begun in England, it was not until 1839 that the government voted the necessary funds. James Clark Ross was put in charge of the expedition and given two ships from the Royal Navy, the *Erebus* and the *Terror.* Both were small, slow, and clumsy and, unlike Wilkes' ships, they were perfect for making their way through the ice. They had sturdy hulls, watertight bulkheads to prevent flooding in case of a collision with an iceberg, and decks of double thickness. Warm clothes were issued to the men. Canned meats and

Right: the *Terror* taking on water during the expedition led by James Clark Ross, in a watercolor by I. E. Davis. The men are cutting into the icecap, which will then be melted.

Right: taking possession of Possession Island in 1841. A landing had to be made to make a proper claim to the land for the British sovereign, but the coast of the mainland was inaccessible because of ice. They therefore made the landing on a little rocky islet.

Above: the Ross Ice Shelf. The shelf is in constant movement, going toward the sea at a rate of about five feet a day. There the tides make large pieces break off at the edge, especially at the end of the Antarctic summer.

vegetables, which were relative innovations at that time, were put in the holds. The staple diet of the sailors on such a voyage was dried meat and dried biscuits, so the addition of properly preserved canned food would provide a welcome variety for the long voyage to the Antarctic.

In September, 1839, the *Erebus* and the *Terror* sailed from the River Thames out into the English Channel and began the first leg of their journey to Australia. This was to take the expedition 11 months to accomplish, and the ships docked at Hobart, Tasmania, in August, 1840.

While they were being refitted and made ready for the Antarctic, Ross received word from London that both d'Urville and Wilkes had been cruising in the region where he was planning to search for the South Magnetic Pole. Angry at the "embarrassing situation" that the two explorers had placed him in, he decided to explore the coast to the east of where the others had investigated.

On November 12, 1840, the *Erebus* and the *Terror* left for Antarctica and in less than two months they were in the great belt of floating icebergs that had almost destroyed Wilkes' ships. The two sturdy ships slowly battered their way through the pack until January 9, when they finally broke out of the crushing pack ice. Ahead of them lay open sea with no land in sight. They were free to continue sailing on toward Antarctica. Ross ordered a course of due south, confident that the South Magnetic Pole was within reach.

Then land was sighted far ahead of the ships. Towering peaks rose for thousands of feet above the sea. The men on board the *Erebus* and the *Terror* saw mountains, "perfectly covered with eternal snow, which rose to elevations varying from seven- to ten-thousand feet above the level of the ocean. The glaciers that filled their intervening valleys, and which descended from the mountains' summits, projected in many places several miles into the sea."

By January 12, Ross was only a few miles off the mainland that he called Victoria Land in honor of Queen Victoria. He and his second-in-command, Francis Crozier, landed on a small island and named it Possession Island. Then continuing on, the *Erebus* and the

Right: Antarctica, showing the routes of the explorers who, in the years between1772 and 1843, succeeded in establishing the approximate size and position of Antarctica.

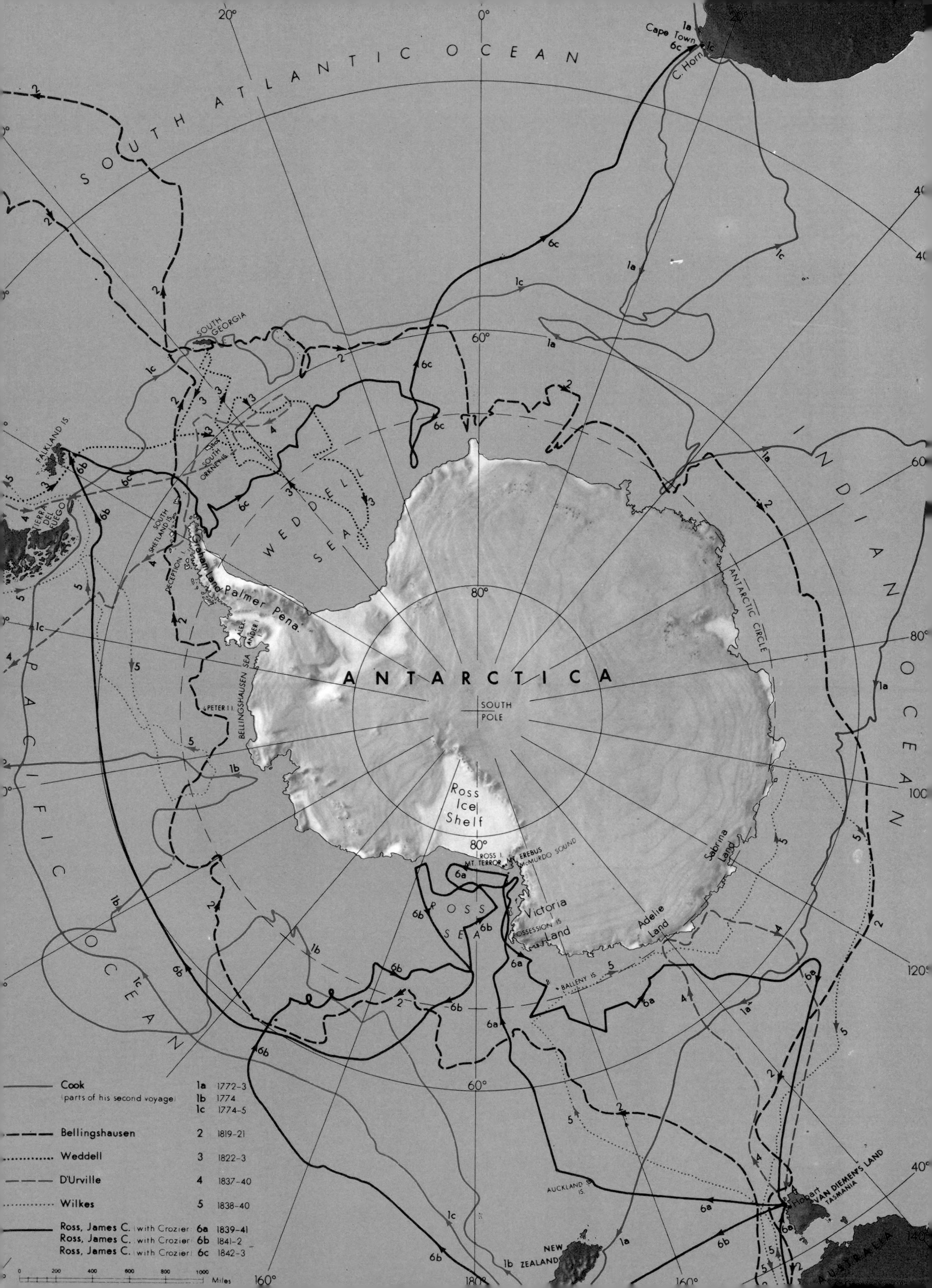
SOUTH ATLANTIC OCEAN
INDIAN OCEAN
PACIFIC OCEAN
ANTARCTICA
SOUTH POLE
WEDDELL SEA
ROSS SEA
BELLINGSHAUSEN SEA
Ross Ice Shelf
Graham Land
Palmer Pena.
ALEXANDER I.
PETER I I.
Victoria Land
Adelie Land
Sabrina Land
ANTARCTIC CIRCLE
ROSS I.
MT. EREBUS
MT. TERROR
McMURDO SOUND
POSSESSION IS.
BALLENY IS.
SOUTH GEORGIA
SOUTH ORKNEY IS.
SOUTH SHETLAND IS.
DECEPTION I.
FALKLAND IS.
TIERRA DEL FUEGO
Cape Town
C. Horn
Hobart
VAN DIEMEN'S LAND
TASMANIA
AUSTRALIA
NEW ZEALAND
AUCKLAND IS.
Cook (parts of his second voyage) 1a 1772–3
1b 1774
1c 1774–5
Bellingshausen 2 1819–21
Weddell 3 1822–3
D'Urville 4 1837–40
Wilkes 5 1838–40
Ross, James C. (with Crozier) 6a 1839–41
Ross, James C. (with Crozier) 6b 1841–2
Ross, James C. (with Crozier) 6c 1842–3
Miles 0 200 400 600 800 1000

Terror reached the southerly position of 74° 20′, thus beating the record Weddell had set a quarter of the way around on the other side of the continent. Open water still stretched ahead of them.

Early on the morning of January 28, another island capped with mountains was sighted. Coming closer, the men on board the two ships stared in disbelief at what they saw in this frigid land of ice and snow. Before them was an active volcano that gave off a stream of black smoke and spurts of flame. Ross named the steaming volcano Mount Erebus. An inactive volcano nearby was named Mount Terror.

Ross sailed along the northern edge of the island, still hoping to find a path toward the elusive South Magnetic Pole. Instead he came upon a sight even more spectacular than the volcano. Eastward from the island Ross saw a low, white line that stretched as far as the eye could see. "It presented an extraordinary appearance, gradually increasing in height as we got nearer to it, and proving to be a perpendicular cliff of ice between 150 and 200 feet above the level of the sea, perfectly flat and level at the top and without any fissures or promontories on its seaward face." Ross had discovered what is now called the Ross Ice Shelf—a vast slab of floating ice 600 to 1,000 feet thick that forms an almost impenetrable barrier to the interior of Antarctica.

From what he could see, Ross concluded that there could be no further progress toward the south and wrote in his log book, "We might with equal chance of success try to sail through the cliffs of Dover." So he decided to sail eastward, hoping to find a channel somewhere along the ice cliff. But by February 5, ice made further movement impossible, and the ships had to turn back toward Victoria Land. At McMurdo Sound, named for one of his officers, Ross gave up completely the idea of finding a way to the South Magnetic Pole. The *Erebus* and the *Terror* turned northward toward Tasmania.

In November, 1841, the British expedition explored almost the entire length of the ice shelf, and by the end of February, 1842, had reached 78° 10′ south latitude, a record that was to stand for the next 60 years. But again the onset of another Antarctic winter forced them to withdraw before they had definitely established its eastern limits.

In November, 1842, Ross received permission from the British government to spend a third and final year in the Antarctic. His ambition this time was to combine a survey of the east coast of Graham Land with an attempt to achieve a record southerly position in the Weddell Sea. But he had not reckoned with the unaccountable changes in Antarctic weather or the position of the ice. The weather that season was one of constant gales, fogs, and snowstorms. At night the men had to keep themselves half awake, listening for the lookout's cry of "berg ahead" followed by the command "all hands on deck." Commander Crozier of the *Terror* never spent a night in his bed throughout that winter, preferring to take short naps in a

Above: the *Erebus* and the *Terror* caught in a storm. For Ross' expedition the weather could not have been worse. The two ships were in almost constant gales and storms. It was fortunate that they were almost perfectly suited for exploration in the polar waters.

chair or to be out on deck. James Weddell in his unprotected sealer had reached 74° 15′ S. in 1823. A little south of 70° was all that could be achieved by the sturdy *Erebus* and *Terror*, which had in the previous year thrust their way through to the Ross Ice Shelf. When his ships were stopped by the ice Ross gave up his ambitions in the Weddell Sea and returned to England.

After a lapse of about 50 years the British resumed their explorations in Antarctica and it was the Ross Sea sector that was chosen as starting point for British inland explorations of the continent. Because this region provided the most accessible and the shortest route to the heart of the continent, Britain's tragic race for the South Pole was to begin in the Ross Sea.

Above: the Cross of the Guelphic Order of Hanover, Franklin's medal that was found in 1848 in the hands of the Eskimos—the first real evidence of the fate of the expedition that had set out to find the Northwest Passage.

The Search for Sir John Franklin

4

On May 19, 1845, the British explorer Sir John Franklin sailed from England with an expedition to search for the legendary Northwest Passage. His ships were the *Erebus* and the *Terror,* which had proved to be so seaworthy on James Clark Ross' expedition to the South Magnetic Pole. They were well stocked with provisions for a three-year journey to the icy wastes of the Arctic and back again. By the summer of 1847 nothing had been heard about the progress of Franklin and his men. Although everyone knew that there were still enough provisions on board, there was already a feeling of anxiety about the complete silence from the *Erebus* and the *Terror*.

The Hudson's Bay Company sent word to the Eskimos who roamed the Arctic to be on the lookout for the men from the expedition. The British government went so far as to offer a reward of £20,000 (worth about $300,000 in today's money) to any man of any nationality who rescued the missing men in Franklin's party.

The chill winter of 1847–1848 descended on Britain and with it still no news of Franklin—not a clue, not a word. Now the anxiety that had stimulated discussions in pubs and at garden parties the summer

CAPT: SIR JOHN FRANKLIN.

COM^DR FITZJAMES.

LIEUT: GRAHAM GORE.

H.D.S. GOODSIR (ASST: SURGEON)

C. OSMER. (PURSER)

H.F. COLLINS (ICEMASTER)

Above: some of the officers of the *Erebus,* which sailed from England on May 19, 1845, and was never heard from again. Franklin is in the middle of the upper row, wearing the medal shown opposite.

before grew into a wave of concern. Inactivity fed the growing fear that all was not well with Franklin and his crew. Something had to be done and soon.

What route had Franklin taken? How might ice, wind, and storms have affected his course? Such questions had to be answered before a rescue mission could be organized and dispatched to the network of straits, bays, channels, and gulfs that made a forbidding maze of the yet-to-be-discovered Northwest Passage. But for every possible route suggested an alternative was proposed. Finally, the British government decided to send a massive rescue expedition.

Two ships would probe the Northwest Passage from the Bering Strait, while an overland expedition would trek northward from Canada. At the same time James Clark Ross would lead a third group that would approach the area from the east by sea. The Bering Strait expedition occupied themselves in exploring the waters north and west of the strait. The overland group, however, was forced to give up the Franklin search because of ice and storms.

James Clark Ross and his expedition got to the northeast end of

Above: the Arctic Council, the group set up to determine the fate of the Franklin expedition, planning the search in a painting by S. Pearce. James Clark Ross is the fourth from the left. On the wall behind them are portraits of Franklin and Sir John Barrow, who backed the expedition. Below: Lady Franklin, who became a popular heroine for her determination to continue the search for her husband.

Somerset Island where they spent the winter of 1848–1849. Traveling by foot and man-hauling their sledges they trekked 200 miles over Somerset Island hunting for signs of Franklin and his men. But it was to no avail and in 1849, when Ross returned to England, no more had been learned about the fate of the *Erebus* and the *Terror*.

Four years had now passed since Franklin had said goodbye to his wife Jane, and though almost all who searched for clues to the mysterious disappearance of Franklin and his men would eventually give up the quest, she continued to feel that somehow someone would eventually find her husband.

The following year more men and ships joined in the search for Franklin. Fifteen vessels and hundreds of men fanned out across ice, land, and water. The complicated maneuvers of the various search expeditions added to the details of Arctic geography and to the development of techniques of polar exploration. But they made no real advances in the evolution of polar exploration.

One of the search parties under the command of Captain Horatio Austin threaded its way through ice flows in Barrow Strait. Austin's small fleet, consisting of nine ships, came upon a barren, rocky bit of land called Beechey Island. Landing parties were sent ashore, although it was hard to believe that anyone would have chosen this forbidding place to camp. One of the parties was led by an American, Lieutenant E. J. De Haven, who commanded two small United States Navy brigs that had joined Austin's squadron. As De Haven scanned the bleak landscape, he saw an unusual object among the unpatterned rubble of rock and earth that formed the island. When he got nearer this obviously man-made feature, he saw that it consisted of a forge, the remains of a shooting gallery, and a storehouse. In the storehouse there were hundreds of cans of meat, stacked neatly in rows, coils of rope were piled up, empty bottles were scattered about. Was this all that remained of the Franklin expedition? Nearby, De Haven and his party found three tombstones. On one was roughly carved the name of John Torrinton, who had been the leading stoker of the *Terror*. The other two stones bore the names of two men from the *Erebus*. But what had become of the other missing men?

In 1853, Dr. John Rae, a Hudson's Bay Company official, set out on foot from northern Canada in search of the answer to this question. Slowly working his way northward, Rae and his companions reached Pelly Bay early in April, 1854. Pelly Bay leads out into the Gulf of Boothia, a body of frigid water that separates Baffin Island on the east from the Boothia Peninsula. From this Arctic area, Eskimos take their sledges over the ice to hunt for food.

When Dr. Rae encountered some of these Eskimos, he talked with them and learned that they had heard, from some other Eskimos, about a group of 40 white men seen several years before as they trudged south about 150 miles west of where Dr. Rae was. The strangers were hauling sledges and a small boat and talked about the

Below: among the many ships searching for Franklin was H.M.S. *Investigator,* here caught in the ice. The captain, Robert McLure, continued eastward by sledge after his ship was frozen into Prince of Wales Strait in 1850. He reached Melville Sound, which earlier explorers had reached coming from the east, and thus discovered the first of what later turned out to be several northwest passages to the Pacific Ocean.

Above: the sledge teams that were landed on Beechey Island from Austin's ships used kites to keep in touch with one another, and even developed an elaborate system of messages, which were dropped from paper balloons.

two large ships they had had to abandon. They were heading for the Back River (also known as Back's "Fish River," or "Great Fish" River), but before they had got very far many of the men dropped in their tracks, apparently victims of exhaustion, scurvy, and hunger. Had any Eskimos seen the abandoned ships? Yes—not only seen but boarded. Where? Off the northwest coast of King William Island.

Any doubt of the truth of the Eskimos' report was quickly laid to rest when they produced cutlery, pieces of clothing, and other objects easily identified as having come from the *Erebus* and *Terror*. Dr. Rae concluded that there was little more to be learned at Pelly Bay and he set out toward the northwest. Along the way he met more Eskimos who gave him bits of information about the missing expedition. One story was particularly disturbing. According to Rae the Eskimos told of discovering "the corpses of some thirty persons and some graves . . . on the continent, and five dead bodies on an island near it, about a long day's journey to the northwest of the mouth of a large stream, which can be no other than Back's Fish River. . . . Some of the bodies were in a tent or tents, others were under the boat, which had been turned over to form a shelter, and some lay scattered about in different directions. . . . From the mutilated state of many of the bodies, and the contents of the kettles, it is evident that our wretched countrymen had been driven to the last dread alternative as a means of sustaining life [cannibalism]. . . ."

When Dr. Rae's report reached England, the news, though tragic, at least answered some of the questions that had been puzzling people for more than seven years. The British government was satisfied—although Dr. Rae pointed out that "None of the Esqi-

maux (Eskimos) with whom I had communication saw the "white men" either while living or after death, nor had they ever been at the place where the corpses were found, but had their information from natives who had been there. . . ." Nevertheless, the Franklin expedition was considered lost, and Dr. Rae was awarded £10,000 (about $150,000 in today's money) by the British government. It is not clear why the original reward of £20,000 was halved—perhaps because Rae had merely found evidence of the death of some of Franklin's men but had not managed to rescue any of them.

For Lady Franklin and for many people there still remained the question of what had become of Franklin himself? What had been the fate of the 100 men still unaccounted for? The British Government decided, however, that further expensive expeditions would not solve the mystery, and Lady Franklin's request for a resumed search was turned down.

She then arranged for a privately sponsored mission and purchased and outfitted a small steamer called the *Fox*. Leopold McClintock, who had been on an earlier search, was put in charge of the *Fox* and was to sail it into the islands that stretched from Atlantic to Pacific above the Arctic Circle.

Left: Dr. John Rae. He was a most successful Arctic traveler, borrowing from the early fur traders the habit of making his journeys with little equipment, but in the company of the natives of the region and using the skills they used to survive. He was a superb hunter and could build an igloo or a stone house if necessary. Below: the cutlery that the Eskimos from Pelly Bay gave Rae in 1854. It was Franklin's own, bearing his crest.

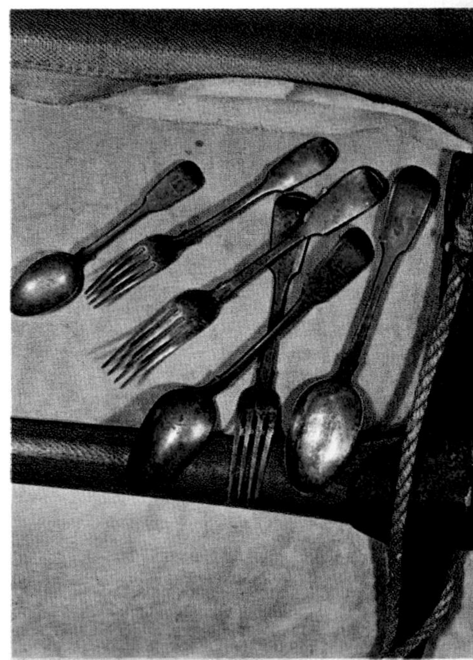

On July 1, 1857, a little more than 12 years after John Franklin had sailed on his ill-fated mission, the *Fox* eased from her berth at Aberdeen, Scotland. By the end of the month she had reached Greenland where 35 dogs and an Eskimo were taken on board in preparation for the time when McClintock and his men would abandon their ship for the search over the ice. Early in August they sailed away from Upernavik, the most northern of the Danish settlements in Greenland.

Only 12 days later when attempting to pass from Melville Bay to Lancaster Sound, through vast accumulations of drift-ice, the *Fox* was stopped by the ice and was soon frozen up for the winter. "Then commenced an ice-drift not exceeded in length by any that I know of," wrote McClintock in his journal. "It was not until April 25, 1858, by which time we had drifted down to latitude 63.5°N, that we were able to escape out of the ice, under circumstances which will long be remembered by all on board. A heavy southeast gale rolled in such an ocean-swell that it broke up all the ice, and threw the masses into violent commotion, dashing them one against the other and against the ship in a terrific manner. We owed our escape, under Providence, to the peculiar wedge-formed bow and steam power of our obedient little vessel." In all, the *Fox* had been adrift for 242 days and had been carried 1,194 miles down Baffin Bay to the southeast.

After returning to Greenland for fresh supplies, the *Fox* turned her bow northwestward again. This time, she succeeded in crossing

Above: the *Fox,* the small steamer commanded by Leopold McClintock, which Lady Franklin purchased and outfitted privately. She obtained McClintock's services from the British Navy with the help of Prince Albert. Below: Leopold McClintock. He had already sailed to the Arctic in 1848 as James Clark Ross' second lieutenant.

Melville Bay and reached Pond Inlet on July 27, 1858. McClintock and a small party of men went ashore and visited an Eskimo village at Kaparoktolic. The Eskimo they had taken on board the *Fox* at Greenland acted as McClintock's interpreter and questioned the Eskimos about whether they had seen Franklin or any of his men. They knew nothing about an expedition. This negative reply led McClintock to assume that the *Erebus* and *Terror* must have passed north of Pond's Inlet and the small island to the north of it. He thought they had then made their way through Lancaster Sound into

Right: the departure of exploring parties from the *Fox.* From his service under Ross, McClintock had learned the value of flexibility in approach when in the Arctic, and was quick to use whatever methods might come to hand.

Barrow Strait where they had spent the winter at Beechey Island.

McClintock's next move was to sail the *Fox* to Beechey Island, which he reached in about 10 days. But he found no more clues at Beechey and decided to sail the *Fox* south toward King William Island. When the *Fox* got to Franklin Strait and only 150 miles away from King William Island, the ice again closed in about the tiny ship and held it in a viselike grip. Impatient to continue the search for Franklin, McClintock decided not to wait for the ice to open and made preparations to trek overland with two other men from the *Fox*. On February 17, 1859, accompanied by an Eskimo and a seaman, McClintock started on his way south over the Boothia Peninsula. They had with them two dog sledges to carry supplies. Eleven days later, they met a group of Eskimos who had been hunting near Cape Victoria, 30 miles across the James Ross Strait from King William Island.

Again the Eskimo who was acting as interpreter asked the usual questions about the Franklin expedition. According to McClintock's account, the Eskimos said that several years before, a ship had been crushed by the ice and sunk off the northwestern shore of King William Island. All the men on board had got safely on to land and then went away to a great river where they died. This report confirmed Dr. Rae's discoveries and convinced McClintock that there was nothing more he could do without more men and provisions. So he turned north again and hurried back to the *Fox*.

Above: the chronometer watch that had been issued to the H.M.S. *Terror,* and which McClintock found on the ship's boat. He was appalled at the amount of useless equipment the weakened men had apparently tried to drag on the sledge—even such things as books and silver plate. The sledge weighed nearly three-quarters of a ton.

On April 2, two search parties left the *Fox,* one commanded by McClintock and the other by a Lieutenant Hobson. Both groups covered the icy miles between the *Fox* and Cape Victoria together, but there they separated. McClintock and his men crossed over the ice of James Ross Strait to King William Island and turned south along the east coast of the island. His destination was Back River. Hobson led his sledges over the same ice bridge, but after reaching King William Island, he turned to the west. He would search the northern and western coasts of the island, where according to the Eskimos, the *Erebus* and *Terror* had foundered.

Swiftly, McClintock and his men cut through the ice toward Back River. While still on King William Island, they met about 40 Eskimos who showed them some disturbing souvenirs—silverware bearing the crests and initials of Franklin and some of his officers. When they finally reached Back River however, they found no sign

Right: the sledges approach a point about 12 miles beyond Cape Herschel, where McClintock's party found the letter left by Lieutenant Hobson reporting his discovery of the two notices by the men of Franklin's party.

Line	Expedition	Route	Dates
———	Franklin (with Back)	1a	1819–22
	Franklin (with Back)	1b	1825–7
	Franklin (with Crozier)	1c	1845–7
	Winter Sledging parties	1D	1847
	Crozier (with remaining members of expedition on foot)	1E	1848
●	Position of ships in successive winters		
– – – –	1st. Search expeditions:		
	Rae (with Richardson)	2a	1847–9
	Ross, James C. (with McClure & McClintock)	2b	1848–9
	McClure	2c	1850–5
	Collinson	2d	1850–4
———	2nd. Search expeditions:		
	British ships (with Austin, McClintock, John Ross, Ommaney & Penny)	3a	1850–1
	Sledging parties from British ships	3b	1851
	American ships (with De Haven & Kane)	3c	1850–1
	Rae	3d	1850–1
—·—·—	3rd. Search expeditions:		
	Rae	4	1853–4
....	Final Search expeditions:		
	McClintock	5a	1857–9
	McClintock & sledging parties	5b	1858–9

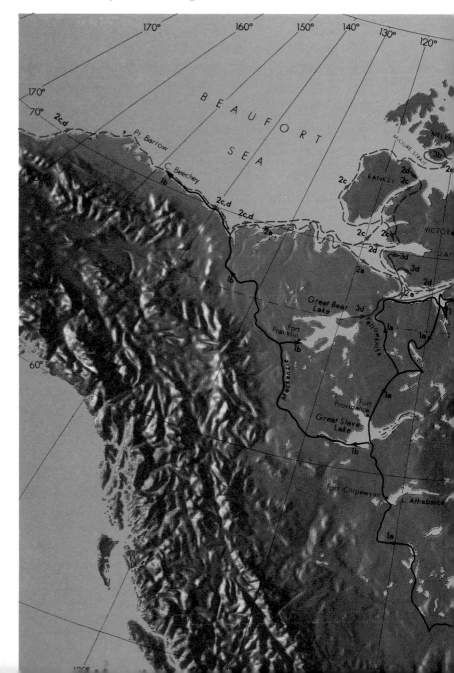

Right: Northeast Canada and Greenland, showing the routes taken by Sir John Franklin on his three Arctic expeditions. Also shown are the routes of the men who between 1847 and 1859 went to find what had happened to Franklin. They never found him, but their searches added greatly to our detailed knowledge of the Arctic.

GREENLAND
MELVILLE BAY
Upernavik
JONES SD.
DEVON I.
LANCASTER SD.
CORNWALLIS I.
BEECHEY I.
BARROW STR.
PEEL SD.
SOMERSET I.
PR. OF WALES I.
BELLOT STR.
FRANKLIN STR.
GULF OF BOOTHIA
Pond Inlet
BAFFIN BAY
DAVIS STR.
C. Herschel
KING WILLIAM
Repulse Bay
Back
HUDSON STRAIT
HUDSON BAY
ATLANTIC OCEAN
York Factory
ARCTIC CIRC

of the Franklin mission. Crossing back to King William Island, they headed up the western coast hoping to meet Hobson.

Time was again running out. It was now May, and McClintock knew the *Fox* would have to make its break for England during the early summer thaw. Then at Cape Herschel, on the southwestern coast of King William Island, a "bleached skeleton was found near the beach, around which lay fragments of European clothing. The snow was most carefully removed, and a small pocket-book containing a seaman's parchment certificate and a few letters were found," but still no record of the ill-fated expedition.

A few days later McClintock's party came across the remains of a

28-foot-long ship's boat. It contained two skeletons, some books and old pocket watches, two double-barreled guns, some clothing, supplies of tea and chocolate—but no records. Another perplexing clue was also the fact that the sledge on which the boat was rested was pointing toward the north. Apparently, the men from the *Erebus* and *Terror* had abandoned their ships and headed southward to find one of the outposts of the Hudson's Bay Company. Then for some reason they had turned back in a vain attempt, at least for some, to reach the safety of the ships.

McClintock ordered his sledges to go north, feeling confident he was near the place where the Franklin mystery might be solved. He was also thinking about Hobson's trek around the northwestern coast of King William Island and what his party might have found. In his log McClintock's own words tell us what happened next.

"A few miles beyond Cape Herschel the land becomes very low; many islets and shingle-ridges lie far off the coast; and as we advanced we met with hummocks of unusually heavy ice . . . we were approaching a spot where a revelation of intense interest was awaiting . . . . About 12 miles from Cape Herschel I found a small cairn built by Hobson's search party, and containing a note for me."

On May 6, Hobson had reached Point Victory on the northwest coast of King William Island. While nearing the spit of land that jutted out into Victoria Strait he and his men had spotted a large cairn. Piles of equipment lay around a heap of rocks—cooking stoves, pickaxes, canvas, shovels, and nautical instruments. Then one of Hobson's men came across a rusty cylinder that had apparently been soldered shut at one time only to be reopened and closed again later. What could this mean? When they broke open the cylinder the men found two separately dated notices:

The main entry had been written on May 28, 1847. It read: "H.M. ships *Erebus* and *Terror* wintered in the ice in lat. 70°05′ N., long. 98°23′ W. Having wintered in 1846–7 at Beechey Island, in lat.

Above: Hobson's party smashes open the cairn on Point Victory, to find the record of Crozier and Fitzjames that reported the death of Franklin.

Right: the medicine chest found by Hobson's party with the last written record of the Franklin expedition. It contained pills, ointments, some bandages and oiled silk, and 25 small bottles. It seems odd that it should have been left at the cairn when the surviving expedition members began their doomed march to Back River.

Above: *The Death of Franklin,* by W. Thomas Smith, painted in 1895. The record left by Crozier and Fitzjames stated clearly that Franklin had died before the ships were abandoned, but in this dramatic version the bodies lie around the lifeboat with Franklin the last man alive. This painting was widely exhibited in England, where the public was stunned by the disaster.

74°43′28″ N., long. 91°39′15″ W., after having ascended Wellington Channel to lat. 77°, and returned by the west side of Cornwallis Island. Sir John Franklin commanding the expedition. All well. Party consisting of two officers and six men left the ships on Monday, 24th May, 1847." Signed, Gm. Gore, Lieut. and Chas. F. Des Voeux, Mate.

The marginal entry was written almost a year later: "April 25, 1848—H.M. ships *Terror* and *Erebus* were deserted on the 22nd April, 5 leagues N.N.W. of this, having been beset since 12 Sept., 1846. The officers and crews, consisting of 105 souls, under the command of Captain F. R. M. Crozier, landed here in lat. 69°37′42″ N., long. 98°41′ W. . . . Sir John Franklin died on the 11th June, 1847; and the total loss by deaths in the expedition has been to this date 9 officers and 15 men." Signed, F. R. M. Crozier, Captain and senior officer and James Fitzjames, Captain H.M.S. *Erebus*. There was a final postcript: "and start tomorrow, 26th, for Back's (Great) Fish River."

There was one inconsistency about dates that Hobson had

immediately spotted. The gravestones at Beechey Island bore dates during the winter of 1845–1846. Yet the main entry stated that the *Erebus* and *Terror* wintered at the island in 1846–1847. Hobson concluded that Lieutenant Gore must have made an incorrect entry. The expedition must have spent its first winter on Beechey Island and the second here.

Where had Franklin died? Why hadn't the men joined up with the Eskimos who could have helped them to survive? Why had they been forced back from Back River? For another 20 years parties of explorers would search in vain for the answers.

Right: the last message, written on one of the official printed forms that discovery ships would throw overboard enclosed in bottles to prove the direction of currents. The finder was requested to send it to the Admiralty with a note of the time and the place where it was found.

H. M. S.hips Erebus and Terror
Wintered in the Ice in
28 of May 1847 Lat. 70° 5′ N Long. 98° 23′ W

Having wintered in 1846—7 at Beechey Island in Lat 74° 43′ 28″ N. Long 91° 39′ 15″ W After having ascended Wellington Channel to Lat 77° and returned by the West side of Cornwallis Island.

Commander.

Sir John Franklin commanding the Expedition.

All well

WHOEVER finds this paper is requested to forward it to the Secretary of the Admiralty, London, *with a note of the time and place at which it was found:* or, if more convenient, to deliver it for that purpose to the British Consul at the nearest Port.

QUINCONQUE trouvera ce papier est prié d'y marquer le tems et lieu ou il l'aura trouvé, et de le faire parvenir au plutot au Secretaire de l'Amirauté Britannique à Londres.

CUALQUIERA que hallare este Papel, se le suplica de enviarlo al Secretario del Almirantazgo, en Londrés, con una nota del tiempo y del lugar en donde se halló.

EEN ieder die dit Papier mogt vinden, wordt hiermede verzogt, om het zelve, ten spoedigste, te willen zenden aan den Heer Minister van de Marine der Nederlanden in 's Gravenhage, of wel aan den Secretaris der Britsche Admiraliteit, te London, en daar by te voegen eene Nota, inhoudende de tyd en de plaats alwaar dit Papier is gevonden geworden.

FINDEREN af dette Papiir ombedes, naar Leilighed gives, at sende samme til Admiralitets Secretairen i London, eller nærmeste Embedsmand i Danmark, Norge, eller Sverrig. Tiden og Stœdit hvor dette er fundet önskes venskabeligt paategnet.

WER diesen Zettel findet, wird hier-durch ersucht denselben an den Secretair des Admiralitets in London einzusenden, mit gefälliger angabe an welchen ort und zu welcher zeit er gefundet worden ist.

Party consisting of 2 Officers and 6 Men left the Ships on Monday 24th May 1847

Gm. Gore Lieut.

Chas. F. Des Voeux Mate

Below: Fridtjof Nansen's watercolor of the polar night, November 24, 1893, He painted it while the *Fram* was slowly drifting with the pack ice north of the New Siberian Islands.

The True Viking

5

Ironically it was the failure of one Arctic expedition in 1881 that was to provide a clue to the eventual conquest of the North Geographic Pole. In 1879, Lieutenant George Washington De Long of the United States Navy sailed from San Francisco aboard a ship named the *Jeannette*. But after being underway for only a few months, the *Jeannette* was caught in the ice near Herald Island. Gradually it drifted westward past Wrangel Island and then in a northwesterly direction for 17 months. By June 1881 the *Jeannette* had been crushed in the ice north of the New Siberian Islands. Its crew managed to reach the estuary of the Lena River in Siberia, but hunger and cold killed De Long and all but two of the men. Three years after the *Jeannette* had sunk, some wreckage from the ship was found on the southwest coast of Greenland. How had an old pair of oilskin trousers and the other remnants from the *Jeannette* got from Siberia to southwest Greenland? Had they perhaps drifted across the North Pole or very close to it?

A newspaper article about the mysterious items from the *Jeannette* was read by a young Norwegian explorer, Fridtjof Nansen. He had previously made trips across the Greenland ice pack and had for several years been speculating about the possibility of a new route to the North Pole. The newspaper account about the wreckage confirmed what Nansen already supposed to be true—that the best route to the North Pole lay along the moving highway of ice that stretched from Siberia to Greenland. There was other evidence to support this theory. One of Nansen's colleagues had received from a Greenlander at Godthåb a remarkable piece of wood, which had been found among the driftwood on the coast. It was one of the "throwing sticks," that Eskimos use in hurling their "bird-darts," but altogether unlike those used by the Eskimos on the west coast of Greenland. This stick must have come from the coast of Alaska in the region of the Bering Strait, as that is the place where that particular kind of throwing stick is used. Furthermore, it was ornamented with Chinese glass beads, very much like those that the Alaskan Eskimos obtain from the people who live along the East Siberian Sea.

Nansen had further evidence of the existence of a current that crossed the North Pole. From his previous voyages he knew that the scrub that grows in Greenland is unsuitable for making the boats and sledges that are such essential items in the lives of the Green-

Above: Fridtjof Nansen at Cape Flora in 1896, photographed by Frederick Jackson, whose hut is in the background. Nansen was a young Norwegian explorer who decided to try out a new route to the North Pole, drifting with the transpolar current.

Left: the discovery of the bodies of the crew of the *Jeannette.* The wreckage of the ship drifted across the North Pole to Greenland, which confirmed Nansen's theory that it was possible to travel on the drifting pack ice.

Below: Nansen's cabin in the *Fram*, with his clothing, as it now appears in the Fram Museum in Oslo, Norway.

Left: the *Fram*, now preserved in the Oslo museum. Nansen designed the ship himself. He planned it to be as small and short as possible, with the sides smooth, so that the crushing ice would slide past them. The bows, stern, and keel were all carefully rounded so that the ice could not secure a grip.

Right: the crew of the *Fram* on the deck after the 1893–1896 expedition. Nansen is in the center of the back row. In front of him at the left is Svedrup, the captain, and on his left is Johansen, who was Nansen's partner on the two-year trek across the ice.

landers. Therefore they must have fashioned these things from driftwood collected along the shoreline. But where did that timber come from? A botanist supplied a feasible answer. In the driftwood that reached Greenland there were pieces of Siberian larch and other kinds of wood that must have drifted over the top of the world from Siberia.

Taken together, these bits of evidence led Nansen to conclude that if timbers could drift across the polar region, that drift might also be used by explorers to get to the North Pole. Nansen was contemplating an expedition aboard a boat that would be properly shaped to allow him to slip through the ice. Using the transpolar current he, like the wreckage from the *Jeannette*, could cross the polar basin. Nansen knew that the current might not carry him exactly across the pole, but at least it would enable him to explore the region.

Nansen's next project was the design and construction of a ship that could ride the ice highway without being crushed. He wanted to have a ship built as small and as strong as possible—"just big enough to contain . . . coal and provisions for 12 men for 5 years. The essential factor was that the ship should be able to withstand the pressure of the ice. The sides should slope sufficiently to prevent the ice from getting a firm hold on the hull. . . . Instead of nipping the ship, the ice should raise it up out of the water."

With the money he received from the Norwegian government for the proposed expedition Nansen had a ship designed and built

according to his conceptions. On June 24, 1893, the small but rugged vessel that Nansen christened the *Fram* ("Forward") was ready to sail from Pepperviken, Norway. Aboard it were 12 Norwegians including Nansen and Otto Sverdrup, the captain.

As the expedition got underway Nansen jotted in his diary, "It was midsummer day. A dull, gloomy day; and with it came the inevitable leave-taking. . . . Behind me lay all I held dear in life. And what before me?" For Franklin and De Long the answer had been hardship and death. For Nansen? He knew quite well the risks that lay waiting. "Like an arrow the little boat sped over Lysaker Bay bearing me on the first stage of a journey on which life itself, if not more, was staked."

For the next few months the *Fram* sailed eastward, along the coast of northern Europe and then into the waters of the Arctic Ocean above Russia. Nansen had planned to take on supplies at the New Siberian Islands before beginning the hazardous drive toward the Arctic ice pack. However, he changed direction northward before reaching them and before September was over, the *Fram* was locked in the ice. From then on it would go where the ice took it.

The men on board resigned themselves to the prospect of isolation and wandering for at least the next two years. As winter approached the ice pack grew, and Nansen and his crew began to wonder whether the *Fram*, like the *Jeannette*, might be crushed by it? One black December evening as they were sitting at supper they heard the sound of cracking ice. The cracking sound became a roar so loud that it was impossible for the crew to hear one another's voices. Then the ship began to rise as the ice squeezed against its sides. Nansen's theory about the design of the *Fram* was correct.

Now began a long succession of monotonous days, weeks, and months of drifting as the ice floes drifted. Nansen, who throve on activity, was particularly affected by the confinement. "I long to return to life," he wrote in his diary. "At times this inactivity crushed one's very soul; one's life seems as dark as the winter night outside. . . . I feel as if I must break through this deadness, this inertia, and find some outlet for my energies. Can't something happen? Could not a hurricane come and tear up this ice, and set it rolling in high waves like the open sea?"

By late December the *Fram* had reached latitude 82° 30′ N. No ship, adrift or under its own power, had poked its bow so close to the North Pole. And none had probably encountered the icy pressure ridge that crept threateningly closer and closer to the helpless, ice-locked ship. Nansen writes, "The floe, seven feet thick, has borne down on us on the port side, forcing itself up on the ice in which we are lying, and crushing it down. Thus the *Fram* was forced down with the ice, while the other floe, packed up on the ice beneath, bore down on her, and took her amidships while she was still frozen fast. As far as I can judge, she could hardly have had a tighter squeeze; it was no wonder that she groaned under it;

Above: the *Fram* locked in the ice during the winter of 1894-1895. As the ice closed in, the *Fram* withstood the pressure and drifted with the slow ice flow, confirming Nansen's ideas.

but she withstood it, broke loose and eased." Again, the *Fram* had proved its ice-worthiness.

Although elated by the behavior of the ship, Nansen and his crew continued to become depressed by the frustratingly slow drift of the ice. Moreover, as each day passed, it became apparent that the ice drift would not carry them across the pole. The *Fram's* northward drift had stopped at about 84° N. latitude. It was now being pulled toward the west. Nansen guessed that they would remain locked in the ice for at least a year—and perhaps for two or three years. He also knew that he could not endure the enforced idleness and began to plan how he could get farther north to the pole, which was only 350 miles away.

For a while he had been calculating that two hardy men, equipped with sledge, dog teams, kayaks, and carrying enough food for 100 days could cover the distance in 50 days—if all went well. Nansen decided that he would try to make this journey, accompanied by one of the young officers on the *Fram,* Hjalmar Johansen. He would leave Captain Sverdrup in charge of the ship.

Below: the *Fram* in the ice in July, 1894. Above the awning over the deck is the windmill. It was designed to drive the generator that would produce electric light for the ship, as the ship's engine would not be running once the *Fram* was frozen in.

Below: the Arctic Ocean, showing the ocean currents and ice drift suggested by the observed movement of driftwood and other objects. Nansen was convinced that the Arctic ice drift shown here could be used to carry a ship, locked in the ice, across the Arctic to the North Pole. The course of the *Fram*, in which he set out to prove his theory, is plotted on the map on page 87.

On March 14, 1895, Nansen and Johansen left the *Fram* and set out for the pole. The first few days of the journey were deceptively easy. The men with their 3 sledges, 27 dogs, and 2 kayaks sped across the flat, smooth ice. But where the ice was broken up into immense jagged ridges, they had to struggle over it.

By April 5, Nansen and Johansen had reached latitude 86°2.8′N.—within 272 miles of the pole. But the going had become so difficult that Nansen began to think about turning back. He reconsidered however, and decided they should at least try to reach 87° N.

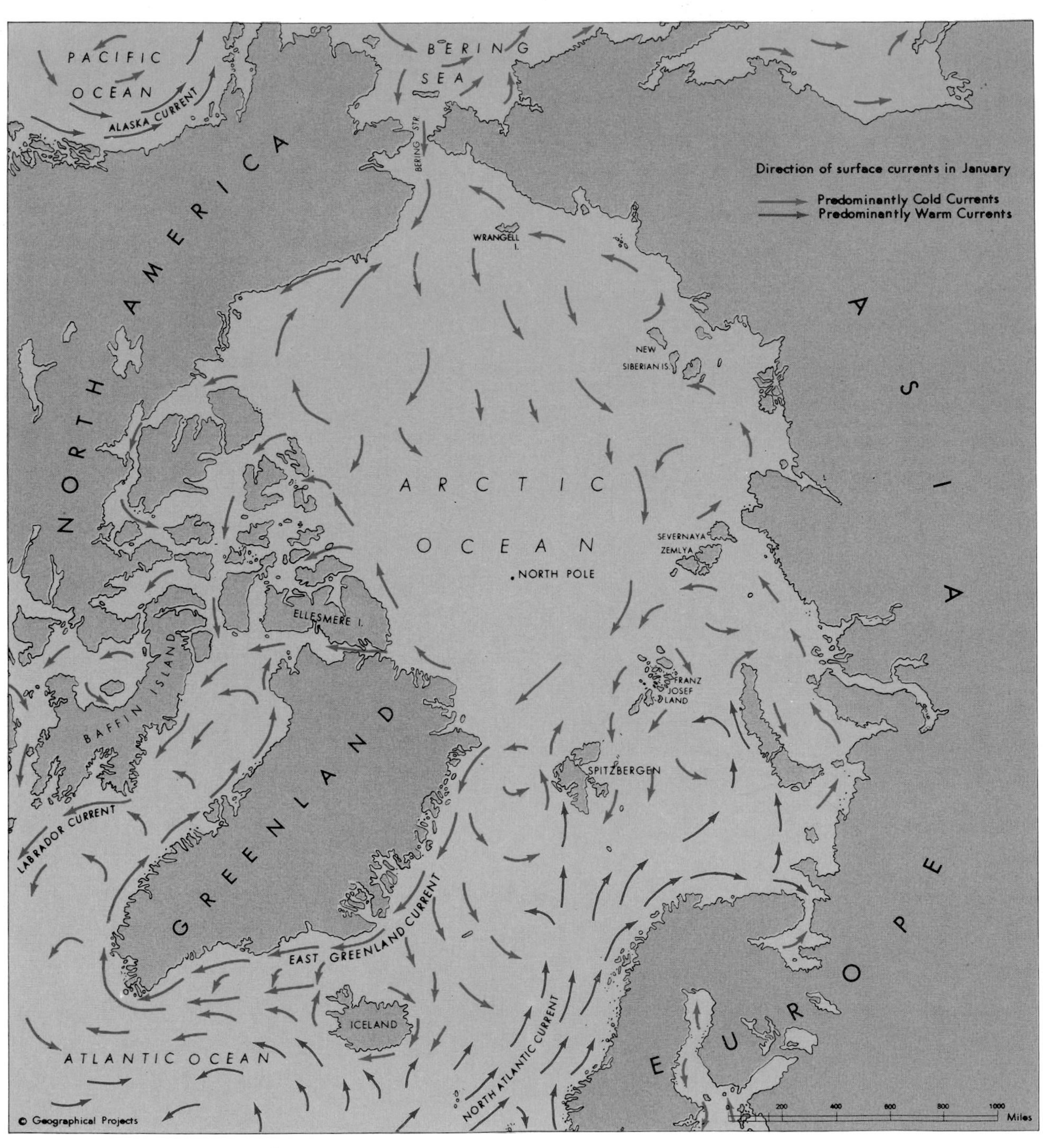

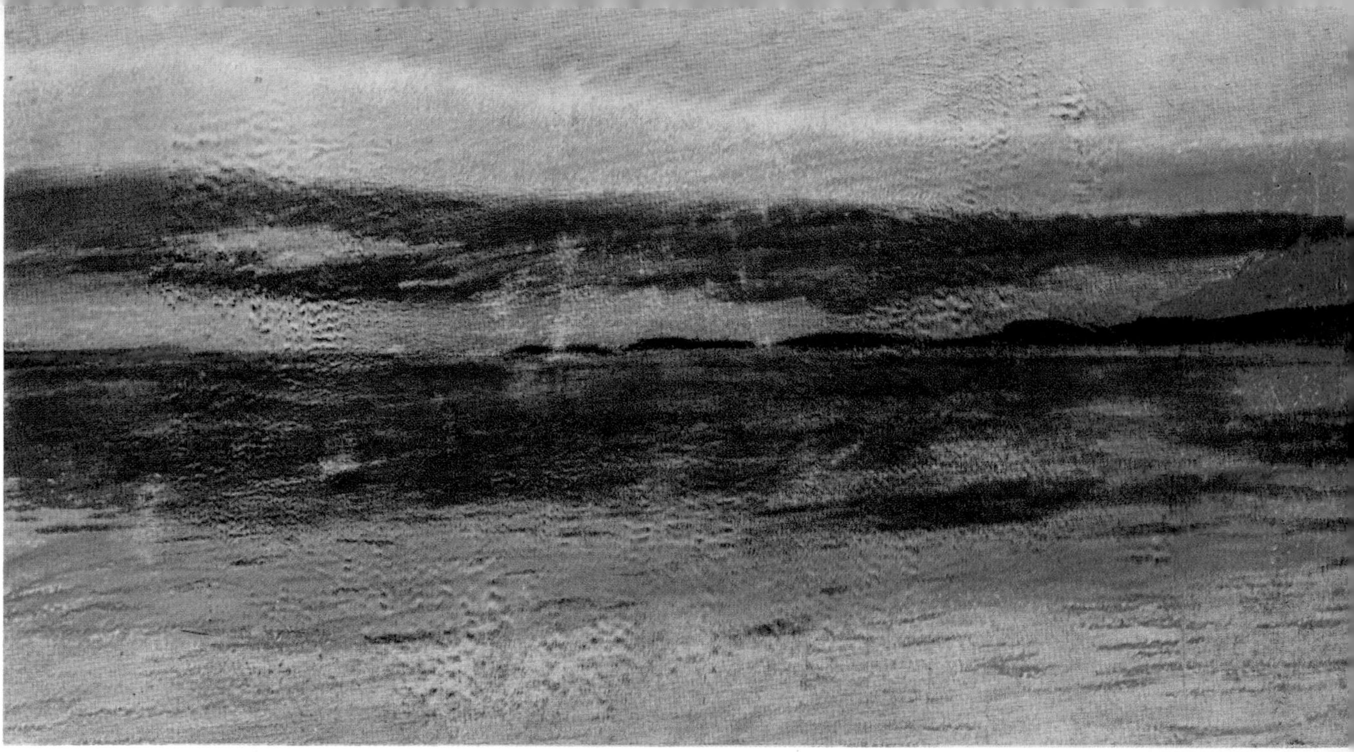

In his diary Nansen recorded his feelings as they pushed on. "Saturday, April 6. Two A.M., −11.4° F. (−24.2°). The ice grew worse and worse. Yesterday it brought me to the verge of despair. . . . I will go on one day longer, however, to see if the ice is really as bad farther northward as it appears to be from the ridge . . . where we are encamped. . . . Lanes, ridges, and endless rough ice, it looks like an endless moraine of ice-blocks; and this continual lifting of the sledges over every irregularity is enough to tire out giants. . . . I am rapidly coming to the conclusion that we are not doing any good here."

Above: a chalk drawing of the northern light at midnight, by Nansen. He was fascinated by the effects of the light. Below: two of the *Fram* crew members with their meteorological "observatory." They took readings every four hours.

Nevertheless, Nansen and Johansen struggled across the almost impenetrable ice for another two days. "Monday, April 8 . . . the ice grew worse and worse and we got no way. Ridge after ridge . . . stretching as far as the horizon. There is not much sense in keeping on longer; we are sacrificing valuable time and doing little. If there be much more such ice between here and [land], we shall, indeed want all the time we have." The Norwegians had managed to get 160 miles farther north than had any explorer before them.

Then began the journey southward to the nearest piece of land, a group of islands called Franz Josef Land. Not long after they had started to go south both men forgot to wind their watches—an oversight that was to make their trek even more difficult. Without an accurate means of measuring time they would be unable to make precise calculations about their position. Nansen and Johansen could do nothing but rely on the compass, even though it might mean that they would end up miles from Franz Josef Land.

As spring began to come to the Arctic, the ice pack became pock-marked with spots of open blue water, over which a thin sheet of

Above: for the first part of their journey after leaving the *Fram* Nansen and Johansen had dog teams. But the conditions became worse, and they had to start killing their dogs one by one to feed those that remained. Above right: Nansen and Johansen with kayaks on their ski-sledges. It was a real feat of endurance to drag the sledges over the ice ridges.

ice would often form. When the water was clear, the men, dogs, and sledges would cross these stretches of water in the kayaks. But when it was crusted with ice, they had to make long and tiring detours.

Food was running short and the dogs were beginning to gnaw almost anything they came across that might satisfy their hunger. Nansen decided that they would have to kill the weaker dogs and keep the others alive on their meat. Although Nansen and Johansen still had a small supply of dried meat and some other rations for themselves, these would not hold out for long. On May 15, they celebrated Johansen's 28th birthday by drinking hot lime juice and sugar. By June 9, they were so low on food that they had to kill all but three of the dogs.

Now the weather added to the misery of the exhausted men. Wind-whipped sheets of rain lashed down from gray skies for the next few days. Nansen had an attack of painful lumbago, which made traveling impossible. They decided to make camp rather than sap their strength in a vain attempt to make progress. After resting for three days Nansen felt better, and they decided to push on.

Summer brought better luck. One day Johansen spotted a seal and shot it for their first meal of fresh meat since they had left the luxury of the *Fram*. The terrain was easier now, even though the days dragged on with no sight of land.

On August 7, the men reached open water that stretched as far as they could see. They tied the kayaks together, rigged a sail, loaded supplies and sledges, and pushed off into the water. As the strange vessel bobbed along the water, a fine, damp mist engulfed it. A gentle breeze pushed them onward, and when the mist suddenly lifted Nansen and Johansen saw in the distance a group of tiny islands—the northernmost islands of Franz Josef Land.

Soon they stepped out on one of the islands—the first solid land they had walked on for two years. It was already late summer and they decided to find a suitable place to wait out the Arctic winter, which descends in this region in September. They made their camp in a sheltered spot near a high cliff on one of the northern islands in Franz Josef Land. Ivory gulls, kittiwakes, skuas, and auks wheeled in the sky above. And bears, seals, and walruses made a playground of the nearby rocks. There would be plenty of fresh meat for the winter.

For shelter, Nansen built a sturdy stone hut roofed with walrus hides. Chinks in the walls and roof were made weather-tight with tiny pebbles, bits of moss, and hide. On October 15, the sun set and the long Arctic night descended for the third time on Nansen and Johansen. Occasionally, one of them would go outside to hunt down a meal or repair a part of the hut, but it would be nine months before they would again be able to move on toward Norway. Finally on May 19, 1896, they took one last look at their winter home and put their kayaks into the water.

The next few weeks were full of unexpected adventures—and misadventures. One day, a walrus ripped open the side of Nansen's kayak. Fortunately, he quickly paddled to a spot over a half-submerged piece of ice where he was able to repair the jagged hole. Another time when the men had stopped to go ashore on an island, their kayaks, which had not been moored firmly enough, began to drift away. Nansen's quick thinking in this sort of situation is best described by his diary entry for that day. "We went up to a hummock close by. As we stood there, Johansen suddenly cried, 'I say, the kayaks are adrift!' " Nansen quickly threw off some clothing and plunged into the water. "The water was icy cold; it was hard work swimming with clothes on. . . . But all our hope was drifting there; all we possessed was on board—we had not even a knife with us: and whether I got cramp and sank here, or turned back without the kayaks, it would come to pretty much the same thing." But Nansen

Above: the Aurora Borealis, by Nansen. He wrote of the Arctic night, "It is dreamland, painted in the imagination's most delicate tints; it is colour etherealised. One shade melts into the other, so that you cannot tell where one ends and the other begins." Below: Nansen and Johansen's boat, made by lashing together two kayaks.

did not drown. He caught the kayaks, which were attached to the same line and hoisted himself into one of them and paddled back to Johansen.

Then one morning when the two men had camped temporarily on another of the Franz Josef Land islands, Nansen heard the distant sound of barking. The last of their own dogs had been killed months ago so the sound was not a familiar one. Nansen immediately forgot the breakfast he was cooking and started walking and running in the direction of the barking.

In his diary Nansen described his emotions at this crucial moment. "It was with a strange mixture of feelings that I made my way in towards land among the numerous hummocks. . . . Suddenly I thought I heard a shout from a human voice, a strange voice, the first for three years. How my heart beat and the blood rushed to my brain as I ran up the hummock and hallooed with all the strength of my lungs! . . . Soon I heard another shout, and saw, too, from an ice-ridge, a dark form moving among the hummocks farther in. It was a dog; but farther off came another figure, and that was a man. . . . We approached one another quickly. I waved my hat; he did the same. I heard him speak to the dog, and I listened. It was English, and as I drew nearer I thought I recognized Mr. Jackson [Frederick Jackson, an English Arctic explorer]. . . ." The two men exchanged greetings, almost unable to believe that their meeting was actually happening and was not a dream.

Then less than a month after this chance meeting the *Windward,* one of the ships in Jackson's expedition, arrived at Cape Flora, one of the southern islands of Franz Josef Land. With Nansen and Johansen aboard, the *Windward* weighed anchor and headed toward Norway on August 7. The news that Nansen had been found alive was telegraphed to Norway. When the two explorers, whom many had thought were dead, arrived in Norway they at last got word about the *Fram,* which had sailed into the port of Skjaervo, Norway on August 20. After drifting for 35 months it had broken out of the ice northwest of Spitzbergen. Not a single man had been lost and the *Fram*, having sustained the battering of the ice, at last set sail for Norway, which it had left more than three years before.

Thus ended one of the greatest Arctic journeys, organized in a scientific way and led by an exceptional man of imagination and intelligence. Although Nansen and Johansen never reached the North Pole they did get to within 272 miles of it. Their observations about the polar region, and those carried out by the *Fram* as it drifted along with the ice were to give future Arctic explorers a basis from which to carry out their work.

Nansen lived and worked during a period when the Scandinavian countries were once again exerting their almost instinctive urge to explore and to cross the unknown world. This impulse can be said to be part of the national heritage that men like Nansen inherited from their Viking ancestors.

Right: the historic meeting of Nansen and Frederick Jackson. Jackson greeted him cordially, but obviously did not recognize him at first. Then he peered at him intently, asked "Aren't you Nansen?" and when Nansen said that he was, seized his hand thankfully and said, "By Jove! I am glad to see you!"

Below: crew members who remained on the *Fram*, celebrating a Norwegian holiday in May, 1896. The *Fram* at last broke loose from the ice after 35 months, northwest of Spitzbergen.

Reaching the North Pole

6

Ten years after his attempt to drift across the polar region, Fridtjof Nansen was asked by the United States President Theodore Roosevelt to recommend the best American explorer to lead an expedition to the North Pole. At that time there were numerous explorers from many countries striving to reach the North Pole, and to Nansen's experienced eye Robert E. Peary, a young naval officer, seemed the most likely one to win the competition.

In 1886, Peary had made the first of many expeditions to Greenland and already he was obsessed by an overriding ambition to conquer the Artic's great geographical prize. Even though Nansen had discovered that the polar region was an ice-covered sea, Peary still wanted to be the first man to get to the North Pole. Unlike the Norwegian, scientific exploration was not his primary aim. He was a naval officer, who considered his attempt on the pole in terms of the tactics and strategy of getting there. Peary's 1886 crossing of the Greenland ice sheet and his subsequent Greenland journeys were really training exercises. Above all he wanted to prove that he could conquer the Arctic. To do this he must rigorously prepare himself and test all kinds of equipment before trying for the pole.

In May, 1893, Peary was again in Greenland. He and one companion drove forward into the icy wasteland. Through swirling snow

Left: the taffeta flag made by Peary's wife, which he took to the North Pole. Peary wore it wrapped around his body, not trusting it to a sledge, and when he reached each expedition's objective would cut a small piece of the flag and bury it at that point. In 1909, when he reached the North Pole, and after the photographs had been taken, he cut a four-inch diagonal strip from the center and buried that.

Right: Robert E. Peary on the *Roosevelt* after his epic achievement. His face is worn and weary with the fatigue of the 1,000 miles he had sledged.

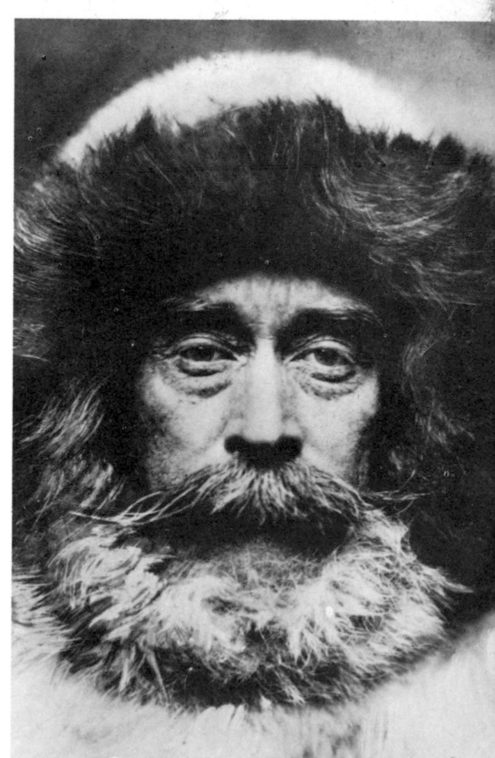

and stinging wind the men struggled forward until they reached the northeast coast of Greenland. This crossing convinced Peary he could get to the North Pole, but not with a large expedition. Only a few men should make the final dash from the base camp.

In the years between 1893 and 1897 Robert Peary spent most of his time in Greenland, striking northward in hopes of finding a suitable place for an advanced base camp that could someday be used for the last crucial phase of getting to the North Pole. These forays into the Greenland ice made him realize, however, that Greenland was not the right place for an advanced camp. The reason

Above: members of Peary's expedition taking a dog team across a lead on a floating cake of ice. One of the constantly recurring problems of Peary's attempts to reach the North Pole was the opening and closing leads. Below: an aerial view of a lead in the ice. These long, narrow water passages through the pack ice constantly shift in position, opening and closing without warning. A hazard of polar bivouacs has always been the possibility of a lead opening at night and carrying away the sleeping men.

for discarding a Greenland route was the comparatively rapid movement of ice in this region as it swung around the northern coast of the island and into the southerly East Greenland Current.

During a trip in 1902, Peary switched his starting point to Grant Land (on the northern edge of Ellesmere Island). The condition of the ice was very bad, and by mid-April he had managed to get only as far north as latitude 84°17′27″. Early in April, at Cape Hecla, he had left land behind him, hoping this time to get across the pack ice to the pole. In parts the snow covering the pack was so soft that the dogs wallowed in it up to their bellies. Very frequently Peary and his companions were forced to double in their tracks and to make exhausting detours to find smoother ground. Then a blizzard caused the pack ice to move, and two wide channels of water opened up across their path.

Even though this journey of 1902 was one more failure for Peary, it had not been entirely unprofitable. The expedition had laid a number of advance depots along this new route to the North Pole, and Peary had learned several invaluable things about the ice pack. Even here, far to the west of the East Greenland Current, the prevailing drift of the ice was from west to east. In order to offset this drift and reach the pole a course of NNW would have to be set. Another lesson Peary had learned was that a rapid return from the North Pole would have to be made if he was to be able to follow the line of his track northward. There were improvements that could also be made in equipment and in the tactics of the assault. Sledges would have to be lighter to ride easily over the hummocky ice and they should also be wider to bridge channels and water leads. Furthermore, a ship would have to be found to penetrate through Smith Sound to the edge of the polar sea, thus reducing the long journey to the advance base camp. From there an advance party would be needed to push on ahead and break a trail. The final

Below: Peary on board the *Roosevelt*, the ship especially built for his 1905 expedition.

assault party for the North Pole would then pass the advance group and thus conserve their energies for the ultimate race to their goal.

In 1902, Peary returned to the United States having spent four years in the Arctic. He devoted himself to the task of raising money for a new expedition that would incorporate his ideas about new equipment and tactics. A group of wealthy New Yorkers formed an organization called the Peary Arctic Club, and by 1904 they had raised enough money for a new ship to be designed and built.

Then in July, 1905, Peary, who was now 50 and had spent nearly 20 years of his life exploring the Arctic, took another crack at the "impossible." His new ship, the *Roosevelt,* which had been especially designed and built to penetrate the ice of Smith Sound, made its way to Greenland where Eskimos and Siberian huskies were taken aboard. The Eskimos would drive the dog teams and build igloos that would be used as supply camps along the route. Eskimo women were taken on to sew clothing for Peary and the six other men in the expedition—the same kind of outfits that the Eskimos fashioned for themselves from the hides of seals and walruses. Peary's respect for the Eskimos' methods of travel and technique of survival was a significant aspect of his eventual success.

The *Roosevelt* battered its way through the ice to Cape Columbia on the northeast coast of Grant Land. Now the expedition was within 90 miles of the advance base camp at Cape Hecla. The first party of Eskimos started out over the ice in February, 1906. Peary's strategy, as explained earlier, was for these advance parties to blaze the trail and establish supply stations along the route, enabling Peary to take a small party of rested men and dogs for the final dash to the pole.

After so many years of planning and careful thought, it seemed only fair that this time Robert Peary would get to the North Pole. But again conditions were unfavorable and temperatures dropped to a record low of −60°F. The bad surface on the ice and the drift of the floe were also against success. Their rate of speed was reduced to five miles a day, and because of this provisions would never hold out for the journey to the North Pole and back. Peary realized that once again he would fail to attain his goal. To help compensate for another failure he decided to push on north until he got as far as any other explorer had. He discarded every possible inessential item from his sledges and with the least exhausted of the dogs plunged on until he got to latitude 87°6′—a new high latitude in the Arctic.

The *Roosevelt* returned to New York with Peary still feeling that he would somehow conquer the North Pole. He soon began organizing a new expedition and in July, 1908, Peary again set out with the *Roosevelt.* The same Britisher, Captain Bob Bartlett, again navigated the ship, and also on board was Peary's devoted servant, Matthew Henson.

The *Roosevelt* docked at Etah, in Greenland, where 50 Eskimos and 250 dogs were engaged for the expedition. By early September

Right: a photograph by Peary of the dog teams walking across the bumpy ridges of the ice hummocks at the beginning of the expedition's march from Cape Columbia. Throughout the winter advance parties stocked the depots on the way to the North Pole.

Left: the expedition moving across the ice, by F. W. Stokes, who went with Peary to the Arctic. The sledges had to travel across the vast, featureless expanses, where each mile looked much like the last, with only the changing pattern of ice ridges or the challenge of the leads opening before them to break the monotonous sameness of the trek through the icy cold of dark days.

Right: a bear walking in the Arctic under the strange brilliant colors of the polar light, by F. W. Stokes.

Captain Bartlett had maneuvered the ship to Cape Sheridan on the Ellesmere coast. During the autumn all the supplies that would be needed for the spring drive to the pole were taken to the advance base at Cape Columbia. By the end of February, 1909, Peary was ready to move over the ice to the North Pole.

Peary describes his feelings on the day he had chosen to start the assault, which was March 1. "When I awoke before light on the morning of March 1, the wind was whistling around the igloo. . . . I looked through the peephole of the igloo and saw that the weather was still clear, and that the stars were scintillating like diamonds. . . . After breakfast, with the first glimmer of daylight, we got outside the igloo and looked about . . . the ice fields to the north, as well as all the lower part of the land, were invisible in that gray haze which, every experienced Arctic traveler knows, means vicious wind. . . . Some parties would have considered the weather impossible for traveling . . . (but) we were all in our new and perfectly dry fur clothes and could bid defiance to the wind.

Above: the "home stretch" of Peary's race to the North Pole, showing the weary men hauling the sledges over pressure ridges that could sometimes be as high as 50 feet. Peary is in the center, and the man holding the dogs is his companion, Matthew Henson.

"One by one the divisions drew out from the main army of sledges and dog teams, took up Bartlett's trail over the ice and disappeared to the northward in the wind haze." (Captain Bartlett, master of the *Roosevelt,* had left Cape Columbia the day before with sledges, dogs, and provisions, as part of Peary's plan of having various support parties in his advance on the Pole.)

Peary's own party, which was the last to leave camp, consisted of 24 men, 19 sledges, and 133 dogs. Their goal was the almost mystical figure of 90°N. latitude, 420 nautical miles to the north.

Peary's party ran into trouble on their second day out. Toward afternoon, Peary "saw ahead of us a dark ominous cloud upon the northern horizon, which always means open water . . . the open water supplies the evaporation, the cold air acts as a condenser, and when the wind is blowing just right this forms a fog so dense that at times it looks as black as the smoke of a prairie fire." Then the party had to stop suddenly to avoid a yawning, quarter-of-a-mile-wide lead that had formed. Peary ordered the men to camp, hoping that if they waited the ice would come together again.

Before dawn the next morning they were awakened by the screech of grinding ice. The lead was closing. After a hurried breakfast, the party set out across the ice, "which was moving

Right: The Arctic Ocean, showing the routes of explorers from De Long in the 1880's, through Peary's successful expedition to the North Pole in 1908–1909, to Wally Herbert and the British Trans-Arctic Expedition in 1968–1969.

De Long 1a 1879-81
De Long (after leaving his ship) 1b 1881-?
Nansen 2a 1882
Nansen (with Sverdrup) 2b 1888
Nansen (with Sverdrup on 'Fram' in open water) 2c
Drift of 'Fram' in polar ice 2C 1893-6
(28 Dec. 1893-13 Aug. 1896)
Nansen (sledge journey with Johansen) 2D
Nansen (with Johansen on 'Windward') 2E
Sverdrup (on 'Fram' in open water) 2F
Peary 3a
Peary 3b
Peary (with Henson) 3c
Peary (with Henson) 3d
Peary 3e
Peary 3f
Amundsen 4
Nautilus 5
Herbert 6
PACIFIC OCEAN
BERING SEA
ALEUTIAN ISLANDS
BERING STRAIT
ARCTIC OCEAN
NORTH POLE
HERALD I.
WRANGELL I.
NEW SIBERIAN IS.
Lena
SEVERNAYA ZEMLYA
FRANZ JOSEF LAND
SPITZBERGEN
NOVAYA ZEMLYA
VICTORIA ISLAND
BARROW STR.
BEECHEY
LANCASTER SD.
SMITH SD.
C. Columbia
C. Hecla
Independence Fj.
BAFFIN BAY
GREENLAND
Godthåb
JAN MAYEN
ICELAND
FAEROE IS.
North Cape
Vardø
Tromsø
ARCTIC CIRCLE
Oslo
Copenhagen
London
ATLANTIC OCEAN
Miles
© Geographical Projects

THE NEW YORK HERALD.

ROBERT E. PEARY, AFTER 23 YEARS SIEGE, REACHES NORTH POLE; ADDS "THE BIG NAIL" TO NEW YORK YACHT CLUB'S TROPHIES; DR. COOK TO SUBMIT RECORDS TO UNIVERSITY OF DENMARK

Discoverer of the Pole Joins in Cheering When Told Mr. Peary's Success

"If He Has Announced He Has Reached the Farthest North, He Has," Is the Physician's First Comment.

"THERE IS HONOR ENOUGH ON IT FOR BOTH OF US," HE ASSERTS TO ADMIRERS

EXPLORER CONFIDENT OF THE VERDICT

DR. COOK CONGRATULATES MR. PEARY

Mr. E. H. Harriman Suffers Setback from Indigestion

Physician Announces That There Is Nothing Alarming in the Condition of the Financier—Nurse Is Called from New York to Care for Him.

MISS STEWART IS MADE A PRINCESS

NO LONGER DEPENDENT ON MR. ROCKEFELLER

Attains Highest Point on April 6, 1909, Year After Dr. Cook's Discovery

Sends First News of His Achievement from Indian Harbor via Cape Ray, on Newfoundland Coast.

FILES MESSAGES OF SUCCESS, THEN SPEEDS AWAY FOR HOME COUNTRY

SAYS THERE IS HONOR ENOUGH FOR TWO

Left: the front page of the *New York Herald,* September 7, 1909, reporting that Peary had reached the North Pole. It was not until five months after his triumph that the news finally reached the United States.

Below: Peary's photograph of his team standing at the North Pole beneath the flag his wife had made. From left to right, they are Ooqueah, Ootah, Matthew Henson, Egingwah, and Seegloo. After the picture, Peary buried a strip cut from the flag.

crushing, and piling up." It was extremely rough going. The sledges were "crossing a river on a succession of gigantic [ice] shingles, one, two, or three feet deep and all afloat and moving." Peary was afraid that, at any moment, one of the sledges would disappear into the icy water, but none did.

Then, after Peary had caught up with Bob Bartlett's advance party, they found themselves stopped again because of a huge lead. This time Peary waited for a week for the lead to freeze over. Then for almost three weeks Peary and various supporting parties plunged ahead. After they had set up supply camps along the route, the supporting groups would one by one make their way back to Cape Columbia, leaving the two most rested groups—Peary's and Bartlett's—to make the dash for the North Pole. When it came time to decide who would go, Peary was the man to lead the party that consisted of 4 Eskimos and Matthew Henson. They had 5 sledges and 40 dogs for the final assault that began on April 2.

In 5 forced marches Peary drove his party over the final 133 miles to the North Pole. By noon of April 6, 1909, they reached the latitude of 89°57′N., just 3 miles south of their goal.

The story of the rest of their journey is one of the greatest success stories of man against the elements of nature. Although exhausted by the strain of the forced marches, Peary managed to use that final spurt of energy to lead his men to the pole and the prize of 300 years of Arctic exploration. There they camped for 30 hours before beginning their race southward back to Cape Columbia. By pushing on to the North Pole and then returning safely to the *Roosevelt,* Robert Peary had proved that it was possible for men to walk 900 miles over the drifting ice floes of the Polar Sea to the spot in the Northern Hemisphere that is farthest from the equator.

Roald Amundsen (1872–1928)

Robert Falcon Scott (1868–1912)

Duel for the South Pole

7

Two men who raced for the South Pole. Below left: Amundsen of Norway. He was the son of a shipowner, and had trained himself for exploration, studying navigation and seamanship. He was the first man to sail through the Northwest Passage and had hoped to be the first at the North Pole. Below: Scott of England, in a photograph taken on October 7, 1911, in his den at McMurdo Sound with pictures of his wife and son. He left on his final journey on November 1.

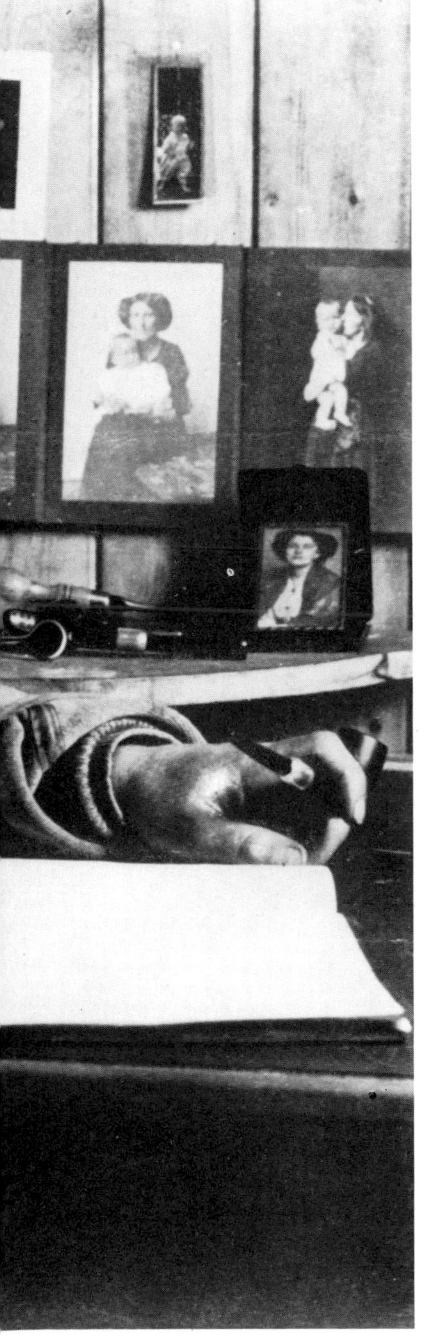

The South Pole is the geographical bottom of the world, 90° south of the equator where all the meridians of longitude come together. Located on the flat, featureless plateau that caps the Antarctic continent, it can only be found by precise astronomical observations. The South Pole cannot otherwise be identified from any other spot on the vast snowfield. Today it is no more than a curiosity, a place for visiting scientists to fly across to say that they have been there. Yet to be the first to reach this icy, undistinguished dot on the map, men suffered incredible privation, showed indomitable courage, and left their frozen bodies to mark the place where, in the end, they failed.

In 1908, an Irishman named Ernest Shackleton led a British expedition to within 97 miles of the pole when lack of food and the approaching Antarctic winter forced him to turn back. It was to be a matter of only a few months before two explorers—Roald Amundsen of Norway and the Englishman Robert F. Scott—were to begin their dramatic race to be first at the pole.

These two men were strikingly different people. As a young naval cadet, Scott was called "old mooney" because of his constant daydreaming. His teachers despaired of his laziness, his slovenly appearance, his uncontrollable temper. As an adult, he was a hard taskmaster and disciplinarian who, despite weak lungs and a less than powerful physique, drove himself harder than he drove his men. He was also a sentimentalist who cried when he heard old hymns, and who could not bear to see a sledge dog killed. He was a brilliant, moody, brave, and iron-willed man who set off for the South Pole at the age of 42.

Amundsen was a simpler and more direct person. Fascinated from boyhood by Sir John Franklin's quest for the Northwest Passage, and by the tales of the expeditions that went to look for the missing Franklin mission, Amundsen was determined to explore the Arctic. Although he had studied to be a medical doctor, at the age of 21 he gave up medicine and began preparing himself for a career as an explorer. He served as a seaman aboard an Arctic merchant vessel and then signed on as first mate aboard the Antarctic-bound *Belgica,* the first ship to spend a winter there. Upon his return to Norway Amundsen bought the 45-foot *Gjoa,* and in a year and eight months managed to make his way through the legendary Northwest Passage. While Scott became a polar explorer comparatively late in

Above left: the Scott expedition ship, the *Terra Nova,* caught in the pack ice that delayed the party on the journey to McMurdo Sound in 1910.

Above: December 17, 1910 in the wardroom of the *Terra Nova.* By this time the men on board knew that Amundsen had changed his objective to the South Pole, and the race was on. Scott is sitting at the head of the table.

life, Amundsen had always known what he wanted to do. His polar experience, skill in planning expeditions, and raw courage were second to none.

After his triumph in the *Gjoa*, Amundsen turned immediately toward his other goal—the North Pole itself. It was not long before he announced his plans for a drifting expedition in Nansen's famous *Fram* across the pole. But funds for even the famous Amundsen were only reluctantly forthcoming from the Norwegian government, and valuable time was slipping away. While the expedition was still in its planning stages, the news that Peary had reached the North Pole flashed around the world in September, 1909. The prize that Amundsen had wanted for himself had been won by someone else. The Norwegian, however, continued to plan for his drift over the pole—or so he claimed.

During the years when Amundsen had been taking the *Gjoa* through the Northwest Passage, Robert Scott had led an expedition to the Antarctic and had managed to get to within 575 miles of the South Pole. He had returned to England a hero, and in 1909 announced his plans to conquer the pole. The ship he selected for the expedition was an old whaler called the *Terra Nova*. Among the men chosen by Scott to accompany him there were half a dozen scientists who would carry out their particular scientific observations in Antarctica. Because he had been disappointed with the performance of the sledge dogs on the previous trip, Scott took aboard the *Terra Nova* 19 sturdy Siberian ponies that he would use to haul supplies for part of the journey to the pole. On June 1,

Right: Fridtjof Nansen's famous ship, the *Fram,* in which Amundsen first planned to drift across the North Pole, After the news of Peary's success reached him, he took the ship south to race Scott to the South Pole.

1910, the *Terra Nova* sailed from London and made its way southeastward to New Zealand.

Two months later Roald Amundsen headed south—his apparent goal Cape Horn and the Pacific gateway to the Arctic Ocean. But, secretly, he had changed his plans and had decided to try for the South Pole. Not until September 9, at Funchal in the Madeira Islands, did he reveal his real plan to the members of his expedition. Scott was not then in New Zealand, but when the *Terra Nova* docked there in October, Scott received this terse cable that Amundsen had sent from Madeira: "BEG LEAVE TO INFORM YOU PROCEEDING ANTARCTICA." When the men on the *Terra Nova* heard this news they were indignant. The race for the South Pole was on.

Scott encountered great difficulties with the pack ice in reaching his old camp on McMurdo Sound at the eastern edge of the Ross Ice Shelf. While the camp was being resupplied, the *Terra Nova* skirted eastward along the great wall of ice to the Bay of Whales. There, Scott's worst fears were confirmed. Amundsen had apparently found the going easy in the *Fram,* which was securely anchored off the ice cliffs of the Bay of Whales. This was a disturbing discovery to the men on board the *Terra Nova*—Amundsen was 60 miles nearer the pole than their camp in McMurdo Sound.

Starting out in October, 1911, Amundsen with his 4 companions,

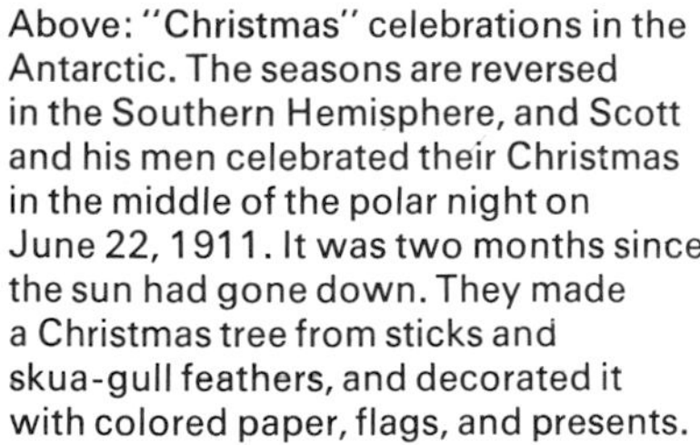

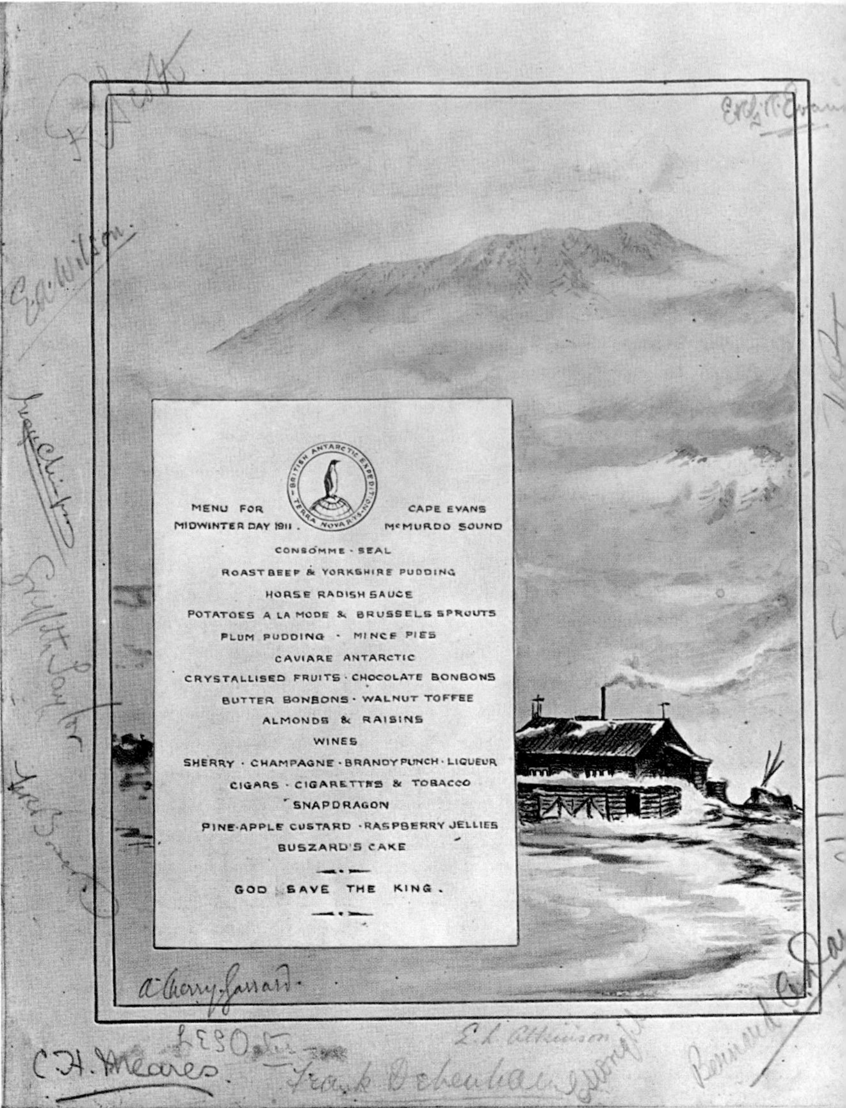

MENU FOR MIDWINTER DAY 1911.

BRITISH ANTARCTIC EXPEDITION · TERRA NOVA 1910

CAPE EVANS McMURDO SOUND

CONSOMMÉ · SEAL
ROAST BEEF & YORKSHIRE PUDDING
HORSE RADISH SAUCE
POTATOES A LA MODE & BRUSSELS SPROUTS
PLUM PUDDING · MINCE PIES
CAVIARE ANTARCTIC
CRYSTALLISED FRUITS · CHOCOLATE BONBONS
BUTTER BONBONS · WALNUT TOFFEE
ALMONDS & RAISINS
WINES
SHERRY · CHAMPAGNE · BRANDY PUNCH · LIQUEUR
CIGARS · CIGARETTES & TOBACCO
SNAPDRAGON
PINE-APPLE CUSTARD · RASPBERRY JELLIES
BUSZARD'S CAKE

GOD SAVE THE KING.

Above: "Christmas" celebrations in the Antarctic. The seasons are reversed in the Southern Hemisphere, and Scott and his men celebrated their Christmas in the middle of the polar night on June 22, 1911. It was two months since the sun had gone down. They made a Christmas tree from sticks and skua-gull feathers, and decorated it with colored paper, flags, and presents.

Above right: the Christmas menu. It includes such diverse delicacies as Caviare Antarctica and Buzzard's Cake. Bordering the menu can be seen the signatures of the expedition members.

4 sledges, and 52 dogs reached their southernmost supply depot on November 3. Scott and his companions left McMurdo Sound on November 1. Amundsen was equipped with Siberian huskies and sledges that he had cleverly managed to reduce in weight from 165 pounds each to only 48. Scott was burdened with the heavy ponies who had already shown that they suffered acutely from the cold and the fine snow that drifted through their shaggy coats. Amundsen was entirely preoccupied with reaching the pole. This ambition was made more pressing because of his fear that, as in the Arctic, he might be yet again forestalled. Scott's situation was somewhat different. The scientists in his party planned to carry out their scientific studies of the Antarctic as they went toward the pole.

Amundsen's greatest advantage was that he knew how to dress himself and his men so that they would be lightly and warmly clad. When he had wintered in the Arctic during the period when he was navigating the Northwest Passage he had adopted the Eskimos' way of dressing in loose-fitting garments made of fur. Thus Amundsen and his companions were warmer in their flexible 10-pound suits than the British expedition would ever be in their specially designed outfits that were of double that weight and that would not stay dry. Another thing that proved very helpful to Amundsen were his excellent dogs, which he had purchased in Greenland and that had arrived in the Antarctic in as good a condition as they were when they left home. Furthermore, Amundsen's men knew how to use the dogs and get them to move along quickly with the sledges. The frisky dogs and light sledges covered 90 miles during the first four days after leaving their main camp at the Bay of Whales. After a two-day rest at the first food depot Amundsen pressed ahead.

On leaving the advance depot at 80° south Amundsen put on skis, fixed a rope to one of the sledges and let himself be pulled along. "And there I stood until we reached 85°05′ S.—340 miles. Yes, that was a pleasant surprise. We had never dreamed of driving on skis to the Pole." They were then only 270 miles away from their goal, and it was only the middle of November. There was plenty of time left for the final stages of the push to the pole.

Scott, who had left his camp after Amundsen had set out from his, found the going across the Ross Ice Shelf slower than expected. Because of a summer blizzard from December 4 to December 9, it was impossible to move at all. When they were finally able to continue, the ponies began to sink up to their bellies in the snow and the men were forced to drive them mercilessly. After 15 hours of very slow progress, Scott had to order that the few remaining animals to survive the cold and exposure be shot.

By this time, all the supplies for the final push to the pole had been brought to the foot of the Beardmore Glacier, a vast river of ice flowing down from the upper plateau. But the four-day layover due to the blizzard had cost Scott dearly. Now he was racing both Amundsen and the on-coming Antarctic winter. He remembered that Ernest Shackleton had returned on February 28, 1909, from his attempt at the pole with barely a day to spare before winter locked the continent in its icy grip. And as he reached the foot of the glacier Scott knew that he was behind Shackleton's schedule.

Amundsen, unable to find a broad avenue like the Beardmore

The interior of Discovery Hut, the last permanent base of the Scott expedition. The stores look exactly as they were left 60 years ago, preserved by the low temperatures of the Antarctic.

Below: Roald Amundsen in his special Antarctic clothing for his bid to reach the South Pole. Amundsen was much better equipped with his light, warm clothing—adapted from the Eskimos' fur garments—and his sledges that were cleverly reduced in weight.

Glacier, to the upper plateau that stretches on to the South Pole, was forced to climb a narrow ice tongue he named the Axel Heiberg Glacier. It was here that he had underestimated the difficulties and distances of the journey. The snow was so deep and loose that the dogs had trouble finding their footing. Repeatedly Amundsen was forced to turn back and find a new route when his way was barred by massive blocks of ice. He was still nevertheless well ahead of Scott. The men in the British expedition were now man-hauling their sledges up the glacier, and on December 22, they established their upper Glacier Depot at an altitude of 8,000 feet. Already the men were showing signs of acute fatigue, and they were less than half way to the pole.

On December 7, Amundsen and his men reached 88° 23′, which had been Shackleton's farthest south point in 1909. To commemorate this achievement Amundsen ordered that the Norwegian flag should be hoisted above one of the sledges. In his book *South Pole,* Amundsen later described his feelings on this occasion. "All the sledges had stopped, and from the foremost of them the Norwegian flag was flying. It shook itself out, waved and flapped so that the silk rustled; it looked wonderfully well in the pure, clear air and the shining white surroundings. . . . No other moment in the whole trip affected me like this. The tears forced their way to my eyes; by no effort of will could I keep them back. Luckily I was some way in advance of the others so that I had time to pull myself together and master my feelings before reaching my comrades."

Just a week later, the Norwegians were at the South Pole. They had camped on December 13 only 15 miles away from it. That night Amundsen was awake off and on "and had the same feeling that I can remember as a little boy of the night before Christmas Eve—an intense expectation of what was going to happen." The next day, the weather was sparklingly clear and by 3 P.M. in the afternoon, they were at 90°S.—the bottom of the world.

Again the Norwegian flag was put up—this time on top of the tent that they planned to leave at the Pole. The men celebrated and gave themselves extra rations. To be certain that they had actually touched the pole itself, they made a 12½ mile circular trek around their camp. Then, on December 17, 1911, they started back to Framheim.

On New Year's Day, 1912, Scott wrote optimistically in his

journal: "Only 170 miles to the Pole and plenty of food." Three days later as he prepared for the final dash he added a fifth man to the group already chosen. The inclusion of one more man was perhaps Scott's most misguided decision, made at a time when he was too absorbed in his ambition to reach the pole to be able to think clearly. The addition of Lieutenant Bowers would mean overcrowding the tent and disorganizing a well-planned routine. Everything was ready—tent, food, and equipment—but of course this meant everything for four men and not five. There was also the matter of skis. Bowers had left his skis behind at the foot of the

Above: a photograph by Scott of his sledge teams drawn by Siberian ponies. Amundsen's attitude toward his animals was strictly matter-of-fact, they were simply part of the expedition supplies. Scott was sentimental, and could not bear the thought of killing and eating dogs that had helped him haul sledges. The ponies that he took instead were completely unsuitable for the journey. Below: a drawing by Dr. Edward Wilson of two of the ponies in a storm. After the ponies had died, the men of the expedition had to man-haul the sledges.

Right: Antarctica, showing the routes of explorers from 1900 to 1931.

Below: Amundsen's expedition members under the Norwegian flag at the South Pole, December 14, 1911. They made the return trip from the pole easily. With plenty of food and the elation of their triumph to keep them going, they reached their home base on January 25, having made the round trip to the pole in 99 days.

glacier, and he would have to trudge along on foot while the others used skis.

Then there were more blizzards. Soft fields of snow made hauling the sledge an agony, and they could cover no more than 10 miles a day. But Scott would not be disillusioned and remained confident that they would be first at the pole. On January 15 he wrote in his journal: "It is wonderful to see that two long marches will land us at the Pole . . . it ought to be a certain thing now, and the only appalling possibility is the sight of the Norwegian flag forestalling ours."

After that date, however, his journal entries became grim and heartrending. "We started off in high spirits in the afternoon, feeling that tomorrow would see us at our destination. About the

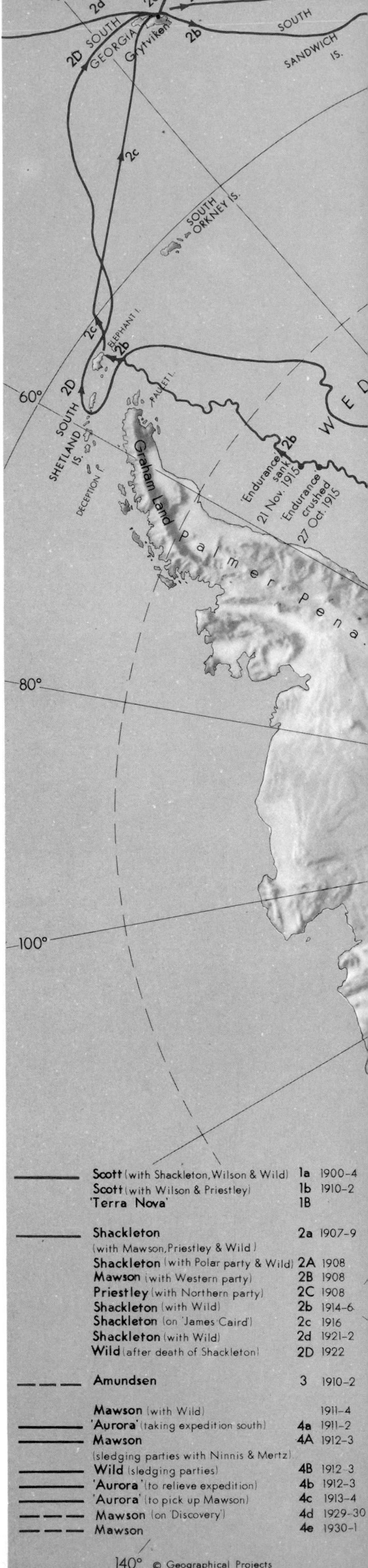

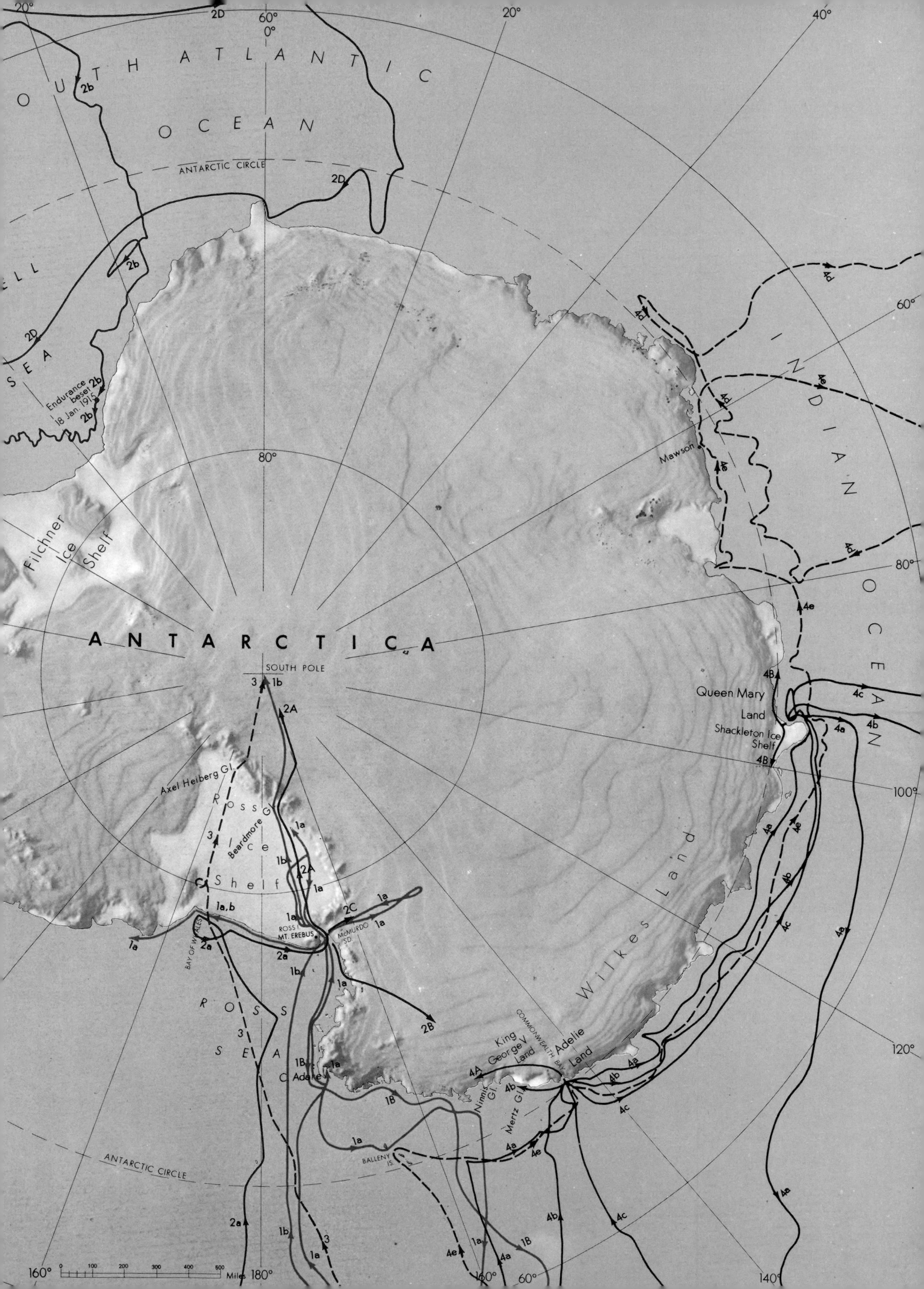

SOUTH ATLANTIC OCEAN
ANTARCTIC CIRCLE
ELL
SEA
Endurance beset 18 Jan. 1915
Filchner Ice Shelf
ANTARCTICA
SOUTH POLE
Axel Heiberg Gl.
ROSS Ice Shelf
Beardmore Gl.
BAY OF WHALES
ROSS I.
MT. EREBUS
McMURDO SD.
ROSS SEA
C. Adare
BALLENY IS.
ANTARCTIC CIRCLE
Ninnis Gl.
Mertz Gl.
King George V Land
COMMONWEALTH BAY
Adelie Land
Wilkes Land
Queen Mary Land
Shackleton Ice Shelf
Mawson
INDIAN OCEAN
Miles
0 100 200 300 400 500
20° 60° 0° 20° 40° 60° 80° 100° 120° 140° 160° 180° 160° 60° 80°

Above: a photograph taken by Bowers on the polar plateau, showing the other four men hauling the sledge. From left to right they are Evans, Oates, Wilson, and Scott. By this time they were weakening, and the task must have been agonizing. Scott wrote, "God help us, we can't keep pulling, that is certain. Amongst ourselves we are unendingly cheerful, but what every man feels in his heart, I can only guess."

second hour of that march, Bowers' sharp eyes detected what he thought was a cairn. . . . Half an hour later he detected a black speck. . . . We marched on and found that it was a black flag tied to a sledge bearer; nearby the remains of a camp . . . this told us the whole story. The Norwegians have forestalled us and are first at the Pole. It is a terrible disappointment for me and I am very sorry for my loyal companions."

On January 17, 1912, Scott reached the pole, where he found Amundsen's tent and the letter he had left behind, addressed to Scott. The exhausted and discouraged Englishmen built a cairn near Amundsen's tent, unfurled their Union Jack and photographed themselves at the Pole. For Scott who had for years dreamed of being the first to stand at the position of the South Pole, it was a bitter experience. "Great God! this is an awful place. . . ." he wrote. "Now for the run home and a desperate struggle. I wonder if we can do it?"

The next day the return journey began—800 miles across the most difficult terrain in the world. The health of the men began to worry Scott, as scurvy, frostbite, and fatigue became constant complaints. On January 25, he wrote: "Only 89 miles to the next

Below: a drawing by Wilson of one of the sledging party getting ready for a night away from the base. In the foreground the sledge can be seen, half-buried by the gale-swept snow. Scott's party was plagued by blizzards.

Above: the Scott party at the pole, their Union Jack fluttering sadly near the Norwegian flag left by the Amundsen expedition. After all their struggles they arrived at the goal to discover that they were simply the second party to reach the pole, that all their grinding fatigue and hardships had been endured for so poor a prize. This photograph, with the others taken on their journey, was developed from negatives found with their bodies eight months later. Left to Right: Oates, Bowers, Scott, Wilson, Evans. Bowers took the photograph by pulling a string attached to the camera-shutter.

depot, but it is time we cleared off this plateau . . . Oates suffers from a very cold foot; Evans' fingers and nose are in a bad state and tonight Wilson is suffering tortures from his eyes . . . I fear a succession of blizzards at this time of year . . . not only stopping our marches but the cold damp air takes it out of us. . . ."

At the same time as Scott wrote these words more than 700 miles deep in the Antarctic solitude, Amundsen was arriving at his base camp near the Bay of Whales. It had taken him 99 days to cover 1,860 miles in his conquest of the pole with an ease that made the feat seem less than it was. Luck had contributed to his success. But his use of dogs rather than ponies, the skill with which he had

placed his food depots, and his determination were equally responsible. Yet even while he and his companions celebrated their safe return tragic events were taking place to the south.

On February 7, Scott and his men reached the head of the Beardmore Glacier where naked rock was exposed by the blasting winds. Even with their disappointment and being completely worn down by the endless days of cold they managed to maintain sufficient morale and strength to collect 30 pounds of rocks from the region. These were to be transported back to the base camp for examination by the expedition geologist. Then on their way down the glacier, they became lost and wasted so much time that food rations

Above: Robert Falcon Scott. In this detail from the photograph opposite his face shows clearly all his tension and bitter disappointment.

had to be reduced. By the time the flag marking the next depot had at last been sighted, there was one meal left for each man. While they were descending the glacier, the seaman in the group, Edgar Evans, fell twice and injured his head. He became dazed and incoherent, and as Scott recorded in his journal, "He (Evans) is absolutely changed from his normal self-reliant self." On February 17, when they reached the bottom of the glacier, Evans became unable to keep pace with the other men, and frequently someone had to stay behind with him. Then one day he dropped to his knees

Above: a charcoal drawing by Edward Wilson of three men cramped together in a tiny tent, drawn on a previous expedition with Scott eight years before the tragic South Pole journey. It must have been very similar to the last sad days when Scott, Wilson, and Bowers lay trapped by the storm after Evans and Oates were gone. It was in that tent that the rescue party found them, lying peacefully in death, with Scott's arm thrown protectively over Wilson, his friend.

Right: Captain Oates walking out into the blizzard on his frostbitten feet, going to his death in an attempt to give his comrades the chance to survive.

with his clothing disarranged, his hands uncovered and badly frostbitten, and "a wild look in his eyes." That night Evans lapsed into a coma and died. The others were still 430 torturous miles from their base camp.

The Army officer, Captain Oates, was the next man to weaken. He could no longer pull a sledge, but trudged alongside despite his painfully frostbitten feet. By March 15, when he realized he could go on no longer, he begged the others to leave him behind to die, which they refused to do. The next day when another blizzard kept

Below: the last page from Scott's diary. When he realized they would not survive, he wrote several moving letters, one of them to Wilson's wife. He said, "If this letter reaches you, Bill and I will have gone out together. We are very near it now and I should like you to know how splendid he was at the end—everlastingly cheerful and ready to sacrifice himself for others, never a word of blame to me for leading him into this mess . . . I can do no more to comfort you than to tell you that he died as he lived, a brave, true man —the best of comrades and staunchest of friends. My whole heart goes out to you in pity. Yours, R. Scott."

Below right: Scott's hut near McMurdo Station and beyond it the cross erected in memory of the unlucky expedition. In Britain the whole nation was plunged into mourning—and Scott and his companions became national heroes.

all four inside the tent, Oates made an excuse for going outside for a few minutes. He shuffled out into the blizzard and was never seen again.

Then the cooking and heating fuel that was vital to their survival began to run low. Somehow, it had evaporated from the cans where it was stored. The danger of freezing to death was now added to the threats of frostbite, hunger, and fatigue. Two days after Oates' disappearance Scott wrote: "We have the last half-fill of oil in our primus and a very small quantity of spirit — this alone between us and. . . ."

On March 21, when they were only 11 miles from their last food depot, yet another blizzard blew up and forced them to make camp. Whirling whiteness and cold pinned the three survivors in their tent. They lay there, knowing that only a short distance away lay thousands of pounds of food.

During this awful period of desolation, Scott still had the strength to record his thoughts in the now-famous journal. "Had we lived, I should have had a tale to tell of the hardihood, endurance, and cour-

We shall stick it out
to the end but we
are getting weaker of
course and the end
cannot be far.
It seems a pity but
I do not think I can
write more—
R. Scott
Last Entry
For God's sake look
after our people

age of my companions that would have stirred the heart of every Englishman. These rough notes and our dead bodies must tell the tale, but surely, surely, a great rich country like ours will see that those who are dependent on us are properly provided for."

About a week later he made this final entry in the journal: "... Every day now we have been ready to start for our depot *eleven miles* away, but outside the door of the tent, it remains a scene of whirling drift. I do not think we can hope for any better things now. We shall stick it out to the end, but we are getting weaker, of course, and the end cannot be far.

"It seems a pity, but I do not think I can write more.

R. Scott.

"For God's sake look after our people."

Eight months passed before their bodies were found. Wilson and Bowers were lying with their sleeping bags closed. Scott's bag was open. One arm was thrown across Wilson, perhaps his closest friend. In a bag lying near the bodies were the 30 pounds of Beardmore rocks the men had carried with them to the end.

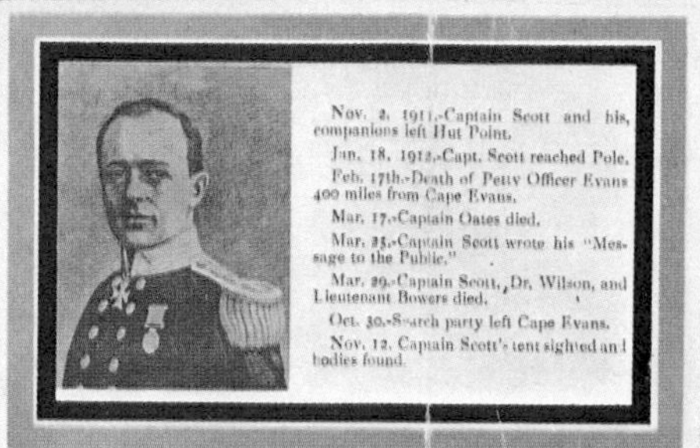

Nov. 2. 1911.-Captain Scott and his, companions left Hut Point.

Jan. 18. 1912.-Capt. Scott reached Pole.

Feb. 17th.-Death of Petty Officer Evans 400 miles from Cape Evans.

Mar. 17.-Captain Oates died.

Mar. 25.-Captain Scott wrote his "Message to the Public."

Mar. 29.-Captain Scott, Dr. Wilson, and Lieutenant Bowers died.

Oct. 30.-Search party left Cape Evans.

Nov. 12. Captain Scott's tent sighted and bodies found.

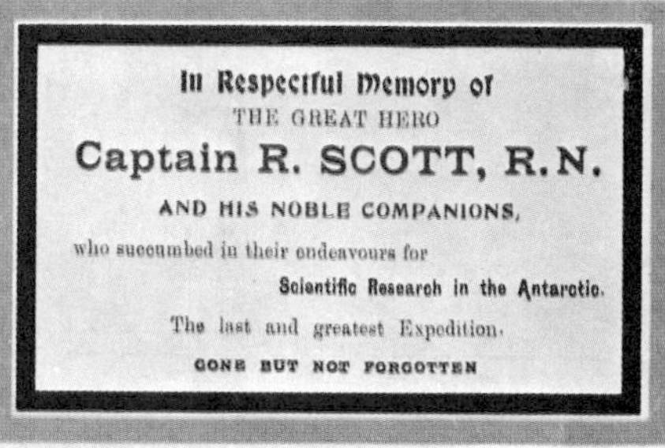

In Respectful Memory of

THE GREAT HERO

Captain R. SCOTT, R.N.

AND HIS NOBLE COMPANIONS,

who succumbed in their endeavours for

Scientific Research in the Antarctic.

The last and greatest Expedition.

GONE BUT NOT FORGOTTEN

Above: In Memoriam cards for Scott.

Right: Douglas Mawson. He was already an experienced Antarctic traveler when in 1911–12 he took the first Australian expedition to the Southern Continent, an expedition not without tragedy.
Below: the interior of an Antarctic building. Unless a building is heated, even the moisture in breath will produce these ice formations hanging from the ceiling—frozen condensation. Mawson named his hut at Commonwealth Bay "The Home of the Blizzard."

The Home of the Blizzard

8

The Antarctic "summer" of 1911–1912 had seen the South Pole conquered twice, with relative ease by Roald Amundsen, tragically by Robert F. Scott. During November and December, 1911, when these two were racing toward the pole, the first Australian expedition to Antarctica was heading for the region between Oates Land and Wilhelm II Land. This was the coastline that had not been visited since the days of Charles Wilkes and Dumont d'Urville and was virgin territory for exploration.

The leader of the Australian group was the English-born Douglas Mawson, an experienced Antarctic traveler and scientist who had climbed Mount Erebus on an earlier expedition. On another journey he had accompanied a Professor T. W. E. David to the South Magnetic Pole. His aim this time was the scientific and geographical exploration of the area between Oates Land and Wilhelm II Land. To make this easier Mawson planned to set up three separate exploring bases on Antarctica that would keep in touch with one another by short-wave radio.

The ship that took the Australians south was an old sealer called the *Aurora*. By January, 1912, it had gone eastward along the Antarctic coast until Mawson saw a suitable site for their main winter base on Cape Denison in Commonwealth Bay.

The area around the camp site was a vast and flat expanse of ice

Below: members of Mawson's expedition gathering ice for water during a blizzard. The power qf the icy wind sweeping over the open expanses of the polar continent knocks men off their feet, so that they must almost crawl about when outdoors.

Above: long crevasses in the Antarctic. Here they are visible, with a thin coat of ice over them that is covered with snow. Frequently the snow covering lies even with the surrounding surface, so that the first indication of their presence is that the ice cracks open when a weight travels over the top.

shelf that got steeper toward the south. Because of the unceasing winds that blew throughout the region Mawson nicknamed their Commonwealth Bay camp "The Home of the Blizzard." Once, a wind speed of 63.6 miles per hour was recorded, and occasionally gusts of up to 200 miles per hour were registered at the weather station set up near the camp. There was always a wind—a screaming gale that dominated the lives of Mawson and his companions. The men had to lean so far forward as they walked into the direction of the wind that a sudden lull would make them lunge forward and fall. Without the 1½-inch spikes attached to the soles of their boots, they would have been unable to make any progress at all against the winds. On one occasion, Mawson saw a 3,000-pound tractor tossed 50 yards into the air by a sudden gust. The constant blizzards brought perpetual darkness, unrelieved by the starlight that in calm weather gives Antarctic winters an eery light.

Despite the furious winds and interminable darkness, Mawson stuck to his intention of making systematic scientific observations. The meteorological hut had to be visited regularly so that records of the weather changes could be made. In his journal Mawson des-

cribed a typical trip to the hut of a man crawling on his hands and knees to keep himself from being blown away. Almost immediately as he emerged from the warmth of a camp building, the man's eyebrows and beard would become frozen and covered with tiny icicles. If he stopped for a moment and put his hand six inches in front of his face, the mittened hand would be hidden by the whirling snow that continually filled the air. When he had crawled along for what seemed to be the distance to the hut, the man would reach out and grope for the door of the hut. Once the door had been found, the man would have to cling to it and with a free hand try to open it enough so that he could squeeze into the hut. Often after such a journey over and back to take a look at the instruments, the man would see that a patch of skin on his face, or a finger, had been frostbitten.

After spending 10 months at the Home of the Blizzard the Australians embarked on their explorations, dividing themselves up into five separate parties. For the next few months four of these groups would concentrate on making systematic explorations of the coastal regions and the inland ice sheet of King George V Land.

Above: Mawson staring in horror down the crevasse into which Ninnis had just disappeared with the sledge that carried most of their food. The hole in the snow was 11 feet across, opening above a crack that went deep below them. There was no sign of him. Mawson and Mertz stayed by the hole calling for hours. No one answered.
Below: Lieutenant B. E. S. Ninnis.

Mawson had two men in his group and they were to explore the coast from Cape Denison to Oates Land. One of them was an Englishman, Lieutenant B. E. S. Ninnis, the other was Dr. Xavier Mertz, a young Swiss mountaineer and skiing champion. The group took three sledges to carry provisions and these were pulled by 17 huskies.

By the end of November Mawson's group had its first setback when one of the sledges, loaded with half the food, dropped into a crevasse. Fortunately they were able to haul it out and continue on. But a few days later, in the midst of a two-day blizzard they were forced to abandon the damaged sledge and had to transfer the food and supplies to the remaining two. Most of the food was loaded on to Ninnis' sledge, which the strongest dogs pulled.

On December 14, with the sun shining brightly, they decided to make one last dash to reach their "farthest east" point before turning back to explore farther inland. Mertz, who was on skis, led the way. Mawson was in the middle with the light sledge, and Ninnis brought up the rear with his heavily laden sledge. Where crevasses threaten, the iron rule of travel across snow is to put the heaviest load in the rear.

About noon, Mertz raised his ski pole, a prearranged signal telling the others that he was passing over a crevasse. Mawson carefully examined the snow at the spot but found no signs of weakness and sledged on. Suddenly, he looked ahead to see Mertz gazing back past him in horror. "Behind me," Mawson wrote, "Nothing met my eyes but my own sledge tracks running back in the distance. Where was Ninnis and his sledge?"

Behind them, there was nothing but a gaping hole where their companion had been. Far below, a crack penetrated deep into the ice, and they could see a badly injured dog whimpering on an ice shelf about 150 feet down. Another dog lay motionless beside the first. Ninnis and his sledge had completely disappeared. For three hours the two men shouted into the crevasse. But no answer came from the depths below. Hours went by, and the injured dog finally died. At last, knowing that Ninnis could not be alive, Mawson read aloud a short burial service.

Mawson and Mertz were in desperate straits. They had lost most of their own rations, all the food for the dogs, and the tent. Worse still was the fact that they were 300 miles from base with no reserve supplies of food on the trail behind them. Their only hope was to make a dash for home, killing and eating the dogs to supplement the 1½-weeks' food supply that remained.

Throwing all precautions aside, they began their race against time and weather, risking snow bridges across crevasses in a way they would have thought suicidal before. Their dogs became so weak from hunger, cold, and overwork that most of them died. The few who managed to keep going were eventually shot for the stringy meat that still remained on their bones.

Then Mertz began to weaken. Lack of food and the killing strain

Above: the icecap with its hummocks and ridges. It was over similar very difficult terrain that Mawson had to haul his sledge alone after Mertz died.

Left: Xavier Mertz. He was a young Swiss mountaineer, who was also a skiing champion. When the expedition had divided into four separate groups for exploration, he went with Mawson.

of manhauling the sledge sapped his strength. He was badly frostbitten but refused to believe it until one day he bit off the end of a finger from which all feeling had gone. By January 1, he could no longer pull the sledge and Mawson had to drag him along on top of it. "Both our chances are going now," wrote Mawson on January 6. The next day Mertz died.

Mawson was alone and still more than 100 miles from the shelter of the Home of the Blizzard. To reduce the weight he had to pull he cut the sledge in half and discarded everything that wasn't essential for survival. By now the skin on his frostbitten feet was beginning to blister, which slowed his pace down to a little more than six miles a day. There seemed little chance that he would ever reach the base camp.

As he was recrossing Mertz Glacier on January 17, Mawson slipped through the snow into a crevasse, dangling on the end of a 14-foot line while the anchoring sledge above inched toward the edge of the crevasse. If it slipped much more, he would be carried to certain death below.

Miraculously the sledge stopped moving. Weakened as he was, Mawson was somehow able to catch hold of a knot in the rope and managed to haul himself up to the rim of the crevasse. But just as he reached the top, the overhanging snow-ledge collapsed. Again, he fell the length of the line.

Somehow Mawson managed to overcome his desperate feelings and the pain of dangling in the rope harness. He climbed up the rope once again, inch by agonizing inch. This time the snow at the top of the crevasse held. He scrambled over the edge and crawled to a safer surface where he lay for an hour, too weak to move. There was very little food left now, but despite his constant hunger Mawson managed to stagger on.

After nearly two more weeks of the most agonising progress he found a cairn that had apparently been left by a search party that had come out from the base camp to look for Mawson, Ninnis, and Mertz. In the cairn Mawson found a bag of food and a note telling him that more supplies had been left 23 miles ahead. The food gave Mawson new strength and he was able to continue his lonely trek to the next food depot, which was only five miles from Commonwealth Bay. As he reached the second cairn, a blizzard struck and prevented him from making any further progress on the five miles between him and the base camp.

Meanwhile, the *Aurora* was being prepared for her return journey to Australia. Even though Mawson had failed to turn up, the captain of the *Aurora* knew that he would have to take the ship on to the Shackleton Ice Shelf to pick up another of the exploring parties that was waiting there. Mawson had told Captain Davis before he had set out with Ninnis and Mertz that Davis should take over command of the expedition if he, Mawson, did not come back. The *Aurora* set sail on February 1, on the very morning that Mawson finally staggered back into the camp at Commonwealth Bay.

Five men were waiting for him there—volunteers who had offered to spend another winter at the Bay in the unlikely hope that Mawson, Ninnis, and Mertz would return. Quickly a message was radioed to the *Aurora* to return. But the ship was unable to get back into the bay because of a hurricane. Furthermore, the party on the Shackleton Ice Shelf, which was led by Frank Wild, an experienced explorer who had been with Robert Scott on an earlier expedition, was unprepared for another winter in the Antarctic. Unless he sailed on, Davis knew that the encroaching winter ice might prevent the *Aurora* from reaching them at all. It was a difficult

Above: the appalling moment when the exhausted Mawson reached Coronation Bay, just in time to see the *Aurora* steaming away. But five expedition members had volunteered to spend another winter in the hut there in the hope that Mawson might return.

Left: Mawson's sledge, cut in half to make it lighter to haul. His ski poles, snow shoes, and sleeping bag are on it.

decision for Davis to make. Mawson would have to spend another winter in the "Home of the Blizzard," on the continent that had killed his two companions and nearly taken his own life.

Another Antarctic winter descended on Mawson and the men who had stayed behind to wait for him. Again the winds were so strong that they had to crawl across the snow to the meteorological hut to record the temperature and wind speeds. One day in July the instruments in the hut showed an average wind speed of 63.5 miles per hour, and for one eight-hour period it got up to 107 miles per hour. As they had done during the previous winter, the men spent some of their idle hours betting on the average monthly velocity of the wind. The prize was usually a bar of chocolate.

Radio contact with Australia was maintained by sending messages via a small substation on Macquarie Island. It was on this hookup that the men learned of the death of Scott and his men, which had occurred almost exactly a year before. Perhaps Mawson better than anyone else was able to appreciate the isolated desperation and pain of their last hours. To help distract themselves from their own feelings of isolation and boredom the men at the Home of the Blizzard produced their own newspaper called *The Adélie Blizzard.* Much of the news, which was typed out on the typewriter, had been picked up from the radio transmissions they received from Australia. Finally, one day in mid-November, the radio informed them that the

Above: the Mawson expedition that was in the Antarctic from 1929 to 1931. Douglas Mawson himself is the third from the right in the center row. He recuperated rapidly from his ordeal and was soon back in the Antarctic.

Aurora had left Australia on its way to pick them up. Several weeks later they saw a faint smudge of smoke on the horizon and knew that the *Aurora* had arrived.

Before they actually set sail for home in mid-December, Mawson asked Captain Davis to take the *Aurora* westward along the coast to the Shackleton Ice Shelf, a glacier-fed platform of ice that extends out into the ocean. This was just another example of Mawson's dedication to science—after an absence of over two years he could still defer his homecoming in order to gain more knowledge about Antarctica. More of the coastline was mapped and more zoological specimens were collected from the ocean. In addition the men on the *Aurora* had a chance to watch the crumbling of a large section of the shelf. As the ship was making its way along the coast about 300 yards out from the cliff, they saw some pieces of ice drop from the top edge of the cliff. Then an enormous slice of the cliff broke off and plunged into the sea with a deep, booming roar. Then it rose again to the surface and began to shed great white masses of itself that pushed toward the ship in an ever-widening field of ice. The main piece of the slice continued to rise high out of the water and then to sink from sight. When this motion ceased the slice had become a beautiful blue iceberg amidst acres and acres of white fragments—the heart of a flower among its fallen petals.

At last in February, 1914, the *Aurora* returned to Australia. Douglas Mawson received worldwide acclaim for his feat. He was still physically broken and it would take years for him to completely recover his strength. But the Antarctic maintained its fascination for Mawson, and he returned for more explorations in 1929.

Below: the *Aurora,* which arrived back at the base camp at Coronation Bay almost a year after Mawson had completed his solitary march.

Above: Vilhjalmur Stefansson, the Canadian explorer who went to the Arctic in 1906 to join the Anglo-American Polar Expedition. Although the expedition never materialized, Stefansson began his lifelong study of the Eskimos. He had an abiding curiosity, an inquiring, original mind, and was to become one of the first scientists to believe in "living off the land"—and to practice his belief.

The Riddle of the Copper Eskimos

9

Charlie Klinkenberg was blessed with boundless energy and fearlessness. As an Arctic sea captain he had few peers. As a ruthless scoundrel he had none. Entrusted with the whaling ship *Olga* by its owner James McKenna, Charlie had one foggy morning in 1905 slipped out of the Yukon port of Herschel without permission and without orders. Steaming eastward, he had looted a storehouse and then sailed farther east to Victoria Island to hunt caribou.

Charlie's adventures might never have been recorded had it not been for the fact that in the spring of 1907 he was to meet with the arctic explorer, Vilhjalmur Stefansson.

In the spring of 1906—a year after Charlie had vanished in the

Above: carved whales' teeth, crafted by a sailor on a whaling ship. The scenes show Eskimo life, hunting bears, reindeer, and seals, traveling in sledges, and living in their igloos.

Arctic fog—this young Canadian explorer had traveled overland from Victoria, British Columbia, then by boat down the Mackenzie River to Herschel Island, which is about 80 miles west of Mackenzie Bay. At Herschel he was to join the Anglo-American Polar Expedition and proceed eastward to Victoria Island aboard the expedition's schooner, the *Duchess of Bedford*. From his book knowledge of the Arctic Stefansson feared that the ship would never reach Herschel Island because it had no auxiliary engines. It was for this reason that he arranged to make his way by rail and river. If the *Duchess of Bedford* failed to get to Mackenzie, Stefansson knew he could spend his time living with the Eskimos of Mackenzie Bay. For a long time

Above: a photograph that Stefansson took of the Mackenzie River Eskimos with whom he lived in the winter of 1906–1907. They were of the Koukgamuit tribe, from the east mouth of the Mackenzie River. By the end of the winter Stefansson had mastered the fundamentals of their language and felt at home in their settlements.

he had been interested in Eskimo life and culture, of which very little was known and even less documented. And he had eagerly accepted an invitation to join the expedition as its anthropologist.

When Stefansson got to Herschel in August there was no sign of the schooner, which of course, did not surprise him. Even though he had always doubted that the ship would come to pick him up, Stefansson had entrusted his entire Arctic outfit to it. If he was going to live with the Eskimos he wanted to do so as one of them—in their houses, dressing like them, and eating what they ate. Thus in August he found himself, in accord with his own plan, set down 200 miles north of the Arctic Circle, with a summer weight suit of clothing, a camera, some notebooks, a rifle, and ammunition. He was facing an Arctic winter, where his only shelter would have to be the roof of some hospitable Eskimo house.

These were ideal conditions for Stefansson who knew that if he had been with an expedition and had lived with the other men in it, he would have lived near the Eskimos, instead of with them. "I should have seen them as an outsider, a stranger. If I had visited

Above: Stefansson was not the first to find the Eskimo pattern of life particularly interesting. This is a drawing by Sir John Ross of an Eskimo village known as North Hendon, near Felix Harbor on the Boothia Peninsula.

them now and then I should have found them wearing their company manners and should have obtained no better insight into their lives than does the ordinary missionary or trader. My very poverty was my greatest advantage; I was not rich and powerful like the whaling captains or mounted policemen, so there was no reason why they should flatter me or show me deference."

The Mackenzie Eskimos of Herschel Island took Stefansson into their houses and treated him hospitably and courteously and exactly as if he were one of them. They gave him clothes to wear and shared their food with him. He in turn helped them with their fishing and hunting and joined in their games until they gradually forgot that he was not one of them. They began to live their lives in front of Stefansson as though he was not there at all.

What Stefansson learned during that winter from October 1906 to March 1907, was to provide him with the incentive to stay five years in the Arctic in order to know more about the Eskimos. Although their language is extremely difficult to learn, by the end of the winter he felt that he had mastered the fundamentals and was able to live among these people without any feeling of isolation.

One day in the spring of 1907 word spread through Herschel that a ship had been sighted. Stefansson thought it might be the *Duchess of Bedford* after all, but when the vessel appeared on the horizon it was seen to be coming from the northeast. The *Duchess* surely would have approached from the west. As the ship approached the harbor on Herschel Island, Stefansson saw the name *Olga* on its bow. The schooner was commanded by Captain Charles Klinkenberg, who met Stefansson when he came ashore.

As the two men talked during the next few days, Klinkenberg had news that particularly interested Stefansson—the *Olga* had wintered on Banks Island to the east of Herschel. Here, Klinkenberg and the men on board had seen Eskimos who were armed with bows and arrows and who used copper tools and who evidently had been in no contact with white men in recent years.

What intrigued Stefansson was the idea that there might really exist on Banks Island and Victoria Island and even on the north shore of the continent of America, Eskimos who had never seen a white man. Perhaps these Eskimos were descendants of men from the Franklin mission or from the many search parties that had gone looking for the lost Englishmen. Stefansson wanted to find out whether human beings really did exist in these remote areas, which were marked with the words "uninhabited" on a map issued by the Canadian government in 1906.

Early in the winter of 1907, Stefansson returned to Canada where he began making plans to go back to the Arctic as soon as possible. (Charlie apparently continued to command the *Olga,* doing some whale hunting to earn money and having an adventurous time.) It was on his return to Canada that Stefansson learned of the fate of the *Duchess of Bedford.* The ice at Point Barrow blocked its farther advance until the beginning of winter and then it had been completely stopped by the floes on the north coast of Alaska at Flaxman Island. The Anglo-American Polar Expedition was now sad history.

Stefansson's keenness to return to the Arctic must have won over the directors of the American Museum of Natural History. They agreed to supply enough money for him to carry out his study of the Eskimos. Then by chance a zoologist and friend of Stefansson's, who was eager to study the birds and animals of the Arctic, was invited to accompany him. This was Dr. Rudolph Martin Anderson.

Right: watercolors of an Eskimo couple, by John White and dated about 1570. The woman (left) is carrying a baby in her hood. Stefansson, exploring the Arctic more than 300 years later, was fascinated by the clothing worn by the Eskimos, which is generally loose-fitting to allow a layer of warm air between clothing and skin.

Right: Eskimos fishing through holes they have made in the ice. Stefansson learned to fish and hunt in the way the Eskimos did, and was very soon able to live in barren surroundings where white men were usually doomed.

Above: an igloo under construction. Stefansson wrote that the Eskimos illuminated their igloos with lamps burning oil. He said the lamps "were set low down in Eskimo fashion but their light was reflected again and again from the million snow crystals in the dome, so that the house was filled with a soft and diffused glow."

In May, 1908, Stefansson and Anderson headed for the Yukon. Their plan was to get to Herschel, pick up some supplies there, and hitch a ride on a whaler for Victoria Island. As before, Stefansson's equipment was of the simplest kind. He and Dr. Anderson each had a camera and supplies of film, a pair of rifles and plenty of ammunition. They also carried half a dozen rifles and shotguns for the Eskimos to use and a small supply of tobacco that they would give to prospective Eskimo employees. They each had a silk tent, writing materials, and a pair of field glasses, and a couple of cooking utensils —all the essentials for Arctic exploration, except for matches.

By mid-August the two men and the Eskimos they had engaged as guides were at Herschel Island where they expected to be able to buy matches from the whaling ships that stop at the island. At Herschel they also planned to join up with any one of the whalers that they expected would be going east to Victoria Island. But only

one whaler arrived, and it had no extra supplies of matches to sell.

Stefansson then went to the Northwest Mounted Police and explained his predicament, asking them to give, lend, or sell him enough matches to last through the winter. This the commanding officer of the police refused to do. He was certain no white men could survive a winter on Victoria Island and he knew that no one would go there without matches. So to "protect" the explorers the police denied them the one absolutely essential item for such a trip. The officer did nevertheless offer to put up the two men for the winter at Herschel. Stefansson's response was typical, "Since we had not come north to study the habits of the police at Herschel, we decided . . . to head for Point Barrow," where matches and supplies might be had.

The explorers had much the same luck at Point Barrow, where they decided to wait out the winter. But the time was not spent in idleness. Stefansson became friendly with Natkusiak, an Eskimo "who turned out to be the best traveling companion I have ever had of any race." Natkusiak was also fluent in many Eskimo dialects and taught these to Stefansson, who picked them up eagerly and quickly. In the meantime, Anderson made frequent side trips into the mountains to collect zoological specimens.

It was not until August, 1909, that Stefansson, Anderson, and Natkusiak left Point Barrow for Herschel. But almost a year was to pass before Stefansson, Natkusiak, and another Eskimo named Tannaumirk went even farther east into the region south of Victoria Island.

Stefansson's goal was still to find the Eskimos he had heard about from Klinkenberg. On April 21, 1910, the party set out along a stretch of mainland coast thought to be uninhabited. (Anderson, who had weathered a bout of pneumonia during the winter, had returned to the Mackenzie delta to continue his work there.)

About eight days out, after rounding Cape Parry, they came upon the remains of an Eskimo village. The place appeared to have been

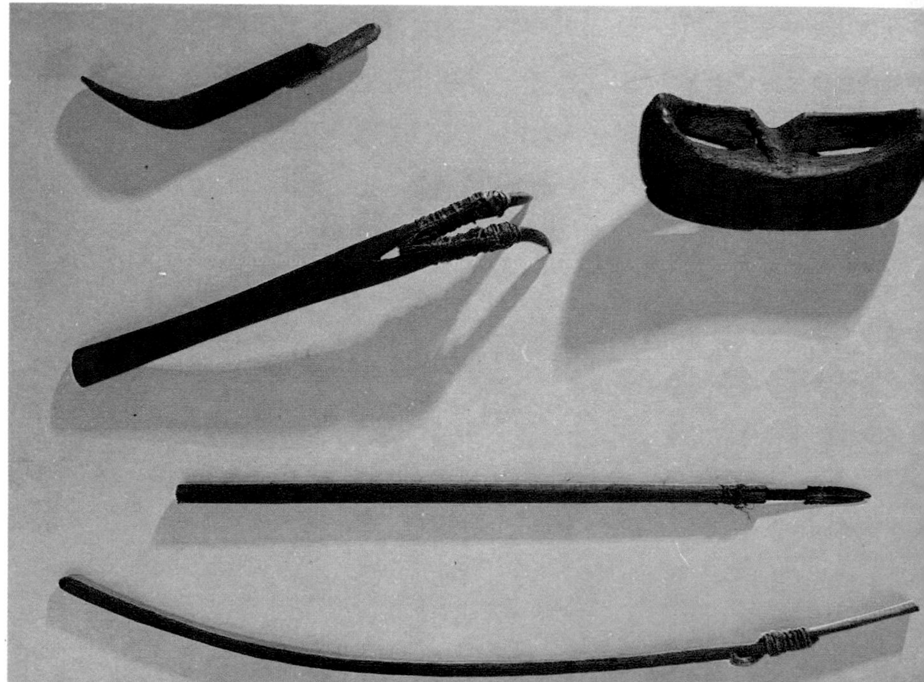

Right: Eskimo hunting equipment that Stefansson collected in the Mackenzie Bay area. Among the implements is a pair of wooden snow goggles, which were worn to prevent snow blindness.

abandoned for a long while, which convinced Natkusiak and Tannaumirk that the region was indeed uninhabited. Stefansson was less certain.

On May 9, they reached Point Wise, where the sea begins to be squeezed between the mainland and the southern shore of Victoria Island. While walking along Stefansson caught sight of a piece of driftwood that seemed to have been hacked by a man-made tool. The next day they saw footprints and sledge tracks. Then during the morning of May 13, they came to a deserted village. Stefansson climbed up on the roof of one of the snow houses to survey the surrounding area. In the distance he saw several men sitting beside some seal holes waiting to spear their prey. After they had driven the sledges nearer to the place where the Eskimo hunters were, Tannaumirk slowly approached them. Suddenly, one of the seal hunters jumped up, holding a long metal knife in his hand. Tannaumirk was quick to explain that he and his companions were friendly. After a while, to convince himself that Tannaumirk was not some sort of evil spirit, the man squeezed Tannaumirk's arm to make sure that he was in fact human. He and the other hunters then invited Tannaumirk, Stefansson, and Natkusiak to come and visit their village.

When they walked into the village, men, women, and children came rushing toward them. After everyone had been introduced, the women hurried off to their houses to cook dinner for their visitors. Then the men got their snow knives and house-building mittens and set about erecting igloos for Stefansson and his two companions.

As he watched and listened Stefansson was hardly able to believe that he was actually seeing not the remains of an ancient civilization but the Stone Age itself. "These people who had never seen a white man until they saw me were completely human men and women, entirely friendly who welcomed us to their homes and bade us stay."

When the snow-house was finished, the Eskimos furnished it with a seal-oil lamp that could be used for cooking and would also provide some warmth to the igloo. Inside they also fashioned a sleeping platform over which were spread reindeer, bear, and musk-ox skins. As the Eskimo men put their final touches to this cozy and comfortable little camp, they told the visitors that their stay in the village was to be a holiday when no hunting would be done.

Right: Vilhjalmur Stefansson in his Eskimo clothing, wearing snow shoes to enable him to move easily across the deep Arctic snows. Throughout his travels from one Eskimo village to another, Stefansson was impressed with the unself-conscious friendliness and the generosity of the people.

Above: while Stefansson was staying with the Mackenzie Bay Eskimos they gave him clothes to wear and taught him how to make his own. This shows the jacket and the hood that he wore.

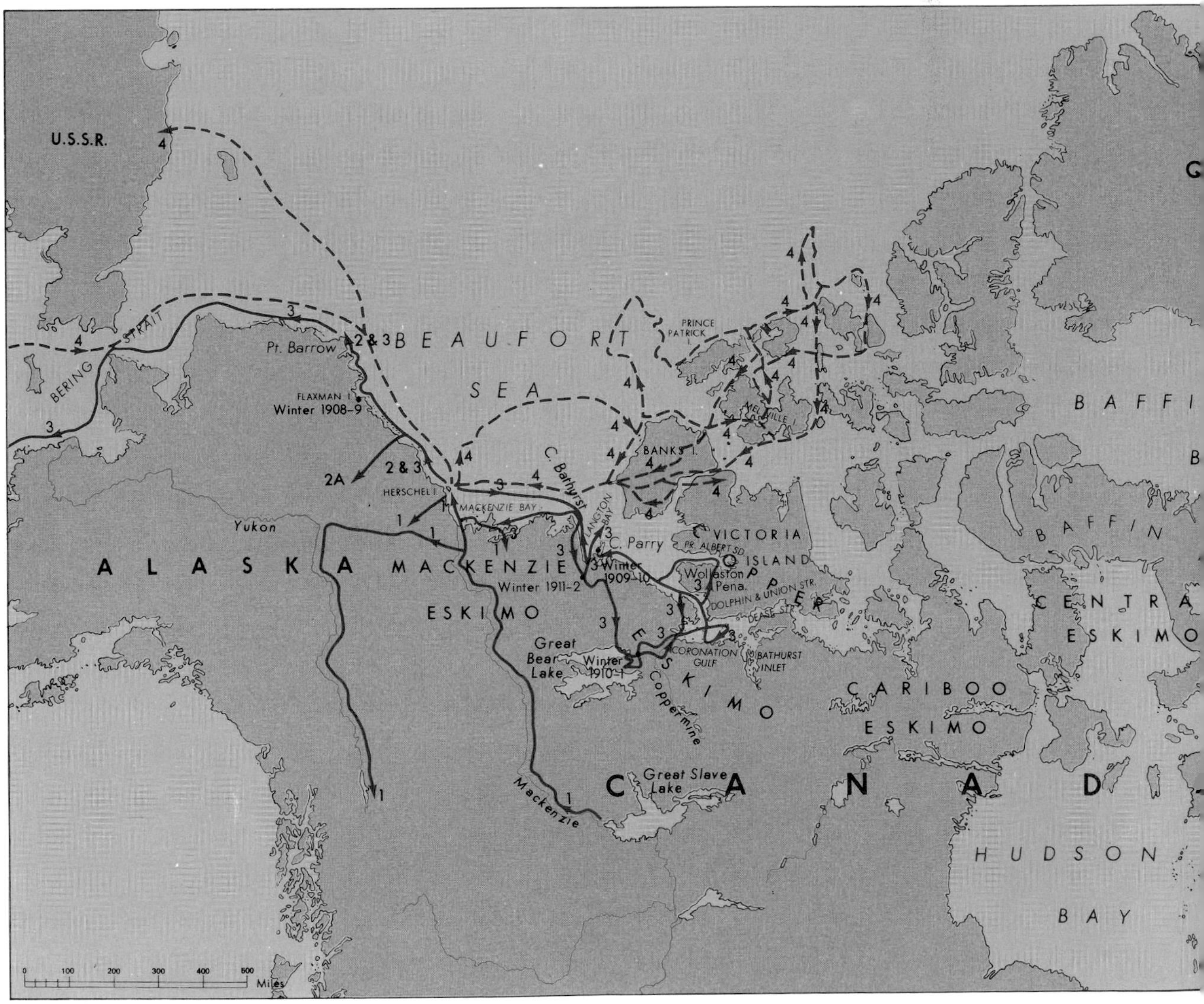

U.S.S.R.
BERING STRAIT
Pt. Barrow
BEAUFORT
SEA
FLAXMAN I.
Winter 1908–9
2A
2 & 3
HERSCHEL I.
MACKENZIE BAY
C. Bathurst
PRINCE PATRICK I.
MELVILLE I.
BANKS I.
LANGTON BAY
C. Parry
VICTORIA ISLAND
PR. ALBERT SD.
Wollaston Pena.
DOLPHIN & UNION STR.
DEASE STR.
Winter 1909–10
Winter 1911–2
Yukon
ALASKA
MACKENZIE ESKIMO
COPPER ESKIMO
Great Bear Lake
Winter 1910–1
CORONATION GULF
BATHURST INLET
Coppermine
CARIBOO ESKIMO
CENTRAL ESKIMO
BAFFIN
Great Slave Lake
Mackenzie
CANAD
HUDSON BAY
0 100 200 300 400 500 Miles

Left: a group of Eskimos carrying their spears, knives, and fishing ropes. The Eskimos have been forced to learn how to make the most efficient use of their slender natural resources. Their superb hunting skills are necessary if their communities are to survive.

This was the first time that they had been visited by people from so great a distance and they wanted to have time to learn about the country from which they had come.

That evening after supper Stefansson showed the Dolphin and Union Straits people how to light a sulfur match and the next day the even greater marvel of his rifle. The language they spoke was very similar to that which he had learned from the Mackenzie River Eskimos, and from the start they were all able to understand one another.

During the next few days as he rested and ate and talked with the Dolphin and Union Straits Eskimos Stefansson tried to find out as much as possible about their customs and beliefs. One of the things that interested him most was their acceptance of his appearance—especially his blue eyes and light brown beard. These were characteristics very unlike the Eskimos' dark eyes and straight black hair. But they told him their neighbors to the north had eyes and beards exactly like his—if he wished they would take him the next day to visit their friends on Victoria Island.

After a journey of 16 miles Stefansson, Tannaumirk, and Natkusjak accompanied by one of the men from the Dolphin and Union tribe came upon another village. Here half of the Haneragmiut people of Victoria Island were camped. Although everyone was asleep, they soon came out of their houses and gathered around Stefansson's guide. There were a few moments of excited questioning, while the Haneragmiuts made sure that they were friendly visitors. Then after some rather formal introductions, Stefansson was again treated to the same unaffected kindliness, the same hospitality and good manners he had become used to in the previous camp. The Haneragmiuts fed their visitors the usual Eskimo dinner of boiled meat and fatty soup with seal or caribou blood in it. Afterward they were invited to sleep in the igloos that had been quickly built for their stay.

For more than a year Vilhjalmur Stefansson lived in the region of the Victoria Island people and their neighbors to the south who had villages near the Coronation Gulf. During this time he had an opportunity to observe very closely their physical characteristics, which suggested that they were of mixed Eskimo and white blood. These people were later to be referred to as the "blond Eskimos," but to Stefansson, who was a trained anthropologist, they were only blond in the sense that the men who did have beards had light-brown ones. (Many Eskimos pulled out their beards by the roots as the North Americans did.) The hair on their heads was a dark, rusty brown color and only ten out of a thousand "blond Eskimos" he saw had blue eyes. It was the proportions of the body and the shape of their heads that led Stefansson to suggest that the people of this region were descended from the Viking colonists of Greenland. In the 1400's, when the Greenlanders seem to have died out, one of two things could have happened. The surviving Norsemen may have intermarried with the Eskimos in Greenland. More probably,

Below: Northern Canada, showing the routes of the Canadian explorer and anthropologist Vilhjalmur Stefansson in the early 1900's.

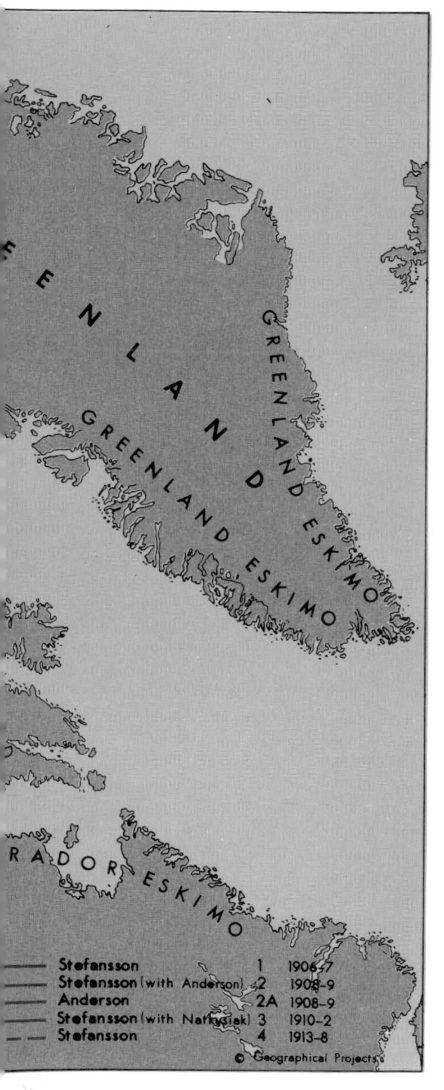

Above: an Eskimo spearing a fish. The Copper Eskimos that Stefansson found lived entirely by fishing and hunting. Many of the white men who died in the Arctic wilderness—such as the men of Sir John Franklin's expedition—might have survived the hostile conditions if they had learned to fish and hunt from the Eskimos they encountered.

according to Stefansson, they may have migrated westward to North America where they settled down with the people they found there.

What interested Stefansson most about the people in the region of Victoria Island—or the Copper Eskimos as he called them—was their way of life. He was continually impressed by their friendliness and by the way in which they had obviously managed to survive the hardships of the Arctic. These people who made for themselves simple copper tools and hunting implements, lived a useful existence relying entirely on their luck at hunting and fishing to keep themselves alive. Their self-reliance made Stefansson think of the needless starving of the Franklin mission. "At the very time when these Englishmen were dying of hunger, there were living about them Eskimo families who were taking care of their aged and bringing up their children, unaided by the rifles and other excellent implements which the Englishmen had in abundance."

Exactly a year after his first discovery of the Copper Eskimos on Victoria Island, Stefansson and Natkusiak took their sledges across the island and crossed the Wollaston Peninsula. They were heading for Prince Albert Sound, where they had been told many tribes of Copper Eskimos gathered in the spring for a trading festival. As they got near the Sound, Stefansson climbed to a high spot of ground. With his binoculars he could see a native village on the ice approximately in the middle of Prince Albert Sound. Stefansson and Natkusiak turned their sledges in the direction of the village which, as they got closer, seemed to be the largest village they had yet come upon. When they arrived Stefansson noted that a greater percentage of these Eskimos looked like Europeans than he had found elsewhere. They were also the most prosperous of the Copper Eskimos. What seemed most remarkable was the extent of their yearly migrations. They had a much greater knowledge of their own country and of others. They also remembered hearing stories from their parents about large sailing ships that had roamed the waters to the east of Victoria Island during the years of the search for Franklin's mission.

In May, 1912, Stefansson and Natkusiak began going westward away from Victoria Island. At Langton Bay they met up again with Dr. Anderson, who with his small party of Eskimos had been continuing his zoological studies. Because Stefansson wanted to visit every Eskimo village along the coast between Langton Bay and Point Barrow, Alaska, he decided not to return with Dr. Anderson to the United States immediately, but to take Natkusiak

Above: seal hunting in Baffin Bay around 1800. Europeans hunted seals in groups like this, but Stefansson found that Eskimos usually hunted alone. Different tribes hunted in different fashions. The Mackenzie Bay people crawled up pretending to be a seal, and then captured their prey by surprise. The Victoria Island men would sit at seal holes for hours, waiting for the seal to come out. Below: an Eskimo mask for dancing.

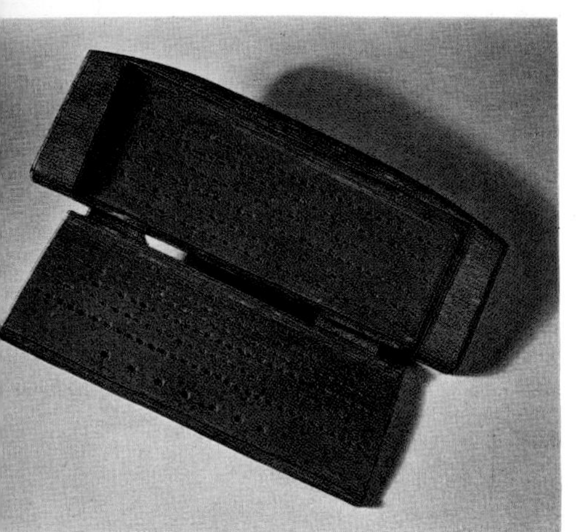

Above- an Eskimo calendar. Each hole represents a day. The seven holes at the front represent one week. The upper 12 rows of holes are days arranged into the months of the year.

with him and make their way slowly up the coast by sledge.

In a sense the results of Vilhjalmur Stefansson's Arctic travels and his meeting the Copper Eskimos were too spectacular. By the time he returned to the United States (via Point Barrow and by boat through the Bering Sea) there was already some controversy about his explorations. A Seattle, Washington, newspaper had heard about the Copper Eskimos and Stefansson's speculations about their origins. One of the paper's reporters wrote an article claiming that they were "a lost tribe of 1,000 white people, who are believed to be direct descendants from the followers of Leif Erikson who came to Greenland from Iceland about the year 100 and a few years later discovered the north coast of America." This story was supposedly based on an interview with Stefansson.

But as we know, Stefansson had merely suggested various theories for the origin of the Eskimos he found on Victoria Island. The story was out—true or not. And Stefansson was consequently criticized by other anthropologists, some of whom doubted that he had actually discovered the Copper Eskimos. Stefansson was hurt by their doubts and accusations—he had never claimed himself the discoverer of these people. Charlie Klinkenberg and the crew of the *Olga* had first seen these Eskimos during the winter of 1906 when they had wintered near Banks Island.

Even though the controversy over the Copper Eskimos would perhaps never be settled, Stefansson was able to produce various copper tools and items of clothing that the Copper Eskimos had given him. There was also the evidence provided by Dr. John Rae who, a half century earlier, had seen "blond Eskimos" who came from the southwest corner of Victoria Island. Sir John Franklin in an 1824 voyage had noticed "blond traits" among the Eskimos he encountered. Even as long ago as 1585 John Davis had referred to blond Eskimos living on Greenland.

For Stefansson, the Copper Eskimo controversy soon became a waste of time. There were more Eskimos to be studied and more regions of the Arctic to be explored. The Arctic should become the servant of man—not his conquerer. Moreover, the identity of its native people should be preserved. These were the principles to which Stefansson dedicated the remaining 50 years of his life, and the principles that guided him as he returned to the Arctic again and again.

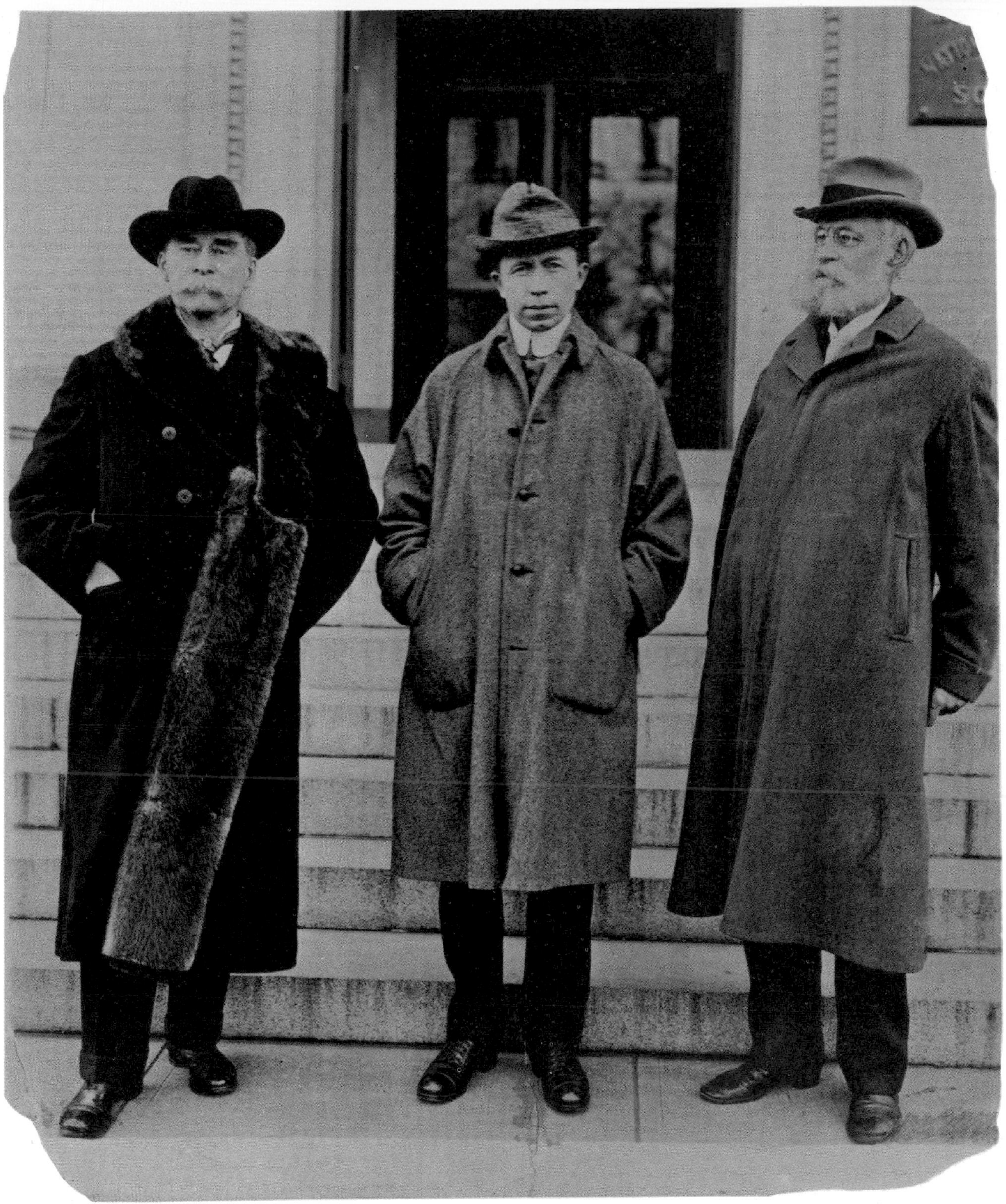

Three veterans of the Arctic: Vilhjalmur Stefansson in the center flanked by Robert Peary and Adolphus Greeley, who had also tried to reach the North Pole. In spite of criticism received from some anthropologists, Stefansson had a very distinguished career. In 1947, he became the Arctic consultant to Dartmouth College, where he remained until his death in 1962. Among the students he trained was Hubert Wilkins, an Australian who tried in 1931 to reach the North Pole in a submarine.

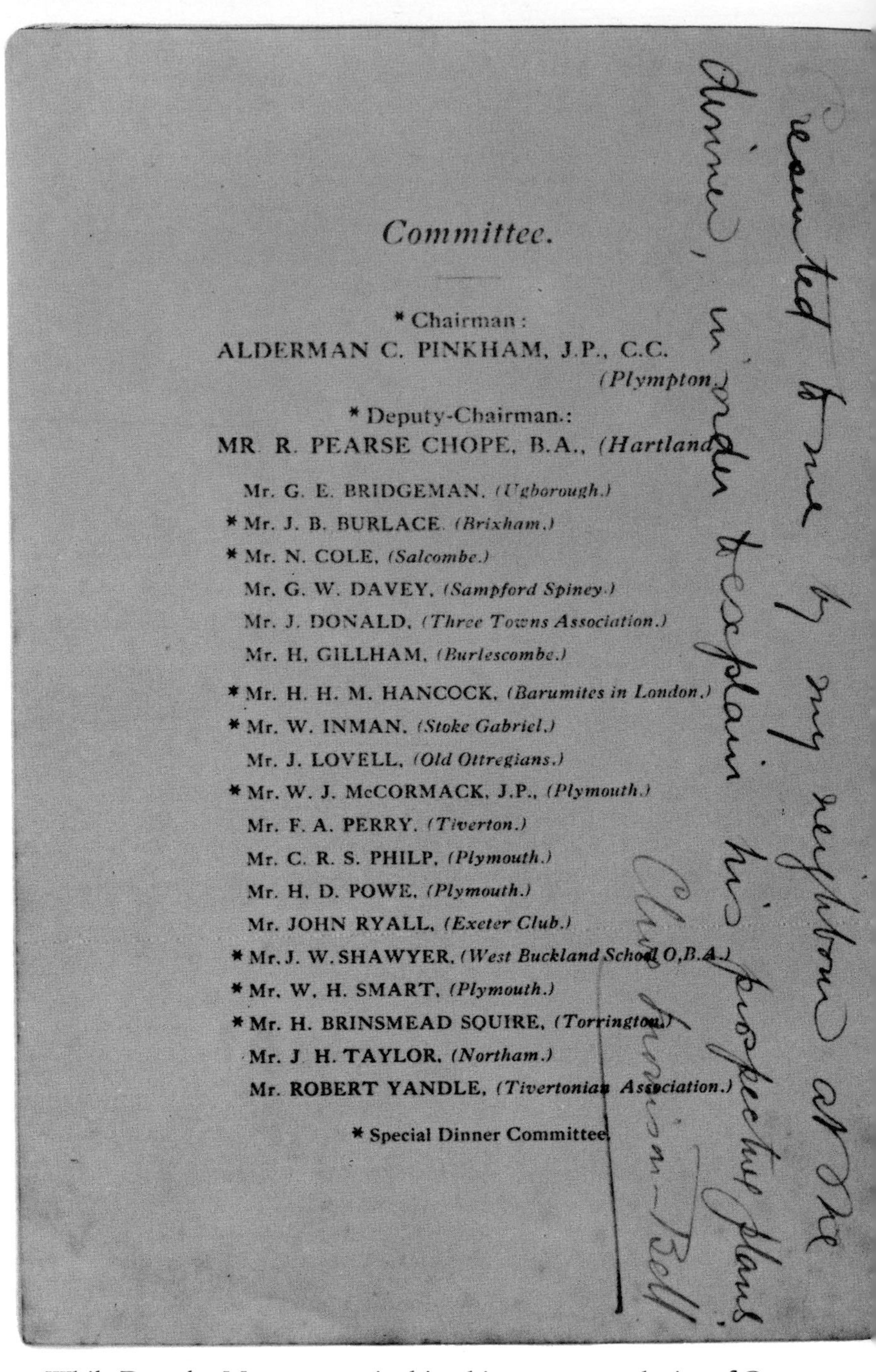

Committee.

* Chairman:
ALDERMAN C. PINKHAM, J.P., C.C.
(Plympton.)

* Deputy-Chairman:
MR. R. PEARSE CHOPE, B.A., (Hartland.)

Mr. G. E. BRIDGEMAN. (Ugborough.)
* Mr. J. B. BURLACE. (Brixham.)
* Mr. N. COLE. (Salcombe.)
Mr. G. W. DAVEY. (Sampford Spiney.)
Mr. J. DONALD. (Three Towns Association.)
Mr. H. GILLHAM. (Burlescombe.)
* Mr. H. H. M. HANCOCK. (Barumites in London.)
* Mr. W. INMAN. (Stoke Gabriel.)
Mr. J. LOVELL. (Old Ottregians.)
* Mr. W. J. McCORMACK, J.P., (Plymouth.)
Mr. F. A. PERRY. (Tiverton.)
Mr. C. R. S. PHILP. (Plymouth.)
Mr. H. D. POWE. (Plymouth.)
Mr. JOHN RYALL. (Exeter Club.)
* Mr. J. W. SHAWYER. (West Buckland School O.B.A.)
* Mr. W. H. SMART. (Plymouth.)
* Mr. H. BRINSMEAD SQUIRE. (Torrington.)
Mr. J. H. TAYLOR. (Northam.)
Mr. ROBERT YANDLE. (Tivertonian Association.)

* Special Dinner Committee.

Shackleton in the Antarctic 10

While Douglas Mawson was inching his way across the ice of George V Land another polar veteran was dreaming of the most ambitious expedition ever launched in Antarctica. An Irishman named Ernest Shackleton planned to cross the South Pole and complete the first transcontinental journey from the Weddell Sea to the Ross Sea. His scheme involved the cooperation of two separate groups of men. While one group braved the Weddell Sea to land on the newly discovered Filchner Ice Shelf, the second one would land on the Ross Ice Shelf and lay a trail of supply depots up the Beardmore Glacier. These depots would be used by Shackleton and five men

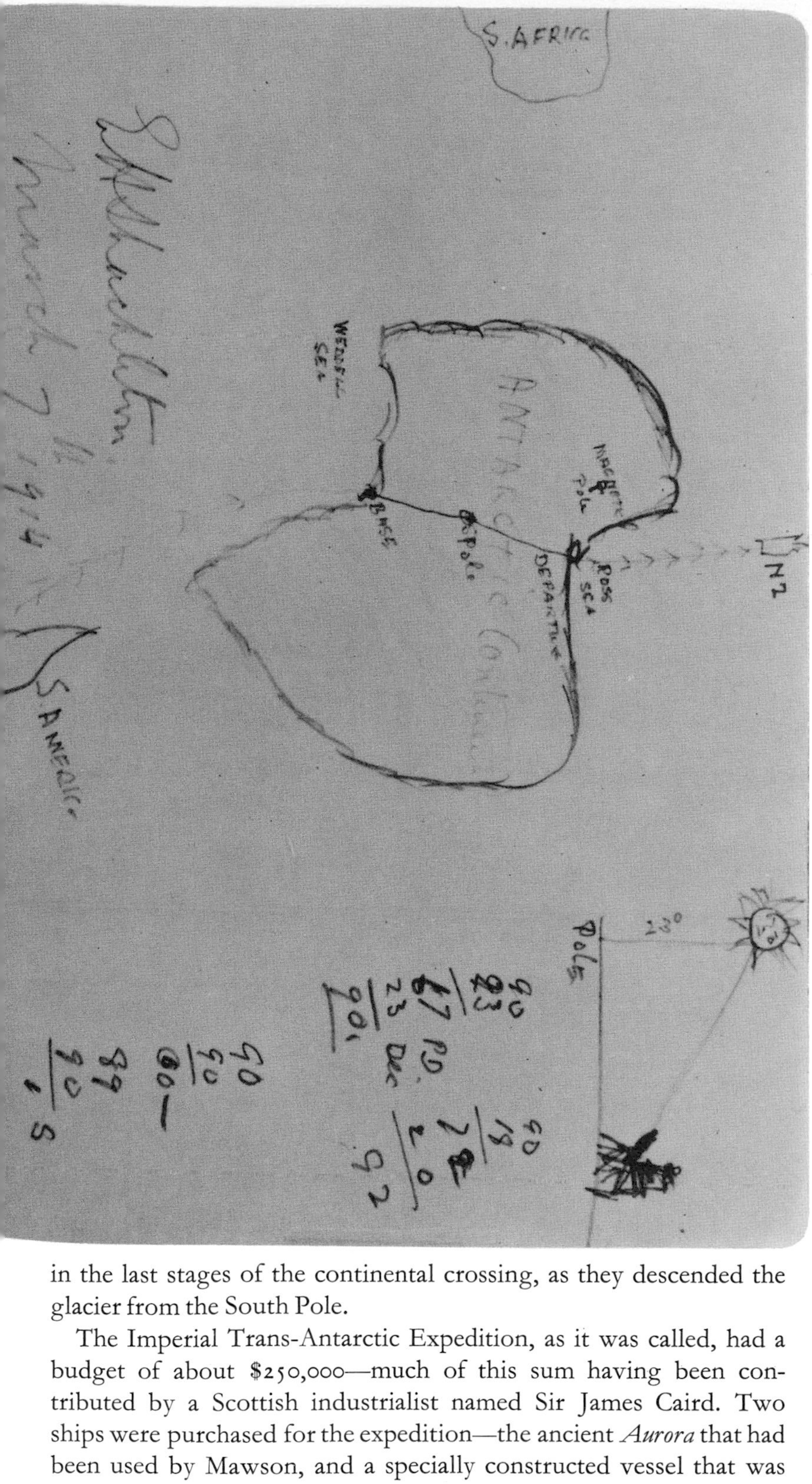

Above: Ernest Shackleton. He was 40 when he decided on his ambitious plan for exploration in Antarctica. He had joined the merchant navy when he was 16, and had gained wide experience at sea. He was said to be a gambler in spirit, always ready to take a chance.

Left: a sketch map that Shackleton drew on a menu for his neighbor at a dinner party to show the route he proposed for crossing the Antarctic continent via the South Pole. He was planning to start from the Weddell Sea and end at the Ross Sea, crossing Antarctica at its narrowest point.

in the last stages of the continental crossing, as they descended the glacier from the South Pole.

The Imperial Trans-Antarctic Expedition, as it was called, had a budget of about $250,000—much of this sum having been contributed by a Scottish industrialist named Sir James Caird. Two ships were purchased for the expedition—the ancient *Aurora* that had been used by Mawson, and a specially constructed vessel that was named *Endurance,* after Shackleton's family motto. The *Aurora,* which was prepared for the expedition in Australia, was to sail from Tasmania to take the Ross Sea party to their allotted task.

Above: crew members of the *Endurance* trying to cut through the ice to a lead ahead in February, 1915. The pack ice in the Weddell Sea moves in a clockwise direction, due to the prevailing winds and water currents and the geography of the sea. The ship was caught in the drift and moved away from her destination. As she drifted the pressure increased. Shackleton wrote, "The effects of the pressure around were awe-inspiring. If the ship was once gripped firmly, her fate would be sealed!"

The *Endurance* set sail from London on August 8, 1914—just four days after the beginning of World War I when England declared war on Germany. Before leaving Shackleton had offered to put his ship and men at the service of the British government. Mr. Winston Churchill, then First Lord of the Admiralty, had thanked him for the offer but instructed Shackleton to proceed with the expedition.

In December, the *Endurance* left South Georgia Island, despite reports from whaling ships of exceptionally bad ice conditions in the Weddell Sea. Only two days out from South Georgia Island the *Endurance* began to run into heavy ice. It became thicker and by January 19, 1915, the pack closed around the ship. It was a helpless prisoner. Two weeks later, a lead of open water appeared near the ship, and the men tried frantically to free the *Endurance*. But the ice refroze as fast as the men could hack their way through it. By mid-February when they were only 60 miles from the Filchner Ice Shelf the *Endurance* became the expedition's official winter station.

It was frozen into a great slab of pack ice almost three miles square that was drifting slowly to the northwest. Three months went by, enlivened only by dog races on the ice and a narrow escape by one of the men from killer whales. Then, around the middle of May, ice floes began to jostle the ship. The ice that had held the *Endurance* in its grip like a giant vise now began to squeeze it. Another two months went by and finally, on August 1, the floe in which they were embedded cracked in two. The border of ice that had protected the *Endurance* for so long was now gone. It was exposed to the full pressure of the ice pack, and destruction seemed inevitable.

At the end of October, after having spent 10 months entrapped by ice, Shackleton ordered that all the boats, sledges, and provisions should be moved off the ship. The next day, the *Endurance* had to be abandoned. A pressure ridge that moved across the pack heaved the ship to the top of the ice like a toy. "At last," Shackleton wrote, "the twisting, grinding floes were working their will on the ship. It was a sickening sensation to feel the decks breaking up under one's feet, the great beams bending and then snapping with a noise like heavy gunfire. . . . The floes, with the force of millions of tons of moving ice behind them, were simply annihilating the ship."

Shackleton and his men were now castaways on the treacherous ice 573 miles from the point where the *Endurance* was first beset in February. The nearest land where they might find shelter was Paulet Island, 346 miles away. So, on December 23, they set out. Unfortunately a rise in temperature softened the ice and made the going difficult. After 7 days of toil, they found they had gone only $7\frac{1}{2}$

Above: a banjo, the last thing to be saved from the *Endurance* as she was crushed by the ice. They took it all the way to the Elephant Island camp. Below: the *Endurance*, caught by the pressure of the ice, heeling over.

miles in a straight line—the drift of the pack was against them.

At their present rate of speed, Shackleton calculated that it would take almost 18 months for them to reach safety—if the ice did not disappear under them during the summer thaw. They had enough food to last for only 1½ months.

Shackleton knew that it was hopeless to go on and decided that they should camp on the ice floe. This was appropriately named Patience Camp and here they lived for 3½ months, occasionally shooting penguins and seals for food when their supplies ran out. They narrowly escaped death when two enormous icebergs moved down through the pack like a pair of scissors, missing the camp by only a few yards. Another day, a fanged leopard seal charged into camp in pursuit of one of the men. The seal was shot to death by Frank Wild—the explorer who had accompanied Mawson to the Antarctic and was now on his fourth trip to the frozen continent.

Early in April, the pack began to break up and the leads of open water became larger. Shackleton decided to make for Deception Island, where they could find some food and where whaling ships occasionally stopped. Loading their supplies into the boats, the men set off through the shifting floes toward the north. The first night they camped on an ice floe that split in two beneath one of the tents. Shackleton pulled one of the men, still in his sleeping bag, out of the water seconds before the edges of the floe crashed together again with sickening force. Later the same night, Shackleton found himself drifting away from the main floe on a small cake of ice. A boat had to be sent through the darkness to bring him back.

In mid-April, 1916, the wind shifted and Shackleton decided to try to get to Elephant Island, 100 miles away. In their haste to leave they forgot to bring along a supply of ice for making water and until they were able to collect some "land" ice the men suffered from thirst. For days they rowed and sailed through a maze of drifting and colliding icebergs until they finally got to Elephant Island. It was a barren and inhospitable place. No one would think of searching for them there. The nearest manned station was at South Georgia Island, 870 miles away across the stormiest seas in the world. Yet someone had to make the desperate attempt to reach it.

Shackleton picked five men to accompany him on the risky voyage, leaving the rest of the men on Elephant Island under the command of Frank Wild. Their boat, the *James Caird,* was an undecked lifeboat from the *Endurance,* only 23 feet long and 6 feet wide. The expedition's carpenter built a crude decking of canvas for it that was battened down with sledge runners, but this was fragile protection against the storms that lay ahead.

On April 24, 1916—almost two years after leaving England—the six men set off on their desperate search for help. Gale after gale raged over them. The salt spray froze as it touched the boat rigging, threatening to tip the craft over with its weight. The men inched their way across the slippery deck to chip away at the ice while waves 50 feet high and 100 yards from crest to crest rolled beneath

Right: the crew members after their landing on Elephant Island, having their first drink and hot food for three days. As Elephant Island is only a large chunk of rock with barren, glacier-capped peaks and cliffs, it took them hours to find a small strip of beach to land on and make their camp. Even then, it was not sheltered enough, and their tents were ripped to shreds by the wind soon after they had been put up. The men spent the rest of their stay in one of the upturned boats.

Right: Shackleton might have remembered his old camps as places of comparative luxury compared to the bleak beach of Elephant Island. The hut he set up in 1907–09 can be seen here covered with snow. One of the dog kennels is still visible in the foreground.

them. Many times it appeared as though the *James Caird* would sink.

On the 11th day out, it seemed that all their agonies were in vain. Shackleton later described the scene in his book *South:* "At midnight I was at the tiller and suddenly noticed a line of clear sky between the south and southwest. I called to the men that the sky was clearing, and then, a moment later, I realized that what I had seen was not a rift in the clouds but the white crest of an enormous wave. During twenty-six years' experience of the ocean in all its moods, I have never seen a wave so gigantic. It was a mighty upheaval of the ocean, a thing quite apart from the big white-capped seas that had been our tireless enemies for many days. I shouted 'For God's Sake, hold on! It's got us!' Then came a moment of suspense that seemed drawn out into hours. . . . We felt our boat lifted and flung forward like a cork in a breaking surf. We were in a seething chaos of tortured water; but somehow the boat lived through it, half full of water, sagging to the dead weight and shuddering under the blow. We bailed with the energy of men fighting for life, flinging the water over with every receptacle that came into our hands; and after ten minutes of uncertainty we felt the boat renew her life beneath us. She floated again and ceased to lurch drunkenly as though dazed by the attack of the sea."

Shackleton and his companions were still to endure the nightmare of thirst when their supply of water got low. "Our mouths were dry and our tongues swollen." Then on May 9, they saw two birds sitting on a mass of floating seaweed. At noontime two days later they sighted the coast of South Georgia—just 14 days after their departure from Elephant Island. A fresh-water stream flowed down to the beach where later that day they landed. As the men climbed stiffly out of the boat they then dropped quickly on their knees to gulp down icy water. It was a wonderful moment.

Their ordeal was still not over, for the *James Caird* had landed on the south side of the island—150 sea miles away from the whaling station on the northern shore. Shackleton knew that neither the *James Caird* nor his men were likely to survive another ocean voyage, and he decided that he and two of them would have to walk across the unexplored island to seek help.

On May 19, they set out, taking with them a compass, a chronometer, a stove, provisions for three days, a tent, and 50 feet of rope. They began this last incredible journey with only the vaguest idea of where the whaling station was located.

During the first day fog shrouded the glacier they had to climb, lifting enough to reveal a vast crevasse only a few feet away. Again and again they scaled ice-covered ridges only to find their way barred by chasms or steep cliffs. Before nightfall they had somehow to reach lower ground where they could put up a tent. A fog-covered cliff lay below them.

There was only one thing to do—trust themselves to the icy slope. They coiled the ropes into three pads, sat down on the pads, and each man locked his legs around the man in front of him. Shackleton

Right: the tiny whaling station on South Goergia Island that Shackleton and his two companions finally reached after their grueling march across the frozen island, climbing the mountains in the photograph on the way.

Below: an Antarctic ice cave, painted by E. L. Greenfield. It was this sort of beautiful but forbidding landscape that lay all around the marooned men, and through which Shackleton made his incredible 1000 mile journey.

Above: the men of Elephant Island when they were rescued. All had survived, although one man had to have his toes amputated because of frostbite. One of them, writing of the rescue, said, "There, just rounding the island . . . we saw a little ship flying the Chilean flag. We tried to cheer, but excitement had gripped our vocal cords . . . Suddenly she stopped, a boat was lowered, and we could recognize Sir Ernest's figure as he climbed down the ladder. Simultaneously we burst into a cheer, and then one said to the other, 'Thank God, the Boss is safe."

was in the lead and pushed off into the unknown. "We seemed to shoot into space. For a moment my hair fairly stood on end. Then quite suddenly I felt a glow and knew I was grinning. I was actually enjoying it. It was most exhilarating. We were shooting down the side of an almost precipitous mountain at nearly a mile a minute. I yelled with excitement and found that the others were yelling too. It seemed ridiculously safe. To hell with the rocks!" Their "toboggan" stopped safely in a soft snowbank.

Now only one more obstacle stood between them and the whaling station. As they made their way through a narrow gorge at the bottom of the mountain they heard the splash of a water fall. As Shackleton was later to explain, they were at the wrong end of the rushing water. Peering down, they saw a drop of 25 to 30 feet with impassable ice cliffs on both sides. Using the same ropes that had brought them down the mountain, they looped one end of each rope securely over a boulder. Then each man swung off on the free end of his rope, through the waterfall. They emerged at the bottom, cold and wet but unhurt.

When Shackleton and his two companions finally staggered into the whaling station, the men who greeted them were astounded. The story of their 1,000 mile journey seemed too incredible to be true.

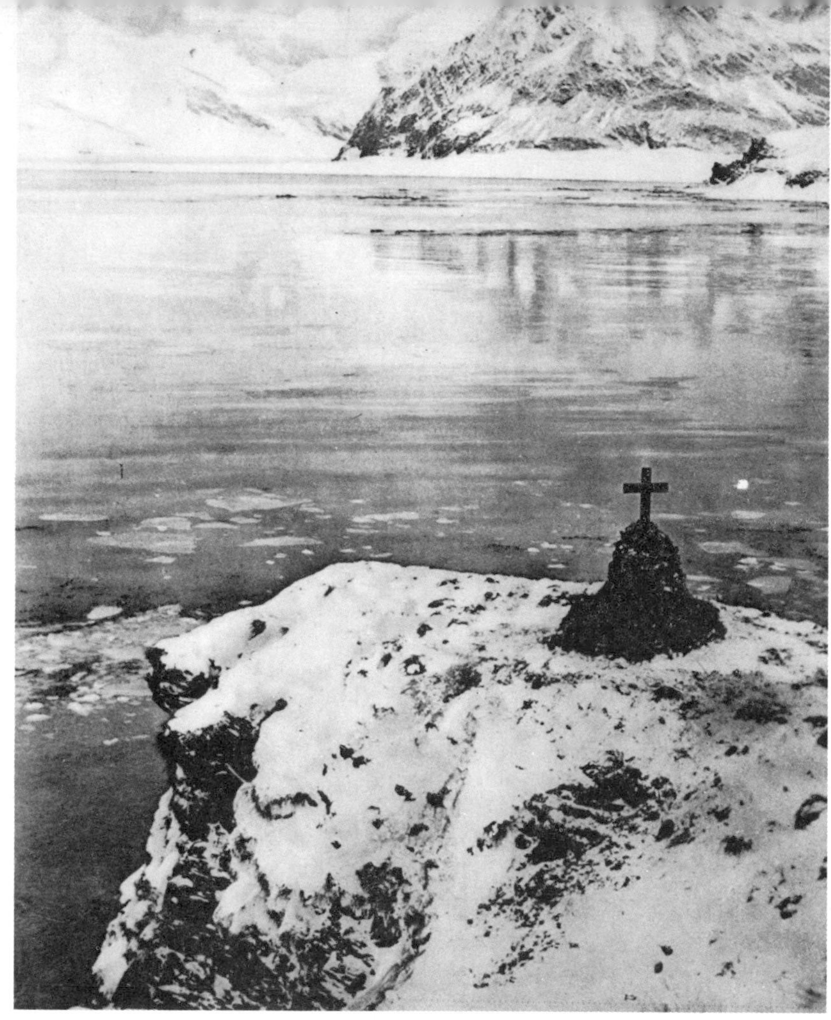

Left: the grave of Ernest Shackleton, just a few miles from the point where he landed on South Georgia Island after his epic voyage from Elephant Island.

Immediately a relief party was organized to sail around to the other side of the island to pick up the three men who had stayed behind with the *James Caird*.

The marooned men on Elephant Island were not so lucky. Three rescue efforts were to be made before a ship was at last able to penetrate the ice that surrounded the island. When they were finally picked up, the men were weak and close to death after having spent 20 weeks on the barren island during yet another Antarctic winter. Quite miraculously they all eventually recovered their strength.

Although the Imperial Trans-Antarctic Expedition had been a failure, the courage and endurance displayed by its members were remarkable. As a heroic achievement, it ranks with Mawson's lonely sledge journey and Scott's fateful polar trek.

Ernest Shackleton was back again in the Antarctic in 1921, this time on an expedition that was to map the unknown Antarctic coast south of the Indian Ocean. Before the expedition actually got underway from South Georgia Island, Shackleton collapsed from a sharp pain in his chest. Within hours, the man who had defied the force of two Antarctic winters was dead of a heart attack. He was buried on South Georgia Island, just a few miles from the rocky shore where he had landed in the *James Caird*.

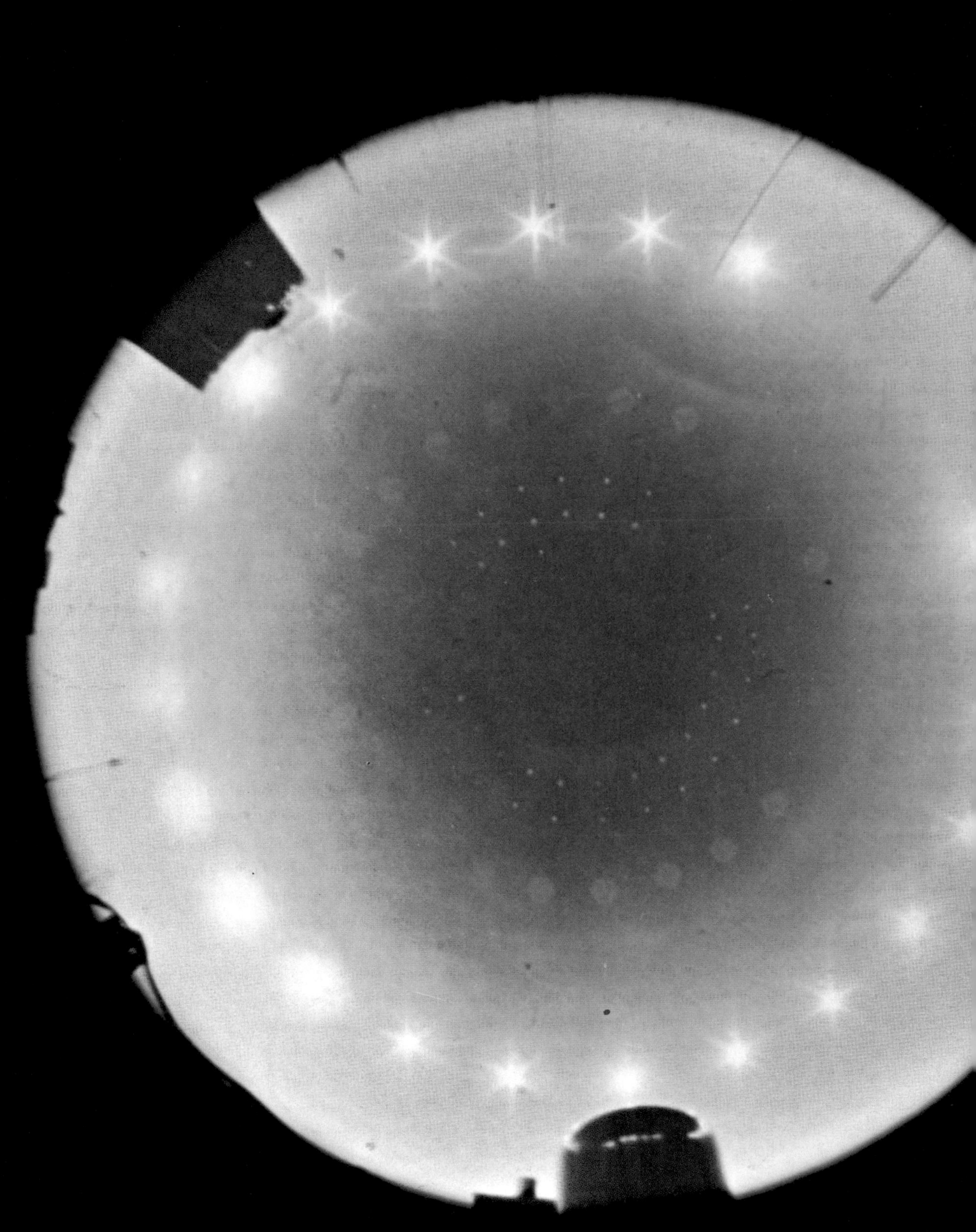

The Poles Today

11

Ernest Shackleton's death in January, 1922, marked the end of the heroic age of polar exploration. When this gay, adventurous, and supremely brave man succumbed to a heart attack the era of exploration with machines was about to begin. No longer would large expeditions make perilous journeys over the ice, carrying their equipment on sledges that they sometimes had to pull themselves.

Perhaps the most important new development in the machine-age conquest of the frozen worlds was the introduction of the airplane. In 1928, the Australian explorer and aviator Hubert Wilkins made the first flight over Antarctica. A year later, Commander Richard E. Byrd of the United States Navy became the first man to fly over the South Pole. Byrd was also the man responsible for the revival of American interest in Antarctic exploration. During the years between 1928–1930 he led an expedition that established an elaborate base of more than a dozen buildings at the Bay of Whales on the Ross Ice Shelf. This was in fact the first major American expedition to Antarctica since Charles Wilkes' voyage 80 years before. Byrd's equipment at Little America, as he called the base, included several airplanes, electricity, telephones, and three tall radio towers to keep in touch with the outside world. Four ships were needed to carry all the equipment and the 74 men to the "city" at Little America. During the first few years of their stay there the men were to carry out extensive geographical and geological work. Richard Byrd, meanwhile, prepared himself for the flight he and two other men were to make over the South Pole.

On November 29, 1929, they set out in their primitive plane to make polar history, thinking that they would follow the route Amundsen and his men had taken. But as the plane approached the icy mountains that separate the polar plateau from the Ross Ice Shelf, Byrd decided to follow the Liv Glacier. He knew that the highest point on the Heiberg Glacier that Amundsen had climbed was 10,500 feet. That would be too high for their overloaded plane to clear. The Liv, he hoped, would be lower.

Left: the sun in its clocklike "midsummer" orbit above the South Pole. An exposure was taken every hour for 22 hours by a camera with a fish-eye lens that had to be treated with special oils to protect it from icing up.

Above left: Richard E. Byrd, the first man to fly over the South Pole, taking a sighting. He, more than any other person, revived interest in the exploration of Antarctica.

Left: Byrd and Bennett returning from their flight over the North Pole in 1926. They had some trouble in navigating over the featureless white expanse of ice and snow, but the flight was otherwise not particularly eventful.

The plane was at full throttle as it climbed steadily and very slowly. Below them, the men could see the tumbled blocks of the glacier, and far ahead in the distance they could just make out the top of the pass. Suddenly the plane no longer responded to the controls. It climbed more and more slowly. Byrd shouted the order for 125 pounds of food (enough to last them for a week) to be pushed out of the plane. Now the aircraft began to climb again. The cliffs on each side of the pass were becoming so narrow that there was no hope of turning back. Another 125 pounds of food was jettisoned. If the plane crashed before their return to Little America, they would starve.

They were now approaching the top of the pass. After several agonizing moments of wondering whether they would actually clear it, the plane hummed over the icy peaks with a few hundred feet to spare. At last! Now they could relax and look down on the featureless, snow-covered plain that leads to the pole.

Before returning to Little America they circled twice over the

Above: the Liv Glacier, photographed from an airplane that flew to the South Pole on the same route that Byrd followed on his way to the pole.

Above: Byrd cooking a meal on the stove that almost brought about his death during his lonely vigil in the weather station 123 miles from Little America. He was alone for more than four months in 1933 while the members of his second expedition continued their exploration of the unknown regions of Antarctica.

South Pole. Byrd dropped two flags out of the plane—the Stars and Stripes, and the Union Jack that he left in honor of Robert Scott and his men.

His next expedition to the Antarctic began in 1933, and wintered as before in the Bay of Whales at Little America. This expedition was primarily a scientific one and the men taking part in it studied meteors, cosmic rays, weather, geography, and the earth's magnetism. In order to take accurate and regular weather measurements, Byrd himself volunteered to man the isolated weather hut that was to be set up 123 miles from Little America. There was no room for three men in the lonely outpost and Byrd thought that two men would have difficulty getting along during the seven dark months of the Antarctic winter.

Above: Mount Erebus, a live volcano, named for the ship of the Ross expedition, seen through the tail rotor of a helicopter. The photograph was taken on Operation Deep Freeze IV, the United States contribution to the International Geographical Year (1957–1958) in the Antarctic, of which Byrd was chief United States representative.

Sections of the prefabricated weather hut were damaged as they were dragged over the ice from Little America, and the door to the hut was so unevenly cut that it never closed completely. The hut itself was set into a pit with the door opening at the top, like a hatch. Some parts of Byrd's stove were missing. Although he tried to make do with repairing the stove himself, it was this essential item that nearly caused his death. Carbon monoxide leaked from the stove, and made him dizzy and sick. One day outside the hut he fell down and injured his arm. Yet throughout these trials he refused to ask the men at Little America for help. He felt that any rescue mission in mid-winter could involve the loss of lives.

As Byrd's radio transmissions became more incoherent, the men at Little America grew suspicious. Finally, against the orders he

Above: Byrd Station, a United States base in Antarctica. Although it is only 5,000 feet above sea level, the ice has been measured at over 7,000 feet thick. Apparently the enormous weight of the icecap has pressed into the crust of the earth so that a large portion of the ice is below sea level.

had given them, a small party set out for the weather hut. They used tractors to haul their supplies, but even so it took them a month to cover the 123 miles. Meanwhile the isolated man in the hut was spending many hours of each day only semi-conscious. The stove that was all that would keep him from freezing to death was also poisoning him.

At last, on August 11, after nearly five months of being alone in the Antarctic, Byrd saw the lights of the tractors approaching. He stood up but did not dare to walk forward. The men who had come to rescue him remember his greeting them and inviting them inside the hut for some hot soup. But Richard Byrd remembered nothing about this moment that was perhaps his narrowest escape from death. He was so weak that it was to be two months before he was

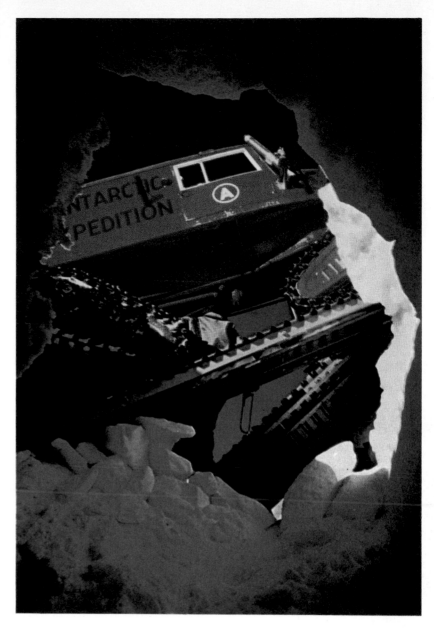

well enough to be taken by plane back to the base at Little America.

Again in 1939, in 1946, and in 1957, Byrd was to return to the Antarctic. The 1946 expedition was the largest exploration of Antarctica ever attempted—Operation Highjump. Byrd had under his command 4,700 men and 13 ships. This great fleet was divided into three groups, which were assigned to various regions of the Antarctic. Fourteen hundred miles of unknown coastline were charted and photographed, new mountain ranges were discovered, and 26 new islands were found.

In 1955, Byrd was again in the Arctic, this time with Operation Deep Freeze, which was to be the basis for the United States participation in the International Geophysical Year. The IGY—involving 12 nations and 50 separate scientific bases on Antarctica—

Above: a Sno-cat tracked vehicle trapped in a crevasse during the 1957 British Commonwealth Trans-Antarctic Expedition. The photograph shows the light metal ramps that were placed under the vehicle. These, and the use of low gears, enabled the explorers to extricate the vehicle from a dangerous situation.

began in July, 1957, and was the most productive scientific venture ever undertaken in the polar regions. The scientists who participated worked together to investigate things like the possible causes of earthquakes. Oceanography (oceans), meteorology (weather), the study of the sun's activity, and the earth's magnetism were some of the subjects they concentrated on. The most spectacular achievement of the IGY was the launching of artificial satellites and high-altitude rockets by Russia and the United States. These devices carried instruments to study cosmic

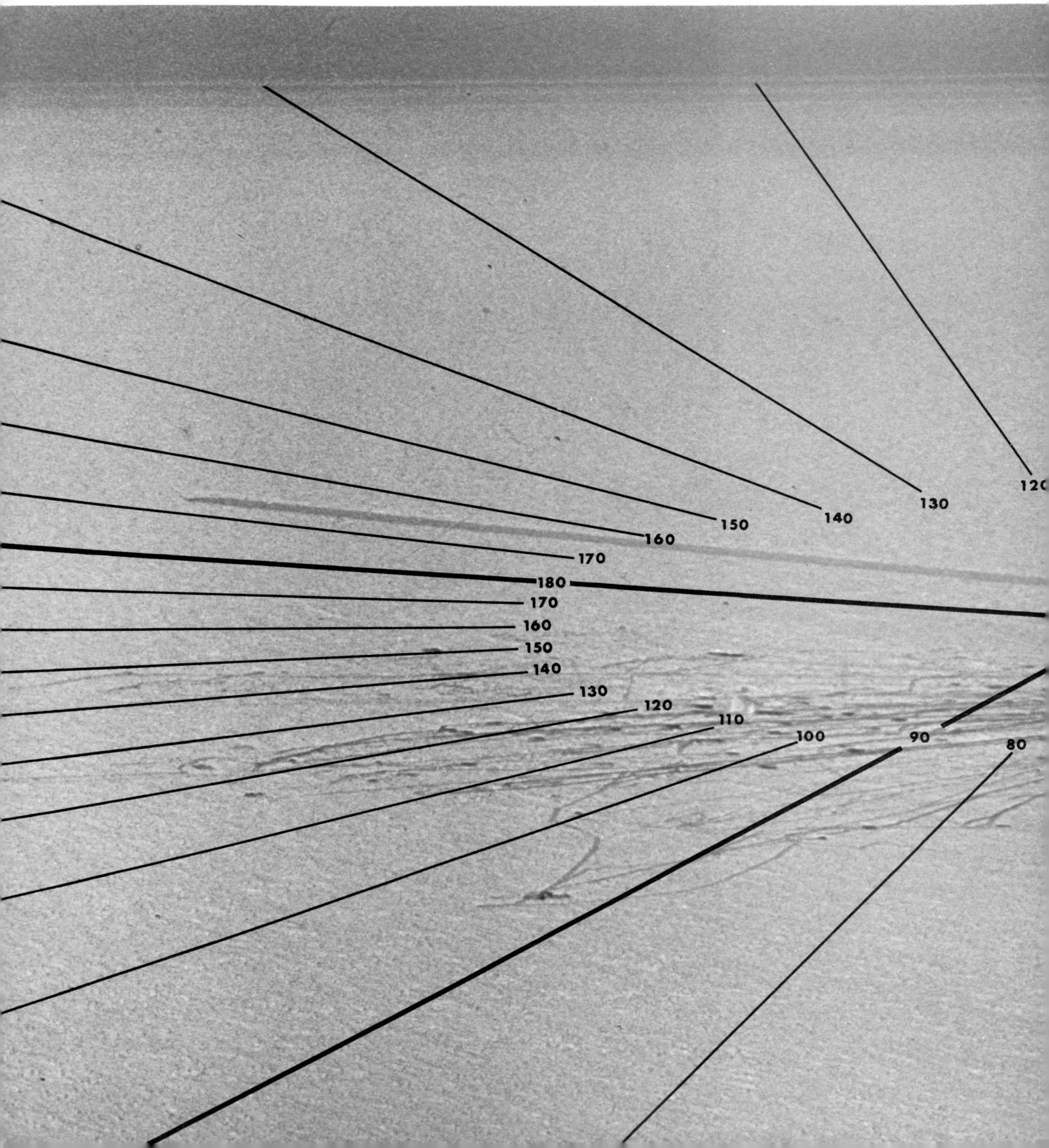

rays, magnetic fields, sunspots, eclipses, meteors, and sunlight.

The year of the IGY was also the time when Ernest Shackleton's dream was accomplished—the crossing of Antarctica from the Weddell Sea to the Ross Sea via the Pole. Early in October, 1957, a British explorer, Dr. Vivian Fuchs, who was the commander of the British Commonwealth Trans-Antarctic Expedition in 1957 and 1958, began breaking a trail toward the pole from his base camp on the Filchner Ice Shelf in the Weddell Sea. At the same time, the New Zealander Sir Edmund Hillary (who in 1953 had shared in the first

Below: the South Pole, photographed from an airplane by Emil Schulthess during the International Geophysical Year. Schulthess has superimposed a diagram that pinpoints the exact geographic pole (black dot at center) to within an area of about 30 feet in diameter. The lines drawn out from the pole are the meridians. The line at the right marked "0" is the Greenwich or Prime Meridian, which passes through Greenwich, England, and from which longitude is measured.

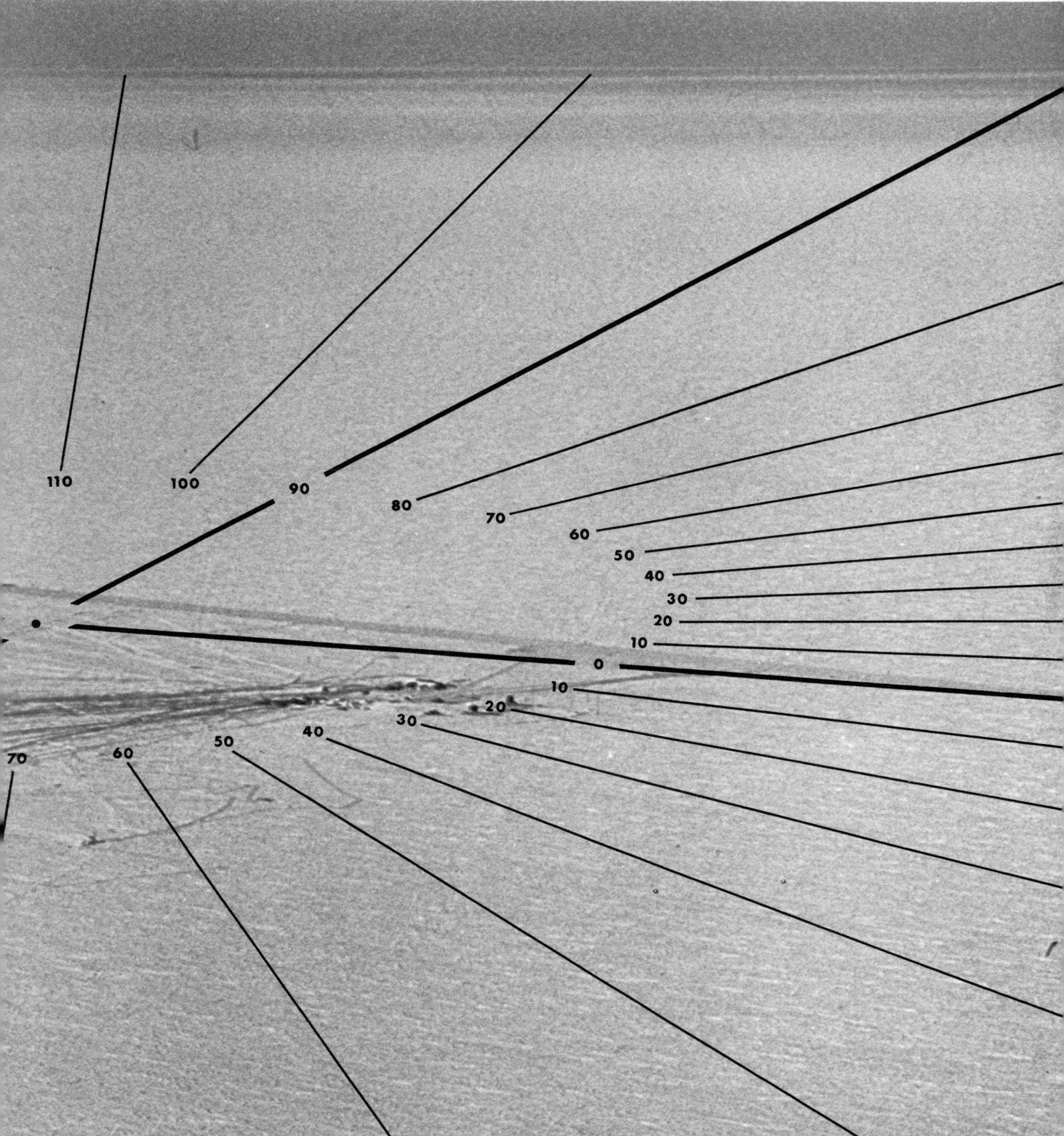

ascent of Mount Everest), and another group of men started pushing southward from their base on McMurdo Sound. Fuchs' plan was to trek across the entire continent via the South Pole and to get supplies from the depots that Hillary's party was to set up on the Ross Ice Shelf.

Below: Antarctica, showing the routes of explorers between 1928 and 1958. Also shown are the territories and bases of the numerous countries that have an interest in Antarctica today.

Even with large Sno-cats and Weasels, Fuchs and his men had a terrible struggle. The tractors were too cumbersome and were constantly getting stuck, as the snow bridges collapsed. Soon, they were behind schedule.

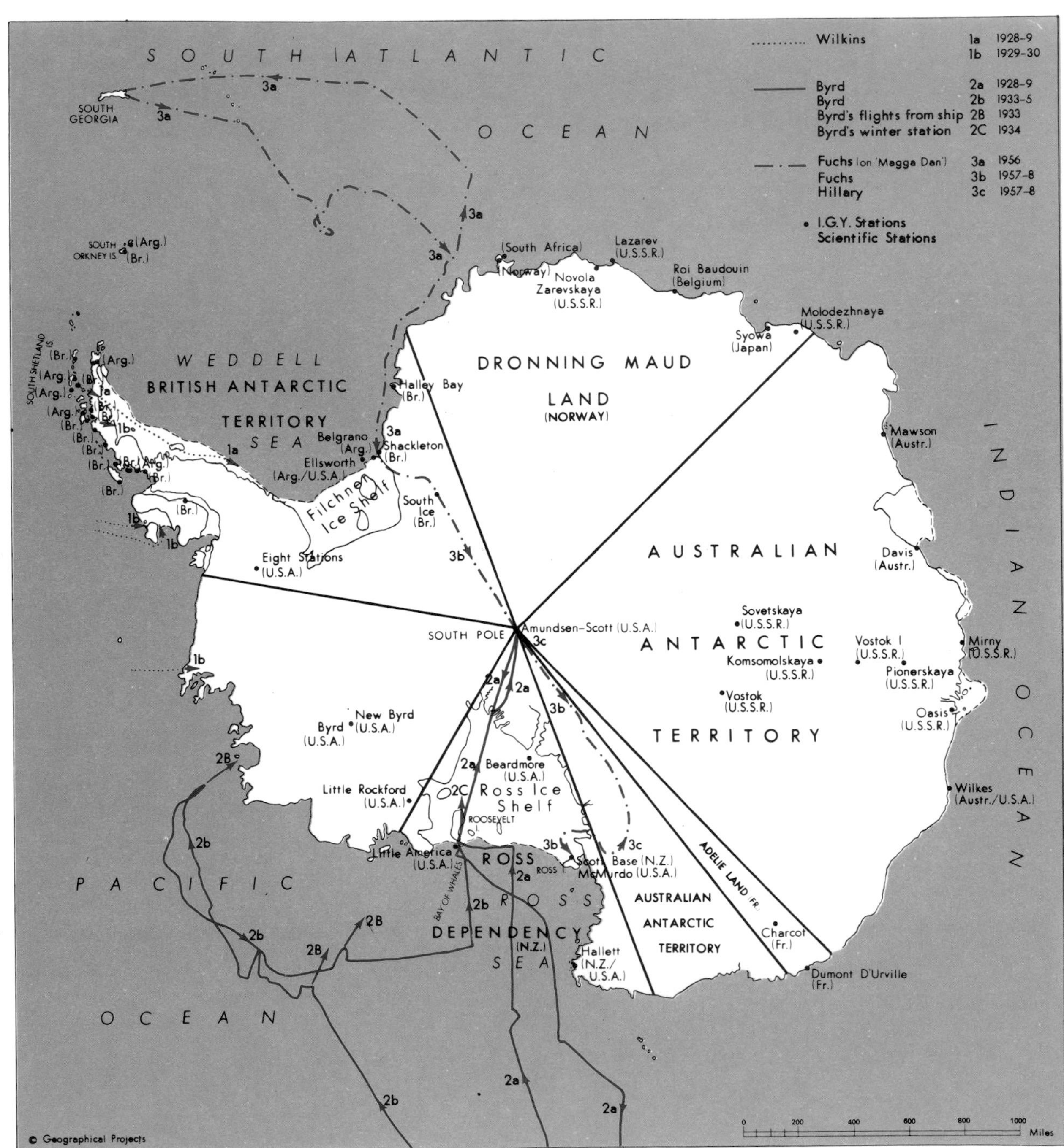

Right: a Sno-cat carrying a crevasse detector: four wooden beams, fitted with large aluminum disks, pushed ahead of the vehicle. They are linked to detectors, which record hollows under the disks on a graph and also make a sound. As soon as a crevasse is discovered the Sno-cat must stop. Despite all precautions, the tractors still break through snow bridges. The surest way—although the slowest—is still a man probing with a metal rod.

Right: a Soviet tractor at Vostok Station in Antarctica. The southern continent is the most international of all, with the hostilities found in the rest of the world suspended for the sake of scientific research. Each year the Russian and American teams exchange a scientist, and many of the expeditions are organized jointly.

Hillary, meanwhile, was having much better luck. With his modified farm tractors, he pushed along at a good pace and was soon ahead of schedule. The original plan had been for Hillary to meet Fuchs at Depot 700, which was only 500 miles from the pole. But when Fuchs radioed that he was behind schedule, Hillary decided to push on to the south.

On January 3, 1958, he and his four companions reached the end of the earth, radioing, "Have hit the Pole bang on." This time a New Zealander had beaten an Englishman to the Pole. Then an argument ensued between the two expedition leaders that would never have occurred if the men had not had short-wave radios to communicate with each other. Because summer was almost over Hillary said to Fuchs and to the expedition authorities in London that Fuchs should abandon his transcontinental trip once he had reached the pole. From there his men and equipment could be flown out to McMurdo.

Above left: a painting of Amundsen's airship the *Norge* over Oslo on its way to the North Pole in April, 1926. Amundsen, and his Italian pilot Umberto Nobile, successfully crossed the pole in May 1926 a few days after Byrd flew over the South Pole.

Above and right: the airship *Italia*, in which Nobile (seen on left in group picture) set out to cross the North Pole two years later. For six weeks nothing was heard from the expedition, and Nobile and his crew were believed dead. Amundsen set out in an airplane with five others to search for him. A short time after they left, Nobile was found alive by another rescue expedition, having survived a crash. But Amundsen and his companions were never seen again.

Fuchs was furious and radioed back that he had no intention of giving up on the last leg of the trip from the Pole to McMurdo Station. Dissention had reached Antarctica. Eventually, through the intervention of the London authorities, it was agreed that Fuchs should continue even though it meant danger. Hillary bowed to their decision and was there to shake Fuchs' hand when he arrived at the South Pole.

Despite the difficulties, Fuchs and his men completed their trek to McMurdo Sound on March 2, 1958—44 years after Shackleton had set out with the ill-fated Imperial Trans-Antarctic Expedition.

There are today more than 50 scientific stations scattered over Antarctica. Hundreds of men—and a few women—still explore there during the short summer from October to March. They keep in touch with one another and the outside world by radio and airplane. At several bases they can even see a movie during their leisure hours. A nuclear power generator operates from the huge American base at McMurdo Sound. Tourist ships now stop there. Today, rescue almost anywhere in Antarctica is only days away.

Thus the last great land mass to be discovered on earth has slowly been revealed and conquered. By the end of this century, geologists,

meteorologists, geophysicists, and other scientists will have discovered more about how our weather is affected by the weather conditions in Antarctica. They will have mapped the land buried beneath its burden of ice, revealed its geological history, and systematically studied the oceans that surround the continent. Satellites in space will be monitoring Antarctic weather conditions and commercial airlines will be taking the southern circle route across its frozen wastes. Inevitably some kinds of industries will be set up in Antarctica.

Most important to the future of Antarctica is its unique status of being the only free continent on earth. A treaty ratified by 12 nations in 1959 guaranteed that no country would be able to exclude any other from performing peaceful or scientific experiments there.

In the Arctic during the 1900's the airplane also replaced the old methods of travel. Before his flight over the South Pole, Richard Byrd and Floyd Bennett became the first men to fly over the North Pole. In about 16 hours they made the round trip journey up and back again to Spitzbergen. Among those on hand to witness their return was Roald Amundsen who had hoped to make the first flight over the pole in the dirigible *Norge*. Three days after Bennett and Byrd had returned he took off in the *Norge* accompanied by an American, Lincoln Ellsworth, and Umberto Nobile of Italy. They completed a perilous flight from Spitzbergen over the pole and on to Alaska.

Another quite different attempt at a transpolar crossing occurred in 1931. This was the attempt by Sir Hubert Wilkins to cross the Arctic Ocean in his submarine the *Nautilus*. Although he failed to do this because of violent storms and damage to diving gear, Wilkins did much to promote the idea of under-ice navigation. However, nearly 30 years were to pass before the U.S. submarine *Nautilus* propelled by atomic power actually achieved the first under-ice crossing. Submerging under the ice off Point Barrow, the *Nautilus* traveled the 1,830 miles to a point near Spitzbergen in only 96 hours.

There nevertheless remains a certain attraction about polar expeditions that involve more than the use of machines to get men safely over the ice. On February 21, 1968, an Englishman, Wally Herbert, and three companions set out from Point Barrow, Alaska to cross the frozen Arctic Ocean on foot. Quite rightly they realized that this could be done only by the marriage of the oldest techniques of Arctic travel with modern air support,

Above: a member of Wally Herbert's Trans-Arctic Expedition with a dog sledge, traveling over good ice. The party left Point Barrow in February, 1968, and arrived north of Spitzbergen in May, 1969, having come over the pole.

Below: members of the Herbert team maneuvering their dogs over an ice ridge. The last part of the journey was a race against time, knowing that they had to reach Spitzbergen before the summer came and the ice began to melt.

radios, and satellite information on weather and ice concentration. They reached the North Pole on April 6, 1969, and from there proceeded in forced marches of 15 hours each in order to reach Spitzbergen before the summer melt of the ice. They had to make speed in order to save their lives, and on June 11, 1969, reached Spitzbergen—3,700 miles from their starting point and 476 days later.

Increasingly, however, emphasis has changed from exploration to economics in the Arctic. The rivalry between various nations to find a Northwest Passage or to be first at the pole has evolved into economic competition with Russia, the United States, and Canada being the principal competitors. The two superpowers, Russia and the United States, confront each other across the Bering Strait only minutes away from each other by rocket. The smaller nations of the Arctic region also claim their triangular wedges of territory extending northward to the Pole. The Soviet Union makes even more sweeping claims. In her sector—nearly half of all the Arctic region—the U.S.S.R. claims control of the sea with its floating ice islands and even the air routes above the ocean itself.

Below: the vast oil tanker, the S.S. *Manhattan,* plows stolidly through the ice during a double voyage through the Northwest Passage in 1969 to test the possibility of carrying oil from the Alaskan fields through this route.

Above: McMurdo Station, Ross Island. It is the largest Antarctic station, with a summer population of 1,000. It has a nuclear reactor to provide heat and electricity, such amenities as a bowling alley and a newspaper called the *McMurdo Sometimes*, and a church named the Chapel of the Snows.

The discovery of huge new deposits of oil along the Arctic coast of Alaska has disturbed relations between Canada and the United States. An international oil company has successfully sent an ice-breaking tanker on a round-trip voyage through the Northwest Passage to test the possibility of transporting oil along this northern route. But the Passage cuts through the islands claimed by Canada, which regards this territory—land and sea—as her own. If one of the giant tankers planned for the Northwest Passage were to sink or be damaged by ice, the oil spewed over the icy water would completely destroy the animal and plant life in the Arctic. An oil pipeline that will run between Anchorage, Alaska, and the northern oilfields may seriously disrupt the delicate balance of life in the tundra. Already, parts of northern Canada and Alaska have been marred by the construction of drilling towers and the massive pieces of equipment used by the oil companies. An influx of people employed in the search for oil and other minerals has drastically changed the life of the Eskimo. They were quick to adapt themselves to a more mechanized way of life and are forgetting the hunting and fishing skills that enabled them to survive for so long in their hostile environment.

The future of the Arctic, like the Antarctic, remains very much an open question. With the successful construction of nuclear power plants man could live the year round in many parts of both polar regions. The possibility of establishing polar colonies where food could be grown and animals could be raised is still extremely remote. Seventy years ago man had not yet managed to get to the poles. Nor, certainly, had he any idea of the potential wealth of the natural resources surrounding them. The next stage in the evolution of the frozen world may be settlement.

Acknowledgments

Aldus Archives 40(TR), 67, 109(B), 111(B), 112, 117, 123(B), 124, 129(T); Photo Carmelo Guadagno, courtesy American Geographical Society 40(TL); H. Aschehoug & C., Oslo 69, 71, 73(T)(B), 76(L)(R), 77(T)(B), 79(T)(B); Baumkotter Antiques/Photo John Webb ©Aldus Books 118(R); Bibliothèque Nationale, Paris/Photo Denise Bourbonnais © Aldus Books 44, 45(L); Emil Schulthess/Black Star, London 50; By permission of the Curators of the Bodleian Library 22(L); Collection André Breton, Paris/Michael Holford Library 131(B); Reproduced by permission of the Trustees of the British Museum 11, 15, 26, 36, 88, 130; British Museum/Photo R. B. Fleming © Aldus Books 20, 22(R), 23, 24(T), 25, 28–29, 123(TL)(TR); British Museum/Michael Holford Library 132; British Museum, courtesy Peter Scott 94(R), 106; British Museum (Natural History/Photo John Webb © Aldus Books 6, 38; Collection Count Brobinskoy/Michael Holford Library 27; Brown Brothers 81, 83, 118(L), 133, 146(T)(B); Courtesy Cavalry Club, London 104–05; Central Office and Museum of National Antiquities, Stockholm/Photo S. Hallgren 12; Reproduced from *Farthest North,* Constable & Co. Ltd., London (1897) 68; Fram Museum/Photo Mittet 70(B), 70–71, 90(L), 93(B); Geographical Projects Limited, London 33, 51, 62–63, 74, 87, 99 129(B), 154; Dr. Georg Gerster 95, 108, 139(B), 144, 160; Courtesy of John Hancock Mutual Life Insurance Company, Boston, Mass. 86; Photo Chauncey C. Loomis 62(T); The Mansell Collection 58, 61(T), 64, 70(T), 98, 109(T), 111(T), 115; Photo Jeremy Whitaker © Aldus Books, courtesy Lord Middleton 21; Ministère de la Guerre, Paris/Photo Giraudon © S.P.A.D.E.M. 16; The Mitchell Library, Sydney, New South Wales/Photo Brian Bird 36–37; Musée Arts Africains et Océaniens, Paris/Photo Giraudon © S.P.A.D.E.M. 42(B); Records of the United States Information Agency, Audiovisual Branch, National Archives, Washington, D.C. 148; Courtesy of National Collection of Fine Arts, Smithsonian Institution 84–85, 85(TR); © National Geographic Society, Courtesy Robert E. Peary Jr. and Marie Peary Kuhne 9, 80, 82(T), 85(B), 89; National Maritime Museum, Greenwich/Photo Michael Holford © Aldus Books 53, 54(L), 59(R), 60(T), 61(B), 65, 66, 137(T); National Maritime Museum, Greenwich/Photo John Webb© Aldus Books 54–55; National Portrait Gallery, London 30, 31(T), 56(T), 58(L), 60(B); National Portrait Gallery, Smithsonian Institution, Washington, D.C. 46(T); © Nationalmuseum, Copenhagen 14; Novosti 41; Oslo Bymuseum 156(T); By kind permission of The Parker Gallery, London 45(R), 57, 131(T); Peabody Museum, Harvard University 120, 125, 127(R); Pitt-Rivers Museum, University of Oxford 29(B); Popperfoto 90–91, 92(TL), 92–93, 94(L), 96(L), 96–97, 100(T), 102, 103; Public Archives of Canada 127(L); Courtesy Queen Victoria Museum and Art Gallery, Launceston, Tasmania 56(B); By kind permission of Mrs. P. E. Quick 107 (T); Rijksmuseum, Amsterdam 24(B); Reprodued by permission of the Royal Geographical Society 40(B), 47(R), 116, 136, 137(B), 139(T), 141(T), 142, 143; Photo John Webb © Aldus Books, reproduced by permission of the Royal Geographical Society 114, 134–35, 135(R), 141(B); Emil Schulthess 19, 149, 150, 152–53, 155(T); Scott Polar Research Institute, Cambridge, England 93(B), 100–01, 104(T); Photo John Webb © Aldus Books, courtesy Scott Polar Research Institute, Cambridge, England 31(B), 34, 35, 38–39, 42–43, 49(T)(B), 121; *Stern* Archiv 156(B), 157; *Sunday Times* Colour Magazine 8, 82(B), 158(T)(B); Charles Swithinbank 10, 13, 18, 107(B), 110, 113, 147, 155(B), 159; Trans-Antarctic Expedition Committee 151; Victoria & Albert Museum, London/Photo John Webb © Aldus Books 17; The Beinecke Rare Book and Manuscript Library, Yale University, courtesy of American Heritage 46–47.

PART TWO

The Roof of the World

PART TWO

The Roof of the World

BY GEOFFREY HINDLEY

Left: it was the Swiss scientist, Horace Bénédict de Saussure, who launched the great age of mountaineering with his passion for Mont Blanc. Here he and his party are seen descending that mountain in 1787.

Right: mountaineering today is an advanced science, but it still demands the utmost skill and courage. Ian Clough, a British climber shown on the south face of Annapurna, was killed on the descent in 1970.

Foreword

Man's conquest of the world's mountains is a comparatively recent enterprise. Until the 1800's, the art of mountaineering was virtually unknown and, indeed, very few mountains had ever been climbed. In the days of the classical world, the lofty peaks were regarded with awe, for gods and spirits were believed to live there. Even during the Christian Middle Ages, little interest was taken in scaling mountains. Then, men were preoccupied with things of the spirit, and nature took second place. Only with the beginning of scientific study of the world during the 1600's did men take any interest in mountains at all.

Once the age of mountaineering opened, however, the bold men who set out to climb mountains soon discovered the fascination that they held. At first, climbing was dangerous, for equipment was virtually nonexistent and rescue in case of accident impossible, but this did not prevent men from making their attempts. As the years passed, techniques were perfected, equipment improved, and mountaineering passed from the realm of art to that of science; but the fascination never diminished. George Leigh Mallory once said that men climb mountains "because they are there", but great as their challenge is, it is not the only reason why men climb.

This part of the book tells the story of man's relationship with the mountains, from the earliest fearful days to the knowledge of today. Now, their wonder is, if possible, greater than ever. For, in a world where man increasingly dominates his environment, the great mountains remain among the last untamed and unspoiled places on earth.

Why Do Men Climb Mountains?

1

A man clings to a precarious hold high on the sheer face of a mountain. Slowly, straining every nerve and muscle, he inches his way upward. One slip, and he could plummet thousands of feet down to the rocks below. But despite the danger, he takes intense pleasure in this struggle to reach the soaring summit above him. Why? What is it that makes men risk their lives to climb mountains?

The question is difficult to answer simply, although many reasons for climbing can be found. One of these, of course, is the desire for conquest. The will to meet and master a significant adversary is as old as man himself. Just as basic is the instinct to explore the unknown—to place one's feet on a lofty portion of the earth never trod before, or to pioneer a new route to a summit already reached.

Love of adventure is another vital part of the climber's motivation. Unforeseen hazards and swiftly changing conditions make every ascent a unique and exciting experience, stretching a man's capacities to the full and giving his life a heightened intensity. Although the

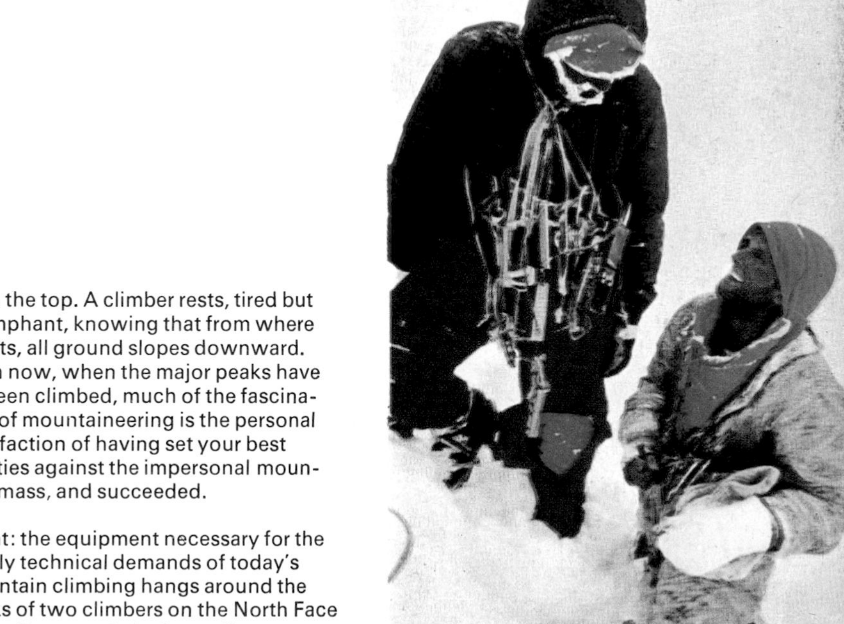

Left: the top. A climber rests, tired but triumphant, knowing that from where he sits, all ground slopes downward. Even now, when the major peaks have all been climbed, much of the fascination of mountaineering is the personal satisfaction of having set your best abilities against the impersonal mountain mass, and succeeded.

Right: the equipment necessary for the highly technical demands of today's mountain climbing hangs around the necks of two climbers on the North Face of the Eiger, ready for immediate use.

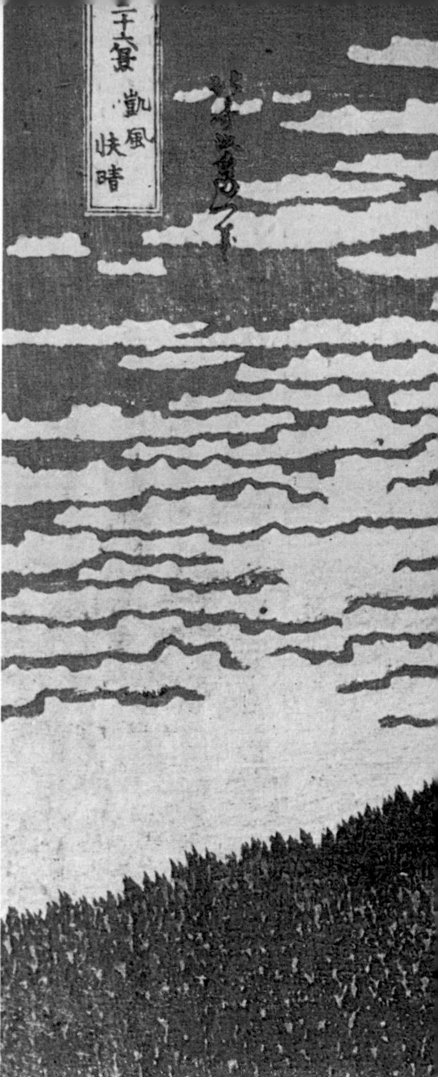

Above: in many of the world's religions, mountains have for centuries been regarded as sacred meeting places for God and man. This painting of the 1300's shows Moses receiving the Ten Commandments on Mount Sinai.

mountaineer does not seek out hardships and perils for their own sake, he willingly accepts them as an integral part of climbing and, in a sense, even welcomes them as a test of his ingenuity, endurance, skill, and courage. And it is the sharing of adventure that draws the members of a team together, forging the strong bond of comradeship that mountaineers so often speak of as one of the great rewards of climbing.

For some men, a successful climb is a matter of personal pride and prestige, quite frankly, something to boast about. For others, it may be that confronting the elemental dangers of the mountains is a way of finding relief and refreshment from the exhausting complexities of everyday life. Indeed, the "call of the wild" plays a large part in the mind and heart of every climber. High above the polluted air and congested streets of the world's cities, he can renew his essential kinship with the natural world. On a deeper level, some mountaineers experience an almost mystical sense of communion with nature amidst the rugged beauty and breathtaking views of the mountains. The Australian climber Herbert Tichy once spoke of this in describing the last few minutes of a Himalayan ascent. "The world

around me showed a kindly benevolence such as I had never before experienced," he wrote. "Snow, sky, the wind, and myself were an indivisible and divine whole."

Mountains have been climbed for reasons as diverse as the pursuit of scientific research and the winning of a wager. And, in the fierce international rivalry of modern times, they have even been climbed in the interests of national prestige. These, like all the other "reasons" for climbing, have been sufficient to spur men on to the highest achievement. Yet none of them alone fully explains the powerful attraction of mountaineering.

Perhaps, as the famed Himalayan climber George Leigh Mallory once remarked, men climb mountains simply, "Because they are there." For the true mountaineer, there is at the heart of it all an obsession that cannot, and need not, be explained. Whatever it may be that starts him climbing, there comes a time when the mountains themselves become his only reason. They take on a personality, and he becomes a part of their world. When this happens, there is no objective worthy of the name but the climb itself, and in that climb, the mountaineer finds fulfillment.

Above: sometimes the mountain itself is regarded as sacred. Mount Fuji, the holy mountain of Japan, has been a source of inspiration—here, for an artist painting during the 1700's—for generations of Japanese people.

Above: one of the most remarkable feats of maneuver in the mountains was accomplished in 218 B.C. when Hannibal, the Carthaginian general, led his army across the Alps to attack the Roman army unexpectedly at the rear.

This being so, another question raises itself: Why have men not always climbed mountains? For until the 1800's, mountaineering as such hardly existed. History records but a scant number of ascents before that time, and even these were mostly undertaken for purely practical reasons. To climb a mountain for pleasure was virtually unheard of, and the rare men who did so risked being thought highly eccentric, if not mad.

From earliest times, mountains were regarded as places of mystery and terror, the source of such frightening and inexplicable phenomena as glaciers, avalanches, and volcanic eruptions. For this reason, early man soon came to believe that mountain summits were the dwelling places of the gods. Peaks such as Mount Olympus and Mount Parnassus in Greece, Popocatépetl in Mexico, Everest on the Tibet-Nepal border, and Mount Fuji in Japan, became the object of reverence. But only in the East were mountains revered for their own sake. In ancient India, China, and Japan, for example, mountains often served as a source of inspiration for poets, artists, and philosophers. But in the Western world, and particularly in ancient

Right: for years men avoided mountains. But in 1336 an Italian poet named Francesco Petrarch, inspired by the paintings of Leonardo da Vinci and spurred on by a stubborn desire to reach the top, climbed Mont Ventoux.

Greece and Rome, men saw nothing beautiful or inspiring about mountains. Far from giving them pleasure or exciting their curiosity, the snowy peaks on their horizons filled them with dread and aversion, and they did their best to ignore all but the handful of peaks to which they had attached religious significance.

Only a few real climbs are known to have been made during classical times. Two of these—the ascent of a Balkan peak by Philip of Macedonia in 350 B.C., and the ascent of Mount Etna by the Emperor Hadrian in the A.D. 100's—were undertaken simply to gratify royal whims. Philip wanted to discover whether both the Adriatic and the Aegean seas could be viewed from a single vantage point, and Hadrian wished to see the sunrise from a mountaintop. A far more heroic undertaking occurred in the winter of 218 B.C., when the Carthaginian general Hannibal led his army across the Alps to launch a surprise attack on the Romans from the north.

But in ancient times, the only known case of a climb made for reasons of curiosity and pleasure was the ascent of Mount Etna, in the 400's B.C., by the philosopher Empedocles. And it was to be many centuries before another such climb was made, for the traditional dislike and disinterest in mountains continued to prevail in the West long after the fall of Rome and the rise of Christendom. In fact, during the early Middle Ages, men became, if possible, even less interested in mountains.

The emphasis placed by Christianity on the relationship between God and man resulted, to a degree, in the devaluing of nature. Mountains, together with all the physical world, were viewed as being less real than the world of spiritual concerns, and were therefore thought unworthy of serious notice. This attitude was reflected not only in medieval paintings, which rarely included landscapes, but also in medieval maps, which frequently omitted to show the locations of even the loftiest peaks in the areas they depicted.

The start of the Renaissance heralded the reawakening of men's interest in the natural world. Scholars began to take a scientific approach to natural phenomena. Artists—chief among them Leonardo da Vinci—began to depict natural scenes with superb accuracy and appreciation. It is perhaps not so surprising, then, that the first known ascent of an Alpine peak should have occurred during this period. The climber was the poet Petrarch, who, on April 26, 1336, ascended Mont Ventoux (6,263 feet) in southern France. From a letter he wrote to his father describing the ascent, it is clear that he made the climb for no other reason than to reach the top, and that he relished both the climb and the glorious view he saw from the summit.

But Petrarch's historic ascent was not emulated by others, and nearly two centuries elapsed before the joys of climbing were discovered by another man, the Swiss scientist Konrad Von Gesner. Perhaps it was in search of botanical specimens that Gesner first began climbing in the mid-1500's. But whatever the reason, he soon became an ardent mountaineer. He made it a rule to climb one

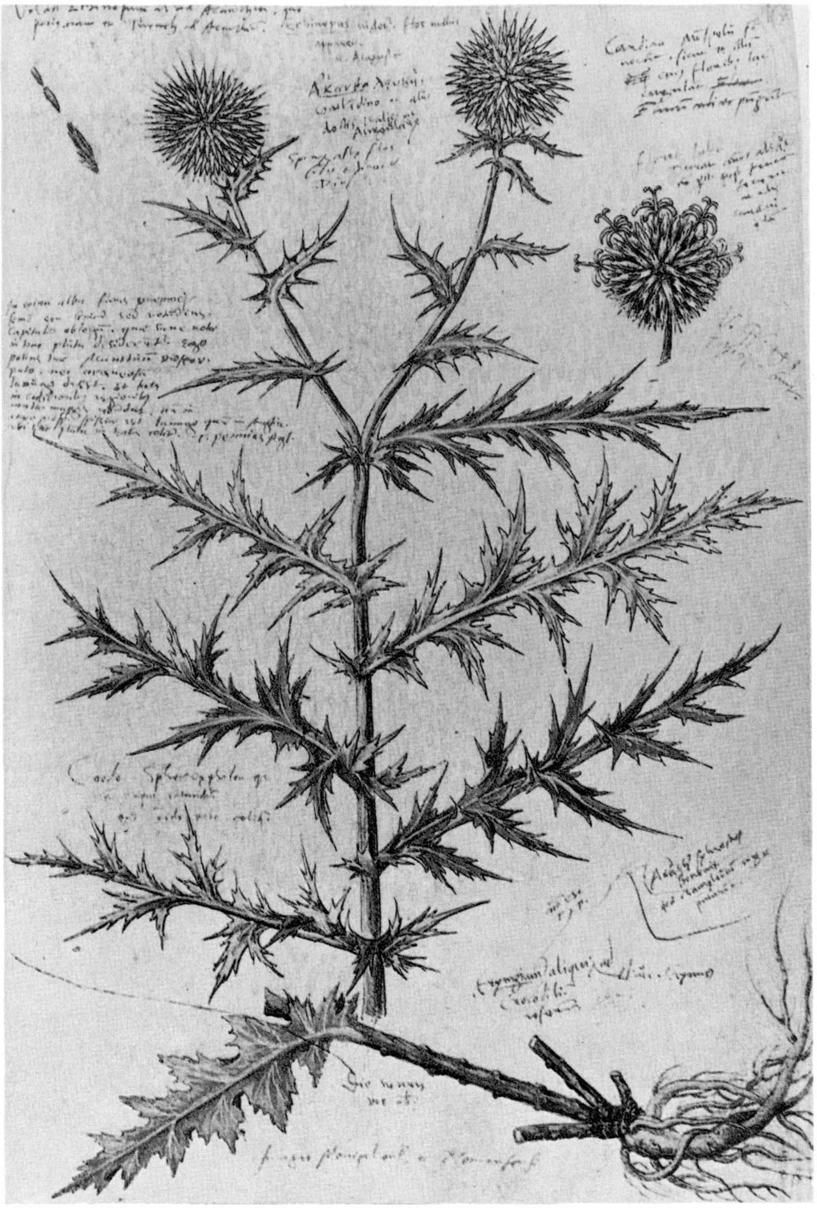

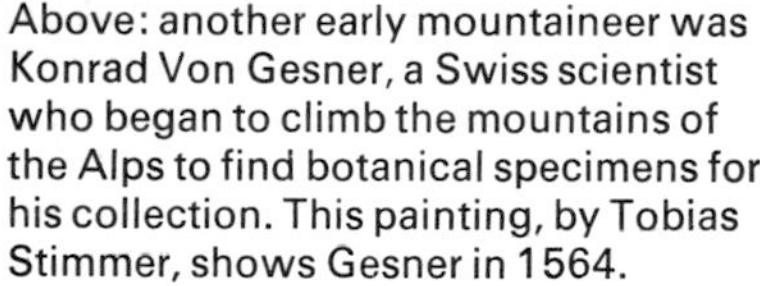

Above: another early mountaineer was Konrad Von Gesner, a Swiss scientist who began to climb the mountains of the Alps to find botanical specimens for his collection. This painting, by Tobias Stimmer, shows Gesner in 1564.

Above right: a thistle *(Echinops Sphaerocephalus)* drawn by Gesner. Having begun climbing to collect plants, Gesner became so interested in the enjoyment of climbing itself that he made it a rule to scale a peak a year.

mountain every year "at the time when the flowers are at their best," and wrote movingly of the rapture that overwhelmed him in the awesome silence of the heights.

In the meantime, at the bidding of Charles VIII of France, the first ascent of the 6,880-foot Alpine peak Mont Aiguille had been made. This climb, led by the king's chamberlain, De Beaupré, in 1492, was an impressive achievement, planned and carried out with much skill. Nonetheless, it was a matter of pure duty. Having done his sovereign's command, De Beaupré never climbed another mountain.

During the next two centuries, an increasing number of European traders and travelers journeyed through the Alps, toiling over the major passes on foot and on horseback. None of these journeys was undertaken for pleasure, but they did contribute substantially to what was then known about Alpine terrain and weather conditions. As early as 1574, a book called *Concerning the Difficulties of Alpine Travel* was written by one Josias Simler of Zurich. In it he offered travelers much useful advice about the avoidance of avalanches and hidden crevasses, and about the use of ropes and crampons as climbing aids.

People listened to the Alpine travelers' tales of blizzards, glaciers, crevasses, and dizzying views with mixed horror and curiosity. By the early 1700's, in search of the picturesque and the "finely horrid," a few people had begun venturing into the mountains. Two such tourists were the Englishmen William Windham and Richard Pococke. These men set forth in 1741 to explore the glaciers in the region of Chamonix, a French mountain village very near the point where the borders of France, Italy, and Switzerland meet. As an "expedition," the venture hardly merits the name, for, despite elaborate preparations, the party went only as far as the Montenvers Pass, to which a path already existed. However, their trip set a fashion for walking in the Alps.

One man who did more than walk in the Alps was Father Placidus á Spescha, a Benedictine monk, who, in the later 1700's, made a series of astonishing climbs there. Many of the peaks he scaled were over 10,000 feet, and all of them he climbed for the sheer joy of it. But although many people today consider him to be the real father of mountaineering, his daring ascents created little stir at the time. Indeed, people's curiosity about mountains might have gone no farther than Alpine "rambles" had it not been for the scientists of the period.

European scholars had first become curious about mountains in the late 1600's. The tales of Alpine travelers intrigued them and they were eager to investigate the phenomena described to them. But beyond this, they sought to understand the very existence of mountains which baffled them by their utter uselessness. Little was known about geology, and scientists were at a loss to explain the whys and wherefores of geographic features.

Today we know that the geography of the earth is the result of continual change and movement over millions of years of geologic time. The world's mountain ranges are the product of these changes. There are four basic types of mountains. *Volcanic mountains* form

Above: one of the earliest Englishmen to be fascinated by the Alpine region was Richard Pococke, seen here in Oriental costume, who set out with a friend, William Windham, to explore the glaciers around Chamonix in 1741.

Below: one of the most frightening hazards for men in the mountains has always been the avalanche, when a wall of snow and rock collapses suddenly and crashes downward, burying everything that lies in its path. This drawing of 1849 shows an avalanche sweeping down a mountainside.

Above: a marine fossil, 130 million years old. It was discovered 18,000 feet up in the Himalaya, showing that this range was once beneath the sea.

when lava and ashes burst through the earth's crust. Some still display the cones of extinct or living volcanoes. *Dome mountains* form when the top section of the earth's crust rises into domes like huge blisters. *Faultblock mountains* form when the earth's crust breaks into great blocks, some of which move upward, while some move downward. *Folded mountains* form when the earth's crust wrinkles into wavelike forms. One of the theories put forward to explain this last phenomenon is that, as the earth's center cools, its surface contracts, causing a wrinkling in the strata beneath the earth's crust. But whatever the cause, the forces are huge and have pushed up mountain peaks of tremendous heights. In the Himalaya, fossil forms of marine life can be found at 18,000 feet—indicating that in some remote past this mountain range was once the floor of a sea.

Once the rock stratum has been thrust above the earth's surface, it becomes subject to weathering. As the softer strata are worn away by the action of massive, slow-moving glaciers, deep valleys are gouged out, leaving jagged peaks. Then these angularities, too, are worn down by wind and rain until, after thousands and thousands

Once the rock layer, the basic material of the mountain, has been thrust up, erosion begins wearing it away. One form of erosion is by massive rivers of slow-moving ice, which carve out deep valleys. The glacier shown in this engraving is the Rheinwald, which is one source of the Rhine River.

of years, a once formidable mountain range has become a series of gently undulating hills. Today, geologists believe that the Russian Urals and the American Appalachians—without mountains in the climber's sense of the word—began to form some 300 million years ago. The formation of the Alps, on the other hand, seems to have begun about 30 million years ago, with the uplift reaching its climax about 1 million years ago. The Himalaya are also quite young and, as a system, may be said to be still developing.

All this was not known in the mid-1700's, when the science of geology was still in its infancy. But a few European thinkers were

beginning to realize—a century before Charles Darwin formulated his theory of evolution—that the history of the earth stretched back many thousands of years and that the world was far older than the Bible's accounts suggested.

One such man, the Swiss scientist Horace Bénédict de Saussure, looked to the mountains for evidence to support his theories. But once in the Alps, his scientific interest in all mountains swiftly changed to a passion for one mountain in particular—Mont Blanc. And it was to be De Saussure's passion for this mountain that launched the great age of mountaineering.

The Beginnings 2

Horace Bénédict de Saussure, the scientist who opened men's eyes to the joys of mountaineering, was born in Geneva in 1740. Very early in his life he showed an extraordinary gift for observation and deduction, and, by the age of 20, was already establishing his reputation as a scientist. In 1760, he went to the Alpine tourist resort of Chamonix to make a study of glaciers. There it was that he first saw Mont Blanc. Towering to a height of 15,781 feet, the mountain's snowy, dome-like summit seemed to beckon to him.

De Saussure's first thought was to establish a scientific research center high on the mountainside, but he could find no one who

Horace Bénédict de Saussure, a Swiss scientist, fulfilled his ambition in 1787 by reaching the summit of Mont Blanc. He was accompanied by 18 guides and supplies, including a basket of bottled wine to celebrate the climb.

would assist him in the project. In fact, his proposed plan to climb the mountain provoked widespread horror and disbelief. Many of the peasants of the region had clambered over the lower slopes and glaciers of Mont Blanc while hunting chamois (a kind of mountain goat), but none had ever dared venture higher than a few thousand feet. They believed that demons and dragons guarded the heights, and despite the young scientist's pleas, they could not be induced to take part in an expedition to the summit.

But De Saussure only became more determined to climb Mont Blanc. Its beauty, as he put it later, had begun to disturb his feelings

Above: De Saussure, a man obsessed by a mountain. Having achieved his goal by conquering Mont Blanc, De Saussure later established a scientific base on the neighboring pass of Col du Géant, and spent two weeks there, engaged in various kinds of research.

like some kind of illness. "I could not even look upon the mountain, which is visible from so many points round about, without being seized with an aching of desire," he wrote later. For a scientist, particularly during the Age of Reason, this was a most unobjective approach, and De Saussure himself could never fully explain the passion that Mont Blanc had inspired in him. In fact, he was at heart a true mountaineer, long before the word itself came into use. Nevertheless, he always found it hard to admit that something more than scientific curiosity lay behind his repeated journeys to the mountains. In the course of these journeys, he did, however, carry on much important research, and his great work, *Voyages in the Alps,*

is recognized as a landmark in the developing science of geology. It was he, for example, who first offered a rational explanation for the movement of glaciers, ascribing it simply to the pull of gravity rather than to any mysterious or magical forces.

While De Saussure was carrying out his Alpine studies, he never ceased to hope that one day he would be able to climb Mont Blanc. He even offered a reward to the first man who would pioneer a route to the summit. Fifteen years went by, and a few attempts were made in the hope of winning the reward, but all were defeated. Nor was it hard to see why. Almost nothing was known at this time about mountain terrain or climbing techniques, and above the familiar lower slopes of Mont Blanc there loomed a world of strange and frightening phenomena. It was a veritable obstacle-course of ice-walls, narrow ledges, and immense, jagged glaciers. The surface of these frozen rivers of ice was split in many places by deep fissures called crevasses. Some of these were masked by a covering of snow; others were spanned by slender ice bridges. Eerie groans could be heard coming out of the depths of these abysses from time to time. And these strange rumblings were occasionally answered by the roar of a mighty avalanche higher up, as tons of ice and snow sheered off the mountainside and crashed down the face of a cliff.

Yet despite the terrors it held, Mont Blanc appeared both incredibly lovely *and* climbable to at least one other man besides De Saussure. This man was a young Chamonix doctor named Michel Gabriel Paccard. He, too, loved the mountain and felt a compulsion to climb it. He made a series of unsuccessful attempts on the summit, but remained determined to master it—for France, for science (he always took his instruments with him), and for his own personal satisfaction.

On August 7, 1786, Paccard set off to make yet another assault on "our" mountain, as he called Mont Blanc. To help him carry his instruments, he took with him a hardy chamois-hunter named Jacques Balmat. Unlike Paccard, Balmat undertook the climb solely in the hopes of winning fame and the reward offered by De Saussure. Nonetheless, he was a strong and fearless man, already well-known for his skill in climbing Mont Blanc's lower slopes.

The two men began their climb early in the afternoon, and by late

Above: Mont Blanc, the mountain which so fascinated De Saussure, and which has beckoned to many other Alpine climbers.

Right: the shoes especially designed by De Saussure for his ascent of Mont Blanc. The soles are studded for more grip when climbing on ice and snow.

Above right: Michel Gabriel Paccard, the young Chamonix doctor who led the first successful assault on Mont Blanc. He and his guide completed the ascent with only the crudest of equipment.

Above: Jacques Balmat, the guide who accompanied Paccard on his summit climb. He later tried to claim all the credit for the historic climb himself.

evening had reached the top of a long ridge of rock called the Montagne de la Côte, where they camped for the night. In the light of early dawn they started off again, and crossed the Jonction, an ice field scored by countless crevasses. The only way they could get across several of the fissures was to lay their two alpenstocks (pointed staves) over it and crawl across them—over empty black space—to the other side. Beyond the Jonction lay a ridge of rocks called the Grands Mulets, and beyond that, two long valleys covered in deep and powdery snow. Sinking up to their hips at every step, they struggled across these valleys (now known as the Petit Plateau and the Grand Plateau) and at 3:30 P.M., reached the last major obstacle between them and the summit. This was a steep incline of ice from which arose two parallel bands of rock, the Rochers Rouges.

By now both men were frostbitten and exhausted. Moreover, they were gasping for breath in the thin air of the heights. But they pressed on, making their way between the two shoulders of rock to the gentle slopes just below the summit.

It was 6:30 P.M., when the two men stood at last, breathless but triumphant, on Mont Blanc's highest point. Tired as he was, Paccard spent an hour taking scientific measurements, and then the two started down. There was a full moon, and they managed to keep going until the early hours of the morning, when they rested again in the Montagne de la Côte, before pushing on to Chamonix. Here, Balmat duly received the reward promised by De Saussure.

For Paccard, however, the success of the climb was reward enough.

Paccard and Balmat's ascent of Mont Blanc is one of the most remarkable in mountaineering history. Not only was it the first ascent of the highest mountain in the Alps; it was achieved by a team of only two men, climbing without the benefit of even the most basic equipment—ropes, crampons (metal spikes on the underside of the boot), or ice-axes. But their triumph was to have a strange sequel. Balmat, not content with his monetary reward, began claiming that all the credit for the climb belonged to him. He boasted that he had led the entire ascent and that Paccard would never have reached the top without his help. In fact, he maintained, he had practically had to carry the doctor up the final slopes to the summit. Balmat was known to be a braggart, and his story would probably never have been believed if a journalist named Marc Bourrit, had not stepped forward to support it. Bourrit—who had tried and failed to climb Mont Blanc himself—was jealous of Paccard's success and only too pleased to spoil the doctor's triumph. He claimed that he had watched the climb through a telescope and seen Balmat take the lead.

Thus, Balmat's version of the climb came to be generally accepted, and it was not until a century later that the record was put straight with the finding of the papers of a certain Baron von Gensdorff. He had also watched the ascent through a telescope, and his notes and sketches of it prove the falsity of Balmat's claims.

For all the controversy surrounding it, and despite the fact that it was the first ascent, Paccard and Balmat's achievement on Mont Blanc was overshadowed by De Saussure's own ascent the following year. The doughty scientist had never given up his dream of climbing the mountain. He had failed on his only previous attempt, but now, after Paccard and Balmat's success, he became more than ever determined to realize his life's ambition. On August 1, 1787, he set out for the summit accompanied by no fewer than 18 guides (including his own valet, who had never even been on a mountain before!). The size of the expedition is partly explained by the number of pieces of scientific equipment that had to be carried up. When, on the afternoon of the second day, the party reached the top, De Saussure spent more than four hours conducting experiments. His only regret was that the difficulty of breathing in the rarified air of the summit forced the party to go back down before he had completed all the work he had planned. Later in the year, he

Marc Bourrit, a journalist who was frustrated many times in his efforts to climb Mont Blanc. He reacted emotionally when he learned of Paccard's successful ascent, and did his best to discredit the climb.

Left: De Saussure, with his son, coming down from the scientific base on the Col du Géant. They became so absorbed with their research that eventually the porters mutinied, and destroyed the food, forcing them down. Below: the Alps are Europe's largest mountain system. They stretch through southeastern France, northern Italy, Switzerland, part of southern Germany, Austria, and Yugoslavia. It was in the Alps that mountaineering as we understand it really began.

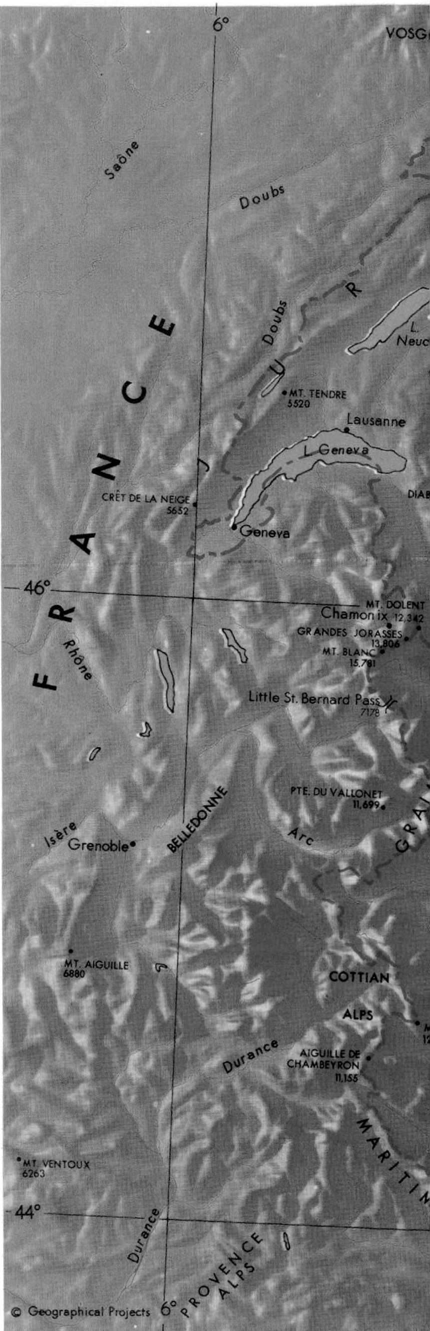

led another large expedition to a height of 10,960 feet on the Alpine pass called the Col du Géant. Once there he and his son, working in shifts, carried out a grueling series of experiments for over two weeks.

Because De Saussure was a distinguished scientist, known throughout Europe, his ascent of Mont Blanc was widely publicized. Reading the accounts of the climb, men in many different countries became fired with the ambition to emulate his achievement. Scientists and adventurers alike began to tackle Alpine peaks, and the next few decades witnessed many first ascents in the mountain chain that arches from southeastern France, through northern Italy, Switzerland, southern Germany, Austria, and into Yugoslavia.

The Alps are really composed of a number of ranges. Mont Blanc, which was climbed with increasing frequency after De Saussure's ascent, lies in the Pennine Alps to the west of the Great Saint Bernard Pass, where the frontiers of Italy, France, and Switzerland converge. From Mont Blanc the mighty Pennine Alps stretch eastward. They include such peaks as the Matterhorn (14,685 feet), the Weisshorn (14,803 feet), and the Monte Rosa (15,200 feet). To the north of the Pennines, is the loftiest of the Alpine ranges, the

Bernese Alps, where the Swiss town of Grindelwald lies surrounded by a number of mighty peaks. One of these, the famous Jungfrau (13,668 feet), was first climbed in 1811 by a wealthy Swiss merchant named Johann Meyer who, with his two sons, had explored many of the glaciers above Grindelwald. Near the Jungfrau stands the Finsteraarhorn (14,026 feet). The loftiest mountain in the Bernese Alps, it was first scaled by two Swiss guides in 1829. Two other towering peaks in the region are the Rosenhorn (12,110 feet), climbed by the German scientist Edouard Desor in 1844, and the

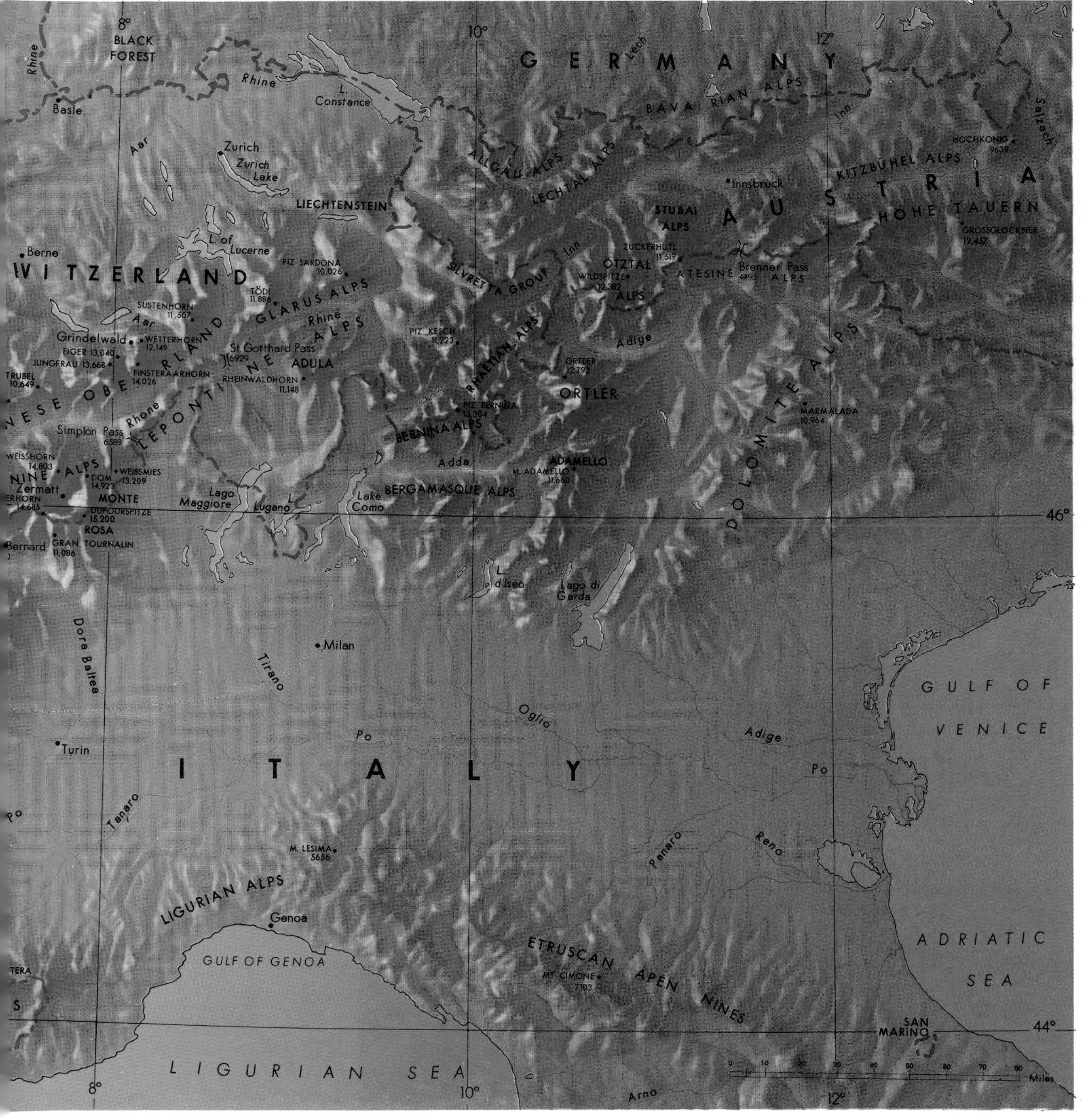

Left: during the early 1800's, most climbing was for scientific reasons. J. D. Forbes, a Scotsman shown here measuring a glacier, was typical of scientist-mountaineers of the period.

Right: the first woman to attempt Mont Blanc was a French countess, Henriette d'Angeville, shown here inspecting her company of guides and porters before setting out. Her stamina was remarkable, and she completed the climb.

Mittelhorn (12,166 feet), first scaled by a Scotsman, Stanhope Templeman Speer in 1845.

The thrill of climbing appealed to women as well as to men. In fact, one of the most daring climbers of this early period of mountaineering was a French countess named Henriette d'Angeville, who climbed Mont Blanc in 1838. She was followed by many other redoubtable women climbers as the century progressed. And perhaps they deserve special credit for their efforts, for not only were they venturing into what was considered a man's realm, but they had to do so in skirts. One woman, Mrs. Aubrey le Blond, who wore trousers under a detachable skirt, was forced to make two ascents of the same peak in one day, when she forgot and left her skirt on the summit. Had she not gone back to retrieve it, she would not have been permitted to enter any of the respectable inns in the valley.

Two of the most important figures in mountaineering at this time were the Scottish scientist James David Forbes and the Swiss naturalist Jean Louis Agassiz. Like De Saussure, both men justified their regular and extensive mountain expeditions on the grounds of

scientific research. But again like De Saussure, both Forbes and Agassiz reveal in their writings a passionate love for the mountains themselves.

Together, Forbes and Agassiz conducted an extensive exploration of the Unteraar Glacier in Switzerland, and, as a result of their findings, published seminal studies on the movement of glaciers. Forbes later climbed the Jungfrau, as well as other peaks in places as widely separated as Scotland, Spain, and Norway. On each of his expeditions, he took numerous scientific instruments—barometers, thermometers, polariscopes, hygrometers, hypsometers, and chronometers—and over the years added a great deal to knowledge of mountain terrain and conditions. Certainly his work was of inestimable value to science. But it was his enthusiasm for climbing that, in the end, had the greater influence on the men of his time. His writings and lectures, as well as his example, did much to encourage the growing British interest in mountaineering.

The late 1700's and early 1800's had seen the development of a literary and aesthetic movement known as Romanticism. Through the works of writers such as Goethe and Rousseau, Wordsworth,

Byron, and Shelley, nature—and mountains in particular—had come to be seen in terms of romantic peril and idyllic beauty. Even after the Romantic movement began to decline, the Romantic attitude toward mountains persisted, and even gained in intensity. The great Victorian art critic John Ruskin, for example, both painted and wrote about the beauties of the Alps with passionate awe.

British interest in mountaineering had been stirred both by the scientific exploits of James Forbes and by the lyrical writings of the Romantics. In mid-century, two events occurred to galvanize this growing interest and launch a historic period of mountaineering.

The first of these events was the well-publicized ascent of Mont Blanc in 1851 by the Englishman Albert Smith. Smith had been consumed with a desire to scale the peak since the moment in his boyhood when he had read a little book called *The Peasants of Chamonix*. He first saw the mountain when, as a student in Paris, he tramped to Chamonix in the hope of joining an expedition as a porter. He had no luck and, as he could not afford to mount an expedition of his own, he had to abandon the project. But he hung on to his dream, and in 1851, after several years of traveling and giving lectures on his experiences, he was back in Chamonix. This time, he joined up with a party of wealthy young Englishmen. They were merely touring, but when they heard that he wanted to scale Mont Blanc, they became determined to do so as well, and offered to pay for the expedition.

Although Mont Blanc had seen almost 40 ascents so far, there were still hazards enough to make the venture exciting. In 1820, three men had been killed in an avalanche on the slopes of the mountain. And even though Smith's party waited for a fine day to begin their adventure, there was still a good deal of danger in their undertaking. The route they took was in fact a very difficult one, and they were ignorant of the importance of roping up. But the weather remained fair and they were spared any serious hardships by their 36 guides and porters, who lifted them over the worst stretches. In fact, the climb went very smoothly and they returned to Chamonix much pleased with themselves.

Albert Smith did not intend to keep his triumph to himself. The very next year, at a large exhibition hall in Piccadilly, London, Smith staged a lecture-cum-picture show called "The Ascent of Mont Blanc." Londoners flocked to see and hear Smith's story, which he recounted as a huge illustrated screen was unrolled, depicting all the incidents and hazards of the adventure. Although many people later accused Smith of "vulgar showmanship," he had seized the public imagination and given an enormous boost to British interest in mountaineering.

The Bernese Alps by Josef Koch. As the mystery of mountains was slowly dispelled by growing numbers of men climbing and living on heights, the writings of early travelers inspired artists to portray their magnificence.

Above: a watercolor by the English art critic and painter John Ruskin, who felt a special reverence for mountains, although he apparently never considered climbing himself.

In 1854, another event—Sir Alfred Wills' ascent of the Wetterhorn—had an even greater impact in Britain than Smith's Mont Blanc epic. Until then, mountain climbing had been seen in terms of science, romance, and adventure. Wills' description of the Wetterhorn ascent raised mountaineering to the status of a heroic endeavor, one that called forth the best in a man and even brought him closer to God.

The Wetterhorn (12,149 feet) is not an impressively difficult climb, but Wills' description of his experience on reaching the summit was both dramatic and inspiring:

"As I took the last step . . . my left shoulder grazed against the angle of an icy embrasure, while on the right, the glacier fell abruptly away beneath me toward an unknown and awful abyss . . . I stepped across, and had passed the ridge of the Wetterhorn!

"I am not ashamed to own that I experienced, as this sublime and wonderful prospect burst upon my view, a profound and almost irrepressible emotion. We felt as in the more immediate presence of Him who had reared this tremendous pinnacle . . . poised, as it seemed, halfway between the earth and sky."

These passages from Wills' book *Wandering Among the High Alps*

Right: Albert Smith, shown here in his climbing oufit, was an Englishman who made a highly-publicized ascent of the formidable Mont Blanc in 1851.

deeply stirred many young men in Victorian England. Here, they felt, was an activity worthy of the highest sacrifice. It was fraught with hardship and peril; it demanded the utmost self-discipline and courage; and it promised a kind of exhilaration and profound satisfaction that no other sport or recreation could do.

Alfred Wills' book came out at a time when mountaineering had already gained many adherents. Nonetheless, it was to prove a landmark in the history of alpinism. For it was with this ascent of the Wetterhorn in 1854 that the so-called Golden Age of mountaineering began.

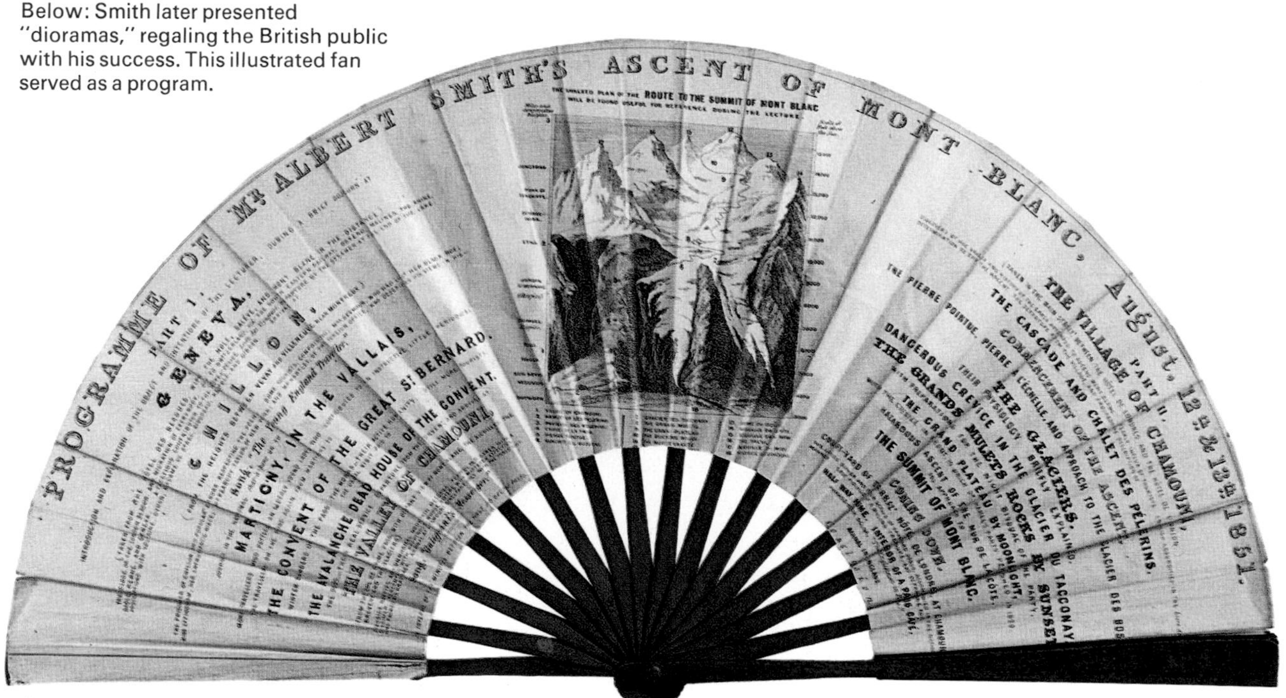

Below: Smith later presented "dioramas," regaling the British public with his success. This illustrated fan served as a program.

Right: the Alpine cottage, the Eagle's Nest, used by the Wills family, some of the most enthusiastic of Victorian mountaineers during the Golden Age. Below: the Wills family at the Eagle's Nest, with Alfred Wills (holding the ice-ax at the extreme left), whose ascent of the Wetterhorn in 1854 began the era when climbing became generally accepted as a sport requiring great courage. The small boy on his mother's lap is E. F. Norton, who was leader of the 1924 attempt on Mount Everest.

The Golden Age

3

The Golden Age that began with Alfred Wills' ascent of the Wetterhorn lasted only a decade—from 1854 to 1865—but it was a decade of extraordinary mountaineering achievement. When it began, the majority of glittering peaks in Europe's mountain arc had never seen the foot of man. By its close, there was hardly a major Alpine summit that had not been climbed at least once. There was nothing planned or coordinated about this all-out assault on the Alps. Public interest and individual enthusiasm simply combined, and a new and thrilling sport was born.

The overwhelming majority of Alpine climbers during the Golden Age were British. Individually, they scored a remarkable number of historic first ascents. As a group they became known for their courage, their determination, and their passionate commitment to the sport itself. In fact, for many British climbers of the period (and for many climbers of all nationalities since then), mountaineering quickly ceased to be a sport and became a way of life. Such men returned to the Alps season after season to pit their skills against ever more difficult peaks. In so doing, they contributed to the growing body of codes and traditions, lore, and jargon that soon became an integral part of mountaineering.

The year 1857 saw a historic development in the formation of the world's first mountaineering association: the Alpine Club. Not surprisingly, the club was set up in London by a group of British climbers. Modestly begun as an association of like-minded enthusiasts, it soon acquired the status of an important society and became the leading body on all Alpine matters. It kept records, tested new equipment, and provided information about Alpine routes and conditions. In addition, it published a regular journal recording the mountaineering experiences of its members. For five years it was the only association of its kind. Then, in 1862, an Austrian counterpart was set up, followed by the formation of a Swiss Alpine Club in 1863. (Since then, hundreds of mountaineering associations have been formed all over the world.)

By and large, the members of these clubs made no pretense of climbing for any other reason than because they enjoyed it. But at least one Victorian mountaineer carried the tradition of the scientific alpinist into the new age. He was Francis Fox Tuckett, a Quaker businessman and amateur scientist who, as a young man, had met the great scientist-mountaineer James Forbes and been inspired by his

Mountaineering quickly became popular. This group of British climbers with their guides shows (back row, left to right) Melchior Anderegg, Macdonald, Grove, Jacob Anderegg, and Young Taugwalder. In the front row, left to right, Leslie Stephen, Short, Buxton, Living, and Francis Fox Tuckett. Stephen and Fox Tuckett were among the British climbers who formed the Alpine Club in London in 1857.

ideals. Between 1856 and 1874, Tuckett climbed more than 160 Alpine peaks and 370 passes. Always he took with him a vast array of scientific instruments, some being of his own invention. Festooned with apparatus, Tuckett cut a strange figure among the new generation of sportsmen climbers. Yet he stuck firmly to his belief that he, and all the other mountaineers of his generation were first and foremost pioneers exploring unknown territory. As such, he said, they were duty-bound to record, measure, and scrutinize everything they might find.

Tuckett was not entirely alone in holding this view. One of the most distinguished climbers of this period, the British physicist John Tyndall, stoutly upheld the value of science in connection with mountaineering. In fact, Tyndall's interest in climbing really came about as a result of his study of glaciers. But once in the mountains, he, like many another man before him, became an ardent alpinist. He made the first ascent of the Weisshorn (14,803 feet) in 1861 and on another occasion climbed the Monte Rosa (15,200 feet) alone, with only a flask of tea and a ham sandwich to keep him going. But even in the midst of these exploits, he never lost sight of his "real" goal—the pursuit of scientific research. And as a result of his careful observations, he made many important contributions to the developing theory of glaciers.

But men like Tuckett and Tyndall were exceptions to the rule. Most of the English mountaineers of the period climbed solely for the pleasure and satisfaction it gave them. Amateur sportsmen in the purest sense, many of them had distinguished careers in fields quite divorced from either sport or natural science. One such man was Sir Leslie Stephen, a philosopher and a leading figure in British literary life, who was also a passionate devotee of mountaineering. In 1871, Stephen turned his pen to his beloved sport and produced a book about Alpine climbing called *The Playground of Europe*. It is still regarded as a classic statement of the mountaineer's attitude.

In being a scholar and an aesthete—as well as a man of some wealth and social standing—Stephen was highly representative of the British climbers of this period. In fact, during the Golden Age, mountain climbing was, perforce, strictly an upper class sport. The cost involved in mounting an Alpine expedition made it impossible for any but men of means and leisure.

Above: Leslie Stephen, the English scholar and philosopher who became a passionate devotee of mountaineering. Below: title page and frontispiece of his book, considered the classic statement of the mountaineer's attitude.

ASCENT OF THE ROTHHORN.

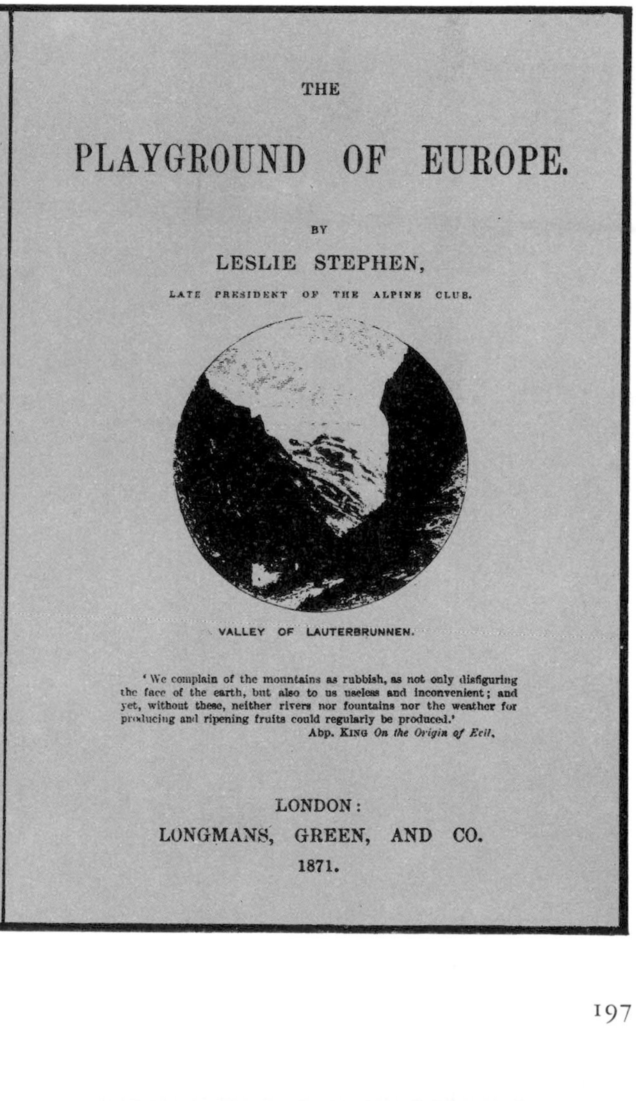

THE

PLAYGROUND OF EUROPE.

BY

LESLIE STEPHEN,

LATE PRESIDENT OF THE ALPINE CLUB.

VALLEY OF LAUTERBRUNNEN.

'We complain of the mountains as rubbish, as not only disfiguring the face of the earth, but also to us useless and inconvenient; and yet, without these, neither rivers nor fountains nor the weather for producing and ripening fruits could regularly be produced.'

Abp. KING *On the Origin of Evil.*

LONDON:
LONGMANS, GREEN, AND CO.
1871.

Above: as mountaineering increased in popularity, a good many Swiss took advantage of their local knowledge and became guides. Several grew quite famous for their daring climbs. This photograph of a group of guides was taken in Zermatt by the Victorian mountain photographer G. P. Abraham.

One of the gentleman climber's chief expenses was the services of professional guides. Although, later on, many mountaineers began climbing without guides, it was at first thought essential to enlist the aid of local men who possessed not only strength and skill, but also a thorough knowledge of mountain terrain and weather conditions. Most of the professional guides of the period were Swiss peasants, one-time herdsmen or chamois-hunters. A good many of them loved mountains and mountain climbing as much as their employers, and more than a few earned themselves an honored place in the history of the sport. Their vital importance to the success of a climb was fully recognized and acknowledged by the amateurs who employed them, and there often grew up between amateur and guide a deep-felt bond of fellowship. The comradeship between guide and amateur early became one of the traditions of the sport.

Of the many leading Swiss guides of the period, one of the best-known was Christian Almer. Born in Grindelwald in 1826, Almer did not begin his climbing career until he was about 28, when he joined Alfred Wills' Wetterhorn ascent party. Two years later he became a professional guide. In the next few years, he took part in many first ascents, including that of the Grandes Jorasses (13,806 feet) near Mont Blanc, and that of the Eiger (13,040 feet) in the

Right: one of the best known of these Swiss guides was Christian Almer. This photograph of him, with his wife Margharitha, was taken just after they had climbed the Wetterhorn to celebrate their 50th wedding anniversary.

Below: Melchior Anderegg, another of the Alpine guides active during the Golden Age, who gained international fame for his superb climbing skill.

Bernese Alps. The famed British climber Edward Whymper once wrote of him that "There is not a truer heart or a surer foot to be found amongst the Alps." Almer was a vigorous and enthusiastic climber to the end of his days. In 1896, he and his devoted wife Margharitha climbed the Wetterhorn to celebrate their Golden Wedding Anniversary. He was then 70 and she 72.

Another well-known Swiss guide of the mid-1800's was Melchior Anderegg, born in 1827. Anderegg began his career as a herdsman, chamois-hunter, and wood-carver. His first opportunity to serve as a guide came when he was in his early 20's, and from then on, mountain climbing became his life. He was Leslie Stephen's favorite guide, and made many first ascents with him. Another distinguished mountaineer with whom he worked was a woman, Lucy Walker. Anderegg was her guide on climbs over a 20-year period and, inevitably, she fell in love with him. Asked why she had never married, she once said, "I love mountains and Melchior, and Melchior already has a wife." Whymper, one of the many other mountaineers who employed Anderegg at one time or another, valued him as highly as he did Almer. "Melchior," he said, "is a very prince among guides."

Guides played a vital part in every major ascent of the Golden

Age. But perhaps in no case was their role so crucial—or so controversial—as in the dramatic episode that marked the end of the decade. This was Edward Whymper's ascent of the Matterhorn, a climb that began with a rivalry, ended in a tragic disaster, and became a legend in its own time.

Born in 1840, Edward Whymper began his career as an apprentice in his father's wood-engraving business, and soon became a master craftsman. At the age of 20, he was commissioned to illustrate the Alpine Club's first series of books, *Peaks, Passes, and Glaciers*. It was this task that first brought him face to face with the Matterhorn.

Situated in the Pennine Alps, the Matterhorn rises to a height of 14,685 feet on the Italian-Swiss border near the town of Zermatt.

Left: the Eiger and Mönsch, painted in watercolor by Edward Whymper, an artist who discovered mountaineering through a commission to illustrate an Alpine Club publication. He became one of those climbers who develop an obsession about a specific mountain – in his case, it was the Matterhorn.

Above: the Matterhorn, for years considered impossible to climb, which came to be so important in the history and legend of Alpine mountaineering.

It is neither the highest nor the most difficult mountain in the Alps, but its four sharp ridges, ending in a peaked summit that seems to overhang its own slopes, give it a forbidding and inaccessible appearance. It is often topped with a plume of billowing cloud that signals the onset of a storm in its upper reaches.

Whymper was not immediately impressed by the towering beauty of this mighty peak. Indeed, his first reaction, as he recorded it in his diary, was to feel contempt for all the writers—Ruskin in particular—who had penned "such precious stuff" about the mountain. This reaction was typical of Whymper, who all his life was an independent, stubborn, and opinionated man.

But if he felt no awe of the mountain, Whymper at once felt a strong ambition to master it. At first he might simply have meant to

Above: Luc Meynet, a little hunchback who overcame his disability to go high in the mountains. He climbed with Edward Whymper on many occasions, but did not take part in the dramatic ascent to the summit of the Matterhorn.

"knock" the growing mystique surrounding alpinism, but once he had formed his resolve to conquer the Matterhorn, it became the dominating factor in his life. His determination to be the first man on its summit drove him to make no fewer than seven attempts between 1861 and 1864.

Whymper was not the only man who wanted to conquer the Matterhorn. A number of other climbers had also begun making attempts. Of these, the only man with as fixed a resolve as Whymper's was an Italian patriot named Jean-Antoine Carrel. Born in 1829 in a little village at the very foot of the Matterhorn, Carrel was determined that the honor of its first ascent should go to an Italian. When, therefore, Whymper began his series of attempts on the summit, Carrel was deeply resentful of the young Englishman. Whymper, however, seems to have been unaware of this, and sought to join forces with the Italian for yet another attempt on the mountain in 1865.

Carrel went so far as to sign up for Whymper's 1865 expedition, but his patriotism was far stronger than any contract. When an Italian party showed up a few days before Whymper's departure and announced their plan of beating the Englishman to the top, Carrel immediately joined them.

Carrel's defection enraged Whymper. For four years the young Englishman had launched repeated assaults on the mountain. Time after time it had defeated him, but he had felt sure that *this* time, particularly with the help of the one man who knew the Matterhorn even better than he himself, he would succeed. But now! Not only were the members of the Italian team blessed with the services of Carrel; they were also superbly equipped and skilled in the most advanced climbing techniques. Worse still, Whymper could find no one willing to join him—even the great-hearted little hunchback guide Luc Keynet, Whymper's loyal companion on earlier attempts, was engaged elsewhere. At the beginning of July, Edward Whymper found himself without an expedition and in danger of losing his coveted prize—the glory of conquering the Matterhorn—to a team of well-prepared rivals.

Yet Whymper refused to be daunted, and within two weeks he was able to assemble an ascent party of seven men. The first to join

Above: photographs of the members of Whymper's party who finally set out to conquer the Matterhorn. In the top row, left to right, Michel Croz, Douglas Hadow, Charles Hudson, and Lord Francis Douglas; lower row, Peter Taugwalder senior, Edward Whymper, and the younger Peter Taugwalder.

Enfin, Monsieur, je regrette beaucoup d'être engagé avec votre compatriote et de ne pouvoir vous accompagner dans vos conquêtes mais dès qu'on a donné sa parole on doit la tenir et être homme.

Ainsi, prenez patience pour cette campagne et espérons que plus tard nous nous retrouverons.

En attendant recevez les humbles salutations de votre tout dévoué

Croz Michel-Auguste

Left: the letter in which the guide Michel-Auguste Croz originally refused Whymper's invitation to join his attempt to conquer the Matterhorn. Croz was killed during the descent.

him was the youthful but experienced English climber Lord Francis Douglas. Douglas was accompanied by his guide, Peter Taugwalder, and by Peter's father, the highly skilled guide Peter Taugwalder senior. Two experienced mountaineers and two good guides were the making of an expedition. And, on the very day that young Peter's father agreed to join the party, Whymper had another stroke of luck.

In his original plans, Whymper had been counting on Michel-Auguste Croz, one of the most expert and sought-after guides of the period. Croz had had to withdraw early on, but now he returned to Zermatt in the employ of the Reverend Charles Hudson, a veteran alpinist, who was also bent on the conquest of the Matterhorn. The two parties joined forces. Hudson was accompanied by a 19-year-old novice climber named Douglas Hadow. Later, Whymper was to claim that he had opposed the inclusion of the youth. Certainly it was hazardous to take a beginner on a climb regarded as one of the Alps' most perilous. However, Hudson had promised his young companion that they would attempt the Matterhorn, and it was probably on his insistence that Hadow was made one of the party.

The climb began on the morning of July 13, 1865 with Whymper and Hudson leading. The ascent of the lower slopes of the ridge was free of incident, and the party camped that night within 3,000 feet of the summit. "Long after dusk," Whymper wrote later, "the cliffs above echoed with our laughter and with the songs of the guides, for we were happy and feared no evil." The precipices of the steep east face still lay before them, but Croz, who had reconnoitered the route before dusk, had reported that they presented no real difficulty. The climbers had ample reason to be in good spirits.

The next morning they set out early and, within a few hours, Whymper and Croz were racing triumphantly up the final ridge of the great peak. At this point, Whymper was still not absolutely sure that he might not yet be beaten to the summit by Carrel. The Italian party had set out before his own and, although they would be slowed down by the heavy gear they were carrying, they might just possibly snatch the victory from him.

A few hundred feet from the summit, Whymper and Croz unroped from the others and made a dash for the highest point. As they neared the top, Whymper, obsessed with the fear that Carrel might have been there before him, anxiously scanned the snow on the summit ahead. There was not a footstep to be seen! He looked down: yes, there was Carrel and his party, still struggling up the south face, hundreds of yards below him. He let out a whoop of delight and, with Croz, rolled a few rocks down the face to signal his victory to his rival.

After they had set up a flag (seen both in Zermatt and in Breuil, where the villagers confidently believed that it was the sign of an Italian victory), the party rested on the summit for nearly an hour. Then, at 2:40 P.M., they began the descent. No doubt the men were exhausted and over excited by their triumph. In any case, they were

Above: the triumphant success, as visualized by the French artist Gustave Doré, as Edward Whymper stands at the summit of his mountain.

Right: disaster struck as the climbers began their jubilant descent. Doré pictures the moment of horror as the fall occurs. On the lower end of the rope is Croz, then Hadow—whose slip caused the fall—the Rev. Hudson, and above him Lord Francis Douglas. Old Peter Taugwalder tenses his body as the rope snaps in two, and those below him on the rope fall to their deaths.

Left: a photograph of Hadow's flimsy and inadequate boot. It was studded with flat-headed nails, and had smooth iron tips round the heels. Douglas Hadow was an inexperienced climber, and his role in the tragedy has often been argued in the search for the cause of Alpine mountaineering's most famous accident.

Below: another subject for controversy has been the ropes used on the ascent of the Matterhorn, pictured below. The one which broke is shown on the left. It was known as the stout sash line.

much less cautious on the way down than they had been on the way up, and they had not gone far before they met with tragedy.

Croz was leading the descent with Hadow immediately following him. Hudson and Lord Francis Douglas came next, with "old" Peter Taugwalder, his son, and Whymper himself bringing up the rear. Roped together, they began moving down the jutting shoulder of rock that had given them their only moment of difficulty on the ascent. Croz was helping Hadow by actually placing the young man's feet in position, step by step. Suddenly, Hadow slipped, and fell against Croz, knocking him off balance. Caught unawares, Hudson and Douglas were dragged down by the falling weight of their companions. Higher up, the three others braced themselves to take the strain as the rope went taut. But the shock never came. The rope spinning out between Douglas and Taugwalder held for only a fraction of a second—and then broke. The four men plunged to their deaths thousands of feet below as the two Taugwalders and Whymper looked on in stunned disbelief.

The three remaining members of the party were too shattered to move for over half an hour. When at last they did begin the descent to Zermatt, it was in a state of shock and near hysteria.

The tremendous publicity given to the Matterhorn disaster led to

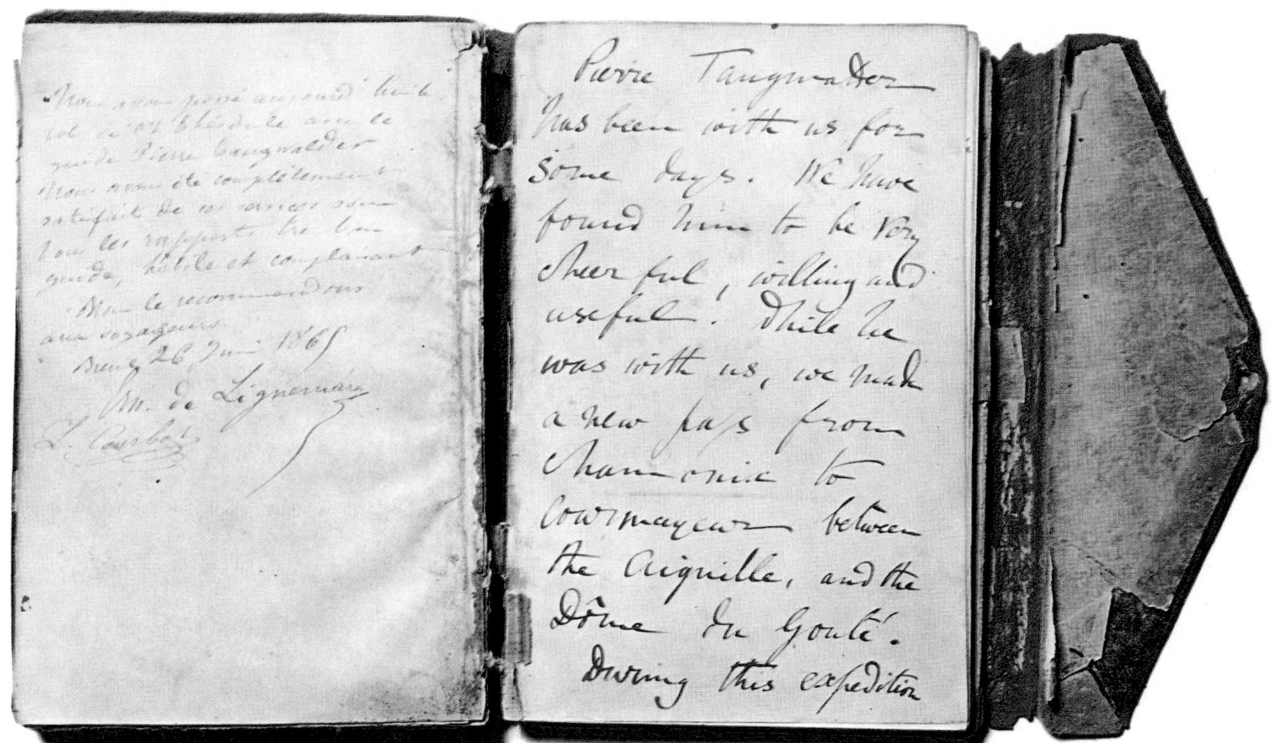
Pierre Taugwalder
has been with us for
some days. We have
found him to be very
cheerful, willing and
useful! While he
was with us, we made
a new pass from
Chamonie to
Courmayeur between
the Aiguille, and the
Dôme du Goûté.
During this expedition

Above: all the mountain guides kept reference books, in which clients wrote recommendations. This is young Peter Taugwalder's book. The Matterhorn climb is missing, since his client, Lord Francis Douglas, was killed and unable to provide him with the usuai reference.

widespread condemnation of the sport in England. Queen Victoria even went so far as to make inquiries about whether mountain climbing could be prohibited by law. But even greater than the disapproval it aroused was the controversy generated by the Matterhorn tragedy. Who was to blame?

The responsibility for the disaster has not and never will be finally settled. Immediately after the event, it was rumored that Peter Taugwalder senior had actually cut the rope to save himself from being dragged down with the others. But even at the time, men doubted whether any climber could have acted quickly enough to sever the rope—particularly in such a way that it would appear to have broken of its own accord as it went taut. Far more damaging was the discovery that the rope used on the descent was old and

Right: the graves of Charles Hudson and Douglas Hadow, two of the victims of the accident which brought to a close the Golden Age of climbing.

Von dem Teütſchen land. cccc

weibern. Jn diſen vier monatẽ Apꝛilis/Mey/Herbſtmonat vñ Wintermonat/ iſt es am aller kommenlichſt. Es ſollen ſich darvoꝛ hüten/ die ein blöd haupt vnd blöden leib haben/vnd ein heiſſe leber vnd heiß nieren. Die mit dem kalten wee beladen ſeind/ſollen des bads an… ſſig ghan.

Leügker bad.

Dis bad ligt gar in eim luſtigẽ ynfang/ghan gerings darūb ſchöne matten/hat zů rucken gegen mitnacht hoch berg/ vñ gegen mittag ein tal/ dardurch man kompt ghen Leugk. Jſt ein groß bad vñ faſt heiß/ das man eyer darin ſieden mag. Dis bad ligt gar nahe ein meil vom flecken Leügk gegẽ mittnacht in dẽ ruwhen gebirg. Vnd wiewol Leügk etwas hoch an einem berg ligt/ můß man doch von dannen on vnderlaß zwüſchen hohen bergen ſteigẽ vñ kl… ttern biß zům bad/ das ligt auff einer groſſen weite/ zwiſchen grauſamen hohẽ bergẽ vnnd felſen/ die diſe weite alſo beſchlieſſen dz man an keim ort darauß kommen mag on groß müh vnd arbeit ſo auff das gäb ſteigenn ghat/ außgenommen den weg ſo ghen Leugk fürt. Gegẽ Occident des bads ſteigent uber ſich biß zům himmel grauſam felſen/die erſchröcklich ſeind an zů ſehen von wegen jrer höhe vnd rühe/ ja an manchen ort ſich laßen anſehen als wöltẽ ſie oben ab her fallen vnd alles ſo hie vnden iſt erſchlagen. Gegen mitnacht keren ſich diſe felſen herūb/ haben vil ſchrundẽ vñ engẽ klufften/ durch wölche ein weg gefundẽ iſt/

ii in dem

The Alps have traditionally been known for their hot water springs which have also attracted tourists. This woodcut shows the spa of Leukerbad, which was so hot that a traveler in 1544 noted it was possible to boil eggs in it.

weak and had been intended only as a reserve. In fact, the party had had with them several coils of sound rope, and both guides came under fire for the decision—if decision it was—to use the weaker rope. The ultimate responsibility for checking the party's equipment before the descent, of course, rested with Whymper as leader of the expedition. Nevertheless, it was not Whymper, but old Taugwalder whose reputation suffered. In fact, the "Lion of Zermatt," as Peter Taugwalder senior was called, never made another great Alpine climb after the Matterhorn. Instead, he spent the rest of his life outside Europe altogether, climbing in Greenland and the Andes.

The Golden Age came to an end with the fatal Matterhorn assault, but not entirely as a result of the tragedy. By this time, mountaineers had climbed nine-tenths of the Alpine peaks—peaks that had remained virgin since the mountains themselves were born. It was only natural that, as the number of remaining "firsts" dwindled, the great dawn of Alpine climbing should draw to a close.

But despite the fact that all the great peaks and many of the lesser ones had been scaled, and despite the sensation caused by the Matterhorn disaster, the popularity of mountaineering continued to race ahead. The next few decades saw a boom in the Swiss tourist industry as more and more men and women traveled to the Alps to climb. For a time, the British kept their lead in Alpine mountaineering, but soon that lead was being challenged by distinguished climbers from many other countries—Switzerland, France, Germany, Austria, and Italy. Non-European mountaineers, too, began to make a name for themselves in the Alps. And indeed, one of the most famous Alpine climbers after the Golden Age was an American, William Augustus Brevoort Coolidge.

Coolidge was not the first American to climb in the Alps, but he was the first American to gain a worldwide mountaineering reputation. Born in New York in 1850, Coolidge was frail and sickly as a child. Doctors recommended mountain air to improve his health and, when he was 14, his devoted aunt, Marguerite Brevoort, took him across the Atlantic to travel in the Alps. The pair embarked on a series of energetic Alpine walks, which became increasingly adventurous as young Coolidge gained in strength and vigor. From these walks it was but a short step to real mountaineering, and in the next few years the two took on greater and greater challenges. Marguerite, "the great Dutch-American miss," as a Swiss contemporary called

All mountaineering was not a serious undertaking. The Alps became attractive to tourists desiring an easy visit to high places. This engraving shows a party on the mountain. Such efforts were called "salon mountaineering."

Queen Margherita of Italy climbed the Monte Rosa in 1893 so that she might be present at the opening of the Capanna Margherita, the highest Alpine hut for the shelter of climbers. The photograph shows the queen and her party, the women wearing face masks to protect their skin from the sun, as a suntan was unseemly for a lady.

her, became the first woman to scale the Matterhorn. And Coolidge, who never returned to America and liked to consider himself a British climber, went on to make no fewer than 600 major ascents. In so doing, he became one of the finest alpinists of his day, and won the accolade of being made an honorary member of the British Alpine Club, a privilege granted to few non-British climbers at that time.

By the last quarter of the century, the Alps had been well and truly tamed. What had once been historic achievements were now standard climbs. Even the Matterhorn might be climbed scores of

times in a single season. For the average amateur the "standard" climbs were sufficiently demanding and rewarding. But for the most expert devotees, something more was needed, some new challenge. With no virgin Alpine summits left to conquer, skilled mountaineers increasingly turned to two new avenues of adventure. One was the conquest of unclimbed peaks elsewhere in the world. The other was the conquest of "impossible" routes and faces in the Alps themselves. The mountaineers who took up this latter challenge made "the route, not the summit," the object of their endeavors. In so doing, they ultimately changed the entire character of alpinism.

New Routes and New Techniques

4

The pioneering of new routes to Alpine summits began as early as 1865, the year of the Matterhorn disaster. In that year, the British mountaineer A. W. Moore climbed to the top of Mont Blanc by way of the Brenva ice-ridge, a far more difficult approach to the summit than that taken by Paccard and De Saussure. In 1877, an even more arduous ascent of Mont Blanc's south face was made by J. Eccles, who reached the top by way of the treacherous Brouillard and Frêney glaciers.

One of the foremost exponents of the "new route" school of mountaineering was Albert Frederick Mummery. He is considered by many to be the founder of this school. Certainly, his example had a profound influence on the whole generation of climbers after the Golden Age. Bold, even reckless in some of his exploits, Mummery nevertheless laid strong emphasis on mountaineering technique, and was one of the first alpinists to climb without guides.

During his long mountaineering career, Mummery pioneered new routes in almost every district of the Alps. Chief among his achievements was his ascent of the Matterhorn's perilous Zmutt Ridge in 1879 and his scaling of the north face of the Grépon (11,423 feet) in 1881. The latter climb, as well as his ascent of Mont Blanc's Brenva Ridge, was made without guides.

Another adventurous pioneer of new routes during this period was Clinton Dent. Of the many assaults he made on difficult Alpine faces, perhaps none was so remarkable as his ascent of the Grand Dru (12,316 feet) in 1878. The sheer face of this peak makes its summit almost unattainable; Dent himself succeeded only after 18 attempts.

Both Dent and Mummery were adept at rock climbing, a mountaineering skill the importance of which came to be fully realized only after the Golden Age. Before the 1870's, most alpinists—though skilled at maneuvering on ice—tended to shy away from rock climbs. Faced with a choice between a short rocky route and a longer, ice-clad route to a summit, they would almost always choose the icy one, even if it meant spending hours hacking out steps in the

Left: Layton Kor, Dougal Haston, and John Harlin standing below the North Face of the Eiger, and spread out in front of them the vast battery of equipment required for them to attempt this most challenging of modern climbs.

Above: Mummery scaling the Crack on the north face of the Grepon. He was the first man to make this climb and went up wearing a white shirt and carrying a rope which was simply looped around his waist.

Above: as the part that rock climbing played in Alpine climbs became more obvious, many climbers took advantage of the mountainous regions of Britain before trying the higher Alpine peaks. This picture was taken in the 1870's.

ice. In fact, one of the reasons why the Matterhorn was not climbed until 1865 was because its ascent entailed so much rock climbing.

But the mountaineer's attitude toward Alpine rock faces changed radically in the decades that followed the Golden Age. The change was due in part to the exploits of men such as Mummery and Dent, in part to the growth of a new sport, and in part to the development of new equipment.

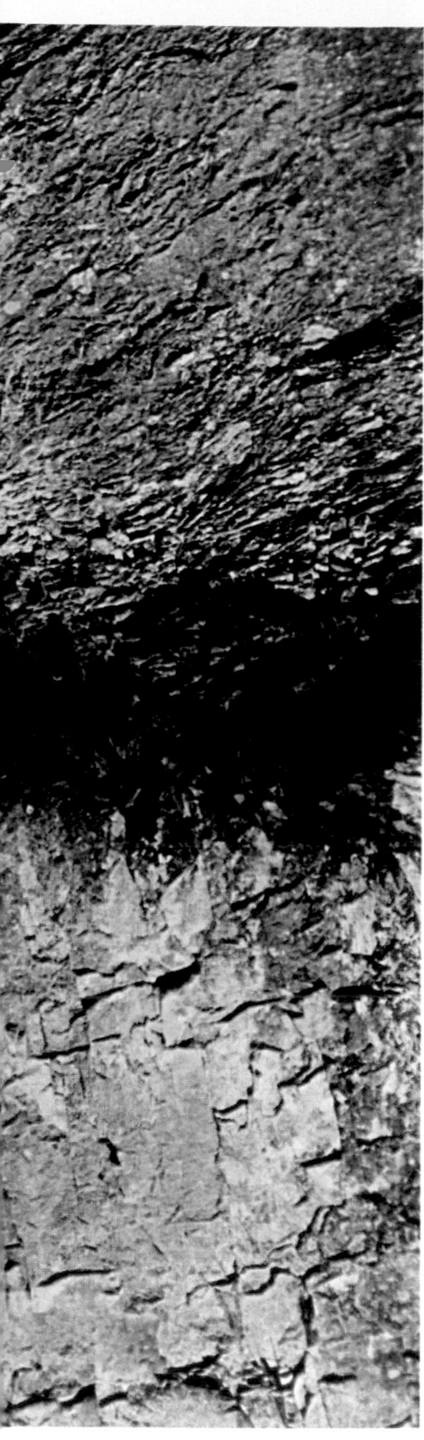

Above: a modern rock climber negotiates a rock overhang in Malham Cove, in England's Yorkshire region. He wears a helmet for protection from falling rock and sits in nylon slings held to the cliff by karabiners attached to pitons in the rock. This sort of sophisticated equipment enables him to make climbs his Victorian counterpart could not possibly have contemplated.

The new sport was rock climbing itself. In the 1870's in Britain, increasing numbers of climbers began traveling to the mountainous regions of Scotland, North Wales, and the Lake District to practice and improve their climbing skills in preparation for later Alpine assaults. Even the highest of Britain's peaks, Ben Nevis (4,406 feet), is lowly by Alpine standards. Nevertheless, the Welsh and Scottish peaks, together with the rocky pinnacles of the Lake District, offer a multitude of taxing and varied climbing problems. This was soon discovered by the men and women who scaled them for practice in the 1870's and 1880's. As they perfected the special rope and balancing techniques required on rock ridges and faces, they found themselves developing a whole new branch of mountaineering. Rock climbing soon came to be recognized as a sport in its own right, and became increasingly popular, not only in Britain, but elsewhere in Europe as well.

It was not long before ardent rock climbers who had mastered all the difficult pinnacles in their own countries were traveling to the Alps to test their skills against the more severe challenges of the rock faces there. The perils of scaling an Alpine peak via a wall of rock are infinitely greater than those of any "standard" Alpine climb. But the mountaineers for whom the route, not the summit, was the objective, were undeterred by the dangers. Soon, men such as Mummery and Dent were pioneering one "impossible" rock route after another. But if improved rock climbing techniques were vital to the success of these "new route" pioneers, so also were the innovations in climbing equipment that came thick and fast in the decades after the Golden Age.

In the early days of Alpine mountaineering, men had assailed the heights armed only with the most basic and primitive climbing aids: long, pointed walking-sticks called *alpenstocks; crampons* to give a surer footing on ice; axes for cutting steps in the ice; and rope for linking the members of a party together. One of the first improvements was the development of the ice-ax, which replaced both the alpenstock and the common ax carried by early mountaineers. Three feet long, the ice-ax has a spike at one end. The other end has a metal head, pointed on one side and adz-shaped on the other. The climber can use the ice-ax as an anchor by driving its spiked end into ice or rock and securing his rope to it. In this way, rope and ice-ax have arrested—and prevented—many a fall. Rope and ice-ax have also been used in combination countless times in the rescue of climbers who have had the terrifying experience of crashing down into the well of a hidden crevasse.

In the early decades of the 1900's, another new piece of mountaineering equipment was developed specifically for rock climbers. This was the *piton*, a metal spike eight inches long with a hole at one end. The spike can be driven into the narrowest of cracks in the rock and a rope passed through the hole to give the safety of a belay where the face offers no natural projection around which to fasten a safety rope. The piton can itself be used as a foothold, or serve as a hook from which to hang a rope foothold, or stirrup, called an *étrier*. In some cases the étrier is a simple sling of rope; in others it is a miniature rope ladder with three wooden rungs. But in all cases, it is secured to the hole in the protruding end of the piton by a metal *karabiner*, or snap-link. Using pitons, snap-links, and a make-shift hammock, the climber may even spend the night on a sheer face of rock.

Even when there are no cracks in the rock face into which pitons can be driven, the climber may still continue the ascent if he has either a "sky-hook" (a form of metal claw which can give a purchase on even the most minute protrusion in the rock), or expansion bolts. To use the latter, the climber must drill a hole in the rock, insert a hollow metal sleeve, and then screw in a threaded piton.

Below: a hunting scene of the 1400's. Left: a detail from the picture showing possibly one of the earliest climbers to use a rope for a safe descent from a rock outcropping.

Right: use of pitons and karabiners on a rock face. A nylon rope has been threaded through the karabiner which is clipped to a piton that has been driven firmly into a crack in the rock.

Far right: Rusty Baillie, an American climber, is shown jumaring, a method of climbing a rope hanging free from the rock face. The picture was taken on the east face of the Old Man of Hoy, a sheer rock pillar in Scotland.

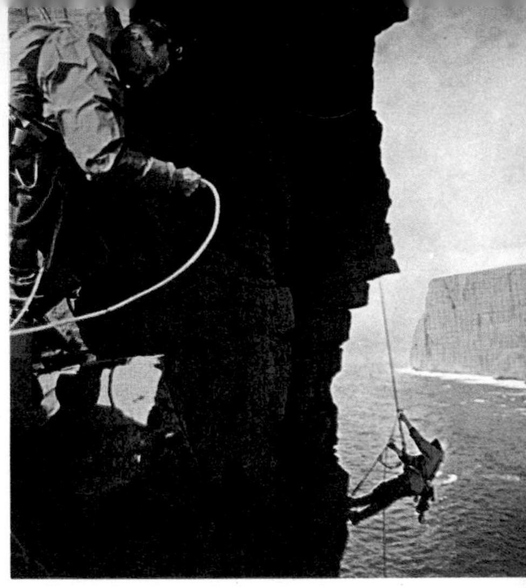

Pitons and expansion bolts enable modern rock climbers to gain hundreds of feet on "impossible" faces, but they do have drawbacks. If the party takes enough of them to cover the whole route up the face, the sheer weight of metal to be carried becomes a formidable handicap. If, on the other hand, each peg and bolt is withdrawn after use, valuable time—and energy—is lost. Still, without these artificial aids, many a near-vertical wall of rock would never have been scaled. It is interesting to note in passing, the conventions surrounding the use of artificial aids. Even today mountaineers would not dream of cutting steps in the rock, much less of actually erecting a fixed scaffold against a difficult face. Yet a battery of pegs and bolts may be driven into a rock face to make an ascent possible where there are no natural holds. The conventions seem inconsistent to the layman, but are clearly understood and accepted by the devotee.

Another major advance in climbing equipment during this century has been the development of nylon rope. It is lighter than hempen rope, does not freeze at high altitudes, and has great elasticity, which reduces the danger of internal injury when a serious fall is arrested by the jerk of the rope. Nylon and the other man-made fibers used in today's mountaineering gear—tents, clothing, and sleeping bags—give the modern climber a tremendous advantage over his predecessors.

Victorian climbers might well have welcomed the development of lighter, warmer clothing and more flexible rope. But they would have been aghast at the elaborate mechanical equipment used by the modern climber. In the early days, mountaineers refused to use any artificial aids that modified the structure of the mountainside. The sole exception to this rule was the cutting of ice-steps. (In the Victorian view, the ice could not reasonably be considered a part of the mountain itself, and could therefore be "modified" with impunity).

As in most things, so in mountaineering, the approach of the younger generation is despised by its elders and its methods regarded as a betrayal of the true faith. In the late 1800's, Mummery, Dent,

Above: a group of climbers during the mid-1800's, roped together. Notice the very short lengths of rope between the climbers—only about six feet—and that the man on the extreme left has the rope tied round his wrist. In case of his companions falling he would be unable to hold them with the rope as it is shown secured here.

and the other pioneers of new routes and the sport of rock climbing were criticized for their "rock gymnastics." And, in the early 1900's, when almost all the "justifiable" Alpine faces had been conquered, and only the most terrifying ascent route remained virgin, the heroic men who tackled them were accused of "suicidal madness." Moreover, when they began to use pitons as the only way to broach these formidable walls, they were criticized for employing "engineering" tactics.

By the 1930's, there were only three great Alpine rock walls that had not yet been conquered. One of these was the north face of the Matterhorn—4,000 feet of ledgeless, crumbling rock. It was first conquered in the summer of 1931 by two young Germans, Franz and Toni Schmid and, as recently as 1953, was the scene of a remarkable solo ascent by the Italian climber, Walter Bonatti. The second of these three formidable rock faces was the north face of the Grandes Jorasses in the Mont Blanc region. An even more difficult climb than the north wall of the Matterhorn, the rock face of the Grandes Jorasses was first mastered in 1935 by Martin Meir and Rudolf Peters.

The third of these "impossible" rock faces, perhaps the most

Above: modern climbers on a mountain. The emphasis has changed to greater safety as mountaineering has become more and more difficult. Notice the length of rope between the climbers—long enough so that each can act independently, and yet offer an anchor should his companion slip. To provide the most stable hold, each has the rope looped around his body.

awesome precipice in the whole of the Alps, was the Eigerwand, the North Face of the Eiger in the Bernese Alps. From other approaches, the mountain itself (13,040 feet) presents no great difficulties. But the Eigerwand approach was for a long time thought to be impossible. The editor of the *Alpine Journal* once described it as "an obsession for the mentally deranged."

The Eigerwand begins at a point some 3,000 feet from the summit and plunges down almost vertically for 6,000 feet. By modern standards, the technical problems of the route are not great, but the conditions on the face in all but the best weather are lethal. Falling rocks and avalanches of ice thunder down the mountainside at frequent intervals; cutting winds, snow squalls, and hail storms are liable to spring up at any moment; rain or melt-water can suddenly freeze on the rock, turning the surface into a wall of glass. These are the factors which have made the north wall of the Eiger one of the most notorious climbs in the world.

Before it was first conquered, in 1938, the Eigerwand claimed eight lives. Four of these tragic deaths occurred on a single climb in 1936—a climb that began with high hopes and ended with one of the most heart-rending dramas in the annals of mountaineering.

The team consisted of Andreas Hinterstoisser, Willy Angerer, Edi Rainer, and Toni Kurz. All four were seasoned climbers, and all four were determined to succeed. The Olympic Games were being held in Berlin that summer and Adolf Hitler himself had promised that the first climbers to conquer the Eigerwand would be rewarded with gold medals.

The first stages of the ascent went well. Using fingers and toes, ropes and pitons, the four worked their way up from one tiny crevice to another, undaunted by the menacing overhangs and almost vertical sections of smooth rock they encountered. By the morning of the third day, they were within 1,000 feet of their goal. But the weather was worsening rapidly. Snow, hail, rain, and melt-water began to stream down the face and soon froze on the rock, making a treacherous surface of *verglas*. Further progress upward became impossible. The team had no choice but to give up the attempt and begin their retreat. But already the surface of the face

Right: a pair of climbing boots with crampons attached. By biting into a snowy or icy surface, crampons enable a climber to move comparatively easily.

Right: the North Face of the Eiger, with the most important routes that have been forced to the summit.

Above: yet another challenge which a few climbers set for themselves is solo climbing. Here Walter Bonatti makes his solo assault on the north face of the Matterhorn, facing 4,000 feet of ledgeless, crumbling rock alone.

had become so wet and glassy that it was as dangerous to move downward as it was to go up. Within a very short time, the four were brought to a complete standstill. They were trapped high up on the face on an exposed section of rock.

Far below, their ascent had been anxiously watched through telescopes. Fear had clutched at the hearts of the watchers when they saw the rain and snow begin to pour down the face. Through the swirling mists they saw the four climbers start to descend, then come to a halt. A rescue party was organized at once, but few believed that it would be able to reach the men while the condition of the face remained so treacherous. Ascending the mountain via the Jungfrau Railway tunnel (which bores right through the Eiger), the rescue team emerged on the outer face about 300 feet below the stranded men. Suddenly, as they began the dangerous traverse toward them, the rescuers heard an agonized cry from above: "Help! The others are all dead—I'm the only one left. Help!"

It was 23-year-old Toni Kurz. Rainer had died of exposure; Hinterstoisser had fallen to his death; and Angerer had been fatally injured by the pull of the rope as his companion fell. Kurz, too, was injured. He was also severely frostbitten and almost at the end of his reserves of strength. Yet he hung on, as the rescue team toiled slowly upward. But a mere 100 feet from him they were stopped by a sheer, ice-covered overhang of rock. They could not get to him; he must somehow get down to them. Following their instructions, he managed to lengthen his own rope with sections from those of his companions. On this rope, a makeshift sling, together with pitons and a hammer, were passed up to him. All this took several hours, but at last, slowly and painfully, he began to lower himself toward his rescuers. Above them in the gathering darkness, they could hear his ice-covered boots scraping against the wall as he moved downward in perilous jerks. Suddenly a knot in the long life-line jammed in one of the snap-links. With his last strength he strove to force it through, but it would not go. Frantically, the rescue team shouted encouragement to him, but Kurz could do no more, and there, only a few feet from safety, the brave young man collapsed and died.

At last, in 1938, the Eigerwand was conquered by another German-Austrian team, consisting of Fritz Kasparek, Heinrich Harrer, Ludwig Vörg, and Andreas Heckmair. Since then, the Eiger's North Face has been scaled a number of times. One of the

1933 Lauper Route
1938 Original (1938) Route
1966 Harlin Route
1968 Polish Route
1968 North East Face Route
1969 Japanese Route
1970 Scottish Route

Above: John Harlin in a helicopter flying low over the Eiger's North Face to survey the uncharted sections of an unclimbed route, the *direttissima*. Harlin was killed during the climb.

Left: Dougal Haston, his face covered with ice, at the summit of the Eiger. Originally a member of the party with Harlin, he joined a German party and went on to complete the assault after the fatal accident.

Right: the North Face of the Eiger has maintained its fascination for climbers of all nations, as one of the most challenging of all climbs, demanding great skill and almost perfect weather for success. Here Chris Bonington, who conquered the face in 1962, stands in front of the Eiger.

most notable of these assaults was that led by the brilliant American climber John Harlin in 1966. It was Harlin's plan to scale the face by the *direttissima,* or direct route. It was an extremely hazardous route, but all went well until the party was within 2,000 feet of the summit. Then, without warning, Harlin's rope broke and he fell to his death. Rather than abandon the climb for which Harlin had given his life, his companion, Dougal Haston, then joined forces with a German party of four that was making the ascent by the ordinary route. Together, the five men reached the summit by the *direttissima,* which they named the John Harlin Route.

Chris Bonington, one of the finest climbers of modern times, made the first British ascent of the Eigerwand in 1962. He has stated that the North Face of the Eiger is now a "justifiable" ascent—but only for those climbers who have proved their skill, determination, and endurance on such faces as the north wall of the Matterhorn and the north wall of the Grandes Jorasses. The Eigerwand is still one of the most formidable climbing problems in the world.

Below: Lenin Peak. In Russia climbing is organized with prizes, proficiency ratings, and penalties. Here mountaineers from the Soviet Union, Poland, and seven other countries gather for a joint climbing expedition.

Beyond the Alps

5

The same impulse that drove some men to seek out ever more difficult routes and faces in the Alps, drove others to seek still-virgin summits elsewhere in the world. And, as more and more of the great Alpine peaks were conquered, more and more mountaineers traveled to faraway ranges to find challenge and adventure.

The first major European mountaineering expedition outside the Alps took place in the Russian Caucasus in 1868. This rugged range, generally considered to be the dividing line between Europe and Asia, stretches from northwest to southeast for some 750 miles between the Black and Caspian Seas. The 1868 expedition was led by the British alpinist and geographer Douglas Freshfield, and included two well-known English climbers, A. W. Moore and C. C. Tucker. As the Caucasus were at that time virtually unknown to Western climbers, the three men spent much of their time simply exploring and mapping the peaks and valleys of the range. Nevertheless, they did make the first ascents to a number of peaks, including Kazbek (16,545 feet) and the lower of the twin summits of Elbrus. (The other of Elbrus' two summits, some 18,481 feet high, was not climbed until 1874.) Freshfield's party was assisted by the local Urusbieh guides, whose skill and toughness greatly impressed them. Indeed, it would seem that these upland tribesmen were by no means inexperienced climbers themselves, for the Englishmen recorded that they were already familiar with a type of crampon.

The next major expedition to the Caucasus was in 1886 when Clinton Dent and W. F. Donkin, accompanied by the well-known Alpine guide Alexander Burgener, scaled Gestola, a peak some

Below: Prince Naurus of Urusbieh with some of his family. His subjects impressed the members of the first expedition to the Caucasus by their climbing ability.

16,000 feet in height. Two years later, Donkin and Dent visited the Caucasus again. On this occasion they were accompanied by a third British climber, Henry Fox. Toward the end of August Donkin and Fox set out from a camp on the Ullauz Glacier to make an attempt on the forbidding heights of Koshtantau (16,875 feet). They were never seen again. For a year there was no news of their fate; rumor had it that they had been waylaid by bandits. But in 1889, a search party led by Douglas Freshfield found their last camp intact; everything was in order and there was no sign of foul play. Although their bodies were never found, it was clear that the men had lost their lives somewhere in the heights of the great mountain they had tried to conquer. In 1887, another expedition did succeed in reaching the summit of Koshtantau, and in 1888, A. F. Mummery scaled the second highest peak in the range, Dykhtau (17,050 feet). In the remaining decades before the outbreak of World War I, many other peaks in the Caucasus range were climbed for the first time.

The highest mountains in Asia, apart from the Himalaya, are the Pamirs of the Soviet Union. In fact, they are sometimes classified as a north-western extension of the Himalayan system. Of the many lofty summits in this Soviet range, Kaufman Peak (23,382 feet) was for a long time thought to be the highest. It was first climbed in 1928 by a Russo-German team led by the German mountaineer W. R. Rickmers. This was a heroic accomplishment—the first complete ascent of a peak over 23,000 feet since 1907. And to celebrate the achievement, the Russians renamed the mountain Lenin Peak.

But four years after this ascent, another peak in the Pamirs was found to be over 1,000 feet higher than Lenin Peak. Stalin Peak (24,590 feet), as the new monarch of the range was named, is situated, like Lenin Peak, in the Tadzhikistan. Skirted by a large glacier, it is one of the world's most beautiful mountains. But its ascent is fraught with terrible hazards, and the Soviet team that first

Above: Russian mountaineers climb over a snow-capped ridge. Climbs once considered difficult are now made annually by large parties of young men and women, as part of a carefully graded series of mountain trials.

Left: high on the slopes of Koshtantau, the abandoned bivouac of Donkin and Fox was found by a search party in 1889. When they failed to return from their attempt on the peak, it was thought that they had been waylaid by bandits.

Above: a group of climbers raise the Soviet flag at the top of Communism Peak. First climbed in 1933, it is one of the most beautiful—and most dangerous—mountains in the world. It was formerly known as Stalin Peak.

climbed it needed no fewer than eight high camps on the mountain itself to ensure success.

In 1962, the mountain was again climbed, this time by an Anglo-Russian party. Since its first ascent in 1932, Stalin Peak's name had been changed (as part of Krushchev's de-Stalinization program) to Communism Peak (Pik Kommunisma). Before tackling the great peak, the expedition climbed a lesser one, Garmo Peak. Here, two members of the British party, Robin Smith and the great climber Wilfrid Noyce, fell 4,000 feet to their deaths. But despite the tragedy, the expedition led jointly by the Russian Anatole Ovchinikov and the Englishman Sir John Hunt, (now Lord Hunt), went on to climb Communism Peak. In a book about the climb, one of the party, Malcolm Slessor, vividly describes the rigors of the climb—the −20°F temperature, the severe winds and blustering snow squalls, and the rarified atmosphere that required the climbers to take several deep breaths before each upward step.

In his account of the expedition, Slessor also touches on a most interesting aspect of Russian mountaineering: its high degree of professionalism. In modern times, mountaineering has been increasingly "professionalized," with many well-known climbs rated on a fixed scale of difficulty. But perhaps nowhere has this process been carried further than in the Soviet Union. The once-arduous ascent of Mount Elbrus is now made every year by large parties of young Russian men and women as one of the lesser trials in a carefully graded series of tests. In the Soviet Union's annual rock-climbing competition, the contestants are required to mark a route on the photograph of an unfamiliar rockface and then scale it without any deviation. Dedicated climbers can win the coveted Master of Sport certificate only after much competition climbing and the step-by-step achievement of various levels of proficiency. Moreover, it is a punishable offense to attempt any climb beyond the level of difficulty a climber has proven himself capable of. In view of the frequent necessity in Western countries of mounting hazardous rescue operations to save novices who have attempted too much, the Russian regulation has much to be said for it. And, in terms of the results achieved, the rigorous training undergone by Soviet mountaineers has some justification. But in the end, however strictly he may have been schooled, the true mountaineer is motivated more by his love of climbing than by any "professional" requirements.

For the mountaineer in Europe, there are, apart from the Alps

Left: the snow-capped summit of Mount Kilimanjaro towers above the plains of Tanzania. An extinct volcano, it is the highest mountain in Africa.

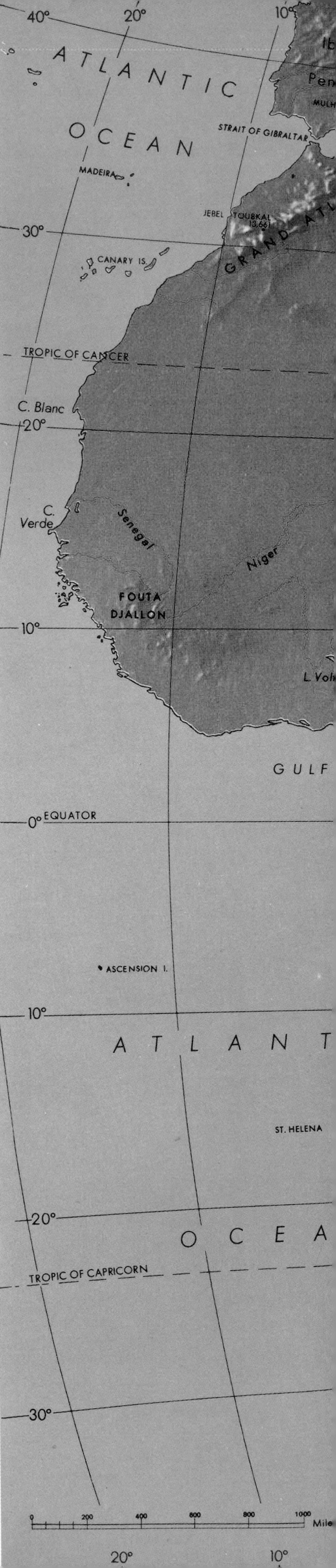

Right: the continent of Africa, showing the mountain ranges and peaks. The highest of Africa's mountains is Kilimanjaro (19,340 feet), situated between Lake Victoria and the Indian Ocean.

Below: the summit of Mount Kilimanjaro. The crater is a mile in diameter, and covered with ice and snow. It is not a difficult climb, and it has been ascended frequently since Meyer first reached the summit in 1889.

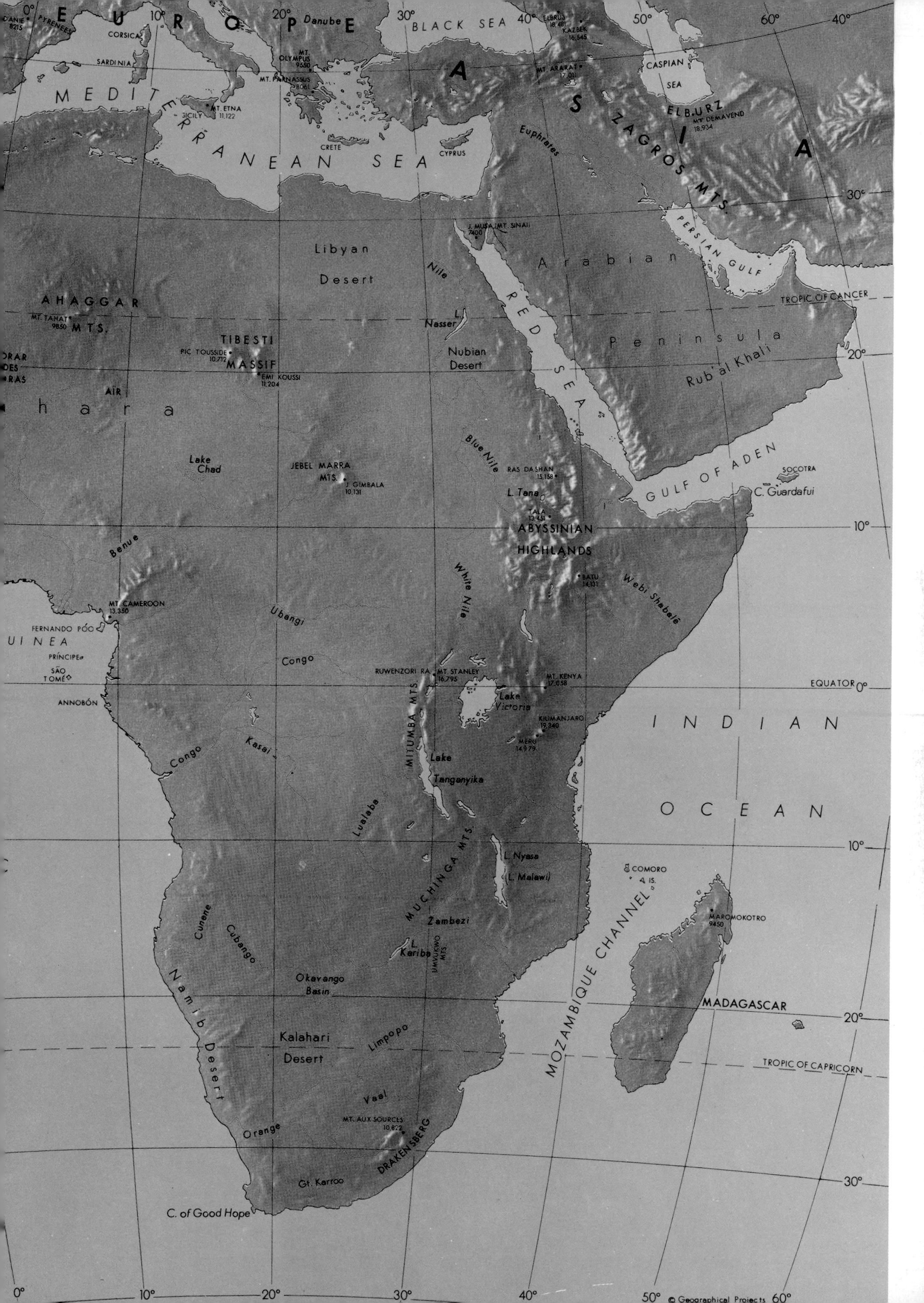
E U R O P E
Danube
BLACK SEA
PYRENEES
CORSICA
SARDINIA
MT. OLYMPUS 9550
MT. PARNASSUS 8061
MT. ETNA 11,122
SICILY
CRETE
CYPRUS
MEDITERRANEAN SEA
ELBRUS 18,481
KAZBEK 16,545
MT. ARARAT 17,011
CASPIAN SEA
ELBURZ
MT. DEMAVEND 18,934
A S I A
ZAGROS MTS.
Euphrates
PERSIAN GULF
J. MUSA (MT. SINAI) 7400
Libyan Desert
Nile
Arabian Peninsula
RED SEA
TROPIC OF CANCER
AHAGGAR MTS.
MT. TAHAT 9850
TIBESTI MASSIF
PIC TOUSSIDE 10,712
EMI KOUSSI 11,204
L. Nasser
Nubian Desert
Rub' al Khali
AIR
Sahara
Blue Nile
GULF OF ADEN
SOCOTRA
C. Guardafui
Lake Chad
JEBEL MARRA MTS.
J. GIMBALA 10,131
RAS DASHAN 15,158
L. Tana
TALA 13,451
ABYSSINIAN HIGHLANDS
BATU 14,131
Webi Shabelē
Benue
White Nile
MT. CAMEROON 13,350
FERNANDO PÓO
Ubangi
GUINEA
PRÍNCIPE
SÃO TOMÉ
ANNOBÓN
Congo
RUWENZORI RA.
MT. STANLEY 16,795
MT. KENYA 17,058
EQUATOR
Lake Victoria
KILIMANJARO 19,340
MERU 14,979
INDIAN OCEAN
Kasai
Congo
MITUMBA MTS.
Lake Tanganyika
Lualaba
MUCHINGA MTS.
L. Nyasa (L. Malawi)
COMORO IS.
MOZAMBIQUE CHANNEL
MAROMOKOTRO 9450
Cunene
Cubango
Zambezi
L. Kariba
UMVUKWE MTS.
Namib Desert
Okavango Basin
MADAGASCAR
Kalahari Desert
Limpopo
TROPIC OF CAPRICORN
Vaal
MT. AUX SOURCES 10,822
Orange
DRAKENSBERG
Gt. Karroo
C. of Good Hope
© Geographical Projects

KENYLON
brand
MEAT and VEGETABLE
RATIONS
UNION SALES COMPANY
OXO (SOUTH AFRICA) LTD.
CAPE TOWN.

This label from a can of meat was carried in his pocket by Felice Benuzzi on the amazing first ascent of Lenana. With two fellow Italian prisoners of war, Benuzzi escaped from their prison camp in 1943 to conquer the mountain, taking food they had saved, and improvised tools. Having achieved their goal, they came back and gave themselves up, spending the remainder of the war in captivity.

and the Caucasus, few great peaks to challenge him. Among the beautiful and dramatic mountains of Norway, for example, the highest, Galdhøpiggen, is only 8,097 feet high and offers few difficulties. And Mulhacén (11,424 feet), although it represents the highest point in Spain's Sierra Nevada range, is of even less interest from a mountaineering point of view.

Just across the Strait of Gibraltar rise the Atlas mountains of northern Africa. This range, familiar to the sailors of the ancient world, extends about 1,500 miles through the deserts of northwest Africa and contains a number of substantial peaks, some of which have not yet been climbed. The highest point is Jebel Toubkal (13,661 feet) and is by no means an easy climb.

But for the mountaineer who journeys to Africa, the real challenges lie in the equatorial zone of East Africa. Here, in Tanzania, is found Kilimanjaro (19,340 feet). An extinct volcano, it is the highest mountain in all of Africa and one of the most beautiful in the world. Kilimanjaro's slopes sweep down majestically from its main peak (Kibo) to the lush equatorial forests below, where its mighty glaciers melt and become rushing torrents. The crater at the top of the main peak is more than a mile in diameter and the upper slopes are covered in a coating of ice about 200 feet thick. Kilimanjaro has been climbed many times since its first ascent, in 1889, by the German scientist and mountaineer Hans Meyer.

The next highest mountain in Africa is Mount Kenya, 200 miles north of Kilimanjaro. Although it, too, is of volcanic origin, its slopes are rugged and precipitous. Mount Kenya possesses two main peaks: Batian and Nelion (both about 17,000 feet) and a lesser peak,

Lenana (16,300 feet). When Batian was first scaled by Sir Halford Mackinder in 1899, his party literally had to fight their way over much of the distance against hostile local tribes. Nelion was first climbed 30 years later by another Englishman, Eric Shipton. Mount Kenya's third summit, Lenana, was not conquered until 1943, and the story of that ascent is one of the most remarkable in the annals of mountaineering.

In 1943, three Italian soldiers who were being held in a British prisoner-of-war camp 50 miles from Mount Kenya made up their minds to climb the mountain. Two of them, Felice Benuzzi and Gíuan Balleto, were amateur mountaineers, the third, Enzo Barsotti, was a complete novice. Gleaning what knowledge they could about the mountain from what they could see of it and from a book in the camp library, they planned their route. For six months they amassed stores and equipment by saving food and improvising tools. They made anoraks from their camp blankets and crampons from the mudguards of a wrecked van. Then one night, they made their escape from the camp and set off for Mount Kenya. Despite inadequate provisions and equipment and despite the extreme conditions they had to endure—from the tropical heat of the lower slopes to the freezing cold and blizzards near the summit—they achieved their objective. Then the three adventurers made their way back to the British camp and gave themselves up. They had no other alternative, for a complete escape from British-occupied Kenya would have been impossible. But, back in the camp, the three endured their punishment—a few weeks of solitary confinement—without complaint, happy in the knowledge of their remarkable conquest of Lenana.

Thirty-seven years before this daring wartime expedition, another Italian party had conquered Africa's third-highest mountain, Margherita Peak (16,763 feet). This peak is the loftiest point in the Ruwenzori chain of mountains, which lie along the frontier between Uganda and Congo (Kinshasa). The whole chain is sometimes known by its romantic English name, the Mountains of the Moon. Storms and mists habitually cloak the summits of this range, and it was not until 1889, when the American explorer Henry Stanley sighted them, that their full extent was revealed. It has been calculated that rain falls on their slopes for 350 days of the year, and early expeditions were always driven back by the difficulties of toiling through the seemingly endless tropical downpours.

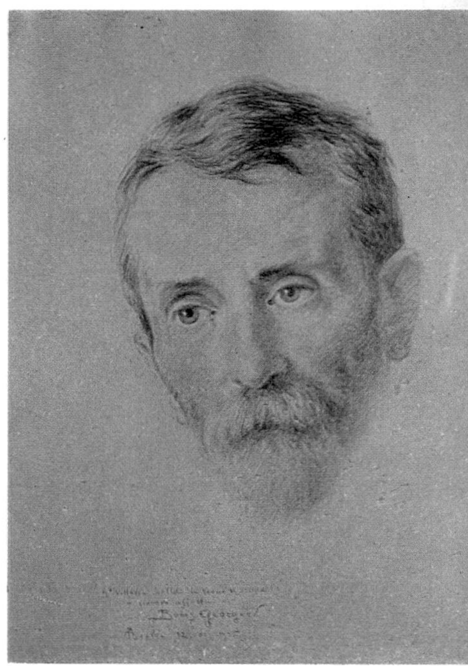

Above: Vittorio Sella, the mountain photographer, who accompanied the Duke of the Abruzzi many times. Below: the camera Sella used in the Caucasus. Earlier, he had an even larger camera, which no longer exists.

In 1906, however, the Duke of the Abruzzi, leading one of the finest and most efficiently organized expeditions of all time, succeeded in reaching the summit of Margherita Peak and of the many lesser peaks in the region as well. In the course of the Margherita Peak ascent, the party encountered one of the strangest and most beautiful mountain phenomena in the world. After days of struggle through rain-lashed gorges, the group emerged on the lower slopes to find them covered as far as the eye could see with gigantically enlarged and dazzlingly hued flowers. Before the climb could begin in earnest, the party had to cut their way through this exotic barrier with their axes.

The Duke was accompanied on this expedition, as he was on several others, by the great mountain photographer Vittorio Sella, who brought back many valuable pictures of the Mountains of the Moon. As a whole, the expedition was undertaken with a number of highly scientific objectives in mind. The Duke hoped not only to climb all the chief peaks of the range, but also to map and survey the entire *massif* (block of mountains). Because of the skill and efficiency of its members, the party was able to carry out all of these objectives, and the whole expedition was crowned with success.

Halfway round the world from the rain-swept Mountains of the Moon lies a range of lower, but far more difficult peaks—the

Right: the vegetation of the Ruwenzori range, where glacier ice and luxuriant jungle crowd closely together. It is through this dense growth that expeditions have to beat a trail before reaching the base of the mountain.

Below: Walter Bonatti on the Nakitawa bridge in the Ruwenzori range.
He followed the route that Abruzzi had taken. Choosing to climb solo, he was alone from the base of the glacier up to the summit of Peak Margherita.

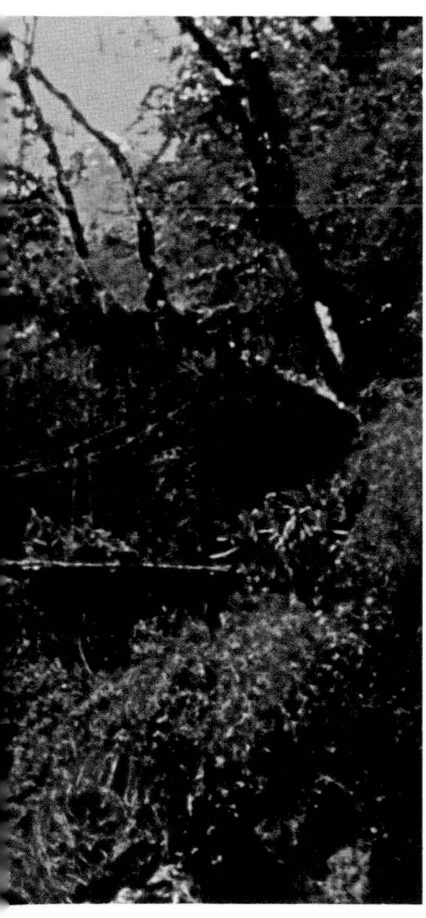

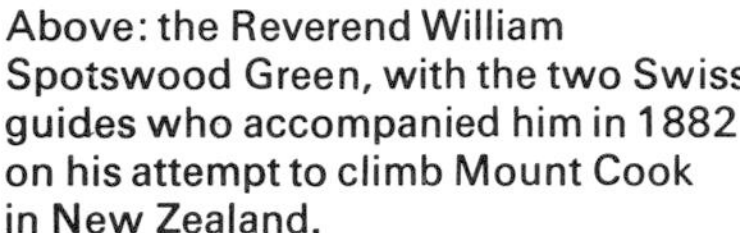

Above: the Reverend William Spotswood Green, with the two Swiss guides who accompanied him in 1882 on his attempt to climb Mount Cook in New Zealand.

so-called Southern Alps of New Zealand's South Island. The highest of these, Mount Cook, is only 12,349 feet above sea level. But its crumbling ledges, frequent avalanches, torturous glaciers, and swiftly changing weather conditions make it a challenge for the most expert mountaineer.

The first man to attempt Mount Cook was William Spotswood Green, a clergyman and member of the British Alpine Club. When, in 1882,the governor of New Zealand offered to help finance any expedition that would tackle the peaks in his country, Green was the first to answer the call. With two Swiss guides, Ulrich Kaufman and Emil Boss, he traveled to New Zealand and set off at once for Mount Cook. Even reaching the mountain was a difficult task, for the three had to make their own trail through the bush to the great Tasman Glacier at the foot of the mountain. Green and his guides, after much arduous reconnoitering, found a route up a spur of this glacier. By the second day of the climb, they had reached a snow shelf high on its upper section. The sky began to take on an ominous yellowish hue, but still they kept on, crawling over rickety rock ledges, and dodging the small ice-avalanches that swept down from above. At last they reached the final ice-wall; the summit lay not more than 200 feet ahead. But suddenly a storm sprang up. High winds swept across the precipice they clung to, lashing them with cold rain and fragments of ice. It was past 6 P.M. and already growing too dark to see. They had to turn back.

The descent was a nightmare. The rain had turned much of the surface snow and ice to slush. As they hurried down, they slipped and slid from one precarious hold to another. At last they were

Mount Erebus in Antarctica was first climbed by members of Shackleton's South Polar expedition. This remarkable first ascent of a polar peak was made with practically no climbing equipment.

enclosed in complete darkness and had to spend the night on a ledge just barely wide enough to stand on. Here they waited for dawn, cold, wet, exhausted, and without anything to eat but a few pieces of dried meat. When morning came, they made their way down to their base camp. They were glad to have escaped with their lives, but deeply disappointed that complete victory had eluded them.

It was not until Christmas Day, 1894, that the first full ascent of Mount Cook was achieved. Appropriately enough, the men who made it—George Graham, Jack Clark, and Tom Fyfe—were New Zealanders. And it was not long before Mount Cook, Mount Tasman (11,475 feet), and others of the Southern Alps became the training ground for hundreds of young New Zealand climbers. The difficult ice, rock, and weather conditions of New Zealand's mountains have schooled many of the world's best mountaineers—among them, of course, Sir Edmund Hillary, the conqueror of Everest.

Mountain climbing began late in New Zealand. It began even later in another mountain region of the world—Antarctica. Here, in 1908, a group of explorers from Ernest Shackleton's South Polar Expedition climbed to the top of Mount Erebus (12,448 feet). In view of the inadequacy of their equipment, this first ascent of a polar peak represents a fine mountaineering achievement. In fact, although exploration of Antarctica proceeded rapidly after 1908, it was not until 1966 that the first explicitly mountaineering expedition to the region was made. Led by the American climber Nicholas Clinch, the 1966 party scaled Vinson Massif (16,864 feet) as well as a number of lesser peaks.

Scaling the North American Peaks 6

After gold was discovered in the Yukon in the year 1896, Alaska became a magnet for thousands of eager prospectors and pioneers. In 1896, one of these "sourdoughs," an American named W. A. Dickey, became the first white man to reach and explore North America's highest mountain. The local Indian tribes called it Denali, "The Great One," but Dickey, proclaiming both his political allegiance and his faith in a Republican victory, renamed it Mount McKinley, for the Republican candidate for the presidency that year. That William McKinley did, in fact, win helped make the name stick. And, thanks to the work of a survey expedition in 1897, the new president had the satisfaction of knowing that "his" mountain was higher than any other on the continent.

The first recorded sighting of Mount McKinley was in 1794, when the English navigator George Vancouver, while sailing off the Alaskan coast, noted "stupendous snow mountains" on the northern horizon. Situated a mere $3\frac{1}{2}°$ below the Arctic Circle,

McKinley and its near neighbor, Mount Foraker, rise in solitary grandeur above a bleak, flat plain. Mount McKinley, whose South Peak is 20,320 feet high, is remarkable not only for its tremendous height, but also for the almost Arctic conditions of its upper reaches. Its flanks are encrusted with manifold layers of ice, and grooved with numerous glaciers. On its upper slopes, the temperature never rises above zero, and the bitter cold is intensified by winds that sometimes exceed 100 miles per hour. These conditions make any ascent of the mountain almost a polar expedition.

The first attempt to climb the mountain took place in 1903, and was led by Judge Wickersham of the little boom town of Fairbanks, 150 miles north of McKinley. His expedition had little hope of success because none of the party possessed even a rudimentary knowledge of mountaineering technique. Instead of planning their route carefully beforehand, the party simply began climbing from the point at which they had arrived on the lower slopes. In no time

Above: the Kashawulsh Glacier in the Saint Elias range in Alaska.

Below: United States President William McKinley in 1899. The highest North American mountain was given his name. National Portrait Gallery, Smithsonian Institution, Washington, D.C.

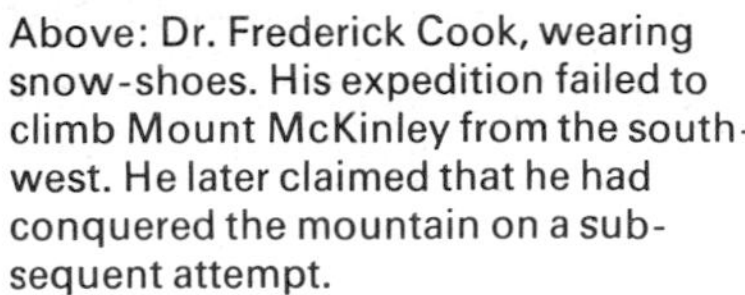

Above: Dr. Frederick Cook, wearing snow-shoes. His expedition failed to climb Mount McKinley from the south-west. He later claimed that he had conquered the mountain on a subsequent attempt.

Above right: Dr. Cook's photograph, which purported to show Burrill, his companion, on the summit. In fact, the picture was taken on a lesser peak.

at all they were defeated by walls of ice they were incapable of traversing. Giving up the attempt, Judge Wickersham went back to Fairbanks and often thereafter was heard to declare that McKinley was unclimbable.

This opinion was not shared by Dr. Frederick Cook, an explorer who had taken part in several polar expeditions in the 1890's. Dr. Cook was highly esteemed by other explorers, and it was thought that if anyone could scale the mountain he was the man. But the saga of Dr. Cook and Mount McKinley was to prove one of the oddest in the history of exploration.

In 1906, Cook, together with Herschel Parker, a physics professor, and Belmore Browne, an artist and naturalist, attempted to scale McKinley from the southwest. But after weeks of struggling to find a way through the maze of glaciers at the base of the mountain, the party was forced to abandon the climb, and return to Tyonek, the small settlement from which they had set out.

It was at this point that the venture took an unusual turn. Leaving Browne and Parker in Tyonek, Cook set off again accompanied only by Edward Barrill, one of the party's pack-carriers. What Cook told his companions was simply that he was going to explore new approaches to McKinley. Something of what he actually had in mind, however, is revealed by a telegram he sent to a friend in New York shortly before he set off: "Am preparing for a last desperate attempt on Mount McKinley."

Cook returned from his expedition within a month, announcing that he had reached McKinley's summit. To prove it, he produced slides and photographs which, he said, he had taken at the top. Over the next few years, chiefly through a book he published about his adventure, called *To the Top of the Continent,* he won considerable public acclaim. But Parker and Browne knew from the outset that Cook's triumph was a hoax. The amount of time he had been away from Tyonek was barely enough to ascend McKinley's glacier-clad lower slopes, let alone attain its summit. Cook, however, stubbornly clung to his grandiose claims until four years later, when another ascent party proved conclusively that his photographs had been taken from one of the lesser peaks near the base of McKinley.

In the meantime, Parker and Browne had not been the only ones to see through Cook's falsehood. Chief among these doubters were

A group of sourdoughs, the prospectors and trappers who lived in the country surrounding Mount McKinley, posing outside a saloon in Fairbanks. Third from the left is Billie McPhee, the bar-keeper who financed the first successful assault on the mountain. He also bet $5,000 that the expedition would reach the top before July 4, 1910.

Above: the Muldrow Glacier, used by the sourdoughs as a route to the summit.

Below: the twin peaks of Mount McKinley appear equal in height, but the South Peak, left, is 850 feet higher.

the trappers, hunters, and gold prospectors in the boom town of Alaska. Although none of them were mountaineers, they possessed a thorough knowledge of the foothills around Mount McKinley, and Cook's claim struck them as preposterous. Their response was to mount an expedition of their own.

One night, in the bitter winter of 1909, a group of "sourdoughs" —prospectors and trappers—were sitting around swapping stories in the bar-room of Billie McPhee, a saloon-keeper in Fairbanks. For the thousandth time, the talk turned to the dubious claims of Dr. Cook. Most of the men held to Judge Wickersham's opinion that the mountain would never be climbed. But two of the party, Tom Lloyd and William Taylor, disagreed. In fact, they said, they could do it themselves. Billie McPhee offered to finance the venture, and even went so far as to make a bet of $5,000 that they would reach the top before July 4, 1910.

Accordingly, on December 20, 1909, Lloyd and Taylor set out to climb Mount McKinley. With them were two hardy trappers, Peter Anderson and Charley McGonagall. None of the four had had any previous mountaineering experience and, of course, they took no

guides. They possessed no professional climbing equipment. All they carried on their two dog sleds was a quantity of rope, their usual camping gear, and sufficient food to last them several weeks. They were also armed with several intangible—and invaluable—advantages: tremendous physical fitness, indomitable pluck, and the trapper's sure instinct for pathfinding.

The men's toughness may be judged by the fact that they thought nothing of setting out in the dead of winter; their skill as pathfinders by the fact that they instinctively hit upon the one comparatively easy route up—the Muldrow Glacier. But the four reached the head of the glacier only after 11 grueling weeks of trekking. Once there, the party established their base camp. They had already climbed to 11,000 feet—much of the way in howling blizzards. Peter Anderson was suffering from a frostbitten toe but, according to the diary kept by Lloyd, he dismissed it as a mere nuisance, remarking that his foot was just "a little bit sore, as a fellow would say."

The men were able to drive their dog sleds up as far as the mountain's razor-backed saddle. There, at 15,000 feet, they discovered that McKinley had two peaks, seemingly of equal height. In fact, the South Peak is the higher of the two by about 850 feet. Unluckily, they picked the North Peak—a choice which ultimately robbed them of the technical "first" ascent of the mountain.

Their last camp before the final assault on the summit was in a hole they carved out of the ice on the steep ridge of the saddle. The next day, they started up the North Peak and kept going, cutting steps for themselves in the ice, until they reached the top. There they raised the flag of the United States on a 14-foot spruce pole which they planted firmly in the ice.

It took them only a few days to retrace their steps down to their

Left: a painting of Mount McKinley by Belmore Browne, who was a well-known artist and naturalist. His fascination with the mountain led him beyond painting the magnificent scene, to attempt the climb to the summit.

Below: Herschel Parker posing with a companion, probably Belmore Browne. They accompanied Dr. Cook on his first unsuccessful assault on Mount McKinley, and were most suspicious of his claim to have conquered the peak.

Above: Hudson Stuck, the Episcopal archdeacon of the Yukon, leader of the expedition that finally conquered the South Peak of Mount McKinley in 1913.

Above: an ice staircase chopped out of the frozen surface of Mount McKinley on the south face, to provide a way to the summit. It was methods like this which enabled the Stuck party to work their way to the top of the peak.

base camp. And in less than two weeks, Lloyd, having made excellent speed in the spring weather, was back in Fairbanks regaling his friends with the tale of their adventure.

For reasons never fully explained, Lloyd claimed that his party had scaled *both* peaks. The most plausible reason for this deception is that Lloyd, fearing that the South Peak just might prove to be the higher of McKinley's peaks, was trying to protect his friend Billie McPhee. The saloon-keeper had, after all, bet $5,000 that they would reach McKinley's *summit*. In any case, it matters little today that Lloyd and his companions scaled the lesser of the two peaks. The mastery of a mountain like McKinley by four complete amateurs remains one of mountaineering's most amazing achievements.

Sadly, few people outside Alaska credited Lloyd's account of the climb. It was not until three years later, when the party's flagstaff was seen on the North Peak by another ascent party, that the achievement of Lloyd and his companions was verified beyond a shadow of doubt.

Two years after the success of the "Sourdough Expedition," the stormy heights of Mount McKinley were the scene of a heroic failure by Herschel Parker and Belmore Browne. They planned their renewed assault on the mountain with meticulous care. Like the sourdoughs, they approached the mountain from the northeast, and were able to drive their dog sleds up to the top of the Muldrow Glacier. Leaving their dogs at the base camp, they then worked their way up the narrow ridge of the saddle. At 16,400 feet they

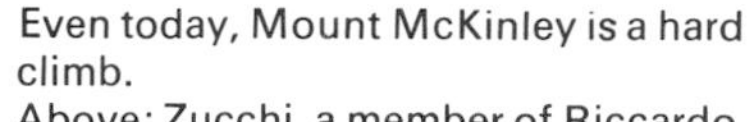

Even today, Mount McKinley is a hard climb.
Above: Zucchi, a member of Riccardo Cassin's Italian expedition, performs ice acrobatics in reaching the next step during the climb of the dangerous south face of Mount McKinley in 1961.

Above right: two members of the Italian expedition, Canali and Zucchi, stand exhausted but safe at the base camp, having returned triumphant from their climb of the "impossible wall."

pitched camp in a glacier basin and prepared to make the final long ascent. But suddenly the weather broke, and for four days they were trapped in their small tent in the midst of a savage blizzard that sent huge avalanches thundering down the mountainside.

When the weather cleared, they set off again. At 19,000 feet, with the angle of the ridge before them decreasing at each step, they felt assured of success. But a few hundred feet from the top, another terrible blizzard struck them. Painfully, they struggled on, but a mere 300 feet below the summit the two men reached the limits of their endurance and had to turn back. They reached their camp only after many arduous hours. Two days afterward, the weather again cleared and they made one last attempt, but again they were driven back by a sudden storm when they were only a short distance from the top.

But if Parker and Browne had been unlucky in one regard, they were miraculously lucky in another. In the late summer of 1912, only a matter of days after they had left McKinley, the entire mountain was shaken by a series of earthquakes. Vast portions of McKinley's slopes were sheered off in a succession of avalanches, and the very crest of the final ridge they had stood on collapsed and fell away. Thus in 1913, when the South Peak was scaled for the first time, McKinley was in a sense a different mountain.

The 1913 ascent was led by Hudson Stuck, the Episcopal archdeacon of the Yukon territory. An experienced mountaineer, he had climbed often in the Rocky Mountains since his arrival in the

Above: an aerial photograph of the sea of snow-capped peaks extending for miles in the incredible expanse of the mountain ranges of Alaska.

United States as an Englishman of 22. When he set out, at the age of 50, to conquer North America's highest peak, he was fulfilling an ambition he had cherished for many years.

Stuck's party included a young missionary named Robert Tatum, a native Alaskan named Walter Harper, and a prospector named Harry P. Karstens. Like the expeditions that had preceded them, Stuck and his party made their way up the Muldrow Glacier and prepared to follow on up the northern ridge that had been described to them. But it was a ridge no longer. The cataclysm of the previous year had so shattered and disrupted the contours of the mountain that the ridge had become a jagged ice-wall of spurs and pinnacles. All the way up this wall, they methodically cut a massive ice staircase, climbing up and down its thousands of steps many times to bring up supplies.

Stuck's party made their final assault on the South Peak on June 6, 1913. At the top, Stuck gave thanks to God for their success. This done, in venerable Alpine tradition he set about taking barometer and thermometer readings. He left one of the thermometers on the mountain to be checked by later expeditions. When it was recovered 19 years later, its indicator had fallen well below the bottom of the scale, the lowest reading of which was −95°F.

In the spring of 1932, Mount McKinley was the object of two expeditions. The first of these, led by Erling Strom and Harry J. Liek was interesting for its extensive use of skis on the ascent of the lower slopes, and for its achievement of the first conquest of *both* peaks. The second, led by the brilliant young climber Allan Carpé, was notable for its highly scientific nature: the study of cosmic rays in higher altitudes.

Carpé's party made use of an airplane to land supplies—the first time such a thing had been attempted on a glacier. This operation was watched by the Strom-Liek party as they climbed high above the glacier on Karstens Ridge. On their descent, they hoped to meet up with Carpé and his colleague Theodore Koven, to compare notes about the climb. But when they reached Carpé's camp, they found the tents deserted. The victims of some inexplicable accident, both men had fallen to their deaths a mile and a half down the mountain.

McKinley was climbed comparatively rarely until shortly after World War II, when the famed Alaskan mountaineer Bradford Washburn proposed several new routes to the summit based on aerial photographs of the mountain. To test these routes, a number of expeditions were launched, and one of them, led by the Italian climber Riccardo Cassin in 1961, achieved the remarkable feat of scaling McKinley's sheer south face—until then known as the "impossible wall."

The Alaska Range, to which McKinley and its neighbor Foraker belong, is but one of numerous ranges in the great mountain system that stretches from Alaska to the tip of South America, taking in the Canadian and American Rockies, the Cascade range, the Sierra Nevada, the Mexican mountains, and the Andes.

One of the most interesting of the northern ranges in this system is the Saint Elias, a chain of volcanic mountains which straddles the border between Alaska and the Yukon Territory. Among

Below: Andy Taylor's dog team. Taylor was the sourdough guide who accompanied Captain MacCarthy on his first ascent of Mount Logan. The dogs took supplies to the base camp.

ASIA
ARCTIC CIRCLE
ARCTIC OCEAN
GREENLAND
PARRY ISLANDS
BANKS I.
VICTORIA I.
BAFFIN ISLAND
BROOKS RANGE
Alaska
Yukon
MT. McKINLEY 20,320
MT. FORAKER 17,395
Fairbanks
ALASKA RA.
ALEUTIAN IS.
WRANGELL MTS.
MT. LUCANIA 17,150
MT. ST. ELIAS 18,008
MT. LOGAN 19,850
MACKENZIE MTS.
Mackenzie
Great Bear L.
Gt. Slave Lake
Laurentian Shield
HUDSON BAY
Ungava Pena.
L. Athabasca
Nelson
ROCKY MOUNTAINS
COAST MOUNTAINS
QUEEN CHARLOTTE ISLANDS
Fraser
MT. ROBSON 12,972
Edmonton
N. Saskatchewan
S. Saskatchewan
MT. ASSINIBOINE 11,870
Lake Winnipeg
Albany
OTISH MTS.
VANCOUVER I.
Vancouver
MT. OLYMPUS 7954
Columbia
MT. RAINIER 14,410
COAST RA.
CASCADE RA.
BLUE MTS.
BITTERROOT RA.
Snake
ABSAROKA RA.
BIG HORN MTS.
DEVIL'S TOWER 5117
BLACK HILLS
Missouri
Lake Superior
Lake Michigan
Huron
Lake Ontario
L. Erie
Mississippi
Chicago
C. Mendocino
MT. SHASTA 14,162
Great Basin
Gt. Salt L.
Yosemite Nat. Park
San Francisco
SIERRA NEVADA
WASATCH RA.
LONGS PK. 14,256
MT. ELBERT 14,431
Platte
Missouri
Ozark Plateau
Ohio
APPALACHIAN
MT. MITCHELL 6684
MT. WHITNEY 14,495
Death Valley -282
SHIPROCK 7178
Grand Canyon
Colorado
Arkansas
BOSTON MTS.
OUACHITA MTS.
Mississippi
Red
Gila
SACRAMENTO MTS.
Rio Grande
Colorado
New Orleans
PACIFIC OCEAN
TROPIC OF CANCER
Lower California
SIERRA MADRE OCCIDENTAL
SA. MADRE ORIENTAL
Rio Grande
GULF OF MEXICO
C. Falso
Yucatan
Mexico City
POPOCATEPETL 17,887
18,701 ORIZABA
0 200 400 600 800 1000 Miles
180° 160° 140° 120° 100° 80° 60° 40° 20°

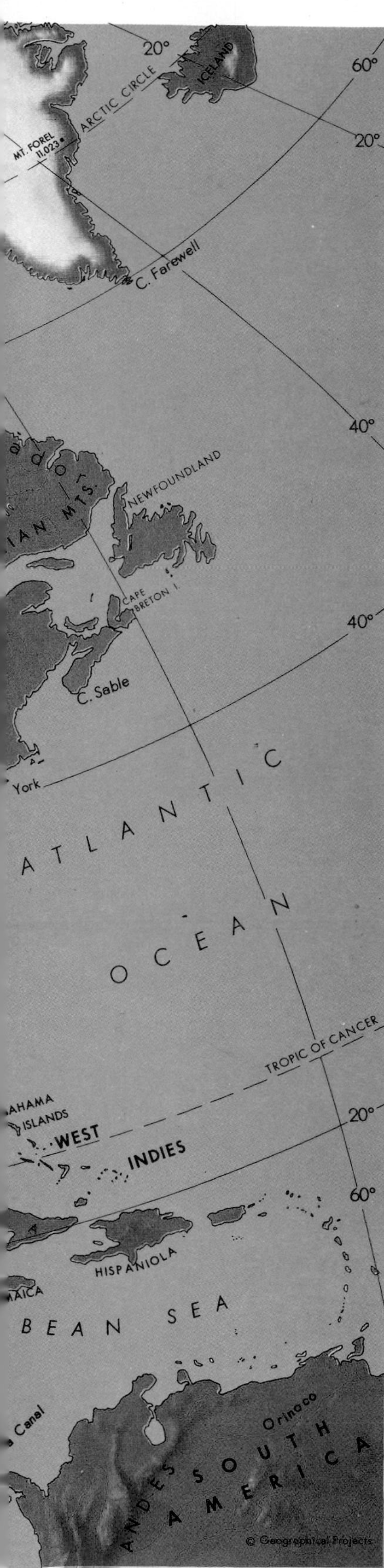

Left: the North American mountain system stretches from Alaska south through the Canadian and American Rockies, the Mexican mountains, and finally links up with the Andes of South America.

Above: the years between the wars saw the majority of North American peaks conquered. One of the leading climbers of this period was Bradford Washburn, standing second from the right here in the Mount Marcus Baker expedition.

the highest peaks in this chain is Mount Saint Elias (18,008 feet). This peak holds a special place in climbing history, for it was with its first ascent, by the Duke of the Abruzzi in 1897, that North American mountaineering really began.

The Duke, a grandson of King Victor Emmanuel II of Italy, was only 24 when he led the ascent of Mount Saint Elias. Nevertheless, wrote Count Aldo Bonacossa, "he was already a leader of men [and although] he was sometimes a little exacting in his demands . . . how striking was his personal example in endurance and in dangers." The Italian expedition he headed included the famous mountain photographer Vittorio Sella, as well as a number of noted Alpine guides and mountaineers. It took the party nearly a month to reach the summit, and the expedition, which carried out a great deal of exploration, took 154 days in all.

The Duke's conquest of Mount Saint Elias provoked a sudden upsurge of interest in climbing in North America, and the three decades that followed saw many brilliant achievements in Alaska, Canada, and the United States. European as well as American mountaineers played an important part in the pioneering climbs of this era. Edward Whymper, for example, spent four years in western Canada at the beginning of the century, and did much to popularize this new area.

By the mid-1920's, most of the major peaks in Canada had been climbed, including Mount Robson, the highest in the Canadian Rockies. Just 12,972 feet high, Robson is not one of the world's highest peaks, but it is certainly one of the most impressive, towering in lordly splendor above the many lesser peaks of the region. First climbed in 1913, it has not often been attempted since then because of the constant danger of avalanches in its upper reaches.

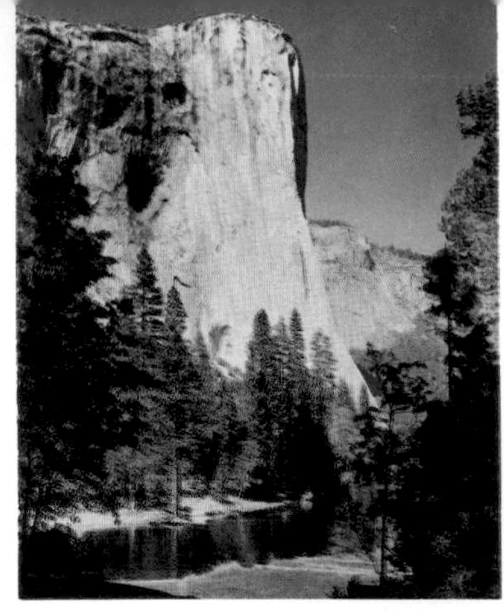

Left: El Capitan and the Merced River in Yosemite Valley, California, the rock climbers' most challenging area. Many of the techniques developed here have had a great influence on methods of international mountaineering.

Right: the tiny figure of a climber can be seen edging his way up the west face of the Leaning Tower, one of the many vast granite outcrops in Yosemite.

Robson's 1913 conqueror was Captain A. H. MacCarthy, one of Canada's most distinguished climbers. MacCarthy had many notable "firsts" to his credit when, in 1925, he led the heroic first assault on Mount Logan (19,850 feet). This mountain, the second highest in North America, is situated in the Saint Elias range, and, like many of the peaks in the region, is almost inaccessible. Before he could begin to plan the ascent, MacCarthy had to spend considerable time locating a route to the lower slopes of the mountain. The next step was to prepare the way for the expedition proper. In the dead of winter, MacCarthy and his sourdough guide, Andy Taylor, pioneered a route up the mountain's outlying glaciers and set up a chain of camps and supply depots for use during the forthcoming assault.

In late May, 1925, the nine members of MacCarthy's assault team at last set off for Mount Logan. The expedition included no porters, and each climber had to carry a 70 pound load of supplies. Their route was almost entirely over snow and ice, and for 44 days, as they fought their way steadily upward, the men were assailed by almost continual blizzards. Visibility was frequently reduced to a mere yard or two, and the high winds piled up drifts of loose snow in which they frequently sank up to their chests.

The party made its last camp at 18,500 feet. The final 1,350 feet to the top took them almost the whole of the next day, and when, at 8 P.M., they stood at last on Canada's highest peak, they had little time for jubilation. Ahead lay the descent, which was to prove a great deal more dangerous than the grueling climb. Within minutes of their setting out on the return journey, another savage blizzard closed in around them. From then on, the trek back to their base camp was one long nightmare of driving snow and freezing ice. At one point they lost their way and discovered to their horror that they were retracing their steps back to the summit. Only after three terrible days—two nights of which they spent in the open—did they reach the safety of their camp. Truly, as the mountaineering historian Arnold Lunn has said of MacCarthy's party, "For endurance and courage, their achievement has rarely been surpassed."

Between the two world wars, North American mountaineering really came of age. One of the foremost mountaineers of this period

was Bradford Washburn, who headed an impressive number of Alaskan expeditions. Many of these had the dual purpose of exploration and scientific investigation. Chief among Washburn's achievements was his ascent of Canada's second highest peak, Mount Lucania (17,150 feet) in the Saint Elias Range in 1937.

Outside Alaska, the highest mountain in the United States is Mount Whitney (14,495 feet), named for the geologist J. Dwight Whitney. Located in the southern Sierra Nevada of California, this lofty peak provides a dramatic contrast to nearby Death Valley, which, at 282 feet below sea level, is the lowest point in the country.

It is somewhat ironic that the United States, with one of the world's most extensive mountain systems, has very few peaks to challenge the mountaineer. The Rocky Mountains, the Cascade range, and the Sierra Nevada cover thousands of square miles, contain many peaks of 13,000 feet and more, yet they can offer nothing to equal the arduous and testing ascents of the Alps. With very few exceptions, these sprawling ranges possess easy contours and gentle gradients, and, although difficult routes can be sought out, the majority of the highest points can be reached with only a stiff uphill walk.

One of the favorite centers for amateur climbers in the United States is Mount Rainier (14,410 feet) in the Cascade Range in Washington state. An extinct volcano, the mountain is snow-capped and covered with no less than 26 glaciers.

But outside Alaska, the most demanding climbs are not on mountains at all, but on the towering rock formations of the American Southwest. Yosemite National Park in central California, for example, offers over 300 rock-climbing routes, of which two-thirds rank among the four highest grades of difficulty. Some of the most exacting of these are the three Cathedral Rocks, the northwest face of the Half Dome, and the Salathé Wall of El Capitan. The difficulties confronting climbers in the Yosemite Valley may be appreciated in terms of the fact that a rock climb here may take anything from 3 to 10 days. In recent years, ever more dangerous climbs have been attempted and achieved in Yosemite.

Another difficult rock climb is offered by Shiprock Butte (1,678 feet), a sheer volcanic outcrop rising out of the New Mexican plateau. Still another is provided by the famous Devils Tower of northeastern Wyoming. Rising perpendicularly 865 feet above the surrounding hills like a prehistoric skyscraper, it was long thought to be unclimbable. However, since it was first scaled in 1937, it has become one of the classic rock climbs of America; during one week in 1956 it was climbed no fewer than 81 times.

Thus, while North America has few mountains to equal the challenges of the Alps, the Andes, or the Himalaya, its Alaskan peaks and its rock pinnacles offer superb training opportunities for the climber. Having served their apprenticeships on their home ground, American mountaineers have gone out to conquer some of the world's greatest peaks.

Meeting the South American Challenge 7

One of the most remarkable incidents in the history of mountaineering occurred in 1521, when a handful of Spanish soldiers climbed to the top of Popocatépetl in central Mexico. Popocatépetl ("The Smoking Mountain") is an inactive volcano. Although its sloping sides do not present serious climbing difficulties, its height alone—17,887 feet—is enough to discourage all but the most strongly-motivated climbers. But we may be sure that the soldiers who made the ascent in 1521 were strongly motivated, for they were acting under the strict orders of their commander, Hernando Cortes. Under the fierce leadership of this man, the Spanish had brought the mighty Aztec empire to its knees. But the Spaniards' continued power in Mexico depended on their superior weaponry, and they were now desperately short of the sulfur they needed to make gunpowder. It was for the purpose of obtaining this vital mineral that Cortes ordered his men to climb Popocatépetl. If they could reach its summit, they could get sulfur from its crater.

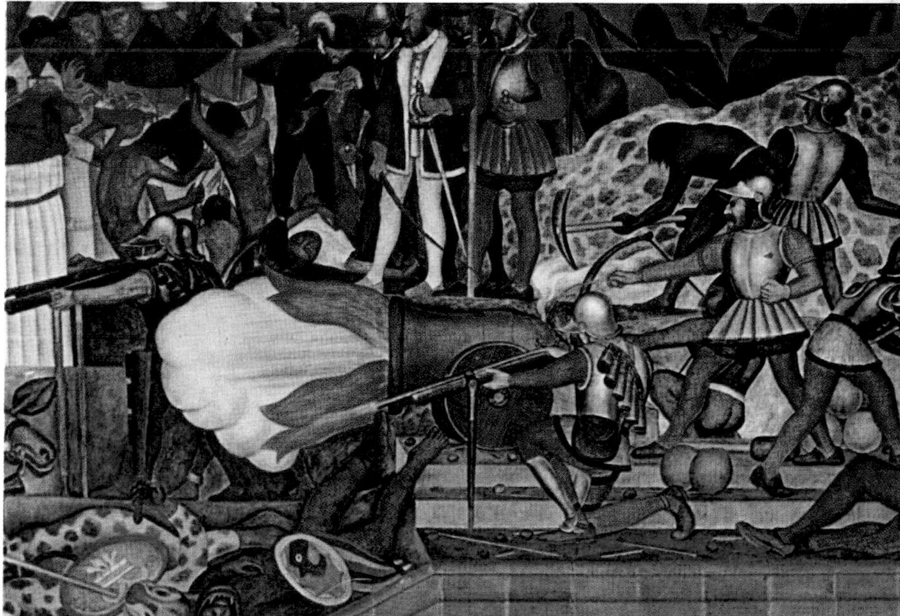

Left: a Mexican family standing at the foot of Popocatépetl. Although nearly 18,000 feet high, the gentle slopes of the volcano present no real challenge to an experienced climber.

Above: Spanish soldiers under Cortes made the first ascent of Popocatépetl in 1521, to collect sulfur from the crater for gunpowder. This mural of the guns in action is by Diego Rivera.

Above: volcanoes have fascinated men since Von Humboldt. Here a climber is seen on Ecuador's Mount Sangay.

Below: Indians of the high Andes have become physically adapted to their life at high altitudes over the centuries.

Cortes' soldiers did not disappoint him. They reached the top and returned to camp laden with quantities of sulfur. No doubt Cortes congratulated himself on having solved his ammunition supply problem in so novel a manner. He little knew that, in carrying out his orders, his soldiers had climbed higher than anyone had ever done before, and had set a height record that remained unbroken for centuries.

Popocatépetl, which today is the dominant feature on the horizon of Mexico City, is but one of many volcanic peaks in the Volcanic Axis, a chain of mountains stretching across Mexico in the south. This mountain chain contains some of the most beautiful peaks in the Americas. Orizaba, for example, which, at 18,701 feet is the third highest mountain in North America, possesses the almost perfect symmetry of Mount Fuji. Unlike Fuji, however, Orizaba and the other volcanic peaks of the Volcanic Axis rise above tropical forest. In fact, the contrast between the cool serenity of their snow-capped summits and the teeming life of the jungle at their feet is one of the most characteristic features of the Mexican mountains. Just as typical, however, is the lack of challenge they offer the experienced mountaineer. Again, Orizaba is a good

example. Despite its height, it affords a remarkably easy ascent. Most of the way up to its snow-line can be accomplished on horseback!

There could be no more dramatic contrast to the gentle slopes of the Mexican mountains than the sheer drops and rugged heights of the Andes. Extending some 4,500 miles down the western coast of South America—all the way from Panama to Cape Horn—the Andes have been called the longest unbroken mountain system in the world. Throughout this great series of mountain ranges, there are lofty and forbidding peaks which have challenged, and continue to challenge, the nerve and endurance of the world's most experienced mountaineers.

The exploration of the Andes began in the early 1700's with a French and Spanish expedition to the mountains of Ecuador. Here, just south of the Equator, the expedition leaders, Bouguer and La Condamine, carried out the first scientific exploration of high altitudes.

The Ecuadorian mountains—most of which are of volcanic origin—were again the subject of investigation in 1802. In that year, Alexander von Humboldt, a German scientist and geographer, went to Ecuador to climb and study two volcanic peaks: Cotopaxi (19,344 feet) and Chimborazo (20,577 feet). In neither case did he succeed in gaining the summit, although he did reach a height of over 19,000 feet on Chimborazo.

Seventy years after Von Humboldt's visit to Ecuador, another German scientist, Wilhelm Reiss, and his companion, A. M. Escobar, made the first complete ascent of Cotopaxi. This mountain is the

Right: Alexander von Humboldt, a German scientist and geographer, in his library. He climbed nearly to the summit of two volcanoes in Ecuador, Cotopaxi and Chimborazo, during his scientific researches in South America.

highest live volcano in the world. Nevertheless, in common with many other volcanic peaks, the slopes leading up to its snow-covered cone slant very gently, at an angle of about 30°.

Chimborazo, the second mountain that Von Humboldt had attempted in 1802, was not fully scaled until 1880. In that year Edward Whymper, then aged 40, in company with his one-time rival Jean-Antoine Carrel, journeyed to South America in search of peaks as yet unclimbed. Having laid to rest the bitter antagonisms of their youth, the two mountaineers made an excellent climbing

Below: a party of English climbers on Popocatépetl in about 1900. They are masked against sunburn. Other common hazards of high altitude climbing are extreme cold, high winds, and oxygen starvation, which causes mountain sickness.

team. Together they made short work of Cotopaxi (theirs was the fifth ascent of the mountain) and scaled several lesser virgin peaks. They then addressed themselves to Chimborazo. Unlike Cotopaxi, this is an inactive volcano, and its flanks are grooved with glaciers which greatly increase the difficulties of the ascent. Whymper and Carrel, however, reached Chimborazo's summit on their first attempt, and, in doing so, far surpassed any of their previous height records.

For 25 years after Whymper and Carrel's ascent, Chimborazo remained the highest mountain ever climbed in South America. Interestingly enough, it had once been erroneously considered the highest mountain on earth as a result of Bouguer and La Condamine's investigations in the 1700's. But "The Watch Tower of the World," as the South American liberator Simón Bolívar called Chimborazo, is not even the highest mountain in South America. That honor is held by Aconcagua, which towers 22,834 feet high in Argentina near the Chile border.

The loftiest peak in the whole of the Western Hemisphere, Aconcagua presents the climber with three deadly hazards: loose rocks, high, bitterly cold winds, and thin air. Because of the howling gales which continually buffet Aconcagua, there is relatively little snow and ice for the climber to contend with. But if the wind sweeps away the snow, it also loosens the rock face, making each foot and hand hold treacherous. Moreover, the icy gusts make it doubly difficult to breathe in the thin air of the heights. For every breath he draws, the climber must struggle against an unseen but powerful enemy—the bitterly cold wind that seems to suck the very oxygen from the air.

The first expedition to be successful in overcoming these hazards was led by the British alpinist, Edward FitzGerald, in 1896-1897. Two years before, he and the famous Swiss guide Mattias Zurbriggen had made the first ascents of Mount Tasman and Mount Sefton in New Zealand. Zurbriggen was again FitzGerald's guide on this expedition. Also in the party was a young English climber named Stuart Vines and an Italian guide named Nicolo Lanti. In addition to these four, the expedition also included a number of other climbers and a host of porters.

The first problem facing the expedition was to locate the base of the mountain itself, for although Aconcagua's upper slopes rise in magnificent isolation from its surrounding foothills, its lower

Above: the hardships of an Andes ascent are often matched by the difficulties of reaching the base of the mountain. Here a climber with a machete cuts down dense growth to reach Mount Sangay.

approaches are obscured by them. After weeks of frustrating detours and minor mishaps, FitzGerald and his party reached their objective —a point 14,000 feet above sea level on Aconcagua's Horcones Glacier. It was nearly Christmas Day—midsummer in the Southern Hemisphere—when the party pitched its first camp on Aconcagua. Above them towered nearly 9,000 feet of windswept snow and crumbling rock, and already a large number of the men who had set out with the expedition had dropped out. Only a few of the porters remained with FitzGerald, Zurbriggen, Vines, and Lanti when, on January 14, 1897, they began the assault.

As they slowly worked their way up the loose shale of the mountainside, the men began to suffer from severe bouts of mountain sickness. Essentially oxygen starvation, this condition can strike the climber at any height over 7,000 feet. It results from there being an inadequate supply of oxygen to the blood and body tissues, and is characterized by weakness, nausea, shortness of breath, and the

Left: as elsewhere in the world, the South American climber finds the local people of invaluable help as guides and porters to help him transport his essential equipment to the mountain. On this expedition to climb Mount Sangay everything had to be carried through forests, prickly grass—as shown here—and even over an area of lava which was still hot enough to burn through the rubber soles of the climbers' shoes.

kind of depression that robs a man of his will-power and concentration. Given a few days, the body can adapt or "acclimatize" itself fairly well to rarified air conditions at heights between 7,000 and 18,000 feet. But at heights of over 18,000 feet, even prolonged rest-stops cannot ensure that a man will not be suddenly and totally incapacitated by an attack of mountain sickness.

Aconcagua's particularly rarified air made FitzGerald's party highly susceptible to the effects of high altitude—and they had now passed the 18,000 foot mark. Nevertheless, though they were trembling with sickness and exhaustion, and chilled to the very marrow by the winds that howled around them, they pressed forward. Sometimes it took several hours to progress a few feet over the precarious scree of the mountainside, and four times they were forced to retreat to a camp lower down to recover their energies. Then the weather cleared slightly, and, on their fifth attempt, they managed to reach a point less than 1,000 feet from the summit with

Below: FitzGerald, leader of the 1896-1897 expedition to Aconcagua, the highest peak in South America.

relative ease. Here, with success seemingly near at hand, they rested and took some food. This proved a disastrous mistake. Once again, FitzGerald, who had been weak throughout the climb, was racked by sickness. There was nothing to be done but to help him back to the last camp. Vines and Lanti undertook this task, leaving Zurbriggen to attempt a solo attack on the mountain top. Once more the Swiss guide set his face to the summit. This time, after several hours of doggedly inching his way forward, he planted his ice-ax on Aconcagua's highest point.

A week afterward, Zurbriggen's success was repeated by Vines and Lanti. FitzGerald, however, remained too ill to attempt the final assault again. It is one of the ironies of mountaineering history that the man who planned and led the first conquest of the Americas' highest peak was denied the satisfaction of experiencing that conquest himself.

Soon after their ascent of Aconcagua, FitzGerald's party made their way to another lofty peak on the Argentina-Chile border.

Right: Lord Conway of Allington, the famous British climber who climbed Aconcagua a year after FitzGerald, and then went on to lead the first assault on Mount Illimani in Bolivia. Conway was a truly international climber who explored mountains the world over.

Far right: a photograph taken by Conway in 1898 of the Harvard Observatory Meteorological Station on the summit of El Misti, the extinct volcano which was important to the ancient Inca civilisation.

Below: Mount Aconcagua towers 22,834 feet above sea level. The altitude and the regular buffeting from icy winds make it one of South America's most difficult peaks to scale. The members of FitzGerald's expedition suffered from the weather, nearly having to give up the assault.

This was Tupungato, 22,310 feet high. FitzGerald himself did not take part in the ascent. Again the final assault was by Mattias Zurbriggen—this time with Stuart Vines, In fact, on this occasion the Swiss guide did not actually lead the way to the summit. As the two men hauled themselves onto the ridge leading to the point that had appeared to be the summit, they were startled to discover that the mountain possessed a still higher peak about an hour's climb away. Overcome by exhaustion and possibly by the depression that so often assails men at high altitudes, Zurbriggen was prepared to give up and go back down. Stuart Vines, however, was not. Picking up his ice-ax, he pushed on again, not stopping until he stood on Tupungato's true summit. Not to be outdone, Zurbriggen then mustered his remaining strength, and followed Vines to the top.

The year after FitzGerald's expedition, another British party arrived in the Andes. This group, led by the explorer-mountaineer Martin Conway, (later Lord Conway), repeated the success of FitzGerald's party by climbing Aconcagua. Conway's team then proceeded to Illimani, the twin-peaked mountain which broods over La Paz, capital of Bolivia. Illimani is one of the highest of the mountains in the Cordillera Real section of the Bolivian Andes. Conway chose to scale the lesser of its two summits. Even so, at 21,151 feet, the peak offered its first climbers an impressive challenge. Nor was it only the mountain that taxed their fortitude and resourcefulness. The native Bolivians, who had been hired to carry their goods and equipment, proved to be both frightened and uncooperative. Conway said later that they were slower than any porters he had ever before encountered. And, when he and the rest of the party reached the ice ridges on the higher slopes of Illimani, the porters flatly refused to go a step farther—even to win the silver coins that until then had served to persuade them over the difficult stretches. This

CARIBBEAN SEA
Panama Canal
PICO CRISTOBAL COLON 18,950
Lake Maracaibo
Caracas
TRINIDAD
SA. NEVADA DE MERIDA
Orinoco
ATLANTIC OCEAN
GUIANA HIGHLANDS
MT. RORAIMA 9219
Guaviare
Orinoco
CORD. OCCIDENTAL
CORD. CENTRAL
CORD. ORIENTAL
EQUATOR
I. DE MARAJÓ
Quito
COTOPAXI 19,344
CHIMBORAZO 20,577
GULF OF JAYAQUIL
Japurá
Negro
Amazon
Amazon Basin
Madeira
Tapajos
Marañón
C. de Roq
Juruá
Purus
Xingu
SA. DO RONCADOR
Araguaia
Tocantins
São Francisco
HUASCARAN 22,205
YERUPAJA 21,758
Lima
SERRA DOS PARECIS
Cuzco
SALCANTAY 20,550
ASUNGATE 20,187
CORD. ORIENTAL
ANDES
Planalto do Mato Grosso
BRAZILIAN HIGHLANDS
NEV. DE ILLIMANI
Lake Titicaca
La Paz
EL MISTI 19,098
CORDILLERA OCCIDENTAL
CORD. CENTRAL
Potosi
Gran Chaco
Paraguay
Paraná
ITATIAIA 9145
Pilcomayo
Rio de Janeiro
TROPIC OF CAPRICORN
SA. DO MAR
Bermejo
LLULLAILLACO
PUNA DE ATACAMA
SA. NEVADA DE CACHI 22,047
CERRO INCAHUASI 21,720
CERRO OJOS DEL SALADO 22,550
MONTE PISSIS 22,240
COCHILHA GRANDE
Uruguay
EL TORO 19,400
SA. DE CÓRDOBA
L. dos Patos
PACIFIC OCEAN
SOUTH ATLANTIC OCEAN
Mirim Lake
ACONCAGUA 22,834
TUPUNGATO 22,310
Santiago
Pampa
Paraná
Buenos Aires
Montevideo
Colorado
Negro
MONTE TRONADOR 11,200
Valdés Pena.
I. DE CHILOE
Patagonia
C. SAN VALENTIN 13,314
Taitao Pena.
FALKLAND ISLANDS
STRAIT OF MAGELLAN
STRAIT OF MAGELLAN
TIERRA DEL FUEGO
SOUTH GEORGIA
80°
60°
40°
200
400
600
800
1000

Left: South America showing the Andes, the world's longest mountain chain. This great range stretches some 4,500 miles down the entire west coast of the continent from Panama to Cape Horn.

"strike" on the part of the men who carried the party's vital supplies might have put an end to the ascent had it not been for Conway's two guides, Antoine Naquiznaz and Louis Pellisier. For the remainder of the climb, these two men generously undertook the duties of the porters, and in so doing made it possible for the expedition to reach Illimani's summit.

Northwest of Illimani, in the Cordillera Blanca region in west-central Peru, stands a mountain called Huascarán. At 22,205 feet, it is the loftiest peak in Peru and is one of the few major peaks in the world first scaled by a woman. Her name was Miss Annie Peck, and the story of her conquest of Huascarán—as she herself recorded it in her book *A Search for the Apex of America*—is a dramatic one. Annie Peck was a school teacher from Providence, Rhode Island. At the age of 45 she traveled to Europe and climbed the Matterhorn. From that moment on, she was passionately addicted to mountaineering. She spent her summer vacations climbing, and within a few years had to her credit an impressive number of ascents—including an assault on Bolivia's 21,490 foot high Mount Illampu (Sorata).

She was a small but exceptionally hardy woman, and possessed a courage and determination that put many of her male colleagues to shame. In 1908, at the age of 58, Miss Peck set her heart on conquering Huascarán. At that time its exact height was not known, but she was convinced, from an earlier reconnaissance of the mountain, that it was at least 24,000 feet high. If that were true, Huascarán's conquerer could claim the first ascent of the highest mountain in the Western Hemisphere. (Aconcagua, whose height was then known, is less than 23,000 feet high).

Huascarán possesses twin peaks. Leading up to the saddle between the two is an enormous glacier, deeply crevassed. The inherent difficulties of the approach—which Annie Peck had decided should be up the glacier—demanded experienced Alpine guides. Accordingly, she enlisted the aid of two Swiss mountaineers, Gabriel and Rudolf Taugwalder, who joined her in New York and traveled with her to Peru.

The initial stages of the climb went well. But at 11,000 feet, Rudolf Taugwalder was suddenly overcome by a debilitating attack of mountain sickness. Too ill to go on with the ascent, he had to return down the mountain with some of the party's Peruvian porters.

Above: Miss Annie Peck, an American schoolteacher who, at 45, began to climb mountains, and became one of the few women to conquer a major unclimbed peak, Mount Huascarán.

Annie Peck and Gabriel Taugwalder, however, continued on over a treacherous surface of sheer ice, powdery snow, and yawning crevasses. Twice they made camp on the steep slope of the glacier. On the third day, they found themselves inching their way up the 80° angle of the final ice-wall to the saddle. It was hard going, for they had to cut steps in the ice to serve as footholds all the way up. On the fourth day, they reached the saddle, a tilted expanse of glittering snow 20,000 feet above sea level. At either end stood a towering peak. Annie Peck chose to make for the northern pinnacle, because it seemed to offer the better ascent route. She could only hope and pray that it was the higher of the two peaks.

Miss Peck and her guide started for the peak at dawn on the morning of the fifth day. A bitterly cold wind began assailing them and Gabriel, who was doing all the cutting of the ice-steps in the towering wall they clung to, was soon trembling with exhaustion. Worse still, he began to show signs of mountain sickness. Ahead of them still lay many hundreds of feet of ice-wall. Behind lay a precipitous staircase of ice. Miss Peck and Taugwalder knew that the descent down that staircase would require all the nerve and strength they could muster. With Gabriel ill, it would be utter recklessness to continue going forward. Reluctantly, they turned their backs on the summit and retraced their steps.

Diminishing food supplies and the continued illness of her guides prevented Annie Peck from making another attempt right away. But she was far from giving up. Ten days after she had left Huascarán, she was back with fresh supplies to try again. And the Taugwalders, by now fully recovered, were as determined as she to succeed.

More familiar with their adversary on this second attempt, the three made rapid progress up the lower part of the mountain. In fact, they reached the ice-wall above the glacier in half the time it had taken them on the first ascent. They proceeded up this precipice at a steady pace and gained the saddle. Here they made their third camp. The following day, in the light of early dawn, they began the final assault on the north peak. The weather was fair, but bitterly cold. They were operating in sub-zero temperatures dressed only in layers of wool—the anorak and other protective gear worn by modern climbers had not yet become standard equipment.

As the three toiled up the glittering spine of the north peak, it seemed that they would be overcome by exhaustion and the numbing cold before they could reach the top. But the way ahead gradually became less steep, and suddenly the summit lay only a few yards away. Staggering toward it, Annie Peck became aware that she had lost the feeling in her left hand. She snatched off her mitten and saw that her fingers had turned unnaturally white. Frostbite! Another few minutes and the tissues would be completely frozen. As she

The Peruvian Andes, seen from the air, stretch away into the distance as an impersonal expanse of indomitable and silent fortresses of snow and ice.

dragged herself forward, she beat her hand against her leg over and over again, and slowly the beginnings of feeling returned to her numbed fingers.

When at last their feet touched the summit, the three climbers were almost too worn out to enjoy their triumph. Before them lay a terrifying descent down the steep ice-staircase to their last camp on the snow-covered saddle. Night had fallen and the remaining food they carried had frozen solid. Shaking with exhaustion, one after the other slipped and almost fell. Most terrible of all, Rudolf

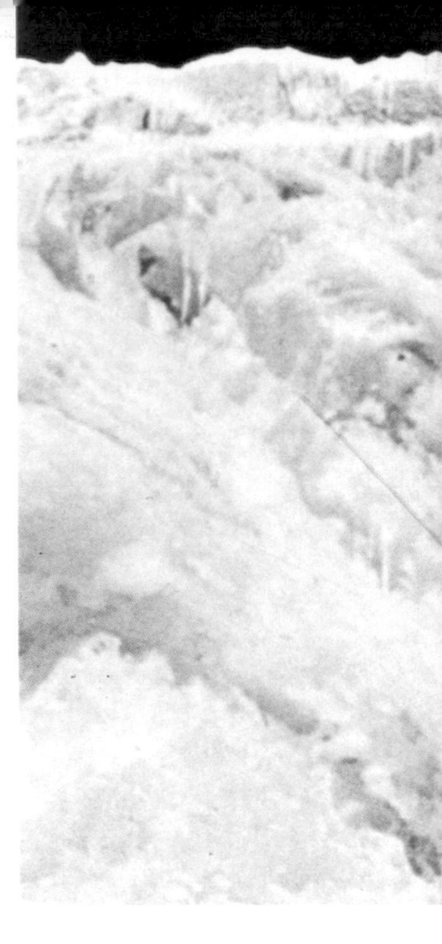

Left: climbers at the base of Mount Yerupajá. The mountain, not one of the world's highest, qualifies as one of the most terrifying to climb. Its summit, an ice ridge with sheer sides, is like the blade of a giant knife.

Taugwalder lost both his gloves, and had to make much of the final descent barehanded. When they finally reached camp, he tried desperately to bring back the feeling in his hands by rubbing them with snow, but it was too late—all of one hand and the fingers of the other later had to be amputated.

Above: an expedition member edges precariously up one of the sharply sloping ice ridges guarding the summit of Mount Yerupajá. The climb was successful, although the descending climbers had to spend an icy night clinging to frozen rock.

On the summit of Huascarán's north peak, Miss Peck had been unable to carry out the tests necessary to determine its height, but she was convinced that it was at least 24,000 feet high. Unfortunately, one year later, a French survey proved it to be no more than 22,205 feet, and even then, the south peak was higher than the one she had climbed. Moreover, in later decades, many mountaineers have been inclined to doubt that she and the Taugwalders actually succeeded in reaching the very top of the north peak. But however that may be, we do know that she made a very gallant attempt on this Andean giant, and deserves the name "The Lady of Huascarán."

Many of the other mountains of Peru have been the subject of daring and eventful climbs. One of these, made by the Americans Dave Harrah and G. Maxwell in 1950, was the first ascent of Yerupajá (21,758 feet). This mountain, although not one of the world's highest, is one of its most terrible. It is often referred to as "The Butcher," because its summit consists, not of a single high point, but of a long, knife-edge ridge, like that of a butcher's cleaver. Almost perpendicular walls of ice fall away from this terrifying knife-edge *arête* (ridge) on both sides.

In many ways, Harrah and Maxwell's experience on Yerupajá was similar to that of Annie Peck and the Taugwalders on Huascarán. After an ascent that had called forth every ounce of their reserves, they found themselves still on the face at nightfall, and had to spend 12 hours clinging to the icy wall in the intense cold before they could get back to their last campsite. Both men suffered frostbite and Harrah later had to have all his toes amputated. It is a measure of the severe conditions in the Andes that frostbite is almost as constant a danger there as it is in the Himalaya.

The Peruvian Andes occupy an important place in history, for it was in these rugged and inaccessible highlands that the ancient civilizations of South America arose and flourished. The last of these great Indian civilizations was that of the Inca, who built their cities and temples in the mountains of Peru, Ecuador, and Chile. It was to these lofty strongholds that the last stubborn Inca people fled when the gold-hungry Spanish conquistadors swept through the Inca empire in the 1500's.

Perhaps the most famous of the final Inca mountain dwelling places is Machu Picchu, discovered by the American scholar-explorer Hiram Bingham in 1912. First and foremost an archeologist, Bingham was also an enthusiastic amateur mountaineer. In 1911, he scaled the awe-inspiring peak of Coropuna (21,700 feet) in Peru. Three years later he led a party to the summit of Salcantay (20,550 feet), which stands near the ancient Inca capital of Cusco in the Cordillera de Vilcanota of southern Peru.

The expeditions Bingham led in search of Inca ruins were sponsored by Yale University. Another university, Harvard, later established an astronomical observatory on Peru's El Misti (19,098 feet), an extinct volcano which once occupied an important place of honor in the Inca religion.

The Andes today are the site of increasing numbers of climbing expeditions by mountaineers from all over the world. One of the most unusual of these expeditions took place in mid-1970, when a team of British climbers attempted to scale the 19,400 foot El Toro in Peru. The highest remaining unscaled peak in all of South America, El Toro is unique among all the world's mountains in being the site of accidentally buried treasure. In 1954, an aircraft carrying 29 people and almost $100,000 worth of gold bullion crashed on its summit. The fate of its passengers was sealed by the impossibility

Machu Picchu, the magnificent fortress-city built by the Incas high in the Peruvian Andes. It was here that many Incas sought refuge as their empire was ravaged by the ruthless Spaniards. Machu Picchu was rediscovered when, in 1912, Hiram Bingham, an American scholar-explorer, stumbled on the site.

of mounting an adequate rescue team in time. But what of its cargo of gold? The 1970 British climbing team hoped to be able to ascertain, in the course of their attempt on the peak, whether it would be possible to recover the bullion.

Unfortunately, a mere 150 feet from El Toro's summit, the expedition was forced to abandon the climb because of the treacherous overhanging cornices of ice on the ridge and the condition of the snow, which was extremely powdery and waist-deep in places. They did discover the fate of the lost bullion, however. They found evidence to indicate that the plane had fallen from the mountainside into the glacier below. There the aircraft and its treasure must remain until the glacier eventually empties itself out, in the foothills of the mountain, hundreds of years from now.

Exploring the Himalaya

8

Nowhere in the world is there another mountain system to compare with the Himalaya. Hundreds of its peaks are similar in height to the loftiest mountains of the Andes or the Pamirs, and scores more are higher again by several thousand feet. The Himalaya are colossal in extent as well as in height. Forming the southern part of the massive central Asian highlands, the successive ranges of the Himalaya stretch the entire length of northern India, and cover most of Nepal, Sikkim, Bhutan, and southern Tibet as well.

Mountain passes through the great walls of peaks and ridges surrounding the Himlayan kingdoms are few and far between, and are rarely less than 15,000 feet high. Moreover, the storms and avalanches that accompany the yearly monsoons make even the existing passes inaccessible except during a few short months of the year. Consequently, although there has always been some trade among the peoples of the Himalaya, the little communities of farmers and herdsmen in the highlands have generally been as cut

Left: one of the fascinations of the Himalayan area is its inaccessibility. There are few routes through the vast mountain chain, and the passes which exist are seldom below 15,000 feet. Outsiders making their way into the isolated villages locked in the high valleys have found the simplicity and warm good humor of the Himalayan people particularly attractive. This 1826 drawing, by James Manson, a British survey officer, shows a Nepalese herdsman with his goats.

Right: the first Europeans to travel in the Himalayan kingdoms were the Jesuits. This painting of the early 1600's shows a prince receiving two of the Portuguese Jesuit missionaries

off from one another as their countries have been from the outside world.

Common to all the peoples of the Himalaya is a deep respect and reverence for the peaks that tower above them. Serene, majestic, and utterly remote from all earthly concerns, these lofty turrets of snow and ice have been held sacred in the highland countries for thousands of years. Many of the individual peaks are accorded special honor as being the homes of gods or goddesses. The very word "Himalaya" comes from an ancient Sanskrit phrase meaning "House of Snow." But it is not only the Himalayan peoples in whom the mountains arouse a feeling of reverence and humility. No mountaineer has traveled to this land of silent, snow-clad peaks without being deeply affected by their almost ethereal purity and massive simplicity.

The first Europeans to enter this awesome terrain and reach the mysterious and romantic kingdoms beyond India were Jesuit missionaries. Indomitable in their crusade to win converts to the faith, they had begun traveling to places as far away as Japan in the early 1500's. In 1624, two Portuguese Jesuits, Father Antonio de Andrade and Brother Manuel Marques, set out from northern India. After a journey of four months, they reached Ladakh in northwestern Kashmir, where they established a church. The church was kept going for several decades by a succession of courageous Jesuit fathers who crossed and recrossed the western Himalaya in the service of the faith. In the meantime, Jesuit missionaries were also venturing into the eastern ranges of the Himalaya, and in 1714, one of them, Father Ippolito Desideri, traveled as far north as Lhasa, the sacred city of Tibet.

But the Jesuits were not map-makers, and despite the missionaries' travels, men still knew almost nothing about the size and scope of the mighty Himalayan ranges, their chief peaks, or the maze of valleys, gorges, foothills, and ridges that guarded them. Real exploration of the Himalaya started only in the mid-1700's, when the British East India Company began extending its control over India and sending out expeditions to explore and map its frontiers. By the close of the century, a few of these expeditions had penetrated the Himalaya as far as Bhutan, Nepal, and Tibet. On the basis of their reports, the Surveyor General of Bengal, Captain James Rennell, was able to publish the first *Map of Hindoostan* in the 1780's.

The need for accurate knowledge of India's geography became more pressing in the years that followed, and soon a major project was underway. It was no less than the mapping of the entire subcontinent, including the 2,000-mile-long arc of mountains along India's northern frontier. This enormous undertaking was to occupy the men of the British Survey Corps for over a century. Moreover, it was to entail all the dangers and hardships of a lengthy military campaign, for the highlands of northern India were inhabited by warlike tribes who were willing to fight to the death to keep the white men out of their domains. The small parties of British soldiers

Captain James Rennell (1742-1830), the Surveyor General of Bengal. In 1783 he produced a notable *Map of Hindoostan*.

Below: a British army camp at Jytock Ridge in the 1840's. The military necessity for accurate maps led many survey officers to climb higher in the Himalaya as part of their job than mountaineers were then climbing in the Alps purely for the sport.

and surveyors who ventured into this uncharted enemy territory risked their lives on every foray. But the surveys were essential, and the work went on. By 1810, maps of the great valley of Nepal had been produced, the source of the Ganges accurately determined, and the first estimates of the most accessible Himalayan peaks made.

In 1823, the Indian Trigonometrical Survey, as the mapping of the sub-continent was called, gained a new surveyor general—Sir George Everest. He it was who first applied the "gridiron," or triangulation, system to large-scale map-making, and he who accurately established the India arc of the meridian (a line of known coordinates running from the southern tip of India to its northern frontier). Everest's innovations made it possible to calculate the relationship between any two geographical points in India. There was now a mathematical basis for determining the relative positions of the great Himalayan peaks, as well as their heights above sea level. To determine the height of an unknown peak, the surveyor traveled to an observation post whose height was known. From there he measured the peak's angle of elevation relative to a horizontal plane. From this he could determine the height of the peak above the observation post, and hence its height above sea level.

Above: Sir George Everest, for whom the highest mountain in the world was named. He was surveyor-general, and applied the triangulation system to the problem of large-scale mapping.

Using these highly scientific methods, the work of the Survey Corps proceeded rapidly, but it was still a dangerous undertaking. Sometimes it was even necessary for the surveyor to travel in disguise, as did the intrepid William Moorcroft, who made his first survey expedition in the garb of an Indian fakir or holy man.

Early in the 1800's, the frontiers of Nepal had been officially closed to foreigners, and until 1947 when this general policy of non-admittance was finally relaxed, Europeans were allowed inside the country only on rare occasions. During the 1800's, the other

Right: outsiders were not admitted in the Himalayan kingdoms. H. Y. Hearsey drew this sketch of himself and William Moorcroft disguised as Indian fakirs during their 1812 expedition to Tibet.

Below: a map taken from a report on the great Trigonometrical Survey shows the scale of the British undertaking. The Great Arc of the Meridian is the line of triangles running due north from the southern tip of India.

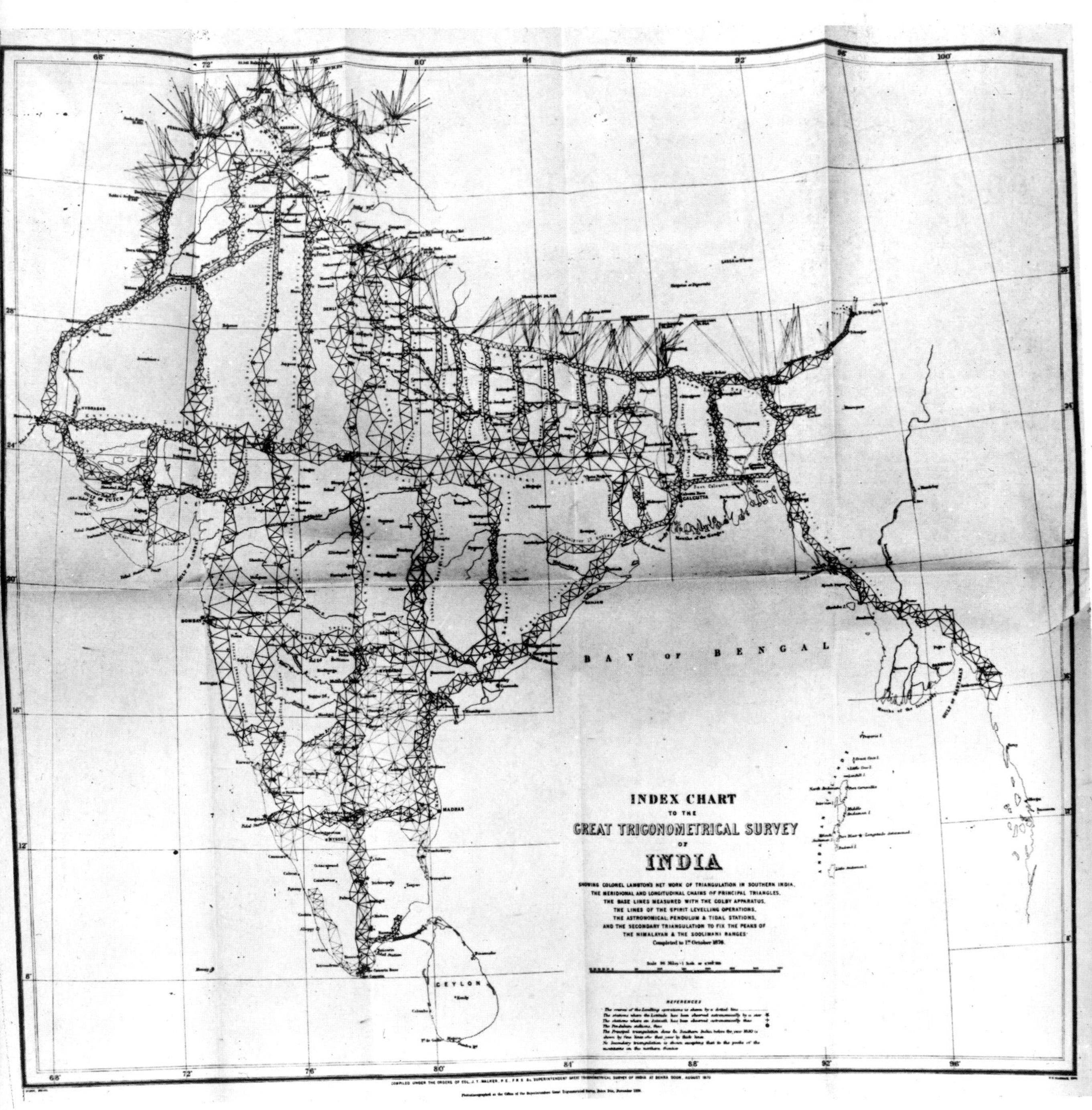

Himalayan states, Tibet, Sikkim, and Bhutan, were only a little less reluctant than Nepal to permit foreigners within their borders. In the mid-1800's, as the British survey teams pushed ever deeper into the Himalaya, the distrust and defensiveness of India's northern neighbors increasingly hampered exploration. At last, finding that all Europeans were to be refused access to these northern regions, the British began training men from the hill tribes to pursue the work of the survey. These so-called "pundit-explorers" soon proved themselves not only hardy enough to withstand the rigors of high-altitude work, but also able to master, with remarkable rapidity, the intricacies of the refined measurement techniques then being used. One of the most famous of these pundits was a man called Nain Singh. On one occasion he made a 1,200 mile journey along the southern trade routes of Tibet to Lhasa and back, taking measurements and making notes all the way. The feat was all the more remarkable in that he had to keep these activities a complete secret from the Tibetan caravan merchants with whom he traveled.

It was another of these pundit-explorers who, in 1852, burst into the head office of the Indian Trigonometrical Survey and announced breathlessly that he had discovered the highest mountain in the world, a peak 29,002 feet high. The news was greeted with disbelief —could so high a mountain actually exist? But his calculations were found to be correct. And later, this mighty peak, number XV on the survey maps, was named Mount Everest, for the surveyor general who had done so much to make the mapping of the world's greatest mountains possible. To the Tibetan people, however, Everest is known as Chomolungma, "Goddess Mother of the Snows." The official height of Everest is set by the Indian government at 29,028 feet.

Below: the prime minister of Nepal, Jung Bahdour Koowar Ranajee. In spite of good personal relations between the British and the Nepalese, the borders of the kingdom remained closed to the British survey teams.

Nain Singh, one of the most famous of the hill tribe surveyors – the Pundits – penetrated deep into territory where Europeans were not admitted. As he traveled he took secret measurements.

As the systematic work of the Survey continued, countless surveyors and explorers, laden with heavy precision equipment, toiled up the peaks and passes of the Himalaya to take their measurements and make their reports. These hardy men had no intention of "mountaineering" in the sense in which that word was being used in the Alps, where the Golden Age of mountaineering was now underway. But while Swiss guides and English gentlemen were winning worldwide acclaim for their Alpine feats, Indian and Gurkha guides, officers, and soldiers of the Observers Corps of the British Army, and civilians employed by the Survey were frequently ascending peaks higher than anything in the "Playground of Europe" as part of their job.

For nearly a century, all the climbing done in the Himalaya had been strictly for scientific purposes—in addition to the surveyors, some few European naturalists and geologists had traveled to the Himalaya in the mid-1800's to carry out research. But the 1880's saw the arrival of a new breed of Himalayan climbers—men who saw in these towering ranges a field for adventure and conquest, rather than for research and discovery. The first European to climb in the Himalaya strictly for "sport and adventure," as he himself put it, was W. W. Graham who, in company with a Swiss guide named Joseph Imboden, traveled extensively in the mountains of Sikkim in 1883. Four years later, a young English lieutenant serving in India made a daring crossing of the perilous Mustagh Pass in the Karakoram range of northwest India. This adventurer, a man who never ceased to love the Himalaya, was Francis Younghusband. He later headed the committee that planned the first assaults on Everest.

The 1890's saw a rising tide in the number of specifically mountaineering expeditions to the Himalaya. In 1892, Martin Conway, already a veteran alpinist, led an expedition to the Karakoram range. In terms of sheer mountaineering, Conway's expedition succeeded in making only one major ascent, that of Pioneer Peak (22,600 feet). But in the course of his extensive exploration of the region, Conway made detailed maps of the Karakoram glaciers and kept careful records of the way in which high altitudes affected both human metabolic rates and the performance of delicate equipment. Both his maps and his notes on the effects of high altitudes were to prove invaluable to later expeditions.

One of the members of Conway's 1892 party was Charles Granville Bruce, a man who soon became one of the most famous and best loved figures in the whole history of Himalayan climbing. When he accompanied Conway to the Karakoram range he was a 26-year-old lieutenant in the British Army. He had already taken part in a number of survey and military expeditions in the Himalaya, and become a passionate addict of mountain climbing for its own sake. His every leave had been spent in the mountains, where he had come to know and love the hill peoples—the Gurkhas and Sherpas of the Kingdom of Nepal. As a result, his knowledge of Himalayan

Above: a drawing by a British survey officer, J. B. Bellasis, of himself conducting a survey from the camp.

Below: Martin Conway was one of the first "amateur" mountaineers in the Karakoram range. His maps and notes on the effects of the high altitude were to prove invaluable to later climbers.

conditions, terrain, languages, and peoples was greater than that of any other man of his time. "Charlie" Bruce was a huge and genial man, courageous and tremendously strong—Conway described him as the "goods-train" of the 1892 expedition. Tradition also has it that Bruce's preferred form of exercise when not mountaineering was running uphill before breakfast with a Gurkha guide under each arm! But that he was loved and revered by the Gurkhas is illustrated by the fact that even as late as the 1950's—years after his death—they were still relishing tales about "the great man Bruce" and his wonderful exploits.

Bruce was to have been part of the first attempt on a major Himalayan peak, Nanga Parbat (26,660 feet) in Kashmir in 1895, but was recalled to duty before the expedition could begin. The Nanga Parbat party was led by Albert F. Mummery, the famous pioneer of new routes and guideless climbing in the Alps. On the first attempt, Mummery and his party reached a height of 20,000 feet before being forced to retreat by the illness of one of the Gurkha guides. An indication of how little even an experienced Alpine climber understood the full realities of a Himalayan ascent is shown by the fact that Mummery believed that another night on the mountain would have been enough to get them up the remaining 6,000 feet. For the next try, the party agreed to separate and reconnoiter two different routes to the summit. Mummery and his two Gurkha guides were never seen again. Almost certainly they were swept away by an avalanche, an accident that may occur at any time in the high

Detail of map produced by Conway's 1892 expedition, this one showing the Baltoro Glacier. The painstaking accuracy of Conway's maps made them essential to later expeditions. This also maps Mount Godwin Austen, the Godwin Austen Glacier, and Mustagh Tower.

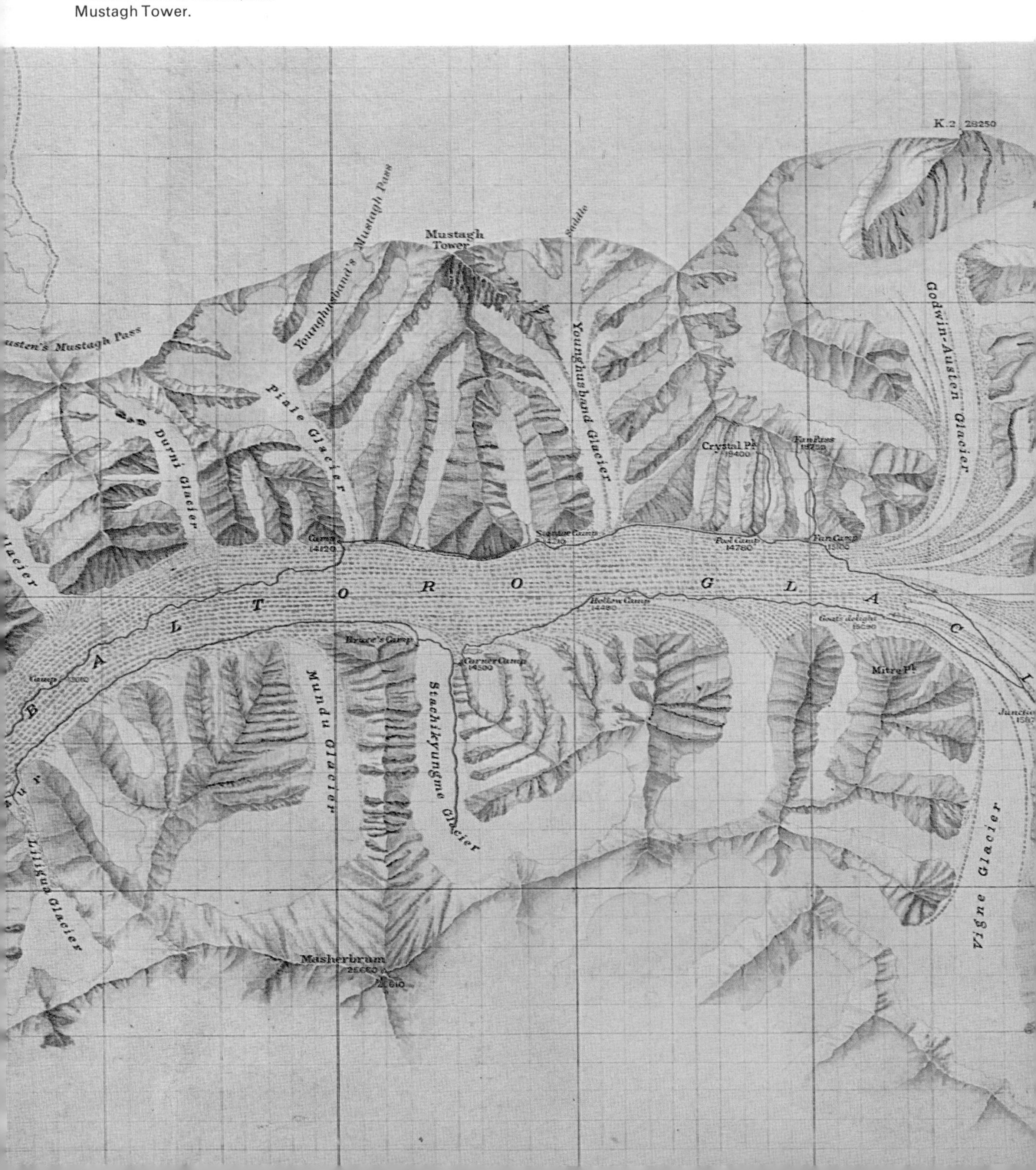

Right: members of the party which conquered Trisul in 1907. Second from the left is Dr. Tom Longstaff, who led the rapid ascent of this lofty peak, and Charles Granville Bruce (seated).

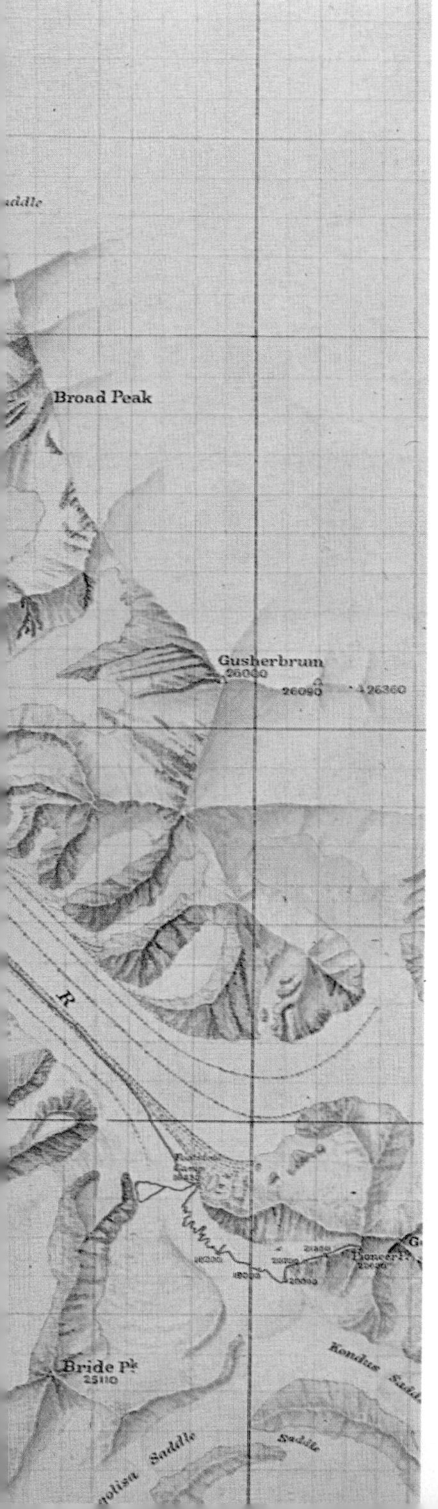

Himalaya. But just as certainly, Mummery had increased the likelihood of the disaster by applying Alpine tactics on the very much more hazardous surfaces of a Himalayan peak. There was still much to be learned about the true dimensions of the daunting Himalayan challenge.

Nevertheless, that great achievements were possible even in these early years of Himalayan mountaineering, was shown by Dr. Tom Longstaff's conquest of Trisul (23,360 feet) in northern India. Longstaff was as much a character in his own way as Charlie Bruce was in his. Small and wiry, with a beaked nose and a red moustache, he was an indefatigable mountaineer and, by the time he made his assault on Trisul, had already climbed in the Alps and the Caucasus and carried out extensive exploration in the mountains of Tibet and Nepal. His ascent of Trisul in 1907 was as much a feat of exploration as it was of mountaineering, for at that time there were no detailed maps of its surrounding glaciers. Luck was with him, however, for he hit on the very route that leads directly up the mountain's northeast face. But at 17,000 feet, Longstaff and his party began to suffer severely from the effects of high altitude. Soon they were gasping for breath and struggling against all the afflictions of mountain sickness—headache, nausea, weakness, and a frightening loss of willpower and concentration. Frozen and exhausted, they had just set up their camp when they were struck by the full force of a blinding blizzard. When at last it abated two days later, Longstaff, fearful of what a continued stay in the rarified atmosphere might do to himself and his men, decided to make a dash for the summit. In fact, his plan was to attempt the very thing on Trisul that Mummery had tried to do on Nanga Parbat—ascend 6,000 feet in one day! Amazingly, in spite of the intense cold, the whipping winds, and the difficulty of breathing, he and his two Swiss guides, Alexis and Henri Brocherel, succeeded in reaching the top after a climb of no more than 12 hours.

Theirs was a historic achievement, not only for the "rush" tactics employed on the final ascent, but for another reason as well. In the words of Kenneth Mason, author of the standard history of Himalayan exploration, and himself long attached to the Indian Survey, this was "the highest summit reached at that time, the height of which was actually known and about the ascent of which there was no doubt."

The Himalaya, the highest of the world's mountain systems, in fact consists of several parallel ranges. They stretch in a 1500-mile curve across southern Asia, from the Pamirs in the west to the great bend of the Brahmaputra River in the east. Mount Everest, at 29,028 feet, the highest mountain, is situated on the frontier between Nepal and Tibet.

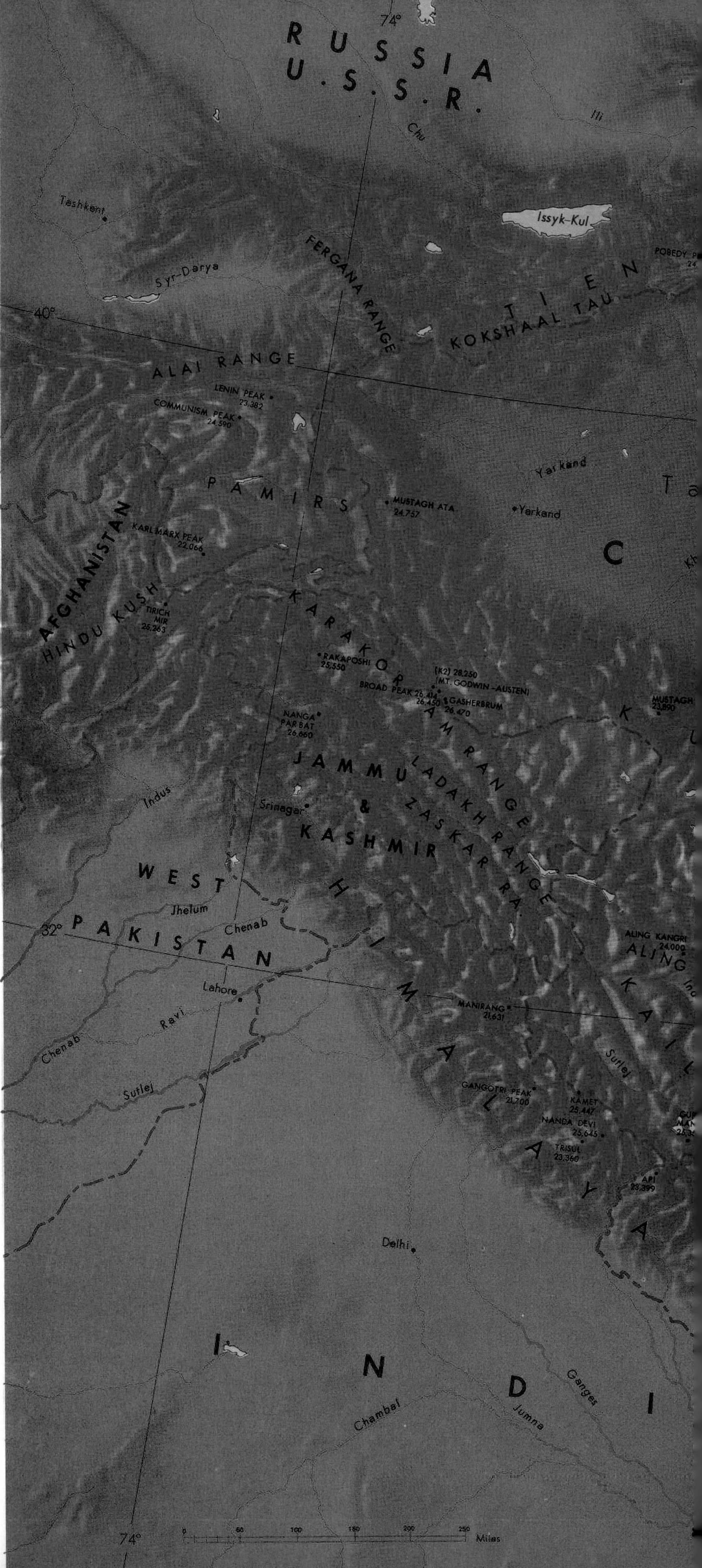

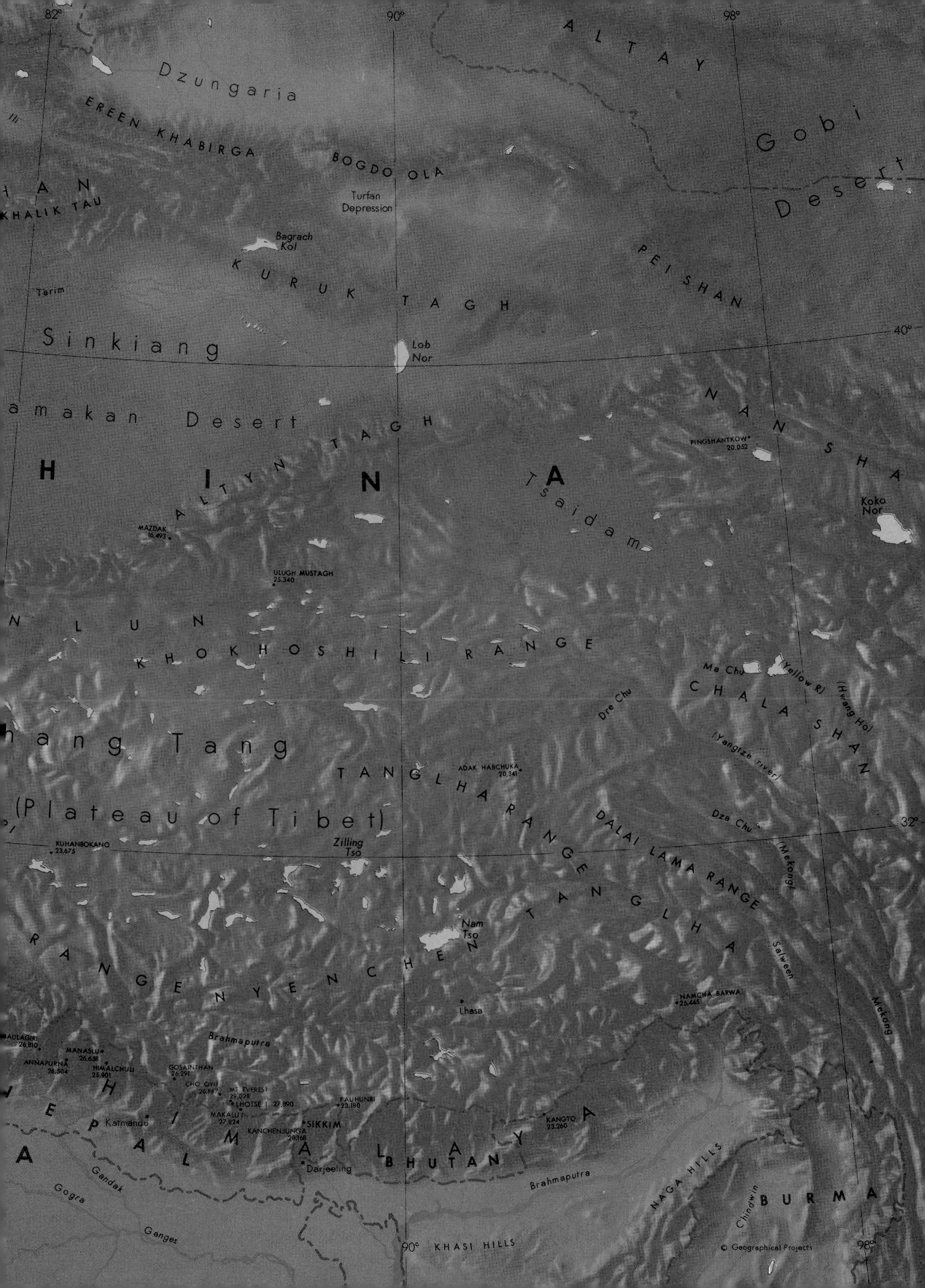

82°
90°
98°
ALTAY
Dzungaria
EREEN KHABIRGA
BOGDO OLA
Gobi
Desert
KHALIK TAU
Turfan Depression
Bagrach Kol
KURUK TAGH
PEI SHAN
Tarim
Sinkiang
Lob Nor
40°
amakan Desert
ALTYN TAGH
NAN SHA
PINGSHANTKOW 20,052
H
I
N
A
Tsaidam
Koko Nor
MAZDAK 16,493
ULUGH MUSTAGH 25,340
N L U N
KHOKHOSHILI RANGE
Ma Chu
(Yellow R.)
(Hwang Ho)
CHALA SHAN
Dre Chu
(Yangtze river)
hang Tang
(Plateau of Tibet)
TANGLHA RANGE
ADAK HABCHUKA 20,341
DALAI LAMA RANGE
Dza Chu
(Mekong)
32°
KUHANBOKANO 23,675
Zilling Tso
TANGLHA
Nam Tso
Salween
Mekong
RANGE NYENCHEN
NAMCHA BARWA 25,445
Lhasa
Brahmaputra
AULAGIRI 26,810
MANASLU 26,658
ANNAPURNA 26,504
HIMALCHULI 25,801
GOSAINTHAN 26,291
CHO OYU 26,867
MT. EVEREST 29,028
LHOTSE I 27,890
MAKALU 27,824
PAUHUNRI 23,180
KANGTO 23,260
KANCHENJUNGA 28,168
SIKKIM
Katmandu
HIMALAYA
NEPAL
BHUTAN
Darjeeling
Gandak
Gogra
Ganges
Brahmaputra
NAGA HILLS
Chindwin
BURMA
KHASI HILLS
90°
98°
© Geographical Projects

Left: Mrs. Fanny Bullock Workman at the door of her tent in a camp in the Karakoram range. With her husband, Dr. William Hunter Workman, she climbed extensively in the Himalaya at the turn of the century. Unfortunately, many of their records have since been found to be inaccurate.

The Duke of the Abruzzi (1873-1933), of the Royal House of Savoy. An enthusiastic mountaineer, he led a large expedition to conquer the mighty Mount Godwin Austen. The expedition was unsuccessful, but reached a height of some 24,000 feet.

These carefully chosen words show the problems not so much of climbing in the Himalaya, but of verifying the claims, sometimes made in good faith, of those who had done so. Perhaps no claims were more difficult to verify than those made by an American husband and wife team who climbed extensively in the Himalaya at the turn of the century. Dr. William Hunter Workman and his wife, Fanny Bullock Workman, made their first expedition to the Karakoram range in 1899. Both on this, and on subsequent expeditions, they were accompanied by competent guides, and succeeded in scaling a number of peaks. But just which peaks, and how high they were, was open to debate, for the Workmans did not consider it necessary to consult the Indian Survey before making their claims. They were prone to be inaccurate in their noting of the exact height and locations of the mountains they explored, and frequently claimed to have made the first ascents of peaks that had been climbed before. To their credit, however, it must be said that on their last expedition to the Karakoram range in 1912, they did take with them an expert cartographer, and with his help produced several useful maps of the region's glaciers.

Another notable contribution to Himalayan exploration was made in 1909, by an expedition led by the famous Italian mountaineer, the Duke of the Abruzzi. Behind him he already had two remarkable expeditions: the ascent of Alaska's Mount Saint Elias in 1897, and the exploration of Uganda's Ruwenzori range in 1906. In the year 1909, he assembled another large and highly professional group of scientists and mountaineers, and set off for the Karakoram range. His objective was Mount Godwin Austen (28,250 feet) on the China-Kashmir border. This mountain, second only to Everest in height, was named for the surveyor Henry Godwin Austen. It is also known as Dapsang (its local name) and K2, the number given it during the survey. Filippo de Filippi, the naturalist on the Duke's expedition,

The Duke's expedition to Godwin Austen included Vittoria Sella, whose photographs—here, of the junction of the Godwin Austen and Baltoro glaciers—are said to be still unmatched.

has described it as a "quadrangular pyramid," made up of four immense ridges which soar upward from the southwest, the northwest, the southeast, and the northeast. The Duke's party reconnoitered all four approaches. In addition, they thoroughly mapped the region surrounding the massive Godwin Austen glacier that sweeps down the mountain's south face. The party made a heroic attempt to reach the summit via a narrow ridge on the south face, but were forced to retreat because they could find no place on the knife-edge of the ridge to establish a camp. Before turning back, however, they did reach a height of some 24,600 feet on the ridge. In their honor, the approach was thereafter known as the Abruzzi Ridge.

One of the members of the Duke's party was the famed mountaineer-photographer Vittorio Sella. In the course of the expedition he took some of the most valuable, and certainly the most beautiful photographs of his career. His numerous pictures of every side of the world's second highest mountain were used in planning every later expedition to the peak.

By the close of the first decade of the 1900's, a score of daring attempts had been made on giants of the Himalaya. As yet, only two peaks over 23,000 feet had been climbed: Trisul (23,360 feet) by Tom Longstaff, in 1907, and Pauhunri (23,180 feet) by Dr. A. M. Kellas, in 1910. But many of the mountaineers who had pitted themselves against the monarchs of the Himalaya had reached heights of 20,000 and more, and all of them had done so armed only with the traditional equipment of the alpinist: crampons, ice-ax, rope, and woolen clothing. Encouraged by the success of these pioneers, men began to dream of conquering Everest itself. The dream was kept alive throughout the grim years of World War I, and, in 1921, the first Everest expedition set off to reconnoiter this, the mightiest of all the world's mountains.

Confronting the Himalayan Giants

9

Before the British expedition to Everest in 1921, no European had ever even reached the base of the mountain, let alone explored its heights. Situated on the frontier between Nepal and Tibet, Everest had long been inaccessible to Westerners because both Nepal and Tibet strictly forbade foreigners within their borders. The only European who had ever succeeded in getting anywhere near the mountain was a young British officer named John Noel. Noel had done some Alpine climbing as a boy. When he was stationed in India in 1913, he spent his first leaves exploring the foothills of the Himalaya. The mystery of the forbidden lands beyond the mountains intrigued him, and he was soon engaged in trying to find a way through to Tibet. Time after time he was turned back by Tibetan soldiers, but at last he located an unguarded pass 20,000 feet high, and managed to penetrate deep into the kingdom of Tibet before being found out and forced to make his way back. It was only after returning to India that he learned that he had come within 40 miles of Everest—closer than any European had ever been before.

After the war, Captain Noel was one of the men chosen to take part in the first expedition to Everest. An Everest Committee had been formed, and the Dalai Lama of Tibet was at last persuaded to permit the expedition to enter his country. The ruler of Nepal, however, would not relent, even for so momentous a project as the first exploration of Everest. As a result, when the expedition at last set out in 1921, it was forced to make a long detour around Nepal before it could arrive at its destination, the valleys at the foot of Everest's glaciers.

Structurally, Everest is an immense pyramid, having three massive faces and three major ridges which soar up to the summit from the north, south, and west. The longest of these huge buttresses is the north ridge. After a thorough reconnaissance, the members of the 1921 expedition concluded that the only feasible route to the summit was by way of this ridge. The ascent plan they suggested was to climb the mighty East Rongbuk Glacier to a pass on the north ridge called the North Col, and from there to proceed along the

The main base camp of the 1922 Everest expedition, on the northern approach to the mountain. The photograph was taken and colored by Captain John Noel, photographer on the 1922 and 1924 expeditions.

Left: Captain Noel and his camera on Everest. His movie camera, a 35 mm Newman Sinclair, had been especially designed to withstand the extremely cold conditions that are a part of any Himalayan photographic enterprise.

main body of the ridge to the summit. As far as they could determine, the chief problem was to reach the North Col itself, which lies at the top of a sheer ice-wall nearly 1,800 feet high.

But whatever purely structural problems the ascent of Everest might entail, one thing was certain: its climbers would have to endure high-altitude conditions more extreme than any mountaineer had ever faced before. Only a comparatively few men had as yet climbed above 20,000 feet, and no one knew what the effects of prolonged work above 25,000 feet might be. Everest was over 29,000 feet, and many people seriously doubted whether the human body could withstand the effects of severe oxygen deprivation at such heights. A kind of oxygen apparatus for use at high altitudes had already made its appearance, but it was still very primitive—heavy, ungainly, and frequently unreliable. Few mountaineers trusted it enough to burden themselves with it on long climbs. Moreover, many mountaineers of this time regarded the use of so artificial a climbing aid with disapproval. Nonetheless, oxygen equipment was taken on the second Everest expedition in 1922.

The 1922 expedition was led by Charles Bruce (at that time a brigadier general in the British Army) and included a number of such highly experienced climbers as John Noel, Tom Longstaff, and Dr. T. H. Somervell. This was to be no mere reconnaissance mission, but rather an all-out assault on the mountain. Accordingly, Bruce moved the team up in easy stages, a strategy which he hoped would conserve the men's energies and give them sufficient time to acclimatize before the final assault. But despite these precautions, the 1922 expedition failed to gain its objective. The first assault

team, having reached a height of 26,700 feet, was forced down by the painful difficulty of breathing in the rarified air. The second, equipped with the cumbersome oxygen apparatus, managed to reach a height of 27,230 feet before being defeated by winds so fierce that the climbers could hardly stand upright. The third and final assault party had barely reached the Col when it was struck by an avalanche. Seven Sherpa porters lost their lives in this tragic accident, and the expedition was brought to a halt.

Despite disaster and defeat, the 1922 expedition produced two

Noel's map of Everest's north face. Until Nepal opened her borders in 1947, this was the only possible way to the summit. The base camp, at the bottom right, was at 16,000 feet. The route up lay along the East Rongbuk Glacier, with a chain of depot camps established at 6-mile intervals. At the head of the glacier, at 21,000 feet, was the advance base camp on a snow field beneath a sheer ice-wall.

positive results. First, the use of oxygen was now seen to be an absolute necessity at heights over 26,000 feet. Using it, men had been able to climb higher—and camp higher—than ever before. Second, the true value of the Sherpa porters was now fully recognized. Tough and energetic, they had proved themselves capable of carrying heavy packs to heights of over 25,000 feet. Moreover, they had shown themselves to be natural mountaineers in the truest sense of the word.

Above: Charles Granville Bruce, leader of the 1922 Everest expedition. Bruce had been greatly loved by the Gurkhas whom he had commanded, and the stories of his strength and courage became folk tales of the mountain people. Thirty years later W. H. Murray was being asked how he was. Murray reported that he hadn't the heart to tell the people that Bruce, in fact, was dead.

The Sherpas belong to a small group of people who inhabit the mountain frontier between Nepal and Tibet. Small, but exceptionally hardy, most are farmers, but some are mountain tradesmen, accustomed from early youth to carrying heavy goods over the high passes of the Himalaya. For this reason they make superb expedition porters. But perhaps even more important than their strength and endurance on a Himalayan expedition is their remarkable temperament. They are a courageous and optimistic people, capable of great feats of heroism, and have a fine sense of humor and a genial tolerance for the ways of foreigners. From the outset, the Sherpas understood the seeming madness of risking life and limb to reach the summit of a mountain. Many of the Sherpas soon became competent mountaineers in their own right, and proved themselves climbing companions as skilled as any of the Swiss guides of the Golden Age. In the history of Himalayan mountaineering, the courage, devotion, and loyalty of the Sherpas have become legendary. On many expeditions, Sherpas have risked their own lives to save those of their employers. And on more than one tragic occasion, they have sacrificed their lives rather than abandon a "sahib" in trouble.

Sherpas made up the majority of the porters on the Everest expedition of 1924. Led by Colonel E. F. Norton, the expedition included some of the finest climbers of the day. Chief among them was a young man named George Leigh Mallory, who had taken part in both the 1921 and the 1922 expeditions. Mallory was a schoolteacher by profession, but had long been an ardent climber, and was well-known in mountaineering circles. All who knew him spoke of his overriding obsession with Everest. From the moment he first saw it, Everest became "his" mountain. Ultimately, the names of Mallory and Mount Everest were destined to become as closely linked in mountaineering legend as those of Edward Whymper and the Matterhorn.

Colonel Norton had worked out a careful plan for the 1924 attack on Everest. After several weeks of staged acclimatization, the party was to work in teams of two, the fittest men working without oxygen, the others with it. The assault was to be made, as before, via the North Col. The party established its base camp on the East Rongbuk Glacier on April 29, and began to prepare for the assault.

The first two attempts were defeated by savage blizzards. Each took weeks of grueling effort, and the men's energies were sorely depleted. But the monsoons were due to begin soon, and when they

The Sherpas, who live in the frontier region between Nepal and Tibet, are accustomed to carrying heavy loads at high altitudes—experience which prepared them well for the part they increasingly played in expeditions, first as skilled porters and then as fellow climbers with the foreigners.

Above: some of the members of the 1924 Everest expedition at the base camp. Standing, left to right, are Irvine, Mallory, Norton (leader), Odell, and MacDonald. Seated, left to right, Shebbeare, Bruce, Somervell, and Beetham.

Left: George Leigh Mallory, the most famous mountaineer of his day. His reason for climbing Everest—"because it is there"—whether he meant it as a serious remark or not, has become the classic rationale for mountaineering.

did, all hope of continuing would have to be abandoned. With time running out, there was nothing to do but strike again at once.

Mallory and Charles Bruce's son, Geoffrey Bruce, went up first and established a camp above the North Col at 25,000 feet. The next team, Norton and Somervell, took over from there. After establishing Camp VI, at 26,800 feet, they made a heroic effort to reach the summit without oxygen. At 28,000 feet, however, breathing became almost unbearably painful, and they were forced to turn back. It was clear that oxygen would have to be used in the ascent of the final 1,000 feet. The third and last assault team was to be Noel Odell and 22-year-old Andrew Irvine. Odell, however, had taken longer to acclimatize than the others, and was not fit enough to undertake the climb. Mallory, still very strong and more than ever determined to conquer "his" mountain, was chosen to take Odell's place.

Early on June 6, Mallory and Irvine, with 30-pound oxygen packs

strapped to their backs, left their companions at Camp IV, a little below the North Col, and set off for the summit. Odell stationed himself at Camp VI, about 3,000 feet below the summit, to watch for them. Mist obscured the upper reaches of the peak for most of the morning, but at 12:50 P.M., the swirling clouds parted, and he caught a glimpse of the two tiny figures. They were only 800 feet from the top and still edging their way forward along the ridge. It could not be long now, he thought, before they reached the summit.

Odell returned to Camp IV where, throughout the long moonlit night, he watched in vain for some sign of Mallory and Irvine. The next day he climbed alone to Camp V, spent the night there, and set off at dawn to search for them. Camp VI was just as he had seen it two days before—empty. He continued upward until he could go no farther, and at last, all hope gone, he returned to Camp VI, where he laid out the two climbers' abandoned blankets in the shape of a T.

Mallory, Irvine, and three Sherpas setting off on one of the stages of their assault on Everest. Mallory and Irvine disappeared on the last stage and their bodies were never found.

The ice-ax, which must have belonged to either Mallory or Irvine, which Wyn Harris found lying at 27,600 feet.

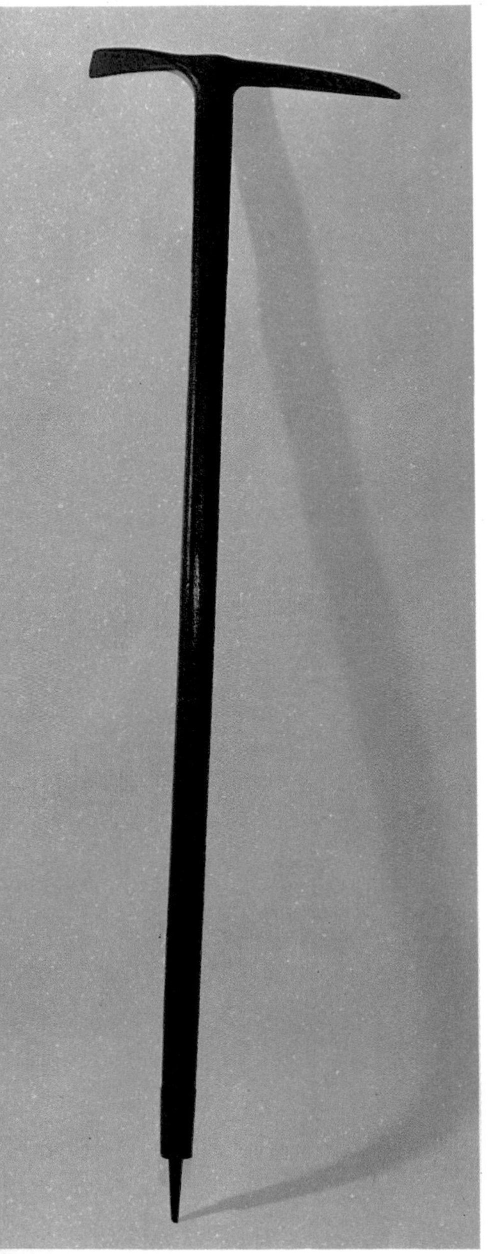

Far below, his teammates saw the signal through their telescopes and read its tragic message: "no trace." Ninety years later, an ice-ax was found 60 feet below the final crest at a height of about 27,600 feet. Whether it was Mallory's or Irvine's is not certain. All that is known is that somewhere, within yards of their cherished goal, the two men lost their footing and plummeted to their deaths.

There were to be no less than four more British attempts on Everest before World War II: in 1933, 1935, 1936, and 1938. All four were made from the North Col on the Tibetan side of the mountain. All failed, and all confirmed the crucial part played by the severe weather conditions on Everest's heights—above all, the howling winds that seemed bent either on tearing the climber from the side of the mountain or driving him back with sprays of blinding snow.

While the decade of the 1930's did not witness a successful assault on Everest, it did see heroic achievements elsewhere in the Himalaya. In 1931, a British expedition led by Frank Smythe conquered Kamet (25,447 feet), in northern India. And, in the next eight years, no less than nine peaks of over 22,000 feet were climbed by teams from Britain, Switzerland, Germany, Japan, and the United States.

American mountaineering in the Himalaya began with a daring expedition to a lofty Chinese mountain, Minya Konka. Situated near Tibet, in the Chinese province of Szechwan, the mountain is part of an outlying spur of the Himalayan system. In 1932, when the American expedition set out to explore it, little was known about Minya Konka. Some believed that it might even be higher than Everest itself. In fact, at 24,900 feet, Minya Konka proved to be about four-fifths of a mile lower than Everest. Nevertheless, this first ascent of the peak was an extremely arduous undertaking. Led by Richard Burdsall, the climb was made during late October in the very teeth of a savage storm. For this reason alone, the climb was a remarkable feat. More important still, it aroused American interest in Himalayan climbing.

The highest mountain scaled during the 1930's was northern India's Nanda Devi (25,645 feet), perhaps the most romantic of all Himalayan peaks. According to legend, it is the sanctuary of the goddess Nanda, who fled to its icy turrets to escape the machinations of an evil prince. Certainly the mountain strikingly resembles a fortress, for it is surrounded on all sides by a towering wall of peaks

Right: the letter Mallory sent down to Noel from the bivouac at 27,000 feet, making arrangements for Noel to film their progress across the skyline. The time should have read "8 A.M."

Dear Noel

We'll probably start early to-morrow (8th) in order to have clear weather. It won't be too early to start looking out for us either crossing the rockband under the pyramid or going up skyline at 8.0 p.m.

Yours ever

G. Mallory

During the 1930's many expeditions were mounted to other parts of the Himalaya. These climbers are members of the 1936 expedition led by Paul Bauer to Mount Siniolchu, called the most beautiful mountain in the world.

and ridges. Within the outer wall there is a second ring of mountains known as the Inner Sanctuary. This second ring was first seen in 1905 by Tom Longstaff who, in the course of exploring the region, climbed to the rim of the outer wall. Longstaff tried, and failed, to gain the Inner Sanctuary, but he did locate the only possible way in: the gorge of the Rishi Ganga River. Perilously steep, the crumbling rock walls of the gorge plunge thousands of feet down to the torrential waters below. The gorge itself is difficult enough to challenge the skills of the most expert mountaineer.

Left: a drawing made in 1851 by Henry Ambrose Oldfield of Nanda Devi, the sacred mountain. In legend it is the sanctuary of the Indian goddess Nanda.

Below: one of the mixed blessings of Himalayan climbing is the necessity for long approach marches to get to the mountains—but sometimes the march is through beautiful forests.

In 1934, a small party consisting of Eric Shipton, H. W. Tilman, and three Sherpas made their way through the magically beautiful forest region of the lower Himalayan valleys, and began a full-scale exploration of the Nanda Devi Ring. After five months of careful reconnoitering and hazardous climbing, they succeeded in forcing a passage through the Rishi Gorge and reached the Inner Sanctuary. Here they surveyed Nanda Devi's slopes from the secluded valleys at its base, and worked out possible routes to its summit. The party was too small to attempt an ascent of the mountain itself, but the groundwork was laid for a later expedition.

Two years later, an Anglo-American team, led jointly by a Welshman, T. Graham Brown, and an American, Dr. Charles Houston, set off to make the first ascent of Nanda Devi. Among the four Americans in the party was Arthur Emmons, who had taken part in the ascent of Minya Konka in 1932. Among the four Englishmen were Noel Odell, who had been on the tragic 1924 Everest expedition, and H. W. Tilman, who, with Shipton, had reconnoitered Nanda Devi in 1934. Ironically, Shipton himself was unable to join the expedition, because he was engaged in the 1936 attempt on Everest.

The climb was an exceptionally difficult one in many respects. Apart from the seasoned climber Pasang Kikuli, the Sherpas of the party were inexperienced. And when they were confronted by a difficult crossing of the Rishi Ganga, the majority of them flatly refused to go any farther. This left the party with a mere handful of porters to carry all the food and equipment necessary for the long siege on the mountain. The only solution was for each of the American and British members of the team to assume the role of carrier as well as climber. Even so, it took countless trips by both "sahibs" and Sherpas to bring everything through the gorge and up to the base camp at 15,000 feet.

By the time they had reached 21,000 feet, the party had suffered further setbacks. Frostbite, snow-blindness, and mountain sickness had forced two of the Americans and the two remaining Sherpas to drop out, and blizzards had halted the progress of the others time after time. But although there were now only six men left to make the final assault, and although the energies of these six were daily being drained by the work of ferrying up their supplies, the four Britons and two Americans were more determined than ever to succeed.

Above: Nanga Parbat, painted by A. D. MacCormick. The mountain has taken a special place in mountaineering history as one of the most dangerous peaks, because several expeditions met disaster on its slopes in the 1930's.

At last they reached 23,000 feet, and Odell and Houston were chosen to make the final assault. But the night before they were to set off, Houston was taken severely ill with food-poisoning. Tilman was chosen to take his place. He and Odell started for the summit at dawn the next day. The expedition carried no oxygen equipment, so the two men had to rely on their reserves of strength and on their determination to keep them going through the increasingly rarified air. Each step forward had to be followed by five or six deep breaths, and their progress was extremely slow. They ploughed through knee-deep powdery snow, ascended a steep ice-wall, and narrowly avoided being swept away by an avalanche. And then, at long last, they reached the final crest of the ridge and strode forward to the mountain's highest point. It was a moment of great triumph but, as Tilman wrote later, "After the first joy in victory came a feeling of sadness that the mountain had succumbed, that the proud head of the goddess was bowed."

But if Nanda Devi could be humbled, it seemed that another great Himalayan peak, Nanga Parbat, could not. In fact this 26,660-foot peak became notorious during the 1930's for the series of disasters which prevented party after party from reaching its summit.

Nanga Parbat is situated in northwest Kashmir, a few miles from the Indus River. Structurally, the mountain resembles Everest—one long major ascending ridge, with a minor peak halfway along. By far the most accessible approach to the summit is via the north face. But, because the ice and snow on the north face is liable to avalanche at frequent intervals, the route to the first snow ridge must be circuitous. This route has been described as "twice as high as the North Col [on Everest] climb, three times as dangerous, and four times as long in point of time." It was on Nanga Parbat that Albert F. Mummery, ignorant of the real problem of Himalayan climbing, lost his life in 1895.

In 1934, a large and highly professional German expedition, led by Willy Merkl, set off to master Nanga Parbat. Merkl had led

Right: the Sherpa Pasang Kikuli is helped back to camp, exhausted and frostbitten, after falling over an ice-wall in his descent from a higher camp during a raging blizzard. This was on the 1934 Nanga Parbat expedition.

another expedition to the mountain two years before, and was well acquainted with the immense difficulties of both the route and the weather conditions on the mountain. The 1934 expedition was rather badly organized, but under his vigorous leadership, it went very well in its early stages. After several weeks of steady climbing and camp-making, 5 Germans and 11 Sherpas reached the "Silver Saddle," a deep depression in the final ridge some 2,000 feet from the summit. Success seemed near at hand. Then, suddenly, the mountain seemed to lash out at the men with diabolical ferocity. A

Above: Willy Merkl, second from the right, leaving Munich in 1934 at the start of the journey to Nanga Parbat, the mountain he hoped to conquer, and on the slopes of which he perished.

Right: camp being set up by the 1937 Nanga Parbat expedition, with the tents sunk partially in the snow for extra protection. The camp was later completely obliterated by an avalanche that struck in the night, killing all 16 climbers who were sleeping there. The negative of this photograph was found when the camp was dug out by would-be rescuers.

raging storm swept down on them and imprisoned all 16 of the advance party in their tents. On the second day, although the blizzard had not let up, Merkl was forced to order a retreat. They were 4,000 feet above the next supply camp and their food was fast running out.

In the terrible few days that followed, all but 7 of the 16 members of the advance party perished in the attempt to reach the safety of the lower camp. Those who survived staggered into the camp one by one, hollow-eyed, frostbitten, and almost dead from exhaustion.

The plains of Katmandu, dominated by the Annapurna range of mountains. It was Annapurna itself which the 1950 French expedition resolved to conquer.

The support party from the lower camp made repeated, frantic efforts to locate those still on the mountain, but were beaten back each time by the storm. On one occasion they made out three tiny figures on the ridge high above them, and even thought they heard a far-off cry for help. Then the blizzard closed in once more and, weeping, they were forced to retreat. The last man to come down from the ridge alive was the Sherpa Ang Tsering. He had been with Merkl and another Sherpa, Gay-Lay, when Merkl collapsed. Gay-Lay had sent Ang Tsering ahead to try and reach the camp. He himself, he said, would remain with the fallen leader. And indeed he did remain, and perished with Merkl in the storm.

German mountaineers were determined to avenge the tragic deaths of their compatriots by conquering this deadly mountain. But in 1937, when the next German expedition made an assault on the mountain, another awesome disaster occurred. In the middle of the night of June 14, a sudden and tremendous avalanche shook the mountain and thundered down on the 7 Germans and 9 Sherpas asleep in their tents. All 16 perished.

Two more German expeditions (one of them led by the great climber Paul Bauer) tried and failed, to reach Nanga Parbat's summit in the late 1930's. But these repeated assaults on the peak had made Nanga Parbat as much "Germany's mountain" as Everest, after many English expeditions, had become "Britain's mountain." And, ultimately, in the great period of Himalayan mountaineering that began after World War II, it was to be a Briton who conquered Everest, and a German who conquered Nanga Parbat. But even before these two great peaks were mastered, another Himalayan monarch—the great Annapurna—was to be the site of a thrilling and historic conquest.

There are only 14 mountains in the world over 26,000 feet high, and Annapurna, in north-central Nepal, is eleventh on this list of giants. In 1950, a French expedition, led by Maurice Herzog, traveled to the Himalaya with the intention of climbing either Annapurna or Dhaulagiri (which at 26,810 feet, is the seventh highest of the mighty 14). After lengthy reconnaissance, they chose to make their assault on Annapurna (26,504 feet).

Louis Lachenal, suffering badly from oxygen starvation and frostbite, is helped down the slopes of Annapurna, exhausted but victorious. Although the descent was harrowing, Lachenal has since said that he did not regret it.

The early stages of the climb went well, and, on June 3, 1950, Herzog set off with Louis Lachenal for the top. They had no oxygen equipment and, as they climbed steadily higher, they had to fight off wave after wave of giddiness and loss of concentration. But they kept struggling forward, and at last, gasping and exhausted, they gained the topmost point. Here they planted the French flag and took pictures of each other. Then they started back down. As they did so, Herzog, his senses numbed by severe oxygen deprivation, somehow managed to lose his gloves.

The loss of Herzog's gloves proved to be only the first of a series of castastrophes that nearly turned triumph into tragedy. Herzog and Lachenal, together with Lionel Terray and Gaston Rébuffat (who had waited for them at the highest camp), were caught in a howling blizzard as they started down together. They were unable to find the next camp, and had to spend the night in a shallow crevasse. Desperately tired but fearful of freezing to death in their sleep, the four huddled together and tried to warm their feet by putting them in their rucksacks. In the morning, the boots they had taken off were buried in the snow. They searched frantically for them, clawing through the snow on their hands and knees, but it took an hour to locate all four pairs—an hour that sealed the fate of the summit team's already badly frostbitten feet.

Miraculously, the four men, by now snowblind as well as frostbitten and pitifully weak, were found later in the day by a rescue party from below. With their teammates' help, they somehow managed to stagger down to the safety of the next camp. There, the expedition doctor gave Herzog and Lachenal massive injections of novaine acetychlorodine to stimulate the flow of blood in their frostbitten limbs. Both men were carried on the backs of the party's devoted Sherpas all the way back to India. There, after a series of operations—in which all of Herzog's fingers and some of both his and Lachenal's toes had to be amputated—the two fearless conquerors of Annapurna slowly recovered their health.

It was a terrible price to pay for victory, but neither Herzog nor Lachenal regretted it. They had become the first men to master a peak over 26,000 feet high, and it was a triumph of historic proportions. It was their climb that launched a whole new era in the history of Himalayan mountaineering, an era which has come to be called "The New Golden Age."

The first of the giants conquered. Maurice Herzog, leader of the 1950 expedition that climbed Annapurna, stands at the summit at the moment of victory, photographed by his companion, Louis Lachenal. They were the first to master a peak over 26,000 feet high, and their achievement began the New Golden Age of climbing.

The New Golden Age

10

Left: the immensity of the Himalayan challenge is dramatically demonstrated by this picture of climbers moving determinedly past an enormous chasm in the Western Cwm, the long, narrow ice valley which proved to offer the best route to the summit of Everest.

That the 1950 ascent of Annapurna had indeed been the herald of great things to come was emphatically confirmed on a warm spring day three years later. On that day, May 29, 1953, the world reverberated with the breathtaking news that Mount Everest had been conquered.

The story of the conquest of Everest, perhaps the most historic event in mountaineering history, goes back to the years immediately following World War II, after Nepal agreed in 1947 to open its frontiers to foreign expeditions. This change in Nepal's policy made it possible for mountaineers to begin exploration of the southern approach to the mountain. In 1951, a British expedition led by Eric Shipton made a thorough reconnaissance of this approach, and located what was to prove the most practical route to the summit. This is the opening, in the *western* ridge of the mountain, through which the vast Khumbu Glacier descends. Farther up, the glacier becomes a steep wall of ice. And at the top of this icefall is a deep crevasse, which separates it from a long, narrow, ice-filled valley called the Western Cwm. At the head of this valley is another ridge, with the summit of Everest at one end, and the summits of its sister peaks, Lhotse I and II, at the other. In between, where the ridge sinks down, is the South Col. The plan of attack suggested by Shipton's party was to climb the Khumbu Icefall and cross the

Below: the British climber Eric Shipton suggested that the best route up Everest was through the Khumbu Glacier, up the Icefall, and across the crevasse to the Western Cwm. These porters were an essential part of the 1953 expedition, which followed that exact route.

Above: Raymond Lambert with Tenzing Norgay. They climbed to 750 feet below the summit before being forced back on the 1952 Swiss attempt. Below: John Hunt, the brilliant leader and organizer who led the successful British assault on Everest. His fine leadership helped produce the victory.

crevasse to the Western Cwm; to continue up the Cwm to Everest's southeast ridge; to attain the South Col from that ridge; and, from the South Col, to stage a final assault directly up to Everest's summit.

In 1952, two successive Swiss expeditions attempted to reach the summit by way of this southern route. On the first attempt, two of the party, Raymond Lambert and the skilled Sherpa climber Tenzing Norgay, came within 750 feet of the summit before being forced to retreat by the paralyzing effects of high altitude. They were equipped with oxygen cylinders, but the effort required to manipulate the flow of air was almost as energy-consuming as climbing without the aid of oxygen. Nonetheless, they had succeeded in establishing a new height record—and this, after spending a sleepless night at 27,500 feet, without sleeping-bags or a stove to ward off the sub-zero cold.

Tenzing and Lambert attempted the final assault again on the second Swiss expedition later that year. Once more, they were defeated by the wind, the cold, and the rarified atmosphere of the heights. But despite their defeat, the Swiss expedition had achieved two important things. First, it had carried out the heroic chore of forging the route. Second, it had demonstrated that even heavily laden porters could make the ascent by this route as far as the slopes directly below the South Col.

In 1953, a British expedition set off to tackle the great peak. In a sense it was a do-or-die mission, for strong Swiss and French teams were already being assembled for Everest assaults in 1954 and 1955. If the British were ever to master "their" mountain, it must be now. Heading the 1953 team was Colonel John Hunt, a man already widely known for his exceptional powers of leadership and organization. Among the 13 other members of the party were three scientists, Tom Bourdillon, Michael Westmacott, and George Band; three doctors, Charles Evans, Michael Ward, and Griffith Pugh; two teachers, Wilfrid Noyce and the New Zealander George Lowe; a professional beekeeper, Edmund Hillary (also from New Zealand); an army officer Charles Wylie; a travel agent, Alfred Gregory; a photographer, Tom Stobart; and the Sherpa *sirdar* or headman, Tenzing Norgay, now a full-fledged expedition member.

As on all major climbs, the ascent party was supported by an army of porters, and the assault had to be methodically prepared for by the establishment of supply depots from the Base Camp, at 18,000 feet, to Camp VIII, on the South Col at 26,000 feet. Hunt brought the expedition up in easy stages, giving both climbers and porters ample time to acclimatize as they progressed from camp to camp. The route up the Khumbu Icefall proved particularly arduous, a veritable obstacle course of chasms and *séracs* (ice-pillars), which soon acquired such nicknames as Hellfire Alley and the Atom Bomb area. As far as the head of the Western Cwm, Hunt followed the route pioneered by the Swiss. But from there, he forged a different route, via the Lhotse Glacier, to the South Col. It was a more indirect approach, but far safer. When Camp VIII had been set up on the Col, two final assault parties were chosen; the first to be Bourdillon and Evans, the second, Hillary and Tenzing.

On May 26, the first pair set off early, and by early afternoon were in sight of the final crest. But here, close as they were to success, the two were forced to turn back by insufficient reserves of oxygen. They were using a new type of oxygen apparatus designed specifically for the expedition. But although it was vastly superior to anything used before, it was still prone to develop defects.

On May 27, a high wind sprang up and storm clouds scudded across the sky. Hillary and Tenzing, poised for their attack on the summit, feared that the weather might close in and put an end to their hopes. But on May 28, the weather suddenly cleared, and they started off. Previously, bivouac equipment had been taken up to a height of 27,900 feet, and it was here that Tenzing and Hillary spent the night. Their tent was pitched on a narrow ledge hacked in the steep slope of the ice-covered ridge. They slept only fitfully, for at that height sleep was only possible with the use of oxygen, and their precious supply had to be conserved for the next day's effort.

The morning dawned bright and clear, and they set off at 6:30 A.M. The surface of the snow on the ridge before them was treacherous, and they were frequently forced off the crest itself by massive cornices of snow. When this happened, they had to inch their way along the sheer ice-wall of the ridge until they had

Part of the plan for the conquest of Everest included a higher base camp than ever before, but this meant long grueling climbs for men burdened with supplies, bringing them up through the hazards of the Icefall.

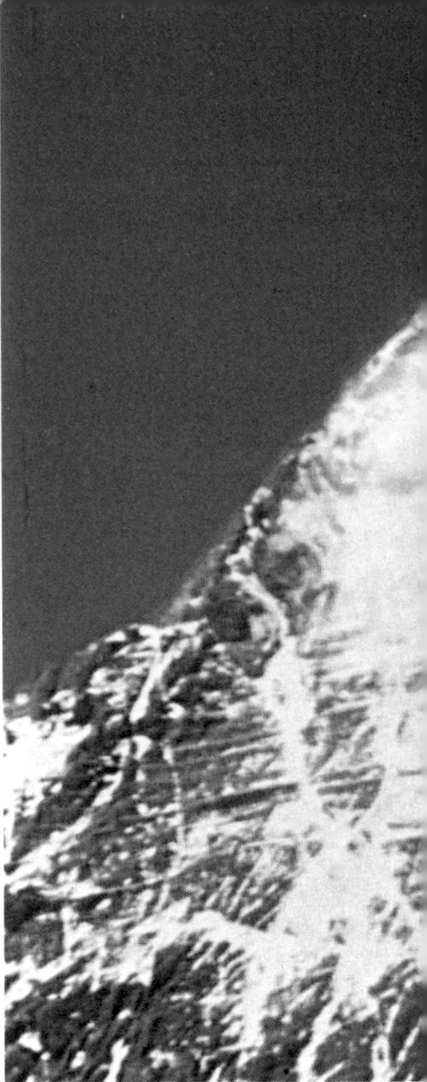

Hillary checks over Tenzing's oxygen equipment as they set out on the last leg of the climb to be first men to stand at the top of the world. Hillary later said he spent much of the climb calculating and recalculating what their oxygen needs would be.

passed the difficult point on the crest. At one point, the oxygen in their cylinders froze up, but they succeeded in getting it started again. As Hillary wrote later, his thoughts were preoccupied with their ever-dwindling supply of oxygen during the whole of the climb: would they have enough, he wondered with increasing anxiety, to get them there *and* back?

On and on they struggled, gaining only one foot per minute. Suddenly there loomed before them a 40-foot pinnacle of rock. One of its sides was a continuation of the sheer wall of the ridge, and from the other there swept outward a huge wing of snow. For a moment, it seemed that this staring face of rock was going to prove one obstacle too many. But perhaps there *was* a way past it. Hillary stepped forward and wedged himself into the narrow gap between the rock and the treacherous white cornice. Slowly, he began hauling himself up. It was like climbing a chimney, one side of which was liable to fall away at any moment. Fortunately, it held until he could force his way to the top and throw down a rope for Tenzing.

It was not long after overcoming this obstacle that the two found themselves taking their final steps to the summit. There, at the top

The south summit, the last obstacle for Hillary and Tenzing. It took them $2\frac{1}{2}$ hours to climb the last 400 feet from there to the summit of Everest.

of the world, they heartily congratulated each other. After resting briefly, they took photographs, and dug a small hole in the snow in which they placed two objects: a little crucifix given by Hunt to Hillary to leave at the summit, and a packet of chocolate brought by Tenzing as a gift to the Buddhist gods.

Their stay at the top of Everest lasted only 15 minutes. It was essential to return before their oxygen ran out. By 2 P.M. they were back at their final bivouac. And late that afternoon they reached the lower camp, where they were met by the support party.

When Hunt, at a still-lower camp, first saw the party of descending climbers, he mistook their wearied postures as a sign of failure. Then spotting him, the men raised their ice-axes, and pointed toward the summit. As they did so, Hunt realized the wonderful truth. "Far from failure," he wrote later, "this was IT. They had made it!"

Victory on Everest was the result of many things: the fine equipment, from sleeping-bags to oxygen systems; the invaluable information about the route provided by the earlier expeditions; the tireless work of the Sherpa porters; the brilliant leadership of John Hunt; and finally, the courage, determination, and teamwork of the

climbers themselves. Reaching the top was a magnificent achievement in itself, but it was all the greater for being accomplished without loss of life or limb. For all these reasons, the first ascent of Everest remains unparalleled in the history of mountaineering.

Just 34 days after the British conquest of Everest, another historic Himalayan ascent took place on Nanga Parbat (26,660 feet). Victory over this, "the killer mountain," was of particular importance to Germany. Of the 31 lives Nanga Parbat had claimed between 1895 and 1950, 26 of them had been lost in the course of German attempts on the peak. There burned in all German climbers a desire to avenge these tragic deaths by mastering the mountain. And, in 1953, a large and highly professional German party set out to do just that. The expedition was led by Dr. Karl Herrligkoffer, the stepbrother of Willy Merkl who had perished in the 1934 assault on the mountain. Among the party was a man named Hermann Buhl, an Austrian mountaineer already well-known for his daring solo climbs.

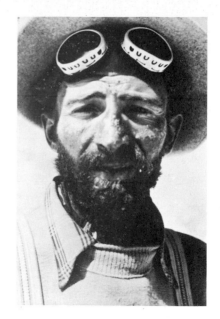

Above: Hermann Buhl after his solo climb to Nanga Parbat's summit, his face showing the exhaustion and strain of his solitary climb. He had been scheduled to climb with Otto Kempter, but they had a disagreement about the time to start, and Buhl went on alone.

The assault was launched with methodical care, and it took eight weeks for the party to reach a point below the famous "Silver Saddle" on the ridge leading to the summit. Here, a team of two men was chosen to make the final ascent: Hermann Buhl and Otto Kempter. Their plan was to start off at 3 A.M., but soon after midnight Buhl was up and anxious to be off. There was an argument, and Buhl set off alone. Kempter attempted to catch up with him later, but soon gave up, exhausted. Meanwhile, Buhl was making rapid progress high above the saddle on the crystalline surface of the steep east face of the mountain. Noon came and went, and still he climbed, driving himself forward hour after hour. He reached the summit at 7 P.M., almost at the end of his strength. Nevertheless, he forced himself to take photographs as proof of his triumph before starting back down in the direction of the camp. But already the sun was going down, and Buhl had to seek shelter on the mountainside—without tent or sleeping-bag—in sub-zero weather. Miraculously, he not only survived that terrible night in the open, but managed, still completely alone, to make his way down to the camp the following day. He was severely frostbitten and almost dead from exhaustion, but he had conquered Nanga Parbat—and done it *alone*.

The year 1953 was to witness yet another feat of human daring and endurance—but it was a feat of a very different kind from Buhl's. This time, the objective was Mount Godwin Austen—at

Left: Tensing Norgay stands truimphant, 29,028 feet above sea level, on the top of Mount Everest, photographed by Edmund Hillary. They reached the top at 11:30 A.M. on May 29, 1953.

Right: Nanga Parbat, the dreaded killer mountain, which was finally conquered by the 1953 expedition led by Dr. Karl Herrligkoffer. Hermann Buhl, climbing alone, succeeded in reaching the top.

28,250 feet, the world's second highest mountain. First attempted in 1909 by the Duke of the Abruzzi, it had been the subject of two assaults in the 1930's, both of them by Americans. The first, in 1938, under the leadership of Dr. Charles Houston, had made a careful reconnaisance of the Abruzzi Ridge and confirmed the practicality of this southeast route to the summit. The entire expedition had been well-planned and carried out with care.

The second American venture, which took place a year later, in 1939, was badly organized and ended in disaster. High on the Abruzzi Ridge, one of the climbers, Dudley Wolfe, fell seriously ill. Believing that a party from lower down the ridge was on its way up and would look after the ailing man, the ascent leader, Fritz Wiessner, and one Sherpa, left him in the high camp and continued with the climb. But as a result of a misunderstanding, no one did come up from the lower camp, and the sick man remained alone for more than a week. By the time the mistake was realized, no member of the party was fit enough to attempt a rescue. The brave Sherpa Pasang Kikuli—a veteran of many a Himalayan climb, including Nanga Parbat and Nanda Devi—volunteered to bring Wolfe down. But the attempt ended in tragedy. Pasang Kikuli and two other Sherpas died with Wolfe in a blizzard high up on the mountain.

In 1953, Dr. Houston led another assault on Godwin Austen with six Americans, Robert Bates, George Bell, Robert Craig, Arthur Gilkey, Dee Molenaar, and Peter Schoening, and an English climber, Tony Streather. The ascent up the steep rise of the Abruzzi Ridge took the party almost two months of hard climbing, and they

Above: a climber negotiates a very difficult wall of sheer ice—ignoring the breathtaking view—on Godwin Austen. He was a member of the 1938 team led by Charles Houston.
Below: in 1953 Houston again led an assault on Godwin Austen. Here he crosses a rope bridge with some of the porters on the way to the expedition base camp.

Right: among the Sherpas on Houston's 1938 expedition was Pasang Kikuli, third from the right in this group photograph taken on the expedition. He was killed the next year while helping the sick Dudley Wolfe down.

had reached only 25,500 feet when they were struck by a week-long storm. When the weather finally improved, young Gilkey was found to be suffering from thrombo-phlebitis. He had a blood-clot in his leg and could not walk. He had to be brought down the mountain somehow, and as quickly as possible, if his life were to be saved. The other men improvised a stretcher for him and began the extremely hazardous task of lowering the helpless man down the sheer, ice-encrusted wall of the ridge. Gilkey weighed 185 pounds, and it took the efforts of all seven of the other men to manoeuver the stretcher on which he lay. Two went ahead to find the route; two held the projecting ends of the stretcher; two more pulled back on the ropes from which the stretcher was suspended; and one served as a relay to pass on the shouted messages of the pathfinders below tc the men steering and holding the stretcher above.

The going became slower and more difficult as the day wore on. The weather worsened, the slope became ever more perilously steep, and the men grew terribly weary. Suddenly, Bell slipped and fell, dragging Streather, to whom he was roped, with him. As they hurtled downward, their rope tangled with the one connecting Houston and Bates, who were torn off the mountain after their companions. In turn, Bates and Houston's rope tangled with the one linking Molenaar to Gilkey and Schoening. Molenaar, too, was dragged down, but Schoening, who had driven his ax deep into the ice-wall, was not. Miraculously, his ax held, and so did the rope which attached it to him and Gilkey. The lives of five men depended on Schoening, and somehow, he was able to hang on until the others—dazed and injured, but alive—could work their way back onto the face. They managed to lash Gilkey to the mountainside, and then stationed themselves on a ledge a few hundred feet away to wait for morning. When dawn came, they discovered to their horror that Gilkey had been swept away by an avalanche during the night. Racked with exhaustion, and in great pain from the injuries they had suffered in the fall, the seven survivors somehow made their way down the mountain. They had not succeeded in conquering Mount Godwin Austen, but they had willingly risked their lives—and almost lost them—to save a dying companion.

Above: Camp VIII, 25,500 feet up on Godwin Austen, where the team was trapped for 7 days by a storm.
Below: Charles S. Houston, who was the leader of the ill-starred 1953 attempt to conquer Godwin Austen.

The following year, the peak was scaled by an Italian party under the leadership of Ardito Desio. Again the ascent was made up the Abruzzi Ridge, again the ascent was a long and hazardous one, and again a man lost his life. One of the climbers, Mario Puchoz, died of pneumonia before he could be brought down to safety.

The year 1955 saw the ascent of yet another of the Himalayan giants that had defied previous attempts. This was Kanchenjunga (28,168 feet), third among the world's highest mountains after Everest and Godwin Austen. Situated on the Sikkim-Nepal border, Kanchenjunga is another of the Himalayan peaks deemed sacred by the people of the highlands, and its name means "The Five Treasures of the Snow." But from the mountaineer's point of view, Kanchenjunga's name might more appropriately be rendered as "The Five Terrors of the Snow," for its most notorious characteristics are its frequent blizzards and avalanches, and its perilous glaciers, icefalls, and séracs. These factors make Kanchenjunga one of the hardest of all the Himalayan peaks to climb. Before the 1955 assault, no fewer than seven expeditions were defeated by the mountain. The two most notable of these attempts were made by German teams in 1929 and 1931. Both were led by the brilliant climber Paul Bauer and both were carried out in the teeth of the worst conditions Kanchenjunga can offer: howling blizzards, incessant avalanches, and diabolically shifting snow surfaces. These savage conditions, despite the heroic, almost superhuman efforts made by Bauer and his teammates, defeated both expeditions a few thousand feet below the summit.

When, under the leadership of Charles Evans, a British expedition set off to conquer Kanchenjunga in 1955, it went armed with the most advanced of modern climbing equipment: aerial reconnaissance photographs of the mountain; radio-relay systems; and three kinds of oxygen apparatus (open-circuit, closed-circuit and a type for use during sleep). This equipment—and the high degree of skill and determination displayed by the team members—enabled

Left: members of the 1955 British expedition to Kanchenjunga, which approached within a few feet of the summit, and then descended. The actual topmost point was left untouched as Charles Evans, the expedition leader, had promised the ruler of Sikkim. The people of Sikkim hold the mountain to be the dwelling place of a deity.

Above: Makalu I (27,824 feet), a near neighbor of Mount Everest. Makalu was first climbed in 1955 by the French.

the party to ascend the difficult lower slopes of the mountain in record time. Nevertheless, the climb from the Yalung Glacier, at the base of the southwest face, to the giant snowfield called the Great Shelf, took them more than six weeks.

Just above the Great Shelf, at a height of about 26,000 feet, they established their last camp. From here, on the morning of May 25, the final ascent pair set off for the summit. They were George Band, who, like Charles Evans, had been in the 1953 Everest expedition, and Joe Brown, the finest ice- and rock-climber of his generation. He and Evans needed all their skill and experience to traverse the difficult approach that brought them at last to within a few feet of the summit. And here they stopped and went back down. Why, after so many weeks of effort, did they turn their backs on the summit when it was within their reach? The answer lies in a promise given by Charles Evans to the ruler of Sikkim before the expedition set out. Knowing that the people of Sikkim believed the summit of the mountain to be the dwelling-place of a deity, Evans gave his word that neither he nor any of his party would desecrate the sanctuary. Thus, despite the men's success in overcoming Kanchenjunga's many challenges, they left the mountain without ever having reached its topmost point. Bare of either footsteps, flags, or other symbols of human conquest, Kanchenjunga's summit remained as virgin after their ascent as it had been since it first reared its glittering head, thousands of years ago.

But such was not the case with 13 others of the Himalayan giants. Already, five of their summits had borne—for however brief a time—the imprint of a climber's crampons. These five were Annapurna,

Left: the treacherous lower reaches of the Khumbu Glacier. During the United States expedition in 1963, one of the climbers, John Breitenbach, was killed in the Khumbu Icefall.

Above: Jim Whittaker and Nawang Gombu, two of the six men that the American expedition in 1963 put on the summit of Everest. The most spectacular result of the expedition was the first-ever Himalayan traverse, when Thomas Hornbein and William Unsoeld climbed the summit by way of the west ridge and descended by the South Col route.

Everest, Nanga Parbat, Godwin Austen, and Cho Oyu (26,867 feet), which was conquered by an Austrian team in 1954. Makalu I (27,824 feet), near neighbor of Everest, was climbed by a French party in 1955. In 1956 there were three first ascents of peaks over 26,000 feet high: Manaslu (26,658 feet), by a Japanese team; Gasherbrum II (26,450 feet), by an Austrian team; and Lhotse I (27,890 feet), by a Swiss team. The Swiss expedition, led by Albert Eggler, followed up their triumph on Lhotse (until then the highest unscaled peak in the world) by making *two* ascents of Everest via the South Col the same season. In 1957, Broad Peak (26,414 feet) was climbed by an Austrian party that included Hermann Buhl, the conqueror of Nanga Parbat, and Gasherbrum I (26,470 feet) was scaled by an American team under the leadership of Nicholas Clinch. A Swiss team mastered Annapurna's near neighbor, Dhaulagiri (26,810 feet) in 1960. The lowliest of the mighty 14, Gosainthan (26,291 feet) was conquered in 1964.

When all 14 of the greatest Himalayan peaks, as well as many of the lesser ones, had been scaled, the search for fresh challenges led inevitably to the forging of new routes. Two of the most exciting of these "new route" ascents were the American conquest of Everest by the west ridge in 1963, and the British conquest of Annapurna by the south face in 1970.

The American objective in the 1963 assault on Everest was nothing less than the traverse of the highest point on earth. The plan was to ascend by the west ridge—a first in itself—and then to descend by way of the traditional South Col route. The party, led by Norman G. Dyhrenfurth, was some 20 men strong, and it required the concerted efforts of the whole team to establish the series of camps along the ridge from which the traverse was to be made.

Tragedy struck early in the assault, when young John Breitenbach was killed by a huge block of falling ice in the Khumbu Icefall. Tragedy almost struck again two months later at 25,500 feet, when the final ascent pair, Thomas F. Hornbein and William F. Unsoeld, with the members of the support team, were camped on a ledge of snow jutting out from the west ridge. In the middle of the night a fierce wind blew up. The gale tugged and pulled at the tents, and at last tore them from their moorings. The tents—with six men still inside—were blown to the very brink of the ice-ledge where, by a miracle, they were stopped by a trough of snow.

Safe, but severely shaken, the party was forced to descend to the camp below. But three days later they were back once more, high on the west ridge. From a camp at 27,250 feet, Hornbein and Unsoeld set out for the summit at 6:30 A.M. on May 22. Twelve hours of unceasing effort in a fiercely cold wind brought them to the top of Everest. There to greet them was the American flag planted by two other members of the expedition—James W. Whittaker and the Sherpa Nawang Gombu—who had reached the summit by the South Col route three weeks before. The same flag, a bit frayed, but still flying bravely, had greeted two other climbers, Luther G. Jerstad and Barry C. Bishop, a mere three hours before Hornbein and Unsoeld reached the top. Like Whittaker and Gombu, Jerstad and Bishop had made the ascent by the South Col route. They were now on their way down, and Unsoeld and Hornbein were able to follow their footsteps for a time.

For the west ridgers, of course, the return by the South Col route was a journey into the unknown. Again and again they lost the tracks they were following and, as darkness closed in, the two men found themselves floundering in a feathery gray world, unsure of their direction. They began to call for help, hoping that they would be heard by members of the support team from Camp VI. At last, miraculously, they heard answering shouts from below. For two

The south face of Annapurna, among the most formidable rock faces in the world, culminating in a wall of ice and rock 12,000 feet high. It was this which the 1970 British expedition, led by Chris Bonington, set out to conquer.

hours, guided by these shouts, they toiled downward in the dark. When they reached the two dim figures waiting for them below, they were astonished to discover that they were Jerstad and Bishop!

All four climbers were by now exhausted and their oxygen supply was dangerously low. Still they pressed on, hour after hour, until they could go no farther. At 12:30 A.M. they found a level place in the ridge and settled down to wait for morning. They had no tent, no sleeping-bags, no food or drink—and no more oxygen. The temperature was −18°F. and they were still above 28,000 feet. Never before had any man remained in the open at that height and

lived to tell the tale. And, had the usual fierce Everest wind been blowing, they would certainly have perished. But luck was with them. The wind died away, and at dawn, after a calm, starlit night, the four men found themselves still alive and still able to move. Two hours after they began to stumble downward again, they were found by the support team and taken to the camp below.

Few expeditions have achieved such a spectacular series of triumphs as did the American Everest team of 1963. Not only did the team accomplish the first west ridge ascent and the first traverse of Everest, but it also managed to put no less than six climbers on the summit, four of whom broke all previous records by surviving a night in the open, without camping gear or oxygen, at 28,000 feet.

The goal of the 1970 British expedition to Annapurna was to

Dougal Haston and Don Whillans on Annapurna. While they were searching for a suitable camp site for the highest camp, the weather suddenly cleared, revealing the summit. They decided to try for the top, although they were unroped and not equipped with oxygen.

achieve the first conquest of the peak by the sheer south face. Led by Chris Bonington, the team consisted of 11 exceptionally skilled climbers. (Tragically, one of them, Ian Clough, was to be killed by a falling ice pillar at the very end of the expedition.)

The south face of Annapurna is one of the most formidable rock faces in the world. Its final 12,000 feet consists of a wall of ice and rock that soars almost vertically to the summit. The British team, like the American team on Everest, had to battle against severe winds most of the way up. Camp VI was established at 24,000 feet. At dawn on May 21, Don Whillans and Dougal Haston set off to reconnoiter a site for Camp VII. The weather cleared and they could see the summit. It was still early, and so they decided to make a try for it. Unroped, and without oxygen, they inched their way up and past the final 50 feet of almost vertical ice-glazed rock. Unbelievably, they stood at last on Annapurna's summit.

When Everest was climed in 1953, much of the nonmountaineering public thought that there would be nothing left for climbers to do. Just how wrong they were was shown in the period of spectacular Himalayan climbs that followed. Now, with the great peaks climbed, mountaineers have begun forging new routes that make more and more difficult demands on their skill and endurance.

The recent Everest expeditions have demonstrated clearly that skill is not enough, however. Even expeditions made up of the finest individual climbers have failed because of haphazard organization, personality clashes among the climbers, and relentlessly bad weather. In 1971, a large international expedition attacked the southwest face of Everest, which has never been climbed. Terrible storms raked the mountain: in one of them Harsh Bahuguna of India was trapped and died. Food ran low, and there were not enough Sherpas to assist in moving supplies higher. While controversy raged among the climbers about which route to pursue, Whillans and Haston—working together again, and supported by Reizo Ito and Naomi Uemura of Japan—went within about 165 feet of the summit of the southwest face. They had to retreat because the expedition could not give them adequate support. The next year a mainly German expedition failed to get any higher on the same route, defeated by lack of adequate organization and planning, and personal rivalries between the climbers. In the post-monsoon season of 1972, Chris Bonington led another British expedition onto the southwest face. They managed to reach 27,000 feet, but appalling storms and cold plagued them. They were unable to reach the summit, and gave up the attempt in the face of approaching winter.

So the challenges remain: Everest's tempting southwest face, hundreds of other unscaled peaks in the Himalaya and elsewhere, thousands of still-undreamed-of routes to find. Like his predecessors, a mountaineer today finds the need to climb as hard to explain as to deny. He climbs for adventure, for exploration, for conquest. Most of all, his final, compelling reason for climbing is simply his deep, abiding love for the mountains themselves.

Acknowledgments

Courtesy Alaska Historical Society Library 239; Aldus Archives 181, 188, 197(B), 202, 203(B), 271(L); Alex Photography 221; The Alpine Club, London 196, 213; The Alpine Club, London/Photo John Webb © Aldus Books 184(L)(R), 186, 193(B), 199(L), 200, 226(B), 290, 294; The American K2 Expedition (1953) 311(B), 312(T)(B); Archiv Deutsche Himalaja Stiftung, München/courtesy Paul Bauer 291(B), 295; Bavaria Verlag, München 182(R), 228(L)(R), 263; Martin Conway, *Climbing in the Karakorann Himalayas*, Ernest Benn Ltd., London 275(B); Bibliothèque Publique et Universitaire, Geneva 189; Courtesy Monsieur Pierre Bourrit/Photo Borel-Boissonnas 185; Musée d'Art et d'Histoire, Geneva (Collection La Foundation Gottfried Keller)/Photo Borel Boissonnas 175; Reproduced by permission of the Trustees of the British Museum 166; British Museum (Natural History)/Photo Michael Holford © Aldus Books 177; Brown Brothers 238(R), 241(R), 242(T); Camera Press 264, 265; J. Allan Cash 244; Photo Riccardo Cassin 242(B), 242–43, 243(R); Photo John Cleare 217(L)(R), 219(B), 223(B); *Daily Telegraph* Colour Library 169, 212, 219(T), 222(B), 222–23, 252(T)(B), 256–57, 256 (L); Photo Glen Denny 248–49; Deutsches Institut fur Auslandsforschung, München 309(T); Photo C. M. Dixon 214–15; Photo Norman Dyhrenfurth 315; Fédération Francaise de la Montagne, Paris 301; Photo George Fisher 198, 214(L); Photo Harrison Forman 309(B); Museum zu Allerhelligen, Schaffhausen/courtesy Orell Füssli Verlag, Zürich 174(L); Universitatsbibliothek, Erlangen/courtesy Orell Füssli Verlag, Zürich 174(R); Geographical Projects Limited, London 187, 229, 246, 260, 278; Gernsheim Collection, Humanities Research Center, The University of Texas at Austin 193 (T); Dr. Georg Gerster 170, 235; Photo Alfred Gregory 302, 303, 305, 307, 314; Belmore Browne, *The Conquest of Mt. McKinley*, Houghton Mifflin Company, Boston, Mass. 241(L); Photo Charles S. Houston 310, 311(T); Reproduced by courtesy of India Office Library and Records, London 272, 242(T); Reproduced by courtesy of India Office Library and Records, London/Photo R. B. Fleming © Aldus Books 268, 269, 273(T)(B), 275(T); Instituto Photographia Alpina V. Sella, San Gerolamo 210–11, 231(T)(B); Photo by Peter Larsen, A.R.P.S., F.R.G.S. 251, 267; Magdalen College, Oxford 199 (R), 236–37; Mansell Collection 234; Courtesy Arnoldo Mondadori Ltd. 220, 232, 289; The Mount Everest Foundation 304(B), 306, 308, 313(L)(R); The Mount Everest Foundation (Annapurna South Face Expedition, 1970) 317, 318, 320; Photo Josef Muench 248(T); Musée d'Histoire des Sciences, Geneva 182(L), 183; National Portrait Gallery, London 197(T); Courtesy Captain John Noel 282, 284, 285, 288(T)(B), 289, 291(T), 292(B); By courtesy of Captain Peter Norton 194, 195; Novosti 224, 226–27(T), 227(B); Österreichische Galerie, Vienna/Photo Erwin Meyer 191; *Paris Match*/Photo Ichac 299; Photoworld 261; Picturepoint, London 298; Galleria Borghese, Rome/Photo Mauro Pucciarelli 173; Museo Navale, La Spezia/Photo Mauro Pucciarelli 280(B); Palazzo dei Conservatori/Photo Mauro Pucciarelli 172; Ronan Picture Library 176; Royal Geographical Society 245, 257, 271(R), 277; Royal Geographical Society/Photo John Webb © Aldus Books 225, 253, 254, 259(L)(R), 270, 274, 276, 280(T), 281, 286; Photo Emil Schulthess 233; Schweizerische PTT Museum, Bern 179, 208, 209, 230; Swiss Foundation for Alpine Research, Zürich 304(T); Swiss National Tourist Office, London 218; Three Lions, Inc. 238(L); Ullstein GMBH/Bilderdienst 296, 297; Universitätsbibliothek, Erlangen-Nürnberg 216(T)(B); Victoria & Albert Museum, London/Photo John Webb © Aldus Books 171, 192; Bradford Washburn 240(L)(R), 247; Ian Yeomans/Susan Griggs Agency 203(T), 204, 205, 206(L)(R), 207(T)(B); Zentrale Farbbild Agentur, Düsseldorf 168, 201, 250, 258.

Left: the 1970 Annapurna expedition was an example of modern mountaineering—showing that even after the highest peaks have been conquered, there are challenges remaining to the dedicated mountaineer. Here Chris Bonington works his way slowly up Annapurna's south face, pioneering a new route.

PART THREE

Secrets of the Sea

Below: deep beneath the sea lies a strange and mysterious world, whose landscape is even greater than that mirrored in its surface. For hundreds of years, this world remained beyond the reach of man, but now its long-hidden secrets are coming to light.

PART THREE

Secrets of the Sea

BY CARL PROUJAN

Right: *Argyropelecus hemigymnus,* a deep-sea hatchet fish, is one of the many grotesque animals that live in the darkness of the deep ocean. This particular deep-sea monster, however, is only 2½ inches long.

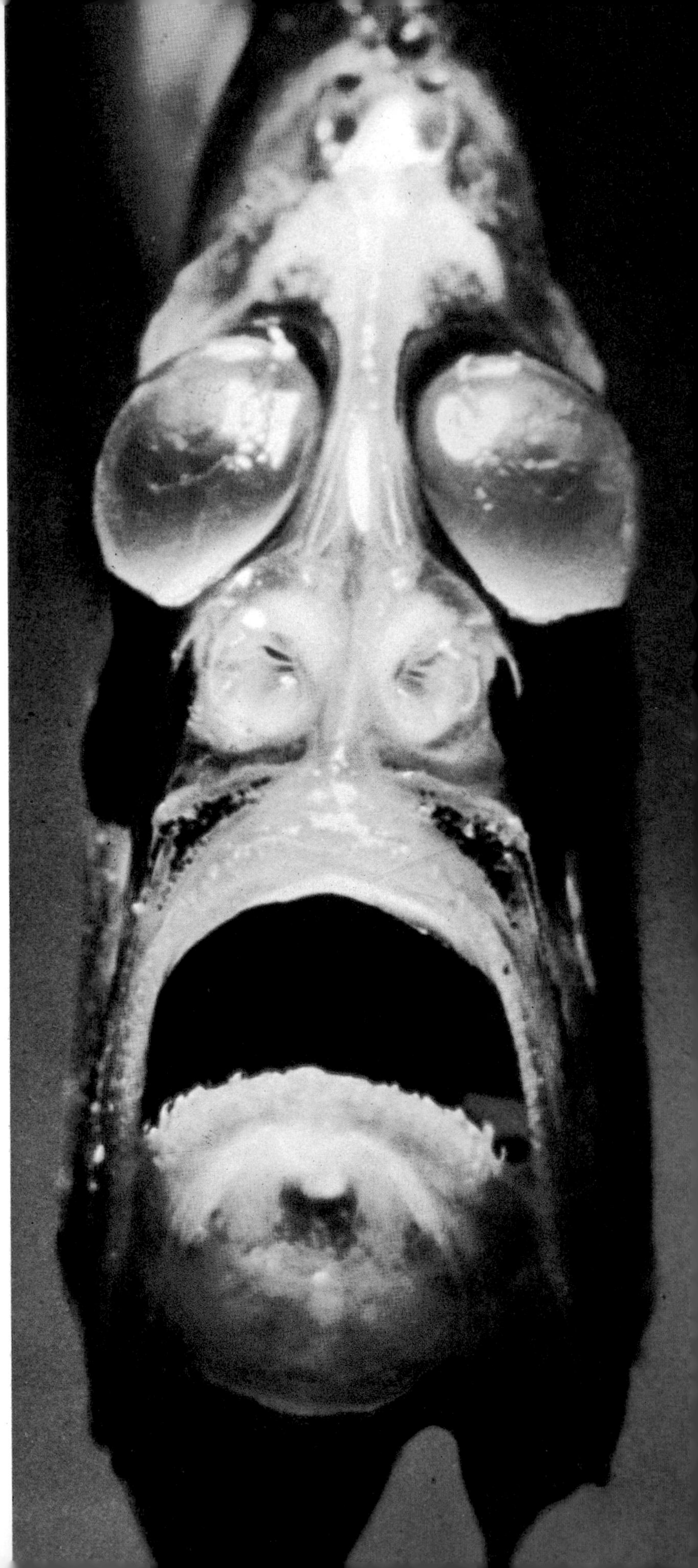

Foreword

The world's continents have been mapped, and her seas charted. Man has traveled to the poles, and climbed the earth's highest mountain peak. But even today, despite the extent of scientific knowledge and the sophistication of techniques, man has not conquered the depths of the sea.

Man's interest in the oceans, and his attempts to learn about them are, however, of long standing, and it is the story of his efforts that this part of the book tells. It begins far back, in the early days of civilization, when sea gods were an integral part of every nation's mythology, and leads through to the great days of the classical world. Then, man was already diving into the sea to bring back treasures from its bed. It was, however, only with the beginnings of true scientific study that the modern world began to take an interest in the waters of the earth.

The study of the oceans centers around two focal points—the investigation and examination of the seabed, of the sea's waters, and of life in them; and man's efforts to live beneath the waves. The first has been carried out principally from ships at the surface, which have used soundings to judge the depth of the water, scientific analysis to prove its composition, and trawls to catch deep-sea fish. Today, techniques are so advanced that from cores drilled from the seabed, much can be learned even about the history of the earth. Man's attempts at undersea living, starting from the skin dives of classical times, have led to many wonderful inventions. They have enabled him to reach the deepest-known spot on earth, and to swim in the sea almost as freely as a fish. Now, scientists look forward to the days of undersea cities, the days when the oceans can be used to solve some of the problems of the world.

TRIESTE
US NAVY
NEL ONR

The Last Great Frontier
1

At dawn on January 23, 1960, two men embarked on one of the most perilous journeys ever undertaken. Locked inside a steel sphere aboard the U.S. Navy's bathyscaph (deep-sea submersible) *Trieste,* Jacques Piccard and Donald Walsh set out to plunge through 35,800 feet of ocean in the deepest-known spot on earth. No one knew what they would find there, or whether they would come back alive.

The *Trieste* pitched and rolled on a stormy sea, watched by the anxious crews of two U.S. Navy escort ships. Far below them lay Challenger Deep in the Mariana Trench, a huge crescent-shaped gorge in the floor of the western Pacific Ocean. Inside their strange craft, in a space three feet across and less than six feet high, Piccard and Walsh waited, their eyes fixed on the depth gauge.

At 8:23 A.M. the signal came. The *Trieste* began to drop into the silence of the depths. It took nearly 40 minutes to reach 800 feet, but at 9 A.M. Piccard accelerated the rate of descent. First they passed through a twilight zone. Then darkness. Piccard flicked on the forward beam. As he peered into the sea, a flurry of tiny marine creatures streamed past.

Deep in the heart of the ocean, the two men were very much alone. A telephone provided their only link with the surface. This contact was reassuring. But Piccard and Walsh were far beyond the reach of assistance.

"9:20, depth 2,400 feet," reported Piccard. "Outside, total blackness. . . . We have entered the abyssal zone—the timeless world of eternal darkness." A chill penetrated the sphere as the temperature dropped rapidly. Thousands of tons of pressure from the surrounding sea gripped the descending craft. At 4,200 feet, the men were alarmed to see a thin trickle of water seeping in.

Black water rushed past as the *Trieste* shot on downward at 180 feet per minute. Piccard noticed with relief that the leak had stopped. At 20,000 feet the sphere began to plunge into the deepest ocean trench in the world.

At 29,150 feet Piccard noted "a vast emptiness beyond all comprehension." With perhaps a mile or more still to go, he was

Left: Donald Walsh (right) and Jacques Piccard in the bathyscaph *Trieste* after diving to the deepest-known part of the sea. They descended 35,800 feet, or nearly seven miles, into the Mariana Trench in the Pacific.

becoming increasingly worried about the moments ahead. At the bottom of the trench was a gap barely a mile in width. The *Trieste* would have to be right on target to avoid colliding with the rocky trench walls that might shatter it to pieces.

At 32,400 feet, there was a sudden explosion. The sphere shook as if it had been caught in a small earthquake. The two men looked anxiously at each other, fearing that they had hit the sea floor too fast and too soon. They waited and listened, but all was silent. After checking out the instruments, Piccard and Walsh agreed to continue the dive. They slowed their descent in preparation for touchdown on the ocean floor.

At 1:06 P.M., the *Trieste* landed gently on a bed of flat, snuff-colored ooze. Piccard and Walsh made "token claim, in the name of science and humanity, to the ultimate depth in all our oceans." But although the *Trieste* was resting on the bottom of the ocean, nearly

7 miles down, it was nearly 400 feet short of the ocean's deepest point at 36,198 feet.

Piccard and Walsh returned safely to the surface. Other daring explorers have sacrificed their lives in pursuit of the sea's secrets. What is it that lures men into the hostile environment of the underwater world? Why, in spite of all the difficulties and dangers, do men *want* to go down into the depths of the oceans?

For some divers, the difficulties and dangers are themselves reason enough. In an age when man has climbed to the peaks of the loftiest mountains, and crossed the frozen wastes of the poles, the depths of the sea remain unconquered. They form the last great frontier on earth.

Allied with the urge for adventure is a basic need to know. Men long to see for themselves what lies beneath the shimmering surface of the oceans. They want to know what it feels like to float in the watery world of *inner space,* the world of the ocean depths. Man hopes to solve the mystery of his own beginnings in the sea from which many scientists believe all life sprang.

But, today, curiosity and a desire for conquest are no longer the only reasons for probing the ocean depths. Man needs the sea if he is to continue to survive. If the population of the world keeps on growing as rapidly as it does now, the natural resources on dry land will run out. Under the sea lie vast unexploited supplies of food and minerals. The need to find and extract these resources has become the most urgent reason for man to explore the oceans.

The earth is a watery planet. More than two-thirds of it lie under the sea. The land masses are no more than islands in this immense watery mass. The oceans contain some 316 million cubic miles of water. If all the exposed land on the earth's surface were engulfed in the sea, the ocean floor would still be covered by an unbroken waste of water about two miles deep. The ocean bottom lies at an average depth of 12,450 feet. This is 4½ times as great as the average height of the land, including the mountains. At its deepest point, the

Above: a shoal of fish swimming over a coral formation. Man has always been fascinated by the life of the sea, but until recently, he had only been able to catch fleeting glimpses of this strange world.

Right: an artist's impression of the *Trieste* nearing the ocean floor. Protected in their steel sphere, the intrepid explorers look out onto the most remote landscape on earth.

ocean could accommodate the world's highest mountain with about $1\frac{1}{2}$ miles to spare.

But the sea is far more than a vast surface and a sheer mass of water. It is a complete world in itself. At shallower depths the scenery can be dramatic, but deeper down the waters are black and silent. The inhabitants of the underwater world are many and startlingly varied, both in appearance and size.

It was probably in search of living things that man first ventured into the sea. He began a relationship that has always contained

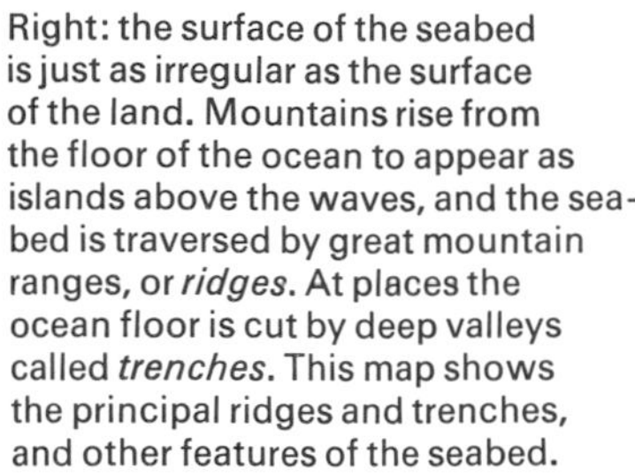

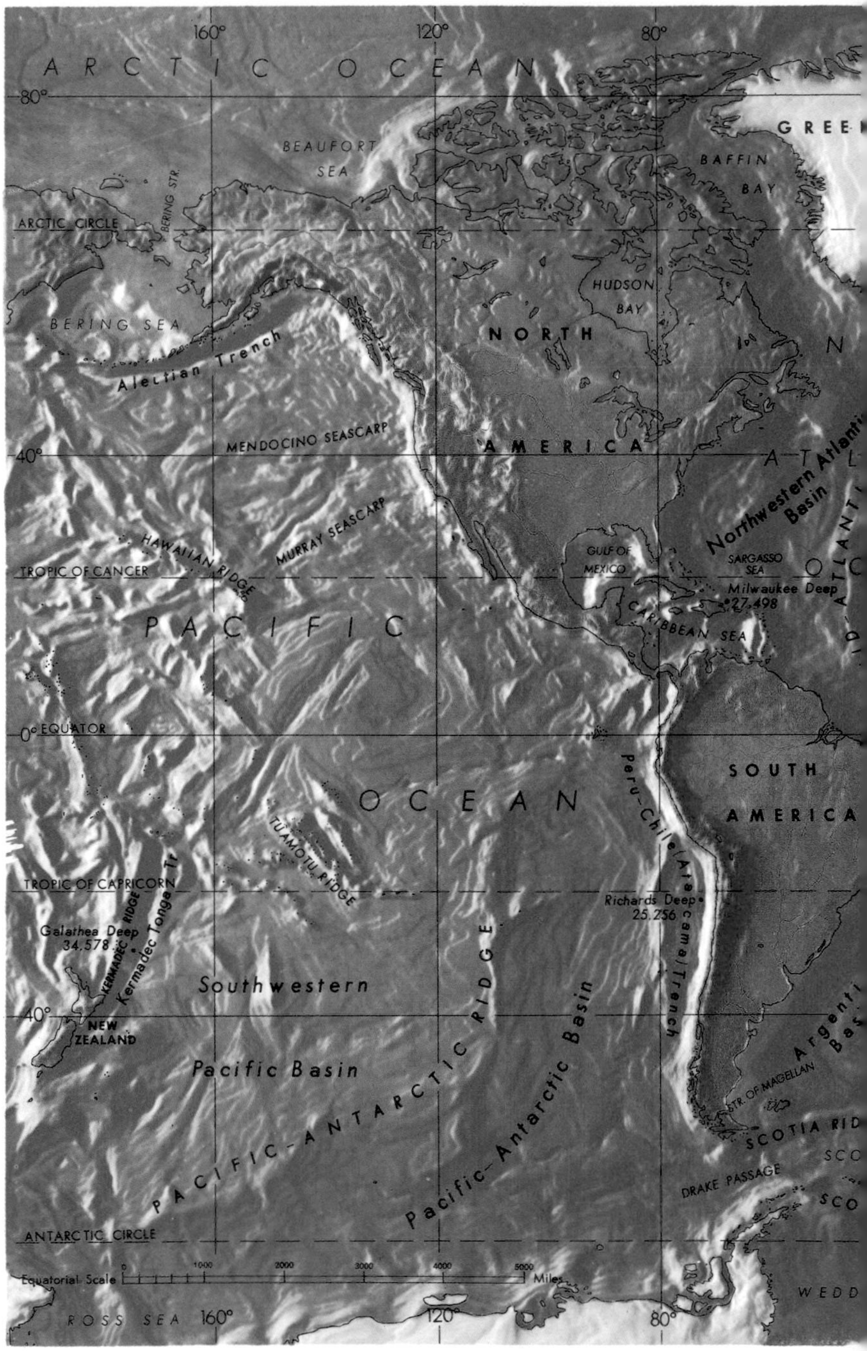

Right: the surface of the seabed is just as irregular as the surface of the land. Mountains rise from the floor of the ocean to appear as islands above the waves, and the seabed is traversed by great mountain ranges, or *ridges*. At places the ocean floor is cut by deep valleys called *trenches*. This map shows the principal ridges and trenches, and other features of the seabed.

Above: an Akkadian seal (about 2300 B.C.) shows Zu the Birdman, being led before Ea, the Babylonian water god. The Babylonians, like other early civilizations, believed that gods controlled the forces of the sea.

elements of fear as well as wonder. Despite an early familiarity with the waters around the coast, the great depths of the open sea remained impenetrable and frightening. For centuries, the dark and shadowy realms of the deep were thought to be inhabited by terrible monsters. To early man it seemed that this must be where the immense forces of the sea lay hidden. And he ascribed these forces to the workings of powerful supernatural beings.

The first records of sea gods come from the Babylonian civilization, which flourished 5,000 years ago, though the myths about

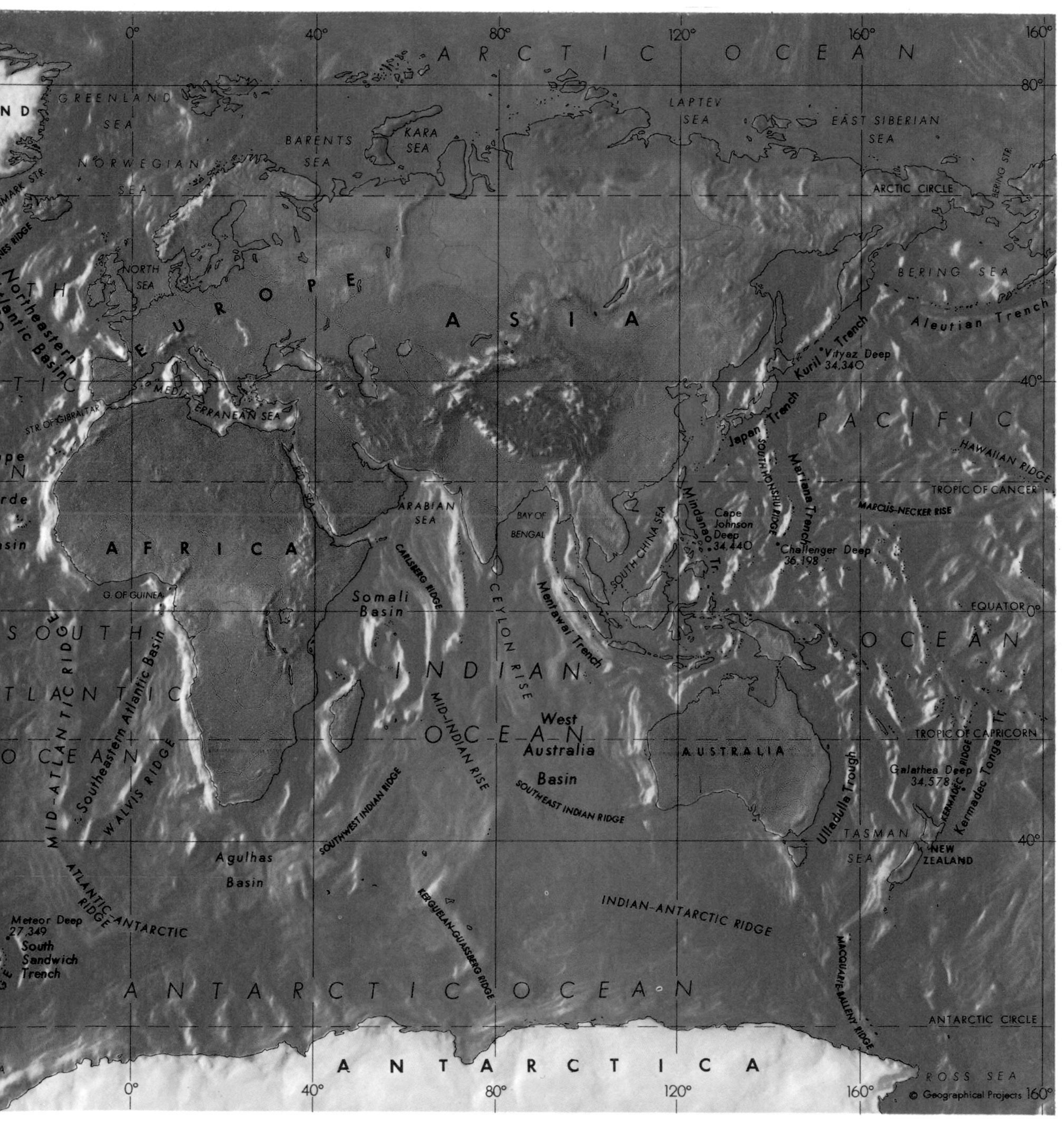

gods of the sea are even older. The Babylonians, who lived in what is now southeastern Iraq, worshiped a god named Ea, "the deity of the watery deep." Ea was a fresh-water god, but the Babylonians had sea gods and goddesses too, some of whom resembled the mermaids found in legends of the sea.

More plentiful evidence of the worship of underwater gods has been found on Minoan frescoes and drinking vessels. The Minoan civilization flourished from 3000 B.C. onward on the island of Crete in the Mediterranean Sea, a clear, warm, and largely tideless sea. Minoans sailed all over the Mediterranean to trade, and they were accomplished swimmers and divers. One of the most famous Minoan heroes was a diver called Glaucus who was said to have learned the secrets of the sea after eating a special kind of seaweed that enabled him to breathe underwater. The sea gods, impressed by his desire to visit the undersea world, made him immortal and he too became a god.

The Greeks, for whom Glaucus was also a god, inherited the Minoan tradition of diving. Among their gods were the most famous underwater deities of antiquity. The chief Greek god of the sea was Poseidon (later to be called Neptune by the Romans). In fits

Left: a French painting of the 1200's showing Alexander the Great (356–323 B.C.) at the bottom of the sea in a glass barrel. The story of his dive into the sea to observe marine life is probably only a legend which grew up long after his death. According to some versions of the story, he is reputed to have seen a monster which took three days to swim past his glass cage. Bibliotheque Royale Albert 1er, Bruxelles. Ms. 11040, f.70v.

Right: an Indian painting of the 1500's illustrating the same legend. Notice how Alexander's appearance has changed from a typical European monarch with ermine and crown to that of a bearded Eastern potentate.

Below: starfish on the seashore. Mariners and divers of the early civilizations around the Mediterranean Sea, such as the Minoans and Greeks, were certainly familiar with these and other shallow-water animals. They had little idea, however, of the vast variety of creatures that lived in the deeper parts of the sea.

of anger, Poseidon was believed to beat the seas into fury with his trident. In an effort to placate him, the Greeks built temples in his honor at dangerous points along the coast.

The records and legends of ancient Greece contain many accounts of underwater exploits. Herodotus, the Greek historian, tells the story of Scyllias, an accomplished diver of the 500's B.C. Scyllias and his daughter Cyana sank at least one enemy ship by cutting its cables under the sea. They also recovered quantities of treasure from Persian ships that had been sunk by the Greeks.

Above: a vase made in the 500's B.C. shows a Greek diver about to enter the sea. In their search for sponges, Greek divers are known to have reached depths of 75 to 100 feet, sometimes using primitive diving bells to replenish their air supplies. During their dives they observed other forms of marine life and so added to the growing knowledge about the sea.

Herodotus also mentions the use of submarine vessels in the 500's B.C. These were cages, made of glass, from which the approach of enemy ships could be sighted. Two centuries later, Alexander the Great is said to have observed marine life from a similar glass barrel, which was suspended into the sea by a golden chain. This story seems to have grown up long after Alexander's death and his submarine adventure probably never happened. But Alexander did use divers to saw through enemy defenses during the siege of the Phoenician city of Tyre in 332 B.C.

One of the most famous legends about warfare and the sea is the story of the "lost continent" of Atlantis, a large mythical island in the Atlantic Ocean. The armies of Atlantis were said to have planned to conquer the Mediterranean countries. They had made some conquests in Europe and Africa when they were defeated in battle by the Greeks. Later Atlantis was swallowed up in the depths of the sea during terrible earthquakes and floods.

Apart from their military exploits, the Greeks dived regularly for peaceful purposes, searching the sea for fish, coral, mother-of-pearl, and sponges. Greek sponge divers are known to have reached depths of 75 to 100 feet. These ventures into the sea were not limited by the air capacity of a diver's lungs. Aristotle, the Greek scientist and philosopher who lived in the 300's B.C., describes primitive diving bells used by sponge divers. The bells were weighted and filled with air. When out of breath, a diver would poke his head into the bell for air. Moreover, the air supply in the bell could be replenished with air delivered in weighted animal skins.

These divers brought back knowledge as well as sponges. Their observations of underwater life were carefully noted by Aristotle. But Aristotle did not confine his studies to the reports of divers and fishermen. He sailed over large areas of the Aegean Sea in his quest for knowledge of marine life. He discovered, named, and described 116 kinds of fish, 24 kinds of crustaceans and marine worms, and 40 kinds of shellfish and *radiolarians*—minute creatures with delicate outer skeletons.

Being sailors, like most island peoples, the Minoans of Crete were the first to explore the sea. But their voyages were confined to the waters of their own familiar Mediterranean Sea. Rumor and superstition persisted about the world that lay beyond. However, by 600 B.C., the Phoenicians had sailed out into the Atlantic Ocean. They reached the British Isles and may even have sailed around Africa.

The first great individual explorer of the sea was Pytheas of Massalia. Pytheas, a Greek astronomer and mathematician as well as an explorer, sailed from Massalia (now the French port of Marseille) in about 325 B.C. Passing through the Strait of Gibraltar into the Atlantic, he made his way northward up the west coast of Portugal and past France and Britain. During a voyage which took him as far as the frozen seas of the Arctic, Pytheas made a number of scientific observations and was the first of the Greeks to suggest that the ebb and flow of the tides is related to the moon.

In the 100's B.C., Posidonius, a Greek philosopher born in Syria,

Left: a ship carved in a rock face at Lindos, on the island of Rhodes. The ship is Greek in design and the carving dates from the Hellenistic Age which began in 323 B.C. and lasted for nearly 200 years. During this period Greek culture spread into Egypt and throughout the Near East. In such ships the Greeks explored the Mediterranean and Atlantic.

Above: an Assyrian relief of about 750 B.C. showing men swimming underwater to attack a city. One of the attackers has an air-filled pig's bladder between his teeth. Some historians see this as an early attempt to provide air for an underwater swimmer. Others point out that the bladder would be too buoyant to keep the diver submerged, and think he is using it as a float.

set sail for Spain to confirm or refute the belief that, as the sun set in the west, it sank into the Atlantic and the sea sizzled with a hissing noise. Although Posidonius never heard the sun plunging into the ocean, he did note that the depth of the sea near the coast of Sardinia was 1,000 fathoms (6,000 feet). No one knows how this measurement was made, but it is a reasonable one. Depths in excess of 8,500 feet have been recorded near Sardinia by modern oceanographic vessels.

The Romans, like the Greeks, used divers in combat. But they appear to have had little other interest in what went on beneath the surface of the sea. Centuries passed, during which the art of diving was kept alive by the Arabs and by pearl divers of the East. Elsewhere, man withdrew from the challenge of the sea and turned his interest inland. The explorations begun by the Minoans and the Greeks ground to a halt and so did the science of oceanography.

Left: a portrait of Constantine John Phipps. Phipps made the first sounding of the deep ocean floor in 1773. Until then all attempts had failed, and many people still thought the sea was bottomless. Aboard H.M.S. *Racehorse* Phipps sounded the seabed between Iceland and Norway and recorded a depth of 683 fathoms. Below: a water color showing H.M.S. *Racehorse* and H.M.S. *Carcass* stuck in pack ice during the voyage they made toward the North Pole in 1773.

The Search Begins

2

The oceanographers of the ancient world had been puzzled by two questions in particular. How deep is the sea? How deep can animals live in it? Aristotle's works, lost and forgotten in the West during the Dark Ages from the 400's to the 900's, had been rediscovered by the 1300's. Although they helped to spark a new interest in the oceans' depths, it was not until the 1700's that a determined bid was made to answer the questions posed more than 2,000 years earlier.

The scientists who undertook this huge task had many problems to overcome. For hundreds of years, explorers had failed to sound (measure) the depth of the bottom in the open ocean. Their sounding lines were not long enough. Currents and surface winds prevented the lines from descending vertically, and on many occasions thousands of feet of line were paid out without touching the bottom. Many people continued to believe that the oceans were bottomless.

The first deep-sea sounding was made in 1773 by a British scientist named Constantine John Phipps aboard H.M.S. *Racehorse*. Using a weighted line, Phipps measured a depth of 683 fathoms (4,098 feet) between Iceland and Norway. This was to remain a record for 35 years.

While Phipps was making his soundings and measuring the temperature of deep water, other scientists were busy investigating underwater life. They captured their specimens with the aid of deep-sea dredges that were dragged across the bottom of the sea by a slow-moving ship. The first scientific dredging missions concentrated on relatively shallow water but, as the scientists scraped up living organisms from ever greater depths, undersea life became a controversial issue. Scientists began to take sides over the question of whether there was a depth beyond which life could not exist.

A French naturalist, François Péron, added to this controversy after returning from an around-the-world journey in 1804. During the trip, Péron had measured the temperature of the ocean at various depths. Because the water became colder and colder with greater depth, he was led to believe that the bed of the ocean was covered with "eternal ice," and that no life could possibly exist there. But there was little hard evidence to support or refute his contention.

Then, in 1818, a British sailor named John Ross (later Sir John), set sail for the Arctic Ocean on a voyage of discovery. Ross took with him a combination sounding and sampling device, which he called the *Deep-sea Clamm*. The Clamm could pick up a portion of

Above: an engraving of Sir John Ross being greeted by Eskimos of Prince Regent Inlet, at the northwest end of Baffin Island, in 1818. The ships in the bay are the *Isabella* and the *Alexander*. During this voyage Ross, commander of the *Isabella,* used the *Deep-sea Clamm* to retrieve a sample of the ocean bed from 6,000 feet. The sample contained living things, proving that life existed on the seabed.

the ocean's floor, and bring it back to the surface of the water.

On September 1, 1819, the Clamm was lowered over the side into the waters of the Atlantic. Fathom after fathom was counted off as the line played out into the sea. At 6,000 feet, the Clamm struck bottom and bit a six-pound chunk out of the ocean floor. Then Ross ordered the line to be hauled in. Throughout the long process, the men aboard the vessel wondered what the Clamm would hold.

Finally, the Clamm broke surface. From its teeth oozed soft mud. And in the mud there wriggled a tangle of tube-worms. Péron had been wrong. Here, at least, the floor of the ocean was not sheathed in ice. More important, it teemed with life. But was this the deepest part of the ocean? Were there depths still undiscovered where life could not exist? Many scientists believed so.

Among the most prominent of these scientists was a British naturalist named Edward Forbes. Forbes was born on the Isle of Man, a spot of land between England and Ireland, washed by the waters of the Irish Sea. As a boy, he had explored the cliffs and beaches that ringed his island home. Later, as a young student,

Above: a lithograph of the British naturalist Edward Forbes. In 1841 Forbes joined the British survey ship *Beacon* on a cruise to chart the Mediterranean and Aegean seas. During the voyage he dredged up animals from the sea floor 1,200 feet below him. What he found then, and in later studies, prompted him to classify marine life by dividing the sea into four principal zones.

Forbes often left the relative safety of the familiar coast to venture into the Irish Sea in a fishing boat.

Like Aristotle, Forbes observed, examined, and dissected the creatures he landed with dredge and trawl. Soon he had become one of the leading naturalists in Great Britain. He was an expert on the animals that dwelled in the waters of the Irish Sea. But the creatures that might lurk in deeper waters also intrigued him. So it was natural that he should jump at the opportunity to join the crew of the British survey ship *Beacon,* whose task it was to chart the waters of the Mediterranean and Aegean seas.

Forbes signed on as ship's naturalist in 1841. During the *Beacon*'s voyage, which lasted a year and a half, he dredged deeper than any scientist had done before him—1,380 feet down. From 1,200 feet, he brought up living starfish and shellfish that had previously been found only as fossils and were thought to be extinct.

From his findings on this journey and other studies, Forbes developed a system of classifying marine life. He divided the waters of the seas into four zones, each having a different *ecosystem* (animal

Left: mussels on a beach. These and other mollusks live between high- and low-water marks, on the edge of the sea. Forbes called this densely populated region the *littoral* zone, from the Latin word *littoralis*, which means seashore.

Above: a sea cucumber in eelgrass. This marine invertebrate is typical of the animals found in the sea to a depth of about 75 feet. This is Forbes' *laminarian* zone, named for the brown algae, *Laminaria*.

and plant populations and the environment in which they live).

The *littoral* zone consisted of shore waters between high-water and low-water marks. Living things in this zone were periodically bathed with air and sunlight. Seaweed flourished. The zone was alive with animals, especially mollusks.

The *laminarian* zone sloped to a depth of 60 to 75 feet below the low-water mark. This was the home of marine invertebrates (animals without backbones) who fed on vast "fields" of brown algae, and other plant food.

Probing below 75 feet, Forbes had found a layer of water crowded with large crustaceans and food fishes such as cod, haddock, and halibut. He named this the *coralline* zone. According to Forbes its lower boundary was marked by a depth of 300 feet.

Next, and seemingly bottomless, Forbes found the zone of deep-sea corals. And he was convinced that somewhere in this zone, pressure, darkness, and cold increased to a point where no life could possibly exist. Plants, which required sunlight, would vanish first, then animals that feed on plants would disappear. Finally, animals that prey on other animals would be lost. Forbes believed that this point would be reached at a depth of 1,800 feet. All the waters below that depth he called the *azoic* (lifeless) zone. But what of the worms found by John Ross at 6,000 feet? Forbes was either unaware of Ross's feat or he doubted that the worms were bottom dwellers.

Top right: a shark glides menacingly through the blue sea. The shark, together with many other fish and large crustaceans, lives in what Forbes called the *coralline* zone. He believed this extended from 75 to 300 feet, the lower limit of *coralline* algae growth.

Right: *Omosudis,* a deep-sea fish up to nine inches in length found below 3,000 feet. Forbes believed below 1,800 feet there was no life in the ocean. No plants or animals, he reasoned, could possibly survive the increasing coldness, darkness, and pressure. He called this region the *azoic* zone.

Right: Charles Wyville Thomson. As a former student of Edward Forbes, Thomson shared his belief that no life existed in the ocean below 1,800 feet. Between 1868 and 1870, however, Thomson proved Forbes, himself, and many other scientists completely wrong. Even the slimy ooze he recovered from the bottom at depths of over 15,000 feet contained living things.

Below: Sir James Clark Ross. Between 1839 and 1843, Ross led an expedition to the Antarctic in H.M.S. *Erebus*. He was a scrupulous scientist and made many careful measurements of weather conditions, sea temperature, and the water depth. One sounding showed that the bottom depth was 14,500 feet, the greatest depth then recorded.

In 1860, 6 years after Forbes died at the age of 39, an event seemingly unrelated to the controversy over deep-sea life occurred. A telegraph cable between Corsica and Sardinia broke on the floor of the Mediterranean, 7,200 feet below the sea's surface. A repair crew was sent to the site of the break. After a considerable amount of work, the crew hauled the cable to the surface. To their amazement, a deep-sea coral clung to the cable at the point of the break. Corals are *sessile* animals—that is, they grow and develop while anchored to a solid object. They are not free swimmers. Therefore, the coral had fastened itself to the cable at a depth of 7,200 feet.

As foot by foot of the cable emerged from the sea, other sessile animals were found clinging to it. This was powerful evidence against Forbes' concept of a lifeless zone below 1,800 feet. Yet preconceived notions of such a lifeless zone lingered on. Many scientists could not conceive of living things spending their lives in total darkness, at temperatures close to the freezing point of water, and, more important, at pressures in excess of 1,000 pounds per square inch. (In the sea, water pressure increases at a rate of 0.442 pounds per square inch for each foot of depth.)

One of those who continued to believe in a lifeless zone was another British naturalist, Charles Wyville Thomson, who was later to make great contributions to the science of oceanography. Thomson, who had been a student of Forbes, decided to put his beliefs to

Above: a water color painted during Ross's voyage to Antarctica between 1839 and 1843 shows H.M.S. *Erebus* and her sister ship, H.M.S. *Terror* off the coast of Antarctica in 1841. Ross, commander of the *Erebus,* named the volcano he saw Mount Erebus.

the test of controlled scientific observation. In 1868, he set sail on a small gunboat, H.M.S. *Lightning*, which had been loaned by the British Admiralty. Equipped with a deep-sea dredge, *Lightning* scraped the Atlantic floor from the Faeroe Islands, about 250 miles north of the Scottish coast, to as far south as Gibraltar. From depths as great as 3,600 feet, the dredge snared myriads of living creatures. In 1869 and 1870, Thomson cruised the Atlantic aboard another borrowed gunboat, H.M.S. *Porcupine*. From its decks, he lowered dredges deeper and deeper into the ocean. And always they came up loaded with living things—even from a depth of more than 15,000 feet. Life did exist in the total darkness of the deep. This part of the sea, where sunlight never penetrates, is known as the *abyss,* or *abyssal* zone. In most parts of the world, its upper boundary lies about 6,600 feet below the surface. Its lower boundary is the ocean floor. The abyssal zone is now known to be the world's largest ecosystem and covers half of the earth's area.

For Thomson, two questions remained unanswered. Although he had hauled living things from a depth of 15,000 feet, was there still a depth at which no living creature could survive? And if no depth was uninhabited, what sort of strange creatures would be found at depths yet unexplored? Thomson determined to dredge all the sea beds of the world, if necessary, until he found the answers, and he began to petition the British Admiralty for their support.

While Forbes and Thomson were busy searching for life in the deep, plans were going ahead to lay an underwater telegraph cable between Europe and America. Such a project called for more efficient methods of measuring the ocean depths and increased knowledge of the physical properties of the sea and the nature of the ocean floor.

In 1839, Sir James Clark Ross, nephew of Sir John Ross, left for the frigid waters of the Antarctic aboard H.M.S. *Erebus*. Pausing on the way south, Ross ordered a boat lowered over the side. The boat carried a simple cargo—a 76-pound lead weight attached to a hemp line that was coiled around a huge reel. When the boat was a few yards from the mother ship, Ross commanded the oarsmen to drop the weight over the side.

The line spun rapidly from the reel, but it was nearly an hour before the weight struck bottom. It had carried 14,550 feet of line into the sea. Thus did James Clark Ross make the first abyssal sounding of "a depression of the bed of the ocean beneath its surface very little short of the elevation of Mont Blanc above it."

During his voyage, Ross also took many temperature readings at the ocean bottom. He found that the temperature at the bottom was the same at all latitudes—about 4°C. However, Ross had overlooked the effect of water pressure on the thermometer bulb. Pressure forced the mercury too far up the stem of the thermometer and gave a reading that was too high.

Wyville Thomson aboard the *Lightning* also measured the temperature of the sea and made a surprising discovery. He found that

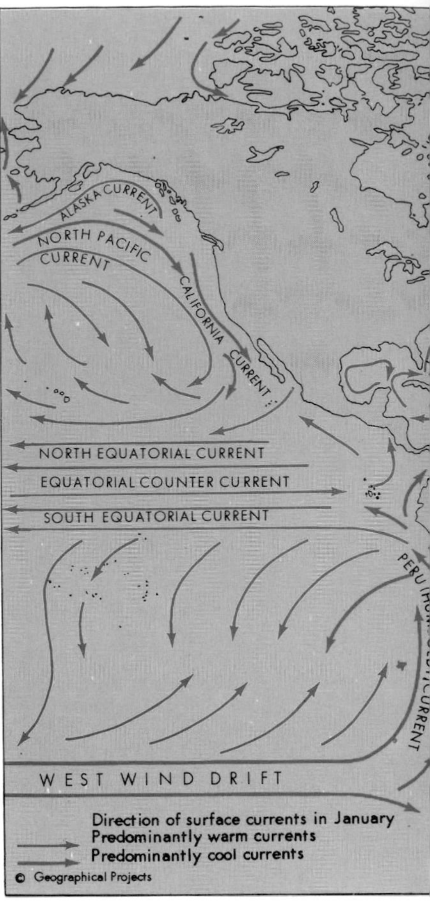

Above: the oceans of the world, showing the most important ocean currents. The currents—which can be either hot or cold—are great rivers in the oceans, set in motion by the winds. In the Northern Hemisphere the currents' flow is generally clockwise and in the Southern Hemisphere counterclockwise. This difference of direction is caused by the rotation of the earth on its axis.

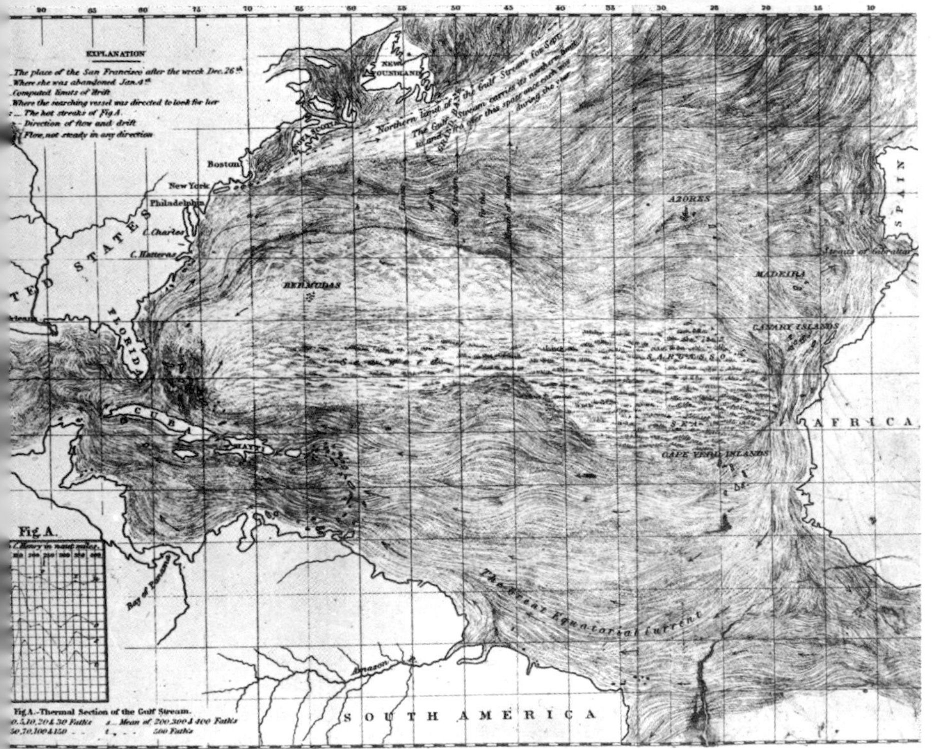

Left: a chart of the Gulf Stream from Matthew Maury's book *Physical Geography of the Sea and its Meteorology,* published in 1855. Maury believed that warm winds from the eastern branch of the Gulf Stream (the North Atlantic Current) caused the relatively mild climate of Britain and western Europe.

Right: Matthew Fontaine Maury. His *Wind and Current Charts* formed the basis of the government's pilot charts.

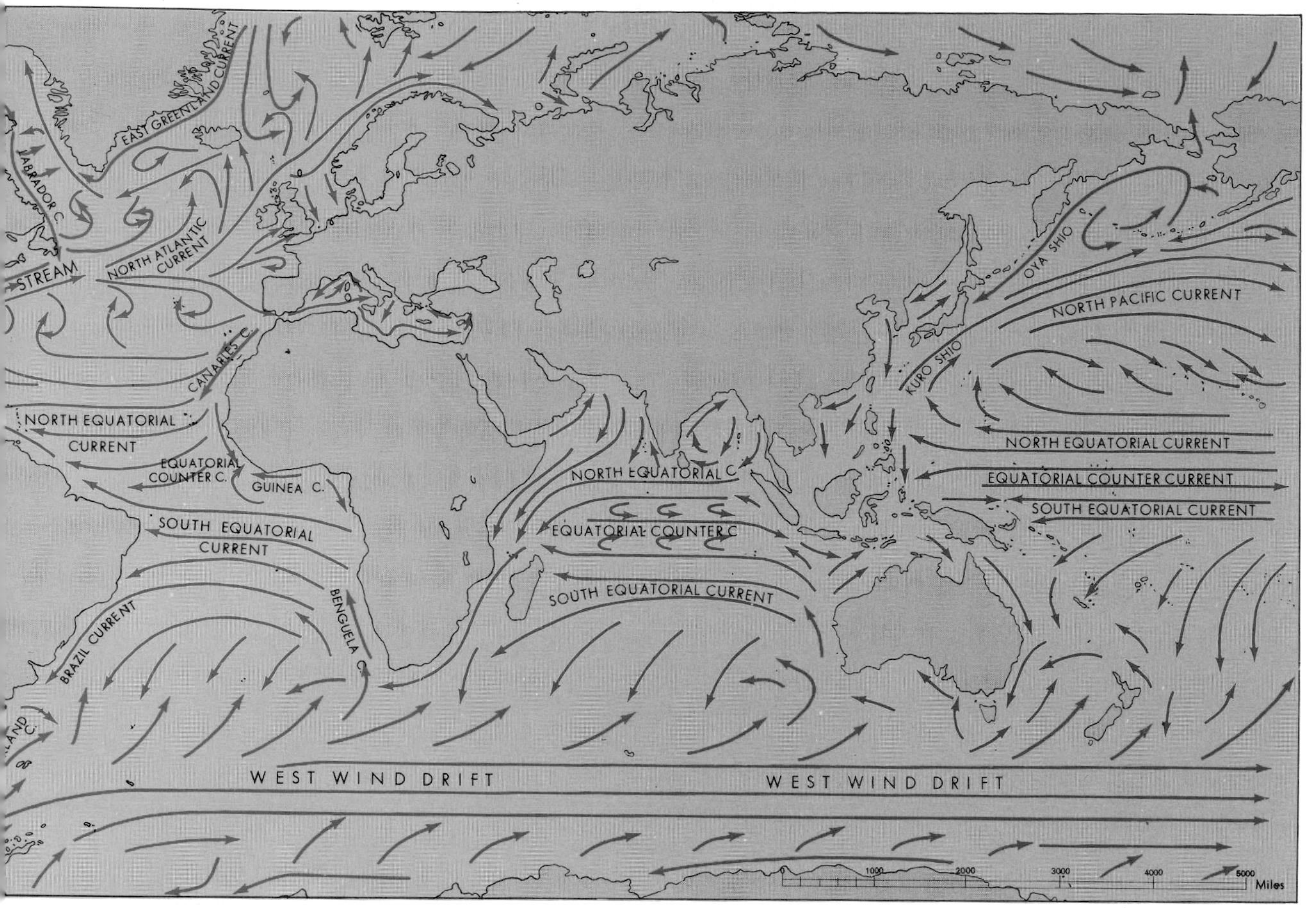

EAST GREENLAND CURRENT
LABRADOR C.
STREAM
NORTH ATLANTIC CURRENT
CANARIES C.
NORTH EQUATORIAL CURRENT
EQUATORIAL COUNTER C.
GUINEA C.
SOUTH EQUATORIAL CURRENT
BRAZIL CURRENT
BENGUELA C.
NORTH EQUATORIAL C.
EQUATORIAL COUNTER C.
SOUTH EQUATORIAL CURRENT
OYA SHIO
KURO SHIO
NORTH PACIFIC CURRENT
NORTH EQUATORIAL CURRENT
EQUATORIAL COUNTER CURRENT
SOUTH EQUATORIAL CURRENT
WEST WIND DRIFT
WEST WIND DRIFT
1000
2000
3000
4000
5000
Miles

"great masses of water at different temperatures (and depths) are moving about, each in its particular course; maintaining a remarkable system of oceanic circulation, and yet keeping so distinct from one another that an hour's sail may be sufficient to pass from the extreme of heat to the extreme of cold."

Others had charted such "rivers" in the sea. Nantucket whaling captain Timothy Folger charted the Gulf Stream in 1770. And in the same year the great American scientist and statesman Benjamin Franklin drew up temperature tables of the Gulf Stream so that a ship's navigator could tell whether he was in or out of its northeastward-flowing current. In 1781, Charles Blagden charted the cold Labrador Current, which flows from the Arctic Ocean and runs into the warm Gulf Stream near the Grand Banks off Newfoundland. Where the warm, moisture-laden air of the Gulf Stream meets the cold Labrador Current, the sea is often shrouded in dense fog.

The work of Folger, Franklin, Blagden and others was expanded into a world-wide system of meteorological observation by Matthew Fontaine Maury, who has been called the *Pathfinder of the Seas*. As a young officer in the U.S. Navy, Maury began to study winds and currents as a means of shortening the journeys of ships across vast expanses of the sea. He took lengthy notes wherever he sailed, and drew graphs and charts of all he observed. Then, in 1839, after 14

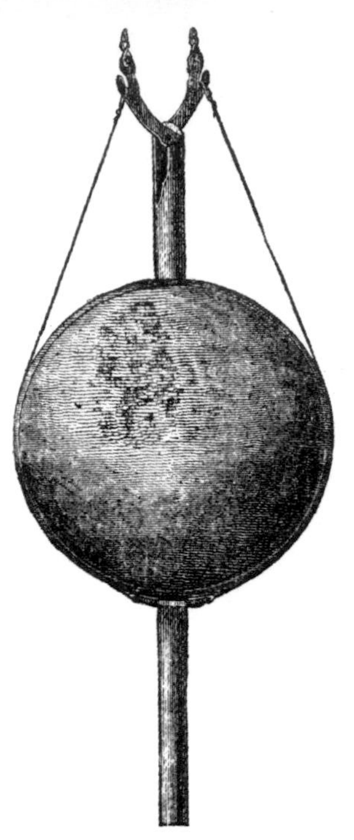

Above: the deep-sea sounding device developed by Maury and Brooke. It consisted of a hollow tube running through a cannon ball. When lowered, the ball was held in place by a collar fixed to two hinged brackets.
Below: when the tube struck bottom the drop in tension on the sounding line tripped the brackets and the ball was released. The tube, with a sample of the seabed, was then reeled in.

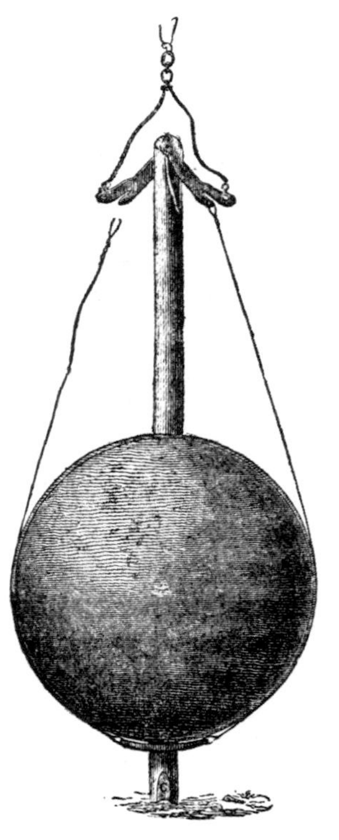

years of sea duty, Maury was lamed in an accident and declared unfit for active service.

But the Navy did not waste Maury's talents. In 1842, he was put in charge of the Depot of Charts and Instruments. Now Maury pored over the records of countless voyages in his search for "short cuts" across the seas. With these in hand, Maury charted the tracks of many ships making identical voyages. He noted the season in which a voyage was made. And he recorded wind and current data reported from each voyage. He even asked that navigators indicate temperatures, barometric pressures, encounters with fog, the sighting of whales, birds, and islands.

During the next 10 years, Maury accumulated data obtained from 265,298 days of observation—the equivalent of almost 727 years of sailing by a single seafarer. From this information, he made charts indicating the prevailing winds and currents at different times of the year, which could be used to find the speediest routes across the seas.

But Maury was not yet satisfied with the feat he had accomplished. In 1853, he sailed to Belgium to attend a conference where he would meet representatives of all the world's maritime nations. Maury knew that to make ocean voyages safe as well as speedy, a world-wide system of meteorological observations would have to be set up. Addressing the conference, he pleaded for the cooperation of scientists throughout the world. The representatives of the seagoing nations agreed to support Maury's scheme. The foundation of today's weather bureaus had been laid.

Maury was also a physical oceanographer—he studied the basic processes at work in the sea. In his famous book, *Physical Geography of the Sea and Its Meteorology,* published in 1855, Maury presented many fascinating concepts and theories. For example, he suggested that ocean currents influence climate. He believed that warm winds from the eastward branch of the Gulf Stream, called the North Atlantic Current, raise the temperature of Britain and western Europe by 20°F over that of other land areas at similar latitudes. To support this contention, Maury noted that Britain, bathed by the North Atlantic Current, is a land of greenery in winter, when Newfoundland, at much the same latitude but gripped by the cold Labrador Current, is covered in ice and snow. He also suggested that currents such as the Gulf Stream spawn destructive storms. And he stated that the fogs of Newfoundland were caused by the condensation of moisture above the Gulf Stream. His theory was that the moisture condensed when the cold temperatures of the southward-sweeping Labrador Current cooled the damp air of the Gulf Stream.

Maury also tried to explain the forces that cause currents to flow. He concluded that many factors played a role. Among these are winds, differences in the density of water, and the earth's rotation.

Maury was involved in practical as well as theoretical oceanography. Together with John M. Brooke, a young naval officer, he developed a new sounding device that could measure depth and bring back a small sample of the seabed. The device was mostly

Brooke's invention but it was Maury who arranged for ships all over the world to use it. By organizing a series of systematic soundings of the North Atlantic, Maury played a leading part in the laying of the first transatlantic telegraph cable.

The successful laying of this cable on July 27, 1866, gave rise to a new wave of interest in oceanography. Six years later, the Royal Society of London charged Wyville Thomson with the task of learning "everything about the sea." This was the chance that Thomson had been waiting for, and he was determined not to return empty-handed.

Above: the steamship *Great Eastern.* This ship laid the first successful transatlantic telegraph cable in 1866. It was the only ship of its time capable of carrying the 2,300 nautical miles of cable needed to traverse the Atlantic. The laying of the telegraph cable had been made possible by Matthew Maury's soundings of the Atlantic Ocean floor. Below: crewmen of the *Great Eastern* splicing the cable after a fault developed in July, 1865. The cable broke and the attempt was abandoned.

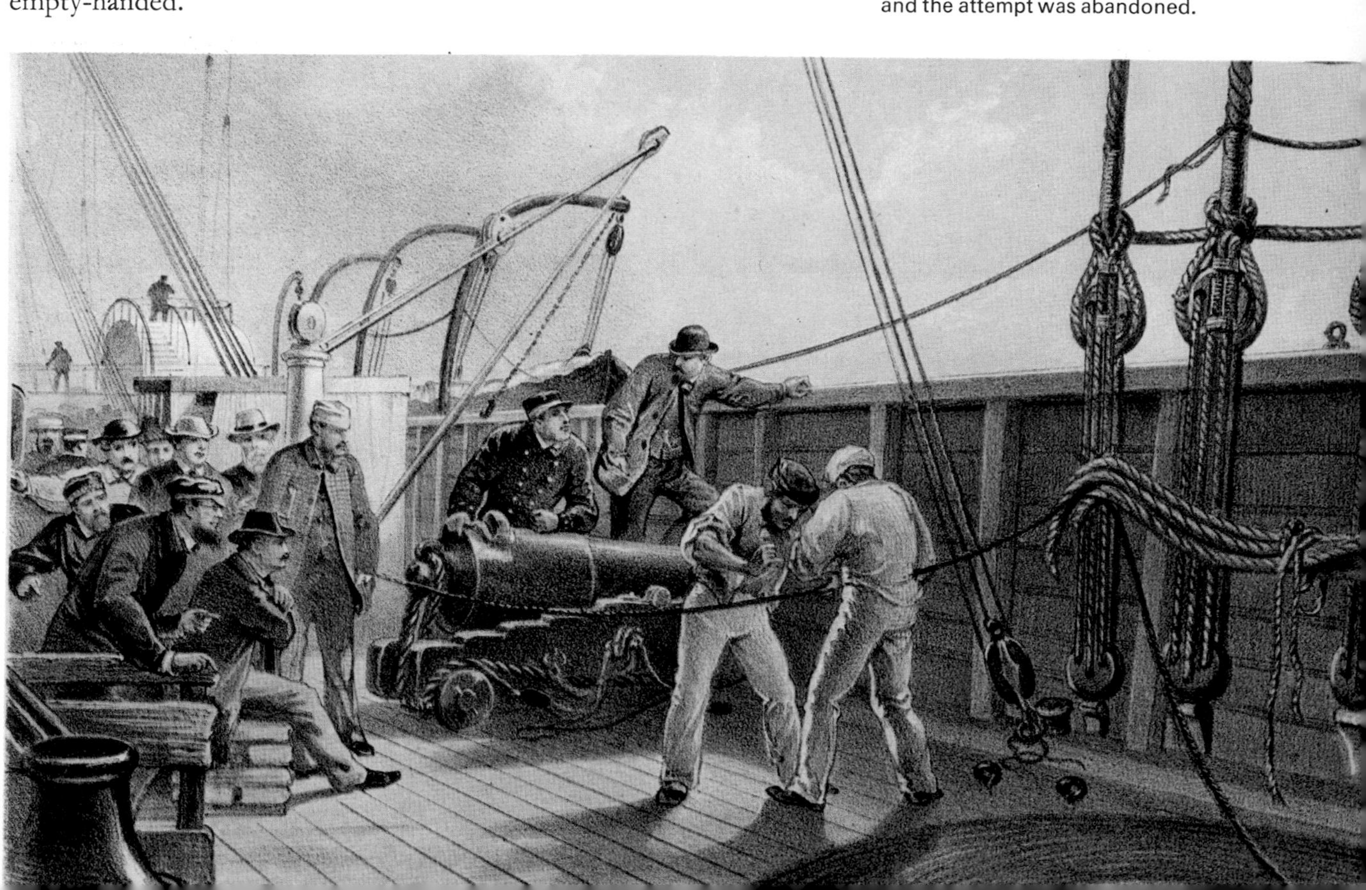

Challenger Faces the Unknown

3

Left: water color of H.M.S. *Challenger.* In December, 1872, this 2,306-ton corvette began a world-wide voyage of scientific research and discovery. The team of scientists on board was headed by Charles Wyville Thomson. The information they collected during the $3\frac{1}{2}$-year voyage laid the foundation of the era of modern oceanography.

On December 7, 1872, a British man-of-war edged from its berth at Sheerness, about 30 miles east of London. It was making for Portsmouth, on the south coast of England, where it would start man's first global oceanographic expedition—an expedition that still holds the record for the longest continuous scientific mission. To the idle passer-by, the ship must have seemed a strange sight. For only 2 of its 18 cannons poked through its gun ports. The rest had been removed to make room for scientific equipment. This ship was not outfitted to do battle with a human enemy. Its only foes during a $3\frac{1}{2}$-year voyage would be winter and rough weather. It would log 68,890 nautical miles in an adventure that would take it through all the world's oceans, except the Arctic. Its commander was George S. Nares of the Royal Navy. But, in a very real sense, the man at the helm was Charles Wyville Thomson.

The vessel was the 2,306-ton corvette H.M.S. *Challenger.* Though it would make most of its journey under sail, it was equipped with an auxiliary steam engine. And it was aptly named. It was on loan from the British Admiralty to the Royal Society of London, which had pleaded for a ship to challenge the unknown reaches of the oceans' depths.

Thomson headed the small scientific team aboard the *Challenger,* which included four naturalists, John Murray, H. N. Moseley,

Below: scientists using microscopes to examine biological samples during research on board H.M.S. *Challenger.*

Right: the dredging and sounding equipment on board H.M.S. *Challenger*. Sounding weights, dredges, and trawls were let down into the sea over the side of the ship. They were reeled in on drums powered by two steam engines near the mainmast. A system of blocks and spring units reduced the strain on the drums during rewinding.

Above: John Murray, one of the four naturalists on the *Challenger* expedition. He was particularly interested in the formation and composition of deep-sea sediments. Through studying material brought up in the *Challenger's* dredges and sample tubes, he began to distinguish two main types of sediment. The classification he devised for these sediments is still used today.

Rudolph von Willemoes-Suhm, and J. J. Wild, and one chemist, J. Y. Buchanan. During the voyage, the researchers would work in two well-equipped laboratories—one designed for analyzing samples of seawater, the other built for the study of animals and plants.

Storerooms below were crammed with bottles to take samples of water from various depths. There were miles of sounding line that would be used to measure the depths of the world's oceans. Dredges and trawls lay ready to scrape the floor of four oceans, snaring animals that had never been seen before. Some of the scientific gear was primitive by modern standards. For example, the sounding lines were made of hemp, a plant fiber. The end of each line was tied securely to a 200-pound lead ball. And the line itself was wound around a drum 10 feet in diameter. When a sounding was to be made, the *Challenger* was put under steam power so that it could be held fairly stationary, against the pull of winds and ocean currents. The weight was dropped over the side, unreeling the line from the drum.

Along the line, marks had been made every 600 feet. As the line was carried into the sea, one of the scientists noted the number of marks that slipped below the surface. However, during early soundings, an unforeseen problem arose. The line would continue to unreel from the drum even after the lead ball had struck bottom.

Apparently, the weight of the line that had uncoiled into the ocean was sufficient to drag more line from the drum. To solve this problem, which threatened to affect the accuracy of deep-sea soundings, the *Challenger* scientists took advantage of a principle developed in the 1600's by the English scientist Robert Hooke.

Hooke had invented a device for measuring depth without a line. The device consisted of a wooden ball connected to a lead ball. The two balls were thrown over the side of a stationary vessel. When the lead ball hit bottom, the wooden one was automatically released by a latch that opened on impact. The wooden ball then rose to the surface.

By trial and error, Hooke discovered how long the ball took to hit the bottom. From this he found that the time that elapsed between the dropping of the device into the water and the reappearance of the wooden ball could be used to measure depth. Knowing that there was a predictable relationship between rate of descent and depth, the *Challenger* scientists timed the rate at which their line unwound into the sea. When the rate began to slow down, the scientists assumed the lead ball had struck bottom. At great depths such soundings could take several hours. Modern sonar techniques, in which a *pulse* of sound is bounced off the bottom, can make them in seconds.

Using line and ball sounding methods, the *Challenger* plumbed a depth of 26,850 feet near the Mariana Islands in the western Pacific. As far as we know, the sea floor in this area of the Pacific is deeper than that of any other ocean bed in the world. A record depth of 36,198 has been measured in Challenger Deep, which is in the

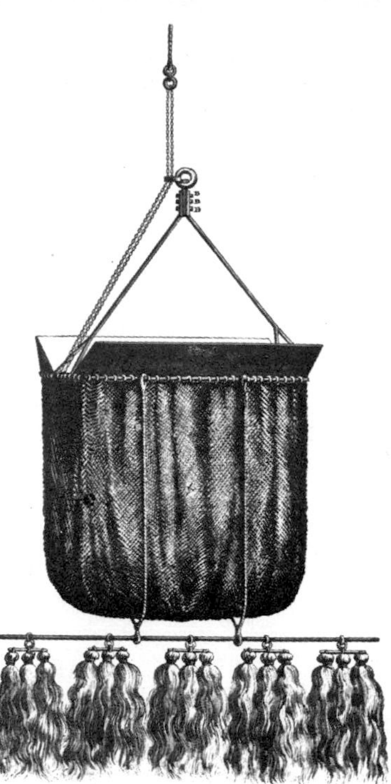

Above: the dredge used by *Challenger.* It consisted of a twine-netting bag held open by a rectangular iron frame. Below: once the dredge was trailing behind the ship the crew sent a "traveler" weight down the line. It stopped at a toggle tied to the rope and carried the dredge to the bottom.

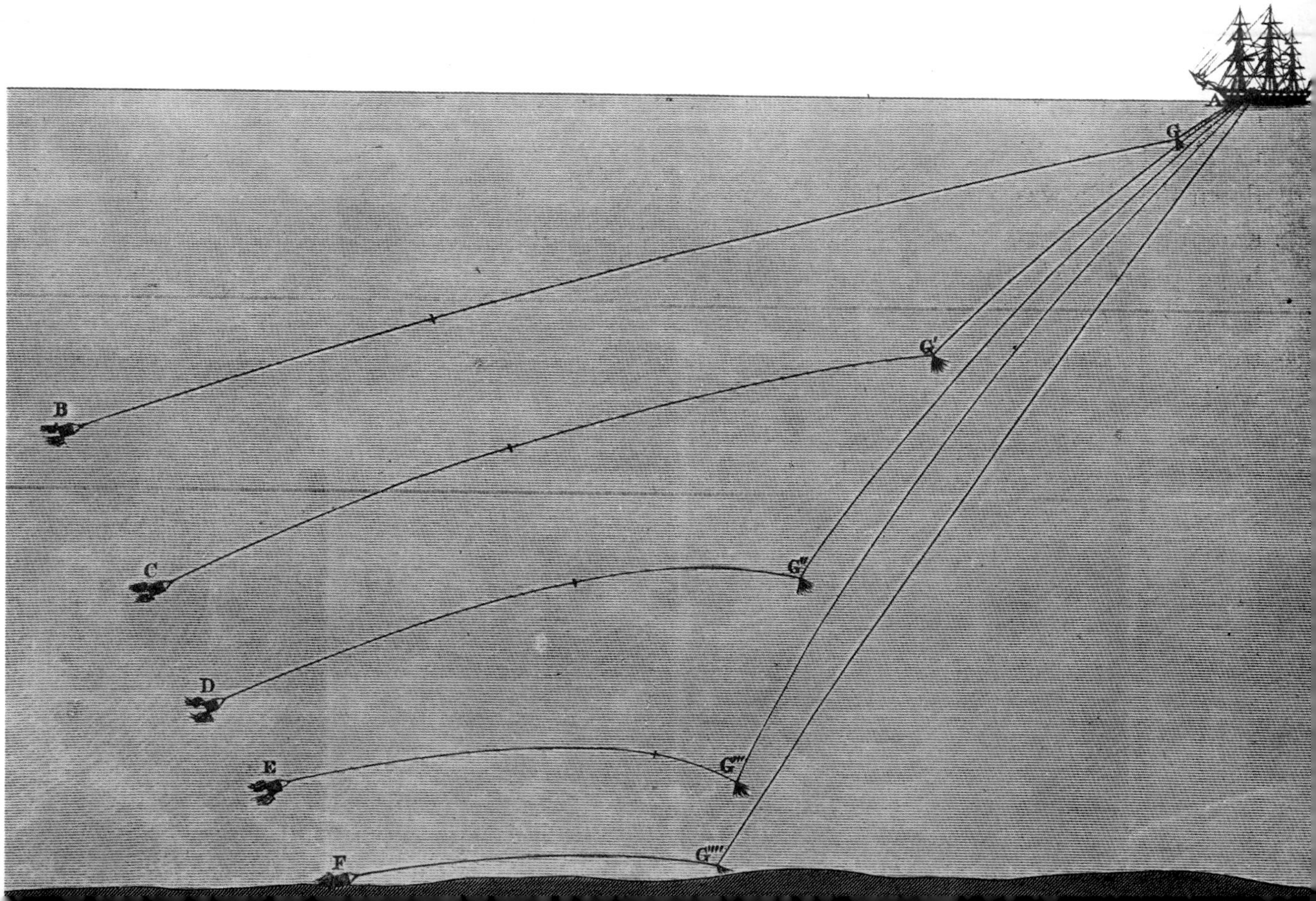

Mariana Trench, 200 miles southwest of Guam in the Mariana Islands.

What of life at great depths? The *Challenger*'s trawls and dredges brought up thousands of animals and plants. Of the animals, 4,717 species and 715 genera (groups of species) had never before been seen by man. Moreover, at no depth were there no living creatures. And the *Challenger* dredged the bottom at depths greater than 19,000 feet. But though animal life seemed to know no bounds, plants were not found beneath about 600 feet.

The *Challenger* scientists also found some explanation of how living things can survive in the cold, dark, high-pressure environment of the deep.

Above: two crewmen empty the dredge net on board the *Challenger*. The closely woven netting around the bottom of the dredge held everything but the finest mud, so the scientists could study even very tiny animals.

One creature, dredged from below 12,000 feet, was found to be equipped with its own light source—a powerful light-emitting organ. Some had huge eyes that could undoubtedly sense the faintest flicker of light. Still others had no eyes at all. They relied on sensitive organs of touch such as delicate antennae.

How did such animals survive the pressure of more than 8,400 pounds per square inch that exists at a depth of about 19,000 feet? An experiment performed by the expedition's chemist, J. Y. Buchanan, provided the answer.

Buchanan sealed both ends of a length of glass tubing, which he ordinarily used for experiments aboard ship. He wrapped the air-filled vial in cloth and placed it in a perforated copper container. Then the container and its contents were lowered over the side to a depth of 12,000 feet. Finally, the container was hauled back up and examined.

Buchanan found that the copper shell had been crushed. And of the glass tube it had held, nothing remained but powder. The perforated copper container was normally used to house thermometers that had measured water temperature at great depths. From past experience, Buchanan knew that the container could survive undamaged from depths greater than 12,000 feet. Yet it had not survived this plunge.

Buchanan had a reasonable, and correct, explanation. The glass tube, sealed at the sea's surface, contained air at atmospheric pressure—14.7 pounds per square inch. At some depth, the pressure outside of the tube so much exceeded that inside, that the tube collapsed. For an instant, there was a hollow space within the container. Before water could rush through the perforations in the container, the enormous water pressure drove the walls of the container inward.

Normally, when such a container was lowered into the sea, water passed through the perforations and equalized the pressure on both sides of the container's wall. The thermometer inside the container, was essentially a solid object. Therefore, it did not collapse. Water pressure, though enormous, remained balanced inside and outside of the container and no damage resulted.

This experiment, reasoned Buchanan and his colleagues, explained how animals survived under great pressure. The fluids inside their

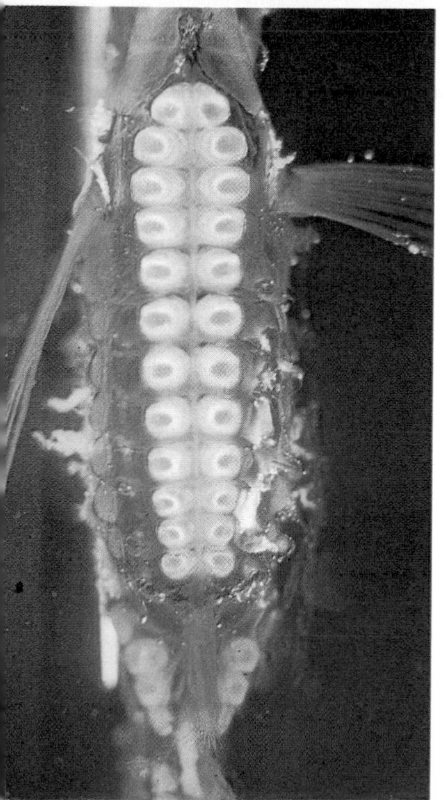

Above: the deep-sea hatchet fish (*Argyropelecus sp.* three inches long), one of the many light-producing marine animals the *Challenger* scientists encountered. Left: the light organs on the underside of the fish. Light is produced in them by a complex chemical reaction. In the darkness of the deep ocean these pinpoints of light serve as recognition patterns and may also attract prey. Below: the well-equipped natural history workroom on H.M.S. *Challenger.*

Above: crew members on *Challenger* retrieving a thermometer from the sea. Below: the thermometer they used. It registered only maximum and minimum temperatures and was housed in a protective perforated copper case (right).

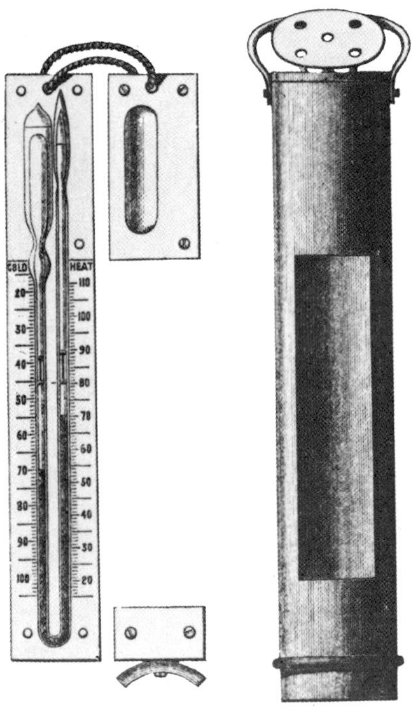

bodies were at the same pressure as was the water outside. Armed with this concept, the *Challenger* scientists concluded that life would be found at any depth, no matter how great. The one remaining factor —cold temperature—would affect only the kind of life present, not the existence of life itself.

Challenger scientists discovered the greatest number of marine living things in the relatively cold waters of the South Atlantic. These animals thrived in a food pyramid whose base consisted of an immense surface carpet of floating microscopic plants and animals that have since come to be known as *plankton* (from the Greek, meaning *wandering*). Plant plankton, mostly diatoms (single-celled algae), utilize sunlight to manufacture food from carbon dioxide, minerals, and water. These plants are the food of animal plankton, which, in turn, are the food of higher animals, and so on up the pyramid to large fish and aquatic carnivorous mammals.

Although questions concerning life in the deep were both intriguing and exciting, the 3½-year voyage of the *Challenger* also shed light on the riddles posed by physical oceanographers. Temperature readings were made at the 362 *stations* (stops) made by the *Challenger*. Self-closing bottles were lowered to various depths at each station to get samples of the water. A sounding was also made on each occasion, and a sample of the bottom was taken. From all the data, a picture of the sea's depths began to develop. In all, *Challenger* charted 140 million square miles of ocean floor.

Bottom temperatures of the abyss were almost always found to be near the freezing point of water. The temperatures were measured by a *self-registering thermometer* developed by Wyville Thomson during the *Lightning* expedition. The instrument recorded only the maximum and minimum temperatures to which it was exposed. A number of these thermometers, each housed in a protective perforated copper case, were attached to a sounding line at various intervals. The line was lowered into the sea to a known depth and then hauled up. Readings were taken of each thermometer and plotted on a graph. This graph provided a temperature *profile* at any given location. Similar instruments were lowered at each station to determine water pressure and water density at various depths.

Another discovery made by the *Challenger* team, which has great significance today, was that, in many places, the ocean floor is littered with manganese nodules. The nodules vary in size from

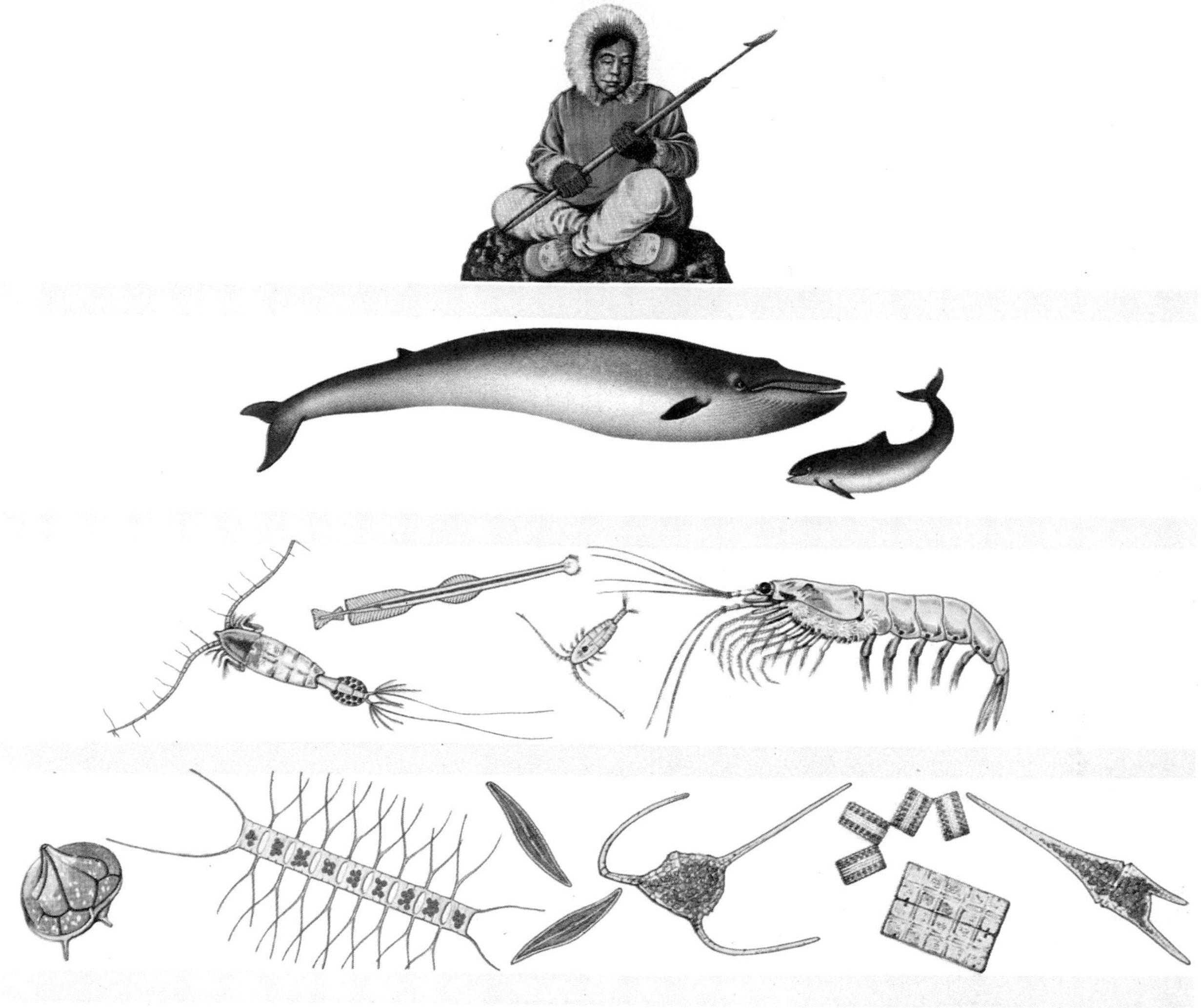

Above: a simplified food pyramid. The abundance of life that the *Challenger* scientists discovered in the sea all depends for its food supply on the tiny plant *plankton* (from the Greek, meaning *wandering*) that floats near the surface. Plant plankton produces food by photosynthesis. It is eaten by animal plankton, which is in turn eaten by higher animals. The whale shown above feeds on the animal plankton and itself provides food for man. The plants and animals forming plankton are so small that most of them can only be studied under a microscope.

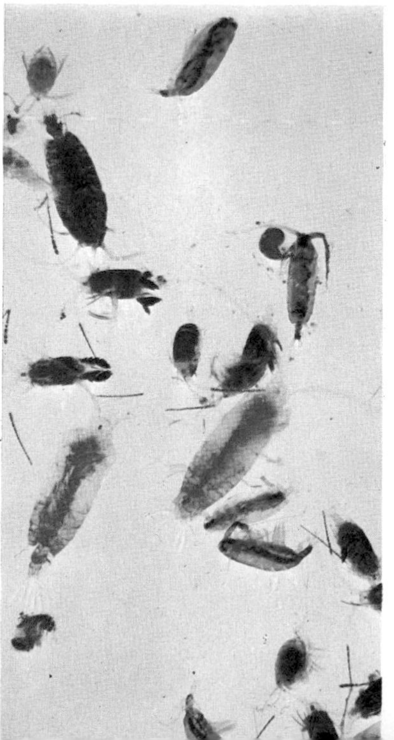

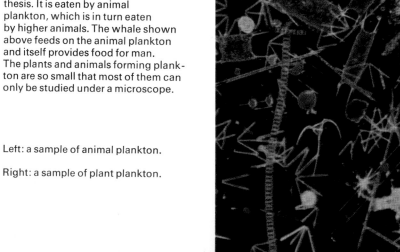

Left: a sample of animal plankton.

Right: a sample of plant plankton.

about 0.5 centimeters to 25 centimeters. In addition to manganese, they are rich in iron and contain significant amounts of aluminum and magnesium, as well as nickel, copper, and cobalt. Some of these nodule beds are at present being tapped by oceanographic mining firms.

While studying bottom samples John Murray developed a system for classifying sediments in the abyss that is still used today. Murray studied the bottom samples brought up by *Challenger* devices, and divided the sediments into two broad categories—*pelagic* sediments

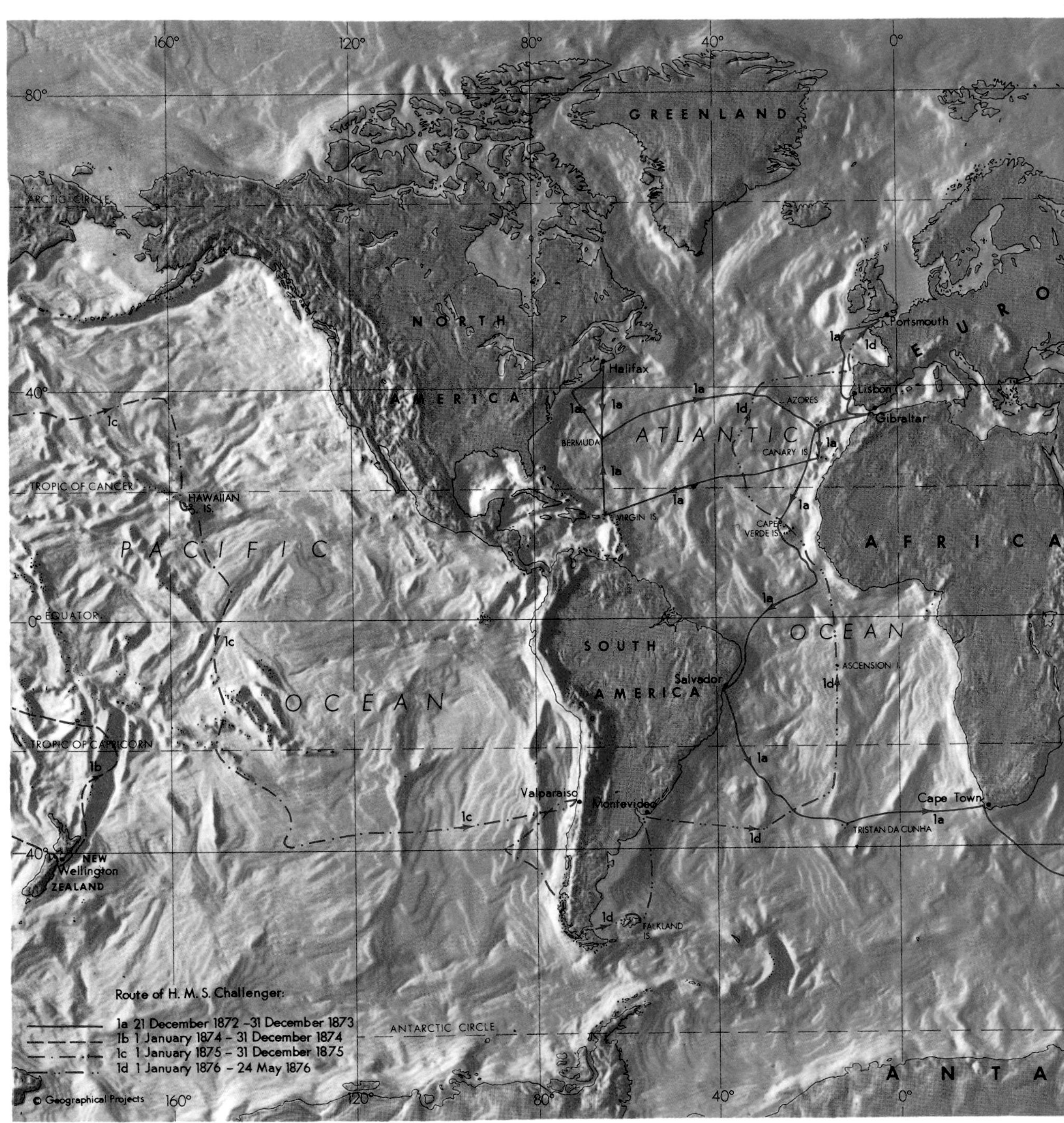

and *terrigenous* sediments. According to Murray's classification, the pelagic sediment consisted of fine-grained material that rides waves, winds, and currents of the sea, and falls as a constant rain on the ocean floor. This material is made up of inorganic red clay or has its origin in organic (once living) material. The terrigenous sediment consists of particles of various sizes that come in the main from nearby continents or islands. Murray subdivided this later category into: blue, green, and red muds; volcanic mud; and coral sand and mud.

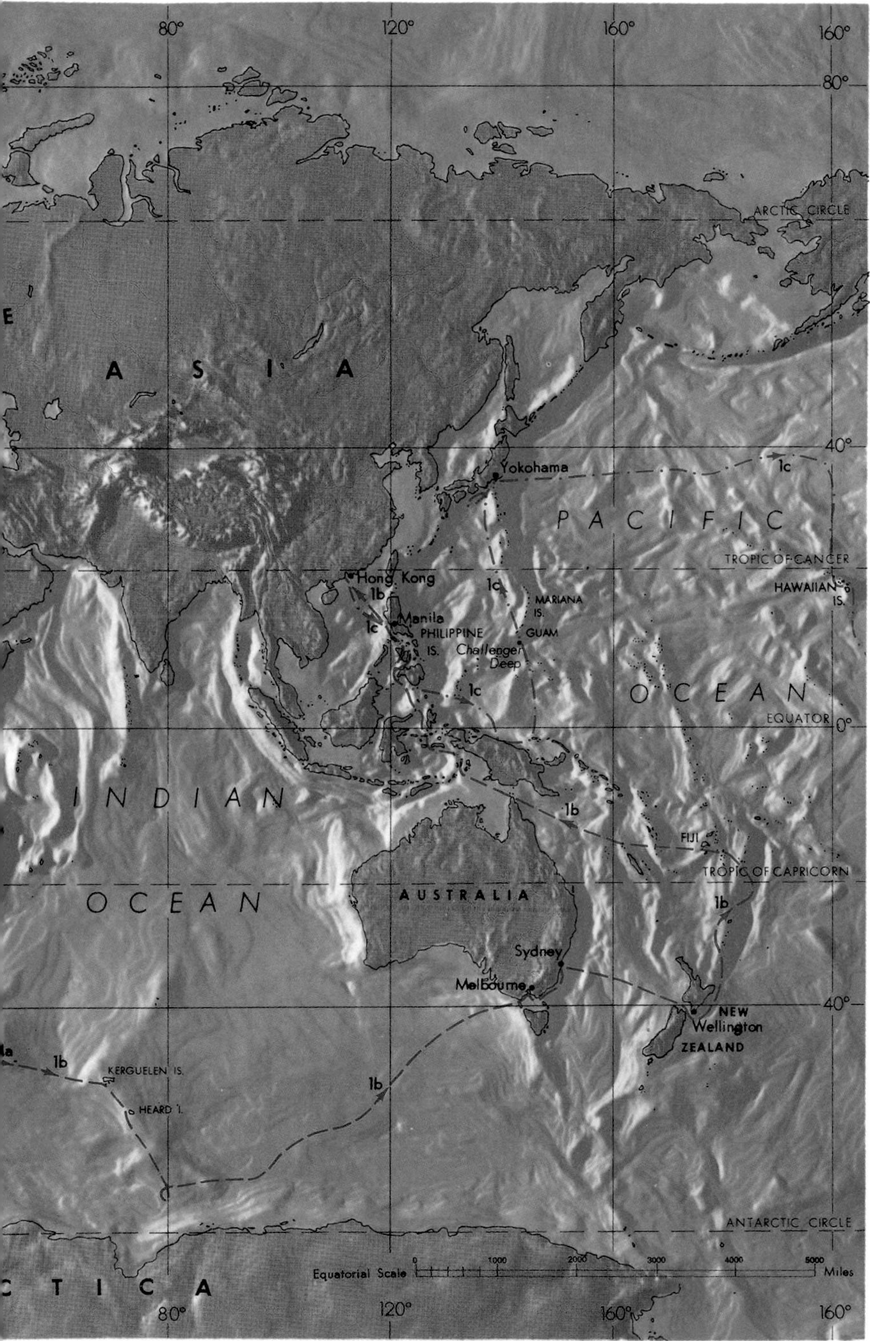

Left: the voyage of H.M.S. *Challenger* between 1872 and 1876 was the first global oceanographic expedition. Commissioned by the Royal Society of London to find out "everything about the sea," the expedition circled the earth, visiting every ocean except the Arctic. The data brought home by the expedition was to fill 50 volumes of the *Challenger Reports*.

Analysis of seawater brought up from various depths at the 362 stations revealed that the waters of the world's oceans have a constant composition of dissolved substances. That is, the proportion of substances in any sample of seawater will be approximately the same regardless of the origin of the sample. But the salinity (concentration of salt) varies at different locations and depths. In general, the parts of the ocean that receive heavy rainfall and those near the mouths of great rivers are less salty than average. In regions where the sun and wind cause a high rate of evaporation of moisture from the surface, the salinity is usually high.

The topography (surface features) of the cauldrons that hold the vast salty seas was also studied on the *Challenger* expedition. Thomson and his colleagues were familiar with the often precipitous contours of the earth's continents—mountains rising sharply from deserts and plateaus, and sheer cliffs plunging into the sea. But beneath the oceans the topography appeared to be different. Over thousands of years, a gentle rain of sediments had softened the contours of the ocean floor.

In May, 1876, the *Challenger* made its way back along the English Channel toward Portsmouth. The epic voyage was drawing to a close. It had cost the lives of two men. Rudolph von Willemoes-Suhm had died of *erysipelas* (a skin disease), and a young sailor had been swept overboard, caught in the line of a descending dredge. But much had been gained. The data brought home by the *Challenger* filled 50 volumes containing 29,500 pages. These reports were to launch the era of modern oceanography and came to be called "the oceanographer's Bible."

Their impact on the scientific world was immediate. Countries all over the globe began to fit out expeditions to follow in the wake of the *Challenger*. Other pioneer oceanographers were soon making their own contributions to the young science.

Among them was Alexander Agassiz, a Swiss-American scientist who had been a member of the *Challenger* team and had written

Left: a scientist emptying a water sample bottle on board *Challenger*. The device was lowered into the sea with its sample compartment open. At the desired depth, or when the device hit the bottom, a sudden jerk on the rope released a cylinder which slid down, sealing off compartment and sample.

two volumes of the *Challenger Reports*. He spent 25 years, from 1877 to 1902, in further exploration of the undersea world. Sailing aboard the *Blake* and the *Albatross,* he made extensive soundings in the Caribbean, the Indian Ocean, and the tropical Pacific. Using improved dredges and trawls he snared creatures from depths between 600 and 14,000 feet. He found that the most populated underwater zone was that between 1,200 and 12,000 feet. And within this zone, there was a 4,200-foot layer (1,800 to 6,000 feet) that harbored the greatest variety of animal species.

Another man who dedicated much of his life to the study of the seas was Prince Albert I of Monaco. Between 1885 and 1915, Prince Albert sailed on expeditions in the Mediterranean and Atlantic aboard his own yachts. He wrote many books about his work and helped to bring oceanography to the attention of the general public. In 1910, he founded one of the world's most famous marine museums at Monaco.

Below: a drawing made on board of a young fish (*Antennarius sp.* which is three inches long) found entangled in weed in mid-Atlantic on March 6, 1873.

Above: the Norwegian explorer Fridtjof Nansen at the bow of his ship, the *Fram*, in the summer of 1894. The *Fram* was specially built to withstand the polar ice floes on this expedition to explore the North Polar basin. When, as Nansen had expected, it became locked in the ice, the men on board were able to make scientific studies of polar conditions.

Although these early pioneers had restricted most of their efforts to relatively warm seas, the vast regions of frigid Arctic water did not go unexplored. In 1893, the 128-foot-long ship *Fram* weighed anchor at Pepperviken, Norway. Under the command of Fridtjof Nansen, a Norwegian explorer with a degree in zoology, the *Fram* sailed northward.

For three years, Nansen struggled against the hostile environment of the Arctic—first aboard the *Fram*, and later on foot trekking across the endless ice. Early in the voyage, the *Fram* became locked in the ice. There she remained for 35 months, while her crew performed various scientific tasks. Surface and water temperatures were taken. Soundings were made through holes cut in the ice. Meteorological conditions were studied. And the position of the ship, held fast in the drifting ice pack, was determined every second day.

Nansen discovered that, contrary to popular belief, the north Arctic waters are not shallow. Some of his soundings struck bottom at depths greater than 12,000 feet. Nor were these waters devoid of life. In May, 1894, the *Fram* crew observed for the first time what has come to be called *the early summer plankton bloom*. Beneath the melting ice, a population explosion was occurring.

Above: a pastel drawing by Nansen showing the midnight sun near the North Pole. In the extreme north in summer, it is never dark and the sun shines through the night.

Uncountable swarms of diatoms were reproducing and forming brown patches on the ice. Algae began to appear as did microscopic animals. The base of a food pyramid was being forged, one that could support whales, fish, and other creatures of the Arctic.

On March 14, 1895, Nansen set out with a companion in an attempt to sledge his way to the North Pole. At the time, the *Fram* was at 83° 47′ north—about 483 miles from the pole. The two explorers came within 272 miles of the most northern spot on earth—no one had come closer—before snow and ice forced them to turn back.

In August, 1895, they reached Franz Josef Land. There they remained for nine bitterly cold months of frozen solitude before being rescued by a British polar expedition. Meanwhile, the *Fram* had broken loose from the grip of the polar ice. On August 20, 1896, she sailed into the port of Skjaervo, Norway, where Nansen was waiting to meet her.

Nansen's exploits showed that oceanographers were ready to challenge the greatest hazards on the surface of the sea in the search for knowledge of its depths. But the greatest test of man's courage and ingenuity remained—would he descend deep into the black abyss to see firsthand what wonders it held?

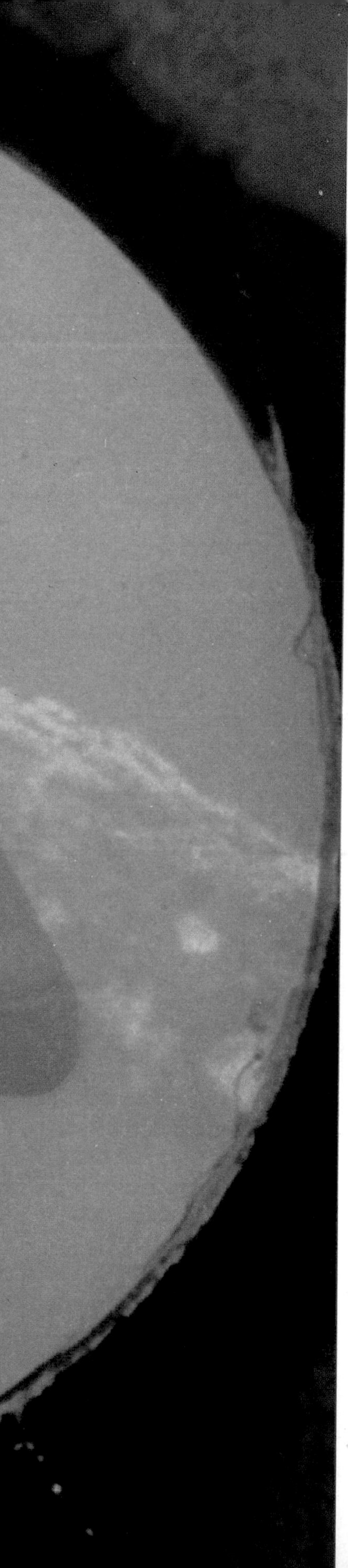

Under the Sea
4

Man is out of his element in water. He cannot swim around under the sea for more than two or three minutes without returning to the surface for a fresh gulp of air. The Greek divers of classic times achieved record dives of $4\frac{1}{2}$ minutes without breathing devices, but only in relatively shallow water and on condition that they did not move at all. When, in the 1300's and 1400's, men turned their attention again to the sea, their first interest lay in providing the diver with the apparatus necessary to breathe and move with ease at great depths and for considerable periods of time.

Among the first thinkers to tackle this problem was Leonardo da Vinci, one of the most brilliant men of the Renaissance (the period of artistic and scientific inquiry in Europe which lasted from the 1300's to the 1500's). His designs for underwater equipment included a headpiece of rigid leather to resist the pressure of water. Fitted to it was a breathing tube topped by a cork float to keep it above the surface. Glass lenses covered the eyeholes and the helmet was equipped with a series of spikes to ward off underwater monsters.

Leonardo also designed webbed gloves and flippers, but he never tried out the equipment he invented. If he had, he would have discovered an unexpected drawback. Equipped with Leonardo's breathing tube, a diver would have suffocated at a depth of little

Left: a diver photographed through the porthole of the U.S. Navy's underwater habitat *Sealab II.* At a depth of 206 feet, he is completely cut off from the surface. However, the sophisticated equipment he is wearing enables him to move freely and safely in the environment of the ocean.

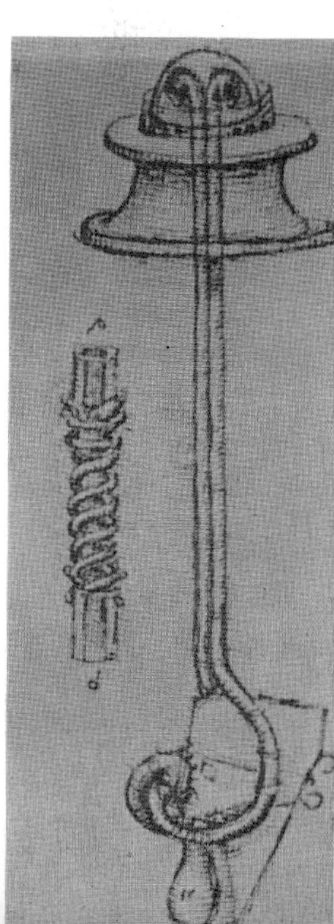

Right: a sketch of a device for breathing underwater made by the artist Leonardo da Vinci (1452–1519). The design shows a mask fitted with breathing tubes leading to a surface float.

more than five feet. The pressure of water on his chest at such a depth would prevent his lungs from expanding sufficiently to inhale the air in the tube.

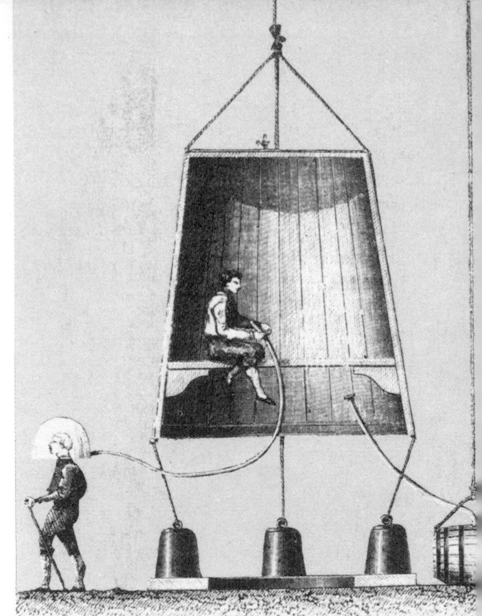

Not until 1690 did Edmund Halley, who discovered the famous comet that bears his name, develop a means of piping pressurized air to a diver in a bell. If the air the diver breathes is at the same pressure as the water surrounding him, his chest is not crushed and he can breathe normally. This is the principle on which the diving bell is based. A diving bell is a container the bottom of which is open to the sea and which is large enough to hold one or two divers. Once the bell is submerged, the weight of the water compresses the air inside the bell and the men are able to breathe for some time. However, the farther the bell descends, the more water will rise in it and the less air will be available. The increasing water pressure

Left: The diving bell invented in 1690 by Edmund Halley. As the volume of air trapped inside decreased with increasing depth, extra air was piped in from casks suspended outside the bell at pressures equal to that of the water surrounding the bell. One of the divers shown here is using an individual bell supplied with air from the main bell. This small bell was the first practicable diving suit.

Below: a more sophisticated diving bell of the mid-1800's. Air was supplied to the men inside the bell from a hand-driven pump at the surface.

compresses the air within the bell, and in so doing raises the air pressure. For example, at a depth of 33 feet, the air within the bell is compressed to half its original volume and the pressure is doubled from 1 atmosphere (14.7 pounds per square inch), to 2 atmospheres (29.4 pounds per square inch). At 66 feet, air volume is reduced to one-third of what it was originally and the pressure is tripled to 3 atmospheres. For every additional 33 feet in depth, the pressure increases by 1 atmosphere. The volume of air in the bell decreases also, but not uniformly. At the relatively shallow depth of 627 feet, the volume of air in the bell would be compressed to one-twentieth of what it had been originally. And the pressure would be 20 atmospheres (294 pounds per square inch).

Assuming that the bell were 10 feet tall, the open space within it at a depth of 627 feet would be only 6 inches deep—hardly enough room to work in, let alone keep instruments functioning. There is a solution to this space problem. By pumping air into the bell from the surface at pressures equal to that of the water surrounding the bell, water can be kept from rising inside it. This was the technique discovered by Halley. He attached two empty casks to a diving bell by means of flexible tubes. A hole in the bottom of each cask let in water, whose pressure drove air from the cask, through the tube and into the bell. The divers inside the bell could let in this air when needed. simply by turning a tap.

Halley himself tested his invention on several occasions and stayed "at the bottom, in 9 or 10 fathoms [54–60 feet] of water, for above an hour and a half at a time, without any sort of ill consequence . . ."

Halley did find one inconvenience in his bell, which he was quick to remedy. Inside the bell was a bench on which the divers remained seated. This meant that they had a very narrow area of vision. Halley's solution was to provide the divers with small, individual bells, attached to their heads and linked by breathing tubes to the main bell. In this way, he invented the first workable diving suit.

Once it was realized that a man could not breathe the ordinary air of the atmosphere when his lungs were under pressure from water, protection of the diver from this hazard of pressure became the prime consideration of diving-suit designers. They began to devise unwieldly, armor-like suits, often reinforced with metal.

One of the first men to use this type of diving suit was the Englishman John Lethbridge, who had a long career as a diver for treasure from sunken wrecks. Lethbridge's diving apparatus consisted of a barrel-like suit, bound with iron hoops and fitted with leather sleeves. Once Lethbridge was inside the barrel it was bolted behind him, and his only means of vision was a four-inch diameter porthole. He was lowered into the sea by a cable and the air in the barrel enabled him to stay down for about half an hour. His assistants would then haul him to the surface and pump fresh air to him from a pair of bellows. In this way, Lethbridge could work for as long as six hours under water, although the rigid shape of the suit forced him to stay face-down all the time. The first of Lethbridge's many

dives was made in 1715, and by 1749 he reported having been down as far as 72 feet.

The prototype of the modern hard hat diving suit was invented in 1819 by Augustus Siebe and in 1837 developed into a full diving suit. This was a rubber watertight suit with a removable copper helmet. The helmet was fitted with intake and outlet valves and pressurized air was pumped into it from the deck of a ship. The Siebe diving suit enabled divers to go down to at least 300 feet. Using Siebe's device, the French zoologist Henri Milne-Edwards became the first scientist to explore the ocean floor in a diving suit. In 1844, he made a descent off the coast of Sicily and collected many specimens of marine life from the Mediterranean. Milne-Edwards repeated this exploit many times but, despite the growing availability of diving suits, few scientists followed his example.

In the mid-1800's, diving suits began to come into general use. But they still had one serious limitation. The diver continued to be dependent on a life line from the surface. In 1865, the Frenchmen Benoît Rouquayrol, a mining engineer, and Auguste Denayrouze, a naval officer, designed an apparatus to make the diver entirely self-sufficient. This was a metal canister, filled with compressed air, which the diver could carry on his back. The air was released by a regulator valve, while another valve removed the air breathed out by the diver.

Above: the diving helmet invented in 1819 by Augustus Siebe. It was supplied with pressurized air from the surface and formed the basis of the modern hard hat diving suit. Below left: a boys' book illustration of the 1930's showing a helmeted diver recovering lost treasure. Below right: a diver seeking pearls.

Although a brilliant invention, the Rouquayrol-Denayrouze apparatus ran into a snag which marred its success. It was impossible at the time to make a canister which could withstand pressure at

Above: a scene from the film based on Jules Verne's book *Twenty Thousand Leagues Under the Sea.* Verne modeled the breathing apparatus on a French invention of 1865. Below right: an illustration from the book, showing divers exploring the seabed.

great depths. Rouquayrol and Denayrouze were obliged to fall back on the use of a tube to pump air into the canister. It was to be another 78 years before divers could dispense entirely with their life lines.

But, if its original design was not wholly successful, the Rouquayrol and Denayrouze device became known all over the world through the writings of Jules Verne. The heroes of his book *Twenty Thousand Leagues Under the Sea* used this apparatus during their underwater excursions.

Jules Verne's book aroused a great deal of public interest toward the close of the 1800's. The adventures of divers and ways of living under the sea became a popular topic for writers, cartoonists, and inventors alike. At the same time, engineers and builders were starting to use diving suits and bells when constructing underwater foundations for bridges and harbors. Then, just as men began to feel more at home underwater, a series of seemingly inexplicable accidents again hindered the progress of diving.

Many of the underwater workers fell ill with a mysterious disease. They complained of severe pains in muscles and joints, of vomiting, fainting, and deafness. Some of them suffered from nervous disorders

Right: a cross-sectional diagram of David Bushnell's submarine *Turtle.* Its intrepid occupant was kept busy cranking two propellers as well as operating a rudder. Bushnell built the craft in 1776 so that it could be used to plant explosives on the hulls of enemy ships during the Revolutionary War in America. The powder charge was housed in a detachable section above the rudder. Below: Bushnell's submarine as it appeared from the outside.

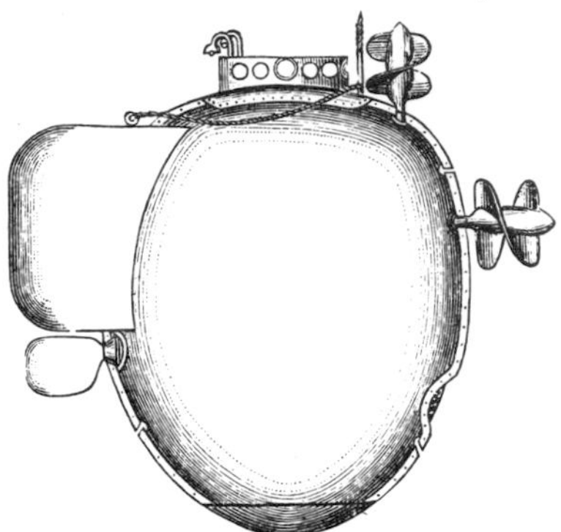

and paralysis. A number of men died suddenly. These men were victims of one of the greatest hazards of diving—the *bends*.

During the time a diver is under water, the nitrogen gas in the air that he breathes is continually being forced into his blood-stream and body tissues. The longer he stays down, and the deeper he goes, the more nitrogen enters his blood. As he returns to the surface, the reverse occurs. The nitrogen is returned to the lung surfaces and breathed out. But if the man ascends too rapidly, pressure drops quickly and the nitrogen trapped in his blood and tissues takes the form of bubbles. These bubbles are the cause of *decompression sickness*. If they block the blood flow to the brain or heart, they can cause permanent injury or death.

This phenomenon was first explained by French physiologist Paul Bert in 1870. Bert also explained that to avoid this decompression sickness a diver must rise to the surface very slowly so that the dissolved nitrogen comes out of his tissues gradually and bubbles do not form. Bert's work eventually led to the drawing up, in 1906, of a decompression table, setting out stages of ascent for divers. But decompression remained a major drawback by limiting the amount of time that divers can work under water and the depth to which they can go. For example, a dive to 600 feet, with 4 minutes spent at that depth, requires $11\frac{1}{2}$ hours of decompression.

This problem was very far from being solved in the early 1900's, when diving was called upon to assume a new and vital role—the rescue of submarine crews.

The development of the submarine had been going on side by side with that of the diving suit ever since the time of Leonardo da Vinci. Leonardo himself is said to have designed an underwater warship but

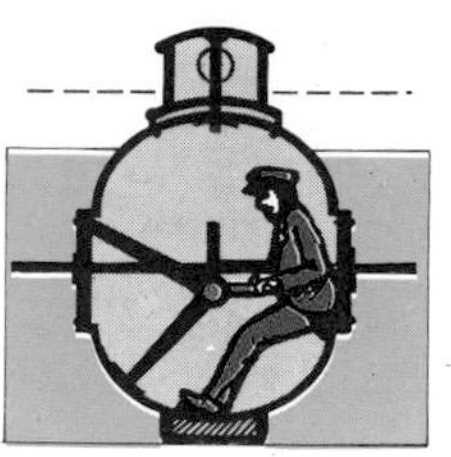

he kept his plans secret. "There is too much wickedness in the hearts of men," he wrote, "to justify my entrusting them with the secret of underwater navigation; they would not hesitate to use it to sow murder in the depths of the seas."

History was to prove him right. In 1776, David Bushnell built an underwater boat for use during the Revolutionary War in America. Bushnell named his submarine *Turtle* because of its shape. It was operated by a single man who hand-cranked two propellors—one to move the vessel forward or backward, the other to move it up or down—and controlled a rudder. Bushnell designed the submarine so that the operator could attach a powder charge to the hull of an enemy vessel. Using an explosive device, *Turtle* attacked a British

Above: diagrams showing two views of the Confederate submarine *Hunley*. It was built in 1863 and, like the *Turtle*, was hand-driven. A crew of eight operated a crankshaft connected directly to the propeller.

Below: an oil painting showing the *Hunley* during the Civil War. This submarine was the first to sink an enemy vessel, the Federal corvette *Housatonic*, on February 17, 1864, in the harbor at Charleston, S.C.

Above: the missile launching chambers on board the U.S. Navy nuclear submarine *George Washington.* Such submarines are important militarily but are of little use for exploration.

man-of-war in the harbor at New York, but was unable to sink it.

The design of the *Turtle* was improved on by American engineer Robert Fulton. In 1800, he built two submarines, the *Nautilus* and the *Mute*. Fulton believed that the submarine would help to end naval warfare and piracy, but neither of his vessels was ever used in war.

The first submarine to sink an enemy vessel was the Confederate *Hunley*. On February 17, 1864, during the Civil War, the *Hunley* sank the *Housatonic,* a Federal corvette that was blockading the harbor at Charleston, South Carolina.

The *Hunley,* like all the early submarines, was propelled by hand. Toward the end of the 1800's, inventors began to experiment with undersea vessels driven by compressed air, steam, and electricity. In 1898, John P. Holland, an Irish immigrant from New Jersey, built a submarine boat called the *Holland,* that used a gasoline engine on the surface and electricity underwater. The *Holland* was bought

by the U.S. Navy in 1900, becoming the Navy's first submarine.

Germany did not build a submarine until 1907, but it was her *Unterseeboten,* or U-boats, which demonstrated the power of submarines in naval warfare during World War I. The war speeded the development of improved submarines. It also revealed the urgency of discovering life-saving apparatus for their crews. Yet, as late as 1958, when America's nuclear-powered *Nautilus* had already made history by sailing under the North Pole, there were still no means of rescuing submarine crews from below 600 feet.

The submarine was designed primarily for military purposes, and as such contributed little to knowledge of the underwater world. The view from inside a submarine was limited and so were the depths to which it could descend. In order to reach and explore the greatest depths of the ocean, a new vehicle was needed. And it had to be a vehicle strong enough to withstand the tremendous pressures of the deep ocean.

Above: the world's first nuclear submarine *Nautilus.* This 3,000-ton ship made history in 1958, when it sailed under the ice at the North Pole charting a navigable route that could save 4,900 miles on an underwater voyage from Japan to Europe.

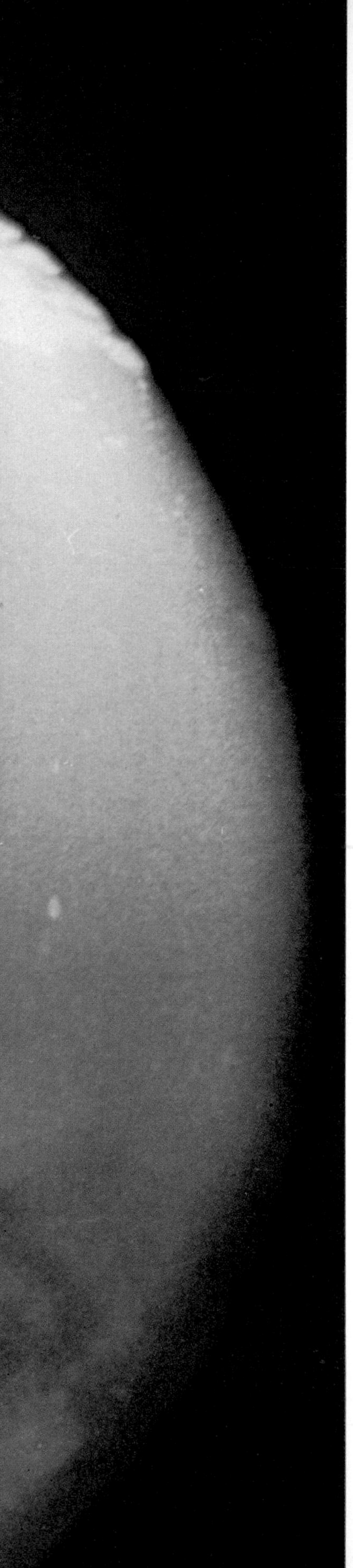

To the Bottom 5

Before 1930, no man had reached an undersea depth of more than about 600 feet. In that year, human beings were at last to penetrate the no man's land of the deep. Their record-breaking achievement was accomplished with the aid of an entirely new underwater vessel. This vessel was the brainchild of William Beebe, an American ornithologist turned marine zoologist.

Beebe had long been drawn to the oceans' depths in search of the living things that it hid. He had dived hundreds of times into the sea—always encased in a diving suit or diving helmet, which limited the depth to which he could go with safety. In the waters off Haiti, Beebe had slid down a rope to a bed of sand 63 feet below the surface. Peering through the glass of his copper helmet, he had walked across the sandy bottom until he had come to the edge of an undersea cliff. Beebe could see strange multicolored fish and other sea creatures darting through the waters below. In his book, *Half Mile Down,* Beebe writes, "As I peered down I realized I was looking toward a world of life almost as unknown as that of Mars or Venus . . . a harvest [of life] which has served only to increase my desire actually to descend into this no man's zone."

Left: a modern bathysphere (depth sphere) being tested in shallow water. When tests are complete the bathysphere will be used to take men thousands of feet down into the ocean.

Right: the American naturalist and writer, William Beebe. With engineer Otis Barton and designer John Butler, Beebe set out to build a bathysphere to break the barrier of the deep. On June 6, 1930 Beebe and Barton descended in their steel sphere to a depth of 800 feet—200 feet deeper than man had ever gone before. It was the first of many successful dives.

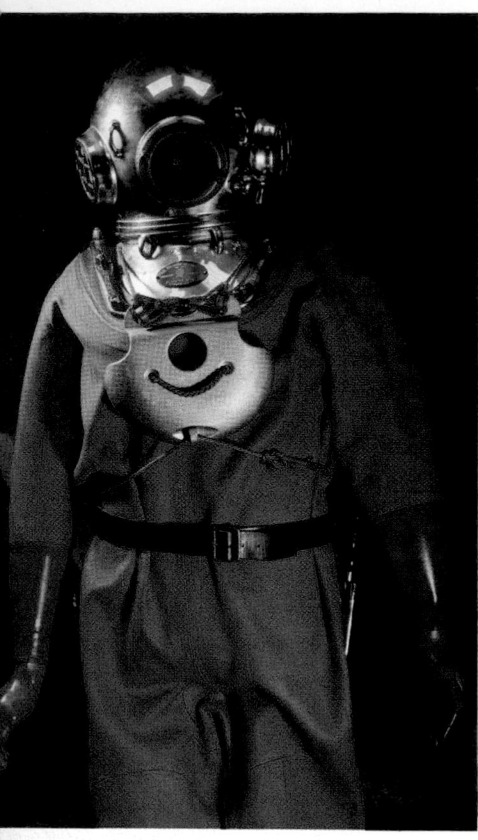

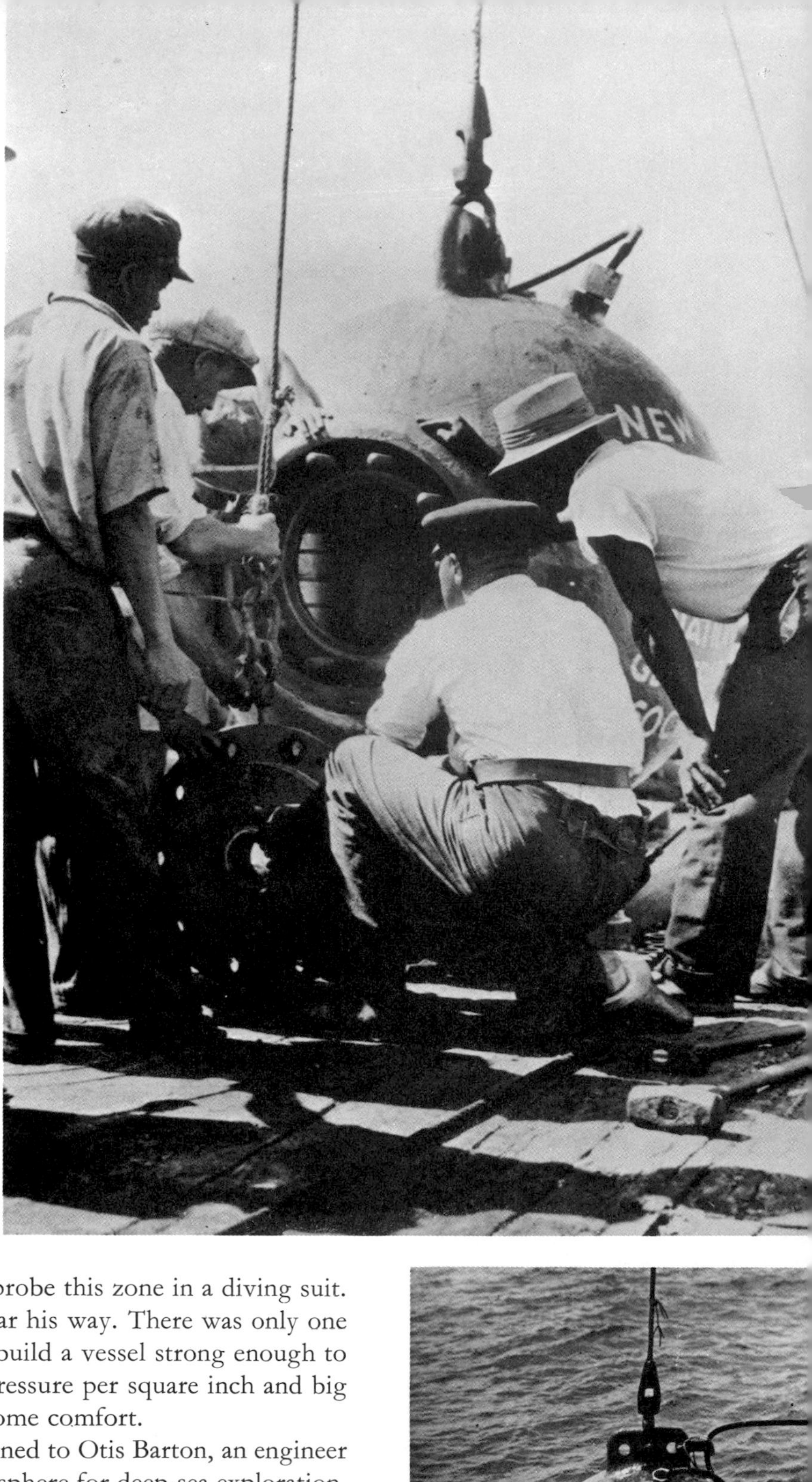

Above: a hard hat diving suit of the 1930's. William Beebe made many dives in a suit of this kind, but he was not content to explore only the shallow waters the suit was designed for. He wanted to go deeper.

Right: the bathysphere at the surface after a record-breaking dive of 2,510 feet, on August 11, 1934. Crew members of the stand-by barge *Ready* open the hatch to release William Beebe and Otis Barton from the sphere.

Below right: the bathysphere breaks surface as it is hauled from the sea.

Beebe realized that he could not probe this zone in a diving suit. Eventually, water pressure would bar his way. There was only one way to break the pressure barrier—build a vessel strong enough to withstand hundreds of pounds of pressure per square inch and big enough to house a man or two in some comfort.

To accomplish this feat, Beebe turned to Otis Barton, an engineer who had already constructed a steel sphere for deep-sea exploration, and to John H. J. Butler, who had designed the vessel. Together, they reconstructed, modified, and outfitted the device. Beebe named it *bathysphere*—depth sphere.

The bathysphere was 4 feet 9 inches in diameter. Its steel walls were $1\frac{1}{4}$ inches thick and strong enough to withstand a pressure in

excess of 1,500 pounds per square inch—equal to that at 3,400 feet below the sea's surface. It weighed 5,400 pounds. Unlike a military submarine, the sphere was equipped with portholes. These were made of three-inch-thick fused quartz, the strongest transparent material known to man and a substance that transmits all wavelengths of light. Each porthole was eight inches across. The bathysphere had a self-contained oxygen supply stored aboard in tanks. Moisture exhaled by the crew would be absorbed by trays of calcium chloride. Trays of soda lime, a mixture of calcium oxide and sodium hydroxide, would be used to remove from the atmosphere of the cabin the carbon dioxide exhaled by the men.

A communication hose would link the bathysphere to a mother ship at the surface. Cables in the hose would bring electricity to power instruments and a searchlight. And a telephone line would allow Beebe to give a "blow-by-blow" account of his plunge into the abyss. Finally, the bathysphere would be lowered on a steel cable, seven-eighths of an inch thick and 3,500 feet long. How deep would the bathysphere descend in its journeys into the sea?

The first answer to this question came on June 6, 1930. On that day, the bathysphere was transported into the warm waters off Bermuda on the deck of a huge barge, the *Ready*. The *Ready* itself was towed to sea by the ocean-going tug *Gladisfen*. During the previous few days, the bathysphere had made the same journey and had been lowered empty into the water a few times to test its seaworthiness. Now it was ready to carry human beings where none had gone before.

Shortly after noon, Beebe and Barton squirmed through the round 14-inch opening that served as a door for the bathysphere. On the outside, the deck crew maneuvered the 400-pound lid over the door opening. Huge bolts and nuts were joined to fasten the lid tightly. Beebe and Barton were sealed in their diving chamber.

The dangers for the two men were tremendous. Prisoners in their steel container, they could do nothing to counteract the jolting of the bathysphere. They were likely to be thrown about by sudden jerking of the cable as the mother ship pitched in the swell above them. At any moment, the strain on the cable could prove too great and the bathysphere plummet like a stone to the ocean bottom.

But danger was temporarily forgotten as Beebe looked out into the world beneath the waves. "At 50 feet," he noted, "I looked out at the brilliant bluish-green haze and could not realize that this was almost my limit in the diving helmet." At 100 feet, the light began to fade. As they sank farther, "motes of life" passed the portholes. Then, at 300 feet, an alarming trickle of water seeped from the door. "I wiped away the meandering stream," wrote Beebe, "and still it came. . . . I knew the door was solid enough . . . and I knew the inward pressure would increase with every foot of depth. So I gave the signal to descend quickly. . . ."

Two minutes later they passed 400 feet, then 500, and 600. The stream did not increase. At 700 feet, Beebe noted "only dead men

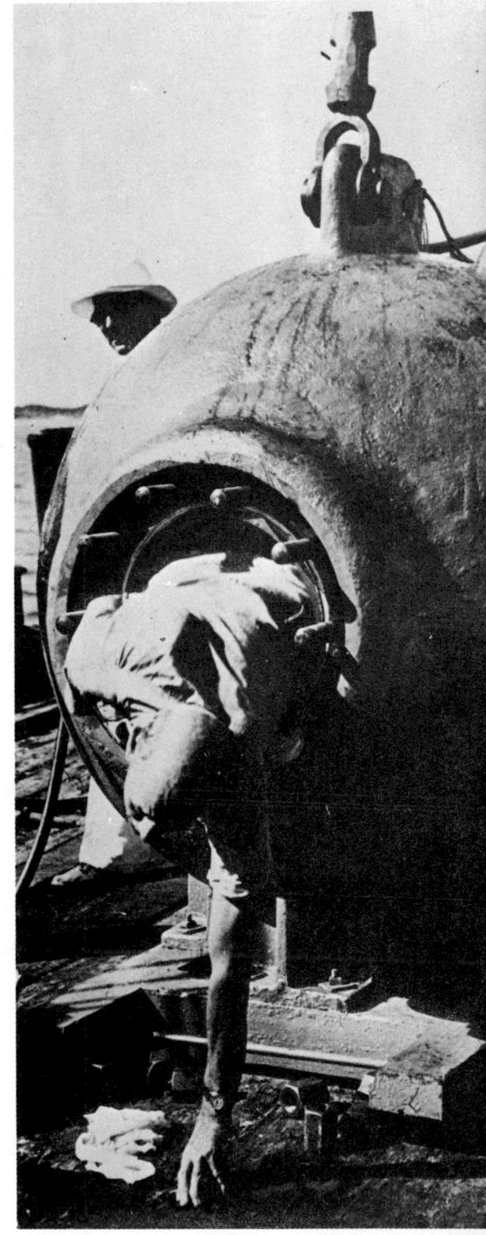

Above: William Beebe clambers out of the bathysphere after descending to 2,510 feet in the sea off Bermuda. This dive was one of a series that he and Otis Barton made during 1934.

Above: a deep-sea red prawn (*Systellaspis sp.*) holding a three-inch-long minnow of the deep *(Cyclothone sp.)*. Both these creatures have light-producing organs and were seen frequently by William Beebe as he descended to depths below the level of 1,000 feet.

have sunk below this." Halting in the journey downward, he described the water outside as "an indefinable translucent blue quite unlike anything I have ever seen in the upper world." As he switched on the searchlight he saw strange fishes darting in and out of the beam. When the light was turned off, luminescent creatures seemed to fill the water with eerie specks of light.

The bathysphere sank deeper into the sea and "the twilight deepened . . . from dark blue to blacker blue." "800 feet," came the call from the surface crew. "Stop!" replied Beebe. The bathysphere had reached "bottom" for this maiden voyage.

During the next 4 years, Beebe and Barton made more than 30 dives in the bathysphere. But none was more dramatic than dive number 32 near Bermuda on August 15, 1934. During the early series of dives in 1930, the two undersea explorers had plumbed the sea to a depth of 1,426 feet. Then the bathysphere had been put on display at the Century of Progress Exposition at Chicago in 1933. Following the exposition, the National Geographic Society offered to sponsor a new series of deep dives. Number 32 was the highlight of Beebe and Barton's final series of probes. It broke all their previous records both for the depth reached and for the number of living creatures observed.

In his account of the dive, Beebe wrote, "Surprises came at every

Above: a saber-toothed viperfish (*Chauliodus* sp.—up to 10 inches long). Beebe reported seeing 7 of them at 1,700 feet. This fish has light-producing organs on its body and inside its mouth. As it opens its mouth the lit interior may act as a lure to crustaceans and small fishes.

few feet . . . the mass of life was totally unexpected, the sum total of creatures seen unbelievable. At 1,000 feet I distinctly saw a shrimp outlined and distinguished several of its pale greenish lights. . . . Large Melanostomiatid dragon-fish with their glowing porthole lights showed themselves now and then [and] we had frequent glimpses of small opalescent copepods [small crustaceans], appropriately called *Sapphirina,* which renewed for us all the spectrum of the sunlight.

"At 1,680 feet. . . . I saw some creature, several inches long, dart toward the window, turn sideways and—explode. . . . At the flash, which was so strong that it illumined my face and the inner sill of the window, I saw the great red shrimp and the outpouring fluid of flame." (This is a defense process of certain shrimps, which confuses predators in a similar way to the ink clouds produced by a threatened octopus.)

"At 1,800 feet I saw a small fish with illumined teeth . . . and ten feet below this my favorite sea-dragons, *Lamprotoxus,* appeared, they of the shining green bow. Only sixteen of these fish have ever been taken. . . . The record size is about eight inches, while here before me were four individuals all more than twice that length, and very probably representing a new species. . . . At 2,450 a very large, dim, but not indistinct outline came into view for a fraction of a

Above: Beebe and Barton after their spectacular dive in the bathysphere on August 15, 1934. On that day they dived to a depth of 3,028 feet.

Below: a deep-sea angler *(Onsirodes carlsbergi)*. At a depth of 1,900 feet William Beebe reported seeing "one of the true giant female angler-fish . . . a full two feet in length. . . ."

second, and at 2,500 a delicately illumined ctenophore jelly throbbed past. Without warning, the large fish returned and this time I saw its complete, shadow-like contour. . . . Twenty feet is the least possible estimate I can give to its full length. . . . For the majority of the 'size-conscious' human race this MARINE MONSTER would, I suppose, be the supreme sight of the expedition. . . . What this creature was I cannot say. A first, and more reasonable guess would be a small whale or blackfish. We know that whales have a special chemical adjustment of the blood which makes it possible for them to dive a mile or more, and come up without getting the 'bends.' So this paltry depth of 2,450 feet would be nothing for any similarly equipped cetacean.

"Soon after [Barton] saw the first living *Stylophthalmus* ever seen by man. . . . This is one of the most remarkable of deep-sea fish, with eyes on the ends of long, periscope stalks, almost one-third as long as the entire body. . . .

"At 11.12 A.M., we came to rest gently at 3,000 feet, and I knew that this was my ultimate floor; the cable on the winch was very near its end. . . . The water . . . seemed to show as blacker than black. It seemed as if all future nights in the upper world must be considered only relative degrees of twilight. I could never again use the word BLACK with any conviction.

"Now and then I felt a slight vibration and an apparent slacking off of the cable. Word came that a cross swell had arisen, and when the full weight of bathysphere and cable came upon the winch, Captain Sylvester let out a few inches to ease the strain. There were only about a dozen turns of cable left upon the reel. . . . We were swinging at 3,028 feet, and, Would we come up?"

They did come up—from the greatest depth reached by a living human being. But the record was not to go long unchallenged.

While Beebe and Barton were making their historic journeys downward, two other pioneers were traveling upward into the unexplored heights of the stratosphere (the second layer of the atmosphere). In 1932, the Swiss physicist Auguste Piccard and his assistant Max Cosyns reached a record height of 53,139 feet in a balloon and gondola of Piccard's invention. (A gondola is an airtight ball in which balloonists travel instead of a basket when exploring the upper atmosphere.)

To Piccard, who had been intrigued by the undersea depths since boyhood, there were clear analogies between the bathysphere and the balloon "In both cases," he wrote, "there is a danger of the cable breaking, with the difference, however, that the aeronaut . . . cannot help wishing: 'If only this rope would break, what a fine trip in a free balloon we should have.' Very much to the contrary, the oceanographer, shut up in his tight cabin, is haunted by the terrifying idea that the cable may break. But can we do without the cable?"

Piccard had long dreamed of an underwater vessel that would need no lifeline to descend to the greatest depths of the ocean. Not long after his balloon ascent, he set about designing just such a device—a bathyscaph, or deep-sea ship. Based on the principle of the balloon, the bathyscaph was intended to float free, up or down. It consisted of two major parts, a cabin and a float. The cabin was very much like a gondola and the float was like a balloon.

The cabin, built to withstand the crushing pressures of the deep ocean, was a steel sphere weighing 10 tons. Its internal diameter was 6$\frac{3}{5}$ feet and its wall was 3.54 inches thick (5.91 inches thick around the 2 cone-shaped portholes). The portholes were made of a newly developed, shatterproof plastic called Plexiglass, which will

Above: the Swiss physicist Auguste Piccard (right) at a balloon meeting with King Leopold of Belgium. Piccard later used the principle of the balloon in the design of his first bathyscaph or deep-sea submersible. Below: Piccard climbing into the steel gondola before a balloon ascent to over 51,000 feet, in 1931.

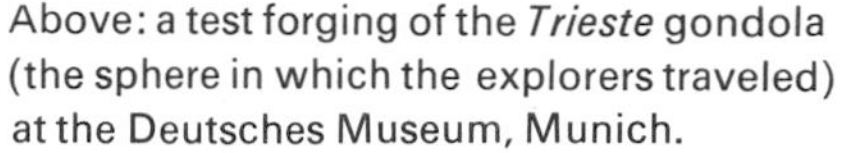

Above: a test forging of the *Trieste* gondola (the sphere in which the explorers traveled) at the Deutsches Museum, Munich.

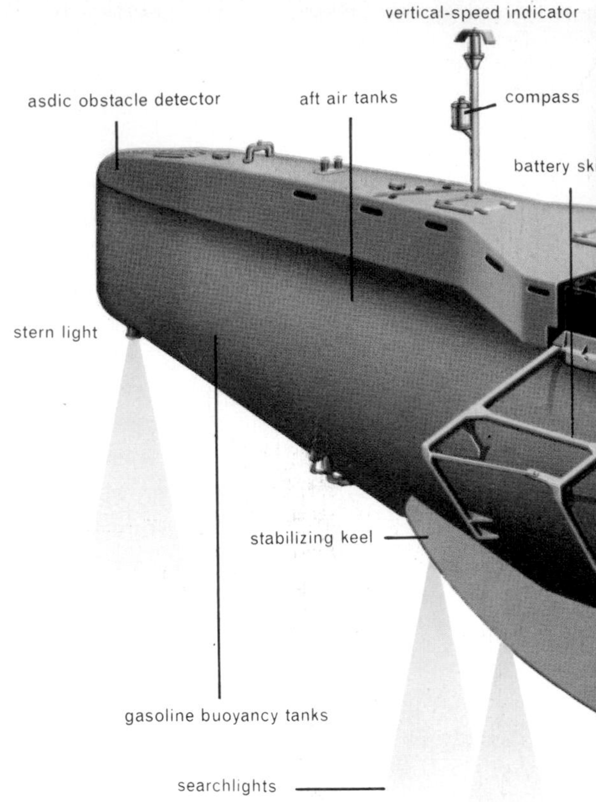

not crack under pressure. Each porthole was 5.91 inches thick, with a 3.94-inch inside diameter, and a 15.75-inch outside diameter.

But how could the descent and ascent of such a sphere be accomplished and, more important, delicately controlled? If the sphere hit bottom too hard, it would be destroyed and its daring passengers killed. To solve this vital problem, Piccard turned to his experience in the air. In simple terms, a balloon rises because it is lighter than the air it displaces. Piccard's balloon had been filled with 100,000 cubic feet of lighter-than-air hydrogen gas. This was enough hydrogen to make the total volume of the balloon and gondola lighter in weight than the same volume of air surrounding it. The balloon would rise until the weights of these two volumes became equal. Because the atmosphere becomes thinner—less dense—with altitude, there is a limit to the height a balloon can soar. To some extent, that limit depends on the volume of hydrogen in the balloon. So there is only one way to bring such a balloon back down—vent hydrogen from it.

Piccard could not fill the float of the bathyscaph with hydrogen or any other gas. Gases are too compressible. As the bathyscaph sank into the ocean depths, increasing pressure would cave in the walls of the float. (The float had to be lighter than water and its walls, therefore, thin-skinned.) After a long search, and a number of experiments, Piccard decided to use common gasoline as the buoyant material in the float. Gasoline had a number of advantages that suited Piccard's needs. It was less dense than water, it was

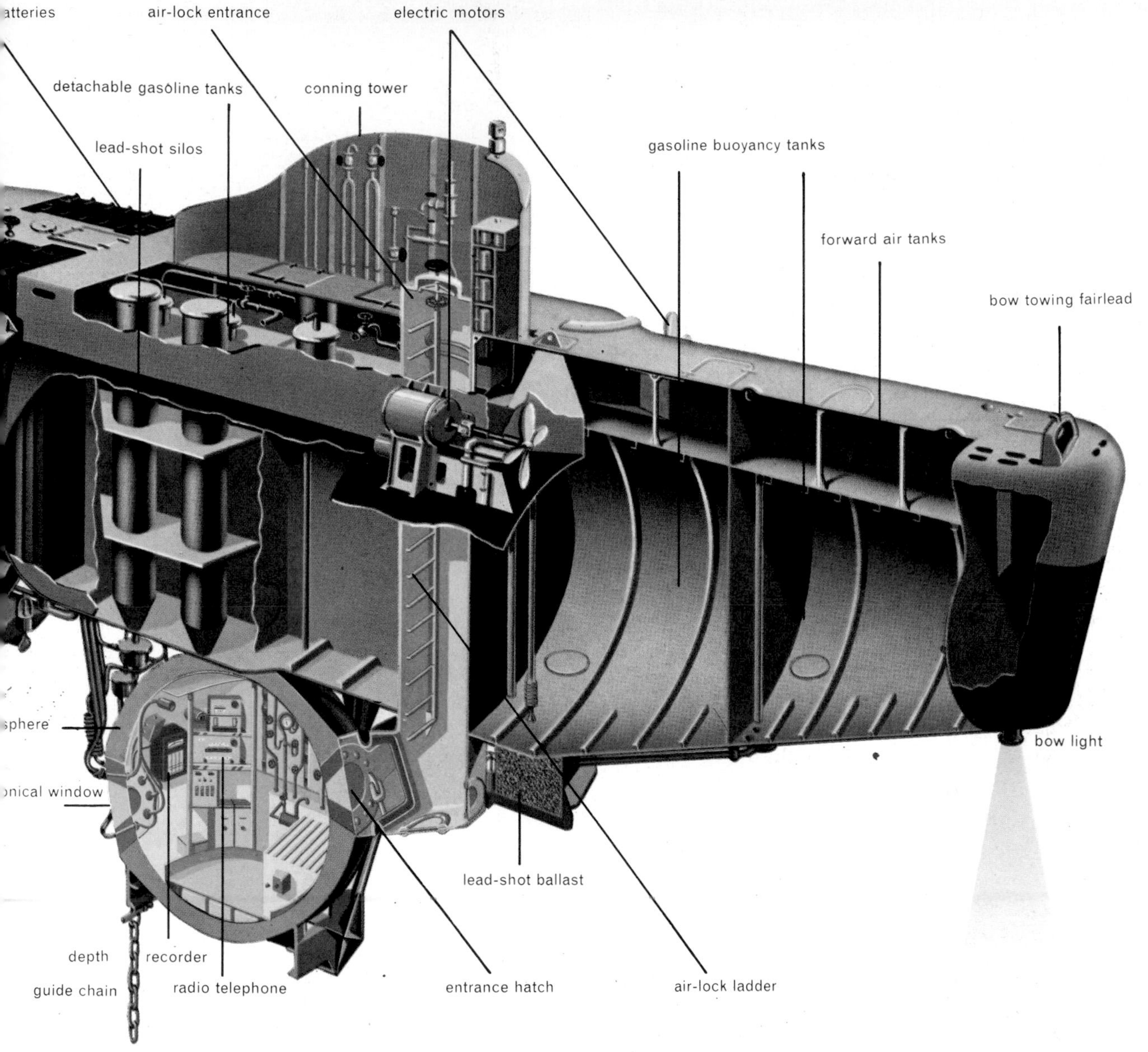

Above: A cutaway diagram of the bathyscaph *FNRS 3*. Based on Piccard's designs, it was built by the French Navy at Toulon. Early in 1954, Georges Houot and Pierre Willm took the *FNRS 3* to the record depth of 13,287 feet below the surface.

Left: Professor Auguste Piccard and his son, Jacques. In 1951, while the *FNRS 3* was still under construction, Piccard received the money to build a new bathyscaph. It was to be named the *Trieste.*

relatively non-compressible, and it was insoluble in water.

In addition to the gasoline tanks, the float was equipped with two air tanks—one at each end of the float—and two ballast hoppers filled with tons of iron shot. When each tank was filled with its appropriate material, the bathyscaph would float on the surface of the sea. However, if water were allowed to enter the air tanks, the bathyscaph would begin a gentle plunge downward. If Piccard wanted to hover, he would drop a small amount of shot. If he wanted to return to the surface, he would drop more shot. The shot was held in the hoppers by the pull of electromagnets situated on top of the float. When the electric current in the electromagnets was cut off from inside the cabin by the pilot—or by some accident—shot would fall out of the hoppers and the craft would rise. To increase the rate of descent, gasoline could be jettisoned from one of the six gasoline tanks.

Left: The Piccards' bathyscaph *Trieste* suspended above the sea. The observation gondola, in which the two men sat, can clearly be seen below the gasoline-filled float.

Pressure was no threat to the float's thin walls because the float was open to the sea. Water could flow freely into the bottom of it. The pressure on the inside of the float always equaled that on the outside. Moreover, because gasoline is less dense than water, the gasoline sat on top of the entering water and could not leak from the openings through which the water entered.

This, essentially, was the ingenious device that was hoisted by winch from the hold of the Belgian cargo ship, *Scaldis,* shortly before

Below: the bathyscaph *Trieste* at the start of a dive. The *Trieste* underwent her first sea trials at Castellammare di Stabia, near Naples in Italy, early in August, 1953.

1 P.M., on November 3, 1948. The *Scaldis,* accompanied by the French oceanographic vessel *Elie Monnier,* had sought out a spot over 4,600 feet deep in the Atlantic Ocean off Dakar (now the capital of Senegal), near the Cape Verde Islands. Here, Auguste Piccard and his 26-year-old son Jacques would put the bathyscaph through its first test dive into the deep ocean. For this unmanned dive, a timing device aboard the bathyscaph would automatically release the iron shot. Piccard had set the depth gauge for 770 fathoms (4,620 feet) and the bathyscaph had 40 minutes to reach it.

It was Jacques Piccard who opened the air tanks of the float while the bathyscaph bobbed on the choppy Atlantic waters. As the seawater rushed in and the bathyscaph began to sink, he jumped clear and joined his father on board the *Scaldis.* The minutes dragged as a tense band of scientist-oceanographers waited anxiously for the moment the bathyscaph would surface again. Clinging to masts and funnels, sailors of the *Scaldis* and *Élie Monnier* joined the watch. At last, a cry came from the *Scaldis.* "*Le voilà!* There it is!"—and the bathyscaph shot through the surface.

Later, readings of the depth gauge in the cabin revealed that the bathyscaph had plumbed the sea to a depth of 4,554 feet. With the exception of a few drops of water in the cabin and a lost radar antenna it had returned in good shape. If it had carried men in its cabin, they would have glimpsed sights never before seen, and returned to tell about them. But the first manned descent was not to be made that day nor for many days. The drops of water, the lost antenna, and an inability to pump off the bathyscaph's gasoline ended the Dakar dives. The first two accidents had to be checked out before men could be allowed to dive in the vehicle. And the gasoline had to be piped into the hold of the *Scaldis* before the bathyscaph could be hoisted aboard for inspection. Unfortunately, through damage or some other inexplicable reason, the hose used to siphon gasoline from the bathyscaph to the *Scaldis* could not be connected properly to the mother ship. Auguste Piccard had no choice but to order the 6,600 gallons of gasoline to be dumped into the sea.

Now came months of frustration. Money was needed for a new supply of gasoline and, more important, for improvements in the design of the bathyscaph. Jacques Piccard scoured Europe for funds. Years passed, but slowly money began to trickle in. Technical problems were eventually solved and a new bathyscaph was constructed. Piccard named it the *Trieste* for the Adriatic seaport where it was built.

The *Trieste* was launched on August 1, 1953, at Castellammare di Stabia, near Naples, in southern Italy. During the next few days preparations were made for shallow test dives in the harbor of Castellammare. Then, on August 11, 1953, Auguste and Jacques Piccard crawled into the cabin of the *Trieste,* sealed themselves in, flooded the float's air tanks, and slowly settled to the bottom of the harbor 26 feet below the surface. After jettisoning iron shot, the *Trieste* gently rose to the surface. The first dive had been successful.

Below: U.S. Navy scientist A. B. Rechnitzer (left) and Jacques Piccard on board *Trieste.* On November 15, 1959 Piccard piloted *Trieste* to a depth of 18,150 feet south of the island of Guam in the Pacific Ocean. It was one of the dives made after *Trieste* was bought by the United States Office of Naval Research.

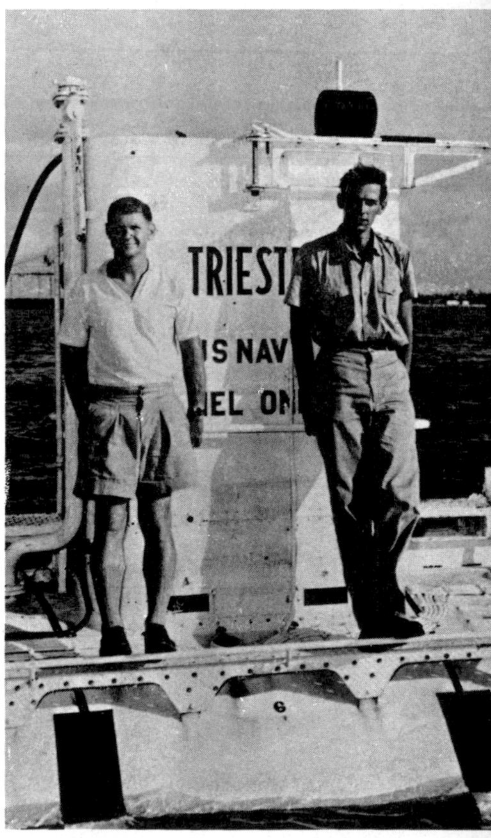

During the years that followed, 64 more dives were logged by the *Trieste*. The Piccards, father and son, rode down 3,540 feet near the island of Capri in the Bay of Naples, and 10,300 feet near the island of Ponza in the Tyrrhenian Sea, west of Naples. In 1958, the *Trieste* was purchased by the United States Office of Naval Research. From then on, Jacques Piccard teamed up with U.S. scientists, engineers, and naval officers to dive to 12,110 feet south of Ponza, to 18,150 feet south of the island of Guam in the Pacific Ocean, and to 23,000 feet, also off Guam. But each of these record-breaking dives was really a dress rehearsal for the most daring dive of all—the attempt to touch down on the bottom of the deepest spot on earth, the Challenger Deep.

The bottom of the Challenger Deep lies 36,198 feet down in the Mariana Trench, southwest of the island of Guam in the Pacific. It was named for H.M.S. *Challenger II,* the British oceanographic research vessel which discovered it in 1951.

Nine years later, on January 23, 1960, the bathyscaph *Trieste* rode the Pacific waters directly above "the basement of the world." It had been towed there by the U.S. naval ship *Wandank*. Aboard the *Wandank* and its destroyer escort, U.S.S. *Lewis,* were Jacques Piccard, his American colleague Donald Walsh of the U.S. Navy, and a team of scientific and naval experts. Walsh had joined Piccard in five previous dives, including number 64 (to 23,000 feet). On this day, he and Piccard would try to reach bottom at the greatest depth ever recorded.

The sea was dangerously rough. Twenty-five-foot waves smashed against the *Wandank* as Piccard jumped aboard a rubber raft and made for the *Trieste*. Once he had reached the bathyscaph, he found to his dismay that the surface telephone, used to communicate from the cabin to the surface just before diving, had been washed overboard. The tachometer, which measures rate of descent, had also been put out of commission by the battering waves, and the dive was in fact made without it.

Walsh joined Piccard aboard the *Trieste* and the two men debated whether or not to risk the dive. Piccard proposed that if all were well in the cabin, they should go ahead. He climbed down to the cabin from the conning tower atop the float and switched on the electromagnets. They worked—and so did the other instruments. The dive was on!

At 8:23 A.M. the *Trieste* began to drift slowly downward. Then at 340 feet, it seemed to go into reverse, bouncing up a few yards. It had struck a common undersea obstacle—a *thermocline,* a body of water separating the warm surface water from the colder depths. The thermocline was colder and therefore denser than the water through which the *Trieste* had just descended—sufficiently dense to buoy the *Trieste* upward. Piccard opened the valve of one of the gasoline tanks. The bathyscaph, heavier now, broke through the thermocline. Down it went at an average speed of four inches per second. By 9 A.M., the *Trieste* had only plunged 800 feet into the sea. At this

Left: the bathyscaph *Trieste* in harbor. After completing many dives—and setting many new depth records—*Trieste* was made ready for the deepest dive of all—into the darkness over 35,000 feet down in the Challenger Deep, southwest of the island of Guam in the Pacific Ocean. Below: life on the soft mud of the deep ocean floor, photographed with a deep-sea camera. Two brittle stars (a type of echinoderm) and a deep-sea fish can clearly be seen.

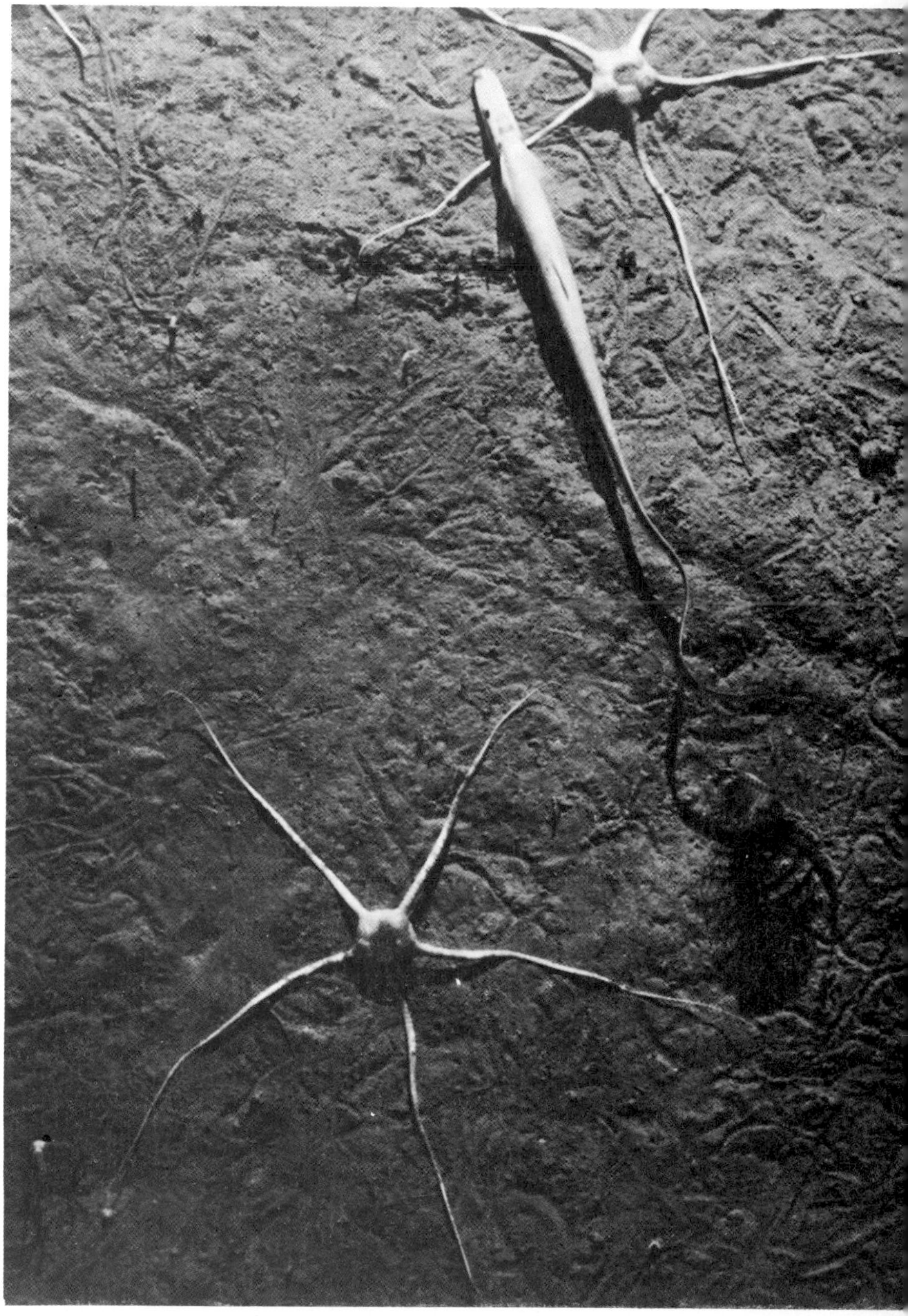

rate, it would not have time to reach bottom and resurface before night, and Piccard would not chance a night-surfacing in calm seas, let alone turbulent ones. More gasoline was vented and the *Trieste* accelerated to three feet per second.

At 1,000 feet, Piccard turned on the outside floodlight. Plankton seemed to swarm upward like a blizzard defying gravity. With the floodlight and cabin lights off, the sea appeared a dark gray-black. At 2,400 feet, total blackness engulfed the bathyscaph. The cold water outside sent a chill into the cabin. Walsh and Piccard changed their wet clothing which had been soaked with seawater when they had boarded the *Trieste,* and the two explorers munched chocolate bars for "lunch."

At 4,200 feet the sphere sprang a leak but sealed itself shortly afterward. Another leak at 18,000 feet abruptly self-sealed. Any slight crack in the sphere was quickly closed by the enormous pressure building up on its surface.

The *Trieste* soon dipped below 23,000 feet, topping record dive number 64. No men had been deeper. At 11:30 A.M., the depth gauge read 27,000 feet. How far to the bottom? Piccard wondered. He dropped some iron shot from the float's hoppers and the *Trieste* sank more slowly. Soon after passing the 29,000-foot level, it was "as deep under the sea as Mount Everest is high above it." The floodlights probed crystal-clear water with no sign of life, large or small. Piccard dumped more iron ballast. The bathyscaph slowed to a descent of one foot per second.

At noon, the *Trieste* reached 31,000 feet. It was rapidly nearing a depth whose pressure had never been tested on its sphere or float. Piccard switched on the echo sounder, which was designed to detect the bottom if it were 600 feet or nearer to the descending bathyscaph. No echo returned. The *Trieste* continued its journey downward—soon it passed 35,000 feet. The men anxiously watched the echo sounder. At last, they received an echo from the bottom—only 252 feet below.

Minutes later, Walsh had counted down the last few fathoms and the *Trieste* touched the ocean floor. Its official depth, given after slight correction of the depth gauges, was 35,800 feet, deeper than any man had yet penetrated and only 398 feet short of the deepest spot in the whole ocean bed.

Two hundred thousand tons of pressure gripped the *Trieste* as the two men scanned the ocean floor. Piccard spotted a flatfish lying on the tan-colored ooze. It was about one foot long and six inches across. Two round eyes protruded from the top of its head. In the enormous pressure of the abyss, there was life.

The two explorers stayed for 20 minutes on the seabed. At 4:56 P.M. they returned to the surface in perfect health. Their historic dive had broken every undersea record. They had reached one of the deepest spots in the earth's oceans and in doing so had proved that man could explore the bottom of the sea and return safely to the surface.

Above: the crew sitting on *Trieste* at sea. On January 23, 1960, rough conditions in the Pacific Ocean threatened to stop Jacques Piccard and Donald Walsh from starting their descent into Challenger Deep. However, all was well in the cabin of the *Trieste* and the dive did take place as originally planned.

Right: a diagrammatic view of the Mariana Trench, showing *Trieste*'s dive into Challenger Deep (H). The diagram also shows: (A) the thermocline; (B) the point where light fades out; (C) the deepest point to which a whale can dive; (D) Beebe's dive in the bathysphere; (E) Barton's benthoscope; (F) the *FNRS 3* bathyscaph, and (G) a deep-sea camera. Pressure increases with depth, and the *Trieste,* resting on the bottom 35,800 feet below the surface, is gripped by 200,000 tons of pressure, or 8 tons per square inch.

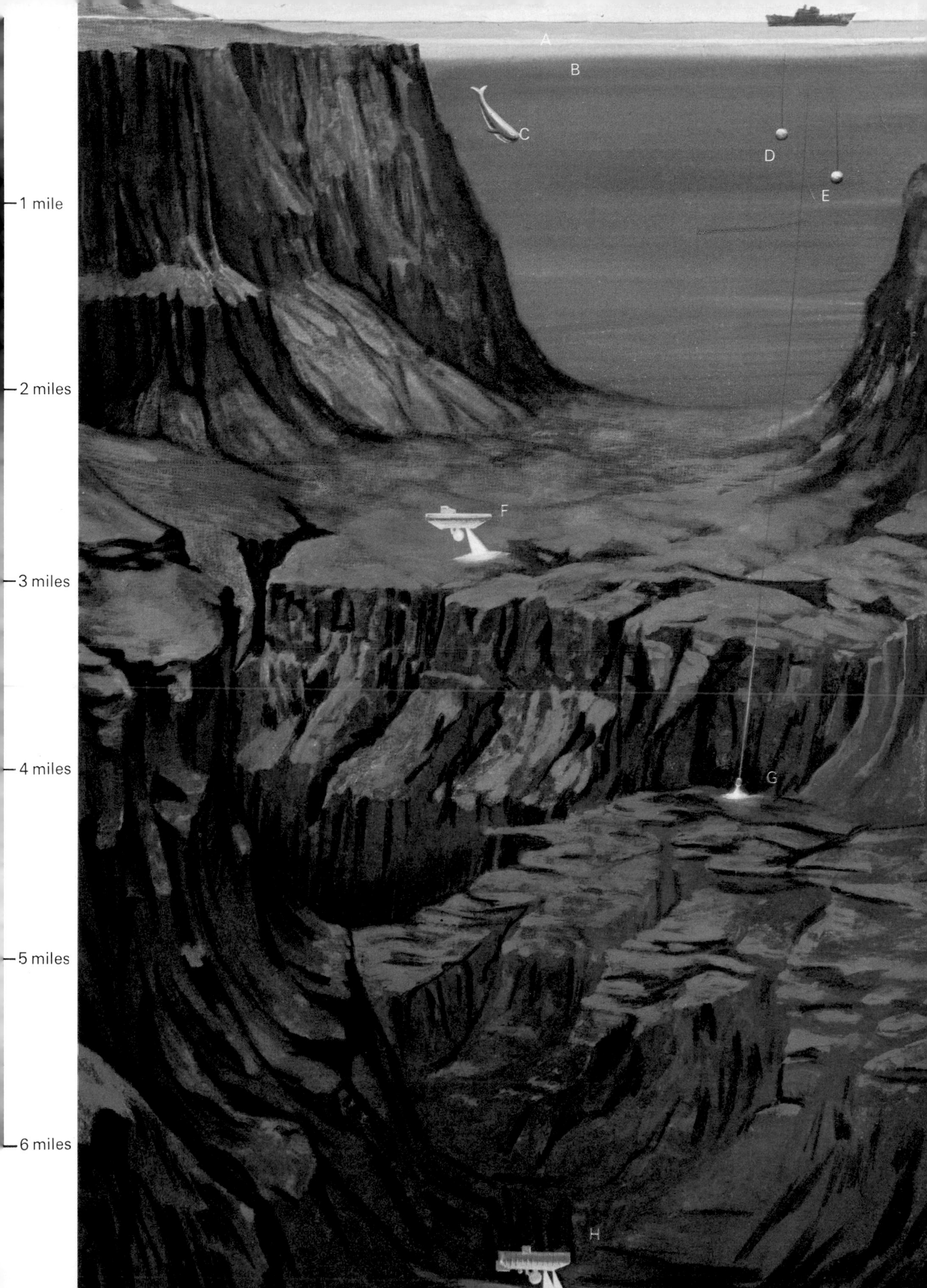

1 mile
2 miles
3 miles
4 miles
5 miles
6 miles
A
B
C
D
E
F
G
H

Above: Benjamin Franklin. In 1770, when Franklin was deputy postmaster general, mail ships from Britain were held up by the Gulf Stream on their way to Massachusetts. Franklin ordered the preparation of a chart showing the current's course, but it was some time before the British captains took advantage of his advice.

Right: the *Ben Franklin,* a research submersible designed by Jacques Piccard and built and operated by the Grumman Aerospace Corporation. On July 14, 1969, the *Ben Franklin* set out on a journey of undersea discovery in the Gulf Stream.

A River in the Sea 6

On July 14, 1969, two days before the liftoff of Apollo 11, crowds of people began gathering near Cape Kennedy to watch the final preparations for man's first landing on the moon. Probably only a handful of these excited onlookers were aware that, a mere 130 miles away, at West Palm Beach, Florida, another historic launching was about to take place. This was the launching of an experimental craft designed by Jacques Piccard and called the *Ben Franklin.* Like Apollo 11, this vehicle was crammed with scientific instruments for a voyage into a strange and hostile environment. But, unlike Apollo 11, the *Ben Franklin*'s voyage was to begin, rather than end, with a

splashdown. This craft, a brand new type of underwater research vessel, was about to undertake the first undersea exploration of the mighty Gulf Stream.

The Gulf Stream is the second largest ocean current in the world. (Only the Antarctic Circumpolar Current is greater.) About 50 miles wide and 3,000 feet deep, it flows from the Gulf of Mexico northeastward through the Atlantic toward the shores of Europe. For centuries, the warm Gulf Stream has intrigued and puzzled both sailors and scientists. But only during the past 200 years has any real progress been made toward understanding the origin of this river

Above: a painting showing the danger and skill involved in whaling in small boats in the mid-1800's. It was during their whaling expeditions that American sea captains became familiar with the Gulf Stream.

in the sea, and learning more about its movement and behavior.

Man's first recorded encounter with the Gulf Stream took place in 1513. In that year, Juan Ponce de León, the Spanish conqueror who explored Florida, was sailing southward down the peninsula's east coast. Suddenly, his three ships, which had been making steady progress before a fresh wind, were brought to a complete halt by a mysterious northward-pushing current. Describing this strange event in his log, Ponce de León wrote, "We held to the south [but] could make no headway. . . . Eventually we had to recognize that despite inflated sails we were being driven backward and that the current was stronger than the wind. Two of the ships, which were somewhat nearer the coast, were able to cast anchor, but the current was so strong that it broke the ropes!"

In the two centuries that followed Ponce de León's voyage, many sailors and explorers crossed the Gulf Stream, bucked its currents or rode with them. These encounters with the river in the sea produced numerous conjectures, theories, and tall tales about its existence and curious characteristics. But it was not until 1770 that the first chart of the great current's path through the Atlantic was made. In that year a complaint was lodged by the customs officials in Boston concerning slow delivery of mail from England to the Massachusetts colony. It seemed to the Bostonians that the mail packets were dawdling on their way across the Atlantic from the Old World to the

Below: Benjamin Franklin's chart of the Gulf Stream. As deputy postmaster general of the colonies, Franklin advised captains of British mail packets sailing west, "Don't fight the Gulf Stream."

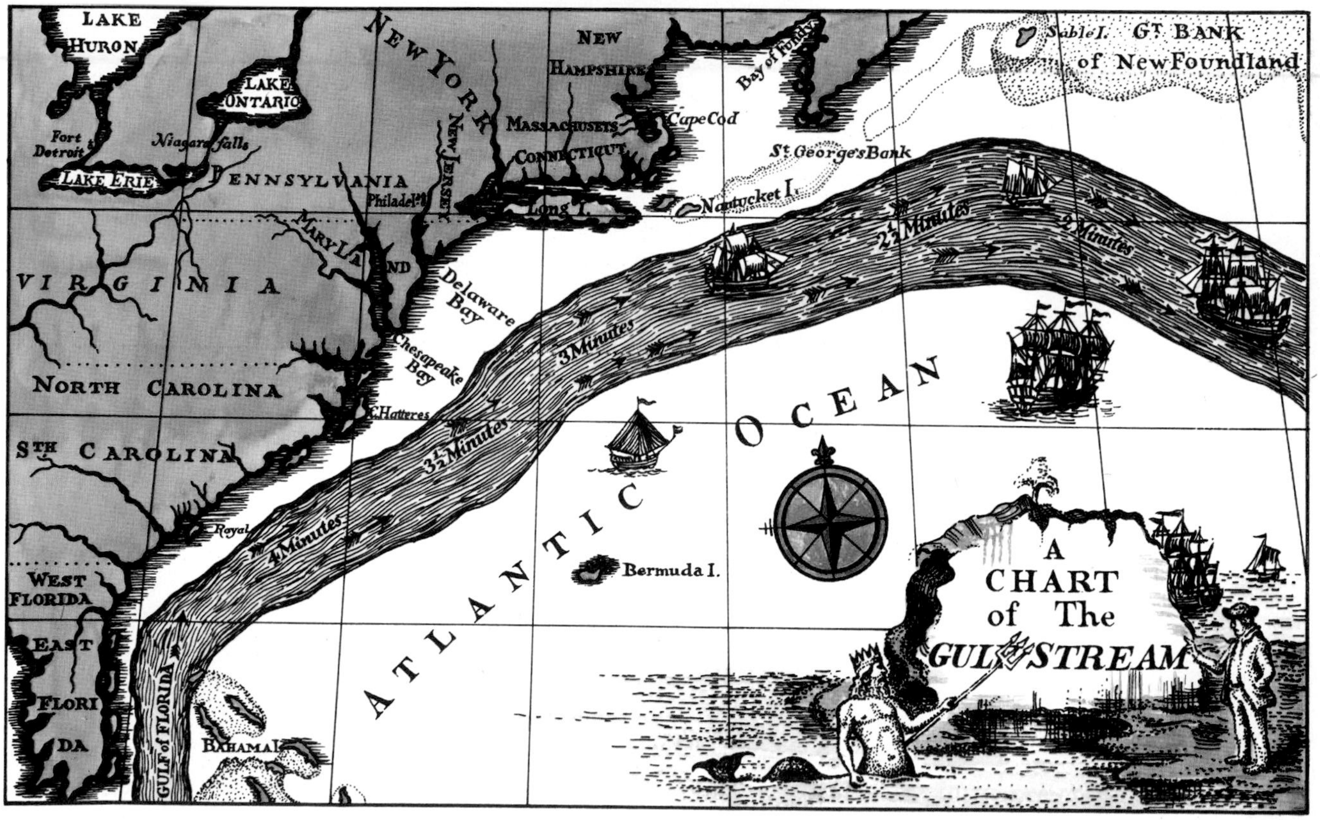

Right: movement of currents in the North Atlantic Ocean. The Gulf Stream is the second largest ocean current in the world. It flows from the Gulf of Mexico northeastward into the Atlantic Ocean. Here it becomes the North Atlantic Current and turns toward the shores of Europe. The Gulf Stream is a warm current, and in winter its influence may help to raise the temperature of the British Isles and western Europe above that of other places at similar latitudes.

Above: the 460-ton ketch *Atlantis.* Launched in 1931, it was outfitted with the latest scientific equipment and used by the newly-formed Woods Hole Oceanographic Institution for research on the Gulf Stream.

New. Why, they wanted to know, should it take the English mail ships two weeks longer to cross the ocean than it did the American vessels going the other way? Benjamin Franklin, who was then deputy postmaster general, put the problem before Nantucket whaling captain Timothy Folger.

Folger's answer was simple—the English captains were not sufficiently familiar with the Gulf Stream. "We are well acquainted with the stream," Folger explained, "because in our pursuit of whales, which keep to the sides of it but are not met within it, we run along the side and frequently cross it to change our side. . . . In crossing it [we] have sometimes met and spoken with those packets who were in the middle of it and stemming it. We have informed them that they were stemming a current that was against them to the value of three miles an hour and advised them to cross it, but they were too wise to be counseled by simple American fishermen."

At Franklin's request, Folger marked out the course of the Gulf Stream on an Atlantic chart. Franklin sent the chart to England, but the English captains are reported to have "slighted it" for some time before realizing its value and following Folger's advice.

On and off during the next 160 years oceanographers ventured into the warm waters of the Gulf Stream in search of its secrets. Using submersible thermometers and sampling bottles, they gathered information about its temperature and density at various depths. *Drift bottles* were labeled and tossed overboard to be recovered later in unexpected places, revealing new eddies and arms of the stream. From this and other information, scientists determined that the stream is created by a combination of winds and currents. Trade winds cause a westerly flow of water where the Atlantic Ocean crosses the equator. This flow passes through the narrow Yucatán Channel into the Gulf of Mexico, where it gathers momentum and flows out through the Straits of Florida.

In 1930, the study of the Gulf Stream took an important step forward with the founding of the Woods Hole Oceanographic Institution at Cape Cod, Massachusetts. One of the primary objectives of the scientists at Woods Hole was to probe the waters of the Gulf Stream. To carry out this mission, they purchased the ketch *Atlantis.* A ship of 460 tons, the *Atlantis* was outfitted with the most modern scientific equipment. and could carry a crew of 25 sailors and oceanographers. Over the next few years, it logged more than half a

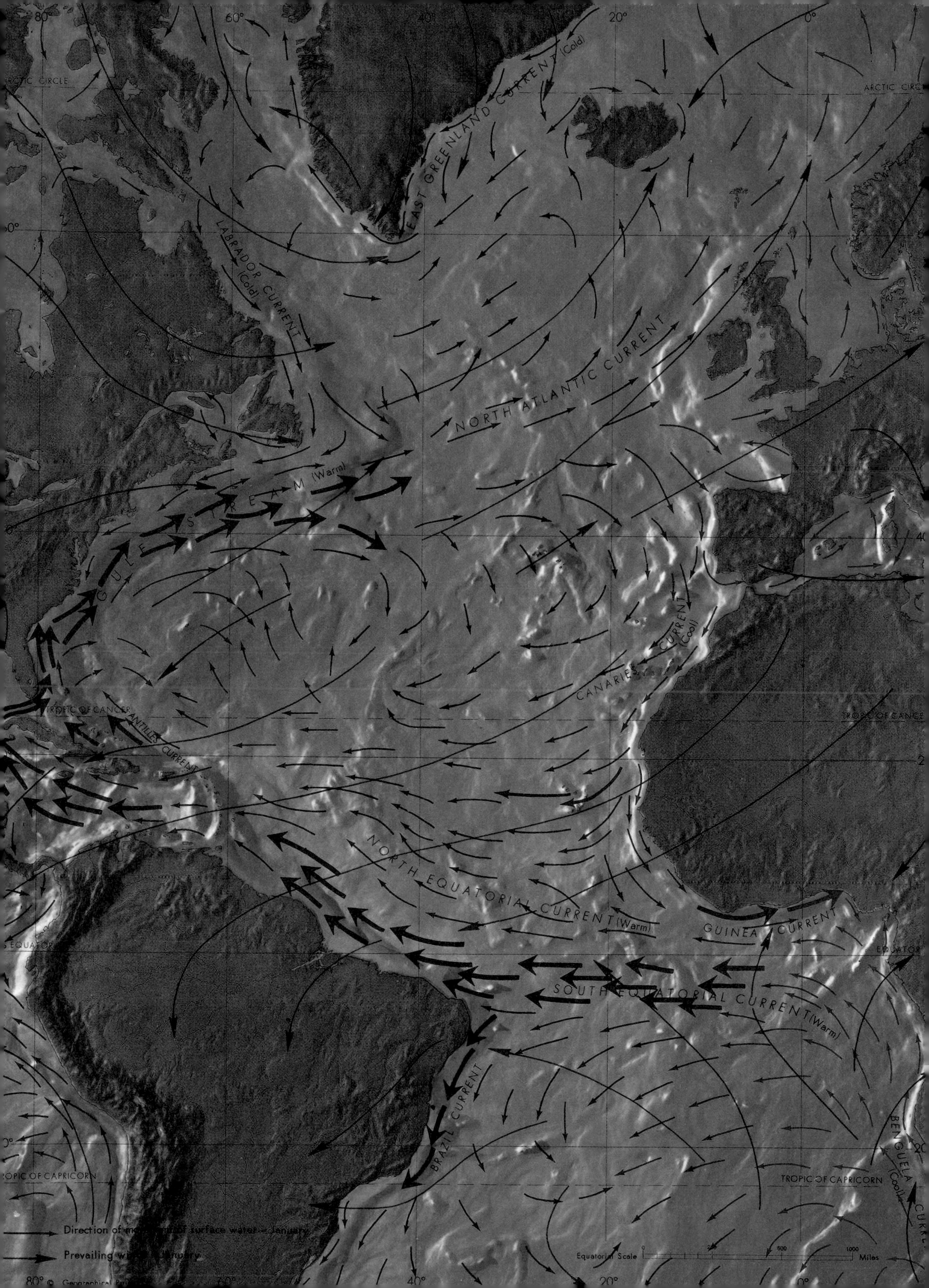

ARCTIC CIRCLE
EAST GREENLAND CURRENT (Cold)
LABRADOR CURRENT (Cold)
NORTH ATLANTIC CURRENT
GULF STREAM (Warm)
CANARIES CURRENT (Cool)
TROPIC OF CANCER
ANTILLES CURRENT
NORTH EQUATORIAL CURRENT (Warm)
GUINEA CURRENT
EQUATOR
SOUTH EQUATORIAL CURRENT (Warm)
BRAZIL CURRENT
BENGUELA CURRENT (Cool)
TROPIC OF CAPRICORN
Direction of surface water – January
Prevailing January
Equatorial Scale
500
1000
Miles
80°
60°
40°
20°
0°

million miles as it sailed to and fro along the stream's pathways.

In the course of their many exploratory missions, the Woods Hole scientists were able to amass an extraordinary amount of information about the Gulf Stream, particularly in regard to the volume of water it carries. Using a variety of sophisticated submersible equipment, they were able to determine that, as the stream heads out into the Atlantic south of New England, it is transporting something like 150-million cubic meters of water a second. (The mightiest river in the United States, the Mississippi, disgorges only about a thousandth of this amount of water at its mouth.) This measurement of the Gulf Stream's tremendous volume becomes even more amazing when we realize that at its source it is carrying only about 30 million cubic meters of water per second. Where the extra water comes from remains a mystery.

Left: the crew of the mesoscaph *Ben Franklin* on deck on July 14, 1969, before the start of their journey in the Gulf Stream. Jacques Piccard is at the right of the group.

This was in part the state of knowledge about the Gulf Stream when the *Ben Franklin* glided out of West Palm Beach on July 14, 1969. A *mesoscaph*—middle boat—it was designed to explore the ocean at depths up to 2,000 feet. Its 49-foot-long hull was filled with scientific and navigational instruments, as well as all the necessary living facilities for its six-man crew.

The *Ben Franklin*'s mission, known as the Gulf Stream Drift Mission, was conceived by Jacques Piccard in 1965. Unlike the bathyscaph project, this idea found almost instant support. The Grumman Aerospace Corporation financed and drew up final plans for the construction of the *Ben Franklin.* The Oceanographic Office of the Department of the Navy (NAVOCEANO) provided about 2,300 pounds of scientific instrumentation for the vessel, and two oceanographers as crew members, as well as a surface support vessel. The National Aeronautics and Space Administration (NASA) supplied an observer to go along on the drift to evaluate crew

Right: a cutaway diagram of the *Ben Franklin.* The 49-foot-long mesoscaph was packed with scientific instruments, including cameras to record the crew's reaction to their 30 days of confinement. During the journey the crew made observations of current velocity, temperature, salinity, animal life, and other characteristics of the Gulf Stream.

1. Ballast tank
2. Scientific control center
3. View port
4. CO_2 filter
5. Hydrophones
6. Surface radio antenna
7. T.V. camera
8. Surface lookout
9. Conning tower
10. Control console
11. Hatch
12. View ports
13. Instrument package, cameras, etc.
14. Propulsion motor
15. Forward oxygen tank
16. Side-looking sonar
17. Batteries
18. Ballast tank
19. Biological sampler
20. Stern oxygen tank

Right: part of the control room on board *Ben Franklin.* The elaborate control systems were vital to the mission. During the journey the submersible was put through many delicate maneuvers, including several trips to investigate the sea bottom at depths of 1,200 to 2,000 feet.

reactions during the month-long voyage. In return, Piccard and his crew were to perform three groups of experiments.

For Grumman, the men of the mesoscaph would search for plankton and minerals in the Gulf Stream waters. NAVOCEANO experiments would cover a wide variety of subjects including periodic measurements of current speed, available light, gravity, magnetic field, natural ocean noises, bottom structure, and animal life. NASA was primarily interested in how men would react to long confinement and isolation—conditions that would exist in space stations. For NASA's experiments, tape recordings were made of crew conversations during meals. Three fixed cameras inside the vessel snapped photographs every two minutes to record the behavior of the submariners, and each member of the crew was required to keep a diary.

In the course of the 30-day 11-hour voyage, the crew of the *Ben Franklin* experienced periods of extreme tension, and occasionally found their enforced captivity and cramped quarters almost unendurable. For the most part, however, their morale remained high and, at the conclusion of their mission, they could point with pride to a record number of achievements.

The Gulf Stream had carried the *Ben Franklin* 1,444 nautical miles

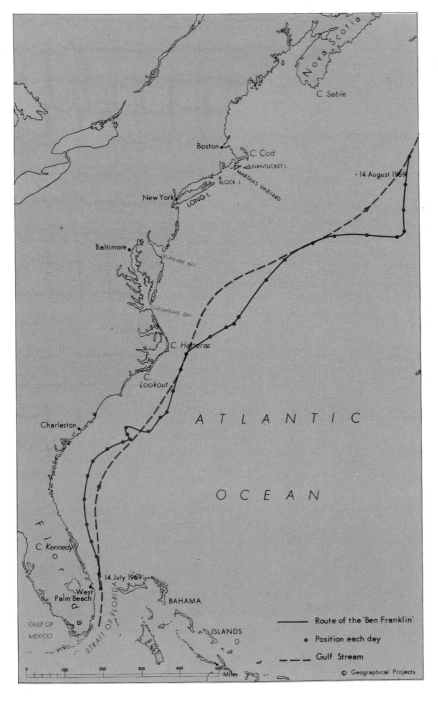

Below: the eastern coastline of the United States, showing the route of the mesoscaph *Ben Franklin* in 1969. The *Ben Franklin* explored the Gulf Stream at depths up to 2,000 feet from West Palm Beach, Florida, to a point 360 miles south of Nova Scotia. Its expedition was known as the Gulf Stream Drift Mission.

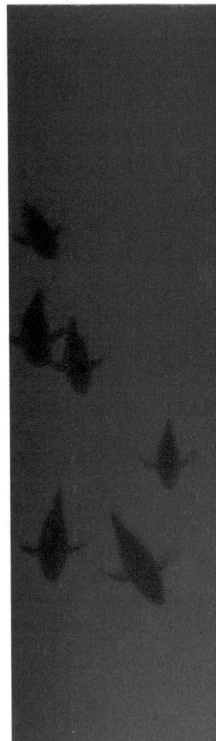

to a spot in the North Atlantic 360 miles south of Nova Scotia. Though it had drifted at an average depth of 650 feet, it had made 10 trips to depths between 1,200 and 1,800 feet—5 of which were ocean bottom surveys. The crew had made more than 900,000 temperature, salinity, and sound velocity (speed) measurements—the latter to determine water density. Sixty thousand photographs of the crew were snapped as the men went about their routine duties. NASA psychologists spent many hours poring over these.

Surprisingly, crew members peering out of the *Ben Franklin*'s

observation ports had spotted relatively few fish and scarcely any plankton in the Gulf Stream. Probes of the stream with pulses of sound had failed to detect a *deep scattering layer* common to many parts of the seas. (The deep scattering layer refers to the dense blanket of marine organisms which reflect back sounds as scattered markings on an echo sounder. Such layers of living things are generally found in depths between 600 and 2,400 feet. And they are usually between 150 and 600 feet thick.) As far as life was concerned, the Gulf Stream was a watery waste.

Below: a photograph taken from the *Ben Franklin* shows a school of tuna swimming overhead. This was an unusual sight for the crew, who saw few signs of life in the Gulf Stream.

Left: Jacques-Yves Cousteau. In 1943 Cousteau tested the first Aqua-Lung, a revolutionary underwater breathing device that enabled divers to explore beneath the sea unencumbered by air-lines linking them to the surface.

Below: a diver wearing a modern Aqua-Lung is able to match the agility of a fish in its natural environment.

Man Lives in the Sea

7

In the summer of 1943, at the height of World War II, a man waded into the Mediterranean off the coast of southern France. The cove in which he waded was sheltered from the eyes of the occupying Axis troops and he had chosen it for that reason. Strapped to his back was a strange apparatus that the enemy armies would have considered priceless.

The man's name was Jacques-Yves Cousteau. The equipment on his back was the first Aqua-Lung—a device that was to revolutionize the exploration of the oceans and open their depths to the individual diver. The Aqua-Lung transformed the old-fashioned diver, with his cumbersome copper helmet and weighted boots, into a *man-fish* who could glide at will beneath the water.

Cousteau and several others had begun skin diving for sport in the Mediterranean in the years before World War II. The small band of underwater pioneers had developed fins, goggles, and fishing spears, and had experimented with several forms of underwater "lungs." But the primitive lungs used pure oxygen and were dangerous at high pressures. On two occasions Cousteau almost drowned when using one of these early devices. What was needed, Cousteau realized, was some kind of compressed-air lung that would automatically release air at the proper pressure on demand from the diver.

The war scattered Cousteau's group of divers. After the signing of the Franco-German armistice in 1940, they came together again. But now their underwater projects had to be carried out in the strictest secrecy. France was occupied by Axis troops, and the French government cooperated to a great extent with the occupying forces, although many Frenchmen, both inside and outside France, continued to fight for French freedom. Cousteau was working for Naval Intelligence against the occupying powers. To cover his activities, he managed to obtain a permit from the occupation authorities enabling him to shoot cultural films in the Mediterranean. But his chief object was to develop his ideas for a self-contained underwater breathing apparatus.

In December, 1942, Cousteau met in Paris with Émile Gagnan, an expert on industrial gas equipment. When Cousteau had finished explaining his needs to the engineer, Gagnan handed him a small mechanism made of plastic. "Something like this?" he asked, "It is a demand valve that I have been working on to feed cooking gas

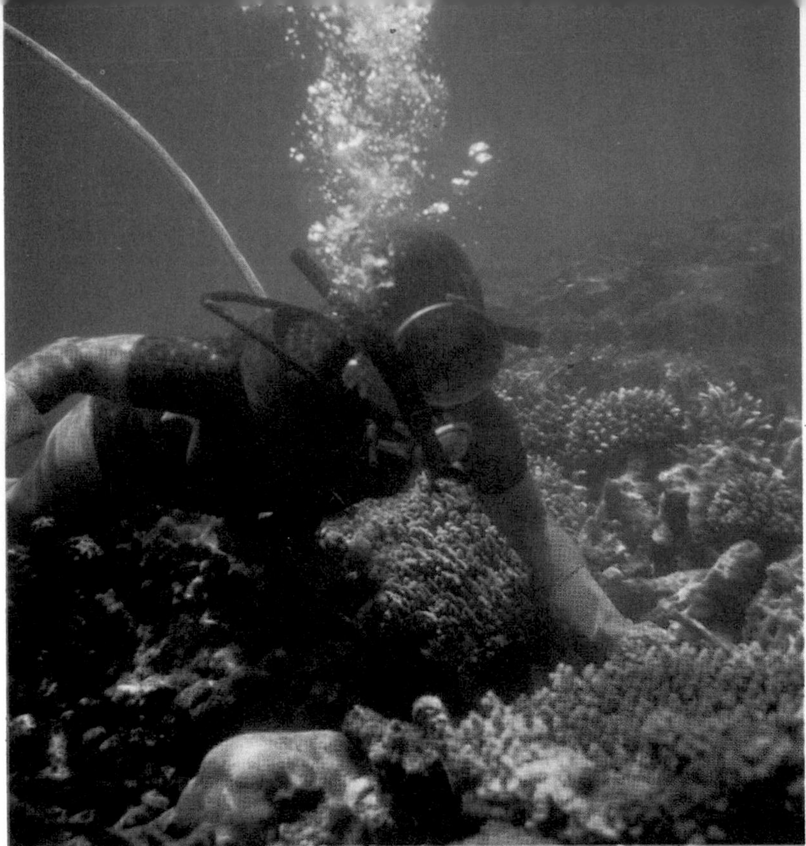

Above left: a diver using a snorkel examines coral in shallow water off the Kenya coast. He can move freely but must return to the surface every two or three minutes for a gulp of air.
Above right: a diver supplied with air from the surface. He can stay down for a long time but can only move within the limits imposed by his life line.

automatically into the motors of automobiles." Gasoline was in short supply in wartime France and many experiments were going on to find a substitute for it.

Within a few weeks Cousteau and Gagnan had completed work on their first demand valve, or regulator, for human breathing. Cousteau tried it out in the wintry waters of the Marne River near Paris. He was able to breathe easily, even though most of the air bubbled wastefully from the regulator. Then Cousteau tried standing on his head. The air supply slowed almost to a halt. Cousteau could not breathe. The first attempt to free man in the sea was a failure.

But in the time it took to drive back to Paris, the two men hit upon a solution to the problem. The exhaust and intake outlets in the experimental regulator were six inches apart. When Cousteau was standing or swimming horizontally, the exhaust was above or at the same level as the air inlet. But when he swam vertically downward, the exhaust was six inches lower, and the tiny difference in pressure blocked the inflow of air. The solution was simple. Place the exhaust as close to the inlet as possible to minimize the pressure difference. It worked—at least in a test tank in Paris. But would the regulator function in the sea at the depths and pressures that Cousteau hoped to penetrate? Only a real dive into the Mediterranean would provide the answer.

On a June morning in 1943, Cousteau went to the railroad station in the tiny town of Bandol on the French Riviera to pick up a wooden case shipped from Paris. Nearby was a large seaside villa that he had rented as a base for diving operations. Cousteau had

Above: a diver wearing an Aqua-Lung. He can move freely like a snorkel diver and yet can stay down for hours at a time. The cylinders of compressed air on his back are connected to his mouthpiece by way of a vital piece of equipment—a demand regulator. As the diver breathes, this feeds him the exact amount of air he needs.

invited his diving companions, Philippe Tailliez and Frédéric Dumas, to join him there. The group had chosen the most obscure site they could find for the first test dive with Cousteau's new apparatus. Germany and Italy were using military frogmen in the war. Their swimming soldiers were equipped with an early type of oxygen lung that was dangerous to use and limited their diving range to 40 feet. The German Admiralty was spending millions of marks on experiments to develop more advanced underwater equipment. If Cousteau's new device worked it would be far superior to any underwater lungs the Germans had so far devised.

As soon as the box arrived, Cousteau rushed it to the Villa Barry where Tailliez and Dumas were waiting. "No children ever opened a Christmas present with more excitement than we did when we unpacked the first 'Aqua-Lung'," says Cousteau, describing the moment in his book *The Silent World*. "We found an assembly of three moderate-sized cylinders of compressed air linked to an air-regulator the size of an alarm clock. From the regulator there extended two tubes, joining on to a mouthpiece. With this equipment harnessed to the back, a watertight glass mask over the eyes and nose, and rubber foot fins, we intended to make unencumbered flights in the depths of the sea."

Cousteau, as head of the group, was to be the first to test the new Aqua-Lung. "Didi" Dumas, whom Cousteau called the best goggle diver in France, was to wait on the beach, ready for an instant rescue if anything went wrong. Cousteau's wife, Simone, was to swim on the surface above him, watching the experiment through her mask.

Dumas and the others strapped the cylinders onto Cousteau's back and attached seven pounds of lead ballast to his belt. Cousteau waded through the surf "with a Charlie Chaplin waddle" and then sank gently into the silent waters of the Mediterranean.

"I breathed sweet, effortless air," wrote Cousteau. "There was a faint whistle when I inhaled and a light rippling sound of bubbles when I breathed out. The regulator was adjusting pressure precisely to my needs.

". . . A modest canyon opened below, full of dark green weeds, black sea urchins and small flowerlike white algae. . . . The sand sloped down to a clear blue infinity. . . . My arms hanging at my sides, I kicked the fins languidly and traveled down, gaining speed, watching the beach reeling past. . . . I reached the bottom in a state of excitement. . . . I looked up and saw the surface shining like a defective mirror. In the center of the looking glass was the trim silhouette of Simone, reduced to a doll. I waved. The doll waved at me. . . ..

"I experimented with all possible maneuvers of the Aqua-Lung—loops, somersaults, and barrel rolls. I stood upside down on one finger and burst out laughing—a shrill distorted laugh. Nothing I did altered the automatic rhythm of air. Delivered from gravity and buoyancy, I flew around in space. . . . I went down to 60 feet. We had been there many times without breathing aids but we did not

Above: Jacques-Yves Cousteau receiving an award for his underwater film *Le Monde Sans Soleil* (sunless world), made in 1964. This is one of the films Cousteau has made of his explorations of the world under the waves.

Right: a diver examines the hull of an old ship. In 1943, Cousteau realized how valuable his diving equipment would be in underwater salvage work. He made a film which he called *Épaves* (sunken ships), photographing underwater wrecks off the coast of southern France. While making the film, he and his team pushed their maximum diving depth beyond the 130-foot mark.

know what happened below that boundary. How far can we go with this strange device?" In the months and years to follow, Cousteau and other divers were to find out.

During that first exciting summer, Cousteau and his team made 500 successful dives to depths between 50 and 100 feet. The Aqua-Lung behaved perfectly and the men had a whole new world to discover. Yet Cousteau still felt apprehensive. "The thing was too easy," he wrote. "Every instinct insisted that we could not so flippantly invade the sea. An unforeseen trap awaited in the deep, any day now, for Dumas, Tailliez, or me."

It was still wartime. The previous year, German troops had invaded the naval base at Toulon, the Mediterranean port in southeast France. The French fleet had destroyed most of its ships in the harbor. The scuttled vessels included two of those on which Cousteau had served. "Sunken ships preyed on our minds," said Cousteau. In 1943, he and his team began to make a film about undersea wrecks. The film was also to serve as proof of the usefulness of the Aqua-Lung in underwater salvage work.

Among the wrecks explored by the divers was the *Dalton*. This British steamer was under charter to a Greek company when she sank off Marseille on Christmas Eve, 1928. Part of the ship lay from 70 to 100 feet down, the stern quarters were about 30 feet deeper. The divers hesitated, wondering whether to take the risk of going

Above: a diver pulling ropes down from the surface during work on wrecks off the coast of England.

Below: a peril for the skin diver, a turkeyfish *(Pterois volitans)*. Its dorsal spines are poisonous.

Above: a diver's back pack opened up to show the cylinders. They contain a mixture of helium and oxygen. This mixture is used for dives deeper than 150 feet because helium under pressure does not affect the nerve cells as does nitrogen—the major constituent of compressed air. Cousteau and his team experienced the narcotic effect of compressed nitrogen. They called this effect "the rapture of the depths."

deep enough to investigate the tantalizing stern section. Cousteau decided that this was the only way to ascertain the limits of the Aqua-Lung. Down they went, deeper than ever before. They reached 132 feet and returned safely.

But Dumas, in particular, believed that the Aqua-Lung could take men deeper still without risk from the crippling effects of the bends. He was ready to test his belief by going down to find out.

On October 17, 1943, preparations were made for an experimental dive. A rope, knotted at regular intervals, was carefully measured and attested by a local official. The rope was lowered to the seabed, about 240 feet down, at the spot where Dumas would attempt a record-breaking dive. Two launches, full of witnesses, accompanied the "condemned man," as Cousteau called him. Dumas was to submerge, heavily weighted, until he reached his limit. Then he was to fix his weights to the line and rise to the surface as quickly as possible.

Dumas dived into a cold and choppy sea. Cousteau, the safety man, dropped to his vantage post 100 feet down on the line, after a breathless struggle against the waves. He wrote, "I followed him [down]. . . . My brain was reeling. Didi did not look up. I saw his fists and head melting into the dun water."

Dumas described his record dive in these words: ". . . . I cannot see clearly. Either the sun is going down quickly or my eyes are weak. I reach the hundred foot knot. My body doesn't feel weak but I keep panting. The damned rope doesn't hang straight. It slants off into the yellow soup . . . . I am anxious about that line, but I really feel wonderful. I have a queer feeling of beatitude. I am drunk and carefree. My ears buzz and my mouth tastes bitter. The current staggers me as though I had had too many drinks.

"I have forgotten Jacques and the people in the boats. My eyes are tired. I lower myself farther, trying to think about the bottom, but I can't. I am going to sleep, but I can't fall asleep in such dizziness. There is a little light around me. I reach for the next knot and miss it. I reach again and tie my belt on it.

"Coming up is merry as a bubble. . . . The drunken sensation vanishes. I am sober and infuriated to have missed my goal. I pass Jacques and hurry on up. I am told I was down seven minutes."

Dumas thought that he had gone no more than 100 feet down. But his weighted belt was tied off 210 feet below the surface. The

Right: the diagram illustrates an experiment performed by Johannes A. Kylstra. It was carried out in the light of Cousteau's suggestion that a type of underwater man could be created, who would breathe in the sea as easily as a fish. Kylstra filled one of a deep-sea diver's lungs with a saline solution that was "breathed" by being pumped in and out. The diver later said that he felt no unpleasant sensations.

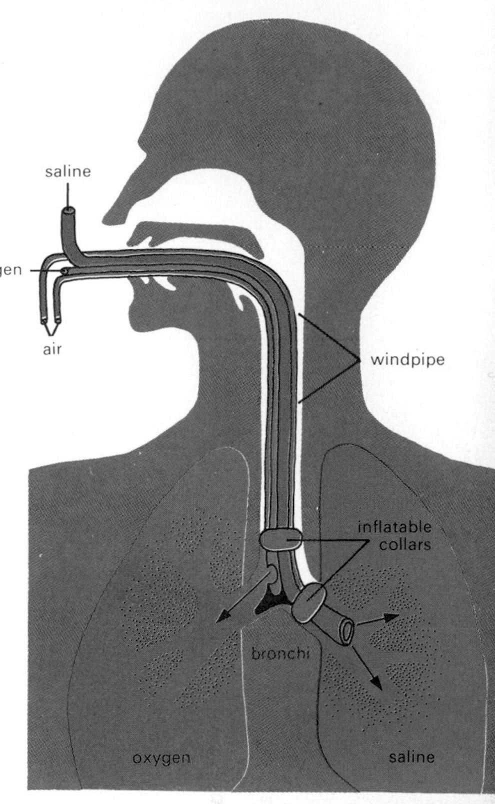

Frenchman had discovered another danger of the sea, one as perilous as the bends. Cousteau's team called it *l'ivresse des grandes profondeurs*—the intoxication, or rapture, of the depths. This "drunkenness" becomes progressively worse with depth. A feeling of elation is succeeded by drowsiness and overwhelming lethargy, while the diver's thoughts become gradually more confused. Feeling perfectly safe, divers have been known to tear off their equipment while "drunk" on nitrogen. Some divers are even reported to have offered their breathing apparatus to a passing fish, lest the creature should drown without air. Others have searched in non-existent pockets to make sure they have brought their cigarettes with them.

This "drunkenness," or nitrogen narcosis, is apparently caused by the effect of nitrogen on the nervous system. Today, deep divers

Left: a close-up of a modern diver's helmet. Compared to the heavy, uncomfortable diving helmets of the 1800's this lightweight version is very comfortable to wear. Good visibility is provided by a large, wrap-around visor. Tubes from the gas cylinders enter the helmet from the sides and are connected to a standard mouthpiece.

use a mixture of helium and oxygen rather than nitrogen and oxygen to guard against the rapture of the depths. But in 1943 the depths of the sea were all too new. Each lesson had to be personally learned.

When the war ended, Cousteau showed his film of sunken ships to the Ministry of the Marine in Paris. As a result, he was given the task of organizing an underwater group to salvage vessels sunk during the war and to carry out diving research. With Tailliez and Dumas, Cousteau set up the Undersea Study and Research Group based on Toulon, where other naval officers and technical experts joined them. Their work was made doubly hazardous by the number of unexploded mines which littered the seabed. Dumas, curious about the effects of explosions underwater, came near to death on more than one occasion during reconnaissance dives.

The group's activities gradually expanded. Other tough assignments came from the Navy. Cousteau and his men continued to dive, film, and experiment, perfecting their techniques as they worked. But the rapture of the depths still fascinated them. In the summer of 1947, the Undersea Research Group decided to challenge the sea

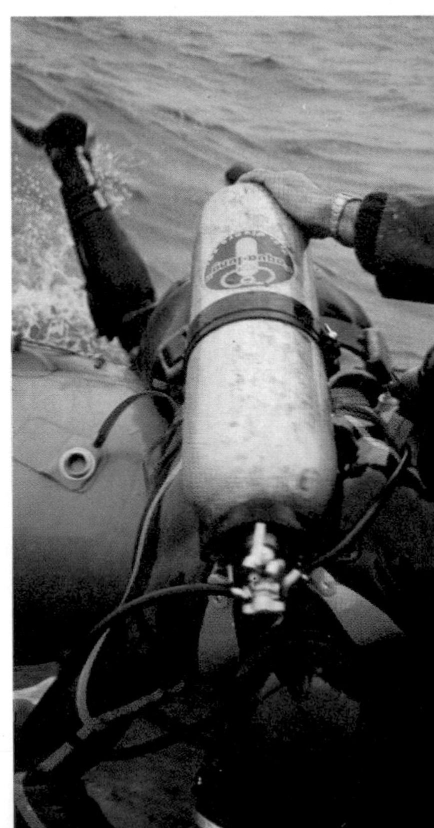

again in a series of even deeper dives. The depth they set for themselves was 300 feet. In the four years since Dumas had dived to 210 feet, no independent diver had beaten his record.

Cousteau was the first to dive. Grasping heavy scrap iron, he plunged down through the water, watching the azure blue of the sunlit surface dim as he neared the lightless depths. At 200 feet, Cousteau "tasted the metallic flavor of compressed nitrogen and was instantaneously and severely struck with rapture." Grabbing the line, Cousteau jotted on one of the small message boards strung along the rope, "Nitrogen has a dirty taste."

"I hung witless on the rope," he wrote later. "Standing aside was a smiling jaunty man, my second self, perfectly self-contained, grinning sardonically at the wretched diver. As the seconds passed, the jaunty man installed himself in my command and ordered that I unloose the rope and go down." Cousteau dropped to the last board, 297 feet down. He signed his name, dropped his load of iron ballast, and shot upward. He had become the deepest free diver in the world.

Then, five more of the group divers visited the deep board. Not

Above: the two center divers are completing tests during Cousteau's first underwater living experiment. Cousteau was fascinated by the idea of men living in the sea. In 1962, he sent down two divers to live for a week in a habitat 33 feet below the surface. The experiment was a complete success and Cousteau followed it up with a series of more ambitious missions.

Left: a diver is helped back into a rubber dinghy. He is one of several divers who surveyed wrecks off England's southwest coast in 1967.

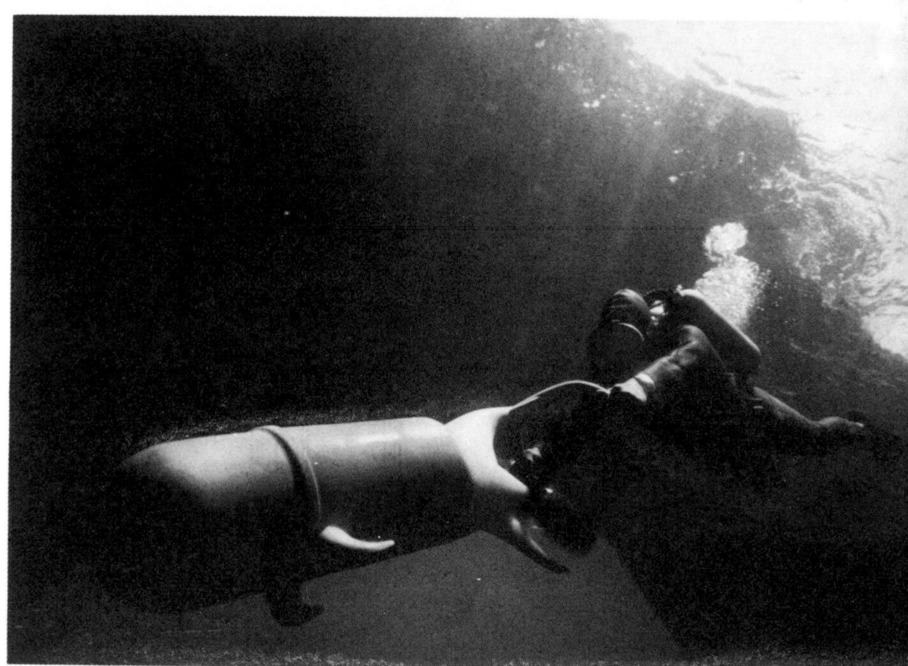

Right: a diver using an underwater scooter. These devices not only provide an exhilarating ride but they also save precious seconds of the limited time a diver has underwater.

one of them was able to scrawl anything intelligible at that depth.

The summer passed and the team decided on another series of dives past the 300-foot mark. The first to go down was Maurice Fargues, a diving master in the group. Down he plunged, occasionally tugging the rope in an "all's well" signal. Suddenly, there was nothing. The safety man dived immediately to meet him at the 150-foot level while others hauled Fargues toward the surface. When the two divers met, Fargues' mouthpiece was dangling on his chest. He was dead. Later, the group examined the boards on the rope and found Fargues' initials scratched at a depth of 396 feet. It was 100 feet deeper than any of the others had ever gone. The group never again challenged the rapture of the depths.

In 1949, Cousteau took command of the *Calypso*. This vessel was designed to undertake a variety of oceanographic research. In 1952, Cousteau took it to Grand Congloué, an islet off Marseille, where he and his team explored one of the most interesting wrecks ever discovered—a 100-ton freighter dating from about 230 B.C.

It was while working on this wreck that Cousteau developed the idea of underwater television. The archaeologists on board the

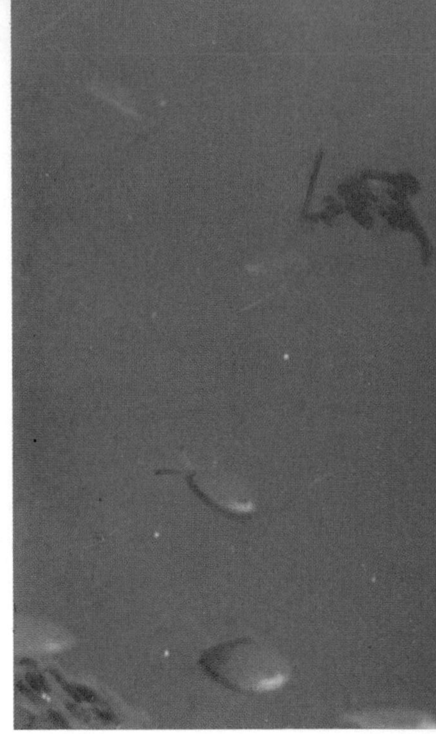

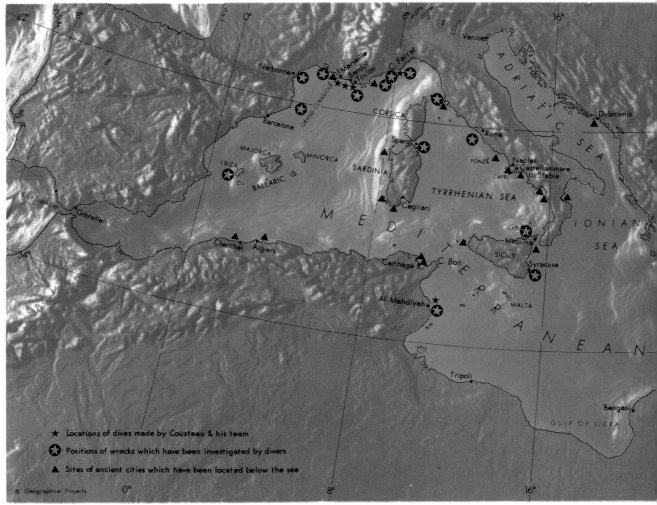

★ Locations of dives made by Cousteau & his team

✪ Positions of wrecks which have been investigated by divers

▲ Sites of ancient cities which have been located below the sea

© Geographical Projects

Above: Cousteau's diving saucer. This free-swimming submersible is propelled by water jets. It can carry two men underwater to a depth of 1,000 feet. Below: an Aqua-Lung diver scoops up a vase from the bottom of the sea.

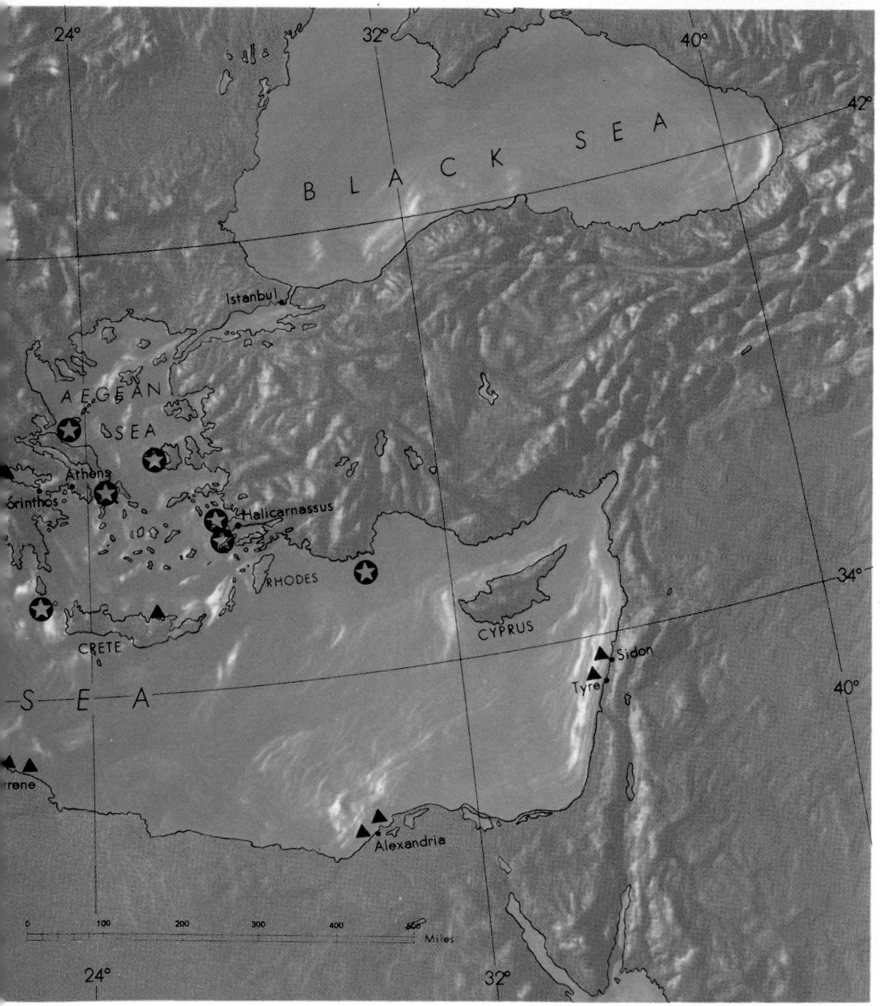

Left: the Mediterranean Sea, showing underwater exploration. At Bandol in 1943 Cousteau and his team tested the first Aqua-Lung, an invention that was to revolutionize deep-sea diving. For the first time, man was able to dive beneath the surface of the waves unencumbered by airlines linking him to the surface.

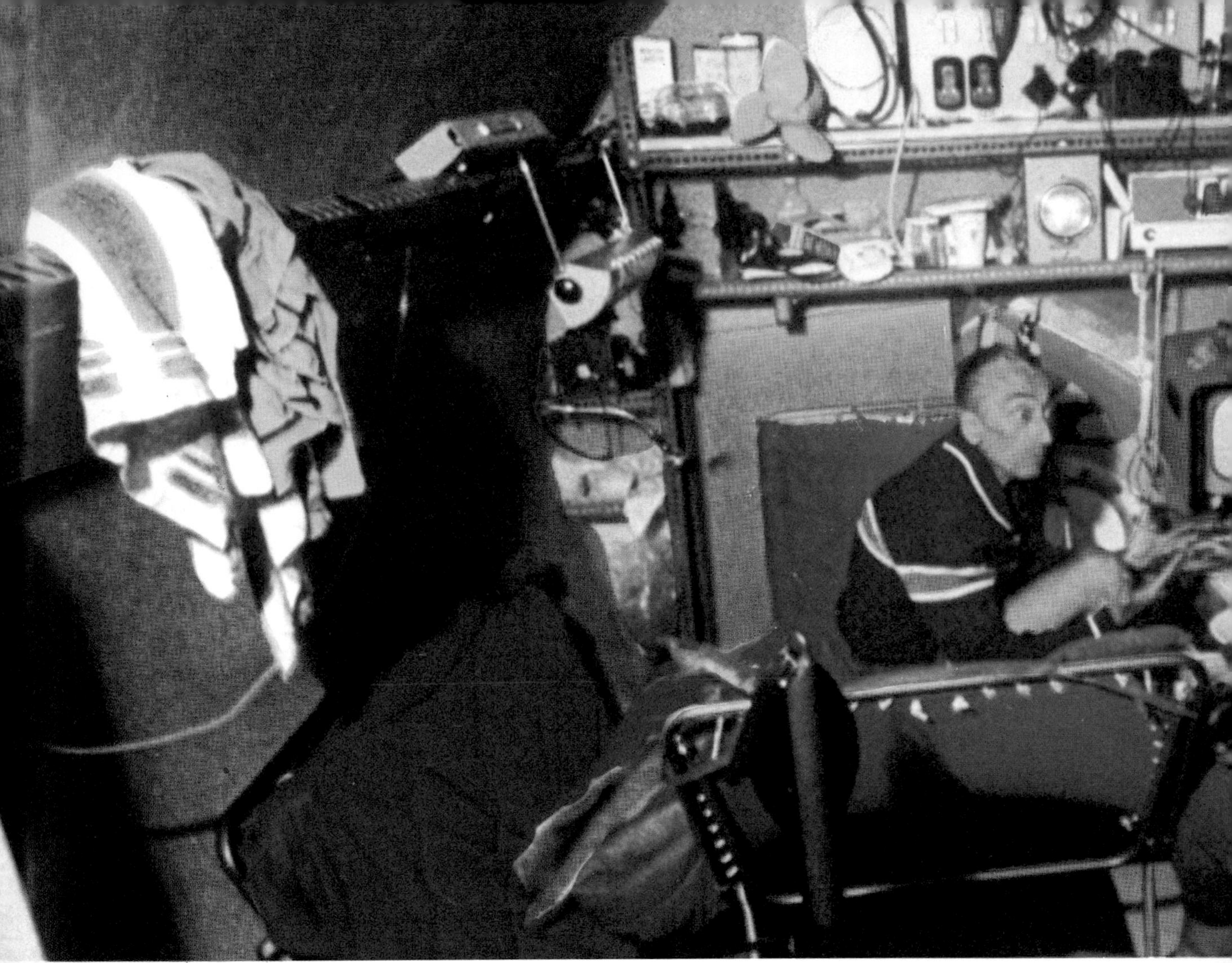

Calypso were anxious to participate more directly in the work of the divers below. Cousteau arranged for the divers to take down a tele-camera, which he borrowed from a large television company. The camera was fitted with a watertight case and could be operated either by the diver or from the surface. Underwater microphones carried instructions down from the *Calypso,* where spectators received a clear picture on their television screen of the activities below.

This was just one of the many devices that Cousteau developed over the years to improve and advance underwater research. Notable among the others is his diving saucer, a two-man submarine. The saucer is equipped with outside mechanical arms and is propelled by water jets.

In the thousands of hours that Cousteau and his men had spent diving under the sea, they had really no more than glimpsed its fascinations. They were men-fish for only a few hours at a time. In a submersible, they could stay longer and dive deeper. Yet, then they would no longer be *in* the sea, but confined within a steel prison. To set up a "home" on the sea floor that would let men live and work

Left: Cousteau inside his first underwater habitat *Conshelf I*. In September 1962, two divers, Albert Falco and Claude Wesley, stayed in *Conshelf I* for a week. The habitat was at a depth of 33 feet and the divers used it as a home base for their daily excursions into the surrounding sea.

Below: a view of the outside of *Conshelf I*. The 17-foot-long cylinder was anchored to the seabed with 34 tons of pig iron. Divers entered and left the habitat through an open hatchway in the bottom of the cylinder. The *Conshelf I* experiment showed that men could live and work underwater.

in comfort there would be the next step in making man into a truly marine creature.

Cousteau was a pioneer in developing such a manned underwater station in the sea. In September, 1962, he set up the world's first underwater habitat. It was called *Conshelf I,* short for Continental Shelf Station Number One. Two aquanauts from his team lived and worked for a week in the habitat, anchored 33 feet underwater off the coast of southern France.

Conshelf I was a steel cylinder 17 feet long and 8 feet in diameter. The entrance to the cylinder was an open hatchway in the floor of the habitat. No door was needed because the air pressure within the cylinder was exactly that of the sea outside. The aquanauts worked for five hours each day to show that men could not only live underwater but also perform useful tasks.

As Cousteau wrote about *Conshelf I*: "They [the divers] were supported—or rather over-supported—by a clutter of vessels and men; as other divers, and just plain well-wishers dropped in, they sometimes felt as if they were living in a bus station." Nevertheless, the divers were reluctant to emerge after their week in the sea, and were in excellent health. The first step had been taken toward living in the sea.

In the same week that Cousteau was carrying out his experiments

Below: *Conshelf II* on the remote Sha'ab Rumi Reef in the Red Sea. Cousteau's second underwater habitat consisted of a starfish-like complex of cylinders that looked more like a village than a house. In 1963, five men stayed in the habitat for a month. Cousteau was not so much interested in breaking depth records—*Conshelf II* was only 36 feet below the surface—as in setting up the forerunner of a possible future "underwater society."

with *Conshelf I,* a Belgian diver, Robert Sténuit, was trying out another underwater home. This was a 3-foot by 11-foot aluminum cylinder designed by American inventor Edwin Link. Sténuit remained for 26 hours at a depth of 200 feet, spending some of that time exploring the sea outside. After his successful stay in the sea, the American program of underwater habitats forged ahead.

Six months later, Cousteau followed his first success with *Conshelf II,* a "village" of five interconnected cylinders and an "advance station" of a single cylinder. His aim this time was to set up a "precursor of underwater society." The main settlement of this colony, 36 feet beneath the sea, housed five men for a month. In the deeper camp at 90 feet two men lived and worked for a week, pushing the depths at which men could do useful work down to 165 feet.

Conshelf II was remarkable for another finding. Cousteau had assembled a group of "average" men for his experiment. He proved that the participants did not have to be expert divers or even young men in top physical condition. Instead, the men of *Conshelf II* were chosen for their individual skills, either as mechanics, cooks, or scientists. And on this second experiment in underwater living, Cousteau took care that the divers were not bothered by underwater sight-seers.

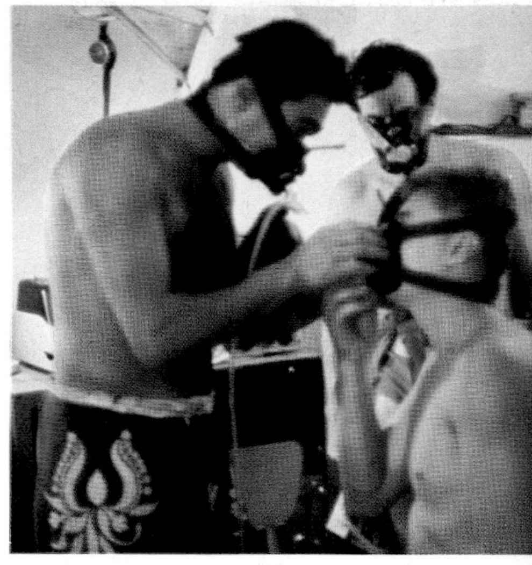

Above: divers fixing each other's masks before swimming out from their underwater home *Conshelf III.* At a depth of 330 feet in the sea their preparations had to be very thorough. If they got into difficulties they had to be able to return to the habitat. To swim to the surface from depth without decompressing would be fatal.

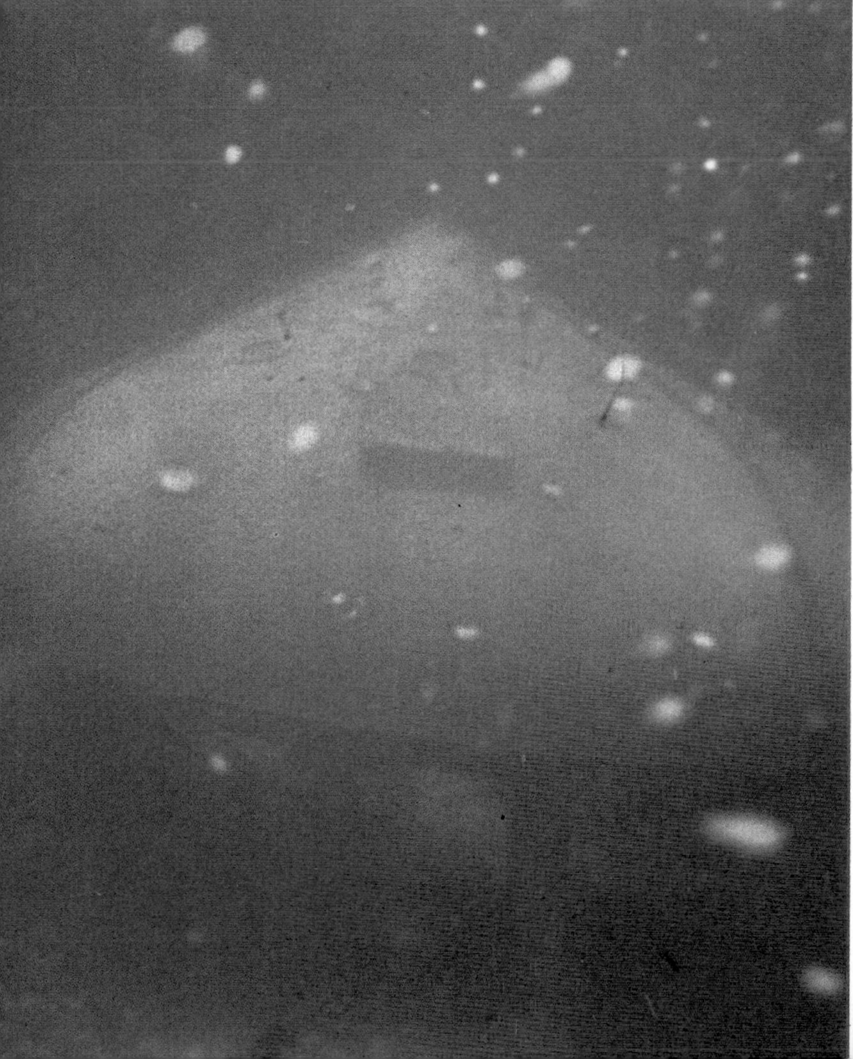

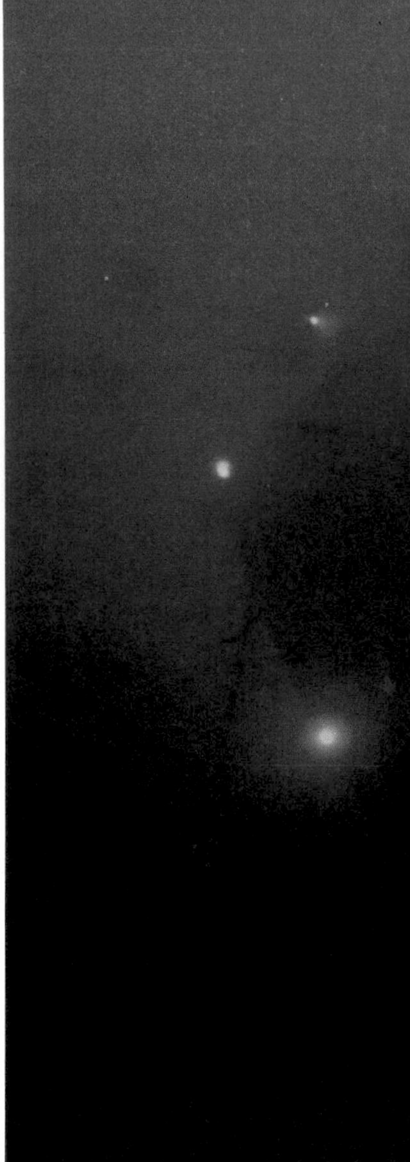

Conshelf III, in 1965, was the deepest and most ambitious of Cousteau's experiments toward the ultimate dream of *Homo aquaticus,* or underwater man. It was to be the most advanced outpost yet established by man in the "offshore wilderness," an attempt to open up hundreds of thousands of square miles of the planet's surface for the use of man. The new habitat was to be located 330 feet down and to house six men, or oceanauts, as Cousteau called them. The plan called for them to live and work in the darkness for more than three weeks.

While conceiving *Conshelf III*, Cousteau decided that the real risk to men living underwater came from the cables and pipes that provided an "umbilical cord" to the surface above. These slender cables providing air to breathe were vulnerable to surface storm damage or some other accident. Better that the men of *Conshelf III* should live in a completely self-contained environment with virtually no reliance on those at the surface except in dire emergency.

The new undersea station was a sphere 18 feet in diameter resting on a 28-foot chassis that held 77 tons of ballast. Before being towed to their destination off Cape Ferrat in the Mediterranean, the six highly-trained oceanauts were pressurized in *heliox*—a helium and oxygen mixture—to a pressure of 11 atmospheres. While still on the surface, they were living under the equivalent of 330 feet of water. But although the heliox mixture protects against the bends and against the rapture of the depths, it poses another problem—that of communication. Helium is so light that it does not "slow down" the vibrations of the vocal cords as does normal air. The speech of people breathing a helium mixture sounds, as one ocean scientist put it, "like Donald Duck in a rage." Cousteau's oceanauts were almost completely unable to understand one another for days.

Cousteau considered that there were two critical periods for *Conshelf III*, apart from unexpected emergencies. One was the descent and precise landing of the huge sphere at a preselected site on the bottom. The other was the return of the habitat to the surface under the control of the oceanauts themselves.

The first critical phase passed successfully. The habitat landed within a foot of its target site. Now came the difficult routine of work with a five-ton mock-up of an oil wellhead, the elaborate system of valves and piping that controls the flow of oil from an underwater well. Conventional divers cannot maintain a wellhead,

Above: *Conshelf III.* Cousteau's third habitat consisted of an 18-foot-diameter sphere divided into two floors, the upper one for eating and scientific work, the lower one for sleeping and diving. Six oceanauts (including Cousteau's son Philippe) lived in *Conshelf III* for three weeks at a depth of 330 feet below the surface.

Right: *Conshelf III* divers working on a mock-up of an underwater oil well-head. One of their main tasks was to discover if divers could maintain these structures at depths below 150 feet.

or *Christmas tree* as it is called, in depths much below 150 feet. For the *Conshelf III* oceanauts to succeed in the difficult job of deepwater maintenance would prove that oil could be produced deeper than ever before—and that such tasks as underwater mining, salvage, and aquaculture (farming the sea) could be done as well.

For three weeks, the six divers went through their daily routine, working with the Christmas tree, observing marine life, and venturing from their base as deep as 370 feet. But then it was time to return. The next critical period was at hand.

Sealed in the sphere, the chief diver turned a crank to release ballast that would free the sphere from the bottom and send it slowly drifting upward. As the iron weights were released, they turned the sea floor into a maelstrom of swirling sediment. But the sphere did not move. The undersea habitat was stuck fast to the bottom.

Cousteau, connected to the habitat by telephone from the command station ashore, suggested that a little compressed air be squirted into the ballast tanks, just enough to loosen the habitat but not enough to send her careering upward. André Laban, commander of the sphere, cracked the compressed air valve for two seconds. "She's not moving," he reported. Cousteau suggested "another gentle injection." There was still no result.

"Here goes a little more," said Laban, twisting the valve again. *Conshelf III* trembled. Then, gently, the sphere began to rise. The habitat was free at last. Minutes later, the huge sphere bobbed on

Above: recent research has shown that glass is as strong as steel in its power to resist the water pressure at great depths in the ocean. But molding and joining pieces of glass to make flawless spheres has always presented problems. The glass sphere shown here rests in a protective cage while being prepared for pressure chamber tests. In use it may be lowered to depths of up to 1,500 feet or may form part of a self-powered submersible. Right: glass is also to be used in the deep-sea city that General Electric hope to start constructing in 1980. Unlike steel, glass does not corrode in seawater, an important consideration in permanent underwater habitats. The drawing shows how standard 12-foot-diameter glass spheres fit together to make a complete self-contained city—12,000 feet down in the Atlantic Ocean. Divers wishing to swim around their home will carry devices in their lungs so that they can "breathe" water.

the surface of the ocean. The divers inside would have to undergo 84 hours of decompression to adjust their bodies slowly to normal air pressure. But they—and the visionary Cousteau—had scored an incredible success.

The *Conshelf* experiments continue today, pursuing ever greater and more ambitious objectives. Each one will mark another milestone on the road to the deep. And each will be a further tribute to the dedicated pioneering of the first aquanaut—Jacques-Yves Cousteau.

Above: the standard sphere—glass segments "seamed" with titanium.

A New History of the Earth

8

Free divers and submersibles are adding every day to man's knowledge of the undersea world. The ability to "go down and see" offers seemingly boundless possibilities for the exploration of the deep. But a great deal of oceanographic research is still carried out from the surface. Ships are playing a vital role in discovering fresh facts about the sea and, through them, gaining a greater understanding of our planet.

One such ship is the *Vema,* possibly the most productive oceanographic vessel in operation and with a long history of valuable research behind it. For the *Vema* has worked in every ocean of the world, logging more miles than any other oceanographic ship of its size.

A 200-foot, 3-masted steel schooner, the *Vema* was built in 1927 as a rich man's yacht. Its varied career later included trade runs between Canada and the West Indies, taking out cargoes of lumber and returning with stocks of West Indian rum. In 1953 the *Vema* was purchased by Columbia University's Lamont-Doherty Geological Observatory and fitted out to serve the cause of oceanography. It was refurbished with a steel deck and deck housings, but is still without proper lifeboats (its Canadian crews claim that dories—narrow, flat-bottomed boats—are far better at sea) or any provision for distilling fresh water. It does not even have watertight bulkheads. Some oceanographers have called the *Vema* and its cramped quarters a floating coffin. Many others think it the most seaworthy ship afloat.

The *Vema*'s early years as a floating laboratory were stormy ones. For months on end it shuddered under the pounding of high explosives that sent showers of water crashing against its steel hull. The oceanographers aboard it became oblivious to the sound. But on another ship, many miles away, the echoes of the explosives were being carefully recorded. After a time the ships would exchange roles—the *Vema* would listen while explosives were set off from the other ship. The scientists on the two ships were engaged on a mission to probe the sea floor with its thick layers of sediment and

Left: an island is born as an erupting volcano breaks surface 150 miles off the Pacific coast of Japan. Scientists know that the earth's crust is thin under the oceans, but only recently have they been able to probe its secrets.

Above: geophysicists examine a profile of the sea bottom produced by seismic soundings. The trace shows underwater mountains called seamounts.

to penetrate the solid rocks below, in search of clues to the earth's past—buried millions, perhaps billions, of years before. With high explosives and film, they were trying to wrest the history of the planet from the depths of the sea.

A charge of high explosives has a tremendously powerful impact in water, far greater than in the comparatively thin air. Energy from the explosion travels outward in all directions. Some of it moves toward the bottom at the speed of sound in water—usually about 4,700 feet a second or around four times faster than in air. When the energy from the explosion reaches the bottom, most of it bounces off. But some of the energy knifes through the bottom until it reaches a layer of different matter beneath the sea floor and part of it bounces off again. Even then the remaining energy manages to penetrate the layer and the successive layers that lie beneath it. At last, the sound may echo off the *basement* itself, the solid rocky bottom of the ocean formed before any material had sifted through the water to cover it.

As the sound energy hits these different layers beneath the sea floor, the sound not only bounces off but also travels along the layer, radiating noise like a plane traveling overhead. This sound broadcasting from the different layers can be picked up by a listening ship equipped with sensitive *hydrophones*—microphones that work in the water. By noting exactly the time it takes for the different echoes to reach the hydrophones of the listening ship, marine geophysicists can tell how deep these layers are, whether they slant up or down or are level, and even make a good guess at what the layers are made of. This technique of reading the layers under the sea bottom requires absolute teamwork between two ships connected only by radio.

The shooting ship, as the ship which drops the explosive charges is called, must put the charges over the side on a precise schedule. The listening ship must know almost to the split second when the charge will go off. This is because any sound—the rumble of a generator, the sound of a pump, even the clank of a wrench dropped on deck—can be picked up by the hydrophones. And this unwanted noise can obscure a vital trace on the film that records the seismic signals—signals caused by an earthquake or an artificial vibration of the earth, in this case the explosion. Absolute silence is the rule on the listening ship.

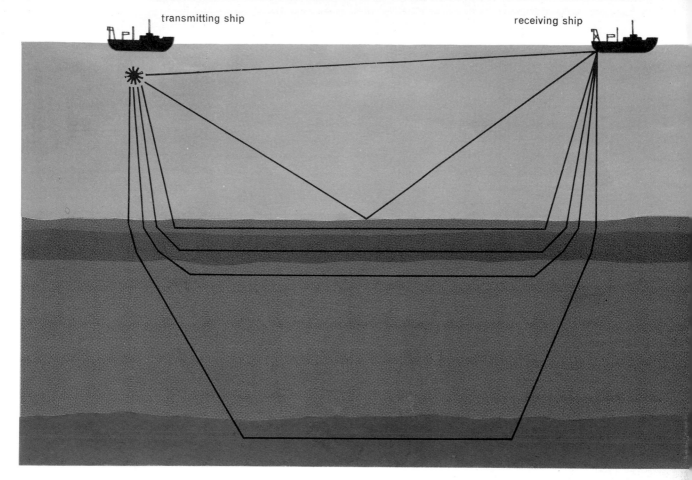

transmitting ship

receiving ship

The same sense of urgency exists on the shooting ship. Handling high explosives at sea is dangerous and the shooting schedule is fast. When the shooting ship is near the listening ship, half-pound blocks of explosives are tossed over the side every 30 seconds or so. To keep up this pace, the man setting off the explosives must cut a six-inch length of fuse, crimp an explosive cap to one end, tape the cap to the charge, and ignite the fuse—twice each minute. But as the ships separate, the rate of shooting drops as the size of the individual charges becomes larger. One-pound charges follow half-pounders, then 3-pounders, 9-pounders, 24-pounders, 100-pounders, and finally, at 20-minute intervals, large depth charges loaded with several hundred pounds of high explosive. When even the depth charges are too weak for the bottom echoes to be heard, the shooting ship heaves to and becomes the listener, the ships move closer together and the series of explosions begins again.

Above: the seismic-refraction method of probing the layers of sediment beneath the sea. One ship releases an explosive charge in the water and another, up to 100 miles away, records the refracted sound waves and measures how long they have taken to arrive. Scientists use the traces produced to tell the depth of the layers beneath the seabed, whether they slant up or down, or are level, and what they are made of.

Below: a section through the floor of the Pacific Ocean. Nicaragua and the Philippine and Marshall island groups are the peaks of undersea mountains. Challenger Deep, at the left, is the deepest known spot on earth.

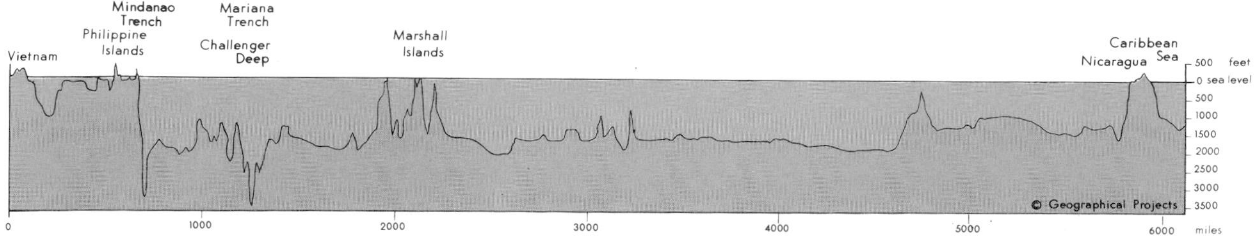

Right: a diagram showing the features beneath the waters of the South Atlantic Ocean, prepared by Bruce Heezen and Marie Tharp of the Lamont-Doherty Geological Observatory. Only recently-developed survey techniques have made such detailed maps possible.

Above: oceanographers of the British research ship *Discovery II* maneuver a sonar "fish" into the water. As it is towed behind the ship the fish "illuminates" the sea floor with sound waves and picks up the returning echoes. On board *Discovery* a display unit translates these echoes into an acoustic "picture" of the sea floor, showing features many thousands of feet below. Using such devices oceanographers have been able to make accurate surveys of the ocean bottom in a fraction of the time taken by more conventional sounding methods.

The *Vema* worked in this way with dozens of other ships, registering thousands of miles of seismic tracks. But in recent years, techniques aboard it have changed. The hazardous high explosives, which caused the death of one oceanographer, are no longer used. Today, an air gun slung from the stern is used instead. The long strands of film used to record the signals have been replaced by an electronic instrument that automatically sketches a picture of the layers below the sea floor.

One piece of the *Vema*'s equipment that has not become obsolete is the Ewing piston corer, named after its designer Maurice Ewing, the director of the Lamont-Doherty Geological Observatory of Columbia University. Ewing, who has sailed regularly aboard the *Vema* since 1953, was the first to use seismic techniques at sea.

The Ewing corer is used for obtaining sediment samples. It consists of a hollow tube that is driven into the bottom sediments by a 2,000-pound weight. Inside the tube is a movable piston that sucks the sample into the tube without disturbing the sediments. The column of layered sediments that is pushed from the tube onto the deck of the *Vema* contains clues to the geological history of the bottom and to the dynamic events taking place on the ocean floor. Some of the many thousands of cores at Lamont are longer than 70 feet and contain material laid down as long as 100 million years ago.

Before Ewing perfected his corer, other marine scientists had tried punching holes in the deep ocean bottom. Their short cores revealed little more than the *Challenger* had discovered in the 1800's. The bottom of the deep sea was thought to be a place of perpetual calm with a constant rain of sediment slowly blanketing it. But Ewing's cores revealed that the ocean floor was far less peaceful than earlier oceanographers had believed. Working with David Ericson of Lamont, Ewing discovered that vast areas of the deep ocean basins had been covered again and again by enormous undersea landslides that swept down from the shelves ringing the continents or from seamounts poking upward from the bottom. Other scientists found that these slides must have rushed across the sea floor at speeds of more than 100 miles an hour, smothering the marine life on and just below the surface of the bottom ooze.

Another veteran instrument aboard the *Vema* is the PDR—the Precision Depth Recorder—which traces a constant graphic outline

PHYSIOGRAPHIC DIAGRAM OF THE
SOUTH ATLANTIC OCEAN
The Caribbean Sea, The Scotia Sea, and the eastern margin of the South Pacific Ocean
BY BRUCE C. HEEZEN AND MARIE THARP
LAMONT GEOLOGICAL OBSERVATORY
Columbia University

Left: a view from the derrick of the drilling ship *Glomar Challenger.* Thousands of feet of drill pipe are laid out in precise order on deck.

Right: the 400-foot-long *Glomar* on station over a drilling site. Named for the original *Challenger,* this remarkable ship has enabled oceanographers to make astounding discoveries about the history of the earth.

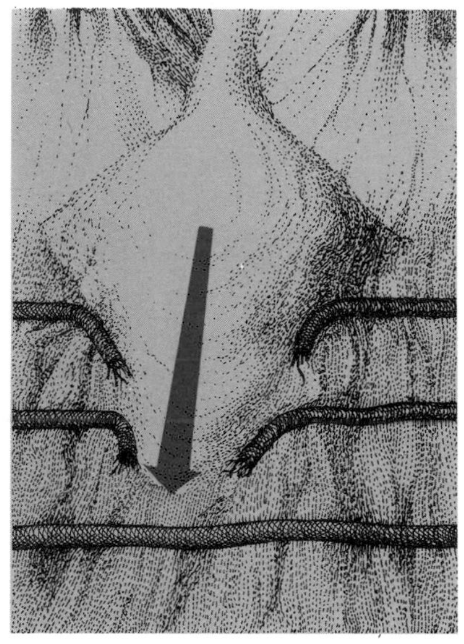

Above: a diagram showing how an underwater landslide snapped a series of telegraph cables off Newfoundland in 1929. By measuring the time interval between the break in each of these cables, oceanographers worked out that the slide was moving at a maximum speed of 50 miles an hour.

of the shape of the sea floor. It was this PDR that helped oceanographers discover one of the strangest features of the undersea world—the vast mid-ocean ridge that forms the greatest mountain range on earth.

As early as the *Challenger* expedition, oceanographers recognized that there was a peculiar rise in the middle of the Atlantic Ocean. As more and more soundings were taken, this hump in the Atlantic gradually took on the shape of an extended mountain chain. Most of the top of the ridge was found to be between 9,000 and 10,000 feet deep, some 5,000 feet above the average depth of the Atlantic Ocean, but in places its peaks rise above the surface of the water to become islands such as the Azores in the North Atlantic, St. Paul Rocks in the South Atlantic about 600 miles northeast of Brazil, and Ascension, Tristan da Cunha, and Bouvet, also in the South Atlantic. The tallest of these peaks is Pico Island in the Azores which is 27,000 feet high, with 7,460 feet above the surface.

Although the main outline of this Atlantic ridge was known by about 1930, no one knew where it began or where it ended. Later, other ridge systems were found in other oceans. But no one thought to connect them into a single giant chain. Then Ewing suggested that all the ridges were part of one enormous "seam around the world" that was of great importance in understanding the deepest secrets of the earth itself. Just how, he was uncertain. But he was sure that the mid-ocean ridge was a vital key to our past. One part of this chain, however, was missing—a ridge to join the peaks of the Atlantic with those in the Indian Ocean. The *Vema* and its PDR were assigned the task of finding this missing link.

The *Vema* picked up the known part of the ridge in the South Atlantic and headed southeast toward the border of the Atlantic and Indian Oceans, south of the Cape of Good Hope. Watch by watch, scientists peering at the PDR saw the missing sections of the mid-ocean ridge gradually unreeling. The *Vema* sailed into Cape

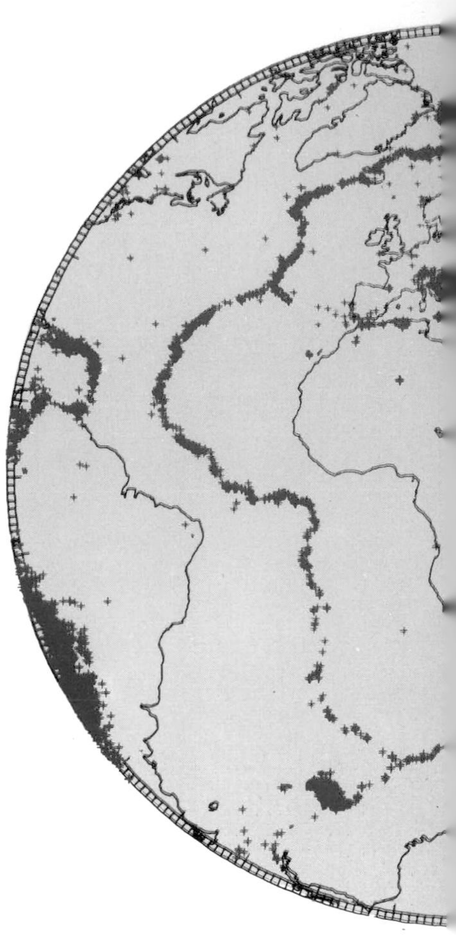

Upper Carboniferous

Eocene

Shallow seas

Deep oceans

Quaternary

Mid-ocean Ridges

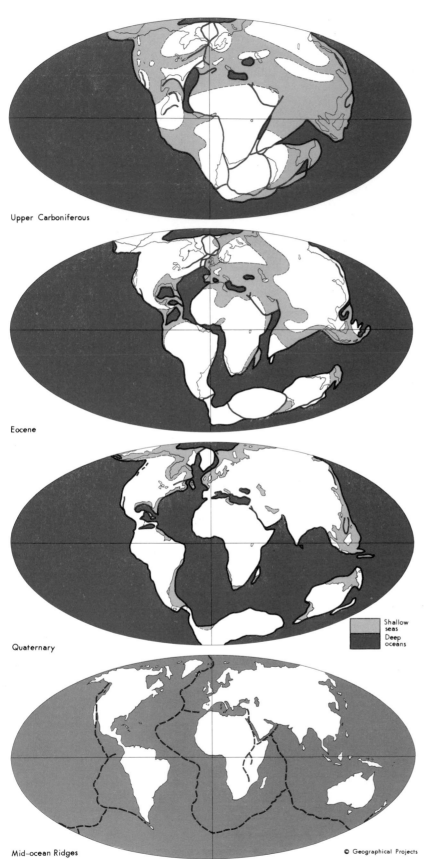

Left: according to certain scientists the continents of the world were once joined together in one huge land mass, but have since drifted apart to their positions today. This theory is known as *Continental Drift*. These maps show how the continents may have drifted apart. From top to bottom: the position of the continents during the Upper Carboniferous Period (310 million to 275 million years ago); during the Eocene Epoch (55 million to 40 million years ago); and during the Quaternary Period ($3\frac{1}{2}$ million years ago to the present day). The bottom map shows the position of the mid-ocean ridges, an undersea mountain chain forming a seam around the earth.

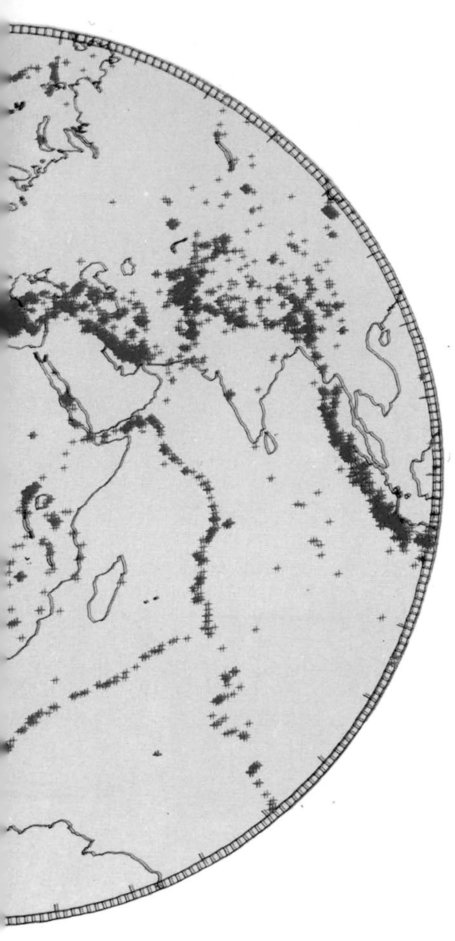

Above: a computer-drawn globe showing the location of earthquakes over a period of several years. The pattern of dots agrees with the theory that the outer crust of the earth is divided into a number of plates that are constantly moving. Accordingly the earthquakes occur where disruption is greatest, at the edges of the plates.

Town, South Africa, for supplies, and then out again, still following the elusive ridge south of Africa around toward the Indian Ocean.

At last, the underwater heights were proved to join others that had already been charted. A few small gaps still existed. But the *Vema* had shown that the globe-girdling chain was a reality. Soon another ship was to show how important the ridge system is to our knowledge of the earth. This vessel, with Maurice Ewing and many other distinguished oceanographers on board, has also furthered the *Vema*'s pioneering studies of the sea floor, revealing the nature of the mysterious layers that lie beneath it. Its work in the deep oceans has made it one of the most important research vessels afloat today.

This remarkable ship is the *Glomar Challenger,* an ungainly-looking, 400-foot-long drilling vessel, topped by a tower of steel. Built in 1968, it was designed expressly to probe through miles of water into the "pages" of the bottom sediments that are the earth's archives, and deeper still into the original floor of the sea. The ship is a worthy descendant of that earlier *Challenger*, which uncovered so many of the secrets of the sea. Manning the *Glomar* is a new breed of seafarer—a rugged crew of deep-ocean drillers who have perfected their skills on demanding and dangerous offshore oil rigs. Teamed with the drillers are seasoned sailor-scientists who have studied the oceans for years. Together, scientists, ship, and crew have penetrated the deep sea floor to answer some of the most fundamental and puzzling questions about our planet.

Ever since the first maps of the world were made, men have been struck by the apparent jigsaw fit of the continents. Africa nestles neatly into the curve of South America. Greenland fits snugly into the top of the joint between North America and Europe. If Antarctica were joined to South America, Australia would fit neatly against its western coast, and India would complete the jigsaw between Africa and Australia.

It was not until 1912, however, that the idea of *Continental Drift* was put forward by Alfred Wegener, an Austrian scientist. Wegener compared the continents to icebergs drifting on a sea of soft rock. He claimed that Australia, Africa, India, South America, and Antarctica were once joined together in a supercontinent which he called Gondwanaland. Eurasia, Greenland, and North America were similarly connected together in another giant continent that Wegener named Laurasia. Earlier still, Wegener suggested, these two supercontinents were joined as a single land mass called Pangaea.

But Wegener was unable to explain the reasons for the drift, and most scientists scoffed at his theory. After all, said his critics, earthquake waves showed clearly that, except for a molten core, the earth was solid rock. How could the continents possibly "drift" through the solid globe? And there the theory of Continental Drift rested, unheralded and unproven, buried for decades in out-of-print geology books.

Gradually, however, impressive evidence began piling up in

Above: a view down the center of the drilling derrick of *Glomar Challenger.* The ship, designed and built by Global Marine Incorporated, was ready to start work in August, 1968. The Scripps Institution of Oceanography at once arranged a voyage of discovery in the Atlantic and Pacific oceans. During two years' drilling, *Glomar Challenger* brought up cores of the ocean bed in many parts of the world. By studying the sediments contained in these cores, some of them 140 million years old, scientists have been able to answer many fundamental questions about the nature of the floor of the oceans.

support of Wegener's idea. When geologists compared the ages and positions of similar kinds of rocks in Africa and South America, they found that the layers of older rocks on both continents matched up perfectly. Identical fossils of plants and animals were found on more than one of the southern continents. The chances of perfectly similar life forms developing at exactly the same time in different places was remote. And the broad oceans that now separate the continents would be an effective barrier to most organisms. Even stronger evidence came from the study of magnetization in rocks of the same age from different continents. Scientists began to take a new look at Wegener's theory.

Meanwhile, oceanographers had been carefully plotting the course of the great mid-ocean ridge. It did not take them long to notice that, if some of the continents were joined together, the ridge would fit exactly between them. What, they wondered, did this seam around the earth have to do with the puzzle of Continental Drift?

Then, in the early 1960's, British scientists discovered the most remarkable feature of the undersea mountain range—a steep-sided valley that cut lengthwise right through the center of it. This discovery led to a new explanation of how the continents might have split apart. More important still, it suggested that the process might be continuing today.

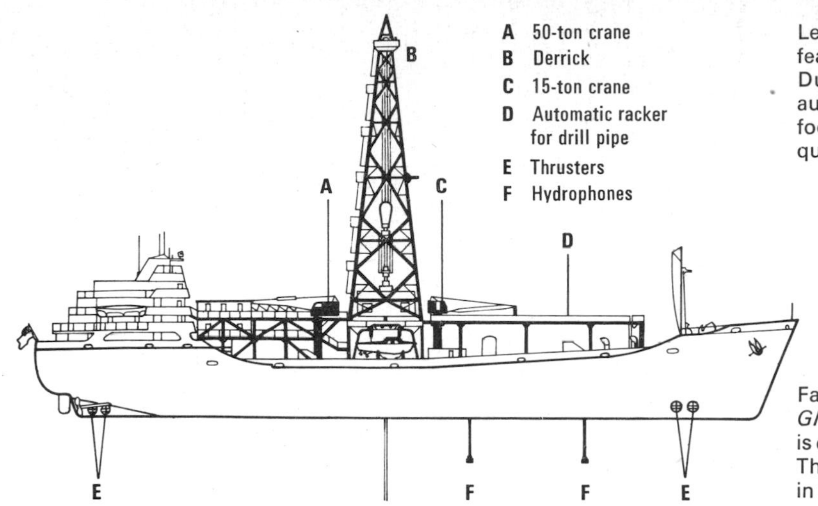

Left: a diagram showing the main features of the *Glomar Challenger.* During drilling operations the automatic racker ensures that the 90-foot lengths of drill pipe are transferred quickly to and from the derrick.

Far left: a scale drawing of the *Glomar*'s drill pipe, when the ship is drilling in 18,000 feet of water. The actual pipe has been increased in thickness so that it shows up.

Scientists proposed that the sea floor itself was spreading apart on both sides of the crack down the middle of the mid-ocean ridge. As the crack widens and fills up with molten rock from deep within the earth, the giant plates of land that form the earth's crust are pushed aside and the continents are borne along with them.

The theory was highly attractive to scientists. But their revolutionary suggestion could only be proved or disproved by drilling through thousands of feet of sediment and into the sea floor on either side of the mid-ocean ridge. The geological evidence obtained in this way would enable them to determine whether or not the continents were drifting, how rapid was their movement, and how old the seemingly timeless oceans really are. The history of the planet seemed there for the taking by adventurous scientists. Thus, the idea of *Glomar Challenger* was born.

On November 14, 1967, Scripps Institution of Oceanography contracted with Global Marine Incorporated to design and build a radical new drilling ship that could penetrate the dark ocean floor 20,000 feet below the surface of the sea. Scripps acted as part of a consortium of five other oceanographic research institutes. Less

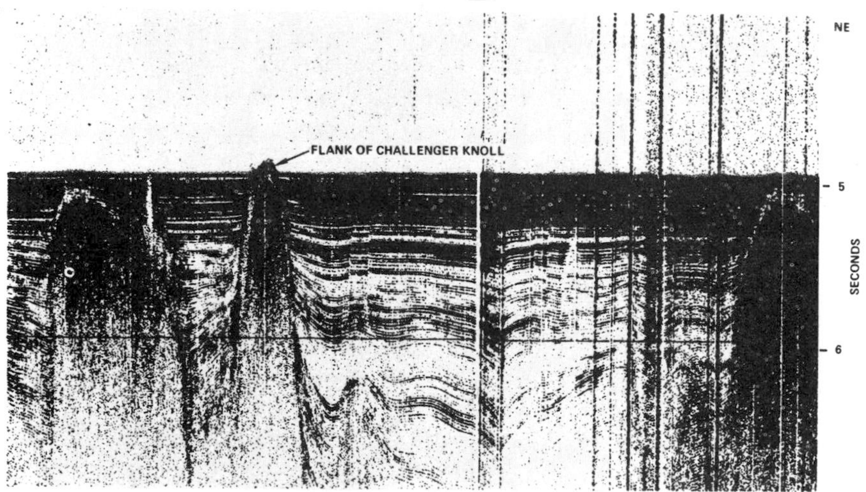

Right: a trace of the sediments below the Sigsbee Knolls in the Gulf of Mexico shows they are the tops of huge, dome-shaped formations extending thousands of feet below the sea floor.

than 10 months later, on August 11, 1968, the ship was officially accepted by the group, and its epoch-making voyage began.

The *Glomar Challenger*'s first adventure came little more than a week after it had put out to sea. Near midnight on August 19, the captain rang "finished with engines" and the ship glided to a halt on the calm waters of the Gulf of Mexico. Below the keel were 11,753 feet of water—one of the deepest areas of the gulf. But it was not the depth that interested the scientists aboard the *Glomar*. On the sea floor itself was one of the greatest puzzles of marine geology, the Sigsbee Knolls. Solving the riddle of these strange, rolling hills that, in the words of one scientist, "shouldn't be there" was to be the ship's first challenge.

The Sigsbee Knolls had been discovered several years before by oceanographers from the Lamont-Doherty Geological Observatory aboard the *Vema*. The knolls lie in a broad belt 200 miles wide that crosses the Sigsbee Deep and trails away toward the southwest. Using instruments that can "see" through the blanket of sediment on the bottom, Lamont scientists had found that the knolls were only the tops of giant, dome-shaped structures that extend thousands of feet beneath the sea floor. Other instruments indicated that these vast domes might be made of salt—exactly like those found in the coastal areas of the Gulf of Mexico. These coastal salt domes often signal the presence of gas and oil and prospectors search for them eagerly.

Most geologists doubted that the domes could be made of salt. It was an accepted fact that the huge deposits of salt required to

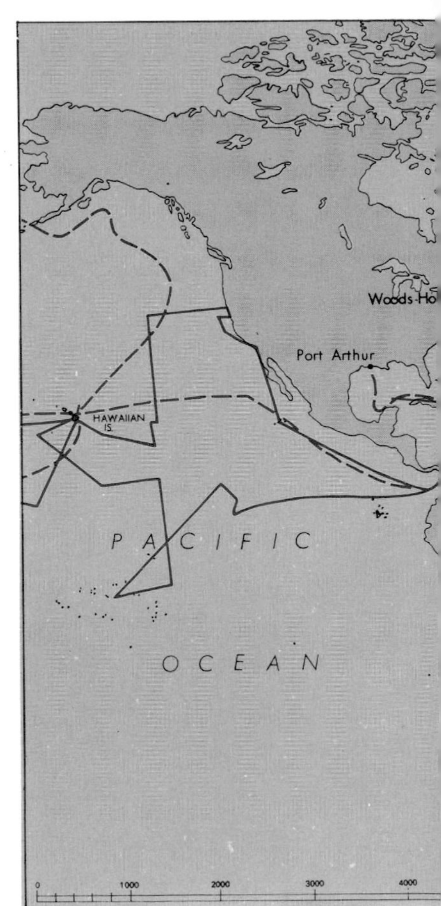

Left: the stern thrusters of *Glomar Challenger.* The *Glomar* has thrusters at both bow and stern—both consist of propellers mounted in tunnels running through the hull. They enable the ship to move sideways so that it can remain precisely over the drill site in the open sea. When drilling starts they are operated automatically as part of the dynamic position-fixing system.

Below: the route of the *Glomar Challenger* on its drilling expeditions between 1968 and 1970. By drilling into the ocean floor much can be learned about the history of the earth. The scientists of the *Glomar Challenger* have studied cores taken from the seabed and made important discoveries about the age of the oceans and about Continental Drift.

form such domes could only be laid down in shallow seas. And the Sigsbee Knolls were more than two miles down.

But at least two scientists aboard the *Glomar Challenger* were certain that the Sigsbee Knolls were indeed salt. These men were Maurice Ewing and J. Lamar Worzel, joint-chief scientists on the pioneering drilling venture of the *Glomar Challenger*. Both were experts in marine geology. Both had checked and rechecked their figures and were certain that they were correct. If the *Glomar* could successfully drill into the bottom, the solution to the riddle might be found.

When the *Glomar Challenger* halted over one of the knolls, electronic technicians went to work. Two sonar beacons were switched on. The beacons were hung over the side and then dropped free, their heavy battery cases dragging them toward the bottom at six feet per second. The sonar beacons are the heart of a dynamic positioning system that permits the *Glomar* to drill in miles of water without anchoring. Signals from the beacons are constantly picked up by four hydrophones hanging in the water beneath the ship's hull. A computer system analyzes these signals, and, as the ship drifts, automatically activates side thrusters to maintain exact position over a hole thousands of feet below.

During the 35 minutes the sonar beacons took to free fall to the

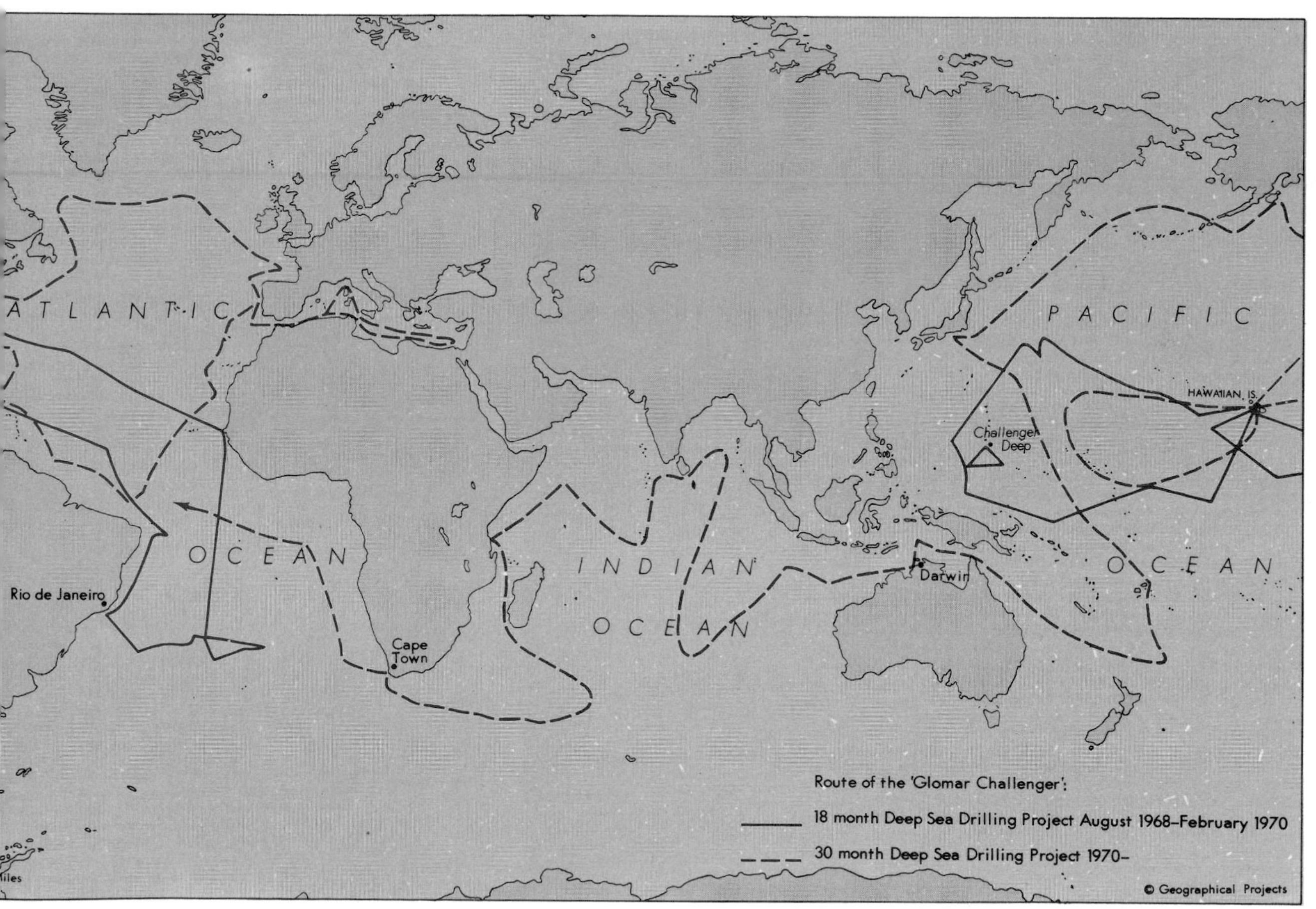

bottom, the expert *Glomar* drillers waited patiently atop the mid-ship derrick that towers 194 feet above the waterline. Finally the go-ahead came. The beacons were down and functioning perfectly. Working through the night, the drillers attached and lowered 90-foot sections of 5-inch drill pipe through the *moon pool*, the center well on the drilling platform that opens to the sea below. No one was certain that the equipment could stand the enormous weight of the steadily lowering drill pipe. But section after section gradually probed downward toward the bottom.

Just after dawn, the drill bit reached a point a few feet above the bottom. Then the chief driller started the 300-horsepower motor assembly that turns the drill pipe from the top of the miles-long string of pipes. Seconds later, the weight indicator signaled that the drill bit had entered the sediment and was starting into the mysterious knoll.

When the bit was 64 feet into the knoll, the driller called a halt. A special coring device was lowered within the string of pipes that now dangled 11,817 feet below the floor of the drilling platform. The scientists aboard anxiously awaited the first core, and when it at last emerged, it was quickly wrapped in plastic and rushed to the laboratory. The driller started up the rig once again. More and more pipe was added to the lengthening strand.

Further cores were taken and retrieved for the scientists. The *Glomar*'s equipment is so sophisticated that they could be taken from deep inside the knoll as well as from the surface. The cores revealed that the knoll was covered with a fine sediment. Then, at 450 feet into the knoll, came a startling discovery. Traces of oil and gas were found in a core. Eleven feet further on, the bit chewed into a typical salt dome cap. It, too, contained traces of oil and gas. Ewing and Worzel were right. Salt domes, and a vast new potential source of oil, had been found on the floor of the deep sea. And, almost as important, the *Glomar Challenger* had proved that it was possible to drill deep into the sea floor while freely floating miles above on the surface of the ocean.

Since that first drill hole, the *Glomar* has drilled hundreds more. After two years of deep-sea drilling, scientists were able to state that the oceans are relatively young—the oldest not much more than 200 million years, compared with the earth's 4,500 million years. They also found very strong evidence for Continental Drift. The earth's crust appears to be spreading aside relatively rapidly. Scientists have estimated that the continents are drifting apart at a rate as high as six inches a year.

Today, the *Glomar Challenger* continues to seek out new information about the history of our planet. Her drilling system has already been improved to enable her to probe ever more deeply into the sea floor. So far, scientists from Great Britain, France, Switzerland, Italy, Australia, the Soviet Union, and Brazil have participated in her mission. Future projects will take the *Glomar Challenger* to every ocean of the world.

Above: the research catamaran *Duplus*, operated by The Netherlands Offshore Company. The range of marine activities is increasing so rapidly that new research ships are designed to be very versatile. The twin-hull design of the catamaran makes it a particularly stable platform that can be used for drilling, surveying, or diving support.

Right: the *Bannock*, the oceanographic research vessel which is operated by the National Research Council of Italy.

Right: the *Atlantis II*, the research ship operated by the Woods Hole Oceanographic Institution, U.S.A. This 280-foot-long vessel was built in 1962 to replace the ketch *Atlantis*.

Life - Large and Small

9

There are now about $3\frac{1}{2}$ billion people in the world. At least $1\frac{1}{2}$ billion of them struggle to stay alive on a meager diet that falls desperately short of human needs. At the present rate of increase, by the year 2000, the world population will probably have almost doubled. There will be about $6\frac{1}{2}$ billion people on earth. How are these people to be fed? The sea may hold the answer, and scientists are seeking to use its resources to the full. But while the oceans abound in protein-rich fish, there is still a danger of overfishing certain species to the point of extinction. Only by careful study of marine animals and of the factors governing their life cycles can the sea's food potential be exploited to give everybody enough to eat.

During the 1800's, fishing became such a large and profitable industry that by the close of the century, stocks of some fish were

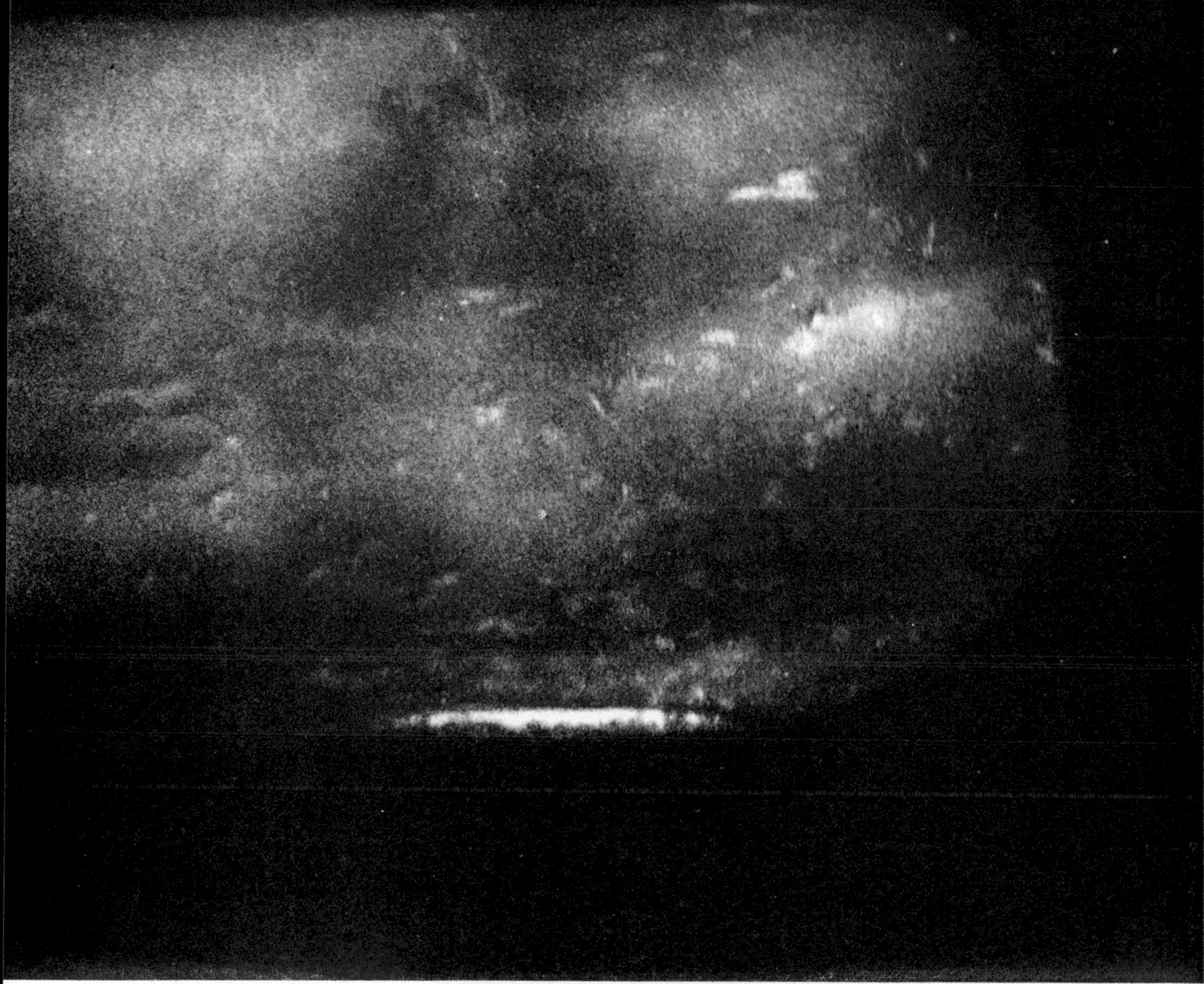

Above: a sperm whale photographed at a depth of 45 feet just off the coast of the Azores. Its broad head contains a reservoir of wax called spermaceti. During the past 100 years whales have been mercilessly hunted for their valuable supply of oil. Today, however, international restrictions on whaling are having a beneficial effect on the numbers of these superb animals.

Right: the shrimp-like crustacean that forms the food of certain baleen whales. These crustaceans, the largest members of the animal plankton, are usually called *krill.*

already seriously depleted. Governments began to realize the need for greater knowledge of marine life. Several nations organized programs of scientific research, and in 1901, the International Council for the Exploration of the Sea was set up. Its aim was to encourage governments to equip research ships and nominate scientists for the study of life and conditions in different areas of the sea.

The Scandinavian countries, whose fisheries were an important source of food, sent out a number of ships. In 1904, a Danish

Below: transparent elvers of the common eel. Eel larvae, returning from the breeding grounds in the Sargasso Sea, change into elvers three inches long when they reach river estuaries.

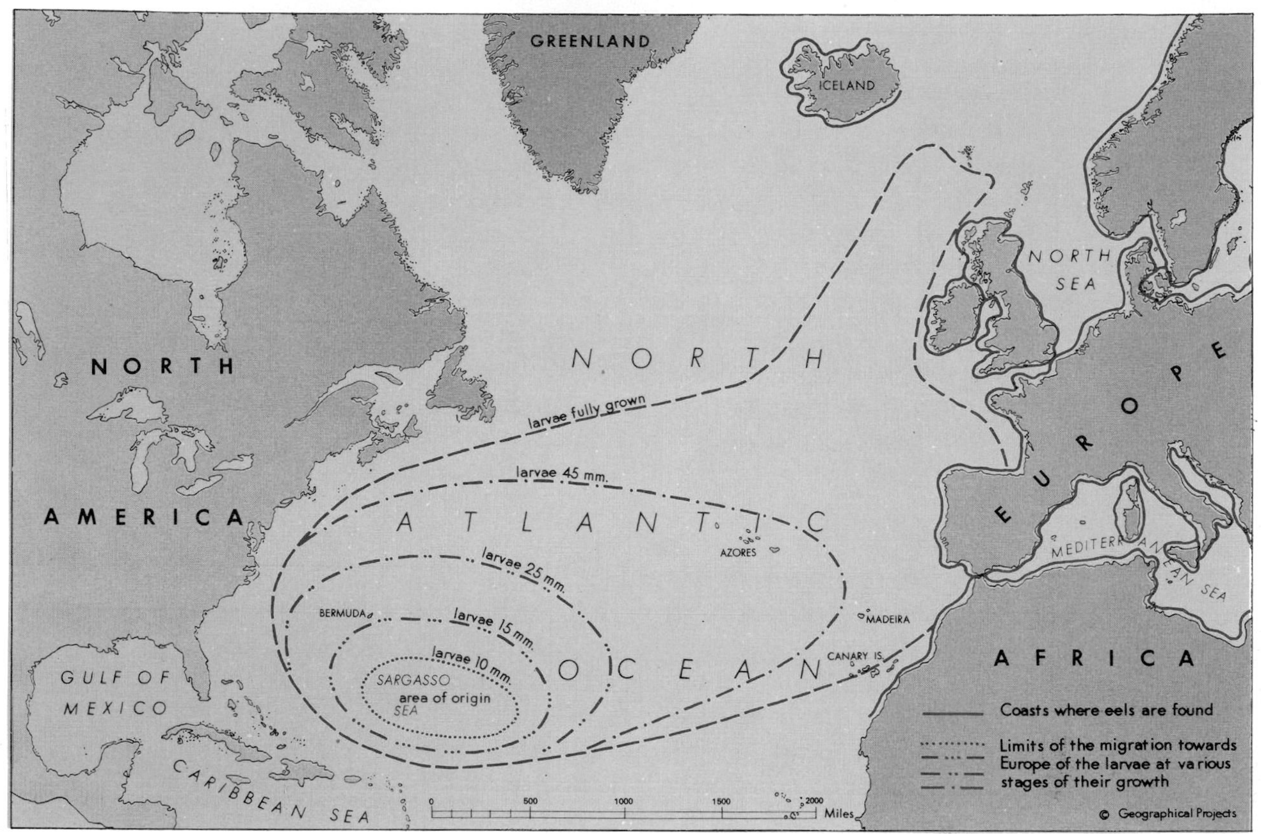

Above: eel migration in the North Atlantic Ocean. Every year, eels from Europe travel to the Sargasso Sea, where they spawn and then die. Their eggs hatch into larvae which swim back across the North Atlantic, growing as they swim, in a journey which lasts three years. Later they, in their turn, set off for the Sargasso Sea to spawn, and so the entire cycle is repeated.

oceanographer, Johannes Schmidt, was working in the North Atlantic on the study of food fishes when he came across a creature that had puzzled and fascinated people for centuries. Schmidt's find was a *Leptocephalus*, or eel larva.

The eel has one of the most curious life stories of all fish. As long ago as the 300's B.C., Aristotle observed and dissected the eels that he found in the Mediterranean and Aegean seas, but he was unable to discover anything about their breeding habits. Aristotle noted that, at certain times, the eels migrated in great numbers to the open sea and apparently disappeared. But where did they go? And was their disappearance in any way linked with the birth of their young?

Over 2,000 years later, Schmidt began to hit on the answers. His discovery of the flat and transparent little *Leptocephalus* led him to believe that the eels' spawning ground might lie somewhere nearby. Although he was mistaken in this belief, his efforts to prove it correct enabled him to put together the true story. After 16 years of patient search in the Atlantic, he was able to piece together the final clues to the mystery of eel migrations. Aboard the research ship *Dana* in 1922, he discovered that the eels migrate to the Sargasso Sea, a large region in the North Atlantic near Bermuda. Millions of eels from America and Europe find their way to this spawning ground—and to death. Every fall, European eels leave the rivers where they have spent five or six years of their life, and swim out to sea. Making their unfailing way across the Atlantic to the Sargasso Sea, the eels show an amazing sense of direction. On arrival, they spawn and die. Their eggs hatch into larval eels (larvae) that return to Europe, growing as they travel on an amazing three-year journey back across the Atlantic. Arriving in springtime, they change into elvers (or young eels) and the female elvers swim up the rivers while the males remain in tidal waters. Several years later, the fully-grown eels set off for the Sargasso Sea again and the cycle is repeated. The same instinct drives the eels of eastern America to the Sargasso Sea to spawn, but the European eel has a longer journey.

While Schmidt was making his discoveries, other oceanographic vessels were also hard at work in the Atlantic. Among these was the Norwegian ship *Michael Sars* which made several cruises under the leadership of oceanographer and fishery scientist Johan Hjort. Hjort had developed a new type of large tow net that could be closed before being hauled to the surface. This meant that the net did not catch animals from many different layers on its way up, and gave an accurate picture of life at a chosen level in the sea.

On one of his voyages, Hjort was joined by a young British zoologist, Alister Hardy. The two men spent three weeks studying whales off Norway and Iceland. Hardy was eager to learn all he could of Hjort's methods and equipment. He was already engaged in the planning of an important mission for the British government. Soon he would set off for the icy waters of the Antarctic in a bid to save the whale from complete extermination at the hand of man.

Man has hunted the whale for centuries, chiefly for the valuable oil it yields. Whale oil used to be a major fuel for lamps and cooking. Now it is used primarily in the production of margarine and, to some extent, in soap making. The sperm whale also provides ingredients for industrial lubricants, beauty creams, and perfume. A by-product of whale oil is glycerin.

Below: *Stranded Whale,* a print by the Japanese artist Kuniyoshi (early 1800's). It shows the mixture of awe and fear with which people regarded these huge animals.

Above: tiles showing Dutch ships whaling in northern waters during the 1600's. A whaling expedition, returning from Spitzbergen in 1611, brought back news of enormous numbers of whales in the area. Competition between English, Dutch, Danes, and Biscayans then became so fierce that, in 1618, the coastline was divided up between the countries.

It was the need for nitroglycerin during World War I that greatly increased the demand for whale oil. To satisfy that demand, whalers slaughtered thousands of whales wherever they could find them. In a single whaling season, nearly 12,000 whales were killed off South Georgia alone. After the war, potential profits from whaling spurred ever more and greater attacks on the whale population of arctic and subarctic waters. Whales were threatened with extinction and so was the whaling industry.

In 1920, the British Parliament agreed on the need for a program of biological exploration to preserve the country's rich whaling industry. A team of researchers was chosen, led by Stanley Kemp and with Alister Hardy as chief zoologist.

An old and sea-scarred vessel was chosen as research ship for the scientific whaling mission. It was the *Discovery*, which had been built in 1901 for Robert Scott's first mission to Antarctica. Later, it was sold to the Hudson's Bay Company and, for many years, plied the frigid arctic waters as a cargo vessel. In 1923, the *Discovery*

Above: the British research ship *Discovery*. It was built in 1901 for Scott's first mission to Antarctica, but later, in 1923, was rebuilt for scientific research work.

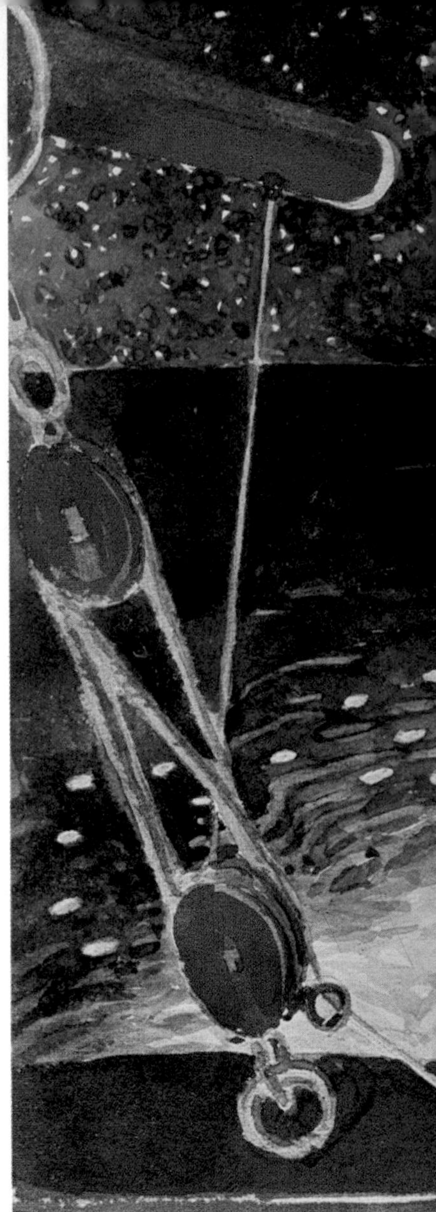

returned to Britain and was almost completely rebuilt. Manned by scientists and sailors, on September 24, 1925, it sailed from southwest England toward the region of its former voyage with Scott, Antarctica. In the South Atlantic lay extensive whaling grounds exploited by Britain from bases on South Georgia and other islands of the Falkland Islands Dependencies whose facilities the *Discovery* scientists could use.

A month out at sea, the *Discovery* met with the largest school of dolphins that the crew had ever seen. Hardy was delighted by these creatures, traditionally regarded as a lucky omen by sailors. "There were certainly no less than a hundred and some estimated . . . two hundred," he noted in his journal. "Many of them kept leaping completely out of the water. . . . Who can doubt that they are leaping in play for the sheer joy of it?"

The old *Discovery* could not be hurried. She made her way slowly southward, often pausing so that the scientists could sample sea

Left: a group photograph taken on board *Discovery* off South Georgia, Christmas, 1926. The director of the research program, Stanley Kemp, is fourth from the left along the seated row. Alister Hardy, chief zoologist, is sixth from the left in the same row. The photograph also includes personnel from the *William Scoresby* (a research ship) and from the Marine Biological Station at South Georgia.

Above: a painting by Alister Hardy showing "a remarkable phosphorescent display of *Pyrosoma* in the wake of the *Discovery* on November 11, 1925, not far from Ascension Island." The crew of *Discovery* saw many such displays during their voyages in the South Atlantic Ocean. Each *Pyrosoma* (Greek *pyro,* fire; *soma,* body) is a colony of sea squirts which glow brightly, especially when disturbed.

water and net the living things it harbored. Fascinated by the creatures he found, Alister Hardy wrote: "Who . . . will ever forget his first catch from 2,000 or 3,000 metres' depth: the tow net bucket filled with fantastically shaped fish, often studded with luminous organs; hosts of scarlet crustaceans, deep-sea medusae, patterned and coloured like Turkey carpets, and many other creatures less easily described." Later, he reported seeing jellyfish "six to nine inches long—made of stiff jelly in which are embedded hundreds of small individual animals, each, when agitated, glowing with a bright blue-green light. For several nights after crossing the equator the ship passed through dense zones of these living lanterns, millions and millions of them, so that a broad patch of light was left behind the ship for half a mile or so."

Gradually, the colorful tropical waters were left behind. Ahead lay whale waters. *Discovery* plowed through a sea dotted with jagged

Above: a school of female sperm whales. Sperm whales are found in all the oceans of the world. They can travel at 12 knots and dive to depths of up to 3,000 feet, staying down for 75 minutes at a time.

icebergs and whipped by hurricane-force winds. Finally, on February 20, 1926, it reached South Georgia. The shore party that greeted the ship included scientists who were already in their second season of whale research. Working under the trying conditions of the whaling station, "amongst the blood, stench, and slime," they had made detailed measurements and observations of more than 1,600 whales. These included the finback whale, the humpback whale, the sei whale, the sperm whale, and the largest animal ever to inhabit the earth, the giant blue whale. (Blue whales have been claimed to measure more than 100 feet in length and to weigh 150 tons. By comparison, the largest dinosaurs are estimated to have weighed about 85 tons, and the largest elephants—the biggest land mammals now in existence—only weigh about 6 tons.)

The scientists had discovered that, with the exception of the sperm whale, these huge aquatic mammals feed on plankton and tiny shrimp-like crustaceans called *krill*. Krill- and plankton-eating whales are baleen whales. They have no teeth in their jaws, but thin plates of whalebone (baleen) extend downward from the upper jaw. The baleen forms a sieve. As the whale glides through the sea, it takes in gulps of water which it squeezes out through the baleen. Krill and plankton are trapped in bristles on the inner edge of the baleen, licked off, and swallowed. Sperm whales, however, have teeth in their jaws and feed almost exclusively on giant squids.

Alister Hardy set foot on South Georgia with high hopes of solving some of the riddles of whale behavior. He knew that whales migrate but was anxious to discover how far they travel and where they go. To track the whales' movements across miles of open sea, Hardy devised an ingenious marking method. The mark, made of silver-

Right: the mammals of the sea, drawn to scale to show their comparative sizes. The tiny man at the left of the diagram gives some indication of the vast size of the blue, finback, and sperm whales.

plated rustless steel, was very much like a huge thumbtack. A number and instructions for its return were engraved on its flat head. The mark was mounted on a wooden arrow and shot into the whale's blubber (the thick fat under the skin) from a light shoulder gun.

The marked whales turned up in widely separated places, yielding new facts to Hardy and his colleagues. Whales, in the same way as many birds, were found to maintain migratory homes in specific areas of the sea. Blues, finbacks, and humpbacks always returned to the same breeding and feeding grounds year after year. It was discovered that whales generally mate in the winter. They then head north to warm waters, where the female gives birth about 12 months later. In the case of the blue whale, the newborn calf weighs $2\frac{1}{2}$ to 3 tons and is about 23 feet long. Feeding on its mother's fat-rich milk, the young blue puts on 200 pounds a day for about 7 months, tipping the scales after weaning at an amazing 23 tons.

Hardy and his colleagues found that whales, like many other large mammals, rarely have more than one offspring at a time. And they give birth only at two-yearly intervals. Often, this relatively slow rate of population growth is not enough to offset the numbers destroyed by whalers.

blue whale
porpoise
killer whale
fin whale
bottle-nosed dolphin
man
beluga or white whale
narwhal
sperm whale
pilot whale

Route of R. R. S. Discovery 1925–7
Route of 'Meteor' 1925–7
GREENLAND
ICELAND
NORTH AMERICA
NORTH ATLANTIC OCEAN
MID ATLANTIC RIDGE
EUROPE
Falmouth
MEDITERRANEAN SEA
BERMUDA
CANARY IS.
GULF OF MEXICO
BAHAMA IS.
SARGASSO SEA
TROPIC OF CANCER
VIRGIN IS.
CARIBBEAN SEA
CAPE VERDE IS.
AFRICA
EQUATOR
SOUTH AMERICA
SOUTH ATLANTIC OCEAN
PACIFIC OCEAN
TROPIC OF CAPRICORN
Cape Town
TRISTAN DA CUNHA
FALKLAND IS.
Stanley
STR. OF MAGELLAN
SOUTH GEORGIA
Grytviken
SCOTIA SEA
Equatorial Scale
Miles
© Geographical Projects

Left: the routes of the *Discovery* and *Meteor* expeditions. The *Discovery* expedition studied whales and their behavior, and the tiny plankton on which whales feed. The German *Meteor* expedition (1925–1927) made observations of the properties of seawater, and other oceanographic surveys, and contributed more to the knowledge of the ocean than any previous expedition.

Right: crew members of the *Discovery* maneuver a continuous plankton recorder over the side of the ship.

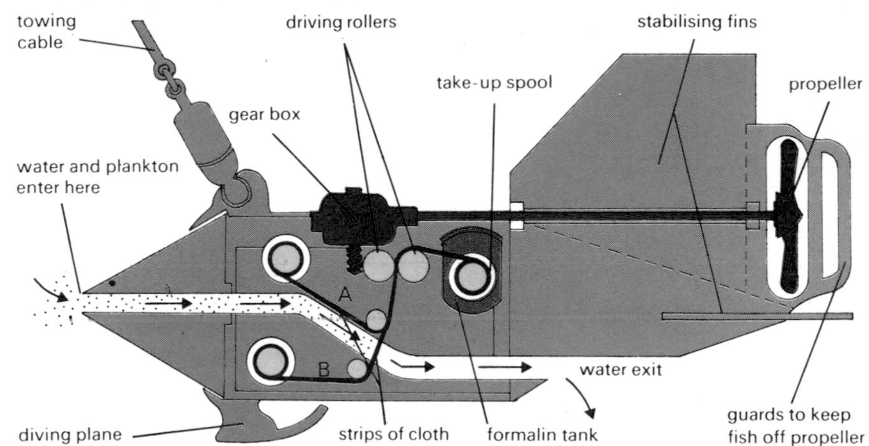

Right: a diagram of the redesigned plankton recorder used on later voyages. As the device moves through the water, plankton is trapped on a roll of silk netting moving across the water channel. The entangled specimens are covered and rolled into a preserving tank full of formalin.

After weaning, mother and calf begin their journey to feeding grounds a thousand or more miles to the south. On the way, the calf gets its first taste of krill and plankton—the foods that will sustain it for the rest of its life. Hardy knew that if the survival of whales was to be guaranteed by man, the biology of the tiny krill would have to yield its secrets to the *Discovery* scientists.

Until the voyage of the *Discovery*, no one had paid much attention to the life history of krill. Hardy had to start from scratch. First, he invented a device, which he called a "continuous plankton recorder," that could snare krill and plankton over long distances and at various depths. The Hardy plankton recorder, as it has come to be called, probed depths up to 600 feet. It revealed that the sea is not covered with a continuous and uniform blanket of plankton, but has patches here and there that the whales must search out in order to survive. As the larger whales can consume as much as 1½ tons of food a day the supply of plankton is extremely important. The impact of this observation was vividly demonstrated to Hardy one summer day as the *Discovery* plowed through the cool waters of the Falkland Islands Dependencies. Just beneath the surface of the water a five-mile-patch of red krill-containing plankton stood out like a beacon beckoning the whales. And they came—150 to 200 whales in search of food. Oblivious of the ship, they strained the plankton from the sea and later played in the sea like puppies, sending spouts of moisture-laden air shooting from their blowholes.

Hardy's findings did not bring about immediate action to curb the slaughter of whales. About 1 million whales have been killed in Antarctic waters since he made his historic voyage. Only recently have whaling nations agreed on adequate protective measures. But to Alister Hardy and whaling scientists like him must go much of the credit for making these reforms possible.

At the same time as the *Discovery* scientists were making their investigations, an important German expedition was also at work in the South Atlantic Ocean. The German team, aboard the *Meteor,* crisscrossed the South Atlantic, making detailed studies of the temperature and chemical composition of sea water. These observations, together with geological and meteorological research carried out from the *Meteor,* contributed a great deal to basic understanding of the ocean.

While knowledge of the ocean itself was increasing, scientists continued to be intrigued by the creatures that live in the underwater world. Hardy had studied the giants of the sea and the plankton upon which they feed. But far below the surface regions populated by plankton, roamed other creatures, as yet undiscovered. It was in search of these that the Danish oceanographic research vessel *Galathea* steamed from Copenhagen on October 15, 1950.

When the *Galathea* expedition was planned, scientists were unsure whether animals lived at depths greater than 19,500 feet. According to Anton Bruun, the scientific leader of the expedition, "The primary purpose of the *Galathea* expedition was to explore the ocean trenches in order to find out whether life occurred under the extreme conditions prevailing there—and if so, to what extent."

For Bruun the voyage was doubly important. As a child, his dearest ambition had been to become a sailor. But this dream could never be realized. Before he was 10 years old, poliomyelitis had left him permanently lame. He could not forget the sea, however, and began a study of marine animals that eventually won him a place as assistant to Johannes Schmidt aboard the *Dana.* Then, at last, the *Galathea* gave him his chance to turn the tables on destiny. The man who could not be a sailor would wrest the secrets of the sea from the deepest ocean abysses.

On the night of July 22, 1951, the *Galathea* was in the Pacific Ocean about 125 miles northeast of the island of Mindanao in the Philippines. Her echo sounder had located a hole 33,678 feet down in the Mindanao Trench, a 540-nautical-mile crevice in the ocean floor. For 110 minutes *Galathea*'s sledge-trawl was dragged along the ocean bottom over six miles down. It was the largest trawl

Above: the water turns red as the men of the Faeroe Islands close in on a school of pilot whales. The islanders drive the 10- to 25-foot-long whales toward shallow water before attacking them with harpoons and knives. Today this massacre is a festival: in former times the whale meat it provided often meant survival through the winter.

Left: a sei whale (foreground) and a finback whale on the deck of a whaling boat. Both are baleen whales whose principal food is plankton.

to reach such a depth and no one knew what it would bring up.

It took several hours to haul the trawl to the surface. Oceanographers and crew gathered around eagerly as the net was opened. Sea anemones, sea cucumbers, clam-like shellfish, an *amphipod* (a burrowing crustacean), and a bristle-worm spilled out among the stones and mud from the deep ocean floor. A whitish sea anemone was discovered which had never before been seen by man. Bruun had found a variety of life in the pressure, darkness, and extreme cold of one of the greatest depths of the ocean.

During the *Galathea*'s two-year voyage in the Pacific, the Caribbean, and the Atlantic, many extraordinary new creatures were discovered. Deep-sea animals depend for food on the life in the ocean layers above them. The open sea is much less rich in life than the area around the coasts. This means that abyssal creatures living a long

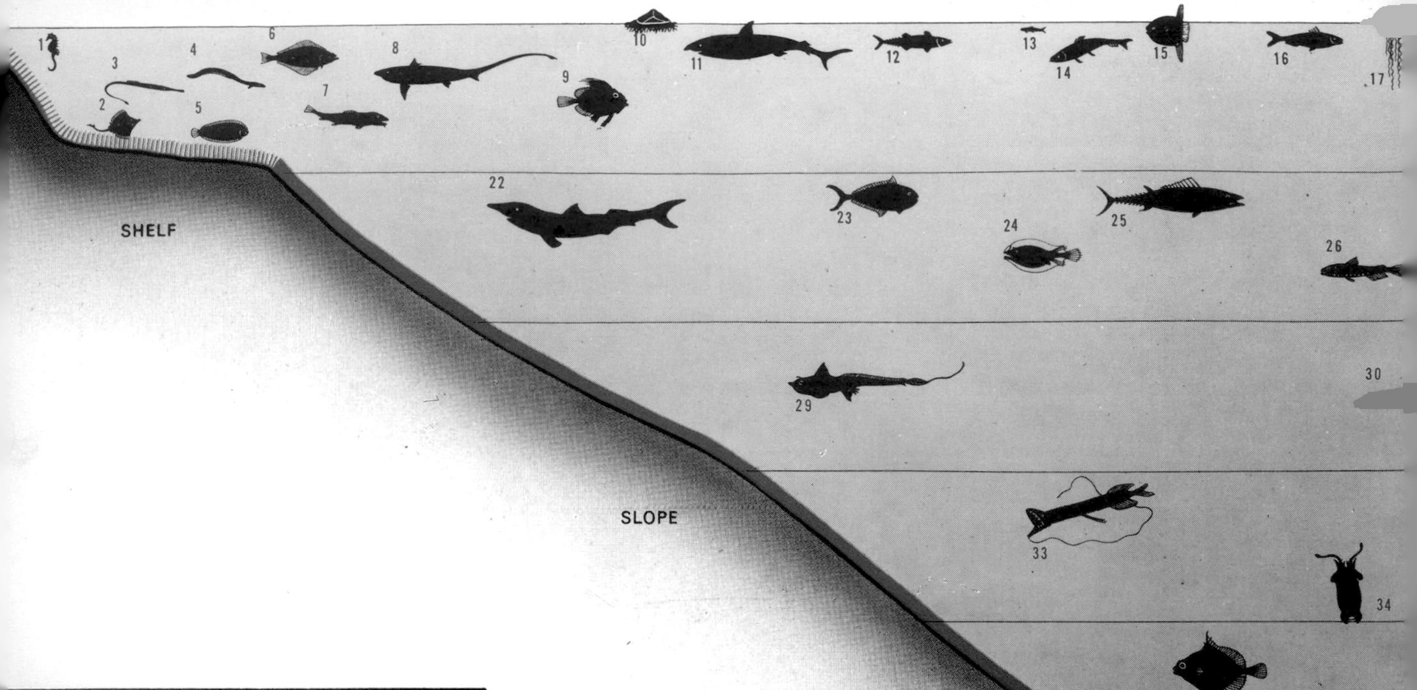

1 2 3 4 5 6 7 8 9 10 11 12 13 14 15 16 17

SHELF

22 23 24 25 26

29 30

SLOPE

33 34

38

Left: a deep-sea prawn *(Sergestes corniculum*—2½ inches). It is among the swiftest of deep-sea crustaceans.

Below: *Sternoptyx,* another type of deep-sea hatchet fish. Its slender, silvery form resembles a hatchet.

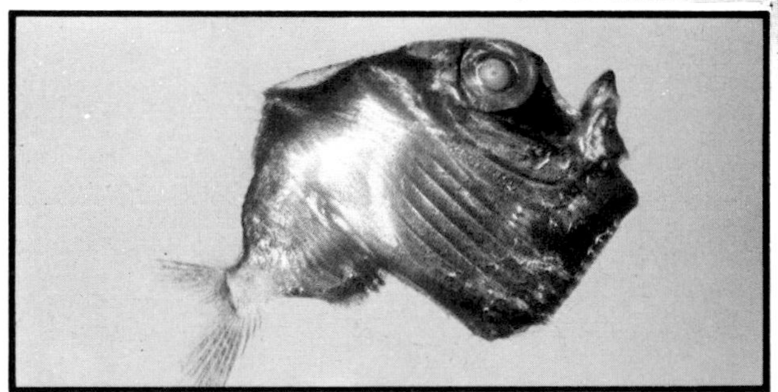

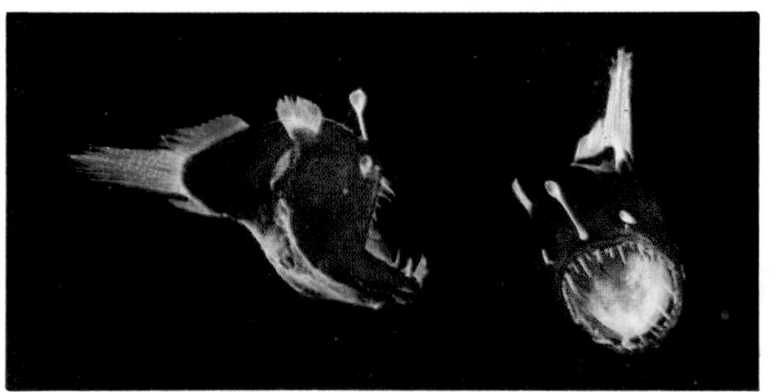

Above: a deep-sea angler (*Melanocetus johnsoni*—four inches). It uses an external light organ to attract prey. Left: the gulper eel *(Eurypharynx* sp.—two feet). Its mouth acts as a fishing net to catch small planktonic organisms.

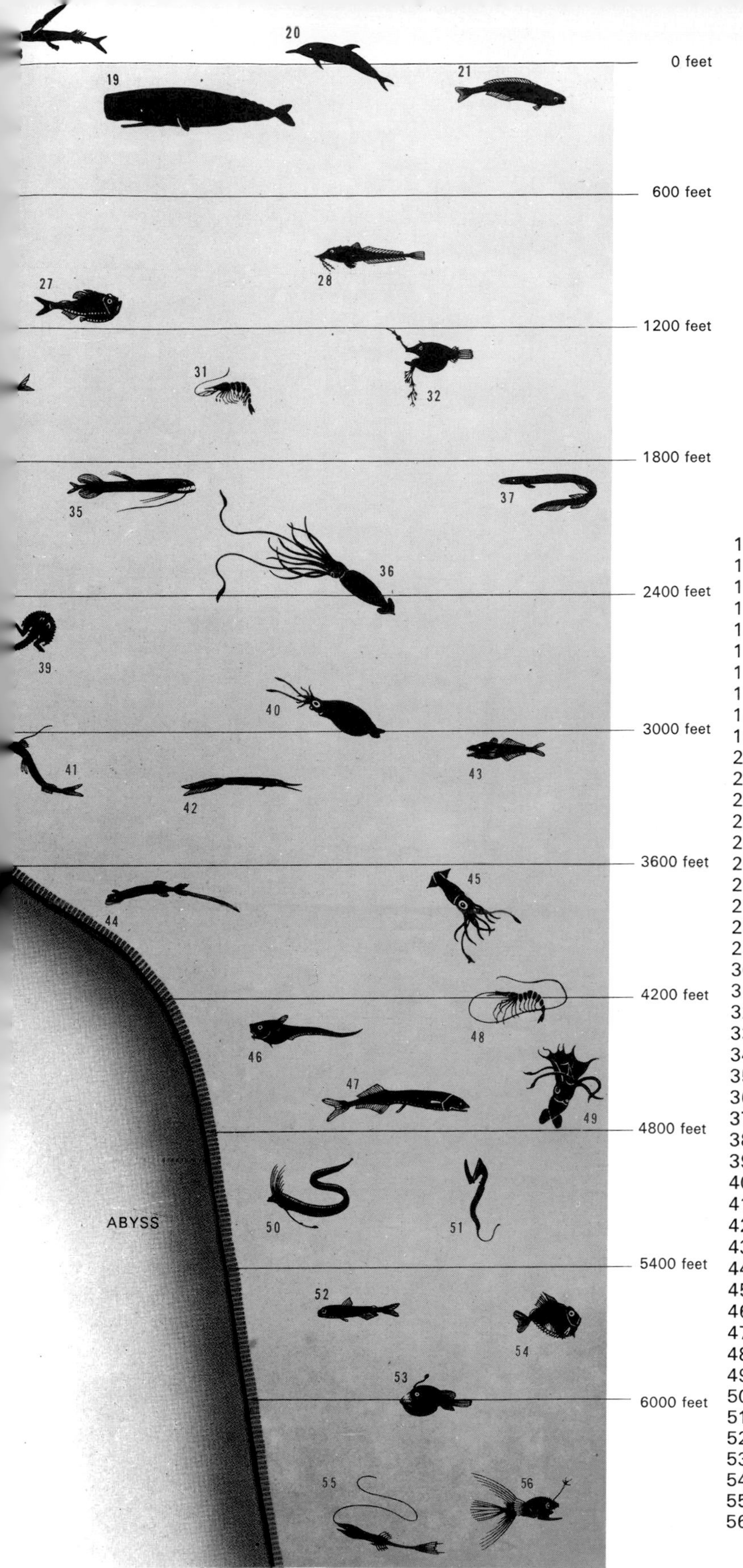

Left: the diagram shows some of the swimming animals of the Atlantic. In the deep ocean, where no light penetrates, many animals have light-producing organs, and some are grotesquely adapted to their environment.

1. Sea horse (*Hippocampus europaeus*) 7 inches
2. Common skate (*Raja batis*) 6 feet wide
3. Broad-nosed pipefish (*Syngnathus typhle*) 12 inches
4. Common eel (*Anguilla anguilla*) 2 feet 6 inches
5. Sole (*Solea solea*) 12 inches
6. Halibut (*Hippoglossus hippoglossus*) 3 feet
7. Cod (*Gadus callarias*) 2 feet 6 inches
8. Thresher shark (*Alopias vulpes*) 15 feet
9. John Dory (*Zeus faber*) 8 inches
10. By-the-wind-sailor (*Velella velella*) 2 inches
11. Basking shark (*Cetorhinus maximus*) 25 feet
12. Mackerel (*Scomber scombrus*) 12 inches
13. Pilchard (*Sardina pilchardus*) 8 inches
14. Herring (*Clupea harengus*) 9 inches
15. Sunfish (*Mola mola*) 8 feet
16. Allis shad (*Alosa alosa*) 9 inches
17. Portuguese man-of-war (*Physalia physalis*) 10 inches
18. Flying fish (*Exocoetus volitans*) 9 inches
19. Sperm whale (*Physeter catodon*) 50 feet
20. Common dolphin (*Delphinus delphis*) 7 feet
21. Black fish (*Centrolophus niger*) 3 feet
22. Blue shark (*Prionace glauca*) 15 feet
23. Ray's bream (*Brama raii*) 1 foot 6 inches
24. Angler (*Haplophryne* species) 1½ inches
25. Bluefin tunny (*Thunnus thynnus*) 8 feet
26. Lantern fish (*Myctophum punctatum*) 4 inches
27. Hatchet fish (*Argyropelecus affinis*) 4 inches
28. Sea robin (*Peristedion miniatum*) 2 feet
29. Ratfish (*Chimaera monstrosa*) 3 feet
30. A stomiatoid fish (*Cyclothone pallida*) 2 inches
31. Prawn (*Acanthephyra multispina*) 3 inches
32. Devilfish (*Linophryne arborifera*) 3 inches
33. A stomiatoid fish (*Ultimostomias mirabilis*) 2 inches
34. Little post-horn squid (*Spirula spirula*) 2 inches
35. A stomiatoid fish (*Bathophilus melas*) 12 inches
36. Giant squid (*Architeuthis princeps*) 40 feet
37. Frilled shark (*Chlamydoselachus anguineus*) 5 feet
38. *Cyttosoma helgae* 9 inches
39. Bat fish (*Malthopsis erinacea*) 5 inches
40. Squid (*Desmoteuthis pellucida*) 5 inches
41. Viperfish (*Chauliodus sloani*) 12 inches
42. Snipe eel (*Cyema atrum*) 12 inches
43. Cross-toothed perch (*Chiasmodus niger*) 5 inches
44. Giant-tail (*Gigantura chuni*) 12 inches
45. Wonder-lamp squid (*Lycoteuthis diadema*) 2 inches
46. Big-headed rat-tail (*Macrourus globiceps*) 12 inches
47. A stomiatoid fish (*Cyclothone microdon*) 3 inches
48. Prawn (*Sergestes corniculum*) 2½ inches
49. Squid (*Histioteuthis bonelliana*) 2 feet
50. Oar fish (*Regalecus glesne*) 12 feet
51. Gulper eel (*Eurypharynx pelecanoides*) 2 feet
52. Lantern fish (*Lampanyctus pusillus*) 4 inches
53. Angler fish (*Melanocetus johnsoni*) 4 inches
54. Hatchet fish (*Sternoptyx diaphana*) 2½ inches
55. Angler fish (*Gigantactis macronema*) 5 inches
56. Devilfish (*Caulophryne acinosa*) 1½ inches

Drawings not to scale. Approximate sizes are given.

distance from the shore often have special adaptations for obtaining food as well as for coping with the other difficulties of their environment. The black swallower, for example, can eat fish up to three times its own size. Others, like the *Stylephorous,* have mouths that shoot out rapidly in front of their heads, or mouths shaped like scoops for digging into the mud in search of food.

Most deep-sea fish belong to the *Brotulidae* family, and the *Galathea*'s nets dredged up large numbers of these blind transparent little creatures. They also found members of the *Mac-*

Above: drawings showing the deep-sea viperfish *(Chauliodus sp.*—10 inches) engulfing prey by swinging its jaws outward and upward. This process allows the fish to swallow animals larger than itself—a useful adaptation to life in the depths of the sea where food is in short supply.

Right: a deep-sea angler fish *(Chaulophryne jordani*—six inches). A parasitic copepod (small crustacean) is attached near the angler's tail.

rouidae, or rat-tail, family who, unlike the brotulids, have sharp eyes. This is because they spend their early days in the light, upper levels of the sea before moving to the perpetual darkness of the deep.

Some animals, however, carry their own portable light with them. A certain type of prawn called *Acanthephydra* produces a mass of "living light" from pores beneath its eyes. The squid also emits a cloud of light in a similar way to an octopus squirting ink. These lights may serve to confuse an enemy, or for communication between animals of the same species. But they can also be used for hunting.

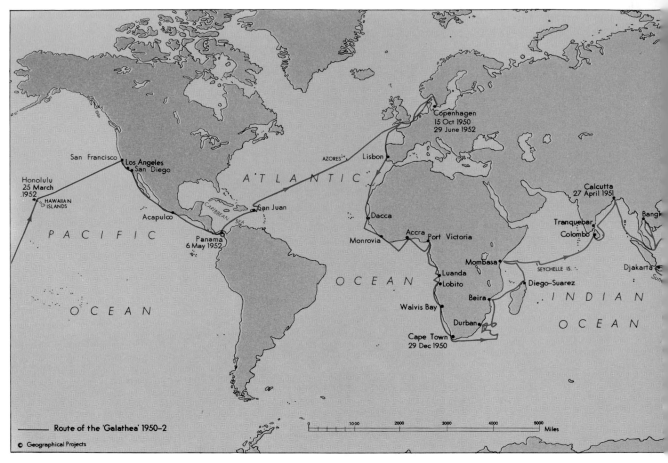

San Francisco
Los Angeles
San Diego
Honolulu 25 March 1952
HAWAIIAN ISLANDS
Acapulco
PACIFIC
OCEAN
Panama 6 May 1952
CARIBBEAN SEA
San Juan
AZORES
ATLANTIC
OCEAN
Copenhagen 15 Oct 1950 29 June 1952
Lisbon
Dacca
Monrovia
Accra
Port Victoria
Luanda
Lobito
Walvis Bay
Cape Town 29 Dec 1950
Durban
Beira
Mombasa
SEYCHELLE IS.
Diego-Suarez
INDIAN
OCEAN
Tranquebar
Colombo
Calcutta 27 April 1951
Djakarta
1000 2000 3000 4000 5000 Miles
Route of the 'Galathea' 1950–2
© Geographical Projects

This use is dramatically demonstrated by the deep-sea angler.

A plump, black, scaleless creature, the deep-sea angler is relatively small but its jaws are armed with many long, inward-curving teeth. Just above its mouth is an arch-shaped light organ—the angler's special hunting apparatus. When a small fish, attracted by the light, ventures too close, it is instantly snapped up in the angler's jaws.

Up until May 6, 1952, this external light organ was the only kind known to be used by the many species of deep-sea anglers. On that day, the *Galathea*'s trawl was scraping along the ocean bottom off the west coast of Central America in waters more than 11,500 feet deep. There it trapped a giant, 18½-inch-long angler. Its size, startling as it was to the scientists, was the least of the surprises presented by the fish. It had no light organ on its head! Where was its "lure"? Had it been knocked off when the animal had been captured? A look inside its gaping mouth revealed the answer.

There, behind the menacing teeth and suspended from the roof of the mouth, was a fork-shaped light organ. The *Galathea* zoologists guessed that this creature rests on the ocean bottom, its mouth open, its light glowing, simply waiting for its prey to dart in. The *Galathea* trawl had brought up one of the laziest hunters of the deep.

Man sometimes takes a tip from the fish world in his own methods

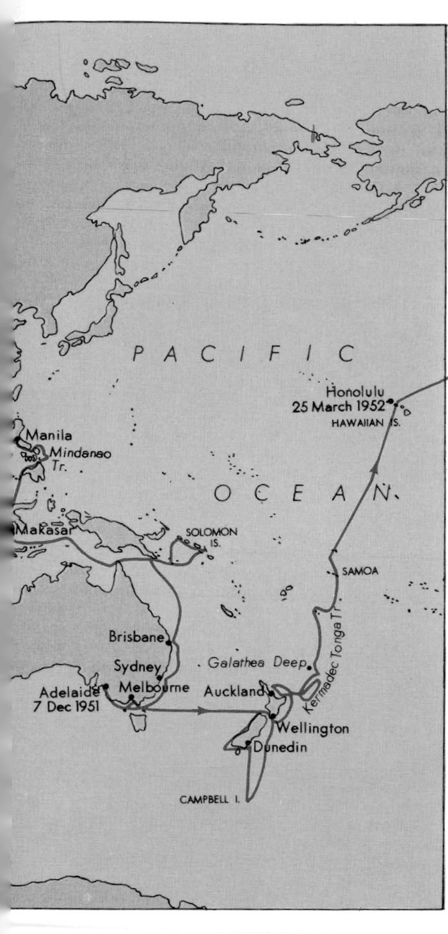

Left: the voyage of the *Galathea*. According to Anton Bruun, the leader of the *Galathea* expedition, the purpose of the expedition was "to explore the ocean trenches in order to find out whether life occurred under the extreme conditions prevailing there—and if so, to what extent." The *Galathea* answered this question when it trawled creatures from the seabed 33,678 feet below the surface.

of hunting food from the sea. It is not unusual for fishermen to use lights to attract fish to their waiting nets. Modern techniques combine this light lure with the use of a suction pump instead of a net. The pump draws the fish up from the sea into the ship's hold.

The fishing industry has been revolutionized in recent years by the invention of technological devices to locate rich fishing grounds, to improve the size and quality of catches, and to process the fish. With these and more traditional methods, the world's fish catch has trebled in the last 20 years to reach an annual total of around 64 million tons. It has been estimated that this could increase to as much as 200 million tons by 1985. But, at the same time, overfishing is still having a disastrous effect on some stocks of fish and will lead to a

Below: the boat in the center has caught a huge shoal of herring with a purse seine. The net was towed around the shoal and then drawn together at the bottom to form a bag.

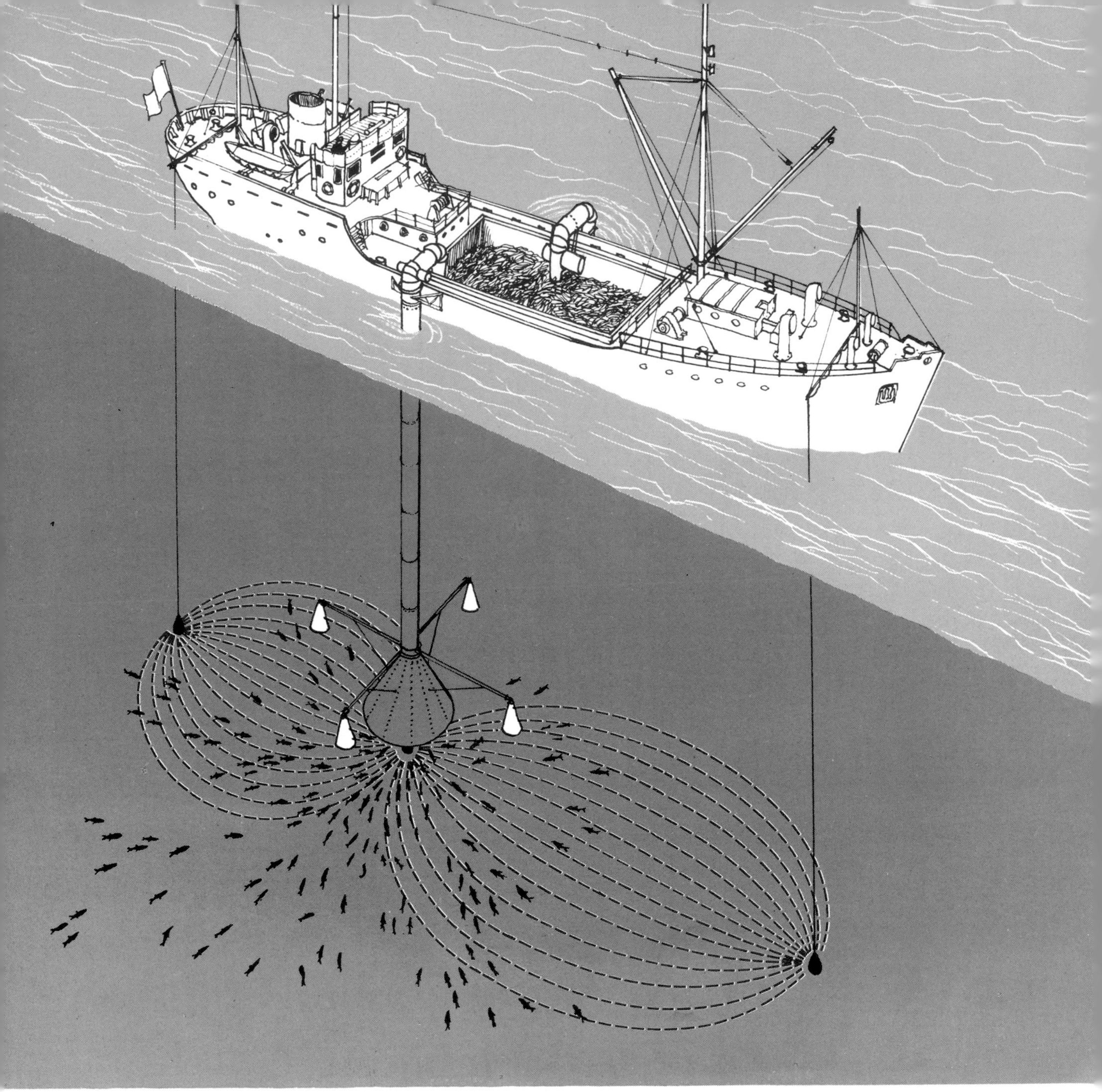

Above: fishing without nets. The fish are attracted by strong underwater lights toward the funnel-shaped opening of a suction pipe. Electrodes suspended in the water set up an electric field, stunning the fish, which are pumped up into the ship's hold.

Right: an underwater fish farm of the future. By the year 2000 the sea will have to produce one-fifth of the world's food. The drawing shows how automated rearing tanks built on the bottom of the sea may make this possible.

decline in future supplies if it is not checked. Just as in the case of the whale, protective measures must be worked out on the advice of marine biologists who are now doing a great deal of research into this problem.

In the meantime, fish farms are providing a substantial new source of food from the sea. These farms work in several different ways. Fish may simply be caught in the ordinary way and held in enclosed areas in or near the sea, for sale when other stocks run low. Alternatively, young fish may be taken from the sea and fattened in enclosures until they are ready for the market. The Japanese have been particularly successful with this technique, producing 20,000 tons of a species of tuna and 13,000 tons of eels from their farms in the course of a single year.

Yet another method involves transferring young fish from overcrowded fishing grounds to fresh areas where there is plenty of food for them. A more advanced technique is to grow fish from eggs in special hatcheries. Once the fish are hatched, they may be released into the open sea to increase existing stocks, or reared to marketable size within the fish farm, where they can be protected from predators and diseases. When the whole process takes place under the controlled conditions of a fish farm, there is also the possibility of breeding new strains of fish.

One of the most successful experiments in marine farming to date is the rearing of prawns. Here again, Japan leads the world with a record 300–400 tons of prawns farmed a year. The Japanese also have extensive oyster farms, capable of producing annually 46,000 pounds of protein-rich sea food per acre of oysters. This is about 200 times as much as the meat production from cattle per acre of pastureland.

The science of aquaculture, as fish farming is known, is being actively developed all over the world. And aquaculturists are not confining their efforts to foods already accepted as "edible" by most of the world's people. They are investigating the possibility of growing and harvesting seaweeds and various kinds of plankton—all rich in vitamins, minerals, and protein. Scientists estimate that the sea's 89 billion acres produce more than 400 billion tons of plant plankton alone during a year. Compared with the 64-million-ton annual fish catch, this represents a huge amount of plant food that might be used to feed the earth's hungry people if such food could be efficiently harvested and made palatable. Some scientists are at work

Above: fish being pumped from the sea Russian fishermen in the Caspian Sea use this technique to catch sardines. Such methods, together with the development of new nets and fish-finding equipment, have boosted the world fish catch, but they may lead to over-fishing of certain vital food fishes.

Right: an octopus on the move. In their search for new drugs and medicines, doctors have discovered that some marine animals and plants yield useful materials. From the octopus they have extracted a medicine used to treat certain heart diseases.
Below: a Japanese fish farm used for rearing tuna. Fishermen catch young fish in the open sea and transfer them first to these floating cages and then to larger enclosures. There they are fattened ready for the market.

trying to develop a plankton flour for making bread or crackers.

In the future, many of our medicines, too, may come from the sea. Scientists have discovered ingredients of certain algae that can be made into highly beneficial drugs. A few of these drugs are already on the market and others are being eagerly sought. One danger of today's widespread use of antibiotics is that bacteria may gradually build up a resistance to them and make them ineffective. This makes it vital for scientists to find new antibiotics.

The American botanist Paul Burkholder has made a detailed study of algae during recent years. Working on 6 species of seaweed, he has discovered at least 15 antibiotic substances. Other specialists have found antibiotics in shellfish such as the clam. Insulin has been extracted from starfish. And the octopus has yielded medicine for the treatment of certain heart diseases. Experiments have shown that some seaweed extracts can prevent the formation of blood clots.

Over 100 years ago, French economist Eugene Noel wrote: "The ocean can be turned into an immense food factory. It can be made into a more fruitful laboratory than the earth. Fertilize it! Seas, rivers, and ponds! Only the earth is cultivated. Where is the art of cultivating the waters? Hear, ye nations!"

Today, the nations have begun to listen—they have no option.

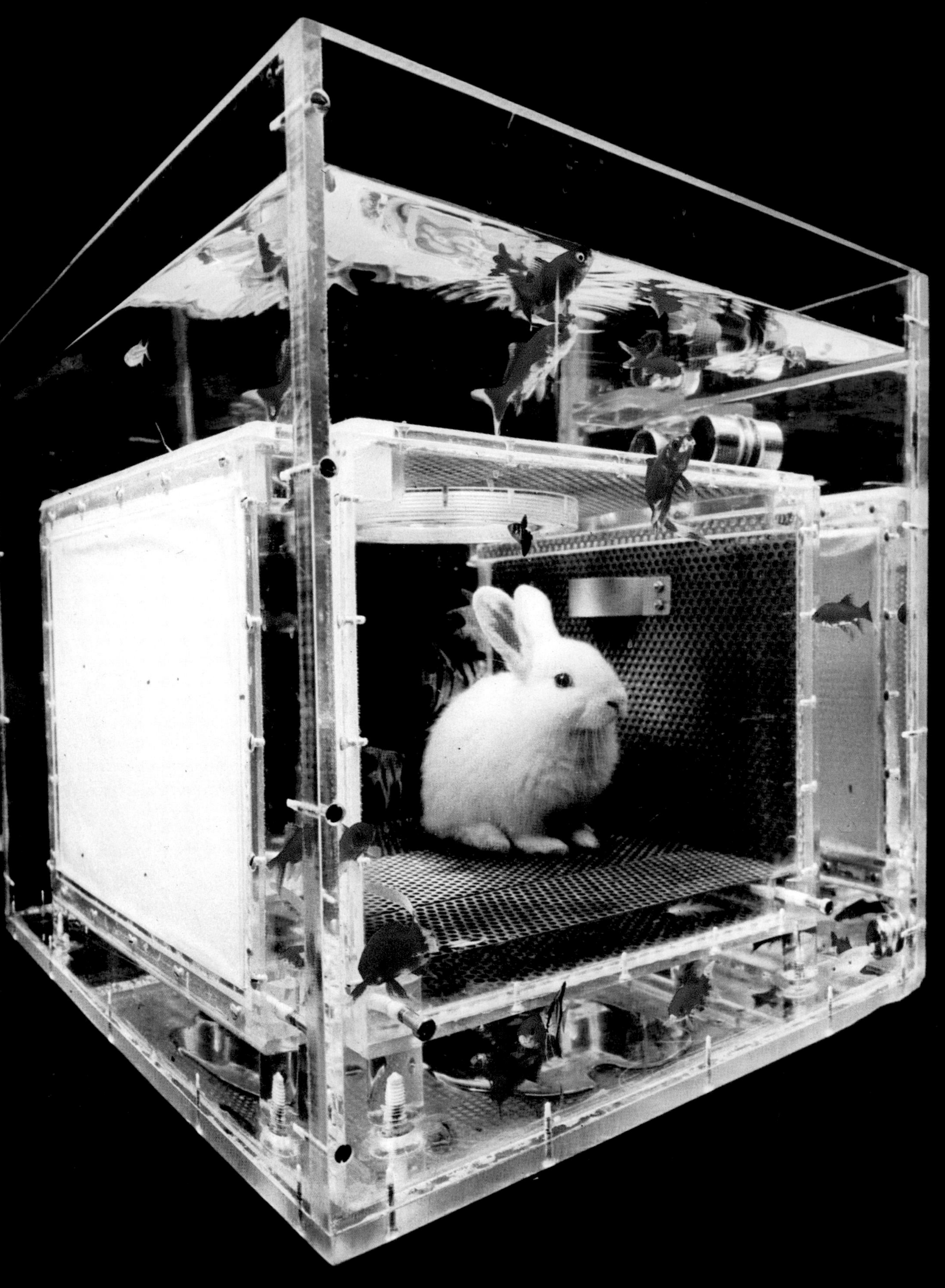

The Conquest of Inner Space

10

Left: this rabbit is in a cage that is completely submerged in water. The air that the rabbit breathes is passing through a membrane stretched over the sides of its cage. The membrane prevents water entering but passes oxygen and carbon dioxide as does the lining of the lung. Diving experts consider that such membranes could be used to construct artificial *gills* for breathing underwater.

Man has come a long way in his understanding of the world oceans since Aristotle first cataloged the marine creatures of the Mediterranean more than 2,000 years ago. Primitive diving gear and submarines have evolved into the Aqua-Lung and undersea submersibles capable of penetrating to the deepest parts of the sea. Life in the ocean, once thought to be confined to the shallow shelves surrounding the land, is now known to exist even in the greatest depths. The great currents, rivers in the ocean, have been charted and measured. The dynamic, constantly changing nature of the sea floor is known, and the history of our planet and its oceans is becoming clearer.

What, then, does the future hold for the exploration of the sea? In 1870 Jules Verne wrote in *Twenty Thousand Leagues Under the Sea,* "One must live within the ocean." And that prediction, now more than 100 years old, seems to point the way toward the next great era of ocean exploration. Man will become—perhaps *must* become—a dweller in the sea.

The first tentative steps toward living in the sea and tapping its riches have already been taken. In the late 1950's and during the 1960's, divers from Europe and the United States pushed the depth limit for diving to 1,000 feet and set up records for time spent underwater. From these achievements came new knowledge about the two greatest problems faced by the deep diver—nitrogen narcosis and the need for decompression.

It was found that, when certain inert, light gases were used,

Right: Waldemar Ayres demonstrates his artificial *gills* on New York's Jones Beach. Each gill consists of two plastic sheets, at the bottom of which is a membrane permeable to gases but not to water. Ayres stayed underwater for 1½ hours, inhaling oxygen directly from the seawater.

nitrogen narcosis did not occur or was greatly reduced. The chief gas now supplied to deep divers is helium. This is combined with a small percentage of oxygen to form an oxy-helium mix suitable at depths of at least 800 feet. Below this depth, however, even this mixture becomes appreciably less easy to breathe. Experts are studying the possibility of replacing helium with hydrogen—the lightest of all known gases. But hydrogen has the disadvantage of being highly flammable and dangerous to handle. Nevertheless, in view of the progress which has been made to date, experienced

Left: the *Seachore* submersible diving chamber, with a decompression chamber behind it. On a routine dive, two divers are sealed in the chamber and winched down to the work site. The chamber is then pressurized to the outside water pressure and the divers leave through a hatchway. When the job is complete, the divers seal themselves into the chamber and return quickly to the surface. There they transfer to a decompression chamber, either to decompress slowly or to wait at pressure until the next dive.

Below: the *Cachalot* diving chamber. This chamber, developed by Westinghouse Underseas Division, is used at depths of below 600 feet. Once at pressure the four-man crew works alternate two-man shifts, remaining in a pressurized chamber between shifts.

divers have predicted dives to 3,000 feet within the next 20 years.

Divers who have taken part in long stays underwater have made another significant discovery, known as *saturation diving,* that helps cut wasteful decompression time. The amount of gas that the body tissues can absorb is limited. Once the saturation limit is reached the gas in the tissues does not increase no matter how long the diver remains at the depth where saturation occurs. As decompression time depends on the degree of saturation, once saturation point is reached, the diver can prolong the time spent at depth for days, weeks, or longer, without increasing the decompression time needed afterward.

Despite the use of saturation diving techniques, decompression is still a lengthy process. A diver might need only 3 minutes to reach a depth of 200 feet, but it will take him more than 2½ hours to return to the surface, decompressing as he comes up. Decompression time cannot be reduced without danger to the diver. This presented a major obstacle to companies wishing to use divers in commercial

Above: the first team of aquanauts to live in the U.S. Navy's *Sealab II* habitat. Second from the left in the front row is ex-astronaut, Commander Scott Carpenter, U.S.N., (NASA).

operations underwater. But how could the diver be brought up rapidly without cutting decompression time?

The answer came from a device known as a submersible diving chamber (SDC) that takes the diver down and carries him back to the surface under pressure. Among the SDCs now in use is Divcon International's *Seachore,* a single chamber that can take two divers down to 600 feet. Inside the chamber, cylinders supply the necessary gas for the divers and for the chamber itself. The divers leave the chamber through a hatchway and return when their work is finished. The *Seachore* is then brought to the surface and locked onto a deck decompression chamber (DDC) to which the divers transfer. The divers may wait in the pressurized DDC until they are needed for further work below. When all tasks are completed, the divers undergo full decompression.

The SDCs provide divers with a valuable work base. But if divers are to work underwater for weeks or months at a time, they need a "home" where they can live in warmth and comfort for the duration of their stay. Since 1962, when Cousteau set up his first underwater habitat, *Conshelf I,* developments in this field have been carried out almost exclusively by American and French teams.

While Cousteau was making his experiments with *Conshelf,* George Bond of the U.S. Navy had been carrying out a series of experiments with divers using pressure simulators in the laboratory to approximate to conditions underwater. The success of this work

Above: an artist's impression of the United States Navy habitat *Sealab III* on the seabed. This habitat is designed to operate at 610 feet and to support five 8-man teams for periods of 12 days. Cables from the shore provide power, fresh water, and emergency communications. Breathing gas and emergency supplies are provided by a surface support ship. During their stay on the ocean floor, the divers test diving suits, communications equipment, and underwater tools.

led to the setting up, in 1964, of the U.S. Navy's Project Sealab.

Sealab I, a cigar-shaped cylinder, 35 feet long and 12 feet in diameter, was sited off the coast of Bermuda. There, 4 men lived for 10 days at a depth of 192 feet, swimming out often to work in the sea. Communications and other facilities reached them through cables from the shore, while breathing gas and emergency supplies were provided by a surface support ship.

The following year, *Sealab II* went into operation at a depth of 206 feet. This was an ambitious project involving three 10-man teams who took turns at staying in the habitat for 15-day periods. Among the men who took part was astronaut Scott Carpenter. He took to inner space so well that he stayed down for 30 consecutive days. Then, in spring 1969, *Sealab III* was developed to operate at 610 feet. For the *Sealab III* mission, divers from Britain, Canada, and Australia were invited to join the five 8-man teams or to act as observers.

The most recent American underwater habitat is *Tektite II,* which consists of two 18-foot high cylinders joined by a tunnel. Within the cylinders are a laboratory, crew quarters, a control center, engine room, and *wet room* (the room by which the divers enter and leave the habitat). A large freezer supplies the crew's store of food. The habitat contains a pressurized breathing mixture and is

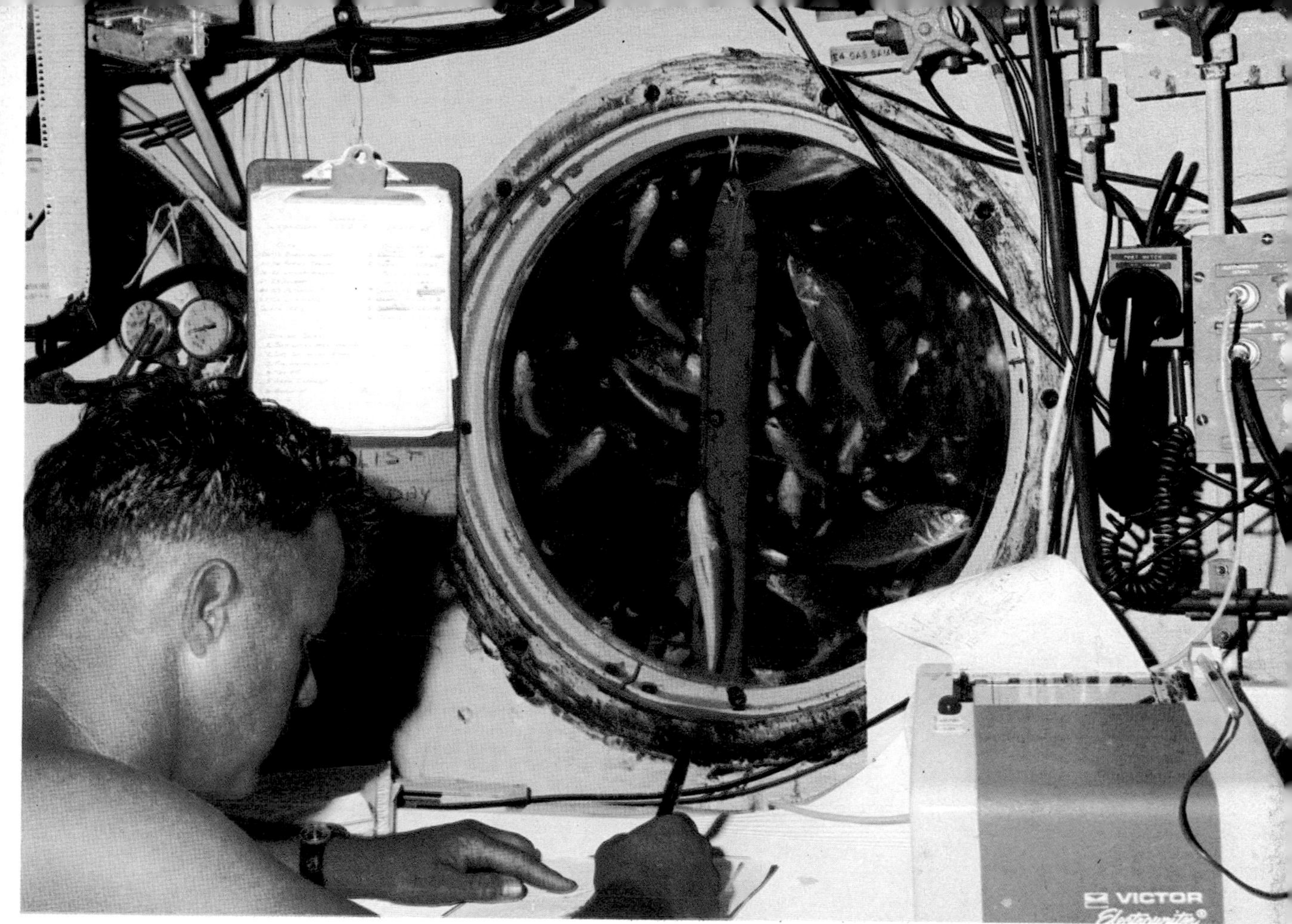

Above: Inside the U.S. Navy habitat *Sealab II*. John Reaves fills out one of the many logs the aquanauts kept during their stay in the habitat, 206 feet deep in the ocean. The light spilling into the sea from the portholes has attracted a shoal of fish.

kept at a temperature of 80°F. A small, two-man *minitat* is also used on the project for work at greater depths. The aquanauts are linked to the surface by television and radio, and surface observers keep a close check on their health and reactions during the long periods spent under confined conditions in an isolated and hostile environment.

One of the difficulties faced by the aquanauts is that of keeping warm. The habitats are well heated but the sea outside is extremely cold. This means that the aquanuats must wear specially insulated diving suits, known as *wet suits*. These are made of a foam material and may be worn over long woolen underwear. A film of water is allowed to circulate between skin and suit. The film of water is warmed by the body and acts as an insulator. Below 200 feet, however, the pressure of the water outside squashes the suit flat against the skin and insulation is lost. The *Conshelf III* divers tried to overcome this problem by wearing incompressible vests made of glass "micro-balloons" filled with carbon dioxide. But these vests were too rigid to allow freedom of movement. Other types of suits are now being tested, some incorporating electrically-heated undersuits or involving an auxiliary heater carried by the diver.

Communication is another problem for the habitat dwellers. The large amounts of helium used in the breathing gas mixtures distort normal speech. The aquanauts gradually become accustomed to this but it slows communication considerably, particularly between the habitat and the people on the surface. Speech deciphering equipment is helping to solve this difficulty.

The greatest obstacle still to be overcome is that of decompression. At the end of their stay in the habitat, the aquanauts have to spend as many as 20 hours in a decompression chamber. A revolutionary solution to this problem came from pioneer aquanaut Jacques-Yves Cousteau. He proposed nothing less than the creation of a new species of man—underwater man, or *Homo aquaticus*. This man, suggested Cousteau, would breathe underwater as naturally as a fish. He would be able to descend to the ocean depths without breathing gas and return to the surface without decompressing. All the equipment *Homo aquaticus* would need would be a small life-support machine plugged directly into his circulatory system. His lungs would be filled with an incompressible fluid and this is what he would breathe.

Cousteau's sensational prediction was made as long ago as the early 1960's. Already considerable advances have been made toward turning his prophesy into reality. A number of experiments with liquid-breathing animals were carried out by Johannes A. Kylstra at the University of Leiden in The Netherlands. In 1963, Kylstra went to the United States and joined with American scientists to make further tests with mice and dogs. Five years later, he was able to report on his first experiment with a human volunteer, deep-sea diver Francis J. Falejczyk. The air in one of Falejczyk's lungs was replaced by a saline solution that was "breathed" by being regularly added and drained off in equal measure. Falejczyk said afterwards that he had felt no discomfort whatsoever. Breathing with the liquid-filled lung had felt no different from breathing normally.

At about the same time, bathers on New York's Jones Beach were witnessing another remarkable experiment in underwater breathing. New Jersey diver and inventor Waldemar Ayres was trying out his synthetic *gills*. With them, he hoped to extract oxygen from the seawater and breathe under the sea just as fishes do. The gills consisted of two plastic sheets on the bottom of which was a *permeable membrane*. The membrane allowed oxygen to pass into the space between the sheets, but kept water out. Connected to this space was a system of rubber hosing through which Ayres could take in the oxygen and breathe out carbon dioxide that would be released into the seawater. Using this apparatus, Ayres stayed underwater for 1½ hours, inhaling oxygen directly from the sea. His breathing came easily. His gills worked perfectly.

Looking into the future, Cousteau has predicted that *Homo aquaticus* will be able to move freely at depths down to about 6,000 feet. He even sees the possibility of a new race of men being born in the depths of the sea and living in huge underwater cities.

The techniques for building small undersea colonies, at least, are already within our grasp. One large corporation has completed an

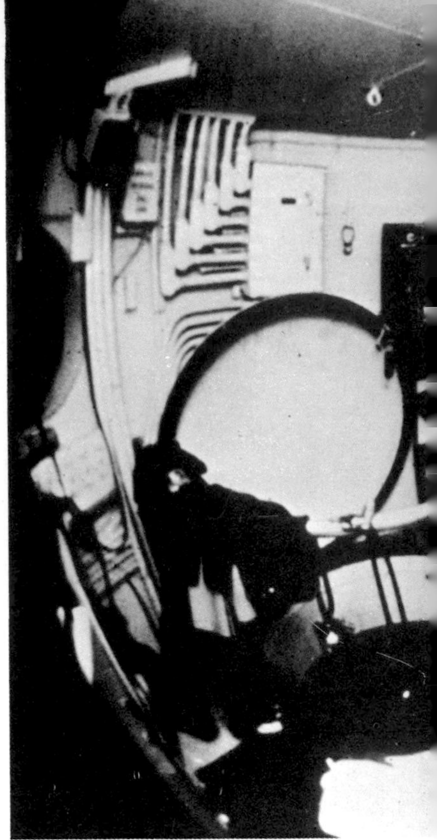

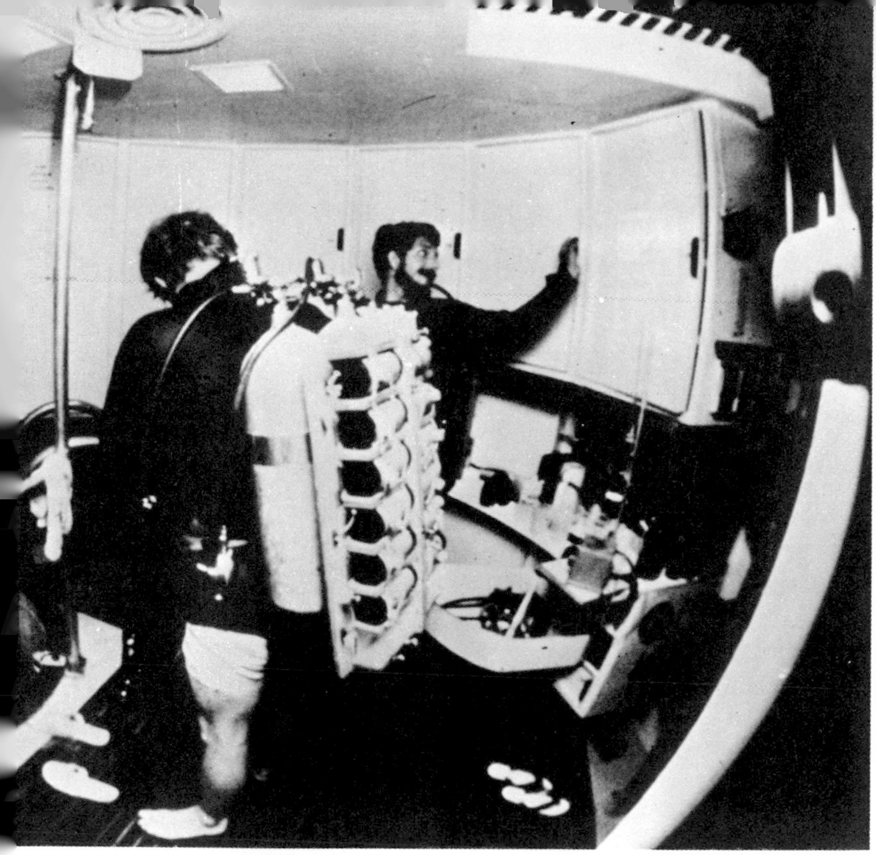

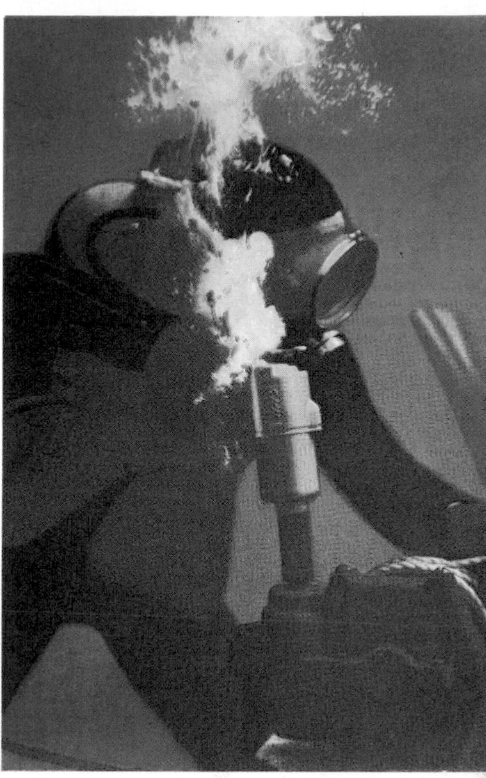

Left: a diver wearing a hot water suit supplied by an umbilical cable. Keeping warm in the sea is one of a diver's main problems. Other suits include one with a closed hot water system and one heated by electricity.

Above: divers prepare to swim out from the *wet room* of *Tektite II.* This American habitat, established during summer, 1970, has provided information on the psychological reactions to complete isolation.

Above: a diver with a powered under-water wrench. Divers underwater can-not exert pressure with normal tools. Below: a diver using a rebreather Aqua-Lung. Exhaled carbon dioxide is scrubbed so that air can be used twice.

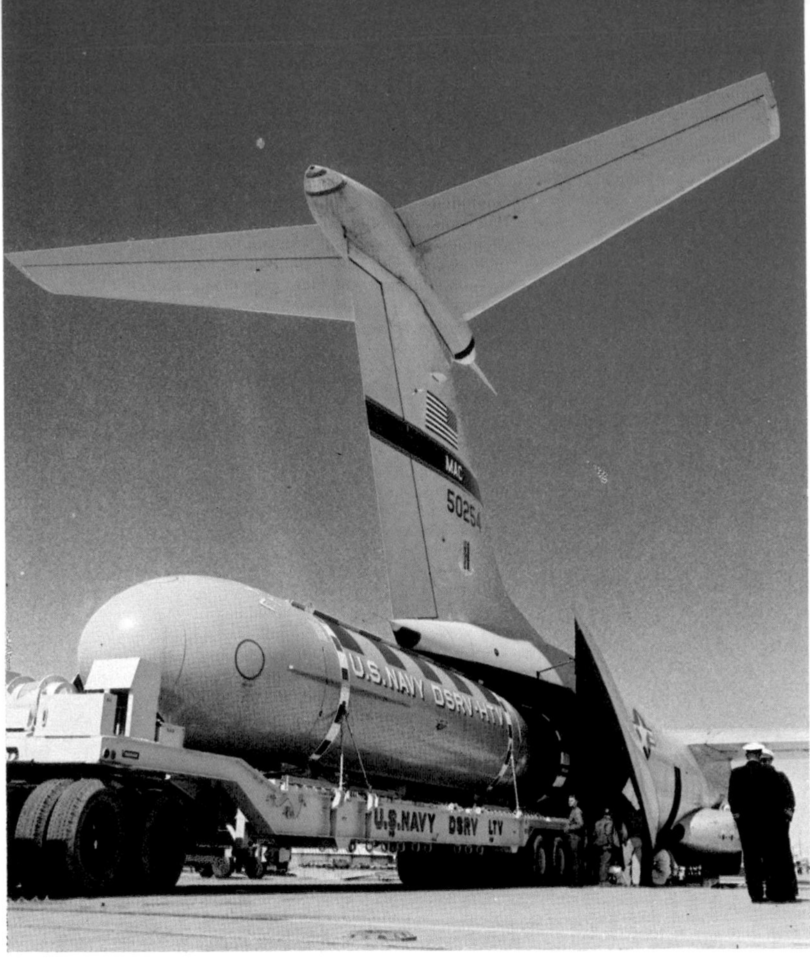

Left: a full-size training model of the Deep Submergence Rescue Vehicle (DSRV) being loaded onto a C-141 aircraft. The DSRV is designed to rescue survivors from wrecked submarines in depths of up to 5,000 feet. It can be flown quickly to the disaster area and taken down to the stricken vessel on another submarine.
Below: an artist's impression shows how the DSRV rescue skirt fits over a submarine's escape hatch. The DSRV can rescue 24 survivors at a time.

engineering study of a sea-floor complex that could house 50 men at depths as great as 1,000 feet. The three-story, starfish-shaped structure is connected with the surface by a pressurized *elevator* hanging from a surface vessel. Cost of the habitat is estimated at about 10 million dollars. Although such habitats are designed for scientific and commercial research, it may not be long before some of them become tourist centers too.

As these undersea hamlets are developed, new kinds of underwater vehicles, called submersibles or submarinos, are also being built for manned and unmanned exploration of the deep. Some of these are designed as scout vessels to reconnoiter the millions of square miles of ocean floor that are still unknown. Others are workboats intended to operate hundreds and thousands of feet down. Future submersibles will act as sub-surface *buses* to transport workers or tourists to and from undersea habitats.

Since 1960, when Piccard and Walsh made their historic dive in the bathyscaph *Trieste,* a large number of submersibles have gone into operation all over the world. More than 40 of these are American. American interest in submersibles, however, came less from the *Trieste's* success than from a disaster which occurred in 1963.

On April 9, 1963, the United States Navy nuclear submarine *Thresher* sank in 8,400 feet of water. High above on the surface, the crew of a rescue ship stood helplessly by. They could hear the

Thresher breaking up but were unable to go to her assistance. No system existed to save submarine crews at depths below 600 feet. All the men of the *Thresher* perished.

Reaction to the disaster was swift. The U.S. Navy set about obtaining funds for one of the most ambitious oceanographic projects ever known. In 1964, they established the Deep Submergence Systems Project to build a fleet of manned submersibles which could be flown anywhere in the world within hours, and would be capable of rescuing submariners from depths of up to 5,000 feet. Though this

Right: *Beaver IV*. This submersible is one of a series built for the offshore oil and gas industry. Using its manipulators it is able to carry out maintenance work on undersea wellheads at a depth of 2,000 feet underwater. Below: the free-swimming submersible *Deepstar 4000*. Since its first dive in 1966, this submersible has been used for many oceanographic studies. The 18-foot-long steel craft carries a crew of 3 to a depth of 4,000 feet, traveling at speeds up to 3 knots.

project could not have helped the men of the *Thresher*, in saving the lives of submariners from these relatively shallow depths techniques may be developed which can be used for deep depth rescues.

Unmanned vehicles may also be used in rescue operations. Controlled from the surface, these vehicles are known as *telechirics*, from the Greek words *tele* (meaning far) and *cheir* (meaning hand). One of the most famous telechirics is the American Cable-controlled Underwater Recovery Vehicle (CURV). This device, used in conjunction with the manned submersibles or submarinos *Alvin* and *Aluminaut*, played an important part in the recovery of an H-bomb that was lost in 2,850 feet of water off the coast of Spain in 1966.

One of the most adaptable modern underwater vessels is the *Deepstar 2000*. The *DS-2000*, as it is known, is one of a family of *Deepstar* undersea vehicles belonging to Westinghouse Electric Corporation. It measures 19 feet long and is built of steel and glass-reinforced plastic. Two men can travel for 45 hours in the *DS-2000* using a self-contained life support system. After taking the submersible down, the men pilot it while lying almost flat on specially adjusted couches.

Inside the *DS-2000* is a wealth of advanced technological equip-

Left: the rig *Orion* burning off natural gas in the North Sea. More than 700 drilling rigs are now probing the seabed for oil or gas. By 1980 a third of the world's oil supply will come from beneath the ocean.

ment. Outside are two sets of mechanical arms, capable of lifting weights up to 50 pounds. These manipulators can collect samples from the ocean bed and put them into a basket, or set up instruments for the crew.

The *DS-2000,* like nearly all existing submersibles, is powered by lead-acid batteries. These are extremely heavy and occupy a large amount of space. Their power output is relatively low. Experiments are now going on to find a more efficient source of power. An obvious choice is nuclear power, and this is already being used in the U.S. Navy submersible *NR-1*. But *NR-1* cost $99.2 million—a price far beyond the reach of most manufacturers.

Industrial need for submersibles that can perform specific tasks has led to the development of a new type of undersea workboat. One such vessel is Perry Submarine's *Deep Diver,* which was designed by Edwin Link. *Deep Diver* can carry both working divers and non-diving observers and advisers. It consists of two compartments—a chamber that can be pressurized for the divers and a chamber kept at atmospheric pressure for the pilot and observers.

Because divers cannot at present work at depths below 1,000 feet in safety, mechanical aids, like the *DS-2000*'s manipulators, must be developed to help them. But it is difficult to carry out very complicated or heavy work with these devices. The average submersible, buoyant in the water, cannot exert sufficient pressure on a manipulator to make it effective. To overcome this difficulty, the vessel must be anchored in a way which will give it the necessary stability.

A British shipbuilding and engineering company, Cammell Laird, has devised an unusual submersible to meet this need. Their manned Sea Bed Vehicle is fitted with four giant wheels that enable it to travel across the sea floor, taking even steep slopes and undersea trenches in its stride. The Sea Bed Vehicle can carry heavy equipment to a depth of 600 feet and is fitted with manipulators controlled from inside by the crew. Its primary use is likely to be the setting up of underwater wellheads to obtain oil and gas from the North Sea.

The production of oil and gas offshore is already big business, in which submersibles and undersea habitats are becoming increas-

Below: an artist's impression of the Cammell Laird Sea Bed Vehicle. Operating at depths of up to 600 feet, it travels along the sea floor on huge hydraulically-driven wheels. Observations are made by means of a pair of T.V. cameras mounted on booms at the front. The vehicle provides a stable platform for heavy engineering work, such as setting up a wellhead. Divers use the rear, pressurized section—the front, at atmospheric pressure, houses pilot and observer.

ingly involved. By 1980, one third of the world's production of petroleum will come from under the ocean. Already much of the oil easily accessible in the shallow continental shelves has been found. As the search goes deeper the task of obtaining the oil by the use of equipment at the surface becomes impossible. In the future, men will need to live and work at an underwater drill site to produce the oil and patrol long pipelines leading back to shore.

There are other ocean riches beside oil. Diamonds, tin, iron, gold, phosphorus, and sulfur have been found in the continental shelves. All are now being commercially extracted by dredging from surface ships. Yet these minerals may well occur deeper than dredges can economically operate. Undersea mining camps may be set up to exploit them.

One last area holds promise of mineral wealth. Scientists think that the broad valley at the center of the giant mid-ocean-ridge system may contain an abundant store of heavy, metallic minerals. Miners living within this volcanic rift could harvest its riches.

The resources of the world's oceans are greater than those of the land. As world population grows and easily accessible land resources shrink, it is to the vast unexploited areas of the sea that man must turn for survival. Properly used, the ocean's riches could meet man's ever increasing demands for a very long time to come. Today, an all-out attempt is being made to locate and exploit those riches. But all man's efforts will come to nothing if he continues to pollute the sea as he is already doing.

Major disasters have focused world attention on the more obvious forms of pollution. In Europe, the tanker *Torrey Canyon* ran aground off southwest England and spilled much of her 117,000 tons of crude oil into the sea. The oil swept over 100 miles of England's lovely Cornish coast and was also carried across the English Channel to Brittany in France. The oil and the detergents used to remove it killed many thousands of seabirds, fish, and other sea creatures. Two years later, in 1969, about 230,000 gallons of oil poured from a leaking oil platform off the Santa Barbara Channel, California. Beaches were polluted and marine life was massacred along 20 miles of the Californian coastline.

Oil pollution kills thousands of sea creatures every year. But this is only a small part of the pollution problem. Already a flood of civilization's by-products has invaded the sea. In addition to oil, these pollutants include raw sewage, dangerous chemicals, radioactive wastes, unwanted explosives, tanks of poison gases left over from wartime, detergents, pesticides, insecticides—the list is, perhaps, more endless than the sea.

This steady flow of waste has begun to make its mark. And, in the Mediterranean, the problem has reached a point that some scientists term "biological suicide." In Italy, an estimated 70 per cent of beaches are polluted and 15 per cent totally poisoned. In Venice, polluted canals are helping to sink the city. And from Italy's holiday playgrounds come reports of dead and poisoned fish

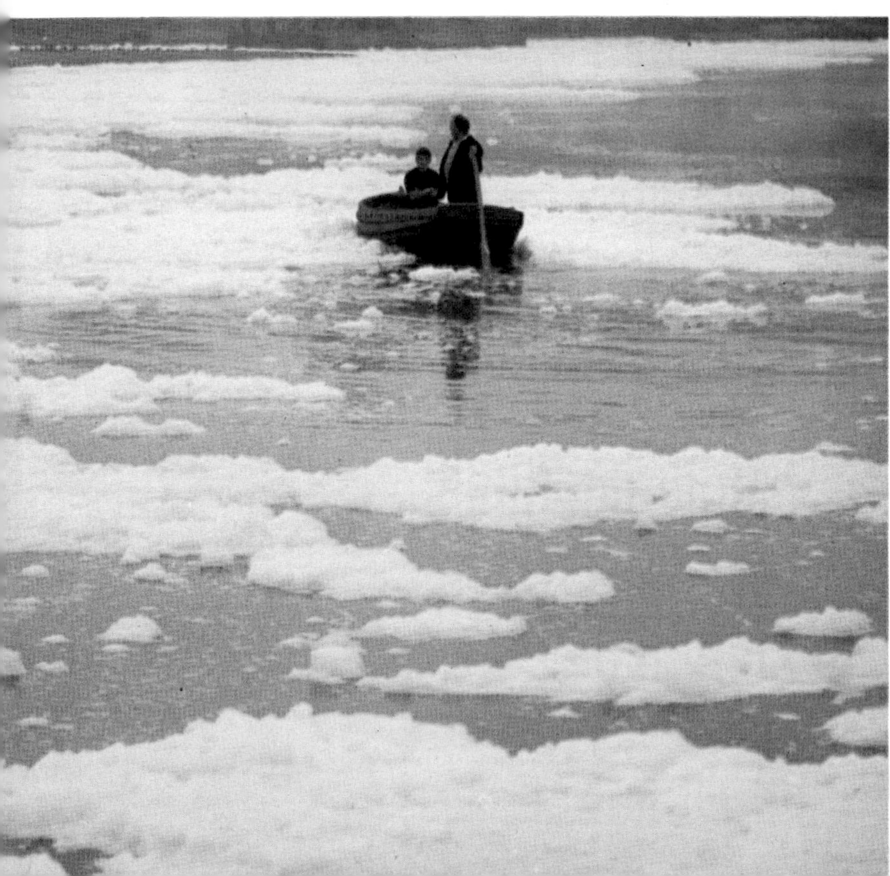

Above: the Liberian oil tanker *Pacific Glory* on fire after a collision in the English Channel, in October, 1970. Some of her 72,000 tons of crude oil spilled into the sea and floated toward the beaches of southern England. Left: pollution of another kind—detergent foam on an English estuary. Below: the sad result of oil pollution in the sea—a dead gannet, its feathers clogged with oil, found washed up on a beach in southern Wales.

and algae, mutilated vegetation, and warnings that bathers must not use certain parts of the coast. According to the secretary of the Mediterranean symposium on marine pollution, "It is not a question as to *when* the sea will be dead. For the Italians it has already happened. The effect on other countries bordering the Mediterranean will only be a matter of time."

Such dire warnings are not confined to the Mediterranean. Pollution is a threat that knows no frontiers. Pollution of one part of one ocean will, sooner or later, pollute all parts of all oceans—from top to bottom. The churning, worldwide system of ocean currents guarantees this.

Already fish caught in many different parts of the world have been found to contain toxic substances. And these include deep-sea fish. Lead from gasoline has been discovered in Arctic snow. The ethnologist Thor Heyerdahl, crossing the Atlantic in his papyrus boat, found huge patches of oil even in the middle of that ocean. And these are but a few examples.

Statistics indicate that pollution is now growing three times faster than world population. In December, 1970, at the close of a conference on marine pollution, 415 scientists from all over the world urged an immediate survey of pollution in the oceans and called for a worldwide monitoring system to control it. In promoting an International Decade of Ocean Exploration for the 1970's, the United States has suggested that special emphasis be placed on "goals of protecting the oceans from the harmful effects of pollution." At the request of Sweden, the United Nations has agreed to organize a conference in Stockholm in 1972 to consider the whole question of man and his environment.

These moves highlight the international nature of the problem and the necessity for international solutions. What is needed is an even greater awareness of the dangers, coupled with a willingness to devote far more organization, equipment, knowledge, and money toward the prevention and control of pollution.

Scientists point out that, if the sea is carefully used, it can be both an important source of food and minerals *and* a safe disposal area for some wastes—particularly those that can be broken down into harmless substances by natural processes. The sea, they say, is man's last storehouse of resources on earth. He cannot afford to upset its life cycles, poison, or pollute it.

The awareness of the sea's importance for man's survival has drawn the nations of the world together in an unprecedented program of oceanic research. The 1970's mark the beginning of a new era in the exploration of the ocean. Now, as never before, man has the means to discover the sea's secrets and to reap its riches. It is up to him to use that ability wisely for the benefit of all mankind.

Right: effluent pours into Lake Erie, U.S.A., destroying the animal and plant life in the water. Where sewage and chemical effluents are pumped into the sea in uncontrolled amounts the balance of nature is similarly disturbed. Only coordinated international action will be able to save the life in the sea.

Index